one Liner taken away from case

Red- who sued whom for what/whatwon/outcome

Black- underline Black letter law applied to help case/what court says

Green- Facts that make Black apply/whatneedsto beproved/statutes/what legislature says

Blue- Issue (Possible it) (answer yes or no), procedural history, dicta

Basic Civil Procedure - *Techniques for Effective Litigation*
Second Revised Edition

Lucy Marsh

Published by:

 Vandeplas Publishing, LLC – July 2017

801 International Parkway, 5th Floor
Lake Mary, FL. 32746
USA

www.vandeplaspublishing.com

ISBN 978-1-60042-294-2

# BASIC CIVIL PROCEDURE
*Techniques for Effective Litigation*

*Second Revised Edition*

LUCY MARSH

# TABLE OF CONTENTS

# INTRODUCTION

Techniques for effective litigation today are based on understanding when, where and how to file a lawsuit; how to make the most of the various tools available for discovering the evidence; and what to do if it appears that a court is making a mistake. The rules of procedure are at the heart of all litigation, so the cases in this book have been selected from a number of different areas of the law, and include a wealth of different fact situations and issues. The cases included are relatively full versions of the actual cases, so that you may come to understand the complexities of actual litigation, and appreciate how different issues within one case may be interrelated. In addition, nearly all of the cases included are good stories in their own right.

Now some basics about the court systems in the United States. To make things challenging, and because of federalism, there are two parallel court systems in the United States — the state system and the federal system. Each of the fifty states has its own sets of courts, and each state has slightly different rules of procedure. (Don't worry — you do not have to learn all of the different sets of rules. You just have to learn when there is likely to be an applicable rule — and how to find the current rules for any particular court when you need them.)

Most state courts are courts of general jurisdiction — meaning that they are authorized to hear almost all types of litigation. The federal courts, on the other hand, are all courts of limited jurisdiction — they can hear only certain types of cases, as authorized by the U.S. Constitution or by specific federal legislation enacted from time to time by Congress.

Within each court system - state or federal - there will probably be at least three levels of courts. First, there will be the trial courts, usually called district courts where nearly all trials take place. Then after the trial is over, an appeal may be taken to a court of appeals. No new evidence is presented at the court of appeals. The judges on the court of appeals just check to be sure that everything was done properly at the trial level. After a decision at the court of appeals it is frequently possible to take one more appeal, to the supreme court. However, usually the supreme court is not obligated to accept all appeals, so the Justices on the supreme court accept only the appeals that seem particularly important, or the ones that they are required by some specific statute to accept.

The majority of the cases in this book are from the U.S. Supreme Court, since that is the ultimate authority on the law. But not all important issues reach the U.S. Supreme Court, so the book also includes important decisions from lower courts — both state and federal.

You will find that in many situations a particular lawsuit could be started in either the *state* court system or the *federal* court system. The two court systems frequently have concurrent jurisdiction. The cases in this book will illustrate some of the reasons why the plaintiff, (the person who starts the lawsuit), may choose one court system over the other. Then, under certain circumstances, it may be possible for the defendant, (the person who is being sued), to remove the case from state court to federal court.

In both court systems — state and federal — there will be a statute of limitations, directing that a suit must be filed within a particular amount of time or it will be too late. Courts simply will not hear a stale dispute. State and federal statutes of limitations specify how much time is allowed for bringing various types of suits.

This book will emphasize the Federal Rules of Civil Procedure, because those are the rules that are applicable in the federal courts that are located in every state. The majority of states have adopted state rules of civil procedure that are very similar to the federal rules — even though there will be slight variations in the rules in each state.

You could get an idea of the basic rules of civil procedure by reading the Federal Rules of Civil Procedure. But that might become somewhat dull, and it is important to remember that the federal rules, like all laws, are subject to being changed from time to time. So studying the following cases will give you a much better idea of the actual complexity of the rules, and of how they are applied in real-life situations. Plus good stories are likely to make the basic rules far more interesting — and more memorable.

As you read the cases be sure to notice the surrounding fact situations and procedural steps involved — in addition to the specific issues that determine the outcome of the particular case. That way, by the end of the course you should have a broad, general understanding of the basics of how litigation is started, how the necessary facts are discovered, and when an appeal may be taken. Using the rules of civil procedure effectively is essential to any civil litigation.

Note: As with all casebooks, the cases included in this book have been extensively edited to try to make them easier for you to read and to understand. The full version of each case is available on Westlaw or Lexis. But for class purposes, these edited versions of the cases will be what you need in order to gain a basic understanding of Civil Procedure.

Enjoy!

# CHAPTER 1

# STARTING A LAWSUIT

## A. STATUTE OF LIMITATIONS/STATUTE OF REPOSE

1. The first thing you need to do when filing a lawsuit is to be sure that the suit is filed on time. No matter how strong your client's case may be, no matter how much work you may have done in preparing the suit, if you do not get the complaint filed in the correct court within the time allowed by the applicable statute of limitations your client will lose. A loss caused entirely by your delay may be difficult to explain to a client.

The following case should provide a memorable illustration of that point.

*[handwritten annotation: One Liner: Equitable tolling is not permittable in a case where an attorney fills late due to personal matters and the suit should be filed before the statute of limitations runs its course]*

**DISTRICT COURT OF APPEAL OF FLORIDA, FIFTH DISTRICT**

**HERBERT WILLIAMS,**[FN1] **APPELLANT,**

**FN1. HERBERT WILLIAMS IS A WOMAN.**

**V.**

**ALBERTSON'S, INC., APPELLEE**

DECIDED AUGUST 6, 2004.

PLEUS, J.

Williams appeals an order dismissing with prejudice her negligence complaint against Albertson's, Inc., for failure to file the complaint within the four year statute of limitations. (Williams filed one day late). Williams argues that the lower court erred in dismissing her complaint because an emergency prevented her attorney from timely filing and therefore, the court should have allowed the complaint under the doctrine of equitable tolling. We conclude that equitable tolling does not apply and that the lower court correctly dismissed the complaint. Accordingly, we affirm.

On or about April 3, 1999, Williams entered Albertson's and allegedly fell on a wet floor. She filed a negligence complaint against Albertson's on April 4, 2003, one day beyond the four year statute of limitations. Albertson's filed a motion to dismiss alleging that the complaint was not filed within the applicable statute of limitations. Williams' counsel filed an objection to the motion to dismiss alleging that:

1. Plaintiff would have filed her case by April 3, 2003, but plaintiff's lawyer was contacted by another lawyer, Charles Barfield, who had the tires slashed on his car, a white Toyota Corolla.

2. Plaintiff's lawyer was there while the Orange County Sheriff's Office through one of his deputies conducted an investigation and then when that was finished Plaintiff's lawyer drove Mr. Barfield's wife, Wendy Barfield to work.

3. Then Plaintiff's lawyer assisted Mr. Barfield during that day.

The trial court granted the motion to dismiss with prejudice for failure to file the complaint within four years.

The standard of review of an order granting a motion to dismiss is de novo.

Section 95.11(3)(a), Florida Statutes, requires an action for negligence to be filed within four years. Williams admits she filed her complaint one day late, but argues that she should have been excused because her attorney was busy helping another attorney in an emergency. She argues that these facts are sufficient to excuse the late filing under the doctrine of equitable tolling.

The doctrine of equitable tolling was developed to permit under certain circumstances the filing of a lawsuit that otherwise would be barred by a limitations period. Generally, the tolling doctrine has been applied when the plaintiff has been misled or lulled into inaction, has in some extraordinary way been prevented from asserting his rights, or has timely asserted his rights mistakenly in the wrong forum.

In the instant case, there were no allegations or evidence that Williams' attorney was misled or lulled into inaction or that he timely asserted his client's rights mistakenly in the wrong forum.

Thus, the only possible basis for asserting this doctrine would be that Williams was "in some extraordinary way prevented from asserting her rights." An example of such an extraordinary circumstance preventing someone from asserting his rights occurred in *Middleton v. Silverman*. In that case, the Dade County Courthouse closed due to a civil disturbance in Miami. The appellate court noted that the plaintiff attempted to file within the limitations period but was frustrated in his attempt by the courthouse closure.

The instant case is clearly distinguishable. Williams' attorney made no attempt to file within the limitations period and the courthouse was open. Instead, the attorney chose to help another attorney with a personal matter on the last day to file. As Albertson's notes, these facts are closer to those in *Whiting v. Florida Department of Law Enforcement* In *Whiting*, the appellant attempted to fax his notice of appeal on the last day to file. After two unsuccessful attempts to fax, the appellant "elected" to try again the next day. This Court held those facts were insufficient to allow the late filing under the doctrine of equitable tolling. Like the appellant in *Whiting*, Williams' attorney "elected" to help a fellow attorney in a personal situation instead of filing a complaint on Williams' behalf.

The remaining cases cited by Williams are also distinguishable because they involve situations where the courthouse was closed on a weekend or holiday on the last day to file.

AFFIRMED.

2. Now that the plaintiff has lost her chance to sue Albertsons – is there anyone else she might sue?

3. Sometimes, either at the beginning of a lawsuit, or at a time much later in the lawsuit, it may appear to someone that there is something very serious going wrong. In that situation the unhappy person might try to get a higher court to intervene promptly, by means of a writ of mandamus. When a higher court issues a writ of mandamus it orders a lower court to take a specific action.

The normal process would be to let the trial court complete the entire trial, and then permit the losing party to take an appeal to a higher court. But all of that takes time, and there are a few situations in which it is important to get an error being made by the trial court corrected much faster than would be the case with a normal appeal. The following case illustrates one such situation – in which the application for a writ of mandamus was successful in preventing the trial court from continuing to consider a paternity issue after the statute of limitations had run.

Note that in a divorce between husband and wife a third person may be brought into the suit by means of a "third party petition." This technique of bringing a third party into a suit is frequently called impleader, and will be covered in more detail in Chapter 6.

At this point just note that the third party in the following case, referred to as S.T., was successful in seeking a writ of mandamus from the Court of Appeals of Texas.

*one liner in Notes*

## 2015 WL 3646990
## COURT OF APPEALS OF TEXAS, FORT WORTH

IN RE S.T.

DECIDED JUNE 12, 2015

TERRIE LIVINGSTON, CHIEF JUSTICE

*asks higher court to judge*

S.T. filed a petition for writ of mandamus in this court seeking relief from a trial court order allowing a suit to adjudicate his paternity of a child to continue in an action joined with a pending divorce and Suit Affecting Parent-Child Relationship (SAPCR) between real parties in interest, referred to in this opinion as Husband and Wife. The primary issue is whether S.T. has a vested right to rely on the statute of limitations in effect at the child's birth in February 2002 and when the child turned four years old, or whether an exception to the statute of limitations—which the legislature did not codify until after the former four-year statute of limitations had run—applies. Based on the particular facts and circumstances of this case, we grant relief.

### Background

Husband filed for divorce from Wife in March 2014. In the petition, Husband denied his paternity of the only child born during the marriage and alleged that he had been precluded from challenging paternity before the statute of limitations ran because Wife's misrepresentations about the child's conception resulted in his mistaken belief that he was the child's father. Husband also sought genetic testing of the child and named an unknown father as respondent. Wife countersued for divorce and alleged that Husband's requested relief was barred on statute of limitations grounds.

*ST doesn't want to adjudicate his paternity*

Husband subsequently filed a third party petition against S.T., the man Husband alleged to be the child's biological father, seeking money damages in "an amount equivalent to what S.T.'s child support obligation would have been if he had been established as the father from the time of birth." Husband also filed a motion seeking genetic testing of S.T.

[Husband attached genetic testing results purporting to show that there is no possibility that he is the child's father. However, we hold that a trial court abuses its discretion by ordering genetic testing if the person seeking the testing is not entitled to maintain a suit to adjudicate paternity.]

In the meantime, Husband and Wife entered into an agreement, in which they agreed (1) to sever the divorce from the SAPCR, (2) that in the final decree Husband would "be adjudicated to not be the father of the child and to have no rights and no duties, including the duty of support," and (3) that if Wife recovered any child support from S.T., she would reimburse Husband for "1/3 of any amount recovered if, as, and when received." S.T. filed an objection to the agreement; he argued that the issues in the divorce and SAPCR were so intertwined that they could not be severed and that adjudicating Husband to not be the child's father in the decree violates public policy. The trial court suspended operation of the agreement.

S.T. filed a third party counterclaim for declaratory judgment, seeking to have the trial court find that any attempt to adjudicate him as the father of the child was barred by the four-year statute of limitations in family code section 160.607 and that Husband is the child's presumed father. S.T. moved for summary judgment on his declaratory judgment claim and on Husband's paternity claims against him. In addition to arguing that Husband's paternity claims were precluded by operation of the applicable statute of limitations, S.T. also claimed that Husband could not sue him for back child support owed.

In October 2014, the trial court granted an agreed partial summary judgment finding that Husband was the child's presumed father "unless he successfully rebuts that presumption" and that Husband would take nothing on his claim for money damages because "there is no cause of action recognized in Texas by a presumed father to recover retroactive child support against a biological father or to recover damages based on fraud and conspiracy with respect to the child's conception." But the trial court denied S.T.'s motion for summary judgment on the limitations issue.

On January 9, 2015, the trial court signed an agreed "Order for Stipulation of Facts," stating that "IT IS ADJUDICATED, ORDERED AND DECREED that no genuine issue exists with respect to the following facts, which are deemed conclusively proven without need of further evidence for proof thereof, in connection with the trial of this cause": (1) Husband is not the father or biological father of the child;

and (2) "facts exist that conclusively establish Husband's right to the relief of being able to challenge his paternity of the child, pursuant to Texas Family Code Section 160.607(b)(2)." Accordingly, the trial court ordered that in the final decree, "it shall be adjudicated that Husband is not the father of the child and that Husband shall have no rights and no duties, including the duty of support, regarding the child and as such, no provisions for the rights or duties will be included in the final decree."

## Applicable Law

When the child was born in February 2002, section 160.607 read as follows:

(a) Except as otherwise provided by Subsection (b), a proceeding brought by a presumed father, the mother, or another individual to adjudicate the parentage of a child having a presumed father shall be commenced not later than the fourth anniversary of the date of the birth of the child.

(b) A proceeding seeking to disprove the relationship between a child and the child's presumed father may be maintained at any time if the court determines that:

(1) the presumed father and the mother of the child did not live together or engage in sexual intercourse with each other during the probable time of conception; and

(2) the presumed father never openly treated the child as his own.

In 2003, the legislature amended section (b)(2) to read, "the presumed father never represented to others that the child was his own." The child turned four in February 2006. No party has contended that either of the exceptions listed in (b)(2) applied then or apply now.

In the 2011 session, the legislature changed sections (b)(1) and (b)(2) of section 160.607 so that the current version of section 160.607(b) provides as follows:

(b) A proceeding seeking to adjudicate the parentage of a child having a presumed father may be maintained at any time if the court determines that:

(1) the presumed father and the mother of the child did not live together or engage in sexual intercourse with each other during the probable time of conception; or

(2) *the presumed father was precluded from commencing a proceeding to adjudicate the parentage of the child before the expiration of the time prescribed by Subsection (a) because of the mistaken belief that he was the child's biological father based on misrepresentations that led him to that conclusion.* (emphasis added).

Husband contends that although the exception in (b)(2) was not in effect when the child was born or when the child turned four years old, he can nevertheless rely on it to defeat the statute of limitations in section 160.607(a).

The enacting legislation for the amendment in (b)(2) states that "the changes in law made by this Act with respect to a proceeding to adjudicate parentage apply only to a proceeding that is commenced on or after the effective date of this Act."

## Analysis

In his response, Husband does not argue that the 2011 amendment to section 160.607(b)(2) applies so that he can rely on that statutory exception; instead, he contends that the 2011 amendment merely codified an already existing application of the common law discovery rule to this type of case. Specifically, Husband argues that because spouses have a fiduciary duty to each other—including the duty of full disclosure of facts affecting the marriage—the common law discovery rule applicable to fraud and breach of fiduciary duty cases operated in this case to toll the four-year statute of limitations.

According to Husband, "the principle of tolling a statute of limitations in the case of fraud or breach of fiduciary duty has been part of Texas case law long before the 2011 amendment." The legislature could have chosen to incorporate the discovery rule into the 2001 and 2003 versions of section 160.607(b), but it did not. Accordingly, we conclude and hold that the trial court abused its discretion by determining that Husband (and by virtue of their agreement, Wife) can rely on the application of either the common law discovery rule or the 2011 amendment to section 160.607(b) to defeat S.T.'s right to summary judgment on the limitations issue.

A presumed father's ability to deny paternity is itself a creature of statute; before former section 12.06 of the family code was enacted in 1983, a presumed father who was married and living with his wife when a child was born could not deny paternity unless he could establish nonaccess to the wife or impotence.

Rightly or wrongly, the legislature had determined when the child was born that a four-year statute of limitations applied to a suit to adjudicate paternity. Thus, S.T.'s right to rely on that limitations period as a defense vested. The Corpus Christi court of appeals has articulated the public policy behind the legislature's determination as follows:

> The purpose of a statute of limitations in cases where a child has a presumed father is to avoid the severance of the parent-child relationship between the child and the presumed father—the psychological father. Section 160.607(a) prevents a mother, a *presumed father*, or any other individual, including the biological father, from destroying the father-child relationship between a presumed father and the child. The purpose of the Uniform Parentage Act, which the Texas Legislature adopted in 2001, *is to protect the child involved in parentage issues.* A statute of limitations in cases where the child has a presumed father usually protects a child because it preserves the established family unit.

This public policy concern is not frustrated in a case such as this one, in which there is a long-term relationship between the child and presumed father, and S.T.'s right to rely on the statute of limitations in effect at the relevant time has long since vested. We conclude and hold that the trial court abused its discretion by denying S.T.'s motion for summary judgment seeking a declaration that Husband's suit to adjudicate paternity was barred by limitations.

S.T. also challenges the trial court's agreed Order of Stipulations. According to Husband, S.T. has no standing to challenge the Order of Stipulations because (1) he is not a party to it, (2) the stipulated facts he challenges relate only to the relationship between Husband and the child, and (3) the stipulated facts do not name S.T. as the presumptive father of the child.

Even though the agreed Order of Stipulations does not directly purport to impose liability on S.T., nor does it adjudicate him the child's biological father, the stipulation that "facts exist that conclusively establish Husband's right to the relief of being able to challenge his paternity of the child, addresses and resolves—contrary to our holding above—S.T.'s challenge to Husband's suit on limitations grounds. Husband and Wife cannot bind S.T. to this stipulation, nor can they resolve this issue by stipulation.

Moreover, the stipulations that Husband is not the father or biological father attempt to adjudicate Husband's nonpaternity by agreement contrary to section 160.204(b), which provides that a presumption of paternity may be rebutted in only two ways: (1) by an adjudication under subchapter G of chapter 160 or (2) by the filing of a denial of paternity along with the filing of a valid acknowledgment of paternity by another person. Tex. Fam. Code Ann. § 160.204(b). A suit under subchapter G cannot be maintained without "a man whose paternity of the child is to be adjudicated" joined as a necessary party. The statutory scheme regarding the establishment of parentage thus contemplates that a child will not be left without a means of support, either by a presumed father or an adjudicated father. *See Gribble v. Layton,* holding that family code section 160.606 furthers public policy of ensuring that child's parents, rather than taxpayers, support the child), *and* Tex. Fam. Code Ann. § 153.001(a)(2) providing that public policy of Texas is to provide safe, stable, and nonviolent environment for child), *A.D.M.* (holding that public policy behind statute of limitations in section 160.607 is to protect the child by preserving an existing family unit); *cf. Goodson v. Castellanos,* ("The destruction of a parent-child relationship is a traumatic experience that can lead to emotional devastation for all the parties involved, and all reasonable efforts to prevent this outcome must be invoked when there is no indication that the destruction of the existing parent-child relationship is in the best interest of the child.").

Husband and Wife's agreements in the Order of Stipulations in this particular situation, therefore, contravene the statutory scheme and directly affect S.T. Consequently, we also conclude and hold that the trial court abused its discretion by including the findings regarding Husband's nonpaternity in the agreed Order of Stipulations.

**Adequacy of Remedy**

Because it is interlocutory, a trial court's denial of summary judgment is generally not a ground for mandamus relief. However, issues involving the rights of parents and children should be resolved expeditiously, and delay in such cases often renders appellate remedies inadequate.

Here, Husband joined the adjudication of paternity action in the underlying proceeding, and Husband and Wife's agreement regarding property division apparently takes the possible future recovery of child support from S.T. into consideration as part of the property division. Thus, whether Husband's suit to adjudicate paternity of S.T. may continue is a factor in Husband's and Wife's negotiations in the divorce proceeding, as evidenced by their agreement and agreed stipulations of fact. Moreover, as we have explained above, allowing Husband and Wife to continue their divorce and SAPCR on the agreed facts contained in the Order of Stipulations would vitiate S.T.'s defense upon the decree's becoming final, regardless of the status of the adjudication proceeding against him. We therefore conclude that S.T. does not have an adequate remedy by appeal.

## Conclusion

For the reasons set forth above, we conditionally grant S.T. the relief he seeks. We order the trial court to (1) vacate its order denying S.T. summary judgment on his declaratory judgment claim that Husband's suit to rebut the presumption of his paternity of the child and to adjudicate S.T.'s paternity of the child is barred by limitations and (2) render summary judgment for S.T. on his claims. We also order the trial court to delete the following from the agreed Order of Stipulations:

4. Petitioner is not the father of the child.

5. Petitioner is not the biological father of the child.

6. Facts exist that conclusively establish Petitioner's right to the relief of being able to challenge his paternity of the child, pursuant to Texas Family Code Section 160.607(b)(2).

Except to the specific relief granted herein, the trial court's orders stand. A writ of mandamus will issue only if the trial court fails to comply with this order. Additionally, this court's order staying proceedings in the trial court will be automatically lifted upon the trial court's compliance with this court's order as set forth above.

4. Long before the founding of this country the doctrine of sovereign immunity was firmly established. Basically, a citizen was prohibited from suing the government. This was frequently enunciated by the statement that, "the King can do no wrong." Surprising as it may seem, that rule of sovereign immunity is still the default rule in the United States. The government cannot be sued – without its consent. There must be a specific waiver of sovereign immunity by the government, for specific situations, before any suit against a governmental entity is allowed.

In the following case you will see a vivid application of that doctrine – and an illustration of the difference between a statute of limitations and a statute of repose.

**2015 WL 1963129**
**COURT OF APPEALS OF TEXAS,**
**EL PASO.**
**CROCKETT COUNTY, TEXAS, APPELLANT,**
**V.**
**KLASSEN ENERGY, INC., APPELLEE.**

DECIDED APRIL 30, 2015

YVONNE T. RODRIGUEZ, Justice

In this interlocutory appeal, Crockett County contends that the trial court erred by denying its plea to the jurisdiction because the county is immune from a suit challenging its decision to close a public road almost two decades ago. We vacate the judgment for want of jurisdiction.

## Background

The facts in this appeal are straightforward. Klassen Energy, Inc., has owned a land-locked oil and gas lease in Crockett County, Texas, since January 30, 1998. From approximately 1995 to 1997, Klassen Energy's predecessor-in-interest could access the leased land by using County Road 309 and used that road as the sole means of ingress and egress. In March 1995, the Crockett County Commissioners Court voted to close County Road 309 to the public. For more than a decade afterward, Klassen Energy apparently continued to use County Road 309, which traverses land owned by the University of Texas System Lands Division ("UT"), to obtain access to its leasehold. In 2013, UT decided to require Klassen Energy to pay for an easement across its land. Klassen Energy purchased the easement, then filed suit against Crockett County, seeking indemnity and a declaration that the 1995 closure order was invalid, or, alternatively, that the county needed to build a road to provide Klassen Energy access to its leased lands.

Crockett County filed a plea to the jurisdiction on sovereign immunity grounds. The trial court overruled the plea, and Crockett County appealed. We have jurisdiction under the interlocutory appeal statute.

## Discussion

In its sole appellate issue, Appellant maintains that Klassen Energy is statutorily barred from challenging the validity of the 1995 commissioners court order on repose ground.

We agree.

### *Standard of Review*

"Sovereign immunity from suit defeats a trial court's subject matter jurisdiction and thus is properly asserted in a plea to the jurisdiction." We review the question of whether the trial court had subject matter jurisdiction *de novo*.

### *Analysis*

At the outset, Klassen Energy contends we should affirm the trial court's order because Appellant improperly presented affirmative limitations and repose defenses in a plea to the jurisdiction when those defenses may only be raised via summary judgment. We disagree. Ordinarily, a defendant must prove an affirmative limitations defense either at trial, or through the traditional summary judgment framework. However, a government entity may properly bring a limitations or repose defense in a plea to the jurisdiction if the applicable statute clearly establishes that timely filing is a statutory prerequisite to suit and, thus, jurisdictional. Here, the statute of repose specifically governing this action states:

> A person must bring suit for any relief from the following acts not later than two years after the day the cause of action accrues:
>
> (2) the adoption by a commissioners court of an order closing and abandoning, or attempting to close and abandon, all or any part of a public road or thoroughfare in the county, other than a state highway.
>
> (b) The cause of action accrues when the order or ordinance is passed or adopted.
>
> (c) If suit is not brought within the period provided by this section, the person in possession of the real property receives complete title to the property by

limitations and the right of the city or county to revoke or rescind the order or ordinance is barred.

TEX. CIV. PRAC. & REM. CODE ANN. § 16.005 (West 2002).

Because the State is immune from suit absent legislative consent, and because legislatively enacted statutory prerequisite conditions to suit are jurisdictional, violation of a statutory requisite is a proper ground for a plea to the jurisdiction. In determining whether a statute is a "statutory prerequisite" to suit, we look to see: (1) whether there is "relevant statutory language" establishing a procedure; (2) whether that procedural prerequisite is required, i.e. "essential" or "necessary" and (3) whether that procedural prerequisite "must be met before the lawsuit is filed."

The statute here mandates that a person seeking to challenge a commissioners court order closing a public road "must bring suit for any relief not later than two years after the day the cause of action accrues." The plain language clearly establishes that compliance with this temporal requirement is mandatory. The two year filing deadline here is a statutory prerequisite to suit.

The parties next dispute whether Section 16.005 constitutes a statute of repose or a statute of limitations. The distinction carries a significant legal difference. A statute of repose, much like a statute of limitations, sets a time limit on a plaintiff's ability to bring a claim. However, unlike a statute of limitations, a statute of repose begins running from a specific point in time, regardless of whether a cause of action has accrued yet. "The essential function of all statutes of repose is to abrogate the discovery rule and similar exceptions to the statute of limitations." Thus, while a litigant may toll a statute of limitations where an injury is undiscoverable, a statute of repose acts as a hard temporal bar and a substantive limit to a plaintiff's right to recovery.

Klassen Energy claims that Section 16.005 does not create a statute of repose, but a statute of limitations that may be tolled by the discovery rule. Appellant correctly notes that the plain language of the statute frames the temporal inquiry in terms of accrual, which would suggest this section is a statute of limitations. However, the statute also states that "the cause of action accrues when the order or ordinance is passed or adopted," and the remaining provisions of the statute provide that once two years elapse from that date, title to real property vests and the commissioners court loses the power to rescind its order. The mechanics of this statute as a whole show that the Legislature intended it to act as a substantive limitation on the right of recovery, not as a claims-processing rule. As such, Section 16.005 is a statute of repose not subject to the discovery rule. The trial court lost jurisdiction to entertain a challenge to the March 1995 commissioners court order two years after its issuance.

Klassen Energy counters that even if the statute of repose creates a jurisdictional bar to suit, Appellant cannot claim immunity under these facts because the commissioners court failed to properly pass the road closure order under Section 2.002(e) of the now-repealed County Road and Bridge Act. We again disagree. The statute of repose covers not only procedurally valid commissioners court orders, but also any order *"attempting* to close and abandon all or any part of a public road." We need not decide whether the Crockett County commissioners issued a procedurally defective order closing County Road 390 in March 1995. The statute of repose insulates Crockett County from any attack on its road closure order, valid or not, after two years. Because the undisputed evidence shows that Klassen Energy and its predecessors in interest failed to file suit to challenge the commissioners court order before March 5, 1997, recovery here is absolutely barred.

The trial court's judgment is vacated for want of jurisdiction.

5. Note: Another situation in which it is frequently the rule that a time limit for bringing suit cannot be extended – for any reason – is in the context of probate. When a person dies, his or her creditors usually have a relatively short time – between two to six months – to file a claim to have the assets of the decedent, (the person who has died), used to pay the valid claims of his or her creditors. If the creditors do not get their claims in on time, those claims, even if they are perfectly valid, simply will not get paid. The surviving relatives have no obligation to pay the debts of the decedent. Statutes limiting the time in which creditors of a decedent can file claims are called non-claim statutes, and they are not subject to equitable tolling – for any reason. The justification for such non-claim statutes is that it is considered important to be able to wrap up the financial affairs of the decedent promptly, and redistribute the assets of the decedent to the survivors – as directed by statute or by a valid will signed by the decedent.

6. Within any particular jurisdiction there will be many different statutes of limitations or statutes of repose – depending on how long the legislature decided that it would be appropriate for a plaintiff to be allowed to sue for a particular type of injury. It is not always easy to determine which statute of limitations or statute of repose applies to a particular fact situation – as illustrated by the following case.

**2015 WL 4541006**
**SUPREME COURT OF MONTANA.**
**JIM HEIN, PLAINTIFF AND APPELLANT,**
**V.**
**JOHN W. SOTT, D/B/A SOTT HOMES, AND KRUDE KUSTOMS,**
**LLC, DEFENDANTS AND APPELLEES.**


DECIDED JULY 14, 2015

Justice BETH BAKER delivered the Opinion of the Court.

This case arises from a dispute between Jim Hein and John Sott and his companies, Sott Homes and Krude Kustoms, LLC (collectively, "Sott"), builders of Hein's home. Hein appeals the Thirteenth Judicial District Court's July 8, 2013 Order partially granting Sott's Motion to Dismiss, and its September 26, 2014 Order granting Sott's Motion for Summary Judgment. We address the following issues on appeal:

> 1. *Whether the District Court correctly concluded that Hein's negligence and negligent misrepresentation claims arising from the 2001 construction of his home and the subsequent inspections and repairs were barred by the statute of repose, § 27–2–208, MCA;*

> 2. *Whether the District Court erred in concluding that Hein's Consumer Protection Act claims arising from the 2001 construction of his home and the subsequent inspections and repairs were barred by the statute of limitations, § 27–2–211, MCA;*

> 3. *Whether the District Court erred in granting summary judgment because Hein did not provide expert testimony on causation for his Consumer Protection Act claim arising from Sott's alleged breach of contract and deceptive billing practices.*

We affirm in part, reverse in part, and remand for further proceedings.

## PROCEDURAL AND FACTUAL BACKGROUND

Sott is a general contractor based in Billings, Montana, and the sole owner of Krude Kustoms, LLC, a metal fabricating and trucking firm. In 2001, Hein hired Sott to construct a log home for him. Sott completed the home that same year.

Each winter following construction of the home, Hein noticed water damage appearing in different areas of the home's tongue and groove ceiling. Each time, Hein asked Sott to do an inspection and, each time, Sott informed Hein that he had repaired the problem. In 2012, after once again noticing water damage, Hein consulted a roofing contractor, Steve Ausen. According to Hein, Ausen discovered that the water damage was caused by improper ventilation in the roof, an issue that Sott never identified.

In 2011, Hein hired Sott to build an addition to the home (hereinafter, "2011 addition"). In 2013, Sott ceased work on the project before completion. The parties dispute the reason behind Sott's decision not to complete the project: Hein alleges that Sott overbilled for services for which Hein already paid, and Sott claims that he stopped working on the addition because Hein was no longer paying him.

On April 19, 2013, Hein filed a complaint alleging three counts against Sott: negligence, negligent misrepresentation, and violation of the Montana Consumer Protection Act. Sott moved to dismiss all of Hein's claims. On July 8, 2013, the District Court issued an order partially granting Sott's motion and dismissing Hein's claims related to the 2001 construction of the home as time-barred under the applicable statute of limitations, and statute of repose. The parties completed discovery and Sott moved for summary judgment on Hein's remaining claims, all arising from the construction of the 2011 addition, on the ground that Hein had not provided expert evidence that Sott's work was either defective or caused Hein damage. On September 26, 2014, the District Court issued an order granting Sott's motion and dismissing Hein's remaining claims. Hein appeals both orders.

## DISCUSSION

The statute of limitations for general tort actions, including negligence and negligent misrepresentation, is three years. Section 27–2–204. The statute of repose for actions for damages arising out of work on improvements to real property, § 27–2–208(1), MCA, provides:

> An action to recover damages resulting from or arising out of the design, planning, supervision, inspection, construction, or observation of construction of any improvement to real property may not be commenced more than 10 years after completion of the improvement.

Accordingly, even if the statute of limitations is tolled, a tort action related to construction damages may not be brought more than ten years after construction is completed.

The District Court determined that Hein's negligence and negligent misrepresentation claims arising from water damage to his home are barred by the statutes of limitations and repose because they relate to Sott's construction of Hein's home in 2001. Hein, however, suggests that each of Sott's acts of inspecting, identifying, and failing to repair the alleged problem constitutes either negligence or negligent misrepresentation. Thus, Hein argues, Sott's later acts are not barred by the statute of limitations or statute of repose. Upon reviewing Hein's complaint, however, it is clear that the only injury it alleges with respect to the home's roof is water damage due to Sott's alleged failure to properly vent the roof. The complaint does not allege that any of Sott's subsequent inspections or repairs created a new or separate injury. Accordingly, the District Court did not err in determining that Hein's negligence and negligent misrepresentation claims derive from his 2001 injury.

The District Court further determined that, even if the statute of limitations was tolled, Hein's claims are barred by the statute of repose because they relate to an injury that occurred more than ten years before Hein filed his complaint. The statute of repose is an absolute bar to bringing a claim for construction-related damages more than ten years after construction is completed. The statute of repose will not be extended even if a party is late in discovering facts.

Hein's complaint, filed on April 19, 2013, states, "The home was completed in 2001."Accordingly, the District Court correctly determined that Hein's negligence and negligent misrepresentation claims arising from water damage to his home are barred by the statute of repose, § 27–2–208.

## CONSUMER PROTECTION ACT

Under Montana's Consumer Protection Act, "unfair or deceptive acts or practices in the conduct of any trade or commerce are unlawful." The statute of limitations for liabilities created by this statute is two years. However, if a defendant "has taken action which prevents the injured party from discovering an injury or its cause," the limitations period does not begin "until the facts constituting the claim have been discovered or, in the exercise of due diligence, should have been discovered by the injured party."

Hein argues that the District Court erred in determining that Hein's Consumer Protection Act claims regarding his allegedly faulty roof were time-barred because Sott's deceptive inspections and repairs prevented Hein from discovering the cause of his injury. In his complaint, Hein alleges that he noticed water seeping into his home each winter between 2001 and 2012. Each spring, Hein asked Sott to inspect and repair the damage, and each winter the problem recurred. Hein waited until 2012—eleven years after construction was completed—to ask for a second opinion from a different contractor. Accordingly, Hein did not exercise due diligence to discover the cause of his injury, and the two-year statute of limitations was not tolled. The District Court did not err in determining that Hein's Consumer Protection Act claims for damages arising before April 19, 2011, two years before Hein filed his complaint, were barred by the statute of limitations.

The District Court also concluded that Hein's claims for damages based on inspections and repairs occurring after April 19, 2011, were barred by the statute of limitations, determining that the limitations period began to run in 2001 when construction was completed. Hein argues that a new Consumer Protection Act claim arose from each of Sott's inspections and repairs because each of Sott's inspections and repairs was deceptive. To the extent his complaint alleges separate acts of deception on separate occasions, Hein's Consumer Protection Act claims were not limited to the 2001 construction of his home, but alleged that Sott deceptively represented that he had performed successful repairs. The limitations period for those claims began to run two years before Hein filed his complaint on April 19, 2013. The District Court erred in determining that Hein's Consumer Protection Act claims based on alleged deceptive acts or practices in the performance of repairs that occurred after April 19, 2011, were barred by the two-year statute of limitations.

In his complaint, Hein alleged that Sott "ceased work on the project in early 2013 and, despite repeated promises to Plaintiff to resume work for which he has already been paid and to remedy deficient work on the current project, has never returned," and that Sott "breached his agreement with Plaintiff." Hein's complaint also alleges, "Since the beginning of the project, Sott has repeatedly billed for 'extras' and work Sott claims were not included in the original bid. Plaintiff felt he had no choice but to pay these charges rather than risk Sott walking off the job."

In his opposition to Sott's summary judgment motion, Hein stated, "The heart of the Consumer Protection Act claim is that Sott accepted deposits and payments for work he did not complete ." The Consumer Protection Act makes unlawful "unfair or deceptive acts or practices in the conduct of any trade or commerce." The Act defines "trade" and "commerce" as "the advertising, offering for sale, sale, or distribution of any services, any property, tangible or intangible, real, personal, or mixed, or any other article, commodity, or thing of value, wherever located." We have defined "unfair act or practice" as "one which offends established public policy and which is either immoral, unethical, oppressive, unscrupulous or substantially injurious to consumers." Hein's allegation that Sott caused him to suffer "actual damages" by billing for work not included in the bid and by failing to perform a service for which Hein paid states a claim for a Consumer Protection Act violation. This claim is separate from Hein's claim that Sott's work was defective.

## CONCLUSION

We affirm the District Court's dismissal of Hein's negligence and negligent misrepresentation claims arising from water damage to his home and its dismissal of Hein's Consumer Protection Act claims arising from Sott's inspections and repairs that occurred before April 19, 2011. We reverse the District Court's dismissal of Hein's Consumer Protection Act claims arising from Sott's inspections and repairs that occurred after April 19, 2011. We also reverse its grant of summary judgment to Sott on Hein's Consumer Protection Act claim arising from Sott's billing on the 2011 addition.

7. Particularly in the medical malpractice area, the application of a statute of repose may seem harsh. For example, what if the patient simply did not discover for several years that a doctor had negligently left sponges inside her abdomen while performing surgery? Should the doctor be protected from suit for his or her negligence? Should the doctor be allowed to get away with that sort of negligence because of the protections offered by a statute of repose? The following case explores those issues.

# SUPREME COURT OF MISSOURI

## SHONDA AMBERS–PHILLIPS AND RICHARD PHILLIPS, II, APPELLANTS,

### V.

## SSM DEPAUL HEALTH CENTER, RESPONDENT.

DECIDED APRIL 28, 2015

Laura Denvir Stith, Judge

Shonda Ambers–Phillips and her husband, Richard Phillips, II, appeal the trial court's dismissal with prejudice of their medical malpractice and related claims against SSM DePaul Health Center for leaving foreign objects in her abdomen during surgery almost 14 years earlier. The Phillipses argue that the trial court erred in not holding that Missouri's 10–year statute of repose for foreign-object medical malpractice claims was equitably tolled until Ms. Ambers–Phillips discovered the wrong, analogizing to the tolling of certain statutes of limitations until the wrong has been discovered. This Court disagrees. While statutes of limitations are subject to equitable tolling in certain circumstances, statutes of repose by their nature are not. They begin to run on the date of the allegedly tortious act and provide an absolute deadline beyond which suit may not be brought. To toll them disregards this basic purpose of statutes of repose—that of providing a final time limit beyond which suit is foreclosed.

This Court also reaffirms its prior cases rejecting the Phillipses' alternative argument that statutes of repose are unconstitutional if not subject to equitable tolling. While the Phillipses are correct that the right to bring suit for medical malpractice is one protected by the right to jury trial and may not be unreasonably foreclosed, this Court rejects the argument that it is a fundamental right to which heightened scrutiny applies. The Phillipses, therefore, must show that the legislature's decision to adopt a statute of repose was without rational basis. They have failed in meeting this burden. Statutes of limitations always have limited the time period for filing suit, and when the legislature extended the statute of limitations for medical malpractice by adopting a discovery rule, its decision also to adopt an absolute limit on the time within which the action could be filed was not unreasonable. Neither did it violate the prohibition against special laws or the guarantee of open courts. For these reasons, the judgment is affirmed.

## I. FACTUAL AND PROCEDURAL HISTORY

On September 13, 1999, Ms. Ambers–Phillips was in a car accident. She underwent an exploratory laparotomy at SSM DePaul. Nearly 14 years later, in June 2013, she underwent another exploratory laparotomy at a different St. Louis-area hospital because she was having pain in her side. According to the petition, during the surgery her doctors found four foreign objects that had been left inside her abdomen during the 1999 surgery. She sued SSM DePaul in 2013, alleging that it committed medical malpractice in failing to account for and remove these four foreign objects during her 1999 laparotomy. Mr. Phillips brought a loss of consortium claim.

SSM DePaul moved to dismiss the Phillipses' claims on numerous grounds, including that they were barred by section 516.105's 10–year statute of repose for claims of medical negligence involving the leaving of foreign objects in the body. The trial court sustained SSM DePaul's motion to dismiss with prejudice, concluding that, because the Phillipses filed their action 14 years after the date of the alleged negligence, the statute of repose applied, making their claims time-barred and subject to dismissal. The trial court also determined that the Phillipses' constitutional claims—that the statute violated due process, equal protection, and the Missouri Constitution's open courts and special legislation provisions—failed to present a "real and substantial" constitutional challenge and were, in any event, not well taken. The Phillipses appeal.

## II. STANDARD OF REVIEW

This Court reviews a trial court's grant of a motion to dismiss a petition de novo. This Court also reviews the constitutional validity of a statute de novo. A statute is presumed to be valid, and the Court will uphold it unless it "clearly and undoubtedly" conflicts with the constitution. The Court "resolves all doubt in favor of the statute's validity."

## III. A STATUTE OF REPOSE IS NOT SUBJECT TO EQUITABLE TOLLING

### A. Historical Treatment of Time for Bringing Foreign Object Cases In Missouri

From 1921 until 1976, cases alleging that a foreign object was left in the body were subject to the general statute of limitations governing certain intentional torts and medical malpractice, which stated in relevant part:

Within two years: An action for libel, slander, assault, battery, false imprisonment or criminal conversation. All actions against physicians, surgeons, or hospitals for damages for malpractice, error, or mistake shall be brought within two years from the date of the act of neglect complained of.

In 1976, the legislature took action that in part addressed the unfairness that had concerned this Court in *Laughlin* by adopting section 516.105, RSMo Supp. 1976. That section sets out a discovery rule for foreign object medical malpractice cases as part of the medical malpractice statute of limitations, stating in relevant part:

All actions against physicians, hospitals, and any other entity providing health care services and all employees of any of the foregoing acting in the course and scope of their employment, for damages for malpractice, negligence, error or mistake related to health care shall be brought within two years from the date of occurrence of the act of neglect complained of, except that *in cases in which the act of neglect complained of is introducing and negligently permitting any foreign object to remain within the body of a living person, the action shall be brought within two years from the date of the discovery of such alleged negligence,* or from the date on which the patient in the exercise of ordinary care should have discovered such alleged negligence, whichever date first occurs....

(Emphasis added). As this Court later noted, by this enactment the legislature provided:

that in cases such as *Laughlin*, in which the act of neglect complained of is introducing and negligently permitting any foreign object to remain within the body of a living person, the statute commences to run from the date of discovery.

Under section 516.105, when the negligent act is discovered, the statute of limitations begins running.

The discovery rule adopted in the 1976 revision to section 516.105 was not unlimited, however. In a classic example of a statute of repose, its final clause provided that no suit could be brought more than 10 years after the foreign object was left in the body, without regard to whether the negligent act had at that point been discovered:

> But in no event shall any action for damages for malpractice, error, or mistake be commenced after the expiration of ten years from the date of the act of neglect complained of.

Section 516.105 was amended in 1999, but the time limit for bringing suit in foreign object cases remained the same.

### B. The Statute of Repose in Section 516.105

This Court first must decide whether the Phillipses' suit was timely brought under section 516.105 as written or as modified by the doctrine of equitable tolling. The Phillipses' suit was filed on November 21, 2013, within two years from the date Ms. Amber–Phillips discovered, in June 2013, that four foreign objects had been left in her body. But this was not within 10 years after she alleges the foreign objects were left in her abdomen during her surgery at DePaul in September 1999. The Phillipses acknowledge that this means that section 516.105's statute of repose appears to bar their claims. But they argue the 10–year repose period should be equitably tolled until the day Ms. Ambers–Phillips discovered the wrong. Neither the cases the Phillipses cite nor the other relevant Missouri cases support their tolling argument.

In support of their argument, the Phillipses note that, when it applies, equitable tolling "pauses the running of, or 'tolls,' a statute of limitations when a litigant has pursued his rights diligently but some extraordinary circumstance prevents him from bringing a timely action." They note that Missouri has recognized the concept of equitable tolling can be applied to statutes of limitations when it is unfair to hold the plaintiff's claim was barred. In *Ross v. Kansas City General Hospital & Medical Center*, this Court explained the fairness principles that supported the legislature's adoption of a discovery rule in section 516.105 in regard to the statute of limitations in foreign object cases, stating:

> One reason why the legislature acted may have been that the legislature considered it particularly unfair that a claimant in whom a foreign object has been left should be barred by the statute of limitations even before there was any discovery of the foreign object, as happened to plaintiff in *Laughlin v. Forgrave*. Or the legislature might have believed it was proper to measure from the time of discovery in the foreign object cases rather than from the time of the act of neglect, because there is less likely to be as great a problem with stale evidence when a foreign object is left in the body than in the other types of malpractice cases.

Combining these principles, the Phillipses argue that the same fairness concerns should be applied here and compel "the intervention of equitable tolling of the statute of repose."

While the Phillipses are correct that this Court's prior cases have recognized the fairness of adopting a discovery rule and of equitable tolling in regard to the statute of limitations, they fail to note that these cases have emphasized that it is up to the legislature to determine whether to adopt a discovery rule or equitable tolling in a particular case because "a 'statute of limitations may be suspended or tolled only by specific disabilities or exceptions enacted by the legislature and the courts are not empowered to extend those exceptions.'"

The Phillipses' argument also fails to consider the philosophical and conceptual differences between statutes of limitations and statutes of repose. Equitable tolling is a term almost universally used in the context of statutes of limitations. This is because, unlike statutes of limitations, statutes of repose "by their nature reimpose on some plaintiffs the hardship of having a claim extinguished before it is discovered, or perhaps before it even exists." The United States Supreme Court itself recently has explained why these differences between statutes of limitations and statutes of repose make the latter incompatible with equitable tolling, stating:

> Statutes of repose, on the other hand, generally may not be tolled, even in cases of extraordinary circumstances beyond a plaintiff's control. Equitable tolling is applicable to statutes of limitations because their main thrust is to encourage the plaintiff to "pursue his rights diligently," and when an "extraordinary circumstance prevents him from bringing a timely action," the restriction imposed by the statute of limitations does not further the statute's purpose. But a statute of repose is a judgment that defendants should "be free from liability after the legislatively determined period of time, beyond which the liability will no longer exist and will not be tolled for any reason."

*CTS Corp. v. Waldburger*, (2014).

Here, the Phillipses cite to nothing in section 516.105 that indicates a legislative intent to equitably toll the statute of repose until a patient discovers a foreign object left in his or her body. To the contrary, the legislature specifically provided that claims of medical malpractice are barred by the statute of repose once 10 years have passed from the time of the negligent act, even if the plaintiff has not at that point discovered the wrong. This is a clear and specific statute of repose, and it bars the Phillipses' claims.

Statutes of repose do not bar the bringing of a valid cause of action. As this Court noted in *Blaske* in considering whether the open courts provision was violated by the 10–year statute of repose for builders and designers set out in section 516.097, RSMo 1986, the failure to bring suit within 10 years extinguishes the cause of action. Therefore, because the substantive statutory law had extinguished any right to sue at the end of 10 years, the plaintiffs had no cause of action to bring by the time they discovered the wrong at a later point.

The open courts guarantee applies only to recognized causes of action; it does not guarantee access to the courts once the statute of repose extinguishes the cause of action. If the Phillipses' right to sue had accrued prior to the time the statute of repose applied, then the open courts provision would be applicable and this Court would examine whether the statute unreasonably restricted their right to bring suit. Similarly, if the legislature had prohibited recovery for personal injury, the due process principles recognized by the United States Supreme Court in *Poindexter v. Greenhow*, (1885), and relied on by the dissent certainly would be implicated. But, here, the legislature provided a reasonable, 10–year period in which to sue. That period concluded before the Phillipses discovered the wrong; as a result, the Phillipses' right to sue never accrued and, therefore, never vested.

As discussed above, the United States Supreme Court has recognized that the effect of a statute of repose is to extinguish an existing cause of action, and it has applied such statutes. A statute of repose is not inconsistent with due process. The open courts provision is inapplicable to the Phillipses' claim, for it applies only to causes of action that have accrued, not to one that, like that of Ms. Ambers–Phillips, was barred before it had a chance to arise under a statute that otherwise allows a reasonable period in which to bring suit.

## DUE PROCESS IS NOT VIOLATED

The Phillipses lastly allege that the statute of repose in section 516.105 violates the provision of the Missouri Constitution guaranteeing that "no person shall be deprived of life, liberty or property without due process of law." In effect, they argue that the section 516.105 violates the due process clause because an individual has a vested property interest in a cause of action that has arisen that cannot be divested by a statute of repose before the person has discovered the foreign object's existence and has had the opportunity to file suit. This argument confuses statutes of limitations with statutes of repose. As discussed earlier, while a statute of limitation allows a cause of action to accrue and then blocks the claim if the suit is not filed within a legislatively determined time period, a statute of repose "eliminates the cause of action altogether after a certain period of time following a specified event," with the specified event in this case being the alleged medical malpractice. Therefore, "the cause of action is *eliminated before* the plaintiffs' injury and thus *before* plaintiffs' cause of action *accrues*." Because the plaintiff's claim is barred by the statute of repose before the claim accrues, the plaintiff never acquires a vested property right to which due process could apply. For these reasons, the statute of repose in section 516.105 did not violate the Phillipses' due process rights.

## CONCLUSION

For the reasons stated above, the judgment is affirmed.

8. Harsh as the application of statutes of limitations or statutes of repose may seem in some circumstances, such statutes are usually left to the discretion of the states. The particular statutes may – and do – vary from state to state.

But in at least one situation Congress has exercised the preemptive power of the federal government to override all state statutes of limitations or statutes of repose on behalf of all members of the military service. The following case explains the basics of the Servicemembers Civil Relief Act.

**481 MICH. 377**

**SUPREME COURT OF MICHIGAN.**

**ROBERT WALTERS, PLAINTIFF–APPELLANT,**

**V.**

**NATHAN NADELL, DEFENDANT–APPELLEE.**

DECIDED JUNE 25, 2008

PER CURIAM.

The issue in this case is whether plaintiff may avail himself of the tolling provision of the Servicemembers Civil Relief Act (SCRA) when he failed to raise that provision in response to a motion for summary disposition by defendant. We hold that he may not. In lieu of granting leave to appeal, we affirm the judgment of the Court of

Appeals, but for a different reason. We vacate that portion of the Court of Appeals judgment holding that the SCRA tolling provision is discretionary; the tolling provision is mandatory. We hold, however, that the Court of Appeals did not err by refusing to consider the issue because the tolling provision may be waived if it is not raised in the trial court.

## I. FACTS AND PROCEDURAL HISTORY

Plaintiff, Robert Walters, was involved in an automobile accident with defendant, Nathan Nadell, on May 11, 2001. Plaintiff filed a complaint on February 26, 2004, that alleged that defendant was negligent. Plaintiff was unable to serve defendant before his original and second summonses expired because defendant was serving in the military. The period of limitations for plaintiff's action expired while he was attempting to perfect service of process.

On October 21, 2004, plaintiff filed a second, separate complaint against defendant, raising the same claims against defendant as those in the first complaint. Plaintiff was issued a summons for the second action that expired on January 20, 2005. Defendant was served with the summons and complaint on December 10, 2004, at Fort Benning, Georgia. Defendant filed a motion seeking dismissal with prejudice on the ground that the period of limitations had expired before plaintiff filed his complaint for the second action. Plaintiff responded to defendant's motion, arguing that the period of limitations was tolled pursuant to MCL 600.5853. The trial court granted summary disposition in favor of defendant and entered an order dismissing plaintiff's complaint with prejudice.

Plaintiff appealed, arguing that the period of limitations was tolled under MCL 600.5853. Plaintiff also argued, for the first time, that the tolling provisions of the SCRA required reversal. The Court of Appeals affirmed the trial court, albeit on different grounds, and declined to address plaintiff's SCRA argument, holding that it was unpreserved for appellate review and that the tolling provision of the SCRA was discretionary.

Plaintiff sought leave to appeal in this Court, arguing only that his claims were timely because the SCRA tolled the period of limitations.

## II. STANDARD OF REVIEW

We review de novo the grant or denial of summary disposition. This case requires us to interpret provisions of the SCRA. Statutory interpretation is a question of law, which we review de novo. When interpreting a federal statute, our task is to give effect to the will of Congress. To do so, we start, of course, with the statutory text, and unless otherwise defined, statutory terms are generally interpreted in accordance with their ordinary meaning. When the words of a statute are unambiguous, judicial inquiry is complete.

## III. THE SCRA'S TOLLING PROVISION IS MANDATORY

Plaintiff argues that the Court of Appeals erred by not addressing his SCRA argument because the tolling provision of the SCRA is mandatory and cannot be waived. We first address plaintiff's contention that the tolling provision of the SCRA is mandatory.

The former Soldiers' and Sailors' Civil Relief Act of 1940 underwent significant amendment in 2003 when Congress enacted the SCRA.

The Court of Appeals opined that the 2003 change from "shall not" to "may not" rendered the tolling discretionary. Although the term "shall" is clearly mandatory, and the term "may" is typically permissive, "may not," in the context of SCRA is not permissive. "May not," as it is used in SCRA has the same meaning and import as "cannot" or its predecessor, "shall not." The provision clearly provides that the time that a servicemember is in military service is excluded from any period of limitations.

The Court of Appeals erred in its conclusion that the amendment rendered the tolling provision discretionary. We hold that the tolling provision, is mandatory. We must next consider whether the act nonetheless permits waiver of the mandatory tolling provision.

## IV. A PLAINTIFF WITH CLAIMS AGAINST A SERVICEMEMBER MAY WAIVE THE SCRA'S MANDATORY TOLLING PROVISION

The SCRA makes clear that the servicemember may waive the protections of the act. 50 USC Appendix 517(a) provides that "a servicemember may waive any of the rights and protections provided by this Act." 517(b) requires written waivers for certain actions that arise from disputes involving certain legal instruments, but in all other actions the rights and protections of the act may be waived by any other means.

Waiver under the SCRA is not limited to servicemembers. Congress set out the purpose of the SCRA in 50 USC Appendix 502:

(1) to provide for, strengthen, and expedite the national defense through protection extended by this Act to servicemembers of the United States

to enable such persons to devote their entire energy to the defense needs of the Nation; and

—(2) to provide for the temporary suspension of judicial and administrative proceedings and transactions that may adversely affect the civil rights of servicemembers during their military service.

Thus, in order to strengthen the national defense, Congress enacted the SCRA to temporarily free servicemembers from the burden of participating in litigation. The tolling of periods of limitations in actions against servicemembers serves to "provide for, strengthen, and expedite the national defense" by protecting the civil rights of servicemembers during their military service. The benefits of the tolling provision to a plaintiff suing a servicemember are merely incidental to the protections that provision provides servicemembers.

Congress enacted the SCRA as a shield to protect servicemembers from having to respond to litigation while in active service, but manifestly indicated that the SCRA's protections may be waived. Here, plaintiff is seeking to transform the SCRA into a sword to preserve his lawsuit without having timely invoked its provisions. It would be incongruent with the purpose of the SCRA to permit a servicemember to waive the rights and protections of the act, but bar a nonservicemember from waiving incidental benefits, and thereby provide, without exception, incidental benefits to a nonservicemember. The express purpose of the act is inconsistent with providing more protections to a nonservicemember than a servicemember. Because the purpose of the act is to protect servicemembers, we conclude that Congress did not intend to prohibit waiver by a nonservicemember. Therefore, we hold that the mandatory tolling provision of SCRA may be waived by a plaintiff asserting a claim against a servicemember during the servicemember's military service.

The final question we must resolve is whether plaintiff waived the tolling of the period of limitations in this case by failing to raise the tolling provision in the trial court.

### V. PLAINTIFF WAIVED THE SCRA'S MANDATORY TOLLING PROVISION

Michigan generally follows the "raise or waive" rule of appellate review. Under our jurisprudence, a litigant must preserve an issue for appellate review by raising it in the trial court. Although this Court has inherent power to review an issue not raised in the trial court to prevent a miscarriage of justice, generally a failure to timely raise an issue waives review of that issue on appeal.

The principal rationale for the rule is based in the nature of the adversarial process and judicial efficiency. By limiting appellate review to those issues raised and argued in the trial court, and holding all other issues waived, appellate courts require litigants to raise and frame their arguments at a time when their opponents may respond to them factually. This practice also avoids the untenable result of permitting an unsuccessful litigant to prevail by avoiding its tactical decisions that proved unsuccessful. Generally, a party may not remain silent in the trial court, only to prevail on an issue that was not called to the trial court's attention. Trial courts are not the research assistants of the litigants; the parties have a duty to fully present their legal arguments to the court for its resolution of their dispute.

Plaintiff's cause of action accrued on May 11, 2001, and plaintiff filed the instant complaint on October 21, 2004. Without tolling, the period of limitations for plaintiff's claim expired on May 12, 2004. Defendant moved to dismiss plaintiff's complaint with prejudice, arguing that plaintiff had filed his complaint after the period of limitations expired. It is undisputed that plaintiff did not raise the tolling provision of the SCRA in response to defendant's motion. Thus, under our "raise or waive" rule, it is undisputed that plaintiff waived the tolling provision.

It could be argued that the tolling provision cannot be waived because it is mandatory. However, as discussed, Congress did not intend to prohibit waiver by a nonservicemember. Moreover, our "raise or waive" rule permits waiver of otherwise mandatory statutory provisions. For example, our statute of limitations provision is mandatory, just like the tolling provision of the SCRA:

> A person *shall not* bring or maintain an action to recover damages for injuries to persons or property unless, after the claim first accrued to the plaintiff or to someone through whom the plaintiff claims, the action is commenced within the period of time prescribed by this section.

It has long been the rule in Michigan that a defendant may waive a statute of limitations defense by failing to raise it in the trial court. Under the Michigan Court Rules, a defendant waives a statute of limitations defense by failing to raise it in his first responsive pleading. The defendant may cure his failure to raise the defense in his first responsive pleading by amending the pleading, but the defendant must, in any event, raise the defense in the trial court.

We hold that a tolling provision may be waived just as a statute of limitations defense may be waived. Consistent with the rule against appellate review of issues not raised in the trial court, a plaintiff may waive the tolling of the period of limitations by failing to raise it in the trial court.

We are aware of decisions in other courts that reach the opposite conclusion, but those decisions are not binding, and we do not find them persuasive. Plaintiff failed to raise his SCRA argument in the trial court, but now seeks belatedly to use it as a sword to defeat dismissal. This would have the perverse effect of rendering the servicemember amenable to suit when the tolling provision was never invoked in the trial court. Therefore, we hold that plaintiff has waived the tolling provision of the SCRA, and the Court of Appeals did not err by not addressing the merits of plaintiff's SCRA argument.

### VI. CONCLUSION

The tolling provision of the SCRA is mandatory but not self-executing. A litigant pursuing a claim against a servicemember has a responsibility to bring the tolling provision to the attention of the trial court if he desires to avail himself of its benefits. Plaintiff failed to raise the tolling provision of the SCRA in the trial court; therefore he has waived his right to raise the provision as grounds for relief on appeal. Affirmed in part and vacated in part.

9. So, when you ascertain that the applicable statutes of limitations or statutes of repose clearly bar any suit by your client as a plaintiff, must you give up? No! That is the beauty of federalism – for a *very* bright attorney.

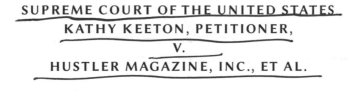

**SUPREME COURT OF THE UNITED STATES**
**KATHY KEETON, PETITIONER,**
**V.**
**HUSTLER MAGAZINE, INC., ET AL.**

DECIDED MARCH 20, 1984

**Justice REHNQUIST delivered the opinion of the Court.**

Petitioner Kathy Keeton sued respondent Hustler Magazine, Inc., and other defendants in the United States District Court for the District of New Hampshire, alleging jurisdiction over her libel complaint by reason of diversity of citizenship. The district court dismissed her suit because it believed that the Due Process Clause of the

Fourteenth Amendment to the United States Constitution forbade the application of New Hampshire's long-arm statute in order to acquire personal jurisdiction over respondent. The Court of Appeals for the First Circuit affirmed, summarizing its concerns with the statement that "the New Hampshire tail is too small to wag so large an out-of-state dog." We granted certiorari, and we now reverse.

Petitioner Keeton is a resident of New York. Her only connection with New Hampshire is the circulation there of copies of a magazine that she assists in producing. The magazine bears petitioner's name in several places crediting her with editorial and other work. Respondent Hustler Magazine, Inc., is an Ohio corporation, with its principal place of business in California. Respondent's contacts with New Hampshire consist of the sale of some 10 to 15,000 copies of *Hustler* magazine in that State each month. Petitioner claims to have been libeled in five separate issues of respondent's magazine published between September, 1975, and May, 1976.

Initially, petitioner brought suit for libel and invasion of privacy in Ohio, where the magazine was published. Her libel claim, however, was dismissed as barred by the Ohio statute of limitations, and her invasion of privacy claim was dismissed as barred by the New York statute of limitations, which the Ohio court considered to be "migratory." Petitioner then filed the present action in October, 1980.

The Court of Appeals, in its opinion affirming the District Court's dismissal of petitioner's complaint, held that petitioner's lack of contacts with New Hampshire rendered the State's interest in redressing the tort of libel to petitioner too attenuated for an assertion of personal jurisdiction over respondent. The Court of Appeals observed that the "single publication rule" ordinarily applicable in multistate libel cases would require it to award petitioner "damages caused in *all* states" should she prevail in her suit, even though the bulk of petitioner's alleged injuries had been sustained outside New Hampshire. The court also stressed New Hampshire's unusually long (6-year) limitations period for libel actions. New Hampshire was the only State where petitioner's suit would not have been time-barred when it was filed. Under these circumstances, the Court of Appeals concluded that it would be "unfair" to assert jurisdiction over respondent. New Hampshire has a minimal interest in applying its unusual statute of limitations to, and awarding damages for, injuries to a nonresident occurring outside the State, particularly since petitioner suffered such a small proportion of her total claimed injury within the State.

The "single publication rule" has been summarized as follows:

> "As to any single publication, (a) only one action for damages can be maintained; (b) all damages suffered in all jurisdictions can be recovered in the one action; and (c) a judgment for or against the plaintiff upon the merits of any action for damages bars any

other action for damages between the same parties in all jurisdictions." Restatement (Second) of Torts § 577A(4) (1977).

We conclude that the Court of Appeals erred when it affirmed the dismissal of petitioner's suit for lack of personal jurisdiction. Respondent's regular circulation of magazines in the forum State is sufficient to support an assertion of jurisdiction in a libel action based on the contents of the magazine. This is so even if New Hampshire courts, and thus the District Court, would apply the so-called "single publication rule" to enable petitioner to recover in the New Hampshire action her damages from "publications" of the alleged libel throughout the United States.

The district court found that "the general course of conduct in circulating magazines throughout the state was purposefully directed at New Hampshire, and inevitably affected persons in the state." Such regular monthly sales of thousands of magazines cannot by any stretch of the imagination be characterized as random, isolated, or fortuitous. It is, therefore, unquestionable that New Hampshire jurisdiction over a complaint based on those contacts would ordinarily satisfy the requirement of the Due Process Clause that a State's assertion of personal jurisdiction over a nonresident defendant be predicated on "minimum contacts" between the defendant and the State. And, as the Court of Appeals acknowledged, New Hampshire has adopted a "long-arm" statute authorizing service of process on nonresident corporations whenever permitted by the Due Process Clause. Thus, all the requisites for personal jurisdiction over Hustler Magazine, Inc., in New Hampshire are present.

We think that the three concerns advanced by the Court of Appeals, whether considered singly or together, are not sufficiently weighty to merit a different result. The "single publication rule," New Hampshire's unusually long statute of limitations, and plaintiff's lack of contacts with the forum State do not defeat jurisdiction otherwise proper under both New Hampshire law and the Due Process Clause.

In judging minimum contacts, a court properly focuses on "the relationship among the defendant, the forum, and the litigation." Thus, it is certainly relevant to the jurisdictional inquiry that petitioner is *seeking* to recover damages suffered in all States in this one suit. The contacts between respondent and the forum must be judged in the light of that claim, rather than a claim only for damages sustained in New Hampshire. That is, the contacts between respondent and New Hampshire must be such that it is "fair" to compel respondent to defend a multistate lawsuit in New Hampshire seeking nationwide damages for all copies of the five issues in question, even though only a small portion of those copies were distributed in New Hampshire.

The Court of Appeals expressed the view that New Hampshire's "interest" in asserting jurisdiction over plaintiff's multistate claim was minimal. We agree that the "fairness" of haling respondent into a New Hampshire court depends to some extent on whether respondent's activities relating to New Hampshire are such as to give that State a legitimate interest in holding respondent answerable on a claim related to those activities. But insofar as the State's "interest" in adjudicating the dispute is a part of the Fourteenth Amendment due process equation, as a surrogate for some of the factors already mentioned, we think the interest is sufficient.

The Court of Appeals acknowledged that petitioner was suing, at least in part, for damages suffered in New Hampshire. And it is beyond dispute that New Hampshire has a significant interest in redressing injuries that actually occur within the State.

> "'A state has an especial interest in exercising judicial jurisdiction over those who commit torts within its territory. This is because torts involve wrongful conduct which a state seeks to deter, and against which it attempts to afford protection, by providing that a tortfeasor shall be liable for damages which are the proximate result of his tort.'"

This interest extends to libel actions brought by nonresidents. False statements of fact harm both the subject of the falsehood *and* the readers of the statement. New Hampshire may rightly employ its libel laws to discourage the deception of its citizens. There is "no constitutional value in false statements of fact."

New Hampshire may also extend its concern to the injury that in-state libel causes within New Hampshire to a nonresident. The tort of libel is generally held to occur wherever the offending material is circulated. *Restatement (Second) of Torts § 577A.* The reputation of the libel victim may suffer harm even in a state in which he has hitherto been anonymous. The communication of the libel may create a negative reputation among the residents of a jurisdiction where the plaintiff's previous reputation was, however small, at least unblemished.

New Hampshire has clearly expressed its interest in protecting such persons from libel, as well as in safeguarding its populace from falsehoods. Its criminal defamation statute bears no restriction to libels of which residents are the victim. Moreover, in 1971 New Hampshire specifically deleted from its long-arm statute the requirement that a tort be committed "against a resident of New Hampshire."

New Hampshire also has a substantial interest in cooperating with other States, through the "single publication rule," to provide a forum for efficiently litigating all issues and damage claims arising out of a libel in a unitary proceeding. This rule reduces the potential serious drain of libel cases on judicial resources. It also serves to protect defendants from harassment resulting from multiple suits. In sum, the combination of New Hampshire's interest in redressing injuries that occur within the State and its interest in cooperating with other States in the application of the "single publication rule" demonstrate the propriety of requiring respondent to answer to a multistate libel action in New Hampshire.

The Court of Appeals also thought that there was an element of due process "unfairness" arising from the fact that the statutes of limitations in every jurisdiction except New Hampshire had run on the plaintiff's claim in this case. Strictly speaking, however, any potential unfairness in applying New Hampshire's statute of limitations to all aspects of this nationwide suit has nothing to do with the jurisdiction of the Court to adjudicate the claims. "The issue is personal jurisdiction, not choice of law." The question of the applicability of New Hampshire's statute of limitations to claims for out-of-state damages presents itself in the course of litigation only after jurisdiction over respondent is established, and we do not think that such choice of law concerns should complicate or distort the jurisdictional inquiry.

Under traditional choice of law principles, the law of the forum State governs on matters of procedure. In New Hampshire, statutes of limitations are considered procedural. There has been considerable academic criticism of the rule that permits a forum State to apply its own statute of limitations regardless of the significance of contacts between the forum State and the litigation. But we find it unnecessary to express an opinion at this time as to whether any arguable unfairness rises to the level of a due process violation.

The chance duration of statutes of limitations in nonforum jurisdictions has nothing to do with the contacts among respondent, New Hampshire, and this multistate libel action. Whether Ohio's limitations period is six months or six years does not alter the jurisdictional calculus in New Hampshire. Petitioner's successful search for a State with a lengthy statute of limitations is no different from the litigation strategy of countless plaintiffs who seek a forum with favorable substantive or procedural rules or sympathetic local populations. Certainly Hustler Magazine, Inc., which chose to enter the New Hampshire market, can be charged with knowledge of its laws and no doubt would have claimed the benefit of them if it had a complaint against a subscriber, distributor, or other commercial partner.

Finally, implicit in the Court of Appeals' analysis of New Hampshire's interest is an emphasis on the extremely limited contacts of the *plaintiff* with New Hampshire. But we have not to date required a plaintiff to have "minimum contacts" with the forum State before permitting that State to assert personal jurisdiction over a non-resident defendant. On the contrary, we have upheld the assertion of jurisdiction where such contacts were entirely lacking. In *Perkins v. Benguet Mining Co.,* none of the parties was a resident of the forum State; indeed, neither the plaintiff nor the subject-matter of his action had any relation to that State. Jurisdiction was based solely on the fact that the defendant corporation had been carrying on in the forum "a continuous and systematic, but limited, part of its general business." In the instant case, respondent's activities in the forum may not be so substantial as to support jurisdiction over a cause of action unrelated to those activities. But respondent is carrying on a "part of its general business" in New Hampshire, and that is sufficient to support jurisdiction when the cause of action arises out of the very activity being conducted, in part, in New Hampshire.

The plaintiff's residence is not, of course, completely irrelevant to the jurisdictional inquiry. As noted, that inquiry focuses on the relations among the defendant, the forum and the litigation. Plaintiff's residence may well play an important role in determining the propriety of entertaining a suit against the defendant in the forum. That is, plaintiff's residence in the forum may, because of defendant's relationship with the plaintiff, enhance defendant's contacts with the forum. Plaintiff's residence may be the focus of the activities of the defendant out of which the suit arises. But plaintiff's residence in the forum State is not a separate requirement, and lack of residence will not defeat jurisdiction established on the basis of defendant's contacts.

It is undoubtedly true that the bulk of the harm done to petitioner occurred outside New Hampshire. But that will be true in almost every libel action brought somewhere other than the plaintiff's domicile. There is no justification for restricting libel actions to the plaintiff's home forum. The victim of a libel, like the victim of any other tort, may choose to bring suit in any forum with which the defendant has "certain minimum contacts ... such that the maintenance of the suit does not offend 'traditional notions of fair play and substantial justice.'

Where, as in this case, respondent Hustler Magazine, Inc., has continuously and deliberately exploited the New Hampshire market, it must reasonably anticipate being haled into court there in a libel action based on the contents of its magazine. And, since respondent can be charged with knowledge of the "single publication rule," it must anticipate that such a suit will seek nationwide damages. Respondent produces a national publication aimed at a nationwide audience. There is no unfairness in calling it to answer for the contents of that publication wherever a substantial number of copies are regularly sold and distributed.

The judgment of the Court of Appeals is reversed and the cause is remanded for proceedings consistent with this opinion.

10. What if the laws of two different states may be involved in a particular lawsuit – and the laws in the two states are not identical? How is the choice made as to which part of the lawsuit is subject to which laws?

## 772 S.E.2D 143
## COURT OF APPEALS OF NORTH CAROLINA.
## MARTIN MARIETTA MATERIALS, INC., PLAINTIFF,
## V.
## BONDHU, LLC, DEFENDANT.

DECIDED MAY 19, 2015

DAVIS, Judge.

Bondhu, LLC ("Defendant") appeals from the trial court's order granting summary judgment in favor of Martin Marietta Materials, Inc. ("Plaintiff") on its action seeking the recovery of $71,947.00 in property taxes paid by Plaintiff on Defendant's behalf and denying Defendant's motion for partial summary judgment. On appeal, Defendant contends that the trial court improperly granted summary judgment in Plaintiff's favor because its claims for reimbursement were barred, in part, by the statute of limitations. After careful review, we affirm.

### Factual Background

This case arises from the parties' joint ownership of a 90–acre tract of real property located in Chesterfield County, Virginia. Property owners in Chesterfield County receive bills for the property taxes they owe from the Chesterfield County Treasurer's Office twice a year. When Plaintiff first acquired its one-half interest in the Property, its then co-tenant, Tamojira, Inc. had already failed to pay its share of the property taxes for the years 2002, 2003, and the first half of 2004. After Plaintiff acquired its interest in the Property, Tamojira failed to pay the taxes for the second half of 2004 and the first half of 2005. Plaintiff brought suit and subsequently obtained a default judgment against Tamojira for the unpaid taxes. Tamojira's interest in the Property was then transferred to Defendant by deed recorded 24 May 2005. Defendant has not paid property taxes on the Property since acquiring its interest in 2005.

On 31 October 2013, Plaintiff filed a verified complaint in Wake County Superior Court alleging that (1) Defendant has failed to pay any property taxes since Defendant acquired its one-half interest in the Property on 24 May 2005; and (2) "as the other one-half owner of the Property, Plaintiff has had to satisfy the tax debts owed by Defendant in the amount of $67,831.60, plus any amounts in taxes, fees, and interest Plaintiff must pay for the property taxes for the second half of 2013." In its complaint,

Plaintiff sought reimbursement from Defendant for the property taxes it had paid on Defendant's behalf.

On 26 February 2014, Defendant filed an answer asserting the statute of limitations as an affirmative defense and seeking the appointment of a receiver. Plaintiff filed a motion for summary judgment pursuant to Rule 56 of the North Carolina Rules of Civil Procedure on 4 February 2014 and an amended motion for summary judgment on 19 February 2014. On 15 May 2014, Defendant filed a motion for partial summary judgment, alleging that the applicable statute of limitations barred Plaintiff's recovery of any property taxes that were paid before the three-year period immediately preceding its 31 October 2013 complaint.

The parties' cross-motions for summary judgment came on for hearing before the Honorable Donald W. Stephens on 20 May 2014. On 22 May 2014, the trial court entered an order granting summary judgment in Plaintiff's favor, denying Defendant's motion for partial summary judgment, and awarding Plaintiff $71,947.00 plus costs and interest. Defendant gave timely notice of appeal to this Court.

Analysis

In this case, no material factual dispute exists as Defendant does not contest (1) its status as a co-owner of the Property during the relevant time period; (2) its nonpayment of property taxes; or (3) the amount of the property tax debt. Rather, the sole issues presented on appeal are (1) which statute of limitations applies to Plaintiff's claims; and (2) whether the applicable statute of limitations serves to render Plaintiff's claims partially time-barred. Defendant contends that the trial court erred in granting Plaintiff's motion for summary judgment because Plaintiff's claims for reimbursement are barred, in part, by the three-year limitations period contained in N.C. Gen. Stat. § 1–52(1). Plaintiff, conversely, asserts that the "catchall" ten-year limitations period contained in N.C. Gen.Stat. § 1–56 is applicable to its action.

Although this case was filed in Wake County, North Carolina, the claims asserted by Plaintiff involve obligations arising from the parties' relationship as co-tenants of the Property in Chesterfield County, Virginia. The Chesterfield County Treasurer's Office—the entity that assessed taxes on the Property—is located in Virginia, and the tax debt on the Property resulting from Defendant's nonpayment of its share of the taxes accrued there as well.

Under North Carolina choice of law rules, we apply the substantive law of the state where the cause of action accrued and the procedural rules of North Carolina. Thus, Virginia's substantive law governs Plaintiff's claims for relief.

Because, however, statutes of limitation are clearly procedural, affecting only the remedy directly and not the right to recover, we must apply the appropriate statute of limitations under North Carolina law to Plaintiff's substantive claims—that is, the limitations period that would apply to such causes of action in this State. "When determining the applicable statute of limitations, we are guided by the principle that the statute of limitations is not determined by the remedy sought, but by the substantive right asserted by plaintiffs." Accordingly, in order to determine the appropriate statute of limitations to apply, we must first identify the nature of the substantive claims asserted by Plaintiff as they exist under Virginia law.

In its complaint, Plaintiff asserted two claims for relief. Without specifically identifying or labeling the first cause of action, Plaintiff made the following allegations in support of this claim:

20. Defendant, as a co-owner of the Property, is liable for its fair share of the property taxes owed on the Property.

21. By virtue of Defendant's failure to pay the taxes owed, and failure to reimburse Plaintiff for such amounts, Plaintiff is entitled to have and recover of Defendant the principal amount of $67,831.60 plus any amount in taxes, fees, and interest Plaintiff must pay for the property taxes for the second half of 2013, plus interest. Plaintiff is also entitled to have and recover of Defendant the costs of this action.

Plaintiff's second claim for relief—pled in the alternative—sought recovery in *quantum meruit* on the theory that Defendant was unjustly enriched by Plaintiff's full payment of property taxes owed on the Property for which Defendant was jointly responsible. It is clear that the statute of limitations for unjust enrichment is three years. ("A claim for unjust enrichment must be brought within three years of accrual under subsection 1 of section 1–52."). However, because the unjust enrichment claim was pled merely as an alternative means of recovery, we must determine the appropriate limitations period that applies to Plaintiff's first cause of action.

The parties differ in their respective positions on this issue. Defendant contends that Plaintiff's right to receive reimbursement as pled in its first claim for relief stems from an implied contract between the parties. Defendant argues that this cause of action is therefore grounded in principles of contract law and more properly denominated as a claim for contribution arising out of a joint debt. Defendant asserts that "when two or more persons are jointly liable to pay a debt, the law *implies a contract* between the co-obligors to contribute ratably toward the discharge of the obligation."

(explaining that right to contribution is based on implied contract "between the parties to contribute ratably toward the discharge of a common obligation"). Consequently, Defendant argues, North Carolina's three-year statute of limitations applicable to an "obligation or liability arising out of a contract, express or implied" applies. N.C. Gen. Stat. § 1–52(1) (2013).

Plaintiff, conversely, contends that its claim against Defendant should be treated as a cause of action for an "accounting in equity" between two tenants in common under Virginia law. As such, Plaintiff argues, its first claim for relief falls under Va.Code Ann. § 8.01–31, which provides that "an accounting in equity may be had against any fiduciary or by one joint tenant, tenant in common, or coparcener for receiving more than comes to his just share or proportion, or against the personal representative of any such party." While North Carolina does not have a statute of limitations expressly addressing claims seeking an equitable accounting, Plaintiff contends that its claim is governed by the ten-year limitations period provided in N.C. Gen.Stat. § 1–56 for "actions for relief not otherwise limited by this subchapter." N.C. Gen.Stat. § 1–56 (2013).

In so arguing, Plaintiff notes that North Carolina courts have previously applied N.C. Gen.Stat. § 1–56 to claims seeking an accounting between the parties.

Both parties cite *Jenkins v. Jenkins*, in which two ex-spouses owned a parcel of real property as tenants in common following their divorce. The plaintiff paid the mortgage payments on the property after the divorce and until the property was sold on 4 October 1968. She then sought reimbursement from the defendant for his portion of the mortgage payments as well as an order requiring the defendant to pay half of the real estate taxes on the property that had accrued. The Virginia Supreme Court determined that the plaintiff was entitled to reimbursement because "unless something more can be shown than the mere fact that one co-tenant is in possession of the premises, each co-tenant should be ratably responsible for taxes and other liens against the property." The *Jenkins* Court noted that "an accounting in equity may be had by one tenant in common against the other as bailiff, for receiving more than comes to his just share or proportion."

While *Jenkins* supports the right of a co-tenant such as Plaintiff to obtain reimbursement from its co-tenant under these circumstances, it does not explain the precise nature and origin of this right under Virginia law. However, in *Grove v. Grove*, (1902), the Virginia Supreme Court held that "the right of a co-tenant, who discharges an incumbrance upon the common property, to ratable contribution from his cotenants, is said to *arise out of the trust relationship which exists among joint owners of property*, rather than by way of subrogation."

Thus, Plaintiff's first claim for relief can also be interpreted as asserting a substantive right stemming from the parties' trust relationship as co-tenants rather than one arising from principles of contract law. Under this theory, Plaintiff's first claim for relief would be governed not by the three-year statute of limitations under N.C. Gen.Stat. § 1–52(1) that is applicable to obligations arising from implied contracts but rather by the ten-year limitations period contained in N.C. Gen.Stat. § 1–56.

Consequently, we are unable to discern a clear answer to the question of which of the two respective limitations periods applies most directly to the substantive claim Plaintiff has pled in its first claim for relief. However, our Supreme Court has held that "where there is doubt as to which of two possible statutes of limitation applies, the rule is that the longer statute is to be selected." Such doubt exists here because the first claim for relief in Plaintiff's complaint can be construed as setting forth either of two distinct, legally cognizable claims under Virginia law: (1) a claim for contribution; or (2) a claim for an accounting in equity. While Plaintiff would be entitled under either legal theory to reimbursement from Defendant for its share of the property taxes, a contribution claim would be governed by the three-year statute of limitations contained in N.C. Gen.Stat. § 1–52(1) because the substantive right underlying such a claim is derived from an implied contract whereas a claim for equitable accounting—grounded in equity and arising from a trust relationship—would be subject to the ten-year limitations period set out in N.C. Gen.Stat. § 1–56.

Thus, because there are two statutes of limitations that are equally applicable to Plaintiff's first claim for relief, we conclude—based on our Supreme Court's decision in *Fowler*—that application of the longer ten-year limitations period is appropriate. As such, because all of the payments for which Plaintiff seeks reimbursement fall within the ten-year period immediately preceding the date Plaintiff filed suit, Plaintiff's first claim for relief is not barred in any respect by the statute of limitations. Accordingly, the trial court did not err in granting Plaintiff's motion for summary judgment and denying Defendant's motion for partial summary judgment.

**Conclusion**

For the reasons stated above, we affirm the trial court's order.

11. Over the years, Congress has enacted various statutes waiving its sovereign immunity in specific, limited circumstances. The Federal Tort Claims Act, the Clayton Act, and the Tucker Act are some of such statutes. Normally, when waiving sovereign immunity for a particular situation the government will also provide some statement as to the statute of limitation involved in the particular waiver. Are

such statutes subject to equitable tolling? It depends. And sometimes not on the wording of the particular statute.

## 135 S.CT. 1625
### SUPREME COURT OF THE UNITED STATES
### UNITED STATES, PETITIONER
### v.
### KWAI FUN WONG,
### UNITED STATES, PETITIONER
### v.
### MARLENE JUNE, CONSERVATOR

DECIDED APRIL 22, 2015

**Justice KAGAN delivered the opinion of the Court.**

The Federal Tort Claims Act (FTCA or Act) provides that a tort claim against the United States "shall be forever barred" unless it is presented to the "appropriate Federal agency within two years after such claim accrues" and then brought to federal court "within six months" after the agency acts on the claim. (Emphasis added.) In each of the two cases we resolve here, the claimant missed one of those deadlines, but requested equitable tolling on the ground that she had a good reason for filing late. The Government responded that § 2401(b)'s time limits are not subject to tolling because they are jurisdictional restrictions. Today, we reject the Government's argument and conclude that courts may toll both of the FTCA's limitations periods.

I

In the first case, respondent Kwai Fun Wong asserts that the Immigration and Naturalization Service (INS) falsely imprisoned her for five days in 1999. As the FTCA requires, Wong first presented that claim to the INS within two years of the alleged unlawful action. The INS denied the administrative complaint on December 3, 2001. Under the Act, that gave Wong six months, until June 3, 2002, to bring her tort claim in federal court.

Several months prior to the INS's decision, Wong had filed suit in federal district court asserting various *non*-FTCA claims against the Government arising out of the same alleged misconduct. Anticipating the INS's ruling, Wong moved in mid-November 2001 to amend the complaint in that suit by adding her tort claim. On April 5, 2002, a Magistrate Judge recommended granting Wong leave to amend. But the District Court did not finally adopt that proposal until June 25—three weeks *after* the FTCA's 6–month deadline.

The Government moved to dismiss the tort claim on the ground that it was filed late. The District Court at first rejected the motion. It recognized that Wong had managed to add her FTCA claim only after § 2401(b)'s 6–month time period had expired. But the court equitably tolled that period for all the time between the Magistrate Judge's recommendation and its own order allowing amendment, thus bringing Wong's FTCA claim within the statutory deadline. Several years later, the Government moved for reconsideration of that ruling based on an intervening Ninth Circuit decision. This time, the District Court dismissed Wong's claim, reasoning that § 2401(b)'s 6–month time bar was jurisdictional and therefore not subject to equitable tolling. On appeal, the Ninth Circuit agreed to hear the case en banc to address an intra-circuit conflict on the issue. The en banc court held that the 6–month limit is not jurisdictional and that equitable tolling is available. It then confirmed the District Court's prior ruling that the circumstances here justify tolling because Wong "exercised due diligence" in attempting to amend her complaint before the statutory deadline.

The second case before us arises from a deadly highway accident. Andrew Booth was killed in 2005 when a car in which he was riding crossed through a cable median barrier and crashed into oncoming traffic. The following year, respondent Marlene June, acting on behalf of Booth's young son, filed a wrongful death action alleging that the State of Arizona and its contractor had negligently constructed and maintained the median barrier. Years into that state-court litigation, June contends, she discovered that the Federal Highway Administration (FHWA) had approved installation of the barrier knowing it had not been properly crash tested.

Relying on that new information, June presented a tort claim to the FHWA in 2010, more than five years after the accident. The FHWA denied the claim, and June promptly filed this action in federal district court. The court dismissed the suit because June had failed to submit her claim to the FHWA within two years of the collision. The FTCA's 2–year bar, the court ruled, is jurisdictional and therefore not subject to equitable tolling; accordingly, the court did not consider June's contention that tolling was proper because the Government had concealed its failure to require crash testing. On appeal, the Ninth Circuit reversed in light of its recent decision in

*Wong,* thus holding that § 2401(b)'s 2–year deadline, like its 6–month counterpart, is not jurisdictional and may be tolled.

We granted certiorari in both cases, to resolve a circuit split about whether courts may equitably toll § 2401(b)'s two time limits. We now affirm the Court of Appeals' rulings.

## II

*Irwin v. Department of Veterans Affairs,* (1990), sets out the framework for deciding "the applicability of equitable tolling in suits against the Government." In *Irwin,* we recognized that time bars in suits between *private* parties are presumptively subject to equitable tolling. That means a court usually may pause the running of a limitations statute in private litigation when a party "has pursued his rights diligently but some extraordinary circumstance" prevents him from meeting a deadline. We held in *Irwin* that "the same rebuttable presumption of equitable tolling" should also apply to suits brought against the United States under a statute waiving sovereign immunity. Our old "ad hoc," law-by-law approach to determining the availability of tolling in those suits, we reasoned, had produced inconsistency and "unpredictability" without the offsetting virtue of enhanced "fidelity to the intent of Congress." Adopting the "general rule" used in private litigation, we stated, would "amount to little, if any, broadening" of a statutory waiver of immunity. Accordingly, we thought such a presumption "likely to be a realistic assessment of legislative intent as well as a practically useful" rule of interpretation.

A rebuttable presumption, of course, may be rebutted, so *Irwin* does not end the matter. When enacting a time bar for a suit against the Government (as for one against a private party), Congress may reverse the usual rule if it chooses. The Government may therefore attempt to establish, through evidence relating to a particular statute of limitations, that Congress opted to forbid equitable tolling.

One way to meet that burden—and the way the Government pursues here—is to show that Congress made the time bar at issue jurisdictional. When that is so, a litigant's failure to comply with the bar deprives a court of all authority to hear a case. Hence, a court must enforce the limitation even if the other party has waived any timeliness objection. And, more crucially here, a court must do so even if equitable considerations would support extending the prescribed time period.

Given those harsh consequences, the Government must clear a high bar to establish that a statute of limitations is jurisdictional. In recent years, we have repeatedly held that procedural rules, including time bars, cabin a court's power only if Congress has "clearly stated" as much. "Absent such a clear statement, courts should treat the restriction as nonjurisdictional." That does not mean "Congress must incant magic words." But traditional tools of statutory construction must plainly show that Congress imbued a procedural bar with jurisdictional consequences.

And in applying that clear statement rule, we have made plain that most time bars are nonjurisdictional. Time and again, we have described filing deadlines as "quintessential claim-processing rules," which "seek to promote the orderly progress of litigation," but do not deprive a court of authority to hear a case. That is so, contrary to the dissent's suggestion, even when the time limit is important (most are) and even when it is framed in mandatory terms (again, most are); indeed, that is so "however emphatically" expressed those terms may be. Congress must do something special, beyond setting an exception-free deadline, to tag a statute of limitations as jurisdictional and so prohibit a court from tolling it.

In enacting the FTCA, Congress did nothing of that kind. It provided no clear statement indicating that § 2401(b) is the rare statute of limitations that can deprive a court of jurisdiction. Neither the text nor the context nor the legislative history indicates (much less does so plainly) that Congress meant to enact something other than a standard time bar.

Most important, § 2401(b)'s text speaks only to a claim's timeliness, not to a court's power. It states that "a tort claim against the United States shall be forever barred unless it is presented to the agency within two years or unless action is begun within six months" of the agency's denial of the claim. That is mundane statute-of-limitations language, saying only what every time bar, by definition, must: that after a certain time a claim is barred. The language is mandatory—"shall" be barred—but that is true of most such statutes, and we have consistently found it of no consequence. Too, the language might be viewed as emphatic—"forever" barred—but (again) we have often held that not to matter. What matters instead is that § 2401(b) "does not speak in jurisdictional terms or refer in any way to the jurisdiction of the district courts." It does not define a federal court's jurisdiction over tort claims generally, address its authority to hear untimely suits, or in any way cabin its usual equitable powers. Section 2401(b), in short, "reads like an ordinary, run-of-the-mill statute of limitations," spelling out a litigant's filing obligations without restricting a court's authority.

Statutory context confirms that reading. This Court has often explained that Congress's separation of a filing deadline from a jurisdictional grant indicates that the time bar is not jurisdictional. So too here. Whereas § 2401(b) houses the FTCA's time limitations, a different section of Title 28 confers power on federal district courts to hear FTCA claims. See § 1346(b)(1) ("district courts ... shall have exclusive jurisdiction" over tort claims against the United States). Nothing conditions the jurisdictional grant on the limitations periods, or otherwise links those separate provisions. Treating § 2401(b)'s time bars as jurisdictional would thus disregard the structural divide built into the statute.

Finally, even assuming legislative history alone could provide a clear statement (which we doubt), none does so here. And so we wind up back where we started, with *Irwin's* "general rule" that equitable tolling is available in suits against the Government. The justification the Government offers for departing from that principle fails: Section 2401(b) is not a jurisdictional requirement. The time limits in the FTCA are just time limits, nothing more. Even though they govern litigation against the Government, a court can toll them on equitable grounds.

## III

The Government balks at that straightforward analysis, claiming that it overlooks two reasons for thinking § 2401(b) jurisdictional. But neither of those reasons is persuasive. Indeed, our precedents in this area foreclose them both.

### A

*Tucker Act*

The Government principally contends that § 2401(b) is jurisdictional because it includes the same language as the statute of limitations governing contract (and some other non-tort) suits brought against the United States under the Tucker Act. That statute long provided that such suits "shall be forever barred" if not filed within six years. And this Court repeatedly held that 6-year limit to be jurisdictional and thus not subject to equitable tolling. When Congress drafted the FTCA's time bar, it used the same "shall be forever barred" language (though selecting a shorter limitations period). "In these circumstances," the Government maintains, "the only reasonable conclusion is that Congress intended the FTCA's identically worded time limit to be a jurisdictional bar." According to the Government, Congress wanted the FTCA to serve as "a tort-law analogue to the Tucker Act" and incorporated the words "shall be forever barred" to similarly preclude equitable tolling.

But the Government takes too much from Congress's use in § 2401(b) of an utterly unremarkable phrase. The "shall be forever barred" formulation was a commonplace in federal limitations statutes for many decades surrounding Congress's enactment of the FTCA. And neither this Court nor any other has accorded those words talismanic power to render time bars jurisdictional. To the contrary, we have construed the very same "shall be forever barred" language in 15 U.S.C. § 15b, the Clayton Act's statute of limitations, to be subject to tolling; nothing in that provision, we found, "restricts the power of the federal courts" to extend a limitations period when circumstances warrant. As the Government itself has previously acknowledged, referring to the "shall be forever barred" locution: "That type of language has more to do with the legal rhetoric at the time the statute was passed" than with anything else, and should not "make a difference" to the jurisdictional analysis. Or, put just a bit differently: Congress's inclusion of a phrase endemic to limitations statutes of that era, at least some of which allow tolling, cannot provide the requisite clear statement that a time bar curtails a court's authority.

Indeed, in two decisions directly addressing the Tucker Act's statute of limitations, this Court dismissed the idea that the language the Government relies on here has jurisdictional significance. Twice we described the words in that provision as not meaningfully different from those in a nonjurisdictional statute of limitations. And twice we made clear that the jurisdictional status of the Tucker Act's time bar has precious little to do with its phrasing.

More recently, *John R. Sand* reaffirmed that conclusion, even as it refused to overturn our century-old view that the Tucker Act's time bar is jurisdictional. No less than three times, *John R. Sand* approvingly repeated *Irwin*'s statement that the textual differences between the Tucker Act's time bar and § 2000e–16(c) were insignificant—*i.e.*, that the language of the two provisions could not explain why the former was jurisdictional and the latter not. But if that were so, *John R. Sand* asked, why not hold that the Tucker Act's time limit, like § 2000e–16(c), is nonjurisdictional? The answer came down to two words: *stare decisis*. The Tucker Act's bar was different because it had been the subject of "a definitive earlier interpretation." And for that reason alone, *John R. Sand* left in place our prior construction of the Tucker Act's time limit. (Observing, in Justice Brandeis's words, that "it is more important that" the rule "be settled than that it be settled right" What is special about the Tucker Act's deadline, *John R. Sand* recognized, comes merely from this Court's prior rulings, not from Congress's choice of wording.

The Government thus cannot show that the phrase "shall be forever barred" in § 2401(b) plainly signifies a jurisdictional statute, as our decisions require. Unlike in *John R. Sand*, here *stare decisis* plays no role: We have not previously considered whether § 2401(b) restricts a court's authority. What we have done is to say, again and again, that the core language in that provision has no jurisdictional significance. It is materially indistinguishable from the language in one nonjurisdictional time bar. Yes, we have held that the Tucker Act's time bar, which includes those same words, constrains a court's power to hear late claims. But as we explained in *Irwin*, that is not because the phrase itself "manifests a ... congressional intent with respect to the availability of equitable tolling." The words on which the Government pins its hopes are just the words of a limitations statute of a particular era. And nothing else supports the Government's claim that Congress, when enacting the FTCA, wanted to incorporate this Court's view of the Tucker Act's time bar—much less that Congress expressed that purported intent with the needed clear statement.

## B

The Government next contends that at the time of the FTCA's enactment, Congress thought that *every* limitations statute applying to suits against the United States, however framed or worded, cut off a court's jurisdiction over untimely claims. On that view, the particular language of those statutes makes no difference. All that matters is that such time limits function as conditions on the Government's waiver of sovereign immunity. In that era—indeed, up until *Irwin* was decided—those conditions were generally supposed to be "strictly observed." That meant, the Government urges, that all time limits on actions against the United States "carried jurisdictional consequences." Accordingly, the Government concludes, Congress "would have expected courts to apply § 2401(b) as a jurisdictional requirement—just as conditions on waivers of sovereign immunity had always been applied."

In the years since, this Court has repeatedly followed *Irwin*'s lead. We have applied *Irwin* to pre-*Irwin* statutes, just as we have to statutes that followed in that decision's wake. To be sure, *Irwin*'s presumption is rebuttable. But the rebuttal cannot rely on what *Irwin* itself deemed irrelevant—that Congress passed the statute in an earlier era, when this Court often attached jurisdictional consequence to conditions on waivers of sovereign immunity. Rather, the rebuttal must identify something distinctive about the time limit at issue, whether enacted then or later—a reason for thinking Congress wanted *that* limitations statute (not all statutes passed in an earlier day) to curtail a court's jurisdiction. On the Government's contrary view, *Irwin* would effectively become only a prospective decision. Nothing could be less consonant with *Irwin*'s ambition to adopt a "general rule to govern the applicability of equitable tolling in suits against the Government."

The Government's claim is peculiarly inapt as applied to § 2401(b) because all that is special about the FTCA cuts *in favor of* allowing equitable tolling. As compared to other waivers of immunity (prominently including the Tucker Act), the FTCA treats the United States more like a commoner than like the Crown. The FTCA's jurisdictional provision states that courts may hear suits "under circumstances where the United States, if a private person, would be liable to the claimant." 28 U.S.C. § 1346(b). And when defining substantive liability for torts, the Act reiterates that the United States is accountable "in the same manner and to the same extent as a private individual." § 2674. In keeping with those provisions, this Court has often rejected the Government's calls to cabin the FTCA on the ground that it waives sovereign immunity—and indeed, the Court did so in the years immediately after the Act's passage, even as it was construing *other* waivers of immunity narrowly. There is no reason to do differently here. As *Irwin* recognized, treating the Government like a private person means (among other things) permitting equitable tolling. So in stressing the Government's equivalence to a private party, the FTCA goes further than the typical statute waiving sovereign immunity to indicate that its time bar allows a court to hear late claims.

## IV

Our precedents make this a clear-cut case. *Irwin* requires an affirmative indication from Congress that it intends to preclude equitable tolling in a suit against the Government. Congress can provide that signal by making a statute of limitations jurisdictional. But that requires its own plain statement; otherwise, we treat a time bar as a mere claims-processing rule. Congress has supplied no such statement here. As this Court has repeatedly stated, nothing about § 2401(b)'s core language is special; "shall be forever barred" is an ordinary (albeit old-fashioned) way of setting a deadline, which does not preclude tolling when circumstances warrant. And it makes no difference that a time bar conditions a waiver of sovereign immunity, even if Congress enacted the measure when different interpretive conventions applied; that is the very point of this Court's decision to treat time bars in suits against the Government, whenever passed, the same as in litigation between private parties. Accordingly, we hold that the FTCA's time bars are nonjurisdictional and subject to equitable tolling.

We affirm the judgments of the U.S. Court of Appeals for the Ninth Circuit and remand the cases for further proceedings consistent with this opinion. On remand in *June,* it is for the District Court to decide whether, on the facts of her case, June is entitled to equitable tolling.

## B. SPECIAL NOTICE REQUIREMENTS FOR SUING THE GOVERNMENT

12. As you have seen, there are always obstacles to be overcome when attempting to sue any governmental entity. The first obstacle is the brick wall of sovereign immunity. You cannot sue the government without its consent. Fortunately, virtually all governmental entities will by now have cut some specific holes in the wall of sovereign immunity – specific waivers of sovereign immunity for specific situations, such as the Federal Tort Claims Act or the Tucker Act.

Once you are able to get through that brick wall of sovereign immunity by fitting your case into one of the specific holes in the wall of sovereign immunity you will be faced with a fence – the applicable statute of limitations. The particular statute of limitations may, or may not, be subject to equitable tolling.

Assuming that you are able to get over the fence of the statute of limitations, you are very likely to find one more obstacle – a very high, razor-wire fence requiring that *notice* must have been given to the governmental entity within a very short time after the particular incident occurred. These notice requirements are frequently very strict – you must have given notice to exactly the right person with the governmental entity within a very short time after the incident occurred – usually only about 90 or 180 *days*!

Thus, after finding a way through the brick wall of sovereign immunity, and having gotten over the fence of the statute of limitations, you may find that you nevertheless are totally barred by the razor-wire fence of the notice requirement.

It does not matter whether or not the governmental entity was at fault. It cannot be sued unless it was given *notice* of the incident within 180 *days* of the time the cause of action first accrued – or within whatever other specific number of *days* is specified in the notice statute.

182 P.3D 687

# SUPREME COURT OF COLORADO

## COLORADO DEPARTMENT OF TRANSPORTATION, PETITIONER

### V.

## BROWN GROUP RETAIL, INC., A PENNSYLVANIA CORPORATION, RESPONDENT.

DECIDED APRIL 14, 2008

Justice COATS delivered the Opinion of the Court.

The Colorado Department of Transportation sought review of the court of appeals' judgment affirming the denial of its motion to dismiss this groundwater contamination case. Although the district court found Brown Group's claims of trespass and negligent storage and disposal of hazardous waste barred by the Colorado Governmental Immunity Act, it denied the Department's motion to dismiss Brown Group's claims for contribution, unjust enrichment, and declaratory relief, finding them to be equitable in nature and not governed by the Act. The court of appeals affirmed.

Because Brown Group's claims for contribution, unjust enrichment, and declaratory relief all assert claims of liability against the Department that either lie in tort or could lie in tort within the meaning of the Governmental Immunity Act, they are governed by it and must meet its prerequisites. Because Brown Group failed to comply with the notice requirement of the Act, the judgment of the court of appeals is reversed and remanded with directions to order dismissal of Brown Group's second, third, and seventh claims for relief.

I

Brown Group Retail, Inc., brought suit against the Colorado Department of Transportation asserting, among other things, various claims arising from the Department's alleged contamination of one of Brown Group's manufacturing sites and its failure to reimburse Brown Group for a portion of the costs incurred in cleaning up the contamination at both that site and a contiguous residential neighborhood. The Department moved to dismiss the complaint for lack of jurisdiction, on grounds that Brown Group failed to comply with the 180-day notice requirement of the Governmental Immunity Act. For purposes of this jurisdictional determination, the court heard testimony from both parties and accepted a joint stipulation of facts and numerous uncontested exhibits.

As a result of environmental assessments done in 1994, Brown Group discovered both soil and groundwater pollution at its Redfield manufacturing site and learned that chlorinated solvents had likely migrated through groundwater to an adjacent residential neighborhood. In May 1997, it advised the Colorado Department of Public Health and Environment ("CDPHE") of its investigation and proposed a remediation program. The CDPHE ultimately determined that Brown Group's proposed remediation program was insufficient and in May 1998 issued a compliance order, directing it to take specific steps to remedy the pollution on both its own and the adjacent property.

Chlorinated solvents disposed of by the Department at its Region 6 Headquarters, adjoining the Redfield site, also migrated by groundwater onto Brown Group's property and from there into the adjacent neighborhood. Although the district court found that Brown Group should have known as early as December 1994 that the contaminants traveling off its property were coming in part from the property owned by the Department, Brown Group failed to give notice to the Department until April 1998, just weeks before receiving the CDPHE's compliance order. Brown Group's April 1998 letter to the Department requested that it share in the expense of investigating and remediating the pollution.

In December 2003, Brown Group filed its complaint, stating eight separate claims for relief. Brown Group alleged that the Department trespassed on its property when contaminants traveled from the Department's property onto the Redfield site, and it sought damages for that trespass. Brown Group also claimed that the Department was negligent in the storage and disposal of industrial solvents and sought damages in the form of reimbursement for that portion of its remediation costs attributable to the Department's negligence.

In addition to these seemingly straightforward tort claims, Brown Group also brought claims for contribution and unjust enrichment, again alleging that the Department was liable for a portion of the substantial costs Brown Group incurred in complying with CDPHE's order. Finally, Brown Group requested a declaration that the Department was responsible for a pro rata share of past, present, and future costs expended in complying with the CDPHE compliance order.

The district court granted the Department's motion to dismiss for failure to comply with the notice requirements of the Governmental Immunity Act with regard to the claims of trespass and negligence, but it denied the motion with regard to the claims of contribution, unjust enrichment, and declaratory judgment. The district court reasoned that the latter claims, which it distinguished as seeking restitution rather than damages, were equitable in nature and therefore not subject to the Act. Both parties appealed various aspects of the district court's ruling, and the court of appeals affirmed. We granted the Department's petition for writ of certiorari to review the denial of its motion regarding its claims seeking contribution, unjust enrichment, and declaratory relief.

## II

*gov cannot be sued w/o its consent*

Although we had never attempted any meaningful theoretical justification, until 1971 this court openly acknowledged the doctrine of sovereign or governmental immunity and applied it to bar nonconsensual court suits against subdivisions of the state or local governments. In that year, primarily for policy reasons, a majority of this court found it appropriate "simply to undo" what we had done and leave to the General Assembly the future existence of any such doctrine or doctrines. We made clear at that time our understanding that it would be within the authority of the legislature to restore sovereign immunity in whole or in part, and if the latter, to place limitations on the actions that might be brought against the state and its subdivisions.

The legislature immediately obliged by enacting the Colorado Governmental Immunity Act. As presently codified, the Act specifically waives sovereign immunity for injuries resulting from dangerous conditions in or along an access to, or from the operation or maintenance of, a host of public facilities, vehicles, roadways, and assets; and it also provides for a further waiver of immunity at the choice of the governing body of any public entity. As a jurisdictional prerequisite to any action claiming injury by a public entity, however, the Act requires that notice be given within 180 days of discovering the injury, and that the public entity be given 90 days to consider and respond before being sued. § 24-10-109.

Unlike those jurisdictions in which the doctrine of sovereign immunity had never been judicially abrogated, however, the Colorado legislature was faced with the task of creating and defining the reach of sovereign immunity in this jurisdiction, before specifying the circumstances in which it would be legislatively waived. As a result, its statutory scheme first broadly defined the nature of the claims to which the Act was intended to apply, and re-imposed a bar to any such claims not falling within one of the Act's enumerated exceptions. To accomplish this objective it therefore extended its coverage to all actions which lie or could lie in tort, regardless of the type of action actually pled by the claimant.

To the extent the legislature has considered subsequent court decisions as too narrowly construing its mandate, it has responded, sometimes redundantly, by reemphasizing the breadth of its initial intent.

While the notion of a "tort" is notoriously difficult to define with any degree of precision, and the expansive statutory phrase "lies in tort or could lie in tort," adds to the difficulty of defining the Act's intended coverage, there can be little doubt that the legislature used this language in reference to the breach of a general duty of care, as distinguished from the breach of a contract or other agreement.

### III

Both the district court and court of appeals appear to have been overly concerned with what they considered to be the equitable nature of Brown Group's claims of contribution, unjust enrichment, and declaratory relief, and most particularly with the fact that they did not seek compensation for damages directly caused by tortious conduct of the Department. When examined in light of their factual allegations, however, there can be no doubt that all three claims are premised upon, and could succeed only upon a demonstration of, the Department's liability for tortious conduct.

Although a right to contribution has long been recognized, in a number of non-tort contexts, as a basis for requiring restitution to the party performing a joint obligation, and at the same time preventing the unjust enrichment of the nonperforming party, Brown Group's claim expressly asserts only a statutory entitlement to "equitable apportionment of damages," as now permitted by the Uniform Contribution Among Tortfeasors Act. Brown Group openly understands that this claim is necessarily contingent upon the Department's joint and several liability as a tortfeasor. It merely relies on the distinction between an action for contribution and one directly seeking recovery by the tort victim himself to support its assertion of noncoverage by the Governmental Immunity Act.

The coverage of the Act, however, is not limited to claims that are presented, or are capable of being presented, directly by the claimant as tort claims. Rather it more broadly encompasses all claims against a public entity arising from the breach of a general duty of care, as distinguished from contractual relations or a distinctly non-tortious statutorily-imposed duty.

Similarly, although the theoretical justification for ordering restitution to prevent unjust enrichment is often couched in terms of constructive or quasi contract, whether a particular claim lies in tort or could lie in tort within the meaning of the Act depends upon the factual basis underlying the claim. Whether a party has been unjustly (or unjustifiably) enriched, however, becomes an issue only if it has been enriched by receiving a benefit at the expense of another. Brown Group's claim of unjust enrichment is premised upon its allegation that the Department has benefited from Brown Group's reparation of damages for which the Department is jointly and severally liable in tort. For virtually the same reasons its claim for contribution falls within the coverage of the Act, so too does its claim of unjust enrichment.

Finally, Brown Group's claim for a declaration that the Department is responsible for a pro rata share of past, present, and future costs expended in complying with the CDPHE order is wholly derivative of its claims for contribution and unjust enrichment. The nature of the relief requested is not dispositive of coverage by the Act, and the mere fact that a claim for relief seeks a declaration of liability resulting from tortious conduct rather than actual damages for the tortious conduct itself has no impact with regard to coverage.

## IV

Because Brown Group's claims for contribution, unjust enrichment, and declaratory relief, all assert claims of liability against the Department that either lie in tort or could lie in tort within the meaning of the Governmental Immunity Act, they are governed by it and must meet its prerequisites. Because Brown Group's notice was held to be untimely for claims based on the same underlying conduct, and that finding is not at issue here, the judgment of the court of appeals is reversed and the case is remanded with directions to order dismissal of Brown Group's second, third, and seventh claims for relief and for further appropriate proceedings on the remaining claims.

# C. SERVICE OF PROCESS – NOTICE

13. Rule 3 of the Federal Rules of Civil Procedure (FRCP) provides that "A civil action is commenced by filing a complaint with the court." That is enough to comply with the statute of limitations. But it is not enough to give the court control over the defendant. In order for the court to establish control over the defendant, the defendant must be served with a copy of the complaint – and a *Summons* – directing the defendant to appear in court and answer the complaint.

   FRCP 4(c)(1) provides that the summons and a copy of the complaint must be served together on the defendant. Service may be made by any person who is over the age of eighteen, and is not a party to the action. (FRCP 4(c)(2)) Normally, service must be made on the defendant within 120 days after the complaint is filed with the court (FRCP 4(m), but that time may be extended by the court under certain circumstances.

   There are limits, however, as to when service of process will be effective to give a court jurisdiction over a defendant. For example, if a defendant who has always lived in Maine is personally served in Maine with a summons and complaint directing her to appear in a specific court in *California* that, alone, will *not* give the California court any jurisdiction over the person who lives in Maine.

14. The following case, *Pennoyer v. Neff*, is the landmark case setting forth when service of process outside the borders of a state will – or will not – give the state jurisdiction over an out-of-state defendant.

   Although modifications have been made over the last 140 years of so to the principles set forth in *Pennoyer v. Neff*, the fundamentals remain the same.

   The case of *Pennoyer v. Neff* included below was really the second of two important lawsuits. In the first lawsuit a lawyer named *Mitchell* had sued Neff, his former client, in order to collect the attorney's fees which Mitchell claimed were owed to him by Neff. Neff was not personally served within the state, and did not respond to Mitchell's suit. So Mitchell got a default judgment against Neff, and had Neff's land sold to pay the judgment. The land was sold to a third party, named Pennoyer.

When Neff found out what had happened, Neff (successfully) sued Pennoyer to get his land back. It is the opinion in that second suit, by Neff against Pennoyer, that is included below. [As you have probably noticed by now, the order of the names in an appellate opinion is frequently not the order of the names in the original lawsuit. It depends on who brought the case to the appellate court.]

The opinion below explains why the original judgment, in the case by Mitchell to collect his attorney's fees, was totally void.

## 95 U.S. 714
### SUPREME COURT OF THE UNITED STATES
### PENNOYER
### V.
### NEFF

OCTOBER TERM, 1877

**MR. JUSTICE FIELD delivered the opinion of the court.**

This is an action to recover the possession of a tract of land, of the alleged value of $15,000, situated in the State of Oregon. The plaintiff in this suit, (Neff) asserts title to the premises by a patent of the United States issued to him in 1866. The defendant in this suit, (Pennoyer) claims to have acquired the premises under a sheriff's deed, made upon a sale of the property on execution issued upon a judgment recovered against Neff in a prior case. This case turns upon the validity of that prior judgment.

It appears from the record that the judgment [in the prior case] was rendered in February, 1866, in favor of J. H. Mitchell, for less than $300, in an action brought by attorney Mitchell against Neff upon a demand for services as an attorney; that, at the time the prior action was commenced and the judgment rendered, the plaintiff here (Neff), was a non-resident of the State, that he was not personally served with process, and did not appear therein; and that the judgment was entered upon his default in not answering the complaint, upon a constructive service of summons by publication.

The Code of Oregon provides for such service when an action is brought against a non-resident and absent defendant, who has property within the State. It also provides, where the action is for the recovery of money or damages, for the attachment of the property of the non-resident. And it also declares that no natural person is subject to the jurisdiction of a court of the State, 'unless he appear in the court, or be found within the State, or be a resident thereof, or have property therein; and, in the last case, only to the extent of such property at the time the jurisdiction attached.' Construing this latter provision to mean, that, in an action for money or damages where a defendant does not appear in the court, and is not found within the State, and is not a resident thereof, but has property therein, the jurisdiction of the court extends only over such property, the declaration expresses a principle of general, if not universal, law. The authority of every tribunal is necessarily restricted by the territorial limits of the State in which it is established. Any attempt to exercise authority beyond those limits would be deemed in every other forum as an illegitimate assumption of power, and be resisted as mere abuse. In the [original] case against [Neff] the property here in controversy was not attached, nor in any way brought under the jurisdiction of the court. Its first connection with the case was caused by a levy of the execution. It was not, therefore, disposed of pursuant to any adjudication, but only in enforcement of a personal judgment, having no relation to the property, rendered against a non-resident without service of process upon him in the action, or his appearance therein. The court below held that the judgment was invalid.

It is insisted here that the judgment in the State court against the plaintiff was void for want of personal service of process on him, or of his appearance in the action in which it was rendered and that the premises in controversy could not be subjected to the payment of the demand of a resident creditor except by a proceeding *in rem;* that is, by a direct proceeding against the property for that purpose. If these positions are sound, the ruling of the Circuit Court as to the invalidity of that judgment must be sustained. That they are sound would seem to follow from two well-established principles of public law respecting the jurisdiction of an independent State over persons and property. The several States of the Union are not, it is true, in every respect independent, many of the rights and powers which originally belonged to them being now vested in the government created by the Constitution. But, except as restrained and limited by that instrument, they possess and exercise the authority of independent States, and the principles of public law to which we have referred are applicable to them. One of these principles is, that every State possesses exclusive jurisdiction and sovereignty over persons and property within its territory. As a consequence, every State has the power to determine for itself the civil *status* and capacities of its inhabitants; to prescribe the subjects upon which they may contract, the forms and solemnities with which their contracts shall be executed, the rights and obligations arising from them, and the mode in which their validity shall be determined and their obligations enforced; and also to regulate the manner and conditions upon which property situated within such territory, both personal and real, may be acquired, enjoyed, and transferred. The other principle of public law referred to follows from the one mentioned; that is, that no State can exercise direct jurisdiction and authority over persons or property without its territory. The several States are of equal dignity and authority, and the independence of one implies the exclusion of power from all others. And so it is laid down by jurists, as an elementary principle, that the laws of one State have no operation outside of its territory, except so far as is allowed by comity; and that no tribunal established by it can extend its process beyond that territory so as to subject either persons or property to its decisions. 'Any exertion of authority of this sort beyond this limit,' says Story, 'is a mere nullity, and incapable of binding such persons or property in any other tribunals.'

But as contracts made in one State may be enforceable only in another State, and property may be held by non-residents, the exercise of the jurisdiction which every State is admitted to possess over persons and property within its own territory will often affect persons and property without it. Thus the State, through its tribunals, may compel persons domiciled within its limits to execute, in pursuance of their contracts respecting property elsewhere situated, instruments in such form and with such solemnities as to transfer the title, so far as such formalities can be complied with; and the exercise of this jurisdiction in no manner interferes with the supreme control over the property by the State within which it is situated.

So the State, through its tribunals, may subject property situated within its limits owned by non-residents to the payment of the demand of its own citizens against them; and the exercise of this jurisdiction in no respect infringes upon the sovereignty of the State where the owners are domiciled. Every State owes protection to its own citizens; and, when non-residents deal with them, it is a legitimate and just exercise of authority to hold and appropriate any property owned by such non-residents to satisfy the claims of its citizens. It is in virtue of the State's jurisdiction over the property of the non-resident situated within its limits that its tribunals can inquire into that non-resident's obligations to its own citizens, and the inquiry can then be carried only to the extent necessary to control the disposition of the property. If the non-resident have no property in the State, there is nothing upon which the tribunals can adjudicate.

'Where a party is within a territory, he may justly be subjected to its process, and bound personally by the judgment pronounced on such process against him. Where he is not within such territory, and is not personally subject to its laws, if, on account of his supposed or actual property being within the territory, process by the local laws may, by attachment, go to compel his appearance, and for his default to appear judgment may be pronounced against him, such a judgment must, upon general principles, be deemed only to bind him to the extent of such property, and cannot have the effect of a conclusive judgment *in personam*, for the plain reason, that, except so far as the property is concerned, it is a judgment *coram non judice.'*

If, without personal service, judgments *in personam*, obtained *ex parte* against non-residents and absent parties, upon mere publication of process, which, in the great majority of cases, would never be seen by the parties interested, could be upheld and enforced, they would be the constant instruments of fraud and oppression. Judgments for all sorts of claims upon contracts and for torts, real or pretended, would be thus obtained, under which property would be seized, when the evidence of the transactions upon which they were founded, if they ever had any existence, had perished.

Substituted service by publication, or in any other authorized form, may be sufficient to inform parties of the object of proceedings taken where property is once brought under the control of the court by seizure or some equivalent act. The law assumes that property is always in the possession of its owner, in person or by agent; and it proceeds upon the theory that its seizure will inform him, not only that it is taken into the custody of the court, but that he must look to any proceedings authorized by law upon such seizure for its condemnation and sale. Such service may also be sufficient in cases where the object of the action is to reach and dispose of property in the State, or of some interest therein, by enforcing a contract or a lien respecting the same, or to partition it among different owners, or, when the public is a party, to condemn and appropriate it for a public purpose. In other words, such service may answer in all actions which are substantially proceedings *in rem.* But where the entire object of the action is to determine the personal rights and obligations of the defendants, that is, where the suit is merely *in personam,* constructive service in this form upon a non-resident is ineffectual for any purpose. Process from  the tribunals of one State cannot run into another State, and summon parties there domiciled to leave its territory and respond to proceedings against them. Publication of process or notice within the State where the tribunal sits cannot create any greater obligation upon the non-resident to appear. Process sent to him out of the State, and process published within it, are equally unavailing in proceedings to establish his personal liability.

The jurisdiction of the court to inquire into and determine his obligations at all is only incidental to its jurisdiction over the property. Its jurisdiction in that respect cannot be made to depend upon facts to be ascertained after it has tried the cause and rendered the judgment. If the judgment be previously void, it will not become valid by the subsequent discovery of property of the defendant, or by his subsequent acquisition of it. The judgment, if void when rendered, will always remain void: it cannot occupy the doubtful position of being valid if property be found, and void if there be none.

The validity of every judgment depends upon the jurisdiction of the court before it is rendered, not upon what may occur subsequently. To give such proceedings any validity, there must be a tribunal competent by its constitution—that is, by the law of its creation—to pass upon the subject-matter of the suit; and, if that involves merely a determination of the personal liability of the defendant, he must be brought within its jurisdiction by service of process within the State, or his voluntary appearance.

Except in cases affecting the personal *status* of the plaintiff, and cases in which that mode of service may be considered to have been assented to in advance, the substituted service of process by publication, allowed by the law of Oregon and by similar laws in other States, where actions are brought against non-residents, is effectual only where, in connection with process against the person for commencing the action, property in the State is brought under the control of the court, and subjected to its disposition by process adapted to that purpose, or where the judgment is sought as a means of reaching such property or affecting some interest therein; in other words, where the action is in the nature of a proceeding *in rem*.

It is true that, in a strict sense, a proceeding *in rem* is one taken directly against property, and has for its object the disposition of the property, without reference to the title of individual claimants; but, in a larger and more general sense, the terms are applied to actions between parties, where the direct object is to reach and dispose of property owned by them, or of some interest therein. Such are cases commenced by attachment against the property of debtors, or instituted to partition real estate, foreclose a mortgage, or enforce a lien. So far as they affect property in the State, they are substantially proceedings *in rem* in the broader sense which we have mentioned.

It follows from the views expressed that the personal judgment recovered in the State court of Oregon against the plaintiff herein, then a non-resident of the State, was without any validity, and did not authorize a sale of the property in controversy.

To prevent any misapplication of the views expressed in this opinion, it is proper to observe that we do not mean to assert, by any thing we have said, that a State may not authorize proceedings to determine the *status* of one of its citizens towards a non-resident, which would be binding within the State, though made without service of process or personal notice to the non-resident. The jurisdiction which every State possesses to determine the civil *status* and capacities of all its inhabitants involves authority to prescribe the conditions on which proceedings affecting them may be commenced and carried on within its territory. The State, for example, has absolute right to prescribe the conditions upon which the marriage relation between its own citizens shall be created, and the causes for which it may be dissolved. One of the

*[handwritten margin note: Oregon can terminate marriage in Oregon]*

*[handwritten note at bottom:]*
in personam = against a person → didn't have b/c wasn't served
in rem = against a thing → didn't have b/c didn't own property

parties guilty of acts for which, by the law of the State, a dissolution may be granted, may have removed to a State where no dissolution is permitted. The complaining party would, therefore, fail if a divorce were sought in the State of the defendant; and if application could not be made to the tribunals of the complainant's domicile in such case, and proceedings be there instituted without personal service of process or personal notice to the offending party, the injured citizen would be without redress.

Neither do we mean to assert that a State may not require a non-resident entering into a partnership or association within its limits, or making contracts enforceable there, to appoint an agent or representative in the State to receive service of process and notice in legal proceedings instituted with respect to such partnership, association, or contracts, or to designate a place where such service may be made and notice given, and provide, upon their failure, to make such appointment or to designate such place that service may be made upon a public officer designated for that purpose, or in some other prescribed way, and that judgments rendered upon such service may not be binding upon the non-residents both within and without the State.

Nor do we doubt that a State, on creating corporations or other institutions for pecuniary or charitable purposes, may provide a mode in which their conduct may be investigated, their obligations enforced, or their charters revoked, which shall require other than personal service upon their officers or members.

In the present case, there is no feature of this kind, and, consequently, no consideration of what would be the effect of such legislation in enforcing the contract of a non-resident can arise. The question here respects only the validity of a money judgment rendered in one State, in an action upon a simple contract against the resident of another, without service of process upon him, or his appearance therein.

*Judgment affirmed.*

15. There are two major reasons for requiring service of process. One is to give the court jurisdiction over the defendant. The other is to give the defendant notice that he is being sued.

In some cases, personal service on a defendant may not be required to give the court jurisdiction over certain property of the defendant. But the plaintiff will always be required to give the defendant enough "notice reasonably calculated, under all the circumstances, to apprise the defendant of the pendency of the action, and afford the defendant an opportunity to present objections."

The following case, decided more than 70 years after *Pennoyer v. Neff*, announces some modifications to the clear-cut rule of *Pennoyer v. Neff*, and sets forth a standard by which the adequacy of notice is to be measured. This still remains the fundamental standard today.

## 70 S.CT. 652
## SUPREME COURT OF THE UNITED STATES
## MULLANE
## V.
## CENTRAL HANOVER BANK & TRUST CO. ET AL.

DECIDED APRIL 24, 1950

**Mr. Justice JACKSON delivered the opinion of the Court.**

This controversy questions the constitutional sufficiency of notice to beneficiaries on judicial settlement of accounts by the trustee of a common trust fund established under the New York Banking Law. The New York Court of Appeals considered and overruled objections that the statutory notice contravenes requirements of the Fourteenth Amendment and that by allowance of the account beneficiaries were deprived of property without due process of law. The case is here on appeal.

Common trust fund legislation is addressed to a problem appropriate for state action. Mounting overheads have made administration of small trusts undesirable to corporate trustees. In order that donors and testators of moderately sized trusts may not be denied the service of corporate fiduciaries, the District of Columbia and some thirty states other than New York have permitted pooling small trust estates into one fund for investment administration. The income, capital gains, losses and expenses of the collective trust are shared by the constituent trusts in proportion to their contribution. By this plan, diversification of risk and economy of management can be extended to those whose capital standing alone would not obtain such advantage.

Statutory authorization for the establishment of such common trust funds is provided in the New York Banking Law. Under this Act a trust company may, with approval of the State Banking Board, establish a common fund and, within prescribed limits, invest therein the assets of an unlimited number of estates, trusts or other funds of which it is trustee. Each participating trust shares ratably in the common fund, but exclusive management and control is in the trust company as trustee, and neither a fiduciary nor any beneficiary of a participating trust is deemed to have ownership in any particular asset or investment of this common fund. The trust company must keep fund assets separate from its own, and in its fiduciary capacity may not deal with itself or any affiliate. Provisions are made for accountings twelve to fifteen months after the establishment of a fund and triennially thereafter. The decree in each such judicial settlement of accounts is made binding and conclusive as to any matter set forth in the account upon everyone having any interest in the common fund or in any participating estate, trust or fund.

In January, 1946, Central Hanover Bank and Trust Company established a common trust fund in accordance with these provisions, and in March, 1947, it petitioned the Surrogate's Court for settlement of its first account as common trustee. During the accounting period a total of 113 trusts participated in the common trust fund, the gross capital of which was nearly three million dollars. The record does not show the number or residence of the beneficiaries, but they were many and it is clear that some of them were not residents of the State of New York.

The only notice given beneficiaries of this specific application was by publication in a local newspaper in strict compliance with the minimum requirements of N.Y. Banking Law. Thus the only notice required, and the only one given, was by newspaper publication setting forth merely the name and address of the trust company, the name and the date of establishment of the common trust fund, and a list of all participating estates, trusts or funds.

At the time the first investment in the common fund was made, however, the trust company, pursuant to the requirements of the Act, had notified by mail each person of full age and sound mind whose name and address was then known to it and who was 'entitled to share in the income therefrom (or) who would be entitled to share in the principal if the event upon which such estate, trust or fund will become distributable should have occurred at the time of sending such notice.' Included in the notice was a copy of those provisions of the Act relating to the sending of the notice itself and to the judicial settlement of common trust fund accounts.

Upon the filing of the petition for the settlement of accounts, appellant was, by order of the court, appointed special guardian and attorney for all persons known or unknown not otherwise appearing who had or might thereafter have any interest in the income of the common trust fund; and appellee Vaughan was appointed to represent those similarly interested in the principal. There were no other appearances on behalf of anyone interested in either interest or principal.

Appellant appeared specially, objecting that notice and the statutory provisions for notice to beneficiaries were inadequate to afford due process under the Fourteenth Amendment, and therefore that the court was without jurisdiction to render a final and binding decree. Appellant's objections were entertained and overruled, the

due process = fair treatment through judicial system : given life, liberty, & property

Surrogate holding that the notice required and given was sufficient. A final decree accepting the accounts has been entered, affirmed by the Appellate Division of the Supreme Court, and by the Court of Appeals of the State of New York.

The effect of this decree is to settle 'all questions respecting the management of the common fund.' We understand that every right which beneficiaries would otherwise have against the trust company, either as trustee of the common fund or as trustee of any individual trust, for improper management of the common trust fund during the period covered by the accounting is sealed and wholly terminated by the decree.

We are met at the outset with a challenge to the power of the State—the right of its courts to adjudicate at all as against those beneficiaries who reside without the State of New York. It is contended that the proceeding is one in personam in that the decree affects neither title to nor possession of any res, but adjudges only personal rights of the beneficiaries to surcharge their trustee for negligence or breach of trust. Accordingly, it is said, under the strict doctrine of *Pennoyer v. Neff* the Surrogate is without jurisdiction as to nonresidents upon whom personal service of process was not made.

Distinctions between actions in rem and those in personam are ancient and originally expressed in procedural terms what seems really to have been a distinction in the substantive law of property under a system quite unlike our own. The legal recognition and rise in economic importance of incorporeal or intangible forms of property have upset the ancient simplicity of property law and the clarity of its distinctions, while new forms of proceedings have confused the old procedural classification. American courts have sometimes classed certain actions as in rem because personal service of process was not required, and at other times have held personal service of process not required because the action was in rem.

Judicial proceedings to settle fiduciary accounts have been sometimes termed in rem, or more indefinitely quasi in rem, or more vaguely still, 'in the nature of a proceeding in rem.' It is not readily apparent how the courts of New York did or would classify the present proceeding, which has some characteristics and is wanting in some features of proceedings both in rem and in personam. But in any event we think that the requirements of the Fourteenth Amendment to the Federal Constitution do not depend upon a classification for which the standards are so elusive and confused generally and which, being primarily for state courts to define, may and do vary from state to state. Without disparaging the usefulness of distinctions between actions in rem and those in personam in many branches of law, or on other issues, or the reasoning which underlies them, we do not rest the power of the State to resort to constructive service in this proceeding upon how its courts or this Court may regard

Due Process Clause: an individual must recieve notice before they can be deprived of life, liberty, or property in a judicial proceeding

this historic antithesis. It is sufficient to observe that, whatever the technical definition of its chosen procedure, the interest of each state in providing means to close
trusts that exist by the grace of its laws and are administered under the supervision
of its courts is so insistent and rooted in custom as to establish beyond doubt the
right of its courts to determine the interests of all claimants, resident or nonresident,
provided its procedure accords full opportunity to appear and be heard.

Quite different from the question of a state's power to discharge trustees is that of
the opportunity it must give beneficiaries to contest. Many controversies have raged
about the cryptic and abstract words of the Due Process Clause but there can be no
doubt that at a minimum they require that deprivation of life, liberty or property by
adjudication be preceded by notice and opportunity for hearing appropriate to the
nature of the case.

In two ways this proceeding does or may deprive beneficiaries of property. It may
cut off their rights to have the trustee answer for negligent or illegal impairments of
their interests. Also, their interests are presumably subject to diminution in the proceeding by allowance of fees and expenses to one who, in their names but without
their knowledge, may conduct a fruitless or uncompensatory contest. Certainly the
proceeding is one in which they may be deprived of property rights and hence notice
and hearing must measure up to the standards of due process.

Personal service of written notice within the jurisdiction is the classic form of
notice always adequate in any type of proceeding. But the vital interest of the State
in bringing any issues as to its fiduciaries to a final settlement can be served only if
interests or claims of individuals who are outside of the State can somehow be determined. A construction of the Due Process Clause which would place impossible or
impractical obstacles in the way could not be justified.

Against this interest of the State we must balance the individual interest sought to
be protected by the Fourteenth Amendment. This is defined by our holding that 'The
fundamental requisite of due process of law is the opportunity to be heard.' This right
to be heard has little reality or worth unless one is informed that the matter is pending and can choose for himself whether to appear or default, acquiesce or contest.

The Court has not committed itself to any formula achieving a balance between
these interests in a particular proceeding or determining when constructive notice
may be utilized or what test it must meet. Personal service has not in all circumstances been regarded as indispensable to the process due to residents, and it has
more often been held unnecessary as to nonresidents. We disturb none of the established rules on these subjects. No decision constitutes a controlling or even a very
illuminating precedent for the case before us. But a few general principles stand out
in the books.

An elementary and fundamental requirement of due process in any proceeding which is to be accorded finality is notice reasonably calculated, under all the circumstances, to apprise interested parties of the pendency of the action and afford them an opportunity to present their objections. The notice must be of such nature as reasonably to convey the required information, and it must afford a reasonable time for those interested to make their appearance. But if with due regard for the practicalities and peculiarities of the case these conditions are reasonably met the constitutional requirements are satisfied. 'The criterion is not the possibility of conceivable injury, but the just and reasonable character of the requirements, having reference to the subject with which the statute deals.'

But when notice is a person's due, process which is a mere gesture is not due process. The means employed must be such as one desirous of actually informing the absentee might reasonably adopt to accomplish it. The reasonableness and hence the constitutional validity of any chosen method may be defended on the ground that it is in itself reasonably certain to inform those affected. Where conditions do not reasonably permit such notice, that the form chosen is not substantially less likely to bring home notice than other of the feasible and customary substitutes.

It would be idle to pretend that publication alone as prescribed here, is a reliable means of acquainting interested parties of the fact that their rights are before the courts. It is not an accident that the greater number of cases reaching this Court on the question of adequacy of notice have been concerned with actions founded on process constructively served through local newspapers. Chance alone brings to the attention of even a local resident an advertisement in small type inserted in the back pages of a newspaper, and if he makes his home outside the area of the newspaper's normal circulation the odds that the information will never reach him are large indeed. The chance of actual notice is further reduced when as here the notice required does not even name those whose attention it is supposed to attract, and does not inform acquaintances who might call it to attention. In weighing its sufficiency on the basis of equivalence with actual notice we are unable to regard this as more than a feint.

Nor is publication here reinforced by steps likely to attract the parties' attention to the proceeding. It is true that publication traditionally has been acceptable as notification supplemental to other action which in itself may reasonably be expected to convey a warning. The ways of an owner with tangible property are such that he usually arranges means to learn of any direct attack upon his possessory or proprietary rights. Hence, libel of a ship, attachment of a chattel or entry upon real estate in the name of law may reasonably be expected to come promptly to the owner's attention. When the state within which the owner has located such property seizes it for some reason, publication or posting affords an additional measure of notification. A state may indulge the assumption that one who has left tangible property in the state either has abandoned it, in which case proceedings against it deprive him of nothing, or that he has left some caretaker under a duty to let him know that it is being jeopardized. As phrased long ago by Chief Justice Marshall in The Mary, 9 Cranch 126, 144, 3 L.Ed. 678, 'It is the part of common prudence for all those who have any interest in a thing, to guard that interest by persons who are in a situation to protect it.'

In the case before us there is, of course, no abandonment. On the other hand these beneficiaries do have a resident fiduciary as caretaker of their interest in this property. But it is their caretaker who in the accounting becomes their adversary. Their trustee is released from giving notice of jeopardy, and no one else is expected to do so. Not even the special guardian is required or apparently expected to communicate with his ward and client, and, of course, if such a duty were merely transferred from the trustee to the guardian, economy would not be served and more likely the cost would be increased.

This Court has not hesitated to approve of resort to publication as a customary substitute in another class of cases where it is not reasonably possible or practicable to give more adequate warning. Thus it has been recognized that, in the case of persons missing or unknown, employment of an indirect and even a probably futile means of notification is all that the situation permits and creates no constitutional bar to a final decree foreclosing their rights. Those beneficiaries represented by appellant whose interests or whereabouts could not with due diligence be ascertained come clearly within this category. As to them the statutory notice is sufficient. However great the odds that publication will never reach the eyes of such unknown parties, it is not in the typical case much more likely to fail than any of the choices open to legislators endeavoring to prescribe the best notice practicable.

Nor do we consider it unreasonable for the State to dispense with more certain notice to those beneficiaries whose interests are either conjectural or future or, although they could be discovered upon investigation, do not in due course of business come to the knowledge of the common trustee. Whatever searches might be required in another situation under ordinary standards of diligence, in view of the character of the proceedings and the nature of the interests here involved we think them unnecessary. We recognize the practical difficulties and costs that would be attendant on frequent investigations into the status of great numbers of beneficiaries, many of whose interests in the common fund are so remote as to be ephemeral; and we have no doubt that such impracticable and extended searches are not required in the name of due process. The expense of keeping informed from day to day of substitutions among even current income beneficiaries and presumptive remaindermen, to say nothing of the far greater number of contingent beneficiaries, would impose a severe burden on the plan, and would likely dissipate its advantages. These are practical matters in which we should be reluctant to disturb the judgment of the state authorities.

Accordingly we overrule appellant's constitutional objections to published notice insofar as they are urged on behalf of any beneficiaries whose interests or addresses are unknown to the trustee.

As to known present beneficiaries of known place of residence, however, notice by publication stands on a different footing. Exceptions in the name of necessity do not sweep away the rule that within the limits of practicability notice must be such as is reasonably calculated to reach interested parties. Where the names and post office addresses of those affected by a proceeding are at hand, the reasons disappear for resort to means less likely than the mails to apprise them of its pendency.

The trustee has on its books the names and addresses of the income beneficiaries represented by appellant, and we find no tenable ground for dispensing with a serious effort to inform them personally of the accounting, at least by ordinary mail to the record addresses. Certainly sending them a copy of the statute months and perhaps years in advance does not answer this purpose. The trustee periodically remits their income to them, and we think that they might reasonably expect that with or apart from their remittances word might come to them personally that steps were being taken affecting their interests.

We need not weigh contentions that a requirement of personal service of citation on even the large number of known resident or nonresident beneficiaries would, by reasons of delay if not of expense, seriously interfere with the proper administration of the fund. Of course personal service even without the jurisdiction of the issuing authority serves the end of actual and personal notice, whatever power of compulsion it might lack. However, no such service is required under the circumstances. This type of trust presupposes a large number of small interests. The individual interest does not stand alone but is identical with that of a class. The rights of each in the integrity of the fund and the fidelity of the trustee are shared by many other beneficiaries. Therefore notice reasonably certain to reach most of those interested in objecting is likely to safeguard the interests of all, since any objections sustained would inure to the benefit of all. We think that under such circumstances reasonable risks that notice might not actually reach every beneficiary are justifiable. 'Now and then an extraordinary case may turn up, but constitutional law, like other mortal contrivances, has to take some chances, and in the great majority of instances, no doubt, justice will be done.'

The statutory notice to known beneficiaries is inadequate, not because in fact it fails to reach everyone, but because under the circumstances it is not reasonably calculated to reach those who could easily be informed by other means at hand. However it may have been in former times, the mails today are recognized as an efficient and inexpensive means of communication. Moreover, the fact that the trust company has been able to give mailed notice to known beneficiaries at the time the common trust fund was established is persuasive that postal notification at the time of accounting would not seriously burden the plan.

In some situations the law requires greater precautions in its proceedings than the business world accepts for its own purposes. In few, if any, will it be satisfied with less. Certainly it is instructive, in determining the reasonableness of the impersonal broadcast notification here used, to ask whether it would satisfy a prudent man of business, counting his pennies but finding it in his interest to convey information to many persons whose names and addresses are in his files. We are not satisfied that it would. Publication may theoretically be available for all the world to see, but it is too much in our day to suppose that each or any individual beneficiary does or could examine all that is published to see if something may be tucked away in it that affects his property interests. We have before indicated in reference to notice by publication that, 'Great caution should be used not to let fiction deny the fair play that can be secured only by a pretty close adhesion to fact.

We hold the notice of judicial settlement of accounts required by the New York Banking Law s 100-c(12) is incompatible with the requirements of the Fourteenth Amendment as a basis for adjudication depriving known persons whose whereabouts are also known of substantial property rights. Accordingly the judgment is reversed and the cause remanded for further proceedings not inconsistent with this opinion.

Reversed.

16. Query: Would the Due Process Clause require that when notice is being given to people who are known to speak only Spanish, then that notice must be required to be given in Spanish?

17. Sometimes a potential defendant will intentionally try to avoid service of process – so that the statute of limitations will run before suit can be properly commenced – and the potential defendant will walk away free. Sometimes the potential defendant gets away with it – and sometimes he or she does not.

Sixty-five years after *Mullane* the adequacy of notice may still be an issue.

342 P.3D 422

# SUPREME COURT OF COLORADO.
## IN-RE: LILLIAN R. MALM, PLAINTIFF,
### v.
## MARION BRIGITTE VILLEGAS, DEFENDANT.

DECIDED JANUARY 20, 2015

**JUSTICE COATS delivered the Opinion of the Court.**

Villegas petitioned for relief from an order of the district court granting Malm's motion to reopen her personal injury lawsuit, some six years after it had been marked inactive and closed. The court denied Villegas's motion to reconsider and dismiss the action for failure to prosecute, despite the passage of more than seven years between the filing and service of the complaint. Relying largely on Malm's self-reported efforts to find and serve Villegas, and Villegas's failure to demonstrate prejudice from the delay, the district court effectively found that service was had within a reasonable time.

Because service following commencement of the action by filing a complaint with the court was delayed for an unreasonable length of time, the district court abused its discretion in declining to dismiss the lawsuit for failure to prosecute. The rule is therefore made absolute, and the matter is remanded to the district court with directions to dismiss the action.

## I

Lillian Malm commenced this action against Marion Villegas by filing a complaint with the district court in December 2005. The complaint alleged that Villegas caused Malm to suffer personal injuries in an automobile accident in 2002, some two years and eleven months earlier. It was undisputed that the complaint was therefore filed approximately one month before expiration of the applicable three-year statute of limitations.

In September 2006, having failed to find and personally serve Villegas, Malm moved for permission to establish quasi in rem jurisdiction by attaching Villegas's insurance policy and accomplishing service through publication. Although the court granted her motion and she demonstrated service by publication, in response to a motion to dismiss for lack of personal jurisdiction by Villegas's insurer, appearing specially, the court ultimately found quasi in rem jurisdiction to be an improper means of acquiring jurisdiction over Villegas's property. Nonetheless, the court denied the motion to dismiss, finding that additional time was warranted to allow Malm to attempt personal service.

In September 2007, Malm filed a status report with the court, noting that she had been unable to locate and personally serve Villegas and requesting that the court take no further action at that time. The court granted the request, marking the case inactive and closed; ordered Malm to provide an updated status report within ninety days, detailing her active attempts to locate and serve the defendant; and invited Malm to move to reopen once service was completed. On December 10, 2007, Malm provided one such status update, indicating that she was continuing her efforts to locate and serve Villegas and would notify the court once service was complete.

No activity of record occurred for the next five years, but on June 27, 2013, Malm moved to reopen, alleging that "in early 2013 investigators retained by Plaintiff's counsel got a 'lead' that Defendant Villegas was living in Germany," and as a result, Villegas was served in Germany "in accordance with the Hague Convention on May 24, 2013." The district court granted the motion in August 2013.

Once the case was reopened, Villegas moved to reconsider, arguing that Malm's failure to make reasonable efforts after the case was closed in 2007 or to serve her within a reasonable time amounted to a failure to diligently prosecute. In a responsive pleading Malm reported her efforts to find and serve Villegas between 2007 and 2013, specifically asserting that she (1) retained the services of a "fourth" private investigator who undertook "expensive and time consuming research" and located Villegas's ex-husband in California, but that this and other leads did not prove productive; (2) attempted to evaluate whether a recently passed statute might allow her to utilize alternative methods of service; (3) retained yet another private investigator in 2012 who utilized "recently developed databases allowing investigators to better access international databases" and obtained some leads that Villegas might be living in Germany; and (4) retained the services of a "sixth" investigator, Ancillary Legal Corporation, which was ultimately able to locate and serve Villegas.

The district court denied the motion to reconsider, finding "that while the lack of 'activity of record' in the case from December 10, 2007 until June 27, 2013 constituted a prima facie failure to prosecute under C.R.C.P. 121 § 1–10," Malm had "evidenced significant activity in furtherance of her prosecution of this case between December 2007 and June 2013." In addition, the court found that no Colorado Rule of Civil Procedure defines a reasonable time in which to accomplish service in a foreign country and that Villegas failed to show she would be prejudiced by the reopening of the case.

Villegas petitioned pursuant to C.A.R. 21, seeking relief from this order, and we issued our rule to show cause why the district court had not abused its discretion in declining to dismiss for failure to prosecute.

II

Rule 3(a) of the Colorado Rules of Civil Procedure permits a civil action to be commenced either by filing a complaint with the court or by service of a summons and complaint on opposing parties. If the action is commenced by service of a summons and complaint, the complaint must be filed within fourteen days thereafter. If, however, the action is commenced by filing a complaint with the court, Rule 3 does not specify any particular period of time within which service must be accomplished. Effective September 5, 2013, C.R.C.P. 4(m) requires the court to dismiss such an action *without prejudice* or order service within a specified time, unless the defendant is served within sixty-three days after filing or good cause is shown for an extension. Rule 4(m) also makes clear that this prescription for dismissal without prejudice is not intended to apply to service in a foreign country as permitted by the civil rules.

Even before the adoption of C.R.C.P. 4(m), however, an action was subject to dismissal *with prejudice* for failure to prosecute if service on the opposing party was not had within a reasonable time after commencing an action by filing. Relying on our own case law concerning failure to prosecute in other contexts, we noted in *Garcia* that the determination whether a delay in serving opposing parties is unreasonable can involve consideration of a number of different factors, such as the length of delay, the reasons for delay, the prejudice that will result to the defendant by allowing the matter to continue, and the nature and extent of the plaintiff's efforts in avoiding or rectifying the delay. In two cases involving a delay between filing and notice to a substituted party that was relatively short, and in fact less than the 120–day delay triggering dismissal without prejudice according to already-existing Fed.R.Civ.P. 4(m), however, we had little difficulty in finding notice to have been within an appropriate time for service of process, without feeling compelled to expressly consider each of the enumerated factors or to specify a particular relationship or balance among them.

We have in the past also noted that this list of factors carried over in *Garcia* was intended to be exemplary and by no means exclusive. Depending upon the nature of and reasons for a plaintiff's inaction, the significance, or even applicability, of any one or more of these factors will undoubtedly differ. Largely because a substantial delay in serving notice on an opposing party puts that party at a severe disadvantage in preparing for litigation, a delay of this kind has typically been considered a particularly serious and unique kind of failure to prosecute.

We have long counted Colorado among those jurisdictions in which service of process can be effected, under certain circumstances, even after the applicable statute of limitations has run. The comprehensive statutory scheme of limitations periods in this jurisdiction is structured to bar the commencement of enumerated actions after designated periods of time. This court has, however, by court rule, defined the point at which an action is commenced as including the point at which a complaint is filed, even though service on opposing parties has not yet been effected. *See* C.R.C.P. 3(a), (filing a complaint tolls the statute of limitations). Because a statute of limitations merely bars the commencement of an action after a designated point in time, in and of itself it imposes no direct limitation on the time for service following commencement by filing.

By contrast, Rule 15, governing amended and supplemental pleadings, permits an amendment changing a named party to relate back to the original claim only if, among other things, that party receives sufficient notice "within the period provided by law for commencing the action against him." Largely to avoid the anomalous situation that would result from permitting less time to serve an amended party than would have been permitted to serve the party originally named, we have eschewed a literal reading of the words "within the period provided by law for commencing the action against him," and instead construed this language of the rule to include a reasonable time to serve opposing parties after filing the complaint, even if that time extends beyond the applicable statute of limitations. In doing so, however, we made clear that this interpretation applied only to the relation back doctrine of Rule 15(c), and in that context, the purposes to be served by a statutory limitations period were adequately protected by the remaining conditions imposed by the rule governing relation back.

While we therefore clarified in *Garcia* that the appropriate inquiry concerning the time allowed for service of process in an action commenced by filing is whether the defendant was served within a reasonable time following the filing date, rather than within a reasonable time following the running of the applicable limitations, *Garcia*, we did not intend to suggest that the statute of limitations for any particular action is unrelated to the time allowed for service of process in the case. Quite the contrary, as various federal courts have expressly recognized, although the statute of limitations for commencing an action may itself be complied with upon the filing of a complaint, the policy considerations supporting a specific limitations period for the particular type of action at issue and those requiring service of process within a reasonable time after filing are largely identical and would be entirely defeated if service could be delayed indefinitely by filing a complaint within the statutory limitations period.

While the equitable doctrine of laches may sooner bar an action as the result of unconscionable delay by the plaintiff combined with prejudicial reliance by the defendant, a legislatively prescribed statute of limitations sets a predetermined time-bar, premised largely on the presumption that lengthy delay in notifying another of the need to defend himself is inherently prejudicial. Not only is it predictable that after lengthy delays, "evidence deteriorates or disappears, memories fade, and witnesses die or move away," but a defendant is also prejudiced simply by the defeat of his right to repose, being exposed as he would then be to surprise litigation long after the statutory limitations period had run. And while even a statute of limitations may be tolled under limited circumstances, such as where the defendant attempts to avoid service by placing himself beyond the power of the jurisdiction to compel attendance, or where "the defendant has wrongfully impeded the plaintiff's ability to bring the claim or truly extraordinary circumstances prevented the plaintiff from filing his or her claim despite diligent efforts," unsuccessful efforts to locate and serve a party cannot alone circumvent a statutory time bar.

For substantially the same policy reasons, a delay between the filing and service of a complaint which actually extends beyond the applicable statute of limitations can be considered reasonable only to the extent that it is the product of either wrongful conduct by the defendant or some formal impediment to service—not simply the inability of the plaintiff to locate the named defendant, no matter how extensive his efforts may be. While a failure to make reasonable efforts to serve may provide a separate basis for finding a delay *unreasonable*, efforts to locate a named defendant alone, whether or not he can make a particularized showing of prejudice or the plaintiff can demonstrate a lack thereof, can no more justify declining to dismiss for failure to prosecute than could they justify a tolling of the statute of limitations in the first place.

In *Garcia*, we characterized the 116 days between the filing of the original complaint and notice to the substituted party as "a relatively short period of time," in part by comparison with the 120–day period permitted for service by federal rule 4(m). At least where we found nothing in the record to suggest that the plaintiff had been dilatory or that the defendant suffered prejudice as a result of the delay, we had no difficulty in concluding that the substituted defendant had received notice within the reasonable time for service required to avoid dismissal for failure to prosecute. We therefore had no cause to consider or suggest precisely what would have amounted to an *unreasonable* delay in service after filing.

Although we have subsequently adopted a similar version of Rule 4(m), with an even shorter grace period for service in the absence of specific justification, it is unnecessary for us to resolve the applicability of that rule to this case because it would, in any event, not displace Rule 41(b)(2)'s provision for dismissal for failure to prosecute, which clearly bars the lengthy delay in this case. As we implied in *Garcia,* even without the benefit of a controlling rule of our own, within some initial period, measured in days rather than years, service after filing will be treated as presumptively reasonable. The significant question for purposes of dismissal for untimely service concerns the justification for longer delay, whether that justification be expressed in terms of good cause for an extension, as contemplated by Rule 4(m), or the reasonableness of inaction that would otherwise amount to a failure to prosecute. Where service after filing is, however, not actually accomplished until a statutory limitations period has passed, any delay in service beyond that "relatively short" initial period cannot be found reasonable simply because the plaintiff made diligent efforts to locate the defendant.

## III

By virtually any standard, the seven-and-a-half years between filing and service in this case far exceeded the relatively short initial period not requiring specific justification. By the same token, permitting the lengthy delay beyond the running of statute of limitations in this case would have effectively tripled the time statutorily contemplated for putting Villegas to her defense of alleged tortious conduct. While certain extraordinary circumstances might excuse even this substantial delay, for the reasons already articulated, the district court's reliance on Malm's efforts to locate and serve Villegas, and Villegas's failure to demonstrate specific prejudice, could not do so.

Notwithstanding Malm's suggestions to the contrary, the district court made no findings to the effect that Villegas had intentionally evaded service, and it explicitly rejected Malm's contention that a voicemail, left by Villegas for plaintiff's counsel after service had been effected, demonstrated that Villegas had actual knowledge of the action sometime prior to being served. Neither did the record suggest, nor the court find, that the lengthy delay in service was attributable to procedural impediments imposed by Villegas's foreign country of residence. To the contrary, the record reflects that service was completed by complying with the Hague Service Convention and C.R.C.P. 4, within approximately two months of Malm's request for service.

Given the complete lack of factual findings to the effect that Villegas deliberately avoided service, or that the lengthy delay was caused by legal obstacles encountered in attempting to serve her in a foreign country, or even that the delay was caused by some reason other than the bona fide and extensive, but unsuccessful, efforts of

Malm to serve her, service was not had within a reasonable time. The district court therefore abused its discretion in declining to dismiss for failure to prosecute.

IV

Because service following commencement of the action by filing a complaint with the court was delayed for an unreasonable length of time, the district court abused its discretion in declining to dismiss the lawsuit for failure to prosecute. The rule is therefore made absolute, and the matter is remanded to the district court with directions to dismiss the action.

18. For an entertaining story about successful service of process on notorious bank robber Jesse Jams, see "The Lawyer Who Took on Jesse James ... and Won," by Stephanie Francis Ward, in the ABA Journal several years ago.

# CHAPTER 2

# PERSONAL JURISDICTION

## A. MINIMUM CONTACTS

1. The case of *Pennoyer v. Neff* raised the issue of personal jurisdiction: Under what circumstances is it legal for a state court to exercise jurisdiction over a defendant who does not reside in the state, and was not served with process in the state? Unfortunately, the answer to that question is still anything but clear.

As you read the following cases, probably the best you can do is to notice the particular circumstances in which the United States Supreme Court has held that a court does – or does not – have personal jurisdiction over a particular defendant. Myriad factors must be considered in reaching each such decision. There is no easy, clear rule that will lead you to the correct answer in every case. The words of the Supreme Court itself are the only valid guide in this area. What factors cause the Supreme Court to find that there is personal jurisdiction in some cases, and not in others?

It will probably work best if you simply read all of the following cases, and then make a list of what turned out to be important. Stopping after each case, to try to make grand generalizations simply will not work. The decision in each case depended on the particular factors involved with that case.

As you will see, the following case, *International Shoe,* although decided in 1945 still remains the fundamental case in the area of personal jurisdiction.

## 66 S.CT. 154

### SUPREME COURT OF THE UNITED STATES

### INTERNATIONAL SHOE CO.

### v.

### STATE OF WASHINGTON, OFFICE OF UNEMPLOYMENT COMPENSATION AND PLACEMENT ET AL.

DECIDED DECEMBER 3, 1945

Mr. Chief Justice STONE delivered the opinion of the Court.

The questions for decision are (1) whether, within the limitations of the due process clause of the Fourteenth Amendment, appellant, a Delaware corporation, has by its activities in the State of Washington rendered itself amenable to proceedings in the courts of that state to recover unpaid contributions to the state unemployment compensation fund exacted by state statutes, and (2) whether the state can exact those contributions consistently with the due process clause of the Fourteenth Amendment.

The statutes in question set up a comprehensive scheme of unemployment compensation, the costs of which are defrayed by contributions required to be made by employers to a state unemployment compensation fund. The contributions are a specified percentage of the wages payable annually by each employer for his employees' services in the state. The assessment and collection of the contributions and the fund are administered by respondents. Section 14(c) of the Act authorizes respondent Commissioner to issue an order and notice of assessment of delinquent contributions upon prescribed personal service of the notice upon the employer if found within the state, or, if not so found, by mailing the notice to the employer by registered mail at his last known address.

In this case notice of assessment for the years in question was personally served upon a sales solicitor employed by appellant in the State of Washington, and a copy of the notice was mailed by registered mail to appellant at its address in St. Louis, Missouri. Appellant appeared specially before the office of unemployment and moved to set aside the order and notice of assessment on the ground that the service upon appellant's salesman was not proper service upon appellant; that appellant was not a corporation of the State of Washington and was not doing business within the state; that it had no agent within the state upon whom service could be made; and that appellant is not an employer and does not furnish employment within the meaning of the statute.

The tribunal denied the motion and ruled that respondent Commissioner was entitled to recover the unpaid contributions. Both the Superior Court and the Supreme Court affirmed.

Appellant is a Delaware corporation, having its principal place of business in St. Louis, Missouri, and is engaged in the manufacture and sale of shoes and other footwear. It maintains places of business in several states, at which its manufacturing is carried on and from which its merchandise is distributed interstate through several sales units or branches located outside the State of Washington.

Appellant has no office in Washington and makes no contracts either for sale or purchase of merchandise there. It maintains no stock of merchandise in that state and makes there no deliveries of goods in intrastate commerce. During the years from 1937 to 1940, now in question, appellant employed eleven to thirteen salesmen under direct supervision and control of sales managers located in St. Louis. These salesmen resided in Washington; their principal activities were confined to that state; and they were compensated by commissions based upon the amount of their sales. The commissions for each year totaled more than $31,000. Appellant supplies its salesmen with a line of samples, each consisting of one shoe of a pair, which they display to prospective purchasers. On occasion they rent permanent sample rooms, for exhibiting samples, in business buildings, or rent rooms in hotels or business buildings temporarily for that purpose. The cost of such rentals is reimbursed by appellant.

The authority of the salesmen is limited to exhibiting their samples and soliciting orders from prospective buyers, at prices and on terms fixed by appellant. The salesmen transmit the orders to appellant's office in St. Louis for acceptance or rejection, and when accepted the merchandise for filling the orders is shipped from points outside Washington to the purchasers within the state. All the merchandise shipped into Washington is invoiced at the place of shipment from which collections are made. No salesman has authority to enter into contracts or to make collections.

The Supreme Court of Washington was of opinion that the regular and systematic solicitation of orders in the state by appellant's salesmen, resulting in a continuous flow of appellant's product into the state, was sufficient to constitute doing business in the state so as to make appellant amenable to suit in its courts. But it was also of opinion that there were sufficient additional activities shown to bring the case within the rule frequently stated, that solicitation within a state by the agents of a foreign corporation plus some additional activities there are sufficient to render the corporation amenable to suit brought in the courts of the state to enforce an obligation arising out of its activities there.

The court found such additional activities in the salesmen's display of samples sometimes in permanent display rooms, and the salesmen's residence within the state, continued over a period of years, all resulting in a substantial volume of merchandise regularly shipped by appellant to purchasers within the state. The court also held that the statute as applied did not invade the constitutional power of Congress to regulate interstate commerce and did not impose a prohibited burden on such commerce.

Appellant's argument that the statute imposes an unconstitutional burden on interstate commerce need not detain us. For 26 U.S.C. 1606(a) provides that 'No person required under a State law to make payments to an unemployment fund shall be relieved from compliance therewith on the ground that he is engaged in interstate or foreign commerce, or that the State law does not distinguish between employees engaged in interstate or foreign commerce and those engaged in intrastate commerce.' It is no longer debatable that Congress, in the exercise of the commerce power, may authorize the states, in specified ways, to regulate interstate commerce or impose burdens upon it.

Appellant also insists that its activities within the state were not sufficient to manifest its 'presence' there and that in its absence the state courts were without jurisdiction, that consequently it was a denial of due process for the state to subject appellant to suit. And appellant further argues that since it was not present within the state, it is a denial of due process to subject it to taxation or other money exaction. It thus denies the power of the state to lay the tax or to subject appellant to a suit for its collection.

Historically the jurisdiction of courts to render judgment in personam is grounded on their de facto power over the defendant's person. Hence his presence within the territorial jurisdiction of court was prerequisite to its rendition of a judgment personally binding him. *Pennoyer v. Neff.* But now that the capias ad respondendum has given way to personal service of summons or other form of notice, due process requires only that in order to subject a defendant to a judgment in personam, if he be not present within the territory of the forum, he have certain minimum contacts with it such that the maintenance of the suit does not offend 'traditional notions of fair play and substantial justice.

Since the corporate personality is a fiction, although a fiction intended to be acted upon as though it were a fact, it is clear that unlike an individual its 'presence' without, as well as within, the state of its origin can be manifested only by activities carried on in its behalf by those who are authorized to act for it. To say that the corporation is so far 'present' there as to satisfy due process requirements, for purposes of taxation or the maintenance of suits against it in the courts of the state, is to beg the question to be decided. For the terms 'present' or 'presence' are used merely to symbolize those activities of the corporation's agent within the state which courts will deem to be sufficient to satisfy the demands of due process. Those demands may be met by such contacts of the corporation with the state of the forum as make it reasonable, in the context of our federal system of government, to require the corporation to defend the particular suit which is brought there. An 'estimate of the inconveniences' which would result to the corporation from a trial away from its 'home' or principal place of business is relevant in this connection.

'Presence' in the state in this sense has never been doubted when the activities of the corporation there have not only been continuous and systematic, but also give rise to the liabilities sued on, even though no consent to be sued or authorization to an agent to accept service of process has been given. Conversely it has been generally recognized that the casual presence of the corporate agent or even his conduct of single or isolated items of activities in a state in the corporation's behalf are not enough to subject it to suit on causes of action unconnected with the activities there. To require the corporation in such circumstances to defend the suit away from its home or other jurisdiction where it carries on more substantial activities has been thought to lay too great and unreasonable a burden on the corporation to comport with due process.

It is evident that the criteria by which we mark the boundary line between those activities which justify the subjection of a corporation to suit, and those which do not, cannot be simply mechanical or quantitative. The test is not merely, as has sometimes been suggested, whether the activity, which the corporation has seen fit to procure through its agents in another state, is a little more or a little less. Whether due process is satisfied must depend rather upon the quality and nature of the activity in relation to the fair and orderly administration of the laws which it was the purpose of the due process clause to insure. That clause does not contemplate that a state may make binding a judgment in personam against an individual or corporate defendant with which the state has no contacts, ties, or relations. Cf. *Pennoyer v. Neff.*

But to the extent that a corporation exercises the privilege of conducting activities within a state, it enjoys the benefits and protection of the laws of that state. The exercise of that privilege may give rise to obligations; and, so far as those obligations arise out of or are connected with the activities within the state, a procedure which requires the corporation to respond to a suit brought to enforce them can, in most instances, hardly be said to be undue.

Applying these standards, the activities carried on in behalf of appellant in the State of Washington were neither irregular nor casual. They were systematic and continuous throughout the years in question. They resulted in a large volume of interstate business, in the course of which appellant received the benefits and protection of the laws of the state, including the right to resort to the courts for the enforcement of its rights. The obligation which is here sued upon arose out of those very activities. It is evident that these operations establish sufficient contacts or ties with the state of the forum to make it reasonable and just according to our traditional conception of fair play and substantial justice to permit the state to enforce the obligations which appellant has incurred there. Hence we cannot say that the maintenance of the present suit in the State of Washington involves an unreasonable or undue procedure.

We are likewise unable to conclude that the service of the process within the state upon an agent whose activities establish appellant's 'presence' there was not sufficient notice of the suit, or that the suit was so unrelated to those activities as to make the agent an inappropriate vehicle for communicating the notice. It is enough that appellant has established such contacts with the state that the particular form of substituted service adopted there gives reasonable assurance that the notice will be actual. Nor can we say that the mailing of the notice of suit to appellant by registered mail at its home office was not reasonably calculated to apprise appellant of the suit.

Only a word need be said of appellant's liability for the demanded contributions of the state unemployment fund. The Supreme Court of Washington, construing and applying the statute, has held that it imposes a tax on the privilege of employing appellant's salesmen within the state measured by a percentage of the wages, here the commissions payable to the salesmen. This construction we accept for purposes of determining the constitutional validity of the statute. The right to employ labor has been deemed an appropriate subject of taxation in this country and England, both before and since the adoption of the Constitution. And such a tax imposed upon the employer for unemployment benefits is within the constitutional power of the states.

Appellant having rendered itself amenable to suit upon obligations arising out of the activities of its salesmen in Washington, the state may maintain the present suit in personam to collect the tax laid upon the exercise of the privilege of employing appellant's salesmen within the state. For Washington has made one of those activities, which taken together establish appellant's 'presence' there for purposes of suit, the taxable event by which the state brings appellant within the reach of its taxing power. The state thus has constitutional power to lay the tax and to subject appellant to a suit to recover it. The activities which establish its 'presence' subject it alike to taxation by the state and to suit to recover the tax.

Affirmed.

Mr. Justice BLACK delivered the following opinion – [which turns out to have been remarkably prescient.]

Congress, pursuant to its constitutional power to regulate commerce, has expressly provided that a State shall not be prohibited from levying the kind of unemployment compensation tax here challenged. We have twice decided that this Congressional consent is an adequate answer to a claim that imposition of the tax violates the Commerce Clause. Consequently that part of this appeal which again seeks to raise the question seems so patently frivolous as to make the case a fit candidate for dismissal. It is unthinkable that the vague due process clause was ever intended to prohibit a State from regulating or taxing a business carried on within its boundaries simply because this is done by agents of a corporation organized and having its headquarters elsewhere.

I believe that the Federal Constitution leaves to each State, without any 'ifs' or 'buts', a power to tax and to open the doors of its courts for its citizens to sue corporations whose agents do business in those States. Believing that the Constitution gave the States that power, I think it a judicial deprivation to condition its exercise upon this Court's notion of 'fair play', however appealing that term may be. Nor can I stretch the meaning of due process so far as to authorize this Court to deprive a State of the right to afford judicial protection to its citizens on the ground that it would be more 'convenient' for the corporation to be sued somewhere else.

There is a strong emotional appeal in the words 'fair play', 'justice', and 'reasonableness.' But they were not chosen by those who wrote the original Constitution or the Fourteenth Amendment as a measuring rod for this Court to use in invalidating State or Federal laws passed by elected legislative representatives. No one, not even those who most feared a democratic government, ever formally proposed that courts should be given power to invalidate legislation under any such elastic standards. Express prohibitions against certain types of legislation are found in the Constitution, and under the long settled practice, courts invalidate laws found to conflict with them. This requires interpretation, and interpretation, it is true, may result in extension of the Constitution's purpose. But that is no reason for reading the due process clause so as to restrict a State's power to tax and sue those whose activities affect persons and businesses within the State, provided proper service can be had. Superimposing the natural justice concept on the Constitution's specific prohibitions could operate as a drastic abridgment of democratic safeguards they embody, such as freedom of speech, press and religion, and the right to counsel. This result, I believe, alters the form of government our Constitution provides. I cannot agree.

True, the State's power is here upheld. But the rule announced means that tomorrow's judgment may strike down a State or Federal enactment on the ground that it does not conform to this Court's idea of natural justice. I therefore find myself moved by the same fears that caused Mr. Justice Holmes to say in 1930:

'I have not yet adequately expressed the more than anxiety that I feel at the ever increasing scope given to the Fourteenth Amendment in cutting down what I believe to be the constitutional rights of the States. As the decisions now stand, I see hardly any limit but the sky to the invalidating of those rights if they happen to strike a majority of this Court as for any reason undesirable.'

2. Thirty-two years later the U.S. Supreme Court was still struggling to ascertain what is a "fair" assertion of state court jurisdiction – this time in a suit brought in the state courts of Delaware, against a director of a company incorporated in Delaware.

## 97 S.CT. 2569
## SUPREME COURT OF THE UNITED STATES
## R. F. SHAFFER ET AL., APPELLANTS,
## V.
## ARNOLD HEITNER, AS CUSTODIAN FOR MARK ANDREW HEITNER.

DECIDED JUNE 24, 1977

**Justice MARSHALL delivered the opinion of the Court.**

The controversy in this case concerns the constitutionality of a Delaware statute that allows a court of that State to take jurisdiction of a lawsuit by sequestering any property of the defendant that happens to be located in Delaware. Appellants contend that the sequestration statute as applied in this case violates the Due Process Clause of the Fourteenth Amendment both because it permits the state courts to exercise jurisdiction despite the absence of sufficient contacts among the defendants, the litigation, and the State of Delaware and because it authorizes the deprivation of defendants' property without providing adequate procedural safeguards. We find it necessary to consider only the first of these contentions.

# I

Appellee Heitner, a nonresident of Delaware, is the owner of one share of stock in the Greyhound Corp., a business incorporated under the laws of Delaware with its principal place of business in Phoenix, Ariz. On May 22, 1974, he filed a shareholder's derivative suit in the Court of Chancery for New Castle County, Del., in which he named as defendants Greyhound, its wholly owned subsidiary Greyhound Lines, Inc., and 28 present or former officers or directors of one or both of the corporations. In essence, Heitner alleged that the individual defendants had violated their duties to Greyhound by causing it and its subsidiary to engage in actions that resulted in the corporations being held liable for substantial damages in a private antitrust suit and a large fine in a criminal contempt action. The activities which led to these penalties took place in Oregon.

Simultaneously with his complaint, Heitner filed a motion for an order of sequestration of the Delaware property of the individual defendants pursuant to Del.Code Ann., Tit. 10, s 366 (1975). This motion was accompanied by a supporting affidavit of counsel which stated that the individual defendants were nonresidents of Delaware. The affidavit identified the property to be sequestered as stock of the Defendant Greyhound Corporation, a Delaware corporation, as well as all options and all warrants to purchase said stock issued to said individual Defendants.

The requested sequestration order was signed the day the motion was filed. Pursuant to that order, the sequestrator "seized" approximately 82,000 shares of Greyhound common stock belonging to 19 of the defendants, and options belonging to another 2 defendants. These seizures were accomplished by placing "stop transfer" orders or their equivalents on the books of the Greyhound Corp. So far as the record shows, none of the certificates representing the seized property was physically present in Delaware. The stock was considered to be in Delaware, and so subject to seizure, by virtue of Del.Code Ann., Tit. 8, s 169 (1975), which makes Delaware the situs of ownership of all stock in Delaware corporations.

All 28 defendants were notified of the initiation of the suit by certified mail directed to their last known addresses and by publication in a Delaware newspaper. The 21 defendants whose property was seized (hereafter referred to as appellants) responded by entering a special appearance for the purpose of moving to quash service of process and to vacate the sequestration order. They contended that the ex parte sequestration procedure did not accord them due process of law and that the property seized was not capable of attachment in Delaware. In addition, appellants asserted that under the rule of *International Shoe* they did not have sufficient contacts with Delaware to sustain the jurisdiction of that State's courts.

The Court of Chancery rejected these arguments. On appeal, the Delaware Supreme Court affirmed the judgment of the Court of Chancery.

We noted probable jurisdiction. We reverse.

## II

As we have noted, under *Pennoyer* state authority to adjudicate was based on the jurisdiction's power over either persons or property. This fundamental concept is embodied in the very vocabulary which we use to describe judgments. If a court's jurisdiction is based on its authority over the defendant's person, the action and judgment are denominated "in personam" and can impose a personal obligation on the defendant in favor of the plaintiff. If jurisdiction is based on the court's power over property within its territory, the action is called "in rem" or "quasi in rem." The effect of a judgment in such a case is limited to the property that supports jurisdiction and does not impose a personal liability on the property owner, since he is not before the court. In *Pennoyer's* terms, the owner is affected only "indirectly" by an in rem judgment adverse to his interest in the property subject to the court's disposition.

The *Pennoyer* rules generally favored nonresident defendants by making them harder to sue. This advantage was reduced, however, by the ability of a resident plaintiff to satisfy a claim against a nonresident defendant by bringing into court any property of the defendant located in the plaintiff's State.

*Pennoyer* itself recognized that its rigid categories could not accommodate some necessary litigation. Accordingly, Mr. Justice Field's opinion carefully noted that cases involving the personal status of the plaintiff, such as divorce actions, could be adjudicated in the plaintiff's home State even though the defendant could not be served within that State. Similarly, the opinion approved the practice of considering a foreign corporation doing business in a State to have consented to being sued in that State. This basis for in personam jurisdiction over foreign corporations was later supplemented by the doctrine that a corporation doing business in a State could be deemed "present" in the State, and so subject to service of process under the rule of *Pennoyer.*

Later, the inquiry into the State's jurisdiction over a foreign corporation appropriately focused not on whether the corporation was "present" but on whether there have been "such contacts of the corporation with the state of the forum as make it reasonable, in the context of our federal system of government, to require the corporation to defend the particular suit which is brought there."

Mechanical or quantitative evaluations of the defendant's activities in the forum could not resolve the question of reasonableness: "Whether due process is satisfied must depend rather upon the quality and nature of the activity in relation to the fair and orderly administration of the laws which it was the purpose of the due process clause to insure. That clause does not contemplate that a state may make binding a judgment in personam against an individual or corporate defendant with which the state has no contacts, ties, or relations."

Thus, the relationship among the defendant, the forum, and the litigation, rather than the mutually exclusive sovereignty of the States on which the rules of *Pennoyer* rest, became the central concern of the inquiry into personal jurisdiction. The immediate effect of this departure from *Pennoyer's* conceptual apparatus was to increase the ability of the state courts to obtain personal jurisdiction over nonresident defendants

No equally dramatic change has occurred in the law governing jurisdiction in rem. There have, however, been intimations that the collapse of the in personam wing of *Pennoyer* has not left that decision unweakened as a foundation for in rem jurisdiction.

Although this Court has not addressed this argument directly, we have held that property cannot be subjected to a court's judgment unless reasonable and appropriate efforts have been made to give the property owners actual notice of the action. *Mullane v. Central Hanover Bank & Trust*. This conclusion recognizes, contrary to Pennoyer, that an adverse judgment in rem directly affects the property owner by divesting him of his rights in the property before the court. Moreover, in *Mullane* we hold that Fourteenth Amendment rights cannot depend on the classification of an action as in rem or in personam, since that is "a classification for which the standards are so elusive and confused generally and which, being primarily for state courts to define, may and do vary from state to state."

It is clear, therefore, that the law of state-court jurisdiction no longer stands securely on the foundation established in *Pennoyer*. We think that the time is ripe to consider whether the standard of fairness and substantial justice set forth in *International Shoe* should be held to govern actions in rem as well as in personam.

III

The case for applying to jurisdiction in rem the same test of "fair play and substantial justice" as governs assertions of jurisdiction in personam is simple and straightforward. It is premised on recognition that "The phrase, 'judicial jurisdiction over a thing', is a customary elliptical way of referring to jurisdiction over the interests of persons in a thing." This recognition leads to the conclusion that in order to justify an exercise of jurisdiction in rem, the basis for jurisdiction must be sufficient to justify exercising "jurisdiction over the interests of persons in a thing." The standard for determining whether an exercise of jurisdiction over the interests of persons is consistent with the Due Process Clause is the minimum-contacts standard elucidated in *International Shoe.*

This does not ignore the fact that the presence of property in a State may bear on the existence of jurisdiction by providing contacts among the forum State, the defendant, and the litigation. For example, when claims to the property itself are the source of the underlying controversy between the plaintiff and the defendant, it would be unusual for the State where the property is located not to have jurisdiction. In such cases, the defendant's claim to property located in the State would normally indicate that he expected to benefit from the State's protection of his interest. The State's strong interests in assuring the marketability of property within its borders and in providing a procedure for peaceful resolution of disputes about the possession of that property would also support jurisdiction, as would the likelihood that important records and witnesses will be found in the State. The presence of property may also favor jurisdiction in cases such as suits for injury suffered on the land of an absentee owner, where the defendant's ownership of the property is conceded but the cause of action is otherwise related to rights and duties growing out of that ownership.

It appears, therefore, that jurisdiction over many types of actions which now are or might be brought in rem would not be affected by a holding that any assertion of state-court jurisdiction must satisfy the *International Shoe* standard. For the type of quasi in rem action typified by *Harris v. Balk* and the present case, however, accepting the proposed analysis would result in significant change. Thus, although the presence of the defendant's property in a State might suggest the existence of other ties among the defendant, the State, and the litigation, the presence of the property alone would not support the State's jurisdiction. If those other ties did not exist, cases over which the State is now thought to have jurisdiction could not be brought in that forum.

We know of nothing to justify the assumption that a debtor can avoid paying his obligations by removing his property to a State in which his creditor cannot obtain personal jurisdiction over him. The Full Faith and Credit Clause, after all, makes the valid in personam judgment of one State enforceable in all other States.

We have never held that the presence of property in a State does not automatically confer jurisdiction over the owner's interest in that property. This history must be considered as supporting the proposition that jurisdiction based solely on the presence of property satisfies the demands of due process, but it is not decisive. "Traditional notions of fair play and substantial justice" can be as readily offended by the perpetuation of ancient forms that are no longer justified as by the adoption of new procedures that are inconsistent with the basic values of our constitutional heritage. The fiction that an assertion of jurisdiction over property is anything but an assertion of jurisdiction over the owner of the property supports an ancient form without substantial modern justification. Its continued acceptance would serve only to allow state-court jurisdiction that is fundamentally unfair to the defendant.

We therefore conclude that all assertions of state-court jurisdiction must be evaluated according to the standards set forth in *International Shoe* and its progeny.

## IV

The Delaware courts based their assertion of jurisdiction in this case solely on the statutory presence of appellants' property in Delaware. Yet that property is not the subject matter of this litigation, nor is the underlying cause of action related to the property. Appellants' holdings in Greyhound do not, therefore, provide contacts with Delaware sufficient to support the jurisdiction of that State's courts over appellants. If it exists, that jurisdiction must have some other foundation.

Appellee Heitner did not allege and does not now claim that appellants have ever set foot in Delaware. Nor does he identify any act related to his cause of action as having taken place in Delaware. Nevertheless, he contends that appellants' positions as directors and officers of a corporation chartered in Delaware provide sufficient "contacts, ties, or relations" with that State to give its courts jurisdiction over appellants in this stockholder's derivative action. This argument is based primarily on what Heitner asserts to be the strong interest of Delaware in supervising the management of a Delaware corporation. That interest is said to derive from the role of Delaware law in establishing the corporation and defining the obligations owed to it by its officers and directors. In order to protect this interest, appellee concludes, Delaware's courts must have jurisdiction over corporate fiduciaries such as appellants.

This argument is undercut by the failure of the Delaware Legislature to assert the state interest appellee finds so compelling. Delaware law bases jurisdiction, not on appellants' status as corporate fiduciaries, but rather on the presence of their property in the State. Although the sequestration procedure used here may be most frequently used in derivative suits against officers and directors, the authorizing statute evinces no specific concern with such actions. Sequestration can be used in any suit against a nonresident.

But as Heitner's failure to secure jurisdiction over seven of the defendants named in his complaint demonstrates, there is no necessary relationship between holding a position as a corporate fiduciary and owning stock or other interests in the corporation. If Delaware perceived its interest in securing jurisdiction over corporate fiduciaries to be as great as Heitner suggests, we would expect it to have enacted a statute more clearly designed to protect that interest.

Moreover, even if Heitner's assessment of the importance of Delaware's interest is accepted, his argument fails to demonstrate that Delaware is a fair forum for this litigation. The interest appellee has identified may support the application of Delaware law to resolve any controversy over appellants' actions in their capacities as officers and directors. But we have rejected the argument that if a State's law can properly be applied to a dispute, its courts necessarily have jurisdiction over the parties to that dispute.

"The State does not acquire jurisdiction by being the 'center of gravity' of the controversy, or the most convenient location for litigation. The issue is personal jurisdiction, not choice of law.

Appellee suggests that by accepting positions as officers or directors of a Delaware corporation, appellants performed the acts required for jurisdiction. He notes that Delaware law provides substantial benefits to corporate officers and directors, and that these benefits were at least in part the incentive for appellants to assume their positions. It is, he says, "only fair and just" to require appellants, in return for these benefits, to respond in the State of Delaware when they are accused of misusing their power.

But like Heitner's first argument, this line of reasoning establishes only that it is appropriate for Delaware law to govern the obligations of appellants to Greyhound and its stockholders. It does not demonstrate that appellants have "purposefully availed themselves of the privilege of conducting activities within the forum State," in a way that would justify bringing them before a Delaware tribunal. Appellants have simply had nothing to do with the State of Delaware. Moreover, appellants had no reason to expect to be haled before a Delaware court. Delaware, unlike some States, has not enacted a statute that treats acceptance of a directorship as consent to jurisdiction in the State. And "it strains reason to suggest that anyone buying securities in a corporation formed in Delaware 'impliedly consents' to subject himself to Delaware's jurisdiction on any cause of action." Appellants, who were not required to acquire interests in Greyhound in order to hold their positions, did not by acquiring those interests surrender their right to be brought to judgment only in States with which they had "minimum contacts."

The Due Process Clause "does not contemplate that a state may make binding a judgment against an individual or corporate defendant with which the state has no contacts, ties, or relations." *International Shoe.*

Delaware's assertion of jurisdiction over appellants in this case is inconsistent with that constitutional limitation on state power. The judgment of the Delaware Supreme Court must, therefore, be reversed.

It is so ordered.

3. What about child support? Does a state have jurisdiction to make or modify child support orders against a non-resident parent who voluntarily sends his or her children to live in a state different from the state in which the parent lives? Would such orders on child support be "fair?"

**98 S.CT. 1690**
**SUPREME COURT OF THE UNITED STATES**
**EZRA KULKO, APPELLANT,**
**V.**
**SUPERIOR COURT OF CALIFORNIA IN AND FOR THE CITY**
**AND COUNTY OF SAN FRANCISCO**
**(SHARON KULKO HORN, REAL PARTY IN INTEREST)**

DECIDED MAY 15, 1978

**Justice MARSHALL delivered the opinion of the Court.**

The issue before us is whether, in this action for child support, the California state courts may exercise *in personam* jurisdiction over a nonresident, nondomiciliary parent of minor children domiciled within the State. For reasons set forth below, we hold that the exercise of such jurisdiction would violate the Due Process Clause of the Fourteenth Amendment.

I

Appellant Ezra Kulko married appellee Sharon Kulko Horn in 1959, during appellant's three-day stopover in California en route from a military base in Texas to a tour of duty in Korea. At the time of this marriage, both parties were domiciled in and residents of New York State. Immediately following the marriage, Sharon Kulko returned to New York, as did appellant after his tour of duty. Their first child, Darwin, was born to the Kulkos in New York in 1961, and a year later their second child, Ilsa, was born, also in New York. The Kulkos and their two children resided together as a family in New York City continuously until March 1972, when the Kulkos separated.

Following the separation, Sharon Kulko moved to San Francisco, California. A written separation agreement was drawn up in New York; in September 1972, Sharon

Kulko flew to New York City in order to sign this agreement. The agreement provided, *inter alia,* that the children would remain with their father during the school year but would spend their Christmas, Easter, and summer vacations with their mother. While Sharon Kulko waived any claim for her own support or maintenance, Ezra Kulko agreed to pay his wife $3,000 per year in child support for the periods when the children were in her care, custody, and control. Immediately after execution of the separation agreement, Sharon Kulko flew to Haiti and procured a divorce there; the divorce decree incorporated the terms of the agreement. She then returned to California, where she remarried and took the name Horn.

The children resided with appellant during the school year and with their mother on vacations, as provided by the separation agreement, until December 1973. At this time, just before Ilsa was to leave New York to spend Christmas vacation with her mother, she told her father that she wanted to remain in California after her vacation. Appellant bought his daughter a one-way plane ticket, and Ilsa left, taking her clothing with her. Ilsa then commenced living in California with her mother during the school year and spending vacations with her father. In January 1976, appellant's other child, Darwin, called his mother from New York and advised her that he wanted to live with her in California. Unbeknownst to appellant, appellee Horn sent a plane ticket to her son, which he used to fly to California where he took up residence with his mother and sister.

Less than one month after Darwin's arrival in California, appellee Horn commenced this action against appellant in the California Superior Court. She sought to establish the Haitian divorce decree as a California judgment; to modify the judgment so as to award her full custody of the children; and to increase appellant's child-support obligations. Appellant appeared specially and moved to quash service of the summons on the ground that he was not a resident of California and lacked sufficient "minimum contacts" with the State under *International Shoe* to warrant the State's assertion of personal jurisdiction over him.

The trial court summarily denied the motion to quash. The appellate court affirmed the denial of appellant's motion to quash, reasoning that, by consenting to his children's living in California, appellant had "caused an effect in the state" warranting the exercise of jurisdiction over him.

The California Supreme Court sustained the rulings of the lower state courts.

We hereby grant the petition for certiorari and reverse.

## II

The Due Process Clause of the Fourteenth Amendment operates as a limitation on the jurisdiction of state courts to enter judgments affecting rights or interests of nonresident defendants. It has long been the rule that a valid judgment imposing a personal obligation or duty in favor of the plaintiff may be entered only by a court having jurisdiction over the person of the defendant. *Pennoyer v. Neff, International Shoe.* The existence of personal jurisdiction, in turn, depends upon the presence of reasonable notice to the defendant that an action has been brought. *Mullane v. Central Hanover Trust,* and a sufficient connection between the defendant and the forum State to make it fair to require defense of the action in the forum. In this case, appellant does not dispute the adequacy of the notice that he received, but contends that his connection with the State of California is too attenuated, under the standards implicit in the Due Process Clause of the Constitution, to justify imposing upon him the burden and inconvenience of defense in California.

The parties are in agreement that the constitutional standard for determining whether the State may enter a binding judgment against appellant here is that set forth in this Court's opinion in *International Shoe:* that a defendant "have certain minimum contacts with [the forum State] such that the maintenance of the suit does not offend 'traditional notions of fair play and substantial justice.'" While the interests of the forum State and of the plaintiff in proceeding with the cause in the plaintiff's forum of choice are, of course, to be considered, an essential criterion in all cases is whether the "quality and nature" of the defendant's activity is such that it is "reasonable" and "fair" to require him to conduct his defense in that forum.

Like any standard that requires a determination of "reasonableness," the "minimum contacts" test of *International Shoe* is not susceptible of mechanical application;  rather, the facts of each case must be weighed to determine whether the requisite "affiliating circumstances" are present. We recognize that this determination is one in which few answers will be written "in black and white. The greys are dominant and even among them the shades are innumerable." But we believe that the California Supreme Court's application of the minimum-contacts test in this case represents an unwarranted extension of *International Shoe* and would, if sustained, sanction a result that is neither fair, just, nor reasonable.

## A

In reaching its result, the California Supreme Court did not rely on appellant's glancing presence in the State some 13 years before the events that led to this controversy, nor could it have. Appellant has been in California on only two occasions, once in 1959 for a three-day military stopover on his way to Korea, and again in 1960 for a 24-hour stopover on his return from Korean service. To hold such temporary visits to a State a basis for the assertion of *in personam* jurisdiction over unrelated actions arising in the future would make a mockery of the limitations on state jurisdiction imposed by the Fourteenth Amendment. Nor did the California court rely on the fact that appellant was actually married in California on one of his two brief visits. We agree that where two New York domiciliaries, for reasons of convenience, marry in the State of California and thereafter spend their entire married life in New York, the fact of their California marriage by itself cannot support a California court's exercise of jurisdiction over a spouse who remains a New York resident in an action relating to child support.

Finally, in holding that personal jurisdiction existed, the court below carefully disclaimed reliance on the fact that appellant had agreed at the time of separation to allow his children to live with their mother three months a year and that he had sent them to California each year pursuant to this agreement. To find personal jurisdiction in a State on this basis, merely because the mother was residing there, would discourage parents from entering into reasonable visitation agreements. Moreover, it could arbitrarily subject one parent to suit in any State of the Union where the other parent chose to spend time while having custody of their offspring pursuant to a separation agreement. As we have emphasized:

"The unilateral activity of those who claim some relationship with a nonresident defendant cannot satisfy the requirement of contact with the forum State. . . . It is essential in each case that there be some act by which the defendant purposefully avails himself of the privilege of conducting activities within the forum State."

The "purposeful act" that the California Supreme Court believed did warrant the exercise of personal jurisdiction over appellant in California was his "actively and fully consenting to Ilsa living in California for the school year ...and sending her to California for that purpose." We cannot accept the proposition that appellant's acquiescence in Ilsa's desire to live with her mother conferred jurisdiction over appellant in the California courts in this action. A father who agrees, in the interests of family harmony and his children's preferences, to allow them to spend more time in California than was required under a separation agreement can hardly be said to have "purposefully availed himself" of the "benefits and protections" of California's laws.

Nor can we agree with the assertion of the court below that the exercise of *in personam* jurisdiction here was warranted by the financial benefit appellant derived from his daughter's presence in California for nine months of the year. This argument rests on the premise that, while appellant's liability for support payments remained unchanged, his yearly expenses for supporting the child in New York decreased. But this circumstance, even if true, does not support California's assertion of jurisdiction here. Any diminution in appellant's household costs resulted, not from the child's presence in California, but rather from her absence from appellant's home. Moreover, an action by appellee Horn to increase support payments could now be brought, and could have been brought when Ilsa first moved to California, in the State of New York; a New York court would clearly have personal jurisdiction over appellant and, if a judgment were entered by a New York court increasing appellant's child-support obligations, it could properly be enforced against him in both New York and California. Any ultimate financial advantage to appellant thus results not from the child's presence in California, but from appellee's failure earlier to seek an increase in payments under the separation agreement. The argument below to the contrary, in our view, confuses the question of appellant's liability with that of the proper forum in which to determine that liability.

B

In light of our conclusion that appellant did not purposefully derive benefit from any activities relating to the State of California, it is apparent that the California Supreme Court's reliance on appellant's having caused an "effect" in California was misplaced. This "effects" test is derived from the Restatement (Second) of Conflict of Laws § 37 (1971), which provides:

"A state has power to exercise judicial jurisdiction over an individual who causes effects in the state by an act done elsewhere with respect to any cause of action arising from these effects unless the nature of the effects and of the individual's relationship to the state make the exercise of such jurisdiction unreasonable."

While this provision is not binding on this Court, it does not in any event support the decision below. As is apparent from the examples accompanying § 37 in the Restatement, this section was intended to reach wrongful activity outside of the State causing injury within the State, e. g. shooting a bullet from one State into another, or commercial activity affecting state residents. Even in such situations, moreover, the Restatement recognizes that there might be circumstances that would render "unreasonable" the assertion of jurisdiction over the nonresident defendant.

The circumstances in this case clearly render "unreasonable" California's assertion of personal jurisdiction. There is no claim that appellant has visited physical injury on either property or persons within the State of California. The cause of action herein asserted arises, not from the defendant's commercial transactions in interstate commerce, but rather from his personal, domestic relations. It thus cannot be said that appellant has sought a commercial benefit from solicitation of business from a resident of California that could reasonably render him liable to suit in state court; appellant's activities cannot fairly be analogized to an insurer's sending an insurance contract and premium notices into the State to an insured resident of the State. Furthermore, the controversy between the parties arises from a separation that occurred in the State of New York; appellee Horn seeks modification of a contract that was negotiated in New York and that she flew to New York to sign. The instant action involves an agreement that was entered into with virtually no connection with the forum State.

Finally, basic considerations of fairness point decisively in favor of appellant's State of domicile as the proper forum for adjudication of this case, whatever the merits of appellee's underlying claim. It is appellant who has remained in the State of the marital domicile, whereas it is appellee who has moved across the continent. Appellant has at all times resided in New York State, and, until the separation and appellee's move to California, his entire family resided there as well. As noted above, appellant did no more than acquiesce in the stated preference of one of his children to live with her mother in California. This single act is surely not one that a reasonable parent would expect to result in the substantial financial burden and personal strain of litigating a child-support suit in a forum 3,000 miles away, and we therefore see no basis on which it can be said that appellant could reasonably have anticipated being "haled before a California court." To make jurisdiction in a case such as this turn on whether appellant bought his daughter her ticket or instead unsuccessfully sought to prevent her departure would impose an unreasonable burden on family relations, and one wholly unjustified by the "quality and nature" of appellant's activities in or relating to the State of California.

## III

In seeking to justify the burden that would be imposed on appellant were the exercise of *in personam* jurisdiction in California sustained, appellee argues that California has substantial interests in protecting the welfare of its minor residents and in promoting to the fullest extent possible a healthy and supportive family environment in which the children of the State are to be raised. These interests are unquestionably important. But while the presence of the children and one parent in California arguably might favor application of California law in a lawsuit in New York, the fact that California may be the "'center of gravity'" for choice-of-law purposes does not mean that California has personal jurisdiction over the defendant. And California has not attempted to assert any particularized interest in trying such cases in its courts by, *e. g.*, enacting a special jurisdictional statute.

California's legitimate interest in ensuring the support of children resident in California without unduly disrupting the children's lives, moreover, is already being served by the State's participation in the Revised Uniform Reciprocal Enforcement of Support Act of 1968. This statute provides a mechanism for communication between court systems in different States, in order to facilitate the procurement and enforcement of child-support decrees where the dependent children reside in a State that cannot obtain personal jurisdiction over the defendant. Thus, not only may plaintiff-appellee here vindicate her claimed right to additional child support from her former husband in a New York court, but also the Uniform Acts will facilitate both her prosecution of a claim for additional support and collection of any support payments found to be owed by appellant. It cannot be disputed that California has substantial interests in protecting resident children and in facilitating child-support actions on behalf of those children. But these interests simply do not make California a "fair forum" in which to require appellant, who derives no personal or commercial benefit from his child's presence in California and who lacks any other relevant contact with the State, either to defend a child-support suit or to suffer liability by default.

IV

The mere act of sending a child to California to live with her mother is not a commercial act and connotes no intent to obtain or expectancy of receiving a corresponding benefit in the State that would make fair the assertion of that State's judicial jurisdiction.

Accordingly, we conclude that the appellant's motion to quash service, on the ground of lack of personal jurisdiction, was erroneously denied by the California courts. The judgment of the California Supreme Court is, therefore,

Reversed.

4. The next case has become one of the landmark cases for personal jurisdiction. Yet it is difficult, on the face of the case, to understand why both sides were fighting so hard on the issue of jurisdiction over a relatively minor defendant. The two major companies named in the initial complaint, Audi and Volkswagen, did not contest the jurisdiction of the Oklahoma court. Surely Audi and Volkswagen would have had sufficient assets to pay any judgment?

**100 S.CT. 559**

SUPREME COURT OF THE UNITED STATES

WORLD-WIDE VOLKSWAGEN CORPORATION ET AL.,
PETITIONERS,

V.

CHARLES S. WOODSON, DISTRICT JUDGE OF CREEK COUNTY,
OKLAHOMA, ET AL.

DECIDED JANUARY 21, 1980

Justice WHITE delivered the opinion of the Court.

The issue before us is whether, consistently with the Due Process Clause of the Fourteenth Amendment, an Oklahoma court may exercise *in personam* jurisdiction over a nonresident automobile retailer and its wholesale distributor in a products-liability action, when the defendants' only connection with Oklahoma is the fact that an automobile sold in New York to New York residents became involved in an accident in Oklahoma.

I

Respondents Harry and Kay Robinson purchased a new Audi automobile from petitioner Seaway, in Massena, N. Y., in 1976. The following year the Robinson family, who resided in New York, left that State for a new home in Arizona. As they passed through the State of Oklahoma, another car struck their Audi in the rear, causing a fire which severely burned Kay Robinson and her two children.

The Robinsons subsequently brought a products-liability action in the District Court for Creek County, Okla., claiming that their injuries resulted from defective design and placement of the Audi's gas tank and fuel system. They joined as defendants the automobile's manufacturer, Audi; its importer Volkswagen; its regional distributor, petitioner World-Wide; and its retail dealer, petitioner Seaway. Seaway and World-Wide entered special appearances claiming that Oklahoma's exercise of jurisdiction over them would offend the limitations on the State's jurisdiction imposed by the Due Process Clause of the Fourteenth Amendment.

The facts presented to the District Court showed that World-Wide is incorporated and has its business office in New York. It distributes vehicles, parts, and accessories, under contract with Volkswagen, to retail dealers in New York, New Jersey, and

Connecticut. Seaway, one of these retail dealers, is incorporated and has its place of business in New York. Insofar as the record reveals, Seaway and World-Wide are fully independent corporations whose relations with each other and with Volkswagen and Audi are contractual only. Respondents adduced no evidence that either World-Wide or Seaway does any business in Oklahoma, ships or sells any products to or in that State, has an agent to receive process there, or purchases advertisements in any media calculated to reach Oklahoma. In fact, as respondents' counsel conceded at oral argument, there was no showing that any automobile sold by World-Wide or Seaway has ever entered Oklahoma with the single exception of the vehicle involved in the present case.

Despite the apparent paucity of contacts between petitioners and Oklahoma, the District Court rejected their constitutional claim, denying petitioners' motion to dismiss. Petitioners then sought a writ of prohibition in the Supreme Court of Oklahoma to restrain the District Judge, respondent Charles S. Woodson, from exercising *in personam* jurisdiction over them.

The Supreme Court of Oklahoma denied the writ, holding that personal jurisdiction over petitioners was authorized by Oklahoma's "long-arm" statute.

We granted certiorari. We now reverse.

II

The Due Process Clause of the Fourteenth Amendment limits the power of a state court to render a valid personal judgment against a nonresident defendant. *Kulko v. California Superior Court.* A judgment rendered in violation of due process is void in the rendering State and is not entitled to full faith and credit elsewhere. *Pennoyer v. Neff.* Due process requires that the defendant be given adequate notice of the suit, *Mullane v. Central Hanover Trust Co.*, and be subject to the personal jurisdiction of the court, *International Shoe.* In the present case, it is not contended that notice was inadequate; the only question is whether these particular petitioners were subject to the jurisdiction of the Oklahoma courts.

As has long been settled, and as we reaffirm today, a state court may exercise personal jurisdiction over a nonresident defendant only so long as there exist "minimum contacts" between the defendant and the forum State. *International Shoe.* The concept of minimum contacts, in turn, can be seen to perform two related, but distinguishable, functions. It protects the defendant against the burdens of litigating in a distant or inconvenient forum. And it acts to ensure that the States through their courts, do not reach out beyond the limits imposed on them by their status as coequal sovereigns in a federal system.

The protection against inconvenient litigation is typically described in terms of "reasonableness" or "fairness." We have said that the defendant's contacts with the forum State must be such that maintenance of the suit "does not offend 'traditional notions of fair play and substantial justice.' " *International Shoe.* The relationship between the defendant and the forum must be such that it is "reasonable ... to require the corporation to defend the particular suit which is brought there." Implicit in this emphasis on reasonableness is the understanding that the burden on the defendant, while always a primary concern, will in an appropriate case be considered in light of other relevant factors, including the forum State's interest in adjudicating the dispute, the plaintiff's interest in obtaining convenient and effective relief, at least when that interest is not adequately protected by the plaintiff's power to choose the forum, the interstate judicial system's interest in obtaining the most efficient resolution of controversies; and the shared interest of the several States in furthering fundamental substantive social policies.

The limits imposed on state jurisdiction by the Due Process Clause, in its role as a guarantor against inconvenient litigation, have been substantially relaxed over the years. As we noted in *McGee v. International Life Ins.:*

> Today many commercial transactions touch two or more States and may involve parties separated by the full continent. With this increasing nationalization of commerce has come a great increase in the amount of business conducted by mail across state lines. At the same time modern transportation and communication have made it much less burdensome for a party sued to defend himself in a State where he engages in economic activity.

Nevertheless, we have never accepted the proposition that state lines are irrelevant for jurisdictional purposes, nor could we, and remain faithful to the principles of interstate federalism embodied in the Constitution. The economic interdependence of the States was foreseen and desired by the Framers. In the Commerce Clause, they provided that the Nation was to be a common market, a "free trade unit" in which the States are debarred from acting as separable economic entities. But the Framers also intended that the States retain many essential attributes of sovereignty, including, in particular, the sovereign power to try causes in their courts. The sovereignty of each State, in turn, implied a limitation on the sovereignty of all of its sister States—a limitation express or implicit in both the original scheme of the Constitution and the Fourteenth Amendment.

Hence, even while abandoning the shibboleth that "the authority of every tribunal is necessarily restricted by the territorial limits of the State in which it is established,"

*Pennoyer v. Neff,* we emphasized that the reasonableness of asserting jurisdiction over the defendant must be assessed "in the context of our federal system of government," and stressed that the Due Process Clause ensures not only fairness, but also the "orderly administration of the laws.

> As technological progress has increased the flow of commerce between the States, the
> need for jurisdiction over nonresidents has undergone a similar increase. At the same
> time, progress in communications and transportation has made the defense of a suit in
> a foreign tribunal less burdensome. In response to these changes, the requirements for
> personal jurisdiction over nonresidents have evolved from the rigid rule of *Pennoyer*
> *v. Neff,* to the flexible standard of *International Shoe.* But it is a mistake to assume that
> this trend heralds the eventual demise of all restrictions on the personal jurisdiction of
> state courts.

Thus, the Due Process Clause "does not contemplate that a state may make binding a judgment *in personam* against an individual or corporate defendant with which the state has no contacts, ties, or relations." *International Shoe.* Even if the defendant would suffer minimal or no inconvenience from being forced to litigate before the tribunals of another State; even if the forum State has a strong interest in applying its law to the controversy; even if the forum State is the most convenient location for litigation, the Due Process Clause, acting as an instrument of interstate federalism, may sometimes act to divest the State of its power to render a valid judgment.

## III

Applying these principles to the case at hand, we find in the record before us a total absence of those affiliating circumstances that are a necessary predicate to any exercise of state-court jurisdiction. Petitioners carry on no activity whatsoever in Oklahoma. They close no sales and perform no services there. They avail themselves of none of the privileges and benefits of Oklahoma law. They solicit no business there either through salespersons or through advertising reasonably calculated to reach the State. Nor does the record show that they regularly sell cars at wholesale or retail to Oklahoma customers or residents or that they indirectly, through others, serve or seek to serve the Oklahoma market. In short, respondents seek to base jurisdiction on one, isolated occurrence and whatever inferences can be drawn therefrom: the fortuitous circumstance that a single Audi automobile, sold in New York to New York residents, happened to suffer an accident while passing through Oklahoma.

It is argued, however, that because an automobile is mobile by its very design and purpose it was "foreseeable" that the Robinsons' Audi would cause injury in Oklahoma. Yet "foreseeability" alone has never been a sufficient benchmark for personal jurisdiction under the Due Process Clause. In *Kulko v. California Superior Court* it was surely "foreseeable" that a divorced wife would move to California from New York, the domicile of the marriage, and that a minor daughter would live with the mother. Yet we held that California could not exercise jurisdiction in a child-support action over the former husband who had remained in New York.

If foreseeability were the criterion, a local California tire retailer could be forced to defend in Pennsylvania when a blowout occurs there, or a Florida soft-drink concessionaire could be summoned to Alaska to account for injuries happening there. Every seller of chattels would in effect appoint the chattel his agent for service of process.

This is not to say, of course, that foreseeability is wholly irrelevant. But the foreseeability that is critical to due process analysis is not the mere likelihood that a product will find its way into the forum State. Rather, it is that the defendant's conduct and connection with the forum State are such that he should reasonably anticipate being haled into court there. The Due Process Clause, by ensuring the "orderly administration of the laws," gives a degree of predictability to the legal system that allows potential defendants to structure their primary conduct with some minimum assurance as to where that conduct will and will not render them liable to suit.

When a corporation "purposefully avails itself of the privilege of conducting activities within the forum State," it has clear notice that it is subject to suit there, and can act to alleviate the risk of burdensome litigation by procuring insurance, passing the expected costs on to customers, or, if the risks are too great, severing its connection with the State. Hence if the sale of a product of a manufacturer or distributor such as Audi or Volkswagen is not simply an isolated occurrence, but arises from the efforts of the manufacturer or distributor to serve directly or indirectly, the market for its product in other States, it is not unreasonable to subject it to suit in one of those States if its allegedly defective merchandise has there been the source of injury to its owner or to others. The forum State does not exceed its powers under the Due Process Clause if it asserts personal jurisdiction over a corporation that delivers its products into the stream of commerce with the expectation that they will be purchased by consumers in the forum State. Cf. *Gray v. American Radiator* 22 Ill.2d 432 (1961).

But there is no such or similar basis for Oklahoma jurisdiction over World-Wide or Seaway in this case. Seaway's sales are made in Massena, N. Y. World-Wide's market, although substantially larger, is limited to dealers in New York, New Jersey, and Connecticut. There is no evidence of record that any automobiles distributed by World-Wide are sold to retail customers outside this tristate area. It is foreseeable that the purchasers of automobiles sold by World-Wide and Seaway may take them to Oklahoma. But the mere "unilateral activity" of those who claim some relationship with a nonresident defendant cannot satisfy the requirement of contact with the forum State.

Financial benefits accruing to the defendant from a collateral relation to the forum State will not support jurisdiction if they do not stem from a constitutionally cognizable contact with that State. In our view, whatever marginal revenues petitioners may receive by virtue of the fact that their products are capable of use in Oklahoma is far too attenuated a contact to justify that State's exercise of *in personam* jurisdiction over them.

Because we find that petitioners have no "contacts, ties, or relations" with the State of Oklahoma, the judgment of the Supreme Court of Oklahoma is

Reversed.

6. The jurisdictional concepts established by the preceding case are very important – enunciating the necessity for "foreseeability" and touching on the concept of "stream of commerce." Yet with both of the major companies involved, Audi and Volkswagen, why did it seem so important – to both sides – to ascertain whether or not there was jurisdiction over the relatively small companies in New England?

It may be because the plaintiff wanted to keep the case in an Oklahoma state court that was considered to be very sympathetic to plaintiffs, rather than giving the major defendants the opportunity to remove the case, under, 28 USC 1441(b) and 28 USC 1332 to a federal court. Because the plaintiffs had not yet reached their intended new domicile of Arizona, they were still considered to be citizens of New York. Since Seaway and World-Wide were also citizens of New York, the federal courts would not have jurisdiction under 28 USC 1332 as long as the two New York defendants remained in the case - so the suit would stay in state court. So perhaps the attempt to stay in state court was an important underlying factor in this dispute. There will be much more about removal, and Diversity jurisdiction in Chapters 3 and 4.

7. In the next case, does it make any legal difference that the defendant is a businessman, rather than a high school student employed to cook the burgers?

# SUPREME COURT OF THE UNITED STATES
## BURGER KING CORPORATION, APPELLANT
### V.
## JOHN RUDZEWICZ.

DECIDED MAY 20, 1985

**Mr. Justice BRENNAN delivered the opinion of the Court.**

The State of Florida's long-arm statute extends jurisdiction to "any person, whether or not a citizen or resident of this state," who, *inter alia,* "breaches a contract in this state by failing to perform acts required by the contract to be performed in this state," so long as the cause of action arises from the alleged contractual breach. The United States District Court for the Southern District of Florida, sitting in diversity, relied on this provision in exercising personal jurisdiction over a Michigan resident who allegedly had breached a franchise agreement with a Florida corporation by failing to make required payments in Florida. The question presented is whether this exercise of long-arm jurisdiction offended "traditional conceptions of fair play and substantial justice" embodied in the Due Process Clause of the Fourteenth Amendment. *International Shoe.*

I

A

Burger King Corporation is a Florida corporation whose principal offices are in Miami. It is one of the world's largest restaurant organizations, with over 3,000 outlets in the 50 States, the Commonwealth of Puerto Rico, and 8 foreign nations. Burger King conducts approximately 80% of its business through a franchise operation that the company styles the "Burger King System"—"a comprehensive restaurant format and operating system for the sale of uniform and quality food products." Burger King licenses its franchisees to use its trademarks and service marks for a period of 20 years and leases standardized restaurant facilities to them for the same term. In addition, franchisees acquire a variety of proprietary information concerning the "standards, specifications, procedures and methods for operating a Burger King Restaurant." They also receive market research and advertising assistance; ongoing training in restaurant management. [Mandatory training seminars are conducted at Burger King University in Miami and at Whopper College Regional Training Centers around the country.]

By permitting franchisees to tap into Burger King's established national reputation and to benefit from proven procedures for dispensing standardized fare, this system enables them to go into the restaurant business with significantly lowered barriers to entry.

In exchange for these benefits, franchisees pay Burger King an initial $40,000 franchise fee and commit themselves to payment of monthly royalties, advertising and sales promotion fees, and rent computed in part from monthly gross sales. Franchisees also agree to submit to the national organization's exacting regulation of virtually every conceivable aspect of their operations. Burger King imposes these standards and undertakes its rigid regulation out of conviction that "uniformity of service, appearance, and quality of product is essential to the preservation of the Burger King image and the benefits accruing therefrom to both Franchisee and Franchisor."

Burger King oversees its franchise system through a two-tiered administrative structure. The governing contracts provide that the franchise relationship is established in Miami and governed by Florida law, and call for payment of all required fees and forwarding of all relevant notices to the Miami headquarters. The Miami headquarters sets policy and works directly with its franchisees in attempting to resolve major problems. Day-to-day monitoring of franchisees, however, is conducted through a network of 10 district offices which in turn report to the Miami headquarters.

The instant litigation grows out of Burger King's termination of one of its franchisees, and is aptly described by the franchisee as "a divorce proceeding among commercial partners." The appellee John Rudzewicz, a Michigan citizen and resident, is the senior partner in a Detroit accounting firm. In 1978, he was approached by Brian MacShara, the son of a business acquaintance, who suggested that they jointly apply to Burger King for a franchise in the Detroit area. Rudzewicz and MacShara finally obtained limited concessions from the Miami headquarters, signed the final agreements, and commenced operations in June 1979. By signing the final agreements, Rudzewicz obligated himself personally to payments exceeding $1 million over the 20-year franchise relationship.

The Drayton Plains facility apparently enjoyed steady business during the summer of 1979, but patronage declined after a recession began later that year. Rudzewicz and MacShara soon fell far behind in their monthly payments to Miami. After several Burger King officials in Miami had engaged in prolonged but ultimately unsuccessful negotiations with the franchisees by mail and by telephone, headquarters terminated the franchise and ordered Rudzewicz and MacShara to vacate the premises. They refused and continued to occupy and operate the facility as a Burger King restaurant.

B

Burger King commenced the instant action in the United States District Court for the Southern District of Florida in May 1981, invoking that court's diversity jurisdiction pursuant to 28 U.S.C. § 1332(a) and its original jurisdiction over federal trademark disputes pursuant to § 1338(a). Burger King sought damages, injunctive relief, and costs and attorney's fees. Rudzewicz and MacShara entered special appearances and argued, *inter alia,* that because they were Michigan residents and because Burger King's claim did not "arise" within the Southern District of Florida, the District Court lacked personal jurisdiction over them. The District Court denied their motions holding that, pursuant to Florida's long-arm statute, "a non-resident Burger King franchisee is subject to the personal jurisdiction of this Court in actions arising out of its franchise agreements." Rudzewicz and MacShara then filed an answer and a counterclaim seeking damages for alleged violations by Burger King of Michigan's Franchise Investment Law.

After a 3-day bench trial, the court again concluded that it had "jurisdiction over the subject matter and the parties to this cause." Finding that Rudzewicz and MacShara had breached their franchise agreements with Burger King and had infringed Burger King's trademarks and service marks, the court entered judgment against them, jointly and severally, for $228,875 in contract damages. The court also ordered them "to immediately close Burger King Restaurant Number 775 from continued operation or to immediately give the keys and possession of said restaurant to Burger King Corporation," found that they had failed to prove any of the required elements of their counterclaim, and awarded costs and attorney's fees to Burger King.

Rudzewicz appealed to the Court of Appeals for the Eleventh Circuit. A divided panel of that Circuit reversed the judgment, concluding that the District Court could not properly exercise personal jurisdiction over Rudzewicz pursuant to Fla.Stat. § 48.193(1)(g) because "the circumstances of the Drayton Plains franchise and the negotiations which led to it left Rudzewicz bereft of reasonable notice and financially unprepared for the prospect of franchise litigation in Florida." Accordingly, the panel majority concluded that "jurisdiction under these circumstances would offend the fundamental fairness which is the touchstone of due process."

We grant Burger King's petition for certiorari and now reverse.

## II

## A

The Due Process Clause protects an individual's liberty interest in not being subject to the binding judgments of a forum with which he has established no meaningful "contacts, ties, or relations." *International Shoe.* By requiring that individuals have "fair warning that a particular activity may subject them to the jurisdiction of a foreign sovereign," the Due Process Clause "gives a degree of predictability to the legal system that allows potential defendants to structure their primary conduct with some minimum assurance as to where that conduct will and will not render them liable to suit."

Although territorial presence frequently will enhance a potential defendant's affiliation with a State and reinforce the reasonable foreseeability of suit there, it is an inescapable fact of modern commercial life that a substantial amount of business is transacted solely by mail and wire communications across state lines, thus obviating the need for physical presence within a State in which business is conducted. So long as a commercial actor's efforts are "purposefully directed" toward residents of another State, we have consistently rejected the notion that an absence of physical contacts can defeat personal jurisdiction there.

Once it has been decided that a defendant purposefully established minimum contacts within the forum State, these contacts may be considered in light of other factors to determine whether the assertion of personal jurisdiction would comport with "fair play and substantial justice." Where a defendant who purposefully has directed his activities at forum residents seeks to defeat jurisdiction, he must present a compelling case that the presence of some other considerations would render jurisdiction unreasonable. Most such considerations usually may be accommodated through means short of finding jurisdiction unconstitutional. For example, the potential clash of the forum's law with the "fundamental substantive social policies" of another State may be accommodated through application of the forum's choice-of-law rules. Similarly, a defendant claiming substantial inconvenience may seek a change of venue. Nevertheless, minimum requirements inherent in the concept of "fair play and substantial justice" may defeat the reasonableness of jurisdiction even if the defendant has purposefully engaged in forum activities. Jurisdictional rules may not be employed in such a way as to make litigation "so gravely difficult and inconvenient" that a party unfairly is at a "severe disadvantage" in comparison to his opponent.

B

(1)

Applying these principles to the case at hand, we believe there is substantial record evidence supporting the District Court's conclusion that the assertion of personal jurisdiction over Rudzewicz in Florida for the alleged breach of his franchise agreement did not offend due process. If the question is whether an individual's contract with an out-of-state party *alone* can automatically establish sufficient minimum contacts in the other party's home forum, we believe the answer clearly is that it cannot. The Court long ago rejected the notion that personal jurisdiction might turn on "mechanical" tests, or on "conceptualistic theories of the place of contracting or of performance." Instead, we have emphasized the need for a "highly realistic" approach that recognizes that a "contract" is "ordinarily but an intermediate step serving to tie up prior business negotiations with future consequences which themselves are the real object of the business transaction." It is these factors—prior negotiations and contemplated future consequences, along with the terms of the contract and the parties' actual course of dealing—that must be evaluated in determining whether the defendant purposefully established minimum contacts within the forum.

In this case, no physical ties to Florida can be attributed to Rudzewicz other than MacShara's brief training course in Miami. Rudzewicz did not maintain offices in Florida and, for all that appears from the record, has never even visited there. Yet this franchise dispute grew directly out of "a contract which had a *substantial* connection with that State." Eschewing the option of operating an independent local enterprise, Rudzewicz deliberately "reached out beyond" Michigan and negotiated with a Florida corporation for the purchase of a long-term franchise and the manifold benefits that would derive from affiliation with a nationwide organization. Upon approval, he entered into a carefully structured 20-year relationship that envisioned continuing and wide-reaching contacts with Burger King in Florida. In light of Rudzewicz' voluntary acceptance of the long-term and exacting regulation of his business from Burger King's Miami headquarters, the "quality and nature" of his relationship to the company in Florida can in no sense be viewed as "random," "fortuitous," or "attenuated." Rudzewicz' refusal to make the contractually required payments in Miami, and his continued use of Burger King's trademarks and confidential business information after his termination, caused foreseeable injuries to the corporation in Florida. For these reasons it was, at the very least, presumptively reasonable for Rudzewicz to be called to account there for such injuries.

The Court of Appeals concluded, however, that in light of the supervision emanating from Burger King's district office in Birmingham, Rudzewicz reasonably believed that "the Michigan office was for all intents and purposes the embodiment of Burger King" and that he therefore had no "reason to anticipate a Burger King suit outside of Michigan." This reasoning overlooks substantial record evidence indicating that Rudzewicz most certainly knew that he was affiliating himself with an enterprise based primarily in Florida. The contract documents themselves emphasize that Burger King's operations are conducted and supervised from the Miami headquarters, that all relevant notices and payments must be sent there, and that the agreements were made in and enforced from Miami. Moreover, the parties' actual course of dealing repeatedly confirmed that decision making authority was vested in the Miami headquarters and that the district office served largely as an intermediate link between the headquarters and the franchisees. When problems arose over building design, site-development fees, rent computation, and the defaulted payments, Rudzewicz and MacShara learned that the Michigan office was powerless to resolve their disputes and could only channel their communications to Miami. Throughout these disputes, the Miami headquarters and the Michigan franchisees carried on a continuous course of direct communications by mail and by telephone, and it was the Miami headquarters that made the key negotiating decisions out of which the instant litigation arose.

Moreover, we believe the Court of Appeals gave insufficient weight to provisions in the various franchise documents providing that all disputes would be governed by Florida law. The franchise agreement, for example, stated:

> This Agreement shall become valid when executed and accepted by BKC at Miami, Florida; it shall be deemed made and entered into in the State of Florida and shall be governed and construed under and in accordance with the laws of the State of Florida. The choice of law designation does not require that all suits concerning this Agreement be filed in Florida.

The Court of Appeals reasoned that choice-of-law provisions are irrelevant to the question of personal jurisdiction - that "the center of gravity for choice-of-law purposes does not necessarily confer the sovereign prerogative to assert jurisdiction." Nothing in our cases suggests that a *choice-of-law provision* should be ignored in considering whether a defendant has "purposefully invoked the benefits and protections of a State's laws" for jurisdictional purposes. Although such a provision standing alone would be insufficient to confer jurisdiction, we believe that, when combined with the 20-year interdependent relationship Rudzewicz established with

Burger King's Miami headquarters, it reinforced his deliberate affiliation with the forum State and the reasonable foreseeability of possible litigation there.

(2)

Nor has Rudzewicz pointed to other factors that can be said persuasively to outweigh the considerations discussed above and to establish the *unconstitutionality* of Florida's assertion of jurisdiction. We cannot conclude that Florida had no legitimate interest in holding Rudzewicz answerable on a claim related to the contacts he had established in that State. Moreover, although Rudzewicz has argued at some length that Michigan's Franchise Investment Law, governs many aspects of this franchise relationship, he has not demonstrated how Michigan's acknowledged interest might possibly render jurisdiction in Florida *unconstitutional.* Finally, the Court of Appeals' assertion that the Florida litigation "severely impaired Rudzewicz' ability to call Michigan witnesses who might be essential to his defense and counterclaim," is wholly without support in the record. And even to the extent that it is inconvenient for a party who has minimum contacts with a forum to litigate there, such considerations most frequently can be accommodated through a change of venue. Although the Court has suggested that inconvenience may at some point become so substantial as to achieve *constitutional* magnitude, this is not such a case.

The Court of Appeals also concluded, however, that the parties' dealings involved "a characteristic disparity of bargaining power" and "elements of surprise," and that Rudzewicz "lacked fair notice" of the potential for litigation in Florida because the contractual provisions suggesting to the contrary were merely "boilerplate declarations in a lengthy printed contract." Rudzewicz presented many of these arguments to the District Court, contending that Burger King was guilty of misrepresentation, fraud, and duress; that it gave insufficient notice in its dealings with him; and that the contract was one of adhesion. After a 3-day bench trial, the District Court found that Burger King had made no misrepresentations, that Rudzewicz and MacShara "were and are experienced and sophisticated businessmen," and that "at no time" did they "act under economic duress or disadvantage imposed by" Burger King. To the contrary, Rudzewicz was represented by counsel throughout these complex transactions and, as Judge Johnson observed in dissent below, was himself an experienced accountant "who for five months conducted negotiations with Burger King over the terms of the franchise and lease agreements, and who obligated himself personally to contracts requiring overtime payments that exceeded $1 million." Rudzewicz was able to secure a modest reduction in rent and other concessions from Miami headquarters; moreover, to the extent that Burger King's terms were inflexible, Rudzewicz presumably decided that the advantages of affiliating with a national organization provided sufficient commercial benefits to offset the detriments.

## III

Notwithstanding these considerations, the Court of Appeals apparently believed that it was necessary to reject jurisdiction in this case as a prophylactic measure, reasoning that an affirmance of the District Court's judgment would result in the exercise of jurisdiction over "out-of-state consumers to collect payments due on modest personal purchases" and would "sow the seeds of default judgments against franchisees owing smaller debts." We share the Court of Appeals' broader concerns and therefore reject any talismanic jurisdictional formulas; "the facts of each case must always be weighed" in determining whether personal jurisdiction would comport with "fair play and substantial justice." The "quality and nature" of an interstate transaction may sometimes be so "random," "fortuitous," or "attenuated" that it cannot fairly be said that the potential defendant "should reasonably anticipate being haled into court" in another jurisdiction. We also have emphasized that jurisdiction may not be grounded on a contract whose terms have been obtained through "fraud, undue influence, or overweening bargaining power" and whose application would render litigation "so gravely difficult and inconvenient that a party will for all practical purposes be deprived of his day in court." Just as the Due Process Clause allows flexibility in ensuring that commercial actors are not effectively "judgment proof" for the consequences of obligations they voluntarily assume in other States, so too does it prevent rules that would unfairly enable them to obtain default judgments against unwitting customers.

For the reasons set forth above, however, these dangers are not present in the instant case. Because Rudzewicz established a substantial and continuing relationship with Burger King's Miami headquarters, received fair notice from the contract documents and the course of dealing that he might be subject to suit in Florida, and has failed to demonstrate how jurisdiction in that forum would otherwise be fundamentally unfair, we conclude that the District Court's exercise of jurisdiction pursuant to Fla.Stat. § 48.193(1)(g) (Supp.1984) did not offend due process. The judgment of the Court of Appeals is accordingly reversed, and the case is remanded for further proceedings consistent with this opinion.

It is so ordered.

8. When United States courts are seeking to exercise jurisdiction over foreign companies, the "fair play" calculations may be somewhat different.

107 S.CT. 1026

## SUPREME COURT OF THE UNITED STATES

### ASAHI METAL INDUSTRY CO., LTD., PETITIONER

v.

### SUPERIOR COURT OF CALIFORNIA, SOLANO COUNTY

### (CHENG SHIN RUBBER INDUSTRIAL CO., LTD., REAL PARTY IN INTEREST).

DECIDED FEBRUARY 24, 1987

Justice O'CONNOR announced the judgment of the Court and delivered the unanimous opinion of the Court with respect to Part I, the opinion of the Court with respect to Part II–B, in which THE CHIEF JUSTICE, Justice BRENNAN, Justice WHITE, Justice MARSHALL, Justice BLACKMUN, Justice POWELL, and Justice STEVENS join, and an opinion with respect to Parts II–A and III, in which THE CHIEF JUSTICE, Justice POWELL, and Justice SCALIA join.

This case presents the question whether the mere awareness on the part of a foreign defendant that the components it manufactured, sold, and delivered outside the United States would reach the forum State in the stream of commerce constitutes "minimum contacts" between the defendant and the forum State such that the exercise of jurisdiction "does not offend 'traditional notions of fair play and substantial justice.'"

## I

On September 23, 1978, on Interstate Highway 80 in Solano County, California, Gary Zurcher lost control of his Honda motorcycle and collided with a tractor. Zurcher was severely injured, and his passenger and wife, Ruth Ann Moreno, was killed. In September 1979, Zurcher filed a product liability action in the Superior Court of the State of California in and for the County of Solano. Zurcher alleged that the 1978 accident was caused by a sudden loss of air and an explosion in the rear tire of the motorcycle, and alleged that the motorcycle tire, tube, and sealant were defective. Zurcher's complaint named, *inter alia,* Cheng Shin Rubber Industrial Co., Ltd. (Cheng Shin), the Taiwanese manufacturer of the tube. Cheng Shin in turn filed a cross-complaint seeking indemnification from its codefendants and from petitioner, Asahi Metal Industry Co., Ltd. (Asahi), the manufacturer of the tube's valve assembly. Zurcher's claims against Cheng Shin and the other defendants were eventually settled and dismissed, leaving only Cheng Shin's indemnity action against Asahi.

California's long-arm statute authorizes the exercise of jurisdiction "on any basis not inconsistent with the Constitution of this state or of the United States." Asahi moved to quash Cheng Shin's service of summons, arguing the State could not exert jurisdiction over it consistent with the Due Process Clause of the Fourteenth Amendment.

In relation to the motion, the following information was submitted by Asahi and Cheng Shin. Asahi is a Japanese corporation. It manufactures tire valve assemblies in Japan and sells the assemblies to Cheng Shin, and to several other tire manufacturers, for use as components in finished tire tubes. Asahi's sales to Cheng Shin took place in Taiwan. The shipments from Asahi to Cheng Shin were sent from Japan to Taiwan. Cheng Shin bought and incorporated into its tire tubes 150,000 Asahi valve assemblies in 1978; 500,000 in 1979; 500,000 in 1980; 100,000 in 1981; and 100,000 in 1982. Sales to Cheng Shin accounted for 1.24 percent of Asahi's income in 1981 and 0.44 percent in 1982. Cheng Shin alleged that approximately 20 percent of its sales in the United States are in California. Cheng Shin purchases valve assemblies from other suppliers as well, and sells finished tubes throughout the world.

In 1983 an attorney for Cheng Shin conducted an informal examination of the valve stems of the tire tubes sold in one cycle store in Solano County. The attorney declared that of the approximately 115 tire tubes in the store, 97 were purportedly manufactured in Japan or Taiwan, and of those 21 valve stems were marked with the circled letter "A", apparently Asahi's trademark. Of the 21 Asahi valve stems, 12 were incorporated into Cheng Shin tire tubes. The store contained 41 other Cheng Shin tubes that incorporated the valve assemblies of other manufacturers. An affidavit of a manager of Cheng Shin whose duties included the purchasing of component parts stated: "'In discussions with Asahi regarding the purchase of valve stem assemblies the fact that my Company sells tubes throughout the world and specifically the United States has been discussed. I am informed and believe that Asahi was fully aware that valve stem assemblies sold to my Company and to others would end up throughout the United States and in California.'" An affidavit of the president of Asahi, on the other hand, declared that Asahi "'has never contemplated that its limited sales of tire valves to Cheng Shin in Taiwan would subject it to lawsuits in California.'" The record does not include any contract between Cheng Shin and Asahi.

Primarily on the basis of the above information, the Superior Court denied the motion to quash summons. The Court of Appeal of the State of California issued a peremptory writ of mandate commanding the Superior Court to quash service of summons. The Supreme Court of the State of California reversed and discharged the writ issued by the Court of Appeal. The court found the exercise of jurisdiction over Asahi to be consistent with the Due Process Clause. It concluded that Asahi knew that some of the valve assemblies sold to Cheng Shin would be incorporated into tire tubes sold in California, and that Asahi benefited indirectly from the sale in California of products incorporating its components. The court considered Asahi's intentional act of placing its components into the stream of commerce—that is, by delivering the components to Cheng Shin in Taiwan—coupled with Asahi's awareness that some of the components would eventually find their way into California, sufficient to form the basis for state court jurisdiction under the Due Process Clause.

We granted certiorari, and now reverse.

II

A

The Due Process Clause of the Fourteenth Amendment limits the power of a state court to exert personal jurisdiction over a nonresident defendant. "The constitutional touchstone" of the determination whether an exercise of personal jurisdiction comports with due process "remains whether the defendant purposefully established 'minimum contacts' in the forum State." Most recently we have reaffirmed the oft-quoted reasoning that minimum contacts must have a basis in "some act by which the defendant purposefully avails itself of the privilege of conducting activities within the forum State, thus invoking the benefits and protections of its laws."

We now find that the "substantial connection," between the defendant and the forum State necessary for a finding of minimum contacts must come about by *an action of the defendant purposefully directed toward the forum State.* The placement of a product into the stream of commerce, without more, is not an act of the defendant purposefully directed toward the forum State. Additional conduct of the defendant may indicate an intent or purpose to serve the market in the forum State, for example, designing the product for the market in the forum State, advertising in the forum State, establishing channels for providing regular advice to customers in the forum State, or marketing the product through a distributor who has agreed to serve as the sales agent in the forum State. But a defendant's awareness that the stream of commerce may or will sweep the product into the forum State does not convert the mere act of placing the product into the stream into an act purposefully directed toward the forum State.

Assuming, *arguendo,* that respondents have established Asahi's awareness that some of the valves sold to Cheng Shin would be incorporated into tire tubes sold in California, respondents have not demonstrated any action by Asahi to purposefully avail itself of the California market. Asahi does not do business in California. It has no office, agents, employees, or property in California. It does not advertise or otherwise solicit business in California. It did not create, control, or employ the distribution system that brought its valves to California. There is no evidence that Asahi designed its product in anticipation of sales in California. On the basis of these facts, the exertion of personal jurisdiction over Asahi by the Superior Court of California exceeds the limits of due process.

B

The strictures of the Due Process Clause forbid a state court to exercise personal jurisdiction over Asahi under circumstances that would offend "'traditional notions of fair play and substantial justice.'"

We have previously explained that the determination of the reasonableness of the exercise of jurisdiction in each case will depend on an evaluation of several factors. A court must consider the burden on the defendant, the interests of the forum State, and the plaintiff's interest in obtaining relief. It must also weigh in its determination "the interstate judicial system's interest in obtaining the most efficient resolution of controversies; and the shared interest of the several States in furthering fundamental substantive social policies."

A consideration of these factors in the present case clearly reveals the unreasonableness of the assertion of jurisdiction over Asahi, even apart from the question of the placement of goods in the stream of commerce.

Certainly the burden on the defendant in this case is severe. Asahi has been commanded by the Supreme Court of California not only to traverse the distance between Asahi's headquarters in Japan and the Superior Court of California in and for the County of Solano, but also to submit its dispute with Cheng Shin to a foreign nation's judicial system. The unique burdens placed upon one who must defend oneself in a foreign legal system should have significant weight in assessing the reasonableness of stretching the long arm of personal jurisdiction over national borders.

When minimum contacts have been established, often the interests of the plaintiff and the forum in the exercise of jurisdiction will justify even the serious burdens placed on the alien defendant. In the present case, however, the interests of the plaintiff and the forum in California's assertion of jurisdiction over Asahi are slight. All that remains is a claim for indemnification asserted by Cheng Shin, a Taiwanese corporation, against Asahi. The transaction on which the indemnification claim is based took place in Taiwan; Asahi's components were shipped from Japan to Taiwan.

Cheng Shin has not demonstrated that it is more convenient for it to litigate its indemnification claim against Asahi in California rather than in Taiwan or Japan.

Because the plaintiff is not a California resident, California's legitimate interests in the dispute have considerably diminished. The Supreme Court of California argued that the State had an interest in "protecting its consumers by ensuring that foreign manufacturers comply with the state's safety standards." The State Supreme Court's definition of California's interest, however, was overly broad. The dispute between Cheng Shin and Asahi is primarily about indemnification rather than safety standards. Moreover, it is not at all clear at this point that California law should govern the question whether a Japanese corporation should indemnify a Taiwanese corporation on the basis of a sale made in Taiwan and a shipment of goods from Japan to Taiwan. The possibility of being haled into a California court as a result of an accident involving Asahi's components undoubtedly creates an additional deterrent to the manufacture of unsafe components; however, similar pressures will be placed on Asahi by the purchasers of its components as long as those who use Asahi components in their final products, and sell those products in California, are subject to the application of California tort law.

*World-Wide Volkswagen* admonished courts to take into consideration the interests of the "several States," in addition to the forum State, in the efficient judicial resolution of the dispute and the advancement of substantive policies. In the present case, this advice calls for a court to consider the procedural and substantive policies of other *nations* whose interests are affected by the assertion of jurisdiction by the California court. The procedural and substantive interests of other nations in a state court's assertion of jurisdiction over an alien defendant will differ from case to case. In every case, however, those interests, as well as the Federal interest in Government's foreign relations policies, will be best served by a careful inquiry into the reasonableness of the assertion of jurisdiction in the particular case, and an unwillingness to find the serious burdens on an alien defendant outweighed by minimal interests on the part of the plaintiff or the forum State. "Great care and reserve should be exercised when extending our notions of personal jurisdiction into the international field."

Considering the international context, the heavy burden on the alien defendant, and the slight interests of the plaintiff and the forum State, the exercise of personal jurisdiction by a California court over Asahi in this instance would be unreasonable and unfair.

## III

Because the facts of this case do not establish minimum contacts such that the exercise of personal jurisdiction is consistent with fair play and substantial justice, the judgment of the Supreme Court of California is reversed, and the case is remanded for further proceedings not inconsistent with this opinion.

It is so ordered.

9. Recall that in 1978, in *Kulko v. Superior Court,* the U.S. Supreme Court held that a father's actions in sending his children to live with their mother in California did not give the California courts jurisdiction over the amount of child support to be paid by the father. How does the following case differ from *Kulko v. Superior Court?* Note that no single part of the following opinion secured enough votes to be the opinion of the court.

**110 S.CT. 2105**

**SUPREME COURT OF THE UNITED STATES**

**DENNIS BURNHAM, PETITIONER**

**v.**

**SUPERIOR COURT OF CALIFORNIA, COUNTY OF MARIN**

**(FRANCIE BURNHAM, REAL PARTY IN INTEREST).**

DECIDED MAY 29, 1990

SCALIA, J., announced the judgment of the Court and delivered an opinion, in which REHNQUIST, C.J., and KENNEDY, J., joined, and in which WHITE, J., joined as to Parts I, II–A, II–B, and II–C. WHITE, J., filed an opinion concurring in part and concurring in the judgment, *post,* p. 2119. BRENNAN, J., filed an opinion concurring in the judgment, in which MARSHALL, BLACKMUN, and O'CONNOR, JJ., joined, *post,* p. 2120. STEVENS, J., filed an opinion concurring in the judgment, *post,* p. 2126.

The question presented is whether the Due Process Clause of the Fourteenth Amendment denies California courts jurisdiction over a nonresident, who was personally served with process while temporarily in that State, in a suit unrelated to his activities in the State.

# I

Petitioner Dennis Burnham married Francie Burnham in 1976 in West Virginia. In 1977 the couple moved to New Jersey, where their two children were born. In July 1987 the Burnhams decided to separate. They agreed that Mrs. Burnham, who intended to move to California, would take custody of the children. Shortly before Mrs. Burnham departed for California that same month, she and petitioner agreed that she would file for divorce on grounds of "irreconcilable differences."

In October 1987, petitioner filed for divorce in New Jersey state court on grounds of "desertion." Petitioner did not, however, obtain an issuance of summons against his wife and did not attempt to serve her with process. Mrs. Burnham, after unsuccessfully demanding that petitioner adhere to their prior agreement to submit to an "irreconcilable differences" divorce, brought suit for divorce in California state court in early January 1988.

In late January, petitioner visited southern California on business, after which he went north to visit his children in the San Francisco Bay area, where his wife resided. He took the older child to San Francisco for the weekend. Upon returning the child to Mrs. Burnham's home on January 24, 1988, petitioner was served with a California court summons and a copy of Mrs. Burnham's divorce petition. He then returned to New Jersey.

Later that year, petitioner made a special appearance in the California Superior Court, moving to quash the service of process on the ground that the court lacked personal jurisdiction over him because his only contacts with California were a few short visits to the State for the purposes of conducting business and visiting his children. The Superior Court denied the motion, and the California Court of Appeal denied mandamus relief, rejecting petitioner's contention that the Due Process Clause prohibited California courts from asserting jurisdiction over him because he lacked "minimum contacts" with the State. The court held it to be "a valid jurisdictional predicate for *in personam* jurisdiction" that the "defendant was present in the forum state and personally served with process."

## II

### A

The proposition that the judgment of a court lacking jurisdiction is void traces back to the English Year Books, see *Bowser v. Collins,* (Ex. Ch. 1482), and was made settled law by Lord Coke in *Case of the Marshalsea,* (K.B. 1612). Traditionally that proposition was embodied in the phrase *coram non judice,* "before a person not a judge"—meaning, in effect, that the proceeding in question was not a *judicial* proceeding because lawful judicial authority was not present, and could therefore not yield a *judgment.* American courts invalidated, or denied recognition to, judgments that violated this common-law principle long before the Fourteenth Amendment was adopted. See, *e.g., Grumon v. Raymond,* (1814). In *Pennoyer v. Neff,* (1878), we announced that the judgment of a court lacking personal jurisdiction violated the Due Process Clause of the Fourteenth Amendment as well.

To determine whether the assertion of personal jurisdiction is consistent with due process, we have long relied on the principles traditionally followed by American courts in marking out the territorial limits of each State's authority. That criterion was first announced in *Pennoyer v. Neff.* In what has become the classic expression of the criterion, we said in *International Shoe* that a state court's assertion of personal jurisdiction satisfies the Due Process Clause if it does not violate traditional notions of fair play and substantial justice. Since *International Shoe,* we have only been called upon to decide whether these "traditional notions" permit States to exercise jurisdiction over absent defendants in a manner that deviates from the rules of jurisdiction applied in the 19th century. We have held such deviations permissible, but only with respect to suits arising out of the absent defendant's contacts with the State. The question we must decide today is whether due process requires a similar connection between the litigation and the defendant's contacts with the State in cases where the defendant is physically present in the State at the time process is served upon him.

### B

Among the most firmly established principles of personal jurisdiction in American tradition is that the courts of a State have jurisdiction over nonresidents who are physically present in the State. The view developed early that each State had the power to hale before its courts any individual who could be found within its borders, and that once having acquired jurisdiction over such a person by properly serving him with process, the State could retain jurisdiction to enter judgment against him, no matter how fleeting his visit. That view had antecedents in English common-law practice, which sometimes allowed "transitory" actions, arising out of events outside the country, to be maintained against seemingly nonresident defendants who were present in England. Justice Story believed the principle, which he traced to Roman origins, to be firmly grounded in English tradition: "By the common law, personal actions, being transitory, may be brought in any place, where the party defendant may be found," for "every nation may ... rightfully exercise jurisdiction over all persons within its domains."

Recent scholarship has suggested that English tradition was not as clear as Story thought. Accurate or not, however, judging by the evidence of contemporaneous or near-contemporaneous decisions, one must conclude that Story's understanding was shared by American courts at the crucial time for present purposes: 1868, when the Fourteenth Amendment was adopted. The following passage in a decision of the Supreme Court of Georgia, in an action on a debt having no apparent relation to the defendant's temporary presence in the State, is representative:

> "Can a citizen of Alabama be sued in this State, as he passes through it?
>
> "Undoubtedly he can. The second of the axioms of *Huberus,* as translated by *Story,* is: 'that all persons who are found within the limits of a government, whether their residence is permanent or temporary, are to be deemed subjects thereof.'
>
> "A citizen of another State, who is merely passing through this State, resides, as he passes, wherever he is. Let him be sued, therefore, wherever he may, he will be sued where he resides."

Decisions in the courts of many States in the 19th and early 20th centuries held that personal service upon a physically present defendant sufficed to confer jurisdiction, without regard to whether the defendant was only briefly in the State or whether the cause of action was related to his activities there. Most States, moreover, had statutes or common-law rules that exempted from service of process individuals who were brought into the forum by force or fraud, or who were there as a party or witness in unrelated judicial proceedings These exceptions obviously rested upon the premise that service of process conferred jurisdiction. Particularly striking is the fact that, as far as we have been able to determine, *not one* American case from the period (or, for that matter, not one American case until 1978) held, or even suggested, that in-state personal service on an individual was insufficient to confer personal jurisdiction.

This American jurisdictional practice is, moreover, not merely old; it is continuing. It remains the practice of, not only a substantial number of the States, but as far as we are aware *all* the States and the Federal Government—if one disregards (as one must for this purpose) the few opinions since 1978 that have erroneously said, on grounds similar to those that petitioner presses here, that this Court's due process decisions render the practice unconstitutional. We do not know of a single state or federal statute, or a single judicial decision resting upon state law, that has abandoned in-state service as a basis of jurisdiction. Many recent cases reaffirm it.

C

Despite this formidable body of precedent, petitioner contends, in reliance on our decisions applying the *International Shoe* standard, that in the absence of "continuous and systematic" contacts with the forum, a nonresident defendant can be subjected to judgment only as to matters that arise out of or relate to his contacts with the forum. This argument rests on a thorough misunderstanding of our cases.

The view of most courts in the 19th century was that a court simply could not exercise *in personam* jurisdiction over a nonresident who had not been personally served with process in the forum. *Pennoyer v. Neff*, while renowned for its statement of the principle that the Fourteenth Amendment prohibits such an exercise of jurisdiction, in fact set that forth only as dictum and decided the case (which involved a judgment rendered more than two years before the Fourteenth Amendment's ratification) under "well-established principles of public law." Those principles, embodied in the Due Process Clause, required (we said) that when proceedings "involve merely a determination of the personal liability of the defendant, he must be brought within the court's jurisdiction by service of process within the State, or his voluntary appearance."

Later years, however, saw the weakening of the *Pennoyer* rule. In the late 19th and early 20th centuries, changes in the technology of transportation and communication, and the tremendous growth of interstate business activity, led to an "inevitable relaxation of the strict limits on state jurisdiction" over nonresident individuals and corporations. States required, for example, that nonresident corporations appoint an in-state agent upon whom process could be served as a condition of transacting business within their borders, and provided in-state "substituted service" for nonresident motorists who caused injury in the State and left before personal service could be accomplished, see, *Hess v. Pawloski* (1927). We initially upheld these laws under the Due Process Clause on grounds that they complied with *Pennoyer*'s rigid requirement of either "consent," or "presence." As many observed, however, the consent and presence were purely fictional. Our opinion in *International Shoe* cast those fictions aside and made explicit the underlying basis of these decisions: Due process does not necessarily *require* the States to adhere to the unbending territorial limits on jurisdiction set forth in *Pennoyer*. The validity of assertion of jurisdiction over a non-consenting defendant who is not present in the forum depends upon whether "the quality and nature of his activity" in relation to the forum renders such jurisdiction consistent with traditional notions of fair play and substantial justice. Subsequent cases have derived from the *International Shoe* standard the general rule that a State may dispense with in-forum personal service on nonresident defendants in suits arising out of their activities in the State. As *International Shoe* suggests, the defendant's litigation-related "minimum contacts" may take the place of physical presence as the basis for jurisdiction.

Nothing in *International Shoe* or the cases that have followed it, however, offers support for the very different proposition petitioner seeks to establish today: that a defendant's presence in the forum is not only unnecessary to validate novel, non-traditional assertions of jurisdiction, but is itself no longer sufficient to establish jurisdiction.

The short of the matter is that jurisdiction based on physical presence alone constitutes due process because it is one of the continuing traditions of our legal system that define the due process standard of "traditional notions of fair play and substantial justice." That standard was developed by *analogy* to "physical presence," and it would be perverse to say it could now be turned against that touchstone of jurisdiction.

D

Petitioner's strongest argument, though we ultimately reject it, relies upon our decision in *Shaffer v. Heitner*, (1977). In that case, a Delaware court hearing a shareholder's derivative suit against a corporation's directors secured jurisdiction *quasi in rem* by sequestering the out-of-state defendants' stock in the company, the situs of which was Delaware under Delaware law. Reasoning that Delaware's sequestration procedure was simply a mechanism to compel the absent defendants to appear in a suit to determine their personal rights and obligations, we concluded that the normal rules we had developed under *International Shoe* for jurisdiction over suits against absent defendants should apply—viz., Delaware could not hear the suit because the defendants' sole contact with the State (ownership of property there) was unrelated to the lawsuit.

It goes too far to say, as petitioner contends, that *Shaffer* compels the conclusion that a State lacks jurisdiction over an individual unless the litigation arises out of his activities in the State. *Shaffer,* like *International Shoe,* involved jurisdiction over an *absent defendant,* and it stands for nothing more than the proposition that when the "minimum contact" that is a substitute for physical presence consists of property ownership it must, like other minimum contacts, be related to the litigation

It is fair to say, however, that while our holding today does not contradict *Shaffer,* our basic approach to the due process question is different. We have conducted no independent inquiry into the desirability or fairness of the prevailing in-state service rule, leaving that judgment to the legislatures that are free to amend it; for our purposes, its validation is its pedigree, as the phrase "*traditional notions* of fair play and substantial justice" makes clear. *Shaffer* did conduct such an independent inquiry, asserting that "traditional notions of fair play and substantial justice" can be as readily offended by the perpetuation of ancient forms that are no longer justified as by the adoption of new procedures that are inconsistent with the basic values of our constitutional heritage. Where, as in the present case, a jurisdictional principle is both firmly approved by tradition and still favored, it is impossible to imagine what standard we could appeal to for the judgment that it is "no longer justified." While in no way receding from or casting doubt upon the holding of *Shaffer* or any other case, we reaffirm today our time-honored approach. For new procedures, hitherto unknown, the Due Process Clause requires analysis to determine whether "traditional notions of fair play and substantial justice" have been offended. But a doctrine of personal jurisdiction that dates back to the adoption of the Fourteenth Amendment and is still generally observed unquestionably meets that standard.

## III

A few words in response to Justice BRENNAN's opinion concurring in the judgment:

Justice BRENNAN lists the "benefits" Mr. Burnham derived from the State of California—the fact that, during the few days he was there, "his health and safety were guaranteed by the State's police, fire, and emergency medical services; he was free to travel on the State's roads and waterways; he likely enjoyed the fruits of the State's economy." Three days' worth of these benefits strike us as powerfully inadequate to establish, as an abstract matter, that it is "fair" for California to decree the ownership of all Mr. Burnham's worldly goods acquired during the 10 years of his marriage, and the custody over his children. We daresay a contractual exchange swapping those benefits for that power would not survive the "unconscionability" provision of the Uniform Commercial Code. Even less persuasive are the other "fairness" factors alluded to by Justice BRENNAN. It would create "an asymmetry," we are told, if Burnham were *permitted* (as he is) to appear in California courts as a plaintiff, but were not *compelled* to appear in California courts as defendant; and travel being as easy as it is nowadays, and modern procedural devices being so convenient, it is no great hardship to appear in California courts. The problem with these assertions is that they justify the exercise of jurisdiction over *everyone, whether or not* he ever comes to California. The only "fairness" elements setting Mr. Burnham apart from the rest of the world are the three days' "benefits" referred to above—and even those do not set him apart from many other people who have enjoyed three days in the Golden State (savoring the fruits of its economy, the availability of its roads and police services) but who were fortunate enough not to be served with process while they were there and thus are not (simply by reason of that savoring) subject to the general jurisdiction of California's courts. In other words, even if one agreed with Justice BRENNAN's conception of an equitable bargain, the "benefits" we have been discussing would explain why it is "fair" to assert general jurisdiction over Burnham-returned-to-New-Jersey-after-service only at the expense of proving that it is also "fair" to assert general jurisdiction over Burnham-returned-to-New-Jersey-*without*-service—which we *know* does not conform with "contemporary notions of due process."

There is, we must acknowledge, one factor mentioned by Justice BRENNAN that *both* relates distinctively to the assertion of jurisdiction on the basis of personal in-state service *and* is fully persuasive—namely, the fact that a defendant voluntarily present in a particular State has a "reasonable expectation" that he is subject to suit there. By formulating it as a "reasonable expectation" Justice BRENNAN makes that seem like a "fairness" factor; but in reality, of course, it is just tradition masquerading as "fairness."

The difference between us and Justice BRENNAN has nothing to do with whether "further progress is to be made" in the "evolution of our legal system." It has to do with whether changes are to be adopted as progressive by the American people or decreed as progressive by the Justices of this Court. Nothing we say today prevents individual States from limiting or entirely abandoning the in-state-service basis of jurisdiction. And nothing prevents an overwhelming majority of them from doing so, with the consequence that the "traditional notions of fairness" that this Court applies may change. But the States have overwhelmingly declined to adopt such limitation or abandonment, evidently not considering it to be progress. The question is whether, armed with no authority other than individual Justices' perceptions of fairness that conflict with both past and current practice, this Court can compel the States to make such a change on the ground that "due process" requires it. We hold that it cannot.

Because the Due Process Clause does not prohibit the California courts from exercising jurisdiction over petitioner based on the fact of in-state service of process, the judgment is

Affirmed.

10. Note the skillful lawyering in the following case. Expecting to be sued by Wine of the Month, ICG decided to seize the home court advantage by initiating the litigation itself. Rather than spending extensive time and money on discovery to try to establish that Wine of the Month had sufficient minimum contacts with Connecticut, an ICG employee simply made one purchase of wine from his Connecticut office, using his credit card that had a Connecticut billing address. Then he watched his e-mails.

**2009 WL 2843261**
**UNITED STATES DISTRICT COURT,**
**D. CONNECTICUT.**
**ICG AMERICA, INC. (D/B/A "FLYING NOODLE," "AMAZING**
**CLUBS," AND "CALIFORNIA REDS"), PLAINTIFF,**
**V.**
**WINE OF THE MONTH CLUB, INC., DEFENDANT.**

DECIDED AUGUST 28, 2009

*RULING ON DEFENDANT'S MOTION TO DISMISS OR TRANSFER*

PETER C. DORSEY, District Judge.

Plaintiff filed this case on January 27, 2009, seeking declaratory judgment that Defendant's trademarks are invalid and unenforceable and that Plaintiff has not infringed the trademarks. On April 10, 2009, Defendant filed the instant Motion to Dismiss Plaintiff's complaint pursuant to Rules 12(b)(2) and 12(b)(3) of the Federal Rules of Civil Procedure for lack of jurisdiction and improper venue. Defendant alternatively moved to transfer the proceedings to the United States District Court for the Central District of California under Federal Rule of Civil Procedure 12(b)(3) and 28 U.S.C. §§ 1404(a) and 1406(a). Defendant also moved pursuant to Federal Rule of

Civil Procedure 12(b)(6) to dismiss Plaintiff's Connecticut Unfair Trade Practices Act ("CUTPA") claim. For the reasons stated herein, Defendant's Motion to Dismiss or Transfer is denied.

## I. BACKGROUND

This dispute concerns whether Plaintiff may continue to advertise the monthly wine products selections it offers on its websites using the phrases "wine of the month club" and "wine of the month." Plaintiff is ICG America, Inc., a Delaware corporation with a place of business in Stamford, Connecticut. Plaintiff does business as Flying Noodle, Amazing Clubs and California Reds and sells wine, beer, coffee, flower arrangements, chocolate and other goods by phone and Internet through its websites. Plaintiff offers merchandise and buying-club memberships to consumers via the Internet and mail order.

Defendant is Wine of the Month Club, Inc., a California corporation with a place of business in Monrovia, California, that sells wine and a variety of wine-related gifts by phone and Internet through its website. Defendant is the record owner of U.S. Trademark Registration No. 1,500,846 for the mark: WINE OF THE MONTH CLUB, registered for "mail order services in distribution of wine", the record owner of U.S. Trademark Registration No. 2,881,828 for the mark: WINE OF THE MONTH CLUB, registered for "newsletters pertaining to food and drink" and the record owner of U.S. Trademark Registration No. 1,246,348 for the mark: WINE OF THE MONTH, registered for "newsletters pertaining to food and drink."

On December 3, 2007, Defendant sent two cease and desist letters (the "December 2007 Cease and Desist Letters") to Plaintiff's offices in Connecticut alleging that Plaintiff, doing business as Amazing Clubs and California Reds, had infringed its trademark and service mark rights. In those letters, Defendant demanded monetary compensation and threatened legal action for the alleged infringement if Plaintiff did not immediately cease its use of Wine of the Month Club's marks and name. Defendant also contended that Plaintiff was guilty of false designation of origin and unfair competition. Plaintiffs did not respond to the December 2007 Cease and Desist letters. On December 10, 2008, Defendant sent Plaintiff, doing business as Flying Noodle, another cease and desist letter (the "December 2008 Cease and Desist Letter") that contained the same allegations as the December 2007 Cease and Desist letters. Plaintiff did not respond. On January 13, 2009, Defendant sent another cease and desist letter to Plaintiff that requested an accounting of revenues, costs and profits so that Defendant could determine monetary damages. Again, Plaintiff did not respond.

On or about November 19, 2008, Plaintiff discovered that the advertisements it had previously purchased from Google to advertise the monthly wine buying clubs offered by California Reds had been disapproved, which prevented Internet users from seeing Plaintiff's advertisements. On or about December 17, 2008, Plaintiff learned that Yahoo had similarly rejected all keyword purchases and advertisements that Plaintiff had previously bought to advertise the monthly wine buying clubs offered by its Flying Noodle brand. Plaintiff contends that Google and Yahoo rejected its advertisements in direct response to Defendant's complaints. Plaintiff alleges that Defendant's actions interfered with its ability to market and advertise the monthly wine buying clubs that it sells through its websites, which resulted in lost revenues and significant injury to Plaintiff.

Plaintiff seeks a declaratory judgment of the invalidity of Defendant's trademark, a declaratory judgment of the unenforceability of Defendant's trademark, and a declaratory judgment of its non-infringement. Plaintiff also seeks a declaratory judgment that its use of Defendant's marks has not violated § 43(a) of the Lanham Act or constituted unfair competition. Plaintiff moves for cancellation of Defendant's trademark and seeks monetary damages for Defendant's alleged violation of CUTPA. Defendant has moved to dismiss Plaintiff's complaint for lack of jurisdiction and improper venue, and alternatively moves to transfer the proceedings to the Central District of California. It has also moved to dismiss Plaintiff's CUTPA claim.

## II. STANDARD OF REVIEW

On a Rule 12(b)(2) motion to dismiss for lack of personal jurisdiction, the plaintiff bears the burden of proving that the court has jurisdiction over the defendant. However, the plaintiff is required only to make a *prima facie* showing that personal jurisdiction exists because the parties have not conducted jurisdictional discovery and the Court has not held an evidentiary hearing. The issue of personal jurisdiction is resolved based on the parties' pleadings, affidavits, and supporting materials "construed in the light most favorable to the plaintiff and with all doubts resolved in the plaintiff's favor." When the proceedings are in their beginning stages, the plaintiff's *prima facie* burden is satisfied by good faith allegations in the pleadings. Plaintiff must eventually prove the jurisdictional facts by a preponderance of the evidence at an evidentiary hearing or trial.

## III. PERSONAL JURISDICTION

To resolve whether the defendant is subject to personal jurisdiction in diversity jurisdiction cases, a federal court must apply the law of the forum state in which it sits.
Connecticut law mandates that to determine whether a court has personal jurisdiction over a foreign defendant, the court must first decide whether it has jurisdiction
under Connecticut's long-arm statute. If so, the court must next consider whether
exercising personal jurisdiction over the defendant comports with constitutional due
process.

### A. Connecticut's Long-Arm Statute

The court must first determine whether the Connecticut long-arm statute authorizes
personal jurisdiction over the defendant. *Conn. Gen.Stat. § 33-929(f)* provides that:

> every foreign corporation shall be subject to suit in this state, by a resident of this state
> or by a person having a usual place of business in this state, whether or not such for-
> eign corporation is transacting or has transacted business in this state and whether or
> not it is engaged exclusively in interstate or foreign commerce, on any cause of action
> arising out of ... (2) repeated business solicited in Connecticut by mail or otherwise; (3)
> the production, manufacture or distribution of goods with the reasonable expectation
> that such goods are to be used or consumed in Connecticut and are so used or con-
> sumed, regardless of how or where the goods were produced, manufactured, marketed
> or sold ...

Defendant submits that it does not ship its wine to Connecticut because state law
prohibits doing so, and that Defendant therefore has not distributed its product for
consumption in Connecticut. Defendant also contends that its website is passive in
relation to the residents of Connecticut because neither the website nor Defendant's
advertisements specifically target Connecticut. Defendant's argument fails because
its website and e-mail campaigns solicit business in Connecticut from Connecticut
residents, and persons in Connecticut do purchase goods from Defendant, even
if the wine is shipped elsewhere. This conduct satisfies the second condition of
the Connecticut long-arm statute, specifically that "repeated business solicited in
Connecticut by mail or otherwise."

Defendant relies on the fact that it does not ship wine to Connecticut to establish
that its website is passive as to Connecticut's residents. However, where a product
is shipped does not dictate whether the website is active or passive. Whether the

exercise of personal jurisdiction is permissible is "directly proportionate to the nature and quality of commercial activity that an entity conducts over the internet." *Best Van Lines, Inc. v. Walker,* 490 F.3d 239, 251 (2d Cir.2007) *(quoting Zippo Mfg. Co. v. Zippo Dot Com, Inc.* 952 F.Supp. 1119, 1124-25 (W.D.Pa.1997)). The standards set in *Zippo* have been applied by many courts to determine in what circumstances the operation of an Internet website serves to establish personal jurisdiction. Internet use has been broken down into three categories to determine whether personal jurisdiction exists:

> At one end of the spectrum are situations where a defendant clearly does business over the Internet. If the defendant enters into contracts with residents of a foreign jurisdiction that involve the knowing and repeated transmission of computer files over the Internet, personal jurisdiction is proper. At the opposite end are situations where a defendant has simply posted information on the Internet Web site which is available to users in foreign jurisdictions. A passive Web site that does little more than make information available to those who are interested in it is not grounds for the exercise of personal jurisdiction. The middle ground is occupied by interactive Web sites where a user can exchange information with the host computer. In these cases, the exercise of jurisdiction is determined by examining the level of interactivity and commercial nature of the exchange of information that occurs on the Web site. *Zippo,* 952 F.Supp. at 1124.

> Interactive, commercial websites permit personal jurisdiction to be exercised over a defendant. "One who uses a web site to make sales to customers in a distant state can thereby become subject to the jurisdiction of that state's courts."

Because Defendant's website sells its products, Defendant's website is interactive and commercial. While stating that it cannot ship to Connecticut, Defendant's website nonetheless explicitly advises consumers that they "may order from any state." Inviting residents of any state to order from its website amounts to a solicitation of business from Connecticut residents. Where the product is shipped does not negate that Defendant has invited Connecticut residents to purchase its products and they have done so. Connecticut courts have found that the state's long arm statute applies to convey personal jurisdiction over a nonresident corporate defendant where:

> the defendant reaches a plaintiff purchaser who actively engages in a transaction from Connecticut to purchase items from defendant's website that has reached them in their living room or office in Connecticut. The store has placed itself in Connecticut and accepted payment from a credit card transaction which has originated in Connecticut,

for the purchase of goods offered by defendant in their online store ... Further, the defendant was doing business in Connecticut at the salient times involved in this case with 2% of its worldwide sales in Connecticut.

Defendant admits that "it is possible that a Connecticut resident could use its website to order wine for someone in another state." Plaintiff demonstrated as much when one of its employees, a Connecticut resident acting from his Connecticut office and using a credit card with a Connecticut billing address, placed an order on Defendant's website in May 2009 for delivery of wine to Texas.

Plaintiff estimates Defendant's Connecticut-related sales to be approximately $18,000 per year, which is one quarter of one percent of the low end of Defendant's estimated yearly revenues of $7.2 million to $9.5 million. While Defendant asserts that Plaintiff's estimation of Defendant's Connecticut-related sales is "disingenuous", Defendant did not provide a corrected figure, as one might have expected had the amount been negligible. In the absence of discovery on the matter, the Court does not rely on Plaintiff's estimate. In any case, the dollar amount of Defendant's Connecticut sales is not dispositive of the jurisdictional question. Courts have found that a defendant's website, if it is active like the one in question here, need not produce significant dollar sales from forum residents in order for the court to find purposeful availment.

Defendant also solicited repeated business within Connecticut. One Connecticut resident, acting at the direction of Plaintiff to order Defendant's product from its website, received at least five promotional e-mails from Defendant in the month after purchasing its products. These e-mails aimed to promote Defendant's products and increase its sales in Connecticut, regardless of the fact that Defendant does not ship its products here. Defendant relies on *Edberg v. Neogen Corp.* for the proposition that personal jurisdiction is not permitted over a foreign defendant whose website is similar to a national advertisement. However, *Neogen* is clearly distinguishable, because the website in that case was passive, meaning that "Internet users could not order products directly from the Web site." In this case, Defendant's interactive, commercial website operates as a virtual store and transacts business within Connecticut. Defendant promoted and sold its products to Connecticut residents through its website, specifically targeting them for repeat business through its e-mail campaigns. Defendant's interactive, commercial website permits the exercise of personal jurisdiction over Defendant under Connecticut's long-arm statute.

## B. Due Process

The second inquiry before the Court is whether exercising personal jurisdiction over Defendant comports with constitutional due process. There are two prongs to this analysis. First, the Court must determine whether a foreign defendant has the necessary "minimum contacts" with the forum state. Second, the Court must consider whether exercising personal jurisdiction over a foreign defendant is reasonable given the circumstances of the case.

### 1. Minimum Contacts and Purposeful Availment

To confer personal jurisdiction, the foreign defendant's action must establish 'certain minimum contacts ... so that the maintenance of the suit does not offend traditional notions of fair play and substantial justice." The defendant must have "purposefully availed itself of the privilege of conducting activities within the forum State, thus invoking the benefits and protections of its laws," such that the defendant should reasonably anticipate being haled into court there."

Defendant maintains that it lacks the minimum contacts with Connecticut necessary to subject it to personal jurisdiction in this state. Defendant asserts that it has purposefully refrained from directing its advertising to Connecticut residents through its website or a direct mail campaign, and that it has no property, personnel or affiliates in Connecticut. Defendant's argument that it has no physical presence in Connecticut fails because if a commercial actor's efforts are "purposefully directed" towards the state, it does not need to have a physical presence there to establish minimum contacts.

Plaintiff also contends that in sending cease and desist letters to Plaintiff in Connecticut alleging trademark infringement, Defendant could reasonably expect to be haled into court in Connecticut.

The due process inquiry focuses on the totality of the circumstances rather than relying on any mechanical criteria. The mere existence of a website accessible from Connecticut does not demonstrate purposeful availment. The level of commercial interactivity of a website determines whether the defendant is transacting business or purposefully availing itself of the privilege of conducting activities within the forum State. Evidence that Connecticut residents accessed the defendant's site, that they purchased products from the website, or that the website targeted Connecticut residents is necessary to find purposeful availment.

Defendant purposefully availed itself of the privilege of doing business in Connecticut. Its interactive, commercial website invites consumers "from any state," including Connecticut, to purchase its products. By operating a commercial website to promote and sell its goods, Defendant has extended itself beyond its home state of California to avail itself of the benefits of doing business in Connecticut. Furthermore, Defendant sold its products to Connecticut residents and profited from such sales. "Although the actual number of sales ... may be small, the critical inquiry in determining whether there was a purposeful availment of the forum state is the quality, not merely the quantity, of the contacts." It is reasonable for Defendant to anticipate being haled into court in Connecticut to defend itself against claims related to the use of its mark because Defendant sold its services there. Purposeful availment is further demonstrated by Defendant's directing email advertisements to Connecticut residents who had made prior purchases of its products. For example, Defendant sent at least five e-mails to a Connecticut resident after that resident made an online purchase, seeking to induce additional sales. Purposeful activity within the state that results in minimum contacts with the forum state may include the solicitation of business by defendants.

Defendant asserts that the cease and desist letters that it sent to Plaintiff's Connecticut offices are insufficient to convey jurisdiction over a declaratory judgment action regarding issues such as validity or non-infringement. However, Defendant's contacts with Connecticut involved more than simply sending cease and desist letters. As discussed above, Defendant maintained a website which permitted direct purchases by Connecticut residents, and Defendant deliberately solicited repeat business from these Connecticut customers through e-mail advertising campaigns. While the Second Circuit has held that sending a cease and desist letter to an alleged infringer is not by itself sufficient to permit the exercise of personal jurisdiction, the numerous cease and desist letters that Defendant sent to Plaintiff's Connecticut offices merely add to Defendant's Connecticut-related activity. The totality of Defendant's conduct in operating an interactive, commercial website, selling its product to Connecticut residents and directing cease and desist letters towards Plaintiff's Connecticut offices constitutes purposeful availment.

Defendant has the requisite minimum contacts with Connecticut and has purposefully availed itself of the privilege of doing business in Connecticut, so as to support the exercise of personal jurisdiction over it.

## 2. Reasonableness

The next step in the constitutional due process inquiry is for the Court to consider the minimum contacts discussed above in conjunction with other factors to determine whether exercising personal jurisdiction over the defendant would "offend the traditional notions of fair play and substantial justice." Personal jurisdiction must be reasonable given the facts of the particular case. The Court evaluates the following factors as part of this "reasonableness" analysis: (1) the burden that the exercise of jurisdiction will impose on the defendant; (2) the interests of the forum state in adjudicating the case; (3) the plaintiff's interest in obtaining convenient and effective relief; (4) the interstate judicial system's interest in obtaining the most efficient resolution of the controversy; and (5) the shared interest of the states in furthering substantive social policies. Once minimum contacts have been established, Defendant "must present a compelling case that the presence of some other considerations would render jurisdiction unreasonable." "Plaintiff's choice of forum is entitled to substantial consideration." "Unless the balance is strongly in favor of defendant, the plaintiff's choice of forum should rarely be disturbed."

Defendant contends that subjecting it to personal jurisdiction in Connecticut would impose a significant burden on it because of the time and expense of having to travel cross-country when the majority of the witnesses and documents are in California, and where the evidence at trial will be about the validity of Defendant's mark. However, "the conveniences of modern communication and transportation ease what would have been a serious burden only a few decades ago." Furthermore, Plaintiff intends to rely on company witnesses and third party witnesses located in Connecticut and the surrounding area. There is no evidence that Defendant will be subjected to undue hardship by defending this suit in Connecticut. "Inconvenience must be substantial to achieve constitutional magnitude." *Burger King*, 471 U.S. at 483. Defendant has not made a "compelling case" that its inconvenience in trying the case in Connecticut would be substantial.

The court must also consider the interests of the forum state in resolving the case. The case involves a state statute, CUTPA, in which Connecticut has an interest. Connecticut has an interest in providing a forum for its companies to obtain convenient relief from injuries allegedly inflicted by foreign defendants. Additionally, as Defendant is a large, national corporation, it should expect to be sued anywhere that it has customers. "It is reasonable for a corporation deriving substantial revenue from interstate commerce, like defendant, to anticipate that its efforts to serve a market with a particular product may subject it to suit there ... even if those efforts have not resulted in much revenue in that market." Defendant could have avoided Connecticut suits by "severing its connection with the state," but chose instead to inform customers that "they may order from any state."

Another factor to consider is Plaintiff's interest in obtaining convenient and effective relief. "The plaintiff's choice of forum is the best indicator of his own convenience." Plaintiff indicates that Connecticut would be convenient because Plaintiff is based in Connecticut, and its marketing, advertising, and financial documents are located here.

With regard to the interstate judicial system's interest in obtaining the most efficient resolution of the controversy, both Defendant and Plaintiff maintain that they have witnesses and evidence in their home states. When witnesses and evidence are in both the forum state and other locations, the interstate judicial system's interest in obtaining the most efficient resolution of the controversy is neutral.

As Defendant has not made a compelling argument that its burden in litigating the case in Connecticut would be significant, the exercise of personal jurisdiction over it in Connecticut comports with due process. Therefore, Defendant's motion to dismiss for lack of jurisdiction is denied.

## IV. VENUE

### A. 28 U.S.C. § 1391

Defendants argue that this action should be dismissed for improper venue under 28 U.S.C. § 1391(b)(2), which provides:

A civil action wherein jurisdiction is not founded solely on diversity of citizenship may, except as otherwise provided by law, be brought only in ... (2) a judicial district in which a substantial part of the events or omissions giving rise to the claim occurred, or a substantial part of property that is the subject of the action is situated.

Defendant contends that since none of the events giving rise to the claim occurred in Connecticut and no property that is the subject of the action is located in Connecticut, venue is improper. However, as Plaintiff is based in Connecticut, its property, including its marketing records and other business information related to this action, is located here, which makes venue proper.

Further, the Court has already determined that it may exercise personal jurisdiction over Defendant in Connecticut. "For purposes of venue under this chapter, a defendant that is a corporation shall be deemed to reside in any judicial district in which it is subject to personal jurisdiction at the time the action is commenced." 28 U.S.C. § 1391(c). "Essentially § 1391(c) equates jurisdiction with venue for corporate defendants." Therefore, because Defendant is a corporation and is subject to personal jurisdiction in Connecticut, it resides here for the purpose of this action and venue is proper in this district.

## B. 28 U.S.C. § 1404(a)

Defendant moves for a transfer of this case to the Central District of California under 28 U.S.C. § 1404(a). Defendant submits that since Plaintiff's trademark claim will be entirely focused on Defendant's commercial activities and its trademarks, and the majority of the witnesses and documents are located in California, the case should be transferred to California. Plaintiff argues that Defendant has not made a convincing showing that the balance of convenience favors Defendant's choice of forum, particularly in light of modern technology. Plaintiff also emphasizes Connecticut's connections to and interest in the action, including the CUTPA claim, and courts' traditional deference to the plaintiff's choice of venue. The Court declines to transfer this action to the Central District of California.

Defendant fails to meet its burden in proving that inconvenience and fairness favor its choice of forum. While Defendant is correct in noting that the presumption in favor of a plaintiff's choice of forum does not apply in declaratory judgment actions to decide enforceability or validity when there is a tenuous material connection between the chosen forum and the issues of the case, here a material connection exists. Plaintiff is located in Connecticut and suffered the alleged economic injury there. The case involves a state statutory claim. Additionally, Defendant directed the cease and desist letters to Plaintiff's Connecticut offices. Therefore, Plaintiff's choice of forum is entitled to deference.

Furthermore, while Defendant contends that the majority of the likely third-party witnesses are located in California, Plaintiff states that it intends to rely on at least seven Connecticut witnesses. However, "it is not the prospective number of witnesses in each district that determines the appropriateness of a transfer, but, rather, the materiality of their anticipated testimony." At this point in the litigation, the Court cannot evaluate the materiality of either party's potential witnesses, and this factor is neutral. Similarly, Plaintiff's documents are in Connecticut, while Defendant's documents are in California. Modern technology, such as e-mail, facsimile, expedited mailing services and electronic storage and transfer techniques "deprive the issue of location of relevant documents of practical or legal weight."

## VI. CONCLUSION

For the foregoing reasons, Defendant Wine of the Month Club's Motion to Dismiss or Transfer is denied.

11. The next case, like *Asahi*, discusses the circumstances under which a foreign corporation may – or may not – be subject to the jurisdiction of courts in the United States. It also includes a discussion of general jurisdiction compared to specific jurisdiction. To what extent do these two forms of jurisdiction actually differ from each other?

## 131 S.CT. 2846
## SUPREME COURT OF THE UNITED STATES
## GOODYEAR DUNLOP TIRES OPERATIONS, S.A., ET AL., PETITIONERS,
### V.
## EDGAR D. BROWN ET UX., CO-ADMINISTRATORS OF THE ESTATE OF JULIAN DAVID BROWN, ET AL.

DECIDED JUNE 27, 2011

**Justice GINSBURG delivered the opinion of the Court.**

This case concerns the jurisdiction of state courts over corporations organized and operating abroad. We address, in particular, this question: Are foreign subsidiaries of a United States parent corporation amenable to suit in state court on claims unrelated to any activity of the subsidiaries in the forum State?

A bus accident outside Paris that took the lives of two 13–year–old boys from North Carolina gave rise to the litigation we here consider. Attributing the accident to a defective tire manufactured in Turkey at the plant of a foreign subsidiary of The Goodyear Tire and Rubber Company (Goodyear USA), the boys' parents commenced an action for damages in a North Carolina state court; they named as defendants Goodyear USA, an Ohio corporation, and three of its subsidiaries, organized and operating, respectively, in Turkey, France, and Luxembourg. Goodyear USA, which had plants in North Carolina and regularly engaged in commercial activity there, did not contest the North Carolina court's jurisdiction over it; Goodyear USA's foreign subsidiaries, however, maintained that North Carolina lacked adjudicatory authority over them.

A state court's assertion of jurisdiction exposes defendants to the State's coercive power, and is therefore subject to review for compatibility with the Fourteenth

Amendment's Due Process Clause. Opinions in the wake of the pathmarking *International Shoe* decision have differentiated between general or all-purpose jurisdiction, and specific or case-linked jurisdiction

A court may assert general jurisdiction over foreign (sister-state or foreign-country) corporations to hear any and all claims against them when their affiliations with the State are so "continuous and systematic" as to render them essentially at home in the forum State. Specific jurisdiction, on the other hand, depends on an "affiliation between the forum and the underlying controversy," principally, activity or an occurrence that takes place in the forum State and is therefore subject to the State's regulation. In contrast to general, all-purpose jurisdiction, specific jurisdiction is confined to adjudication of "issues deriving from, or connected with, the very controversy that establishes jurisdiction."

Because the episode-in-suit, the bus accident, occurred in France, and the tire alleged to have caused the accident was manufactured and sold abroad, North Carolina courts lacked specific jurisdiction to adjudicate the controversy. Were the foreign subsidiaries nonetheless amenable to general jurisdiction in North Carolina courts? Some of the tires made abroad by Goodyear's foreign subsidiaries had reached North Carolina through "the stream of commerce"; that connection, the Court of Appeals believed, gave North Carolina courts the handle needed for the exercise of general jurisdiction over the foreign corporations.

A connection so limited between the forum and the foreign corporation, we hold, is an inadequate basis for the exercise of general jurisdiction. Such a connection does not establish the "continuous and systematic" affiliation necessary to empower North Carolina courts to entertain claims unrelated to the foreign corporation's contacts with the State.

I

Goodyear Luxembourg, Goodyear Turkey, and Goodyear France, petitioners here, were named as defendants. Incorporated in Luxembourg, Turkey, and France, respectively, petitioners are indirect subsidiaries of Goodyear USA, an Ohio corporation also named as a defendant in the suit. Petitioners manufacture tires primarily for sale in European and Asian markets. Their tires differ in size and construction from tires ordinarily sold in the United States. They are designed to carry significantly heavier loads, and to serve under road conditions and speed limits in the manufacturers' primary markets.

The parent company, Goodyear USA, does not contest the North Carolina courts' personal jurisdiction over it. Petitioners, incorporated abroad, do contest jurisdiction.

Petitioners are not registered to do business in North Carolina. They have no place of business, employees, or bank accounts in North Carolina. They do not design, manufacture, or advertise their products in North Carolina. And they do not solicit business in North Carolina or themselves sell or ship tires to North Carolina customers. Even so, a small percentage of petitioners' tires (tens of thousands out of tens of millions manufactured between 2004 and 2007) were distributed within North Carolina by other Goodyear USA affiliates. These tires were typically custom ordered to equip specialized vehicles such as cement mixers, waste haulers, and boat and horse trailers. Petitioners state, and respondents do not here deny, that the type of tire involved in the accident, a Goodyear Regional RHS tire manufactured by Goodyear Turkey, was never distributed in North Carolina.

Petitioners moved to dismiss the claims against them for want of personal jurisdiction. The trial court denied the motion, and the North Carolina Court of Appeals affirmed.

The North Carolina Supreme Court denied discretionary review.

We granted certiorari to decide whether the general jurisdiction the North Carolina courts asserted over petitioners is consistent with the Due Process Clause of the Fourteenth Amendment.

## II

The Due Process Clause of the Fourteenth Amendment sets the outer boundaries of a state tribunal's authority to proceed against a defendant. The canonical opinion in this area remains *International Shoe,* in which we held that a State may authorize its courts to exercise personal jurisdiction over an out-of-state defendant if the defendant has "certain minimum contacts with the State such that the maintenance of the suit does not offend 'traditional notions of fair play and substantial justice.' "

Jurisdiction unquestionably could be asserted where the corporation's in-state activity is "continuous and systematic" and *that activity gave rise to the episode-in-suit.* Further, the commission of certain "single or occasional acts" in a State may be sufficient to render a corporation answerable in that State with respect to those acts, though not with respect to matters unrelated to the forum connections. Adjudicatory authority is "specific" when the suit "arises out of or relates to the defendant's contacts with the forum."

On the other hand, "general jurisdiction" arises in "instances in which the continuous corporate operations within a state are so substantial and of such a nature as to justify suit against a defendant on causes of action arising from dealings entirely distinct from those activities." For an individual, the paradigm forum for the exercise of general jurisdiction is the individual's domicile; for a corporation, it is an equivalent place, one in which the corporation is fairly regarded as at home. See Brilmayer (identifying domicile, place of incorporation, and principal place of business as "paradigm" bases for the exercise of general jurisdiction).

Since *International Shoe,* this Court's decisions have elaborated primarily on circumstances that warrant the exercise of specific jurisdiction, particularly in cases involving "single or occasional acts" occurring or having their impact within the forum State. As a rule in these cases, this Court has inquired whether there was "some act by which the defendant purposefully availed itself of the privilege of conducting activities within the forum State, thus invoking the benefits and protections of its laws."

In only two decisions postdating *International Shoe* has this Court considered whether an out-of-state corporate defendant's in-state contacts were sufficiently "continuous and systematic" to justify the exercise of general jurisdiction over claims unrelated to those contacts.

B

To justify the exercise of general jurisdiction over petitioners, the North Carolina courts relied on the petitioners' placement of their tires in the "stream of commerce." The stream-of-commerce metaphor has been invoked frequently in lower court decisions permitting "jurisdiction in products liability cases in which the product has traveled through an extensive chain of distribution before reaching the ultimate consumer." Typically, in such cases, a nonresident defendant, acting *outside* the forum, places in the stream of commerce a product that ultimately causes harm *inside* the forum.

Many States have enacted long-arm statutes authorizing courts to exercise specific jurisdiction over manufacturers when the events in suit, or some of them, occurred within the forum state. For example, the "Local Injury; Foreign Act" subsection of North Carolina's long-arm statute authorizes North Carolina courts to exercise personal jurisdiction in "any action claiming injury to person or property within this State arising out of the defendant's act or omission outside this State," if, "in addition, at or about the time of the injury," "products manufactured by the defendant were used or consumed, within this State in the ordinary course of trade." As the North Carolina Court of Appeals recognized, this provision of the State's long-arm statute "does not apply to this case," for both the act alleged to have caused injury (the fabrication of the allegedly defective tire) and its impact (the accident) occurred outside the forum.

The North Carolina court's stream-of-commerce analysis elided the essential difference between case-specific and all-purpose (general) jurisdiction. Flow of a manufacturer's products into the forum, we have explained, may bolster an affiliation germane to *specific* jurisdiction. But ties serving to bolster the exercise of specific jurisdiction do not warrant a determination that, based on those ties, the forum has *general* jurisdiction over a defendant.

A corporation's "continuous activity of some sorts within a state," is not enough to support the demand that the corporation be amenable to suits unrelated to that activity."

Measured against our prior cases, such as *Perkins v. Benguet Mining,* North Carolina is not a forum in which it would be permissible to subject petitioners to general jurisdiction. Unlike the defendant in *Perkins,* whose sole wartime business activity was conducted in Ohio, petitioners are in no sense at home in North Carolina. Their attenuated connections to the State fall far short of "the continuous and systematic general business contacts" necessary to empower North Carolina to entertain suit against them on claims unrelated to anything that connects them to the State.

C

Respondents belatedly assert a "single enterprise" theory, asking us to consolidate petitioners' ties to North Carolina with those of Goodyear USA and other Goodyear entities. In effect, respondents would have us pierce Goodyear corporate veils, at least for jurisdictional purposes Neither below nor in their brief in opposition to the petition for certiorari did respondents urge disregard of petitioners' discrete status as subsidiaries and treatment of all Goodyear entities as a "unitary business," so that jurisdiction over the parent would draw in the subsidiaries as well.

For the reasons stated, the judgment of the North Carolina Court of Appeals is

*Reversed.*

# B. CONSENT TO JURISDICTION

12. Regardless of the presence or absence of minimum contacts, an individual or a corporation may voluntarily consent to personal jurisdiction. That could be done accidentally, if the defendant fails to raise the lack of personal jurisdiction at the very beginning of the lawsuit, as required by FRCP 12(b)(2). If a defendant fails to raise the lack of personal jurisdiction by motion before filing an answer to the complaint, or in the answer itself, then the lack of personal jurisdiction is *waived.* (FRCP 12(h)(1)(A). Just as the statute of limitations defense is waived if it is not raised in the answer. (FRCP 8(C)). Good defenses like lack of personal jurisdiction or the running of the statute of limitations should never be waived by accident. But it happens.

Another way in which an individual or corporation may consent to personal jurisdiction is by entering into a contract in which the party specifically consents in advance to submit to personal jurisdiction in a designated forum, should problems arise later.

The following is a rather troubling example of consent to personal jurisdiction when two individuals entered into contracts with a large corporation.

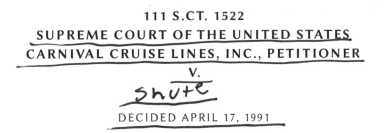

**111 S.CT. 1522**
**SUPREME COURT OF THE UNITED STATES**
**CARNIVAL CRUISE LINES, INC., PETITIONER**
**V.**
## Shute
**DECIDED APRIL 17, 1991**

**Justice BLACKMUN delivered the opinion of the Court.**

In this admiralty case we primarily consider whether the United States Court of Appeals for the Ninth Circuit correctly refused to enforce a forum-selection clause contained in tickets issued by petitioner Carnival Cruise Lines, Inc., to respondents Eulala and Russel Shute.]

I

The Shutes, through an Arlington, Wash., travel agent, purchased passage for a 7-day cruise on petitioner's ship, the *Tropicale*. Respondents paid the fare to the agent who forwarded the payment to petitioner's headquarters in Miami, Fla. Petitioner then prepared the tickets and sent them to respondents in the State of Washington. The face of each ticket, at its left-hand lower corner, contained this admonition:

"SUBJECT TO CONDITIONS OF CONTRACT ON LAST PAGES
**IMPORTANT!** PLEASE READ CONTRACT-ON LAST PAGES 1, 2, 3"

The following appeared on "contract page 1" of each ticket:

"TERMS AND CONDITIONS OF PASSAGE CONTRACT TICKET

"3. (a) The acceptance of this ticket by the person or persons named hereon as passengers shall be deemed to be an acceptance and agreement by each of them of all of the terms and conditions of this Passage Contract Ticket.

"8. It is agreed by and between the passenger and the Carrier that all disputes and matters whatsoever arising under, in connection with or incident to this Contract shall be litigated, if at all, in and before a Court located in the State of Florida, U.S.A., to the exclusion of the Courts of any other state or country."

The last quoted paragraph is the forum-selection clause at issue.

II

Respondents boarded the *Tropicale* in Los Angeles, Cal. The ship sailed to Puerto Vallarta, Mexico, and then returned to Los Angeles. While the ship was in international waters off the Mexican coast, respondent Eulala Shute was injured when she slipped on a deck mat during a guided tour of the ship's galley. Respondents filed suit against petitioner in the United States District Court for the Western District of Washington, claiming that Mrs. Shute's injuries had been caused by the negligence of Carnival Cruise Lines and its employees.]

[Petitioner moved for summary judgment, contending that the forum clause in respondents' tickets required the Shutes to bring their suit against petitioner in a court in the State of Florida. Petitioner contended, alternatively, that the District Court lacked personal jurisdiction over petitioner because petitioner's contacts with the State of Washington were insubstantial. The District Court granted the motion, holding that petitioner's contacts with Washington were constitutionally insufficient to support the exercise of personal jurisdiction.]

[The Court of Appeals reversed. Reasoning that "but for" petitioner's solicitation of business in Washington, respondents would not have taken the cruise and Mrs. Shute would not have been injured, the court concluded that petitioner had sufficient contacts with Washington to justify the District Court's exercise of personal jurisdiction.]

We granted certiorari to address the question whether the Court of Appeals was correct in holding that the District Court should hear respondents' tort claim against petitioner. Because we find the forum-selection clause to be dispositive of this question, we need not consider petitioner's constitutional argument as to personal jurisdiction.

## III

We begin by noting the boundaries of our inquiry. First, this is a case in admiralty, and federal law governs the enforceability of the forum-selection clause we scrutinize. Second, we do not address the question whether respondents had sufficient notice of the forum clause before entering the contract for passage. Respondents essentially have conceded that they had notice of the forum-selection provision. ("The respondents do not contest the incorporation of the provisions nor [sic ] that the forum selection clause was reasonably communicated to the respondents, as much as three pages of fine print can be communicated"). Additionally, the Court of Appeals evaluated the enforceability of the forum clause under the assumption, although "doubtful," that respondents could be deemed to have had knowledge of the clause.

## IV

### A

Both petitioner and respondents argue vigorously that the Court's opinion in *The Bremen* governs this case, and each side purports to find ample support for its position in that opinion's broad-ranging language. This seeming paradox derives in large part from key factual differences between this case and *The Bremen*, differences that preclude an automatic and simple application of *The Bremen*'s general principles to the facts here.

In *The Bremen,* this Court addressed the enforceability of a forum-selection clause in a contract between two business corporations. An American corporation, Zapata, made a contract with Unterweser, a German corporation, for the towage of Zapata's oceangoing drilling rig from Louisiana to a point in the Adriatic Sea off the coast of Italy. The agreement provided that any dispute arising under the contract was to be resolved in the London Court of Justice. After a storm in the Gulf of Mexico seriously damaged the rig, Zapata ordered Unterweser's ship to tow the rig to Tampa, Fla., the nearest point of refuge. Thereafter, Zapata sued Unterweser in admiralty in federal court at Tampa. Citing the forum clause, Unterweser moved to dismiss. The District Court denied Unterweser's motion, and the Court of Appeals for the Fifth Circuit affirmed.

This Court vacated and remanded, stating that, in general, "a freely negotiated private international agreement, unaffected by fraud, undue influence, or overweening bargaining power, such as that involved here, should be given full effect." The Court further generalized that "in the light of present-day commercial realities and expanding international trade we conclude that the forum clause should control absent a strong showing that it should be set aside." The Court did not define precisely the circumstances that would make it unreasonable for a court to enforce a forum clause. Instead, the Court discussed a number of factors that made it reasonable to enforce the clause at issue in *The Bremen* and that, presumably, would be pertinent in any determination whether to enforce a similar clause.

In this respect, the Court noted that there was "strong evidence that the forum clause was a vital part of the agreement, and that it would be unrealistic to think that the parties did not conduct their negotiations, including fixing the monetary terms, with the consequences of the forum clause figuring prominently in their calculations." Further, the Court observed that it was not "dealing with an agreement between two Americans to resolve their essentially local disputes in a remote alien forum," and that in such a case, "the serious inconvenience of the contractual forum to one or both of the parties might carry greater weight in determining the reasonableness of the forum clause." The Court stated that even where the forum clause establishes a remote forum for resolution of conflicts, "the party claiming unfairness should bear a heavy burden of proof."

In contrast, respondents' passage contract was purely routine and doubtless nearly identical to every commercial passage contract issued by petitioner and most other cruise lines. In this context, it would be entirely unreasonable for us to assume that respondents-or any other cruise passenger-would negotiate with petitioner the terms of a forum-selection clause in an ordinary commercial cruise ticket. Common sense dictates that a ticket of this kind will be a form contract the terms of which are not subject to negotiation, and that an individual purchasing the ticket will not have bargaining parity with the cruise line. But by ignoring the crucial differences in the business contexts in which the respective contracts were executed, the Court of Appeals' analysis seems to us to have distorted somewhat this Court's holding in *The Bremen*.

In evaluating the reasonableness of the forum clause at issue in this case, we must refine the analysis of *The Bremen* to account for the realities of form passage contracts. As an initial matter, we do not adopt the Court of Appeals' determination that a nonnegotiated forum-selection clause in a form ticket contract is never enforceable simply because it is not the subject of bargaining. Including a reasonable forum clause in a form contract of this kind well may be permissible for several reasons: First, a cruise line has a special interest in limiting the fora in which it potentially could be subject to suit. Because a cruise ship typically carries passengers from many locales, it is not unlikely that a mishap on a cruise could subject the cruise line to litigation in several different fora. Additionally, a clause establishing *ex ante* the forum for dispute resolution has the salutary effect of dispelling any confusion about where suits arising from the contract must be brought and defended, sparing litigants the time and expense of pretrial motions to determine the correct forum and conserving judicial resources that otherwise would be devoted to deciding those motions. Finally, it stands to reason that passengers who purchase tickets containing a forum clause like that at issue in this case benefit in the form of reduced fares reflecting the savings that the cruise line enjoys by limiting the fora in which it may be sued.

We also do not accept the Court of Appeals' "independent justification" for its conclusion that *The Bremen* dictates that the clause should not be enforced because "there is evidence in the record to indicate that the Shutes are physically and financially incapable of pursuing this litigation in Florida." We do not defer to the Court of Appeals' findings of fact. In dismissing the case for lack of personal jurisdiction over petitioner, the District Court made no finding regarding the physical and financial impediments to the Shutes' pursuing their case in Florida. The Court of Appeals' conclusory reference to the record provides no basis for this Court to validate the finding of inconvenience. Furthermore, the Court of Appeals did not place in proper context this Court's statement in *The Bremen* that "the serious inconvenience of the contractual forum to one or both of the parties might carry greater weight in determining the reasonableness of the forum clause." The Court made this statement in evaluating a hypothetical "agreement between two Americans to resolve their essentially local disputes in a remote alien forum." In the present case, Florida is not a "remote alien forum," nor-given the fact that Mrs. Shute's accident occurred off the coast of Mexico-is this dispute an essentially local one inherently more suited to resolution in the State of Washington than in Florida. In light of these distinctions, and because respondents do not claim lack of notice of the forum clause, we conclude that they have not satisfied the "heavy burden of proof," required to set aside the clause on grounds of inconvenience.

It bears emphasis that forum-selection clauses contained in form passage contracts are subject to judicial scrutiny for fundamental fairness. In this case, there is no indication that petitioner set Florida as the forum in which disputes were to be resolved as a means of discouraging cruise passengers from pursuing legitimate claims. Any suggestion of such a bad-faith motive is belied by two facts: Petitioner has its principal place of business in Florida, and many of its cruises depart from and return to Florida ports. Similarly, there is no evidence that petitioner obtained respondents' accession to the forum clause by fraud or overreaching. Finally, respondents have conceded that they were given notice of the forum provision and, therefore, presumably retained the option of rejecting the contract with impunity. In the case before us, therefore, we conclude that the Court of Appeals erred in refusing to enforce the forum-selection clause.

The judgment of the Court of Appeals is reversed.

*It is so ordered.*

# C. WAIVER OF LACK OF PERSONAL JURISDICTION

13. In addition to finding itself subject to personal jurisdiction because of consent – either accidentally, or intentionally, as part of a contract, a party may find itself subject to personal jurisdiction as a sanction for bad behavior. After all of the cases earlier in this chapter about the necessity for minimum contacts, may a court simply decide that a defendant is subject to personal jurisdiction *without* first establishing minimum contacts? The answer is yes!

## 102 S.CT. 2099
## SUPREME COURT OF THE UNITED STATES
## INSURANCE CORP. OF IRELAND, LTD. ET AL., PETITIONERS,
## V.
## COMPAGNIE DES BAUXITES DE GUINEE.

### DECIDED JUNE 1, 1982

**Justice WHITE delivered the opinion of the Court.**

Rule 37(b), Federal Rules of Civil Procedure, provides that a district court may impose sanctions for failure to comply with discovery orders. Included among the available sanctions is:

> "An order that the matters regarding which the order was made or any other designated facts shall be taken to be established for the purposes of the action in accordance with the claim of the party obtaining the order." Rule 37(b)(2)(A).

The question presented by this case is whether this Rule is applicable to facts that form the basis for personal jurisdiction over a defendant. May a district court, as a sanction for failure to comply with a discovery order directed at establishing jurisdictional facts, proceed on the basis that personal jurisdiction over the recalcitrant party has been established?

I

Respondent Compagnie des Bauxites de Guinee (CBG) is a Delaware corporation, 49% of which is owned by the Republic of Guinea and 51% is owned by Halco (Mining) Inc. CBG's principal place of business is in the Republic of Guinea, where it operates bauxite mines and processing facilities. Halco, which operates in Pennsylvania, has contracted to perform certain administrative services for CBG. These include the procurement of insurance.

In 1973, Halco instructed an insurance broker, Marsh & McLennan, to obtain $20 million worth of business interruption insurance to cover CBG's operations in Guinea. The first half of this coverage was provided by the Insurance Company of North America (INA). The second half, or what is referred to as the "excess" insurance, was provided by a group of 21 foreign insurance companies, 14 of which are petitioners in this action.

Once the offering was fully subscribed, Bland Payne issued a cover note indicating the amount of the coverage and specifying the percentage of the coverage that each excess insurer had agreed to insure. No separate policy was issued; the excess insurers adopted the INA policy "as far as applicable."

Sometime after February 12, CBG allegedly experienced mechanical problems in its Guinea operation, resulting in a business interruption loss in excess of $10 million. Contending that the loss was covered under its policies, CBG brought suit when the insurers refused to indemnify CBG for the loss. Whatever the mechanical problems experienced by CBG, they were perhaps minor compared to the legal difficulties encountered in the courts.

In December 1975, CBG filed a two-count suit in the Western District of Pennsylvania, asserting jurisdiction based on diversity of citizenship. The first count was against INA; the second against the excess insurers. INA did not challenge personal or subject-matter jurisdiction of the District Court. The answer of the excess insurers, however, raised a number of defenses, including lack of *in personam* jurisdiction. Subsequently, this alleged lack of personal jurisdiction became the basis of a motion for summary judgment filed by the excess insurers. The issue in this case requires an account of respondent's attempt to use discovery in order to demonstrate the court's personal jurisdiction over the excess insurers.

Respondent's first discovery request—asking for "copies of all business interruption insurance policies issued by Defendant during the period from January 1, 1972 to

December 31, 1975"—was served on each defendant in August 1976. In January 1977, the excess insurers objected, on grounds of burdensomeness. Several months later, respondent filed a motion to compel petitioners to produce the requested documents. In June 1978, the court orally overruled petitioners' objections. This was followed by a second discovery request in which respondent narrowed the files it was seeking to policies which "were delivered in... Pennsylvania ... or covered a risk located in ... Pennsylvania." Petitioners now objected that these documents were not in their custody or control; rather, they were kept by the brokers in London. The court ordered petitioners to request the information from the brokers, limiting the request to policies covering the period from 1971 to date. That was in July 1978; petitioners were given 90 days to produce the information. On November 8, petitioners were given an additional 30 days to complete discovery. On November 24, petitioners filed an affidavit offering to make their records, allegedly some 4 million files, available at their offices in London for inspection by respondent. Respondent countered with a motion to compel production of the previously requested documents. On December 21, 1978, the court, noting that no conscientious effort had yet been made to produce the requested information and that no objection had been entered to the discovery order in July, gave petitioners 60 more days to produce the requested information. The District Judge also issued the following warning:

> "If you don't get it to him in 60 days, I am going to enter an order saying that because you failed to give the information as requested, that I am going to assume, under Rule of Civil Procedure 37(b), subsection 2(A), that there is jurisdiction."

A few moments later he restated the warning as follows: "I will assume that jurisdiction is here with this court unless you produce statistics and other information in that regard that would indicate otherwise."

On April 19, 1979, the court, after concluding that the requested material had not been produced, imposed the threatened sanction, finding that "for the purpose of this litigation the Excess Insurers are subject to the in personam jurisdiction of this Court due to their business contacts with Pennsylvania." Independently of the sanction, the District Court found two other grounds for holding that it had personal jurisdiction over petitioners. First, on the record established, it found that petitioners had sufficient business contacts with Pennsylvania to fall within the Pennsylvania long-arm statute. Second, in adopting the terms of the INA contract with CBG—a Pennsylvania insurance contract —the excess insurers implicitly agreed to submit to the jurisdiction of the court.

Except with respect to three excess insurers, the Court of Appeals for the Third Circuit affirmed the jurisdictional holding, relying entirely upon the validity of the sanction.

Because the decision below directly conflicts with the decision of the Court of Appeals for the Fifth Circuit in *Familia de Boom v. Arosa Mercantil,* we granted certiorari.

## II

In *McDonald v. Mabee,* (1917), another case involving an alleged lack of personal jurisdiction, Justice Holmes wrote for the Court, "great caution should be used not to let fiction deny the fair play that can be secured only by a pretty close adhesion to fact." Petitioners' basic submission is that to apply Rule 37(b)(2) to jurisdictional facts is to allow fiction to get the better of fact and that it is impermissible to use a fiction to establish judicial power, where, as a matter of fact, it does not exist. In our view, this represents a fundamental misunderstanding of the nature of personal jurisdiction.

The validity of an order of a federal court depends upon that court's having jurisdiction over both the subject matter and the parties. The concepts of subject-matter and personal jurisdiction, however, serve different purposes, and these different purposes affect the legal character of the two requirements. Petitioners fail to recognize the distinction between the two concepts—speaking instead in general terms of "jurisdiction"—although their argument's strength comes from conceiving of jurisdiction only as subject-matter jurisdiction.

Federal courts are courts of limited jurisdiction. The character of the controversies over which federal judicial authority may extend are delineated in Art. III, § 2, cl. 1. Jurisdiction of the lower federal courts is further limited to those subjects encompassed within a statutory grant of jurisdiction. Again, this reflects the constitutional source of federal judicial power: Apart from this Court, that power only exists "in such inferior Courts as the Congress may from time to time ordain and establish." Art. III, § 1.

Subject-matter jurisdiction, then, is an Art. III as well as a statutory requirement; it functions as a restriction on federal power, and contributes to the characterization of the federal sovereign. Certain legal consequences directly follow from this. For example, no action of the parties can confer subject-matter jurisdiction upon a federal court. Thus, the consent of the parties is irrelevant, principles of estoppel do not apply, and a party does not waive the requirement by failing to challenge jurisdiction early in the proceedings. Similarly, a court, including an appellate court, will raise lack of subject-matter jurisdiction on its own motion. "The rule, springing from the nature and limits of the judicial power of the United States is inflexible and without exception, which requires this court, of its own motion, to deny its jurisdiction, and, in the exercise of its appellate power, that of all other courts of the United States, in all cases where such jurisdiction does not affirmatively appear in the record."

None of this is true with respect to personal jurisdiction. The requirement that a court have personal jurisdiction flows not from Art. III, but from the Due Process Clause. The personal jurisdiction requirement recognizes and protects an individual liberty interest. It represents a restriction on judicial power not as a matter of sovereignty, but as a matter of individual liberty. Thus, the test for personal jurisdiction requires that "the maintenance of the suit ... not offend 'traditional notions of fair play and substantial justice.' *International Shoe.*

Because the requirement of personal jurisdiction represents first of all an individual right, it can, like other such rights, be waived. Regardless of the power of the State to serve process, an individual may submit to the jurisdiction of the court by appearance. A variety of legal arrangements have been taken to represent express or implied consent to the personal jurisdiction of the court. In *National Equipment Rental, Ltd. v. Szukhent*, we stated that "parties to a contract may agree in advance to submit to the jurisdiction of a given court." In addition, lower federal courts have found such consent implicit in agreements to arbitrate. Furthermore, the Court has upheld state procedures which find constructive consent to the personal jurisdiction of the state court in the voluntary use of certain state procedures. Finally, unlike subject-matter jurisdiction, which even an appellate court may review *sua sponte* under Rule 12(h), Federal Rules of Civil Procedure, "a defense of lack of jurisdiction over the person ... is waived" if not timely raised in the answer or a responsive pleading.

In sum, the requirement of personal jurisdiction may be intentionally waived, or for various reasons a defendant may be estopped from raising the issue. These characteristics portray it for what it is—a legal right protecting the individual. The plaintiff's demonstration of certain historical facts may make clear to the court that it has personal jurisdiction over the defendant as a matter of law—*i.e.*, certain factual showings will have legal consequences—but this is not the only way in which the personal jurisdiction of the court may arise. The actions of the defendant may amount to a legal submission to the jurisdiction of the court, whether voluntary or not.

The expression of legal rights is often subject to certain procedural rules. The failure to follow those rules may well result in a curtailment of the rights. Thus, the failure to enter a timely objection to personal jurisdiction constitutes, under Rule 12(h)(1), a waiver of the objection. A sanction under Rule 37(b)(2)(A) consisting of a finding of personal jurisdiction has precisely the same effect. As a general proposition, the Rule 37 sanction applied to a finding of personal jurisdiction creates no more of a due process problem than the Rule 12 waiver. Although "a court cannot conclude all persons interested by its mere assertion of its own power," not all rules that establish legal consequences to a party's own behavior are "mere assertions" of power.

Rule 37(b)(2)(A) itself embodies the standard established in *Hammond Packing Co. v. Arkansas*, (1909), for the due process limits on such rules. There the Court held that it did not violate due process for a state court to strike the answer and render a default judgment against a defendant who failed to comply with a pretrial discovery order. Such a rule was permissible as an expression of "the undoubted right of the lawmaking power to create a presumption of fact as to the bad faith and untruth of an answer. The preservation of due process was secured by the presumption that the refusal to produce evidence material to the administration of due process was but an admission of the want of merit in the asserted defense."

The situation in *Hammond* was specifically distinguished from that in *Hovey v. Elliott*, (1897), in which the Court held that it did violate due process for a court to take similar action as "punishment" for failure to obey an order to pay into the registry of the court a certain sum of money. Due process is violated only if the behavior of the defendant will not support the *Hammond Packing* presumption. A proper application of Rule 37(b)(2) will, as a matter of law, support such a presumption. If there is no abuse of discretion in the application of the Rule 37 sanction, as we find to be the case here, then the sanction is nothing more than the invocation of a legal presumption, or what is the same thing, the finding of a constructive waiver.

Petitioners argue that a sanction consisting of a finding of personal jurisdiction differs from all other instances in which a sanction is imposed, including the default judgment in *Hammond Packing*, because a party need not obey the orders of a court until it is established that the court has personal jurisdiction over that party. If there is no obligation to obey a judicial order, a sanction cannot be applied for the failure to comply. Until the court has established personal jurisdiction, moreover, any assertion of judicial power over the party violates due process.

This argument again assumes that there is something unique about the requirement of personal jurisdiction, which prevents it from being established or waived like other rights. A defendant is always free to ignore the judicial proceedings, risk a default judgment, and then challenge that judgment on jurisdictional grounds in a collateral proceeding. See *Baldwin v. Traveling Men's Assn.* By submitting to the jurisdiction of the court for the limited purpose of challenging jurisdiction, the defendant agrees to abide by that court's determination on the issue of jurisdiction: That decision will be res judicata on that issue in any further proceedings. As demonstrated above, the manner in which the court determines whether it has personal jurisdiction may include a variety of legal rules and presumptions, as well as straightforward fact finding. A particular rule may offend the due process standard of *Hammond Packing*, but the mere use of procedural rules does not in itself violate the defendant's due process rights.

## III

Even if Rule 37(b)(2) may be applied to support a finding of personal jurisdiction, the question remains as to whether it was properly applied under the circumstances of this case. Because the District Court's decision to invoke the sanction was accompanied by a detailed explanation of the reasons for that order and because that decision was upheld as a proper exercise of the District Court's discretion by the Court of Appeals, this issue need not detain us for long. What was said in *National Hockey League v. Metropolitan Hockey Club, Inc.* (1976), is fully applicable here: "The question, of course, is not whether this Court, or whether the Court of Appeals, would as an original matter have applied the sanction; it is whether the District Court abused its discretion in so doing" For the reasons that follow, we hold that it did not.

Rule 37(b)(2) contains two standards—one general and one specific—that limit a district court's discretion. First, any sanction must be "just"; second, the sanction must be specifically related to the particular "claim" which was at issue in the order to provide discovery.

In holding that the sanction in this case was "just," we rely specifically on the following. First, the initial discovery request was made in July 1977. Despite repeated orders from the court to provide the requested material, on December 21, 1978, the District Court was able to state that the petitioners "haven't even made any effort to get this information up to this point." The court then warned petitioners of a possible sanction. Confronted with continued delay and an obvious disregard of its orders, the trial court's invoking of its powers under Rule 37 was clearly appropriate. Second, petitioners repeatedly agreed to comply with the discovery orders within specified time periods. In each instance, petitioners failed to comply with their agreements. Third, respondent's allegation that the court had personal jurisdiction over petitioners was not a frivolous claim, and its attempt to use discovery to substantiate this claim was not, therefore, itself a misuse of judicial process. The substantiality of the jurisdictional allegation is demonstrated by the fact that the District Court found, as an alternative ground for its jurisdiction, that petitioners had sufficient contacts with Pennsylvania to fall within the State's long-arm statute. Fourth, petitioners had ample warning that a continued failure to comply with the discovery orders would lead to the imposition of this sanction. Furthermore, the proposed sanction made it clear that, even if there was not compliance with the discovery order, this sanction would not be applied if petitioners were to "produce statistics and other information" that would indicate an absence of personal jurisdiction. In effect, the District Court simply placed the burden of proof upon petitioners on the issue of personal jurisdiction. Petitioners failed to comply with the discovery order; they also failed to make any attempt to meet this burden of proof. This course of behavior, coupled with the ample warnings, demonstrates the "justice" of the trial court's order.

Neither can there be any doubt that this sanction satisfies the second requirement. CBG was seeking through discovery to respond to petitioners' contention that the District Court did not have personal jurisdiction. Having put the issue in question, petitioners did not have the option of blocking the reasonable attempt of CBG to meet its burden of proof. It surely did not have this option once the court had overruled petitioners' objections. Because of petitioners' failure to comply with the discovery orders, CBG was unable to establish the full extent of the contacts between petitioners and Pennsylvania, the critical issue in proving personal jurisdiction. Petitioners' failure to supply the requested information as to its contacts with Pennsylvania supports "the presumption that the refusal to produce evidence ... was but an admission of the want of merit in the asserted defense." The sanction took as established the facts—contacts with Pennsylvania—that CBG was seeking to establish through discovery. That a particular legal consequence—personal jurisdiction of the court over the defendants—follows from this, does not in any way affect the appropriateness of the sanction.

## IV

Because the application of a legal presumption to the issue of personal jurisdiction does not in itself violate the Due Process Clause and because there was no abuse of the discretion granted a district court under Rule 37(b)(2), we affirm the judgment of the Court of Appeals.

# CHAPTER 3

# FEDERAL SUBJECT MATTER JURISDICTION

1. *Subject matter* jurisdiction, as contrasted with *personal* jurisdiction, can *never* be established by consent – in any court – either federal courts or state courts. If a court does not have authority to hear a specific type of case then it cannot hear that case – no matter what any of the parties may do or say. Subject matter jurisdiction cannot be granted by consent.

The lack of subject matter jurisdiction may be raised at any time, by any party, or by the court itself. *Whenever* it is found that the court does not have subject matter jurisdiction the case *must* be dismissed.

Within the state court system there is usually quite broad subject matter jurisdiction. State courts are frequently courts of *general* jurisdiction. They are authorized to hear almost any kind of dispute. Subject matter jurisdiction of the federal courts is much more limited.

It is frequently said that all federal courts are courts of limited jurisdiction. To be able to bring a lawsuit in any federal court the plaintiff must first have a "key to the courthouse." Thus, every complaint filed in a federal court must state at the outset which specific statutory section – or specific Constitutional provision – gives the federal court subject matter jurisdiction over the issue at hand.

There are many different "keys to the courthouse" that create subject matter jurisdiction in various federal courts. Any specific federal statute *might* contain a key to the courthouse for particular issues or entities covered by that statue.

However, the primary keys to the federal courthouse are:

(1) Original jurisdiction in the U.S. Supreme Court for cases "in which a State shall be a Party," (Constitution, Art. III, Sec. 2);
(2) Admiralty jurisdiction, (28 USC 1333);
(3) Federal Question jurisdiction (28 USC 1331); and

(4) Diversity jurisdiction, (28 USC 1332).

Each of these forms of jurisdiction will be discussed below.

# A. ORIGINAL JURISDICTION OF THE SUPREME COURT

2. Article III, Section II, clause 2 of the U.S. Constitution provides that "In all Cases affecting Ambassadors, other public Ministers and Consuls, and those in which a State shall be a Party, the Supreme Court shall have original Jurisdiction. In all other cases ... the Supreme Court shall have appellate Jurisdiction, both as to Law and Fact, with such Exceptions, and under such Regulations as the Congress shall make."

So when states sue each other – over boundaries, or water, or various other matters – litigation *starts in the U.S. Supreme Court*. Needless to say, the justices on the Supreme Court do not act as trial judges. They refer the matter to a Special Master, who then makes recommendations on what the results should be.

The following case is a sample of a recent dispute in which the Supreme Court exercised original jurisdiction. Note in Part II the way the Supreme Court declares that is has much more flexibility in a case like this than it would normally have in litigation between private parties.

**135 S.CT. 1042**
**SUPREME COURT OF THE UNITED STATES**
**STATE OF KANSAS, PLAINTIFF**
**V.**
**STATES OF NEBRASKA AND COLORADO.**

DECIDED FEBRUARY 24, 2015

**Justice KAGAN delivered the opinion of the Court.**

For the second time in little more than a decade, Kansas and Nebraska ask this Court to settle a dispute over the States' rights to the waters of the Republican River Basin, as set out in an interstate compact. The first round of litigation ended with a settlement agreement designed to elaborate on, and promote future compliance with, the Compact's terms. The States now bring new claims against each other arising from the implementation of that settlement. Kansas seeks exceptional relief—both partial disgorgement of gains and an injunction—for Nebraska's conceded overconsumption of water. For its part, Nebraska requests amendment of a technical appendix to the settlement, so that allocations of water will faithfully reflect the parties' intent as expressed in both the body of that agreement and the Compact itself. We referred the case to a Special Master and now accept his recommendations as to appropriate equitable remedies: for Kansas, partial disgorgement but no injunction; and for Nebraska, reform of the appendix.

I

The Republican River originates in Colorado; crosses the northwestern corner of Kansas into Nebraska; flows through much of southwestern Nebraska; and finally cuts back into northern Kansas. Along with its many tributaries, the river drains a 24,900-square-mile watershed, called the Republican River Basin. The Basin contains substantial farmland, producing (among other things) wheat and corn.

During the Dust Bowl of the 1930's, the Republican River Basin experienced an extended drought, interrupted once by a deadly flood. In response, the Federal Government proposed constructing reservoirs in the Basin to control flooding, as well as undertaking an array of irrigation projects to disperse the stored water. But the Government insisted that the three States of the Basin first agree to an allocation of its water resources. As a result of that prodding, the States negotiated and ratified the Republican River Compact; and in 1943, as required under the Constitution, Art. I, § 10, cl. 3, Congress approved that agreement. By act of Congress, the Compact thus became federal law.

The Compact apportions among the three States the "virgin water supply originating in"—and, as we will later discuss, originating *only* in—the Republican River Basin. Compact Art. III. "Virgin water supply," as used in the Compact, means "the water supply within the Basin," in both the River and its tributaries, "undepleted by the activities of man." The Compact gives each State a set share of that supply—roughly, 49% to Nebraska, 40% to Kansas, and 11% to Colorado—for any "beneficial consumptive use." See Art. II (defining that term to mean "that use by which the water supply of the Basin is consumed through the activities of man"). In addition, the Compact charges the chief water official of each State with responsibility to jointly administer the agreement. Pursuant to that provision, the States created the Republican River Compact Administration (RRCA). The RRCA's chief task is to calculate the Basin's annual virgin water supply by measuring stream flow throughout the area, and to determine (retrospectively) whether each State's use of that water has stayed within its allocation.

All was smooth sailing for decades, until Kansas complained to this Court about Nebraska's increased pumping of groundwater, resulting from that State's construction of "thousands of wells hydraulically connected to the Republican River and its tributaries." Kansas contended that such activity was subject to the Compact: To the extent groundwater pumping depleted stream flow in the Basin, it counted against the pumping State's annual allotment of water. Nebraska maintained, to the contrary, that groundwater pumping fell outside the Compact's scope, even if that activity diminished stream flow in the area. A Special Master we appointed favored Kansas's interpretation of the Compact; we summarily agreed, and recommitted the case to him for further proceedings. The States then entered into negotiations, aimed primarily at determining how best to measure, and reflect in Compact accounting, the depletion of the Basin's stream flow due to groundwater pumping. During those discussions, the States also addressed a range of other matters affecting Compact administration. The talks bore fruit in 2002, when the States signed the Final Settlement Stipulation (Settlement).

The Settlement established detailed mechanisms to promote compliance with the Compact's terms. The States agreed that the Settlement was not "intended to, nor could it, change their respective rights and obligations under the Compact." Rather, the agreement aimed to accurately measure the supply and use of the Basin's water, and to assist the States in staying within their prescribed limits. To smooth out year-to-year fluctuations and otherwise facilitate compliance, the Settlement based all Compact accounting on 5–year running averages, reduced to 2–year averages in "water-short" periods. That change gave each State a chance to compensate for one (or more) year's overuse with another (or more) year's underuse before exceeding its allocation. The Settlement further provided, in line with this Court's decision, that groundwater pumping would count as part of a State's consumption to the extent it depleted the Basin's stream flow. And finally, the Settlement made clear, in accordance with the Compact, that a State's use of "imported water"—that is, water farmers bring into the area (usually for irrigation) that eventually seeps into the Republican River—would not count toward the State's allocation, because it did not originate in the Basin. Once again, the Settlement identified the Accounting Procedures and Groundwater Model as the tools to calculate (so as to exclude) that consumption.

But there were more rapids ahead: By 2007, Kansas and Nebraska each had complaints about how the Settlement was working. Kansas protested that in the 2005–2006 accounting period—the first for which the Settlement held States responsible—Nebraska had substantially exceeded its allocation of water. Nebraska, for its part, maintained that the Accounting Procedures and Groundwater Model were charging the State for use of imported water—specifically, for water originating in the Platte River Basin. The States brought those disputes to the RRCA and then to non-binding arbitration, in accordance with the Settlement's dispute resolution provisions. After failing to resolve the disagreements in those forums, Kansas sought redress in this Court, petitioning for both monetary and injunctive relief. We referred the case to a Special Master to consider Kansas's claims. In that proceeding, Nebraska asserted a counterclaim requesting a modification of the Accounting Procedures to ensure that its use of Platte River water would not count toward its Compact allocation.

After two years of conducting hearings, receiving evidence, and entertaining legal arguments, the Special Master issued his report and recommendations. The Master concluded that Nebraska had "knowingly failed" to comply with the Compact in the 2005–2006 accounting period, by consuming 70,869 acre-feet of water in excess of its prescribed share. To remedy that breach, the Master proposed awarding Kansas $3.7 million for its loss, and another $1.8 million in partial disgorgement of Nebraska's still greater gains. The Master, however, thought that an injunction against Nebraska was not warranted. In addition, the Master recommended reforming the Accounting Procedures in line with Nebraska's request, to ensure that the State would not be charged with using Platte River water.

Kansas and Nebraska each filed exceptions in this Court to parts of the Special Master's report. Nebraska objects to the Master's finding of a "knowing" breach and his call for partial disgorgement of its gains. Kansas asserts that the Master should have recommended both a larger disgorgement award and injunctive relief; the State also objects to his proposed change to the Accounting Procedures. In reviewing those claims, this Court gives the Special Master's factual findings "respect and a tacit presumption of correctness." But we conduct an "independent review of the record," and assume "the ultimate responsibility for deciding" all matters. Having carried out that careful review, we now overrule all exceptions and adopt the Master's recommendations.

II

The Constitution gives this Court original jurisdiction to hear suits between the States. See Art. III, § 2. Proceedings under that grant of jurisdiction are "basically equitable in nature." When the Court exercises its original jurisdiction over a controversy between two States, it serves "as a substitute for the diplomatic settlement of controversies between sovereigns and a possible resort to force." That role significantly "differs from" the one the Court undertakes "in suits between private parties. In this singular sphere, "the court may regulate and mould the process it uses in such a manner as in its judgment will best promote the purposes of justice."

Two particular features of this interstate controversy further distinguish it from a run-of-the-mill private suit and highlight the essentially equitable character of our charge. The first relates to the subject matter of the Compact and Settlement: rights to an interstate waterway. The second concerns the Compact's status as not just an agreement, but a federal law. Before proceeding to the merits of this dispute, we say a few words about each.

This Court has recognized for more than a century its inherent authority, as part of the Constitution's grant of original jurisdiction, to equitably apportion interstate streams between States. In *Kansas v. Colorado,* (1902), we confronted a simple consequence of geography: An upstream State can appropriate all water from a river, thus "wholly depriving" a downstream State "of the benefit of water" that "by nature" would flow into its territory. In such a circumstance, the downstream State lacks the sovereign's usual power to respond—the capacity to "make war, grant letters of marque and reprisal," or even enter into agreements without the consent of Congress. "Bound hand and foot by the prohibitions of the Constitution, a resort to the judicial power is the only means left" for stopping an inequitable taking of water.

This Court's authority to apportion interstate streams encourages States to enter into compacts with each other. When the division of water is not "left to the pleasure" of the upstream State, but States instead "know that some tribunal can decide on the right," then "controversies will probably be settled by compact." And that, of course, is what happened here: Kansas and Nebraska negotiated a compact to divide the waters of the Republican River and its tributaries. Our role thus shifts: It is now to declare rights under the Compact and enforce its terms.

But in doing so, we remain aware that the States bargained for those rights in the shadow of our equitable apportionment power—that is, our capacity to prevent one State from taking advantage of another. Each State's "right to invoke the original jurisdiction of this Court is an important part of the context" in which any compact is made. And it is "difficult to conceive" that a downstream State "would trade away its right" to our equitable apportionment if, under such an agreement, an upstream State could avoid its obligations or otherwise continue overreaching. Accordingly, our enforcement authority includes the ability to provide the remedies necessary to prevent abuse. We may invoke equitable principles, so long as consistent with the compact itself, to devise "fair ... solutions" to the state-parties' disputes and provide effective relief for their violations, (supplying an "additional enforcement mechanism" to ensure an upstream State's compliance with a compact).

And that remedial authority gains still greater force because the Compact, having received Congress's blessing, counts as federal law. "Congressional consent transforms an interstate compact ... into a law of the United States"). Of course, that legal status underscores a limit on our enforcement power: We may not "order relief inconsistent with [a compact's] express terms." But within those limits, the Court may exercise its full authority to remedy violations of and promote compliance with the agreement, so as to give complete effect to public law. As we have previously put the point: When federal law is at issue and "the public interest is involved," a federal court's "equitable powers assume an even broader and more flexible character than when only a private controversy is at stake." ("Courts of equity may, and frequently do, go much farther" to give "relief in furtherance of the public interest than they are accustomed to go when only private interests are involved").[5] In exercising our jurisdiction, we may "mould each decree to the necessities of the particular case" and "accord full justice" to all parties. These principles inform our consideration of the dispute before us.

III

We first address Nebraska's breach of the Compact and Settlement and the remedies appropriate to that violation. Both parties assent to the Special Master's finding that in 2005–2006 Nebraska exceeded its allocation of water by 70,869 acre-feet—about 17% more than its proper share. They similarly agree that this overconsumption resulted in a $3.7 million loss to Kansas; and Nebraska has agreed to pay those damages. But the parties dispute whether Nebraska's conduct warrants additional relief. The Master determined that Nebraska "knowingly exposed Kansas to a substantial risk" of breach, and so "knowingly failed" to comply with the Compact. Based in part on that finding, he recommended disgorgement of $1.8 million, which he described as "a small portion of the amount by which Nebraska's gain exceeds Kansas's loss." But he declined to grant Kansas's request for injunctive relief against Nebraska. As noted previously, each party finds something to dislike in the Master's handling of this issue: Nebraska contests his finding of a "knowing" Compact violation and his view that disgorgement is appropriate; Kansas wants a larger disgorgement award and an injunction regulating Nebraska's future conduct. We address those exceptions in turn.

2

After determining that Kansas lost $3.7 million from Nebraska's breach, the Special Master considered the case for an additional monetary award. Based on detailed evidence, not contested here, he concluded that an acre-foot of water is substantially more valuable on farmland in Nebraska than in Kansas. That meant Nebraska's reward for breaching the Compact was "much larger than Kansas' loss, likely by more than several multiples." Given the circumstances, the Master thought that Nebraska should have to disgorge part of that additional gain, to the tune of $1.8 million. In making that recommendation, he relied on his finding—which we have just affirmed—of Nebraska's culpability. He also highlighted this Court's broad remedial powers in compact litigation, noting that such cases involve not private parties' private quarrels, but States' clashes over federal law.

We thus reject Nebraska's exception to the Master's proposed remedy.

B

Kansas assails the Special Master's recommended disgorgement award from the other direction, claiming that it is too low to ensure Nebraska's future compliance. Notably, Kansas does not insist on all of Nebraska's gain. It recognizes the difficulty of ascertaining that figure, given the evidence the parties presented. And still more important, it "agrees" with the Master's view that the Court should select a "fair point on the spectrum" between no profits and full profits, based on the totality of facts and interests in the case. In setting that point, however, Kansas comes up with a higher number—or actually, a trio of them. The State first asks us to award "treble damages of $11.1 million," then suggests that we can go "up to roughly $25 million," and finally proposes a "1:1 loss-to-disgorgement ratio," which means $3.7 million of Nebraska's gains.

We prefer to stick with the Master's single number. As an initial matter, we agree with both the Master and Kansas that disgorgement need not be all or nothing. In exercising our original jurisdiction, this Court recognizes that "flexibility [is] inherent in equitable remedies," and awards them "with reference to the facts of the particular case." So if partial disgorgement will serve to stabilize a compact by conveying an effective message to the breaching party that it must work hard to meet its future obligations, then the Court has discretion to order only that much.

And we agree with the Master's judgment that a relatively small disgorgement award suffices here. That is because, as the Master detailed, Nebraska altered its conduct after the 2006 breach, and has complied with the Compact ever since.

Truth be told, we cannot be sure why the Master selected the exact number he did—why, that is, he arrived at $1.8 million, rather than a little more or a little less. The Master's Report, in this single respect, contains less explanation than we might like. But then again, any hard number reflecting a balance of equities can seem random in a certain light—as Kansas's own briefs, with their ever-fluctuating ideas for a disgorgement award, amply attest. What matters is that the Master took into account the appropriate considerations—weighing Nebraska's incentives, past behavior, and more recent compliance efforts—in determining the kind of signal necessary to prevent another breach. We are thus confident that in approving the Master's recommendation for about half again Kansas's actual damages, we award a fair and equitable remedy suited to the circumstances.

For related reasons, we also reject Kansas's request for an injunction ordering Nebraska to comply with the Compact and Settlement. Kansas wants such an order so that it can seek contempt sanctions against Nebraska for any future breach. But we agree with the Master that Kansas has failed to show, as it must to obtain an injunction, a "cognizable danger of recurrent violation." Nebraska is now on notice that if it relapses, it may again be subject to disgorgement of gains—either in part or in full, as the equities warrant. That, we trust, will adequately guard against Nebraska's repeating its former practices.

## IV.

The final question before us concerns the Special Master's handling of Nebraska's counterclaim. This Court's authority to devise "fair and equitable solutions" to interstate water disputes encompasses modifying a technical agreement to correct material errors in the way it operates and thus align it with the compacting States' intended apportionment.

## V.

Nebraska argues here for a cramped view of our authority to order disgorgement. Kansas argues for a similarly restrictive idea of our power to modify a technical document. We think each has too narrow an understanding of this Court's role in disputes arising from compacts apportioning interstate streams. The Court has broad remedial authority in such cases to enforce the compact's terms. Here, compelling Nebraska to disgorge profits deters it from taking advantage of its upstream position to appropriate more water than the Compact allows. And amending the Accounting Procedures ensures that the Compact's provisions will govern the division of the Republican River Basin's (and only that Basin's) water supply. Both remedies safeguard the Compact; both insist that States live within its law. Accordingly, we adopt all of the Special Master's recommendations.

# B. ADMIRALTY JURISDICTION 28 USC 1333

3. 28 USC 1333 provides, in full, that "The district courts shall have original jurisdiction, exclusive of the courts of the States, of:

(1) Any civil case of admiralty or maritime jurisdiction, saving to suitors in all cases all other remedies to which they are otherwise entitled.

(2) Any prize brought into the United States and all proceedings for the condemnation of property taken as a prize."

The first case in this section is not of earth-shaking importance, but the writing style is too good to miss. Enjoy.

## 147 F. SUPP. 2D 668
## UNITED STATES DISTRICT COURT FOR THE SOUTHERN DISTRICT OF TEXAS, GALVESTON DIVISION
## JOHN W. BRADSHAW, PLAINTIFF,
## V.
## UNITY MARINE CORPORATION, INC.; CORONADO, IN REM; AND PHILLIPS PETROLEUM COMPANY, DEFENDANTS.

### DECIDED JUNE 26, 2001

**OPINION BY:** SAMUEL B. KENT
**ORDER GRANTING DEFENDANT'S MOTION FOR SUMMARY JUDGMENT**

Plaintiff brings this action for personal injuries sustained while working aboard the M/V CORONADO. Now before the Court is Defendant Phillips Petroleum Company's ("Phillips") Motion for Summary Judgment. For the reasons set forth below, Defendant's Motion is **GRANTED**.

# I. DISCUSSION

Plaintiff John W. Bradshaw claims that he was working as a Jones Act seaman aboard the M/V CORONADO on January 4, 1999. The CORONADO was not at sea on January 4, 1999, but instead sat docked at a Phillips' facility in Freeport, Texas. Plaintiff alleges that he "sustained injuries to his body in the course and scope of his employment." The injuries are said to have "occurred as a proximate result of the unsafe and unseaworthy condition of the tugboat CORONADO and its appurtenances while docked at the Phillips/Freeport Dock." Plaintiff's First Amended Complaint, which added Phillips as a Defendant, provides no further information about the manner in which he suffered injury. However, by way of his Response to Defendant's Motion for Summary Judgment, Plaintiff now avers that "he was forced to climb on a piling or dolphin to leave the vessel at the time he was injured." This, in combination with Plaintiff's Complaint, represents the totality of the information available to the Court respecting the potential liability of Defendant Phillips.

Defendant now contends, in its Motion for Summary Judgment, that the Texas two-year statute of limitations for personal injury claims bars this action. Plaintiff suffered injury on January 4, 1999 and filed suit in this Court on September 15, 2000. However, Plaintiff did not amend his Complaint to add Defendant Phillips until March 28, 2001, indisputably more than two-years after the date of his alleged injury. Plaintiff now responds that he timely sued Phillips, contending that the three-year federal statute for maritime personal injuries applies to his action. See *46 U.S.C. § 763a*.

Before proceeding further, the Court notes that this case involves two extremely likable lawyers, who have together delivered some of the most amateurish pleadings ever to cross the hallowed causeway into Galveston, an effort which leads the Court to surmise but one plausible explanation. Both attorneys have obviously entered into a secret pact--complete with hats, handshakes and cryptic words--to draft their pleadings entirely in crayon on the back sides of gravy-stained paper place mats, in the hope that the Court would be so charmed by their child-like efforts that their utter dearth of legal authorities in their briefing would go unnoticed. Whatever actually occurred, the Court is now faced with the daunting task of deciphering their submissions. With Big Chief tablet readied, thick black pencil in hand, and a devil-may-care laugh in the face of death, life on the razor's edge sense of exhilaration, the Court begins.

Summary judgment is appropriate if no genuine issue of material fact exists and the moving party is entitled to judgment as a matter of law. When a motion for summary judgment is made, the nonmoving party must set forth specific facts showing that there is a genuine issue for trial. Therefore, when a defendant moves for summary judgment based upon an affirmative defense to the plaintiff's claim, the plaintiff must bear the burden of producing some evidence to create a fact issue as to some element of defendant's asserted affirmative defense.

Defendant begins the descent into Alice's Wonderland by submitting a Motion that relies upon only one legal authority. The Motion cites a Fifth Circuit case which stands for the whopping proposition that a federal court sitting in Texas applies the Texas statutes of limitations to certain state and federal law claims. That is all well and good--the Court is quite fond of the *Erie* doctrine; indeed there is talk of little else around both the Canal and this Court's water cooler. Defendant, however, does not even cite to *Erie*, but to a mere successor case, and further fails to even begin to analyze why the Court should approach the shores of *Erie*. Finally, Defendant does not even provide a cite to its desired Texas limitation statute.[2] A more bumbling approach is difficult to conceive--but wait folks, There's More!

2 Defendant submitted a Reply brief, on June 11, 2001, after the Court had already drafted, but not finalized, this Order. In a regretful effort to be thorough, the Court reviewed this submission. It too fails to cite to either the Texas statute of limitations or any Fifth Circuit cases discussing maritime law liability for Plaintiff's claims versus Phillips.

Plaintiff responds to this deft, yet minimalist analytical wizardry with an equally gossamer wisp of an argument, although Plaintiff does at least cite the federal limitations provision applicable to maritime tort claims. Naturally, Plaintiff also neglects to provide any analysis whatsoever of why his claim versus Defendant Phillips is a maritime action. Instead, Plaintiff "cites" to a single case from the Fourth Circuit. Plaintiff's citation, however, points to a nonexistent Volume "1886" of the Federal Reporter Third Edition and neglects to provide a pinpoint citation for what, after being located, turned out to be a forty-page decision. Ultimately, to the Court's dismay after reviewing the opinion, it stands simply for the bombshell proposition that torts committed on navigable waters (in this case an alleged defamation committed by the controversial G. Gordon Liddy aboard a cruise ship at sea) require the application of general maritime rather than state tort law. See *Wells v. Liddy, 186 F.3d 505, 524 (4th Cir. 1999)* (What the . . .)?! The Court cannot even begin to comprehend why this case was selected for reference. It is almost as if Plaintiff's counsel chose the opinion by throwing long range darts at the Federal Reporter (remarkably enough hitting a nonexistent volume!). And though the Court often gives great heed to dicta from courts as far flung as those of Manitoba, it finds this case unpersuasive.

There is nothing in Plaintiff's cited case about ingress or egress between a vessel and a dock, although counsel must have been thinking that Mr. Liddy must have had both ingress and egress from the cruise ship at some docking facility, before uttering his fateful words.

Further, as noted above, Plaintiff has submitted a Supplemental Opposition to Defendant's Motion. This Supplement is longer than Plaintiff's purported Response, cites more cases, several constituting binding authority from either the Fifth Circuit or the Supreme Court, and actually includes attachments which purport to be evidence. However, this is all that can be said positively for Plaintiff's Supplement, which does nothing to explain why, on the facts of this case, Plaintiff has an admiralty claim against Phillips (which probably makes some sense because Plaintiff doesn't). Plaintiff seems to rely on the fact that he has pled Rule 9(h) and stated an admiralty claim versus the vessel and his employer to demonstrate that maritime law applies to Phillips. This bootstrapping argument does not work; Plaintiff must properly invoke admiralty law versus each Defendant discretely. Despite the continued shortcomings of Plaintiff's supplemental submission, the Court commends Plaintiff for his vastly improved choice of crayon--Brick Red is much easier on the eyes than Goldenrod, and stands out much better amidst the mustard splotched about Plaintiff's briefing. But at the end of the day, even if you put a calico dress on it and call it Florence, a pig is still a pig.

Now, alas, the Court must return to grownup land. As vaguely alluded to by the parties, the issue in this case turns upon which law--state or maritime--applies to each of Plaintiff's potential claims versus Defendant Phillips. And despite Plaintiff's and Defendant's joint, heroic efforts to obscure it, the answer to this question is readily ascertained. The Fifth Circuit has held that "absent a maritime status between the parties, a dock owner's duty to crew members of a vessel using the dock is defined by the application of state law, not maritime law. Specifically, maritime law does not impose a duty on the dock owner to provide a means of safe ingress or egress. Therefore, because maritime law does not create a duty on the part of Defendant Phillips *vis-a-vis* Plaintiff, any claim Plaintiff does have versus Phillips must necessarily arise under state law.[3]

> 3 Take heed and be suitably awed, oh boys and girls--the Court was able to state the issue and its resolution in one paragraph . . . despite dozes of pages of gibberish from the parties to the contrary!

The Court, therefore, under *Erie*, applies the Texas statute of limitations. Texas has adopted a two-year statute of limitations for personal injury cases. Plaintiff failed to file his action versus Defendant Phillips within that two-year time frame. Plaintiff has offered no justification, such as the discovery rule or other similar tolling doctrines, for this failure. Accordingly, Plaintiff's claims versus Defendant Phillips were not timely filed and are barred. Defendant Phillips' Motion for Summary Judgment is **GRANTED** and Plaintiff's state law claims against Defendant Phillips are hereby **DISMISSED WITH PREJUDICE**. A Final Judgment reflecting such will be entered in due course.

## II. CONCLUSION

After this remarkably long walk on a short legal pier, having received no useful guidance whatever from either party, the Court has endeavored, primarily based upon its affection for both counsel, but also out of its own sense of morbid curiosity, to resolve what it perceived to be the legal issue presented. Despite the waste of perfectly good crayon seen in both parties' briefing (and the inexplicable odor of wet dog emanating from such) the Court believes it has satisfactorily resolved this matter. Defendant's Motion for Summary Judgment is **GRANTED**.

At this juncture, Plaintiff retains, albeit seemingly to his befuddlement and/or consternation, a maritime law cause of action versus his alleged Jones Act employer, Defendant Unity Marine Corporation, Inc. However, it is well known around these parts that Unity Marine's lawyer is equally likable and has been writing crisply in ink since the second grade. Some old-timers even spin yarns of an ability to type. The Court cannot speak to the veracity of such loose talk, but out of caution, the Court suggests that Plaintiff's lovable counsel had best upgrade to a nice shiny No. 2 pencil or at least sharpen what's left of the stubs of his crayons for what remains of this heart-stopping, spine-tingling action.[4]

> 4 In either case, the Court cautions Plaintiff's counsel not to run with a sharpened
> writing utensil in hand--he could put his eye out.

**IT IS SO ORDERED.**
DONE this 26th day of June, 2001, at Galveston, Texas.
SAMUEL B. KENT, UNITED STATES DISTRICT JUDGE

4. The following case *is* of major significance. Who would have guessed that when a plane crashes on land, just short of the runway, that is a matter of *admiralty* jurisdiction?

UNITED STATES COURT OF APPEALS,
SEVENTH CIRCUIT
LU JUNHONG, ET AL., PLAINTIFFS–APPELLEES,
V.
THE BOEING COMPANY, DEFENDANT–APPELLANT.

DECIDED JULY 8, 2015

EASTERBROOK, Circuit Judge.

On July 6, 2013, a Boeing 777 hit the seawall that separates the ocean from the end of a runway at San Francisco International Airport. The plane's tail broke off, 49 persons sustained serious injuries, and three of the passengers died, though the other 255 passengers and crew aboard suffered only minor or no injuries. The flight, operated by Asiana Airlines, had crossed the Pacific Ocean from Seoul, Korea. The National Transportation Safety Board concluded that the principal cause of the accident was pilot error: the pilots approached too low and too slow, and by the time they attempted to add power and execute a missed approach, it was too late. Only three seconds remained until the impact, the plane was about 90 feet above the ground, and the "airplane did not have the performance capability to accomplish a go-around." *Aircraft Accident Report: Descent Below Visual Glidepath and Impact with Seawall, Asiana Airlines Flight 214* (NTSB June 24, 2014) at 126. The Board believed that the pilots would have had to act eight or nine seconds earlier (a total of 11 or 12 seconds before reaching the seawall) to avoid hitting it.

Suits brought in federal courts in California, and some other district courts, were consolidated by the Panel on Multidistrict Litigation in the Northern District of California under 28 U.S.C. § 1407(a). Some passengers filed suit against Boeing in state courts of Illinois, contending that the plane's auto throttle, autopilot, and low-airspeed-warning systems contributed to the pilots' errors. Boeing removed these suits to federal court, asserting two sources of jurisdiction: admiralty, plus federal officials' right to have claims against them resolved by federal courts. 28 U.S.C. §§ 1333, 1442. The Panel on Multidistrict Litigation then decided that these suits, too, should be transferred to California to participate in the consolidated pretrial proceedings. But before receiving the Panel's formal directions to transfer the suits to California, the district court remanded them for lack of subject-matter jurisdiction. The court concluded that Boeing did not act as a federal officer for the purpose of §

1442 and that the tort occurred on land, when the plane hit the seawall, rather than over navigable water. Boeing appealed, as it is entitled to do: removal under § 1442 is an exception to 28 U.S.C. § 1447(d), which makes most remands non-reviewable. We stayed the remand orders.

I

First in line is the question whether Boeing was entitled to remove under § 1442(a)(1), which offers a federal forum to "the United States or any agency thereof or any officer (or any person acting under that officer) of the United States or of any agency thereof, in an official or individual capacity, for or relating to any act under color of such office."

We agree with the district court that § 1442 does not support removal.

II [omitted]

III

The relation between aviation accidents and the admiralty jurisdiction has been fraught ever since *Executive Jet Aviation, Inc. v. Cleveland,* 409 U.S. 249,(1972), modified the former situs requirement and asked, not where a wreck ended up (land or water), but whether the events leading to the accident have enough connection to maritime activity. A plane had taken off from an airport adjoining Lake Erie, collided with a flock of gulls that gathered at the garbage dump off the end of the runway, settled back to earth in the heap of garbage, and was carried by its inertia into the lake, where it sank. The Justices thought that this had nothing to do with maritime affairs, even though the gulls may have made their living eating fish (in addition to refuse), and held the admiralty jurisdiction unavailable.

But the approach articulated in *Executive Jet* has caused problems. The price of throwing out one case that did not seem connected to maritime commerce was to unsettle the rules for many other cases with stronger connections. *Sisson v. Ruby,* (1990), suggested that the Justices had begun to rue the *Executive Jet* decision, and though it was not overruled the Court did hold that damage caused by a fire in the washer/dryer of a yacht tied up at a dock was within the admiralty jurisdiction. A few years later, the Court responded to the Great Chicago Flood—a hole in the bottom of the Chicago River introduced water to tunnels that carried it to basements throughout the Loop, causing injury inland—by holding that this event, too, was within the admiralty jurisdiction because the cause was maritime. *Jerome B.*

*Grubart, Inc. v. Great Lakes Dredge & Dock Co.*, 513 U.S. 527, (1995). Again the result of Executive Jet survived, though the applicable legal standard changed.

The parties and the district court read the interaction of these decisions (and there are others that need not be mentioned) in three ways. Plaintiffs maintain that aviation accidents are outside the admiralty jurisdiction (unless perhaps a flying boat or float plane is involved); as fallbacks they contend that when the injury occurs on land there cannot be admiralty jurisdiction and that in any event a defendant cannot remove under the admiralty jurisdiction. Boeing contends that admiralty jurisdiction is available when an accident has a maritime cause, which Boeing understands to mean a cause that occurred while the plane was over navigable waters. The district court did not accept any of these approaches. Instead it held that admiralty jurisdiction is available only when an accident becomes inevitable while the plane is over water.

We start with the inevitability standard, which as far as we can tell lacks a provenance in the Supreme Court's decisions or in any appellate opinion. And it has the further problem of not supporting the judgment, because the choice between "cause" (Boeing's argument) and "inevitable cause" (the district court's holding) cannot affect the outcome.

As the district judge saw things, until the crash the pilots had only to rev the engines, pull up on the yoke, and execute a missed approach. Their failure to do this caused the accident, but hitting the seawall never became inevitable over water. When Boeing asked the district judge to reconsider, contending that the record did not support the judge's understanding of the facts, the judge replied that the record did not show beyond all doubt that the plane was doomed at any moment while it was over navigable water.

Both the district judge's opinion and his order denying reconsideration were issued before the NTSB released its report, which concluded that by 10 seconds before impact a collision *was* certain; a 777 aircraft lacks the ability to accelerate and climb fast enough, no matter what the pilots did in the final 10 seconds. This means that, while the plane was over San Francisco Bay (part of the Pacific Ocean), an accident became inevitable. And the plaintiffs' own theory of liability pins a portion of the blame on Boeing because, about 4.5 nautical miles from the seawall, the auto throttle system disengaged—apparently without the pilots recognizing what had happened—and caused the plane to descend faster than the pilots appreciated. *NTSB Report* at 79–84.

The auto throttle system did exactly what it had been programmed to do. We have nothing to say about whether it should have been programmed differently, whether its design played a role in the accident, or whether Boeing should have done more to educate airlines (and their pilots) about how it would react when pilots issued the commands that Asiana's pilots did on the descent into San Francisco. But, if Boeing is liable at all, it must be because something about how this system was designed or explained created an unacceptable risk of an accident—and the system's performance (including the interaction between pilots and the automation design) occurred before the plane hit the seawall.

The district judge may have thought that federal jurisdiction depends on a high degree of certainty that jurisdictional facts exist. That seems to be the point of an "inevitability" approach, coupled with insistence on proof that relevant facts and inferences be established beyond dispute. Yet the rules are otherwise. Jurisdictional allegations control unless it is legally impossible for them to be true (or to have the asserted consequences). That's equally true of a defendant's allegations in support of removal. See *Dart Cherokee Basin Operating Co. v. Owens*, --- U.S. ----, 135 S.Ct. 547, 553–54, (2014). Given the NTSB's findings, it is possible for Boeing to show that this accident was caused by, or became inevitable because of, events that occurred over navigable water.

Is that sufficient? *Grubart* says that admiralty jurisdiction is available when an "injury suffered on land was caused by a vessel on navigable water", if the cause bears a "substantial relationship to traditional maritime activity." This plane crossed the Pacific Ocean, a traditional maritime activity, and the cause of the accident likely occurred over the water. But an airplane is not a "vessel" and it was "over" rather than "on" the water. Does that make a difference?

Not functionally. An airplane, just like an ocean-going vessel, moves passengers and freight from one continent to another. It crosses swaths of the high seas that are outside of any nation's territory, and parts of the seas adjacent to the United States but outside any state's territory. It is a traditional, and important, function of admiralty law to supply a forum and a set of rules for accidents in international commerce. And *Executive Jet* itself said as much, though with a hedge, in remarking that a trans-ocean flight "might be thought to bear a significant relationship to traditional maritime activity because it would be performing a function traditionally performed by waterborne vessels".

Before the Wright Brothers, admiralty jurisdiction necessarily was limited to vessels on navigable waters. Perhaps the invention of the submarine (under rather than on the water) was its first logical extension. When aircraft came along, courts had a lot of difficulty classifying them for many purposes. But just as judges have not doubted that Congress can establish an air force even though the Constitution mentions only an army and a navy, so judges have concluded that airplanes over navigable waters should be treated the same as vessels—when a connection to maritime activity exists, as it didn't in *Executive Jet.*

*Executive Jet* treated it as settled that airplanes are within the scope of the Death on the High Seas Act, 46 U.S.C. § 30302, which brings within the admiralty jurisdiction any death that is "caused by wrongful act, neglect, or default occurring on the high seas" more than three nautical miles from shore. *Offshore Logistics, Inc. v. Tallentire,* (1986), later applied that statute when a helicopter went down in the ocean. If accidents that occur because of a cause *over* the water are treated as *on* the water for the purpose of this statute, it is hard to see any stopping point—provided that the accident meets the functional requirements articulated in *Grubart.* For 28 U.S.C. § 1333(1), which creates admiralty jurisdiction, does not mention vessels or demand that the cause or injury be "on" the water. It says only that district courts have jurisdiction of: "Any civil case of admiralty or maritime jurisdiction, saving to suitors in all cases all other remedies to which they are otherwise entitled." This is close to circular. District courts have admiralty jurisdiction in "any civil case of admiralty or maritime jurisdiction". That leaves only the *Grubart* standard, which as we have said is satisfied functionally.

True, we have in this litigation an accident apparently caused by events over water, but producing injury on land, and there's no tort without injury. Yet neither § 1333(1) nor § 30302 requires the whole tort to occur on the water. Section 30302 speaks of a *cause* on the water (or, after *Offshore Logistics,* over the water), and so does *Grubart*—for even if admiralty did not initially cover water-based causes of injury on land, it has done so ever since the Extension of Admiralty Jurisdiction Act, 46 U.S.C. § 30101, on which *Grubart* relied to bring harm from the flooding of Chicago's basements within admiralty jurisdiction.

We are not saying that the Death on the High Seas Act applies to these cases. The plaintiffs do not rely on it. Section 30307(c) creates an exception to the Act for deaths that occur within 12 nautical miles of shore. Nor are we saying that a flight scheduled to take off and land within the United States drifts in and out of admiralty as it crosses lakes and rivers along the way. The Justices remarked in *Executive Jet* that for "flights within the continental United States, which are principally over land, the fact that an aircraft happens to fall in navigable waters, rather than on land, is wholly fortuitous." That opinion wrapped up this way: "we hold that, in the absence of legislation to the contrary, there is no federal admiralty jurisdiction over aviation tort claims arising from flights by land-based aircraft between points within the continental United States."

But Asiana 214 was a trans-ocean flight, a substitute for an ocean-going vessel—as flights from the contiguous United States to and from Alaska, Hawaii, and overseas territories also would be—and thus within the scope of *Executive Jet's* observation that this situation "might be thought to bear a significant relationship to a traditional maritime activity". The Supreme Court's holding in *Offshore Logistics* that an accident caused by problems in airplanes *above* water should be treated, for the purpose of § 30302, the same as an accident caused *on* the water carries the implication that the general admiralty jurisdiction of 28 U.S.C. § 1333(1) also includes accidents caused by problems that occur in trans-ocean commerce. Admiralty then supplies a uniform law for a case that otherwise might cause choice-of-law headaches.

Most appellate decisions on this subject since *Executive Jet* agree. See *Miller v. United States*, 725 F.2d 1311, 1315 (11th Cir.1984) (flight from Bahamas to Florida is within admiralty jurisdiction); *Williams v. United States*, 711 F.2d 893, 896 (9th Cir.1983) (flight from California to Hawaii is within admiralty jurisdiction); *Roberts v. United States*, 498 F.2d 520, 524 (9th Cir.1974) (flight from California to Vietnam is within admiralty jurisdiction). The one exception, *United States Aviation Underwriters, Inc. v. Pilatus Business Aircraft, Ltd.*, 582 F.3d 1131 (10th Cir.2009) (flight between Japan and Russia), stressed that the flight was not commercial; maybe the Tenth Circuit would find admiralty jurisdiction for commercial aviation such as Asiana 214. It is enough for us to say that we accept the majority position.

Plaintiffs tell us that, even if the events come within § 1333(1), Boeing still was not allowed to remove the suits under 28 U.S.C. § 1441(a). Yet that section permits removal of any suit over which a district court would have original jurisdiction—and, if these suits are within the admiralty jurisdiction, that condition is satisfied. Plaintiffs' brief asserts: "admiralty jurisdiction does not provide a basis for removal absent an independent basis for federal jurisdiction." There plaintiffs stop; they don't explain why.

In 2011 Congress amended § 1441(b) to read:

(b) REMOVAL BASED ON DIVERSITY OF CITIZENSHIP.—(1) In determining whether a civil action is removable on the basis of the jurisdiction under section 1332(a) of this title, the citizenship of defendants sued under fictitious names shall be disregarded. (2) A civil action otherwise removable solely on the basis of the jurisdiction under section 1332(a) of this title may not be removed if any of the parties in interest properly joined and served as defendants is a citizen of the State in which such action is brought.

Federal Courts Jurisdiction and Venue Clarification Act of 2011, § 103, Pub.L. No. 112–63, 125 Stat. 759. This amendment limits the ban on removal by a home-state defendant to suits under the diversity jurisdiction.

Perhaps it would be possible to argue that the saving-to-suitors clause itself forbids removal, without regard to any language in § 1441. But plaintiffs, who have not mentioned the saving-to-suitors clause, do not make such an argument. We do not think that it is the sort of contention about subject-matter jurisdiction that a federal court must resolve even if the parties disregard it. Our conclusion that § 1333(1) supplies admiralty jurisdiction shows that subject-matter jurisdiction exists. Plaintiffs thus could have filed these suits directly in federal court (as many victims of this crash did). If the saving-to-suitors clause allows them to stay in state court even after the 2011 amendment, they are free to waive or forfeit that right—which given the scope of § 1333(1) concerns venue rather than subject-matter jurisdiction. Boeing therefore was entitled to remove these suits to federal court.

## IV

One observation in closing. Our conclusions about admiralty jurisdiction, and the appellate-jurisdiction ruling that allowed us to consider the admiralty question, are compatible with the Multiparty, Multiforum Trial Jurisdiction Act of 2002, codified in 28 U.S.C. § 1369 and § 1441(e). This statute supplies federal jurisdiction when an accident with multistate features entails the deaths of 75 or more persons. Like most other grants of federal jurisdiction, it does not say that it is an exclusive means to federal court. A law granting one sort of jurisdiction does not implicitly negate others. No one doubts, for example, that if an air crash has only one victim, that person's estate could sue the plane's manufacturer under the diversity jurisdiction, 28 U.S.C. § 1332, if they were citizens of different states. Likewise with the admiralty jurisdiction. Federal litigation in most air crashes will continue to rely on the diversity jurisdiction (potentially including the Class Action Fairness Act, § 1332(d), if more than 100 injured persons pursue a class action or a mass action) or the Multiparty, Multiforum Trial Jurisdiction Act; adding the possibility of admiralty jurisdiction when the cause of an accident occurs during a trans-ocean flight does not change the forum in which most aircraft suits are litigated.

The district court's decision is reversed, and the case is remanded with instructions to rescind the remand orders and transfer these cases to the Northern District of California for consolidated pretrial proceedings under 28 U.S.C. § 1407, consistent with the decision of the Panel on Multidistrict Litigation.

5. Now that you have read the case, why do you think that Boeing was working so hard to have this case held to be a matter of admiralty jurisdiction? [Hint: The corporate headquarters of Boeing are located in Chicago, Illinois.]

# C. FEDERAL QUESTION JURISDICTION 28 USC 1331

6. We now come to federal question jurisdiction which, with diversity jurisdiction, is one of the two most often used "keys" to the courthouse. The federal question "key," 28 USC 1331 provides, in full, that "The district courts shall have original jurisdiction of all civil actions arising under the Constitution, laws, or treaties of the United States."

Note first that Sec. 1331, unlike Sec 1333 (Admiralty jurisdiction), does not give the federal courts *exclusive* jurisdiction on federal question cases. Sec. 1331 creates *concurrent* jurisdiction with state courts. Litigation involving interpretation of the U.S. Constitution, or federal laws, may be brought in *either* federal or state courts. State courts, on a routine basis, interpret the U.S. Constitution and a wide assortment of federal statutes.

Sec. 1331 just gives a plaintiff who would like to have her case tried in federal court a "key to the courthouse." Note that this is, in effect, a one-sided key: the only thing the plaintiff has to allege is that the matter at issue is based on a federal question. All of the parties involved could be from the same state. The state courts would have full authority to hear a case based on a federal question. But if the plaintiff would prefer to have her case heard in a federal court, Sec. 1331 gives her the opportunity to do so.

The following case involves some very skillful lawyering. To help you understand what is going on, just remember that a plaintiff files a complaint to start a lawsuit. Then the defendant files an answer. In her answer the defendant may include a counterclaim against the plaintiff – if the defendant feels that she has some claim against the plaintiff that arose out of the same transaction.

# UNITED STATES COURT OF APPEALS THIRD CIRCUIT.
## GREAT LAKES RUBBER CORPORATION, APPELLANT,
### V.
## HERBERT COOPER CO., INC.

DECIDED FEBRUARY 8, 1961

Before BIGGS, Chief Judge, and GOODRICH and FORMAN, Circuit Judges.

BIGGS, Chief Judge.

This is an appeal from an order of the court below dismissing a counterclaim of Great Lakes Rubber Corporation (Great Lakes), made against Herbert Cooper Co., Inc. (Cooper), on the ground that the court lacked jurisdiction of the subject matter of the counterclaim. Because the question presented on appeal is whether Great Lakes' counterclaim arises out of the transaction or occurrence that is the subject matter of a claim asserted by Cooper a detailed analysis of the pleadings is necessary.

On May 12, 1959, Great Lakes filed an amended complaint naming Cooper as defendant. Jurisdiction was allegedly based on diversity. The allegations fall roughly into three groups. First, it was alleged that Howard Cooper and Joseph Herbert had been employed by Great Lakes for periods of approximately four and two years, as foreman and supervisor, respectively and that they left Great Lakes' employ taking with them certain information relating to the flexible rubber tubing manufactured by Great Lakes, and lists disclosing Great Lakes' customers; that shortly thereafter they, with others, founded Cooper; that Cooper competed for and obtained customers that were, until then, customers of Great Lakes; and, that Cooper's 'offering to sell, and manufacturing and selling flexible tubing made and offered for sale with utilization of knowledge and information acquired (by Howard Cooper and Joseph Herbert) while these men were in a fiduciary relationship with plaintiff' constituted 'acts of unfair competition and unfair business practices'.

Second, it was alleged that Great Lakes manufactures flexible tubing covered by patents held by Fred T. and Robert E. Roberts; that Great Lakes is a licensee of the Roberts; that Cooper, after failing to obtain a similar license, submitted bids to the United States Army and Air Force, customers of Great Lakes, offering to manufacture and sell flexible rubber tubing of a type, the manufacture and sale of which would constitute Cooper an 'infringer' of the Roberts' patents; that Cooper, as low bidder, was awarded several contracts by the Government; that Cooper was enabled to underbid Great Lakes because unlike Great Lakes it was not paying royalties as a licensee under the Roberts' patents; and, that by reason of Cooper's operation as an 'unlicensed infringer' it 'is and has been in an unfair competitive position' relative to Great Lakes.

Third, it was alleged that Cooper implied to customers of Great Lakes that the quality of the tubing manufactured by Great Lakes was inferior; that Cooper represented to the United States Air Force that no validly patented ideas, processes or inventions held by others would be utilized in fulfilling its contracts for flexible tubing, that their representations were false; and, that these acts have damaged and imminently threaten Great Lakes' business operations.

Great Lakes referred to various contracts with the United States Army and Air Force which it alleged it had failed to obtain but which Cooper did obtain, and further specified an Air Force contract on which it was then being underbid by Cooper and which it would not obtain if Cooper's acts of 'unfair competition' were not enjoined. Great Lakes asked for relief in the form of an injunction, an accounting for profits and an award of damages.

On June 23, 1959, Cooper filed an answer to the amended complaint and a counterclaim which asserted that Great Lakes, Fred T. and Robert E. Roberts, the R. E. Darling Company, which like Great Lakes is a licensee of the Roberts, and various unnamed companies and individuals 'have been and still are * * * conspiring together and attempting both individually and in concert to restrain and monopolize interstate commerce' in violation of Sections 1 and 2 of the Sherman Act, 15 U.S.C.A. §§ 1 and 2. The conspiracy was alleged to include, without limitation, the making of false representations to certain of Cooper's material suppliers that they were guilty of contributory infringement when the conspirators knew that the supplied items were staple articles of commerce and could not be the basis of such liability.

The counterclaim also alleged, and this is of prime importance in the instant case, 'the bringing of a series of unjustified lawsuits by the conspirators in bad faith and without color of right with the sole object of harassing and preventing defendant (Cooper) from competing in the manufacture and sale of flexible hose and thus eliminating defendant as a competitor, including this action (i.e., the action brought by the filing of the amended complaint by Great Lakes) * * * to prevent defendant from seeking the patronage of its principal customer, the United States, (and) an action brought in another court against the United States Secretary of Defense by Fred T. and Robert E. Roberts to prevent the Secretary from buying defendant's hose, and a patent infringement suit brought against defendant in * * * (the court below) by Fred T. and Robert E. Roberts to prevent defendant from manufacturing flexible hose and a temporary restraining order obtained therein, both the action and the restraining order * * * being in violation of 28 U.S.C.A. § 1498 which forbids infringement actions and injunctive restraints against government contractors * * *.' The counterclaim asked treble damages, costs and attorneys' fees.

On July 2, 1959, Cooper moved to dismiss Great Lakes' amended complaint on the ground that there was no diversity of citizenship between the parties. By order dated December 9, 1959, the court granted Cooper's motion to dismiss. Jurisdiction of Cooper's counterclaim was retained on the ground that it had an independent basis of jurisdiction in that it asserted a claim arising under the laws of the United States. No appeal was taken from that order and no question regarding it has been raised on this appeal.

On December 28, 1959, Great Lakes filed an answer and a counterclaim to Cooper's counterclaim. Great Lakes' counterclaim repeated in substance the allegations of its amended complaint. The counterclaim is distinguishable from the amended complaint only in that it is more specific and in that it alleges further that Cooper, with knowledge of the amounts of royalties required to be paid by Great Lakes under the Roberts patents, has underbid Great Lakes on various contracts offered by agencies of the United States by approximately the amount of the royalties required to be paid by Great Lakes to the Roberts; that Herbert and Cooper had induced 'key' employees of Great Lakes to leave it and to become employed by Cooper; and that Cooper's charges in the court below were baseless and untrue and have resulted in damaging Great Lakes unfairly.

On June 6, 1960, Cooper moved to dismiss the Great Lakes counterclaim on the ground that the court below lacked jurisdiction of the subject matter. In opposition to this motion Great Lakes contended that the court had ancillary jurisdiction of its counterclaim as a compulsory counterclaim arising out of the same transaction and occurrences that were the subject matter of Cooper's claim arising under the Federal antitrust laws. On May 5, 1960, the court granted Cooper's motion to dismiss on the ground that Great Lakes' counterclaim was not a compulsory counterclaim. This appeal followed.[FN1]

A federal court has ancillary jurisdiction of the subject matter of a counterclaim if it arises out of the transaction or occurrence that is the subject matter of an opposing party's claim of which the court has jurisdiction. Similarly, a counterclaim that arises out of the transaction or occurrence that is the subject matter of an opposing party's claim is a 'compulsory counterclaim' within the meaning of Rule 13(a) of the Federal Rules of Civil Procedure. It is stated frequently that the determination of ancillary jurisdiction of a counterclaim in a federal court must turn on whether the counterclaim is compulsory within the meaning of Rule 13(a). Such a statement of the law relating to ancillary jurisdiction of counterclaims is not intended to suggest that Rule

13(a) extends the jurisdiction of the federal courts to entertain counterclaims for the Federal Rules of Civil Procedure cannot expand the jurisdiction of the United States courts. What is meant is that the issue of the existence of ancillary jurisdiction and the issue as to whether a counterclaim is compulsory are to be answered by the same test. It is not a coincidence that the same considerations that determine whether a counterclaim is compulsory decide also whether the court has ancillary jurisdiction to adjudicate it. The tests are the same because Rule 13(a) and the doctrine of ancillary jurisdiction are designed to abolish the same evil, viz., piecemeal litigation in the federal courts.

We have indicated that a counterclaim is compulsory if it bears a 'logical relationship' to an opposing party's claim. The phrase 'logical relationship' is given meaning by the purpose of the rule which it was designed to implement. Thus, a counterclaim is logically related to the opposing party's claim where separate trials on each of their respective claims would involve a substantial duplication of effort and time by the parties and the courts. Where multiple claims involve many of the same factual issues, or the same factual and legal issues, or where they are offshoots of the same basic controversy between the parties, fairness and considerations of convenience and of economy require that the counterclaimant be permitted to maintain his cause of action. Indeed the doctrine of res judicata compels the counterclaimant to assert his claim in the same suit for it would be barred if asserted separately, subsequently.

Cooper alleges that the claims originally asserted in Great Lakes' amended complaint, reiterated in substance in its counterclaim, are 'unjustified' and were brought in 'bad faith and without color of right with the sole object of harassing and preventing defendant (Cooper) from competing in the manufacture and sale of flexible hose.' These are the only allegations set out by Cooper's counterclaim which demonstrate a relationship within the purview of Rule 13(a) to Great Lakes' amended complaint or counterclaim. But that they do demonstrate a relationship is unquestionable. It is clear that a determination that Cooper's claims that the claims asserted in Great Lakes' amended complaint and reiterated in substance in its counterclaim are harassing and entail an extensive airing of the facts and the law relating to Great Lakes' counterclaim. It follows that the court below was in error in dismissing Great Lakes' counterclaim on the ground that it was permissive. We hold that Great Lakes' counterclaim was a compulsory one within the meaning of Rule 13(a).

We point out that we express no opinion as to whether any of the pleadings in the present case, whether those of Cooper or those of Great Lakes, state claims upon which relief can be granted. Only the question of jurisdiction is raised on this appeal. There can be no doubt that the court below possesses the power, the jurisdiction, to ascertain whether or not causes of action are stated by the respective parties. The issues of whether or not the respective parties have stated causes of action and their nature will be before the court below and can be decided on remand after briefing and argument. If an appeal be taken from the ensuing decision this court will have the benefit of the views of the lower court.

The judgment will be reversed and the cause will be remanded with the direction to proceed in accordance with this opinion.

## 125 S.CT. 2363
## SUPREME COURT OF THE UNITED STATES
## GRABLE & SONS METAL PRODUCTS, INC., PETITIONER,
## V.
## DARUE ENGINEERING & MANUFACTURING.

JUNE 13, 2005

**Justice SOUTER delivered the opinion of the Court.**

The question is whether want of a federal cause of action to try claims of title to land obtained at a federal tax sale precludes removal to federal court of a state action with nondiverse parties raising a disputed issue of federal title law. We answer no, and hold that the national interest in providing a federal forum for federal tax litigation is sufficiently substantial to support the exercise of federal-question jurisdiction over the disputed issue on removal, which would not distort any division of labor between the state and federal courts, provided or assumed by Congress.

I

In 1994, the Internal Revenue Service seized Michigan real property belonging to petitioner Grable & Sons Metal Products to satisfy Grable's federal tax delinquency. Title 26 U.S.C. § 6335 required the IRS to give notice of the seizure, and there is no dispute that Grable received actual notice by certified mail before the IRS sold the property to respondent Darue Engineering. Although Grable also received notice of the sale itself, it did not exercise its statutory right to redeem the property within 180 days of the sale, and after that period had passed, the Government gave Darue a quitclaim deed to the land.

Five years later, Grable brought a quiet title action in state court, claiming that Darue's record title was invalid because the IRS had failed to notify Grable of its seizure of the property in the exact manner required by § 6335(a), which provides that written notice must be "given by the Secretary to the owner of the property [or] left at his usual place of abode or business." Grable said that the statute required personal service, not service by certified mail.

Darue removed the case to Federal District Court as presenting a federal question, because the claim of title depended on the interpretation of the notice statute in the federal tax law. The District Court declined to remand the case at Grable's behest after finding that the "claim does pose a 'significant question of federal law,' and ruling that Grable's lack of a federal right of action to enforce its claim against Darue did not bar the exercise of federal jurisdiction. On the merits, the court granted summary judgment to Darue, holding that although § 6335 by its terms required personal service, substantial compliance with the statute was enough.

The Court of Appeals for the Sixth Circuit affirmed. We granted certiorari on the jurisdictional question on whether *Merrell Dow Pharmaceuticals Inc. v. Thompson*, (1986), always requires a federal cause of action as a condition for exercising federal-question jurisdiction. We now affirm.

## II

Darue was entitled to remove the quiet title action if Grable could have brought it in federal district court originally, 28 U.S.C. § 1441(a), as a civil action "arising under the Constitution, laws, or treaties of the United States," § 1331. This provision for federal-question jurisdiction is invoked by and large by plaintiffs pleading a cause of action created by federal law. There is, however, another longstanding, if less frequently encountered, variety of federal "arising under" jurisdiction, this Court having recognized for nearly 100 years that in certain cases federal-question jurisdiction will lie over state-law claims that implicate significant federal issues. *E.g., Hopkins v. Walker* (1917). The doctrine captures the commonsense notion that a federal court ought to be able to hear claims recognized under state law that nonetheless turn on substantial questions of federal law, and thus justify resort to the experience, solicitude, and hope of uniformity that a federal forum offers on federal issues

But even when the state action discloses a contested and substantial federal question, the exercise of federal jurisdiction is subject to a possible veto. For the federal issue will ultimately qualify for a federal forum only if federal jurisdiction is consistent with congressional judgment about the sound division of labor between state and federal courts governing the application of § 1331. Thus, the appropriateness of a federal forum to hear an embedded issue [may] be evaluated only after considering the "welter of issues regarding the interrelation of federal and state authority and the proper management of the federal judicial system." Because arising-under jurisdiction to hear a state-law claim always raises the possibility of upsetting the state-federal line drawn (or at least assumed) by Congress, the presence of a disputed federal issue and the ostensible importance of a federal forum are never necessarily dispositive; there must always be an assessment of any disruptive portent in exercising federal jurisdiction.

These considerations have kept us from stating a "single, precise, all-embracing" test for jurisdiction over federal issues embedded in state-law claims between nondiverse parties. We have not kept them out simply because they appeared in state raiment, but neither have we treated "federal issue" as a password opening federal courts to any state action embracing a point of federal law. Instead, the question is, does a state-law claim necessarily raise a stated federal issue, actually disputed and substantial, which a federal forum may entertain without disturbing any congressionally approved balance of federal and state judicial responsibilities.

## III

### A

This case warrants federal jurisdiction. Grable's state complaint must specify "the facts establishing the superiority of [its] claim," and Grable has premised its superior title claim on a failure by the IRS to give it adequate notice, as defined by federal law. Whether Grable was given notice within the meaning of the federal statute is thus an essential element of its quiet title claim, and the meaning of the federal statute is actually in dispute; it appears to be the only legal or factual issue contested in the case. The meaning of the federal tax provision is an important issue of federal law that sensibly belongs in a federal court. The Government has a strong interest in the "prompt and certain collection of delinquent taxes," and the ability of the IRS to satisfy its claims from the property of delinquents requires clear terms of notice to allow buyers like Darue to satisfy themselves that the Service has touched the bases necessary for good title. The Government thus has a direct interest in the availability of a federal forum to vindicate its own administrative action, and buyers (as well as tax delinquents) may find it valuable to come before judges used to federal tax matters. Finally, because it will be the rare state title case that raises a contested matter of federal law, federal jurisdiction to resolve genuine disagreement over federal tax title provisions will portend only a microscopic effect on the federal-state division of labor.

B

*Merrell Dow*, on which Grable rests its position, is not to the contrary. *Merrell Dow* considered a state tort claim resting in part on the allegation that the defendant drug company had violated a federal misbranding prohibition, and was thus presumptively negligent under Ohio law. The Court assumed that federal law would have to be applied to resolve the claim, but after closely examining the strength of the federal interest at stake and the implications of opening the federal forum, held federal jurisdiction unavailable. Congress had not provided a private federal cause of action for violation of the federal branding requirement, and the Court found "it would ... flout, or at least undermine, congressional intent to conclude that federal courts might nevertheless exercise federal-question jurisdiction and provide remedies for violations of that federal statute solely because the violation ... is said to be a ... 'proximate cause' under state law."

Because federal law provides for no quiet title action that could be brought against Darue, Grable argues that there can be no federal jurisdiction here, stressing some broad language in *Merrell Dow* (including the passage just quoted) that on its face supports Grable's position. But an opinion is to be read as a whole, and *Merrell Dow* cannot be read whole as overturning decades of precedent, as it would have done by converting a federal cause of action from a sufficient condition for federal-question jurisdiction into a necessary one.

In the first place, *Merrell Dow* disclaimed the adoption of any bright-line rule, as when the Court reiterated that "in exploring the outer reaches of § 1331, determinations about federal jurisdiction require sensitive judgments about congressional intent, judicial power, and the federal system."

Accordingly, *Merrell Dow* should be read in its entirety as treating the absence of a federal private right of action as evidence relevant to, but not dispositive of, the "sensitive judgments about congressional intent" that § 1331 requires. The absence of any federal cause of action affected *Merrell Dow's* result two ways. The Court saw the fact as worth some consideration in the assessment of substantiality. But its primary importance emerged when the Court treated the combination of no federal cause of action and no preemption of state remedies for misbranding as an important clue to Congress's conception of the scope of jurisdiction to be exercised under § 1331. The Court saw the missing cause of action not as a missing federal door key, always required, but as a missing welcome mat, required in the circumstances, when exercising federal jurisdiction over a state misbranding action would have attracted a horde of original filings and removal cases raising other state claims with embedded federal issues. For if the federal labeling standard without a federal cause of action could get a state claim into federal court, so could any other federal standard without a federal cause of action. And that would have meant a tremendous number of cases.

One only needed to consider the treatment of federal violations generally in garden variety state tort law. "The violation of federal statutes and regulations is commonly given negligence per se effect in state tort proceedings." *Merrell Dow* thought it improbable that the Congress, having made no provision for a federal cause of action, would have meant to welcome any state-law tort case implicating federal law "solely because the violation of the federal statute is said to create a rebuttable presumption of negligence under state law." In this situation, no welcome mat meant keep out. *Merrell Dow's* analysis thus fits within the framework of examining the importance of having a federal forum for the issue, and the consistency of such a forum with Congress's intended division of labor between state and federal courts.

As already indicated, however, a comparable analysis yields a different jurisdictional conclusion in this case. Although Congress also indicated ambivalence in this case by providing no private right of action to Grable, it is the rare state quiet title action that involves contested issues of federal law. Consequently, jurisdiction over actions like Grable's would not materially affect, or threaten to affect, the normal currents of litigation. Given the absence of threatening structural consequences and the clear interest the Government, its buyers, and its delinquents have in the availability of a federal forum, there is no good reason to shirk from federal jurisdiction over the dispositive and contested federal issue at the heart of the state-law title claim.

IV

The judgment of the Court of Appeals, upholding federal jurisdiction over Grable's quiet title action, is affirmed.

7. Prior to 2005 it was generally agreed that federal question jurisdiction was available only when the federal question appeared in the plaintiff's "well-pleaded complaint." *Grable v. Darue* has now changed that. The full effect of the ruling in *Grable v. Darue* remains to be seen.

# D. FEDERAL DIVERSITY JURISDICTION 28 USC 1332

## 1. GENERAL ISSUES

125 S.CT. 2611
SUPREME COURT OF THE UNITED STATES
EXXON MOBIL CORPORATION, PETITIONER,
V.
ALLAPATTAH SERVICES, INC., ET AL.
MARIA DEL ROSARIO ORTEGA, ET AL., PETITIONERS,
V.
STAR-KIST FOODS, INC.

DECIDED JUNE 23, 2005

**Justice KENNEDY delivered the opinion of the Court.**

These consolidated cases present the question whether a federal court in a diversity action may exercise supplemental jurisdiction over additional plaintiffs whose claims do not satisfy the minimum amount-in-controversy requirement, provided the claims are part of the same case or controversy as the claims of plaintiffs who do allege a sufficient amount in controversy.

We hold that, where the other elements of jurisdiction are present and at least one named plaintiff in the action satisfies the amount-in-controversy requirement, § 1367 does authorize supplemental jurisdiction over the claims of other plaintiffs in the same Article III case or controversy, even if those claims are for less than the jurisdictional amount specified in the statute setting forth the requirements for diversity jurisdiction.

## I

[The discussion of the Exxon v. Allapattah case is omitted.]

The other case now before us, Ortega v. Star-Kist Foods was decided by the Court of Appeals for the First Circuit. In that case, a 9–year–old girl sued Star–Kist in a diversity action in the United States District Court for the District of Puerto Rico, seeking damages for unusually severe injuries she received when she sliced her finger on a tuna can. Her family joined in the suit, seeking damages for emotional distress and certain medical expenses. The District Court granted summary judgment to Star–Kist, finding that none of the plaintiffs met the minimum amount-in-controversy requirement. The Court of Appeals for the First Circuit, however, ruled that the injured girl, but not her family members, had made allegations of damages in the requisite amount.

The Court of Appeals then held that § 1367 authorizes supplemental jurisdiction only when the district court has original jurisdiction over the action, and that in a diversity case original jurisdiction is lacking if one plaintiff fails to satisfy the amount-in-controversy requirement.

## II

### A

The district courts of the United States, as we have said many times, are "courts of limited jurisdiction. They possess only that power authorized by Constitution and statute," In order to provide a neutral forum for what have come to be known as diversity cases, Congress has granted district courts original jurisdiction in civil actions between citizens of different States, between U.S. citizens and foreign citizens, or by foreign states against U.S. citizens. § 1332. To ensure that diversity jurisdiction does not flood the federal courts with minor disputes, § 1332(a) requires that the matter in controversy in a diversity case exceed a specified amount, currently $75,000.

Although the district courts may not exercise jurisdiction absent a statutory basis, it is well established—in certain classes of cases—that, once a court has original jurisdiction over some claims in the action, it may exercise supplemental jurisdiction over additional claims that are part of the same case or controversy.

We have consistently interpreted § 1332 as requiring complete diversity: In a case with multiple plaintiffs and multiple defendants, the presence in the action of a single plaintiff from the same State as a single defendant deprives the district court of original diversity jurisdiction over the entire action. *Owen Equipment & Erection Co. v.*

*Kroger.* The complete diversity requirement is not mandated by the Constitution, *State Farm Fire & Casualty Co. v. Tashire,* or by the plain text of § 1332(a). The Court, nonetheless, has adhered to the complete diversity rule in light of the purpose of the diversity requirement, which is to provide a federal forum for important disputes where state courts might favor, or be perceived as favoring, home-state litigants. The presence of parties from the same State on both sides of a case dispels this concern, eliminating a principal reason for conferring § 1332 jurisdiction over any of the claims in the action. Incomplete diversity destroys original jurisdiction with respect to all claims.

B

Whatever we say regarding the scope of jurisdiction conferred by a particular statute can of course be changed by Congress." In 1990, Congress passed the Judicial Improvements Act, 104 Stat. 5089, which enacted § 1367, the provision which controls these cases.

Section 1367 provides, in relevant part:

"(a) Except as provided in subsections (b) and (c) or as expressly provided otherwise by Federal statute, in any civil action of which the district courts have original jurisdiction, the district courts shall have supplemental jurisdiction over all other claims that are so related to claims in the action within such original jurisdiction that they form part of the same case or controversy under Article III of the United States Constitution. Such supplemental jurisdiction shall include claims that involve the joinder or intervention of additional parties.

"(b) In any civil action of which the district courts have original jurisdiction founded solely on section 1332 of this title, the district courts shall not have supplemental jurisdiction under subsection (a) over claims by plaintiffs against persons made parties under Rule 14, 19, 20, or 24 of the Federal Rules of Civil Procedure, or over claims by persons proposed to be joined as plaintiffs under Rule 19 of such rules, or seeking to intervene as plaintiffs under Rule 24 of such rules, when exercising supplemental jurisdiction over such claims would be inconsistent with the jurisdictional requirements of section 1332."

Section 1367(a) is a broad grant of supplemental jurisdiction over other claims within the same case or controversy, as long as the action is one in which the district courts would have original jurisdiction. The last sentence of § 1367(a) makes it clear that the grant of supplemental jurisdiction extends to claims involving joinder or intervention of additional parties. The single question before us, therefore, is whether a diversity case in which the claims of some plaintiffs satisfy the amount-in-controversy requirement, but the claims of other plaintiffs do not, presents a "civil action of which the district courts have original jurisdiction."

We now conclude the answer must be yes. When the well-pleaded complaint contains at least one claim that satisfies the amount-in-controversy requirement, and there are no other relevant jurisdictional defects, the district court, beyond all question, has original jurisdiction over that claim. The presence of other claims in the complaint, over which the district court may lack original jurisdiction, is of no moment. If the court has original jurisdiction over a single claim in the complaint, it has original jurisdiction over a "civil action" within the meaning of § 1367(a), even if the civil action over which it has jurisdiction comprises fewer claims than were included in the complaint.

It follows from this conclusion that the threshold requirement of § 1367(a) is satisfied in cases, like those now before us, where some, but not all, of the plaintiffs in a diversity action allege a sufficient amount in controversy.

The judgment of the Court of Appeals for the First Circuit is reversed, and the case is remanded for proceedings consistent with this opinion.

## 2. CHOICE OF LAW ISSUES – ERIE

### (a) ERIE V. TOMPKINS

8. When a plaintiff has a cause of action created by state law, the plaintiff will often have a choice as to whether to file the lawsuit in state court or in federal court. If the plaintiff and defendant are from different states, and the amount in controversy meets the statutory requirements, (currently $75,000), then the plaintiff may be able to bring the suit in either state or federal court – based on diversity jurisdiction in the federal court. The issue then becomes what law should be applied to the suit – state or federal?

Each state has its own independent set of laws and rules of procedure. As you have seen, the statute of limitations, for example, may not be exactly the same in every state. Similarly, there are frequently differences between state and federal substantive laws.

Because of this variation in law, there is unlikely to be uniformity within all courts – state and federal – within the United States. The issue then becomes: shall we strive for unity within a single state; or shall we strive for unity among all the different federal courts in the nation?

And what about the problem that the state may not have a specific statute or case that is exactly on point? Should the federal court then be entitled to create the necessary common law?

The next case, *Erie v. Tompkins,* sets forth the basic answer to this issue. *Erie v. Tompkins* remains the fundamental case for determining whether state law or federal law should be used in federal courts that are exercising jurisdiction based on diversity of citizenship between the parties.

## 58 S.CT. 817
## SUPREME COURT OF THE UNITED STATES.
## ERIE RAILROAD CO
## V.
## TOMPKINS

DECIDED APRIL 25, 1938

**On Certiorari to the United States Circuit Court of Appeals for the Second Circuit.**

Justice BRANDEIS delivered the opinion of the Court.

Tompkins, a citizen of Pennsylvania, was injured on a dark night by a passing freight train of the Erie Railroad Company while walking along its right of way at Hughestown, Pennsylvania. He claimed that the accident occurred through negligence in the operation, or maintenance, of the train; that he was rightfully on the premises as licensee because on a commonly used beaten footpath which ran for a short distance alongside the tracks; and that he was struck by something which looked like a door projecting from one of the moving cars. To enforce that claim he brought an action in the federal court for Southern New York, which had jurisdiction because the company is a corporation of that state. It denied liability; and the case was tried by a jury.

The Erie insisted that its duty to Tompkins, and hence its liability, should be determined in accordance with the Pennsylvania law; that under the law of Pennsylvania, as declared by its highest court, persons who use pathways along the railroad right of way are to be deemed trespassers; and that the railroad is not liable for injuries to undiscovered trespassers resulting from its negligence, unless it be wanton or willful. Tompkins denied that any such rule had been established by the decisions of the Pennsylvania courts; and contended that, since there was no statute of the state on the subject, the railroad's duty and liability is to be determined in federal courts as a matter of general law.

The jury brought in a verdict of $30,000; and the judgment entered thereon was affirmed by the Circuit Court of Appeals. Because of the importance of the question whether the federal court was free to disregard the alleged rule of the Pennsylvania common law, we granted certiorari.

First. *Swift v. Tyson* held that federal courts exercising jurisdiction on the ground of diversity of citizenship need not, in matters of general jurisprudence, apply the unwritten law of the state as declared by its highest court; that they are free to exercise an independent judgment as to what the common law of the state is—or should be.

Second. Experience in applying the doctrine of *Swift v. Tyson*, had revealed its defects, political and social; and the benefits expected to flow from the rule did not accrue. Persistence of state courts in their own opinions on questions of common law prevented uniformity

The mischievous results of the doctrine had become apparent. Diversity of citizenship jurisdiction was conferred in order to prevent apprehended discrimination in state courts against those not citizens of the state. *Swift v. Tyson* introduced grave discrimination by noncitizens against citizens. It made rights enjoyed under the unwritten "general law" vary according to whether enforcement was sought in the state or in the federal court; and the privilege of selecting the court in which the right should be determined was conferred upon the noncitizen. Thus, the doctrine rendered impossible equal protection of the law. In attempting to promote uniformity of law throughout the United States, the doctrine had prevented uniformity in the administration of the law of the state.

The injustice and confusion incident to the doctrine of *Swift v. Tyson* have been repeatedly urged as reasons for abolishing or limiting diversity of citizenship jurisdiction. If only a question of statutory construction were involved, we should not be prepared to abandon a doctrine so widely applied throughout nearly a century. But the unconstitutionality of the course pursued has now been made clear, and compels us to do so.

Third. Except in matters governed by the Federal Constitution or by acts of Congress, the law to be applied in any case is the law of the state. And whether the law of the state shall be declared by its Legislature in a statute or by its highest court in a decision is not a matter of federal concern. There is no federal general common law. Congress has no power to declare substantive rules of common law applicable in a state whether they be local in their nature or "general," be they commercial law or a part of the law of torts. And no clause in the Constitution purports to confer such a power upon the federal courts.

Notwithstanding the great names which may be cited in favor of the doctrine, and notwithstanding the frequency with which the doctrine has been reiterated, there stands, as a perpetual protest against its repetition, the constitution of the United States, which recognizes and preserves the autonomy and independence of the states,—independence in their legislative and independence in their judicial departments. Supervision over either the legislative or the judicial action of the states is in no case permissible except as to matters by the constitution specifically authorized or delegated to the United States. Any interference with either, except as thus permitted, is an invasion of the authority of the state, and, to that extent, a denial of its independence.

The fallacy underlying the rule declared in *Swift v. Tyson* is made clear by Mr. Justice Holmes. The doctrine rests upon the assumption that there is "a transcendental body of law outside of any particular State but obligatory within it unless and until changed by statute," that federal courts have the power to use their judgment as to what the rules of common law are; and that in the federal courts "the parties are entitled to an independent judgment on matters of general law."

But law in the sense in which courts speak of it today does not exist without some definite authority behind it. The common law so far as it is enforced in a State, whether called common law or not, is not the common law generally but the law of that State existing by the authority of that State without regard to what it may have been in England or anywhere else.

The authority and only authority is the State, and if that be so, the voice adopted by the State as its own (whether it be of its Legislature or of its Supreme Court) should utter the last word.

Thus the doctrine of *Swift v. Tyson* is, as Mr. Justice Holmes said, "an unconstitutional assumption of powers by the Courts of the United States which no lapse of time or respectable array of opinion should make us hesitate to correct."

Fourth. The defendant contended that by the common law of Pennsylvania as declared by its highest court in *Falchetti v. Pennsylvania R. Co.*, the only duty owed to the plaintiff was to refrain from willful or wanton injury. The plaintiff denied that such is the Pennsylvania law. In support of their respective contentions the parties discussed and cited many decisions of the Supreme Court of the state. The Circuit

Court of Appeals ruled that the question of liability is one of general law; and on that ground declined to decide the issue of state law. As we hold this was error, the judgment is reversed and the case remanded to it for further proceedings in conformity with our opinion.

Reversed.

9. Basically, it has now been held that each tribunal, state or federal, is allowed to apply its own rules of procedure, but that federal courts sitting in diversity must apply state substantive law. This sounds clear enough. However, is service of process a matter of substance or of procedure?

## (b) SERVICE OF PROCESS

### 85 S.CT. 1136
### SUPREME COURT OF THE UNITED STATES
### EDDIE V. HANNA, PETITIONER,
### V.
### EDWARD M. PLUMER, JR., EXECUTOR

DECIDED APRIL 26, 1965

**Mr. Chief Justice WARREN delivered the opinion of the Court.**

The question to be decided is whether, in a civil action where the jurisdiction of the United States district court is based upon diversity of citizenship between the parties, service of process shall be made in the manner prescribed by state law or that set forth in Rule 4(d)(1) of the Federal Rules of Civil Procedure.

On February 6, 1963, petitioner, a citizen of Ohio, filed her complaint in the District Court for the District of Massachusetts, claiming damages in excess of $10,000 for personal injuries resulting from an automobile accident in South Carolina, allegedly caused by the negligence of one Louise Plumer Osgood, a Massachusetts citizen deceased at the time of the filing of the complaint. Respondent, Mrs. Osgood's executor and also a Massachusetts citizen, was named as defendant. On February 8, service was made by leaving copies of the summons and the complaint with respondent's wife at his residence, concededly in compliance with Rule 4(d)(1), which provides:

> The summons and complaint shall be served together. The plaintiff shall furnish the person making service with such copies as are necessary. Service shall be made as follows:
>
> (1) Upon an individual other than an infant or an incompetent person, by delivering a copy of the summons and of the complaint to him personally or by leaving copies thereof at his dwelling house or usual place of abode with some person of suitable age and discretion then residing therein.'

Respondent filed his answer on February 26, alleging, inter alia, that the action could not be maintained because it had been brought 'contrary to and in violation of the provisions of Massachusetts General Laws Chapter 197, Section 9.' That section provides:

> Except as provided in this chapter, an executor or administrator shall not be held to answer to an action by a creditor of the deceased unless before the expiration [of the one year allowed] the writ in such action has been served by delivery in hand upon such executor or administrator or service thereof accepted by him or a notice stating the name of the estate, the name and address of the creditor, the amount of the claim and the court in which the action has been brought has been filed in the proper registry of probate.

On October 17, 1963, the District Court granted respondent's motion for summary judgment, in support of its conclusion that the adequacy of the service was to be measured by sec. 9, with which, the court held, petitioner had not complied. On appeal, petitioner admitted noncompliance with sec. 9, but argued that Rule 4(d)(1) defines the method by which service of process is to be effected in diversity actions. The Court of Appeals for the First Circuit, unanimously affirmed. Because of the threat to the goal of uniformity of federal procedure posed by the decision below, we granted certiorari.

We conclude that the adoption of Rule 4(d)(1), designed to control service of process in diversity actions, neither exceeded the congressional mandate embodied in the Rules Enabling Act nor transgressed constitutional bounds, and that the Rule is therefore the standard against which the District Court should have measured the adequacy of the service. Accordingly, we reverse the decision of the Court of Appeals.

The Rules Enabling Act, 28 U.S.C. 2072, provides, in pertinent part:

> The Supreme Court shall have the power to prescribe, by general rules, the forms of process, writs, pleadings, and motions, and the practice and procedure of the district courts of the United States in civil actions.

> Such rules shall not abridge, enlarge or modify any substantive right and shall preserve the right of trial by jury.

Under the cases construing the scope of the Enabling Act, Rule 4(d)(1) clearly passes muster. Prescribing the manner in which a defendant is to be notified that a suit has been instituted against him, it relates to the "practice and procedure of the district courts."

The test must be whether a rule really regulates procedure,—the judicial process for enforcing rights and duties recognized by substantive law and for justly administering remedy and redress for disregard or infraction of them.

In *Mississippi Pub. Corp. v. Murphree,* this Court upheld Rule 4(f), which permits service of a summons anywhere within the State (and not merely the district) in which a district court sits:

> We think that Rule 4(f) is in harmony with the Enabling Act. Undoubtedly most alterations of the rules of practice and procedure may and often do affect the rights of litigants. Congress' prohibition of any alteration of substantive rights of litigants was obviously not addressed to such incidental effects as necessarily attend the adoption of the prescribed new rules of procedure upon the rights of litigants who, agreeably to rules of practice and procedure, have been brought before a court authorized to determine their rights

Thus were there no conflicting state procedure, Rule 4(d)(1) would clearly control. However, respondent, focusing on the contrary Massachusetts rule, calls to the Court's attention another line of cases, a line which—like the Federal Rules—had its birth in 1938. *Erie R. Co. v. Tompkins* held that federal courts sitting in diversity cases, when deciding questions of "substantive" law, are bound by state court decisions as well as state statutes. The broad command of *Erie* was therefore identical to that of the Enabling Act: federal courts are to apply state substantive law and federal procedural law. However, as subsequent cases sharpened the distinction between substance and procedure, the line of cases following *Erie* diverged markedly from the line construing the Enabling Act. *Guaranty Trust* made it clear that *Erie*-type problems were not to be solved by reference to any traditional or common-sense substance-procedure distinction:

And so the question is not whether a statute of limitations is deemed a matter of 'procedure' in some sense. The question is does it significantly affect the result of a litigation for a federal court to disregard a law of a State that would be controlling in an action upon the same claim by the same parties in a State court?

Respondent, by placing primary reliance on *York* and *Ragan*, suggests that the *Erie* doctrine acts as a check on the Federal Rules of Civil Procedure, that despite the clear command of Rule 4(d)(1), *Erie* and its progeny demand the application of the Massachusetts rule. Reduced to essentials, the argument is: (1) *Erie*, as refined in *York,* demands that federal courts apply state law whenever application of federal law in its stead will alter the outcome of the case. (2) In this case, a determination that the Massachusetts service requirements obtain will result in immediate victory for respondent. If, on the other hand, it should be held that Rule 4(d)(1) is applicable, the litigation will continue, with possible victory for petitioner. (3) Therefore, *Erie* demands application of the Massachusetts rule. The syllogism possesses an appealing simplicity, but is for several reasons invalid.

In the first place, it is doubtful that, even if there were no Federal Rule making it clear that in-hand service is not required in diversity actions, the Erie rule would have obligated the District Court to follow the Massachusetts procedure. Outcome-determination' analysis was never intended to serve as a talisman. *Byrd v. Blue Ridge Rural Elec.* Indeed, the message of *York* itself is that choices between state and federal law are to be made not by application of any automatic, 'litmus paper' criterion, but rather by reference to the policies underlying the *Erie* rule. *Guaranty Trust.*

The *Erie* rule is rooted in part in a realization that it would be unfair for the character of result of a litigation materially to differ because the suit had been brought in a federal court. Diversity of citizenship jurisdiction was conferred in order to prevent apprehended discrimination in state courts against those not citizens of the state.

The decision was also in part a reaction to the practice of "forum-shopping." That the *York* test was an attempt to effectuate these policies is demonstrated by the fact that the opinion framed the inquiry in terms of "substantial" variations between state and federal litigation. Not only are nonsubstantial, or trivial, variations not likely to raise the sort of equal protection problems which troubled the Court in *Erie*; they are also unlikely to influence the choice of a forum.

The difference between the conclusion that the Massachusetts rule is applicable, and the conclusion that it is not, is of course at this point "outcome-determinative" in the sense that if we hold the state rule to apply, respondent prevails, whereas if we hold that Rule 4(d)(1) governs, the litigation will continue. But in this sense every procedural variation is "outcome-determinative." For example, having brought suit in a federal court, a plaintiff cannot then insist on the right to file subsequent pleadings in accord with the time limits applicable in state courts, even though enforcement of the federal timetable will, if he continues to insist that he must meet only the state time limit, result in determination of the controversy against him. So it is here. Though choice of the federal or state rule will at this point have a marked effect upon the outcome of the litigation, the difference between the two rules would be of scant, if any, relevance to the choice of a forum. Petitioner, in choosing her forum, was not presented with a situation where application of the state rule would wholly bar recovery. Rather, adherence to the state rule would have resulted only in altering the way in which process was served. Moreover, it is difficult to argue that permitting service of defendant's wife to take the place of in-hand service of defendant himself alters the mode of enforcement of state-created rights in a fashion sufficiently "substantial" to raise the sort of equal protection problems to which the Erie opinion alluded.

There is, however, a more fundamental flaw in respondent's syllogism: the incorrect assumption that the rule of *Erie* constitutes the appropriate test of the validity and therefore the applicability of a Federal Rule of Civil Procedure. The *Erie* rule has never been invoked to void a Federal Rule. It is true that there have been cases where this Court has held applicable a state rule in the face of an argument that the situation was governed by one of the Federal Rules. But the holding of each such case was not that *Erie* commanded displacement of a Federal Rule by an inconsistent state rule, but rather that the scope of the Federal Rule was not as broad as the losing party urged, and therefore, there being no Federal Rule which covered the point in dispute, *Erie* commanded the enforcement of state law.

Here, of course, the clash is unavoidable; Rule 4(d)(1) says—implicitly, but with unmistakable clarity—that in-hand service is not required in federal courts. The line between "substance" and "procedure" shifts as the legal context changes. "Each implies different variables depending upon the particular problem for which it is used." *Guaranty Trust.* It is true that both the Enabling Act and the *Erie* rule say, roughly, that federal courts are to apply state "substantive" law and federal "procedural" law, but from that it need not follow that the tests are identical. For they were designed to control very different sorts of decisions. When a situation is covered by one of the Federal Rules, the question facing the court is a far cry from the typical, relatively unguided *Erie* Choice: the court has been instructed to apply the Federal Rule, and can refuse to do so only if the Advisory Committee, this Court, and Congress erred in their prima facie judgment that the Rule in question transgresses neither the terms of the Enabling Act nor constitutional restrictions.

We are reminded by the *Erie* opinion that neither Congress nor the federal courts can, under the guise of formulating rules of decision for federal courts, fashion rules which are not supported by a grant of federal authority contained in Article I or some other section of the Constitution; in such areas state law must govern because there can be no other law. But the opinion in Erie, which involved no Federal Rule and dealt with a question which was "substantive" in every traditional sense (whether the railroad owed a duty of care to Tompkins as a trespasser or a licensee), surely neither said nor implied that measures like Rule 4(d)(1) are unconstitutional. For the constitutional provision for a federal court system (augmented by the Necessary and Proper Clause) carries with it congressional power to make rules governing the practice and pleading in those courts, which in turn includes a power to regulate matters which, though falling within the uncertain area between substance and procedure, are rationally capable of classification as either. Neither York nor the cases following it ever suggested that the rule there laid down for coping with situations where no Federal Rule applies is coextensive with the limitation on Congress to which *Erie* had adverted.

One of the shaping purposes of the Federal Rules is to bring about uniformity in the federal courts by getting away from local rules. This is especially true of matters which relate to the administration of legal proceedings, an area in which federal courts have traditionally exerted strong inherent power, completely aside from the powers Congress expressly conferred in the Rules. The purpose of the *Erie* doctrine, even as extended in *York* and *Ragan*, was never to bottle up federal courts with "outcome-determinative" and "integral-relations" stoppers—when there are affirmative countervailing (federal) considerations and when there is a Congressional mandate (the Rules) supported by constitutional authority.

*Erie* and its offspring cast no doubt on the long-recognized power of Congress to prescribe housekeeping rules for federal courts even though some of those rules will inevitably differ from comparable state rules. When, because the plaintiff happens to be a non-resident, such a right is enforceable in a federal as well as in a State court, the forms and mode of enforcing the right may at times, naturally enough, vary because the two judicial systems are not identic. Thus, though a court, in measuring a Federal Rule against the standards contained in the Enabling Act and the Constitution, need not wholly blind itself to the degree to which the Rule makes the character and result of the federal litigation stray from the course it would follow in state courts, it cannot be forgotten that the *Erie* rule, and the guidelines suggested in *York*, were created to serve another purpose altogether. To hold that a Federal Rule of Civil Procedure must cease to function whenever it alters the mode of enforcing state-created rights would be to disembowel either the Constitution's grant of power over federal procedure or Congress' attempt to exercise that power in the Enabling Act. Rule 4(d)(1) is valid and controls the instant case.

Reversed.

## (c) ISSUES TO BE DECIDED BY A JURY

10. Is use of a jury a matter of substance or procedure?

## 72 S.CT. 312
## SUPREME COURT OF THE UNITED STATES
## DICE
## V.
## AKRON, CANTON & YOUNGSTOWN R. CO.

DECIDED FEBRUARY 4, 1952

**Opinion of the Court by Mr. Justice BLACK, announced by Mr. Justice DOUGLAS.**

Petitioner, a railroad fireman, was seriously injured when an engine in which he was riding jumped the track. Alleging that his injuries were due to respondent's negligence, he brought this action for damages under the Federal Employers' Liability Act, in an Ohio court of common pleas. Respondent's defenses were (1) a denial of negligence and (2) a written document signed by petitioner purporting to release respondent in full for $924.63. Petitioner admitted that he had signed several receipts for payments made him in connection with his injuries but denied that he had made a full and complete settlement of all his claims. He alleged that the purported release was void because he had signed it relying on respondent's deliberately false statement that the document was nothing more than a mere receipt for back wages.

After both parties had introduced considerable evidence the jury found in favor of petitioner and awarded him a $25,000 verdict. The trial judge later entered judgment notwithstanding the verdict. In doing so he reappraised the evidence as to fraud, found that petitioner had been "guilty of supine negligence" in failing to read the release, and accordingly held that the facts did not "sustain either in law or equity the allegations of fraud by clear, unequivocal and convincing evidence." This judgment notwithstanding the verdict was reversed by the Court of Appeals of Summit County, Ohio, on the ground that under federal law, which controlled, the jury's verdict must stand because there was ample evidence to support its finding of fraud. The Ohio Supreme Court, one judge dissenting, reversed the Court of Appeals' judgment and sustained the trial court's action, holding that: (1) Ohio, not federal, law governed; (2) under that law petitioner, a man of ordinary intelligence who could read, was bound by the release even though he had been induced to sign it by the deliberately false statement that it was only a receipt for back wages; and (3) under controlling Ohio law factual issues as to fraud in the execution of this release were properly decided by the judge rather than by the jury. We granted certiorari because the decision of the Supreme Court of Ohio appeared to deviate from previous decisions of this Court that federal law governs cases arising under the Federal Employers' Liability Act.

First. We agree with the Court of Appeals of Summit County, Ohio, and the dissenting judge in the Ohio Supreme Court and hold that validity of releases under the Federal Employers' Liability Act raises a federal question to be determined by federal rather than state law. Congress in Sec.1 of the Act granted petitioner a right to recover against his employer for damages negligently inflicted. State laws are not controlling in determining what the incidents of this federal right shall be. Manifestly the federal rights affording relief to injured railroad employees under a federally declared standard could be defeated if states were permitted to have the final say as to what defenses could and could not be properly interposed to suits under the Act. Moreover, only if federal law controls can the federal Act be given that uniform application throughout the country essential to effectuate its purposes. Releases and other devices designed to liquidate or defeat injured employees' claims play an important part in the federal Act's administration. Their validity is but one of the many interrelated questions that must constantly be determined in these cases according to a uniform federal law.

Second. In effect the Supreme Court of Ohio held that an employee trusts his employer at his peril, and that the negligence of an innocent worker is sufficient to enable his employer to benefit by its deliberate fraud. Application of so harsh a rule to defeat a railroad employee's claim is wholly incongruous with the general policy of the Act to give railroad employees a right to recover just compensation for injuries negligently inflicted by their employers. And this Ohio rule is out of harmony with modern judicial and legislative practice to relieve injured persons from the effect of releases fraudulently obtained. We hold that the correct federal rule is that announced by the Court of Appeals of Summit County, Ohio, and the dissenting judge in the Ohio Supreme Court—a release of rights under the Act is void when the employee is induced to sign it by the deliberately false and material statements of the railroad's authorized representatives made to deceive the employee as to the contents of the release. The trial court's charge to the jury correctly stated this rule of law.

Third. Ohio provides and has here accorded petitioner the usual jury trial of factual issues relating to negligence. But Ohio treats factual questions of fraudulent releases differently. It permits the judge trying a negligence case to resolve all factual questions of fraud "other than fraud in the factum." The factual issue of fraud is thus split into fragments, some to be determined by the judge, others by the jury.

It is contended that since a state may consistently with the Federal Constitutional provide for trial of cases under the Act by a nonunanimous verdict, Ohio may lawfully eliminate trial by jury as to one phase of fraud while allowing jury trial as to all other issues raised. The argument might be more in point had Ohio abolished trial by jury in all negligence cases including those arising under the federal Act. But Ohio has not done this. It has provided jury trials for cases arising under the federal Act but seeks to single out one phase of the question of fraudulent releases for determination by a judge rather than by a jury.

We have previously held that "The right to trial by jury is a basic and fundamental feature of our system of federal jurisprudence and that it is part and parcel of the remedy afforded railroad workers under the Employers' Liability Act." We also recognized in that case that to deprive railroad workers of the benefit of a jury trial where there is evidence to support negligence is to take away a goodly portion of the relief which Congress has afforded them. It follows that the right to trial by jury is too substantial a part of the rights accorded by the Act to permit it to be classified as a mere "local rule of procedure" for denial in the manner that Ohio has here used.

The trial judge and the Ohio Supreme Court erred in holding that petitioner's rights were to be determined by Ohio law and in taking away petitioner's verdict when the issues of fraud had been submitted to the jury on conflicting evidence and determined in petitioner's favor. The judgment of the Court of Appeals of Summit County, Ohio, was correct and should not have been reversed by the Supreme Court of Ohio. The cause is reversed and remanded to the Supreme Court of Ohio for further action not inconsistent with this opinion.

It is so ordered.

Reversed and remanded with directions.

11. Does that mean that the right to a jury trial is a matter of substantive law, not procedural law?

## 78 S.CT. 893
## SUPREME COURT OF THE UNITED STATES
## JAMES EARL BYRD, PETITIONER,
## V.
## BLUE RIDGE RURAL ELECTRIC COOPERATIVE, INC.

DECIDED MAY 19, 1958

Justice BRENNAN delivered the opinion of the Court.

This case was brought in the District Court for the Western District of South Carolina. Jurisdiction was based on diversity of citizenship. 28 U.S.C.A. s 1332. The petitioner, a resident of North Carolina, sued respondent, a South Carolina corporation, for damages for injuries allegedly caused by the respondent's negligence. He had judgment on a jury verdict. The Court of Appeals for the Fourth Circuit reversed and directed the entry of judgment for the respondent. We granted certiorari.

The respondent is in the business of selling electric power to subscribers in rural sections of South Carolina. The petitioner was employed as a lineman in the construction crew of a construction contractor. The contractor, R. H. Bouligny, Inc., held a contract with the respondent in the amount of $334,300 for the building of some 24 miles of new power lines, the reconversion to higher capacities of about 88 miles of existing lines, and the construction of 2 new substations and a breaker station. The petitioner was injured while connecting power lines to one of the new substations.

One of respondent's affirmative defenses was that under the South Carolina Workmen's Compensation Act, the petitioner—because the work contracted to be done by his employer was work of the kind also done by the respondent's own construction and maintenance crews—had the status of a statutory employee of the respondent and was therefore barred from suing the respondent at law because obliged to accept statutory compensation benefits as the exclusive remedy for his injuries. Two questions concerning this defense are before us: (1) whether the Court of Appeals erred in directing judgment for respondent without a remand to give petitioner an opportunity to introduce further evidence; and (2) whether petitioner, state practice notwithstanding, is entitled to a jury determination of the factual issues raised by this defense.

I.

The Supreme Court of South Carolina has held that there is no particular formula by which to determine whether an owner is a statutory employer under Sec. 72–111. In *Smith v. Fulmer*, the State Supreme Court said:

> The opinion in *Marchbanks v. Duke Power Co.* (said to be the 'leading case' under the statute) reminds us that while the language of the statute is plain and unambiguous, there are so many different factual situations which may arise that no easily applied formula can be laid down for the determination of all cases. In other words, 'it is often a matter of extreme difficulty to decide whether the work in a given case falls within the designation of the statute. It is in each case largely a question of degree and of fact.

The credibility of the manager's testimony, and the general question whether the evidence in support of the affirmative defense presented a jury issue, became irrelevant because of the interpretation given Sec. 72–111 by the trial judge in striking respondent's affirmative defense at the close of all the evidence.

The Court of Appeals disagreed with the District Court's construction of Sec. 72–111. Relying on the decisions of the Supreme Court of South Carolina, among others, in *Marchbanks v. Duke Power* the Court of Appeals held that the statute granted respondent immunity from the action if the proofs established that the respondent's own crews had constructed lines and substations which, like the work contracted to the petitioner's employer, were necessary for the distribution of the electric power which the respondent was in the business of selling. We ordinarily accept the interpretation of local law by the Court of Appeals, cf. *Ragan v. Merchants Transfer & Warehouse Co.* and do so readily here since neither party now disputes the interpretation.

However, instead of ordering a new trial at which the petitioner might offer his own proof pertinent to a determination according to the correct interpretation, the Court of Appeals made its own determination on the record and directed a judgment for the respondent. The court resolved the uncertainties in the manager's testimony in a manner largely favorable to the respondent.

The court found that the respondent financed the work contracted to the petitioner's employer with a loan from the United States, purchased the materials used in the work, and entered into an engineering service contract with an independent engineering company for the design and supervision of the work, concluding from these findings that "the main actor in the whole enterprise was the Cooperative itself."

Finally, the court held that its findings entitled the respondent to the direction of a judgment in its favor.

While the matter is not adverted to in the court's opinion, implicit in the direction of verdict is the holding that the petitioner, although having no occasion to do so under the District Court's erroneous construction of the statute, was not entitled to an opportunity to meet the respondent's case under the correct interpretation, and thus deprives him of his constitutional right to a jury trial on a factual issue.

We believe that the Court of Appeals erred. The petitioner is entitled to have the question determined in the trial court. The jury might reasonably reach an opposite conclusion from the Court of Appeals as to the ultimate fact whether the respondent was a statutory employer.

## II

The respondent argues on the basis of the decision of the Supreme Court of South Carolina in *Adams v. Davison-Paxon Co.*, that the issue of immunity should be decided by the judge and not by the jury. This is to contend that the federal court is bound under *Erie R. Co. v. Tompkins* to follow the state court's holding to secure uniform enforcement of the immunity created by the State.

First. It was decided in *Erie R. Co. v. Tompkins* that the federal courts in diversity cases must respect the definition of state-created rights and obligations by the state courts. We must, therefore, first examine the rule in *Adams v. Davison-Paxon Co.* to determine whether it is bound up with these rights and obligations in such a way that its application in the federal court is required.

The Workmen's Compensation Act is administered in South Carolina by its Industrial Commission. The South Carolina courts hold that, on judicial review of actions of the Commission under Sec. 72–111, the question whether the claim of an injured workman is within the Commission's jurisdiction is a matter of law for decision by the court, which makes its own findings of fact relating to that jurisdiction. The South Carolina Supreme Court states no reasons in *Adams v. Davison-Paxon* why, although the jury decides all other factual issues raised by the cause of action and defenses, the jury is displaced as to the factual issue raised by the affirmative defense under Sec. 72–111. The decisions cited to support the holding are those listed in footnote 8, which are concerned solely with defining the scope and method of judicial review of the Industrial Commission. A State may, of course, distribute the functions of its judicial machinery as it sees fit. The decisions relied upon, however, furnish no reason for selecting the judge rather than the jury to decide this single affirmative defense in the negligence action. They simply reflect a policy, that administrative determination of "jurisdictional facts" should not be final but subject to judicial review. The conclusion is inescapable that the Adams holding is grounded in the practical consideration that the question had theretofore come before the South Carolina courts from the Industrial Commission and the courts had become accustomed to deciding the factual issue of immunity without the aid of juries. We find nothing to suggest that this rule was announced as an integral part of the special relationship created by the statute. Thus the requirement appears to be merely a form and mode of enforcing the immunity, *Guaranty Trust Co. of New York v. York*, and not a rule intended to be bound up with the definition of the rights and obligations of the parties. The situation is therefore not analogous to that in *Dice v. Akron*, where this Court held that the right to trial by jury is so substantial a part of the cause of action created by the Federal Employers' Liability Act, that the Ohio courts could not apply, in an action under that statute, the Ohio rule that the question of fraudulent release was for determination by a judge rather than by a jury.

Second. Cases following *Erie* have evinced a broader policy to the effect that the federal courts should conform as near as may be—in the absence of other considerations—to state rules even of form and mode where the state rules may bear substantially on the question whether the litigation would come out one way in the federal court and another way in the state court if the federal court failed to apply a particular local rule. E.g., *Guaranty Trust*. Concededly the nature of the tribunal which tries issues may be important in the enforcement of the parcel of rights making up a cause of action or defense, and bear significantly upon achievement of uniform enforcement of the right. It may well be that in the instant personal-injury case the outcome would be substantially affected by whether the issue of immunity is decided by a judge or a jury. Therefore, were 'outcome' the only consideration, a strong case might appear for saying that the federal court should follow the state practice.

But there are affirmative countervailing considerations at work here. The federal system is an independent system for administering justice to litigants who properly invoke its jurisdiction. An essential characteristic of that system is the manner in which, in civil common-law actions, it distributes trial functions between judge and jury and, under the influence—if not the command—of the Seventh Amendment, assigns the decisions of disputed questions of fact to the jury. The policy of uniform enforcement of state-created rights and obligations cannot in every case exact compliance with a state rule—not bound up with rights and obligations—which disrupts the federal system of allocating functions between judge and jury. Thus the inquiry here is whether the federal policy favoring jury decisions of disputed fact questions should yield to the state rule in the interest of furthering the objective that the litigation should not come out one way in the federal court and another way in the state court.

We think that in the circumstances of this case the federal court should not follow the state rule. It cannot be gainsaid that there is a strong federal policy against allowing state rules to disrupt the judge-jury relationship in the federal courts.

Third. We have discussed the problem upon the assumption that the outcome of the litigation may be substantially affected by whether the issue of immunity is decided by a judge or a jury. But clearly there is not present here the certainty that a different result would follow, or even the strong possibility that this would be the case. There are factors present here which might reduce that possibility. The trial judge in the federal system has powers denied the judges of many States to comment on the weight of evidence and credibility of witnesses, and discretion to grant a new trial if the verdict appears to him to be against the weight of the evidence. We do not think the likelihood of a different result is so strong as to require the federal practice of jury determination of disputed factual issues to yield to the state rule in the interest of uniformity of outcome.

Reversed and remanded.

12. So, is the question of whether a particular issue is to be determined by a judge or by a jury a matter of substance or of procedure? Does the answer appear to vary, depending on the circumstances of the particular case? Are there situations in which a plaintiff might have to choose between the potential benefits of a jury trial, compared to the potential benefits of being in a federal court instead of a state court? Is that consistent with the aims of *Erie v. Tompkins?* Are there any situations in which a lawyer could be certain that a particular law would be considered to be a matter of procedure?

Note that in the following case, only a relatively small portion of the opinion actually had enough votes to be considered to be the judgment of the court.

## (d) CLASS ACTION RULES

130 S. CT. 1431

SUPREME COURT OF THE UNITED STATES

SHADY GROVE ORTHOPEDIC ASSOCIATES, P. A., PETITIONER

V.

ALLSTATE INSURANCE COMPANY

DECIDED MARCH 31, 2010

JUSTICE SCALIA announced the judgment of the Court and delivered the opinion of the Court with respect to Parts I and II-A, an opinion with respect to Parts II-B and II-D, in which THE CHIEF JUSTICE, JUSTICE THOMAS, and JUSTICE SOTOMAYOR join, and an opinion with respect to Part II-C, in which THE CHIEF JUSTICE and JUSTICE THOMAS join.

New York law prohibits class actions in suits seeking penalties or statutory minimum damages. We consider whether this precludes a federal district court sitting in diversity from entertaining a class action under *Federal Rule of Civil Procedure 23*.[2]

2 *Rule 23(a)* provides:

"(a) Prerequisites. One or more members of a class may sue or be sued as representative parties on behalf of all members only if:

"(1) the class is so numerous that joinder of all members is impracticable;

"(2) there are questions of law or fact common to the class;

"(3) the claims or defenses of the representative parties are typical of the claims or defenses of the class; and

"(4) the representative parties will fairly and adequately protect the interests of the class."

*Subsection (b)* says that "[a] class action may be maintained if Rule 23 (a) is satisfied and if" the suit falls into one of three described categories (irrelevant for present purposes).

# I

The petitioner's complaint alleged the following: Shady Grove Orthopedic Associates, P. A., provided medical care to Sonia E. Galvez for injuries she suffered in an automobile accident. As partial payment for that care, Galvez assigned to Shady Grove her rights to insurance benefits under a policy issued in New York by Allstate Insurance Co. Shady Grove tendered a claim for the assigned benefits to Allstate, which under New York law had 30 days to pay the claim or deny it. Allstate apparently paid, but not on time, and it refused to pay the statutory interest that accrued on the overdue benefits (at two percent per month).

Shady Grove filed this diversity suit in the Eastern District of New York to recover the unpaid statutory interest. Alleging that Allstate routinely refuses to pay interest on overdue benefits, Shady Grove sought relief on behalf of itself and a class of all others to whom Allstate owes interest. The District Court dismissed the suit for lack of jurisdiction. It reasoned that *N. Y. Civ. Prac. Law Ann. § 901(b)*, which precludes a suit to recover a "penalty" from proceeding as a class action, applies in diversity suits in federal court, despite *Federal Rule of Civil Procedure 23*. Concluding that statutory interest is a "penalty" under New York law, it held that *§ 901(b)* prohibited the proposed class action. And, since Shady Grove conceded that its individual claim (worth roughly $ 500) fell far short of the amount-in-controversy requirement for individual suits under *28 U.S.C. § 1332(a)*, the suit did not belong in federal court.[3]

3 Shady Grove had asserted jurisdiction under *28 U.S.C. § 1332(d)(2)*, which relaxes, for class actions seeking at least $ 5 million, the rule against aggregating separate claims for calculation of the amount in controversy.

The Second Circuit affirmed. We granted certiorari.

# II

The framework for our decision is familiar. We must first determine whether *Rule 23* answers the question in dispute. If it does, it governs -- New York's law notwithstanding -- unless it exceeds statutory authorization or Congress's rulemaking power. We do not wade into *Erie*'s murky waters unless the federal rule is inapplicable or invalid.

A

The question in dispute is whether Shady Grove's suit may proceed as a class action. *Rule 23* provides an answer. It states that "[a] class action may be maintained" if two conditions are met: The suit must satisfy the criteria set forth in *subdivision (a)* (*i.e.*, numerosity, commonality, typicality, and adequacy of representation), and it also must fit into one of the three categories described in *subdivision (b)*. *Fed. Rule Civ. Proc. 23(b)*. By its terms this creates a categorical rule entitling a plaintiff whose suit meets the specified criteria to pursue his claim as a class action. (The Federal Rules regularly use "may" to confer categorical permission, as do federal statutes that establish procedural entitlements. Thus, *Rule 23* provides a one-size-fits-all formula for deciding the class-action question. Because *§ 901(b)* attempts to answer the same question -- *i.e.*, it states that Shady Grove's suit "may *not* be maintained as a class action" (emphasis added) because of the relief it seeks -- it cannot apply in diversity suits unless *Rule 23* is ultra vires.

The Second Circuit believed that *§ 901(b)* and *Rule 23* do not conflict because they address different issues. *Rule 23*, it said, concerns only the criteria for determining whether a given class can and should be certified; *section 901(b)*, on the other hand, addresses an antecedent question: whether the particular type of claim is eligible for class treatment in the first place -- a question on which *Rule 23* is silent. Allstate embraces this analysis.

We disagree. To begin with, the line between eligibility and certifiability is entirely artificial. Both are preconditions for maintaining a class action. Allstate suggests that eligibility must depend on the "particular cause of action" asserted, instead of some other attribute of the suit. But that is not so. Congress could, for example, provide that only claims involving more than a certain number of plaintiffs are "eligible" for class treatment in federal court. In other words, relabeling *Rule 23(a)*'s prerequisites "eligibility criteria" would obviate Allstate's objection -- a sure sign that its eligibility-certifiability distinction is made-to-order.

There is no reason, in any event, to read *Rule 23* as addressing only whether claims made eligible for class treatment by some *other* law should be certified as class actions. Allstate asserts that *Rule 23* neither explicitly nor implicitly empowers a federal court "to certify a class in each and every case" where the Rule's criteria are met. But that is *exactly* what *Rule 23* does: It says that if the prescribed preconditions are satisfied "[a] class action *may be maintained*" (emphasis added) -- not "*a class action may be permitted*." Courts do not maintain actions; litigants do. The discretion suggested by *Rule 23*'s "may" is discretion residing in the plaintiff: He may bring his claim in a class action if he wishes. And like the rest of the *Federal Rules of Civil Procedure*, *Rule 23 automatically* applies "in all civil actions and proceedings in the United States district courts," *Fed. Rule Civ. Proc. 1.*

Allstate points out that Congress has carved out some federal claims from *Rule 23*'s reach, which shows, Allstate contends, that *Rule 23* does not authorize class actions for all claims, but rather leaves room for laws like *§ 901(b)*. But Congress, unlike New York, has ultimate authority over the Federal Rules of Civil Procedure; it can create exceptions to an individual rule as it sees fit -- either by directly amending the rule or by enacting a separate statute overriding it in certain instances. The fact that Congress has created specific exceptions to *Rule 23* hardly proves that the Rule does not apply generally. In fact, it proves the opposite. If *Rule 23* did *not* authorize class actions across the board, the statutory exceptions would be unnecessary.

Allstate next suggests that the structure of *§ 901* shows that *Rule 23* addresses only certifiability. *Section 901(a)*, it notes, establishes class-certification criteria roughly analogous to those in *Rule 23* (wherefore it agrees *that* subsection is pre-empted). But *§ 901(b)*'s rule barring class actions for certain claims is set off as its own subsection, and where it applies *§ 901(a)* does not. This shows, according to Allstate, that *§ 901(b)* concerns a separate subject. Perhaps it does concern a subject separate from the subject of *§ 901(a)*. But the question before us is whether it concerns a subject separate from the subject of *Rule 23* -- and for purposes of answering *that* question the way New York has structured its statute is immaterial. *Rule 23* permits all class actions that meet its requirements, and a State cannot limit that permission by structuring one part of its statute to track *Rule 23* and enacting another part that imposes additional requirements. Both of *§ 901*'s subsections undeniably answer the same question as *Rule 23*: whether a class action may proceed for a given suit.

The dissent argues that *§ 901(b)* has nothing to do with whether Shady Grove may maintain its suit as a class action, but affects only the *remedy* it may obtain if it wins. Whereas "*Rule 23* governs procedural aspects of class litigation" by "prescribing the considerations relevant to class certification and post certification proceedings," *§ 901(b)* addresses only "the size of a monetary award a class plaintiff may pursue." Accordingly, the dissent says, *Rule 23* and New York's law may coexist in peace.

We need not decide whether a state law that limits the remedies available in an existing class action would conflict with *Rule 23*; that is not what *§ 901(b)* does. By its terms, the provision precludes a plaintiff from "maintaining" a class action seeking statutory penalties. Unlike a law that sets a ceiling on damages (or puts other remedies out of reach) in properly filed class actions, *§ 901(b)* says nothing about what remedies a court may award; it prevents the class actions it covers from coming into existence at all.[4] Consequently, a court bound by *§ 901(b)* could not certify a class action seeking both statutory penalties and other remedies even if it announces in advance that it will refuse to award the penalties in the event the plaintiffs prevail; to do so would violate the statute's clear prohibition on "maintaining" such suits as class actions.

> 4 Contrary to the dissent's implication, we express no view as to whether state laws that set a ceiling on damages recoverable in a single suit, are pre-empted. Whether or not those laws conflict with *Rule 23*, *§ 901(b)* does conflict because it addresses not the remedy, but the procedural right to maintain a class action. As Allstate and the dissent note, several federal statutes also limit the recovery available in class actions. But Congress has plenary power to override the Federal Rules, so its enactments, unlike those of the States, prevail even in case of a conflict.

The dissent asserts that a plaintiff can avoid *§ 901(b)*'s barrier by omitting from his complaint (or removing) a request for statutory penalties. Even assuming all statutory penalties are waivable, the fact that a complaint omitting them could be brought as a class action would not at all prove that *§ 901(b)* is addressed only to remedies. If the state law instead banned class actions for fraud claims, a would-be class-action plaintiff could drop the fraud counts from his complaint and proceed with the remainder in a class action. Yet that would not mean the law provides no remedy for fraud; the ban would affect only the procedural means by which the remedy may be pursued. In short, although the dissent correctly abandons Allstate's eligibility-certifiability distinction, the alternative it offers fares no better.

The dissent all but admits that the literal terms of *§ 901(b)* address the same subject as *Rule 23* -- i.e., whether a class action may be maintained -- but insists the provision's *purpose* is to restrict only remedies. ("While phrased as responsive to the question whether certain class actions may begin, *§ 901(b)* is unmistakably aimed at controlling how those actions must end"). Unlike *Rule 23*, designed to further procedural fairness and efficiency, *§ 901(b)* (we are told) "responds to an entirely different concern": the fear that allowing statutory damages to be awarded on a class-wide basis would "produce overkill." The dissent reaches this conclusion on the basis of (1) constituent concern recorded in the law's bill jacket; (2) a commentary suggesting that the Legislature "apparently feared" that combining class actions and statutory penalties "could result in annihilating punishment of the defendant," ; (3) a remark by the Governor in his signing statement that *§ 901(b)* "' provides a controlled remedy,'" (4) a state court's statement that the final text of *§ 901(b)* "'was the result of a compromise among competing interests.'"

This evidence of the New York Legislature's purpose is pretty sparse. But even accepting the dissent's account of the Legislature's objective at face value, it cannot override the statute's clear text. Even if its aim is to restrict the remedy a plaintiff can obtain, *§ 901(b)* achieves that end by limiting a plaintiff's power to maintain a class action. The manner in which the law "could have been written," has no bearing; what matters is the law the Legislature *did* enact. We cannot rewrite that to reflect our perception of legislative purpose. The dissent's concern for state prerogatives is frustrated rather than furthered by revising state laws when a potential conflict with a Federal Rule arises; the state-friendly approach would be to accept the law as written and test the validity of the Federal Rule.

The dissent's approach of determining whether state and federal rules conflict based on the subjective intentions of the state legislature is an enterprise destined to produce "confusion worse confounded," It would mean, to begin with, that one State's statute could survive pre-emption (and accordingly affect the procedures in federal court) while another State's identical law would not, merely because its authors had different aspirations. It would also mean that district courts would have to discern, in every diversity case, the purpose behind any putatively pre-empted state procedural rule, even if its text squarely conflicts with federal law. That task will often prove arduous. Many laws further more than one aim, and the aim of others may be impossible to discern. Moreover, to the extent the dissent's purpose-driven approach depends on its characterization of *§ 901(b)*'s aims as substantive, it would apply to many state rules ostensibly addressed to procedure. Pleading standards, for example, often embody policy preferences about the types of claims that should succeed -- as do rules governing summary judgment, pretrial discovery, and the admissibility of certain evidence. Hard cases will abound. It is not even clear that a state supreme court's pronouncement of the law's purpose would settle the issue, since existence of the factual predicate for avoiding federal pre-emption is ultimately a federal question. Predictably, federal judges would be condemned to poring through state legislative history -- which may be less easily obtained, less thorough, and less familiar than its federal counterpart.

But while the dissent does indeed artificially narrow the scope of *§ 901(b)* by finding that it pursues only substantive policies, that is not the central difficulty of the dissent's position. The central difficulty is that even artificial narrowing cannot render *§ 901(b)* compatible with *Rule 23*. *Whatever* the policies they pursue, they flatly contradict each other. Allstate asserts that we can (and must) *interpret Rule 23* in a manner that avoids overstepping its authorizing statute. If the Rule were susceptible of two meanings -- one that would violate *§ 2072(b)* and another that would not -- we would agree. But it is not. *Rule 23* unambiguously authorizes *any* plaintiff, in *any* federal civil proceeding, to maintain a class action if the Rule's prerequisites are met. We cannot contort its text, even to avert a collision with state law that might render it invalid. What the dissent's approach achieves is not the avoiding of a "conflict between *Rule 23* and *§ 901(b)*," but rather the invalidation of *Rule 23* (pursuant to *§ 2072(b)* of the Rules Enabling Act) to the extent that it conflicts with the substantive policies of *§ 901*. There is no other way to reach the dissent's destination. We must therefore confront head-on whether *Rule 23* falls within the statutory authorization.

B

*Erie* involved the constitutional power of federal courts to supplant state law with judge-made rules. In that context, it made no difference whether the rule was technically one of substance or procedure; the touchstone was whether it "significantly affects the result of a litigation." *Guaranty Trust Co. v. York*. That is not the test for either the constitutionality or the statutory validity of a Federal Rule of Procedure. Congress has undoubted power to supplant state law, and undoubted power to prescribe rules for the courts it has created, so long as those rules regulate matters "rationally capable of classification" as procedure. In the Rules Enabling Act, Congress authorized this Court to promulgate rules of procedure subject to its review, *28 U.S.C. § 2072(a)*, but with the limitation that those rules "shall not abridge, enlarge or modify any substantive right," *§ 2072(b)*.

We have long held that this limitation means that the Rule must "really regulate procedure, -- the judicial process for enforcing rights and duties recognized by substantive law and for justly administering remedy and redress for disregard or infraction of them." The test is not whether the rule affects a litigant's substantive rights; most procedural rules do. What matters is what the rule itself *regulates*: If it governs only "the manner and the means" by which the litigants' rights are "enforced," it is valid; if it alters "the rules of decision by which [the] court will adjudicate [those] rights," it is not.

Applying that test, we have rejected every statutory challenge to a Federal Rule that has come before us. We have found to be in compliance with *§ 2072(b)* rules prescribing methods for serving process, and requiring litigants whose mental or physical condition is in dispute to submit to examinations, (*Fed. Rule Civ. Proc. 35*); Likewise, we have upheld rules authorizing imposition of sanctions upon those who file frivolous appeals, or who sign court papers without a reasonable inquiry into the facts asserted, see *Business Guides, Inc. v. Chromatic Communications Enterprises, Inc., 498 U.S. 533 (1991)* (*Fed. Rule Civ. Proc. 11*). Each of these rules had some practical effect on the parties' rights, but each undeniably regulated only the process for enforcing those rights; none altered the rights themselves, the available remedies, or the rules of decision by which the court adjudicated either.

Applying that criterion, we think it obvious that rules allowing multiple claims (and claims by or against multiple parties) to be litigated together are also valid. See, e.g., *Fed. Rules Civ. Proc.* 18 (joinder of claims), 20 (joinder of parties), 42(a) (consolidation of actions). Such rules neither change plaintiffs' separate entitlements to relief nor abridge defendants' rights; they alter only how the claims are processed. For the same reason, *Rule 23* -- at least insofar as it allows willing plaintiffs to join their separate claims against the same defendants in a class action -- falls within § 2072(b)'s authorization. A class action, no less than traditional joinder (of which it is a species), merely enables a federal court to adjudicate claims of multiple parties at once, instead of in separate suits. And like traditional joinder, it leaves the parties' legal rights and duties intact and the rules of decision unchanged.

Allstate contends that the authorization of class actions is not substantively neutral: Allowing Shady Grove to sue on behalf of a class "transform[s] [the] dispute over a five *hundred* dollar penalty into a dispute over a five *million* dollar penalty." Allstate's aggregate liability, however, does not depend on whether the suit proceeds as a class action. Each of the 1,000-plus members of the putative class could (as Allstate acknowledges) bring a freestanding suit asserting his individual claim. It is undoubtedly true that some plaintiffs who would not bring individual suits for the relatively small sums involved will choose to join a class action. That has no bearing, however, on Allstate's or the plaintiffs' legal rights. The likelihood that some (even many) plaintiffs will be induced to sue by the availability of a class action is just the sort of "incidental effect" we have long held does not violate § 2072(b).

Allstate argues that *Rule 23* violates § 2072(b) because the state law it displaces, § 901(b), creates a right that the Federal Rule abridges -- namely, a "substantive right . . . not to be subjected to aggregated class-action liability" in a single suit. To begin with, we doubt that that is so. Nothing in the text of § 901(b) (which is to be found in New York's procedural code) confines it to claims under New York law; and of course New York has no power to alter substantive rights and duties created by other sovereigns. As we have said, the *consequence* of excluding certain class actions may be to cap the damages a defendant can face in a single suit, but the law itself alters only procedure. In that respect, § 901(b) is no different from a state law forbidding simple joinder. As a fallback argument, Allstate argues that even if § 901(b) is a procedural provision, it was enacted "for *substantive reasons.*" Its end was not to improve "the conduct of the litigation process itself" but to alter "the outcome of that process."

The fundamental difficulty with both these arguments is that the substantive nature of New York's law, or its substantive purpose, *makes no difference.* A Federal Rule of Procedure is not valid in some jurisdictions and invalid in others -- or valid in some cases and invalid in others -- depending upon whether its effect is to frustrate a state substantive law (or a state procedural law enacted for substantive purposes).

In sum, it is not the substantive or procedural nature or purpose of the affected state law that matters, but the substantive or procedural nature of the Federal Rule. We have held since *Sibbach*, and reaffirmed repeatedly, that the validity of a Federal Rule depends entirely upon whether it regulates procedure. If it does, it is authorized by § 2072 and is valid in all jurisdictions, with respect to all claims, regardless of its incidental effect upon state-created rights.

## C [Omitted]

## D

We must acknowledge the reality that keeping the federal-court door open to class actions that cannot proceed in state court will produce forum shopping. That is unacceptable when it comes as the consequence of judge-made rules created to fill supposed "gaps" in positive federal law. For where neither the Constitution, a treaty, nor a statute provides the rule of decision or authorizes a federal court to supply one, "state law must govern because there can be no other law." But divergence from state law, with the attendant consequence of forum shopping, is the inevitable (indeed, one might say the intended) result of a uniform system of federal procedure. Congress itself has created the possibility that the same case may follow a different course if filed in federal instead of state court. The short of the matter is that a Federal Rule governing procedure is valid whether or not it alters the outcome of the case in a way that induces forum shopping. To hold otherwise would be to "disembowel either the Constitution's grant of power over federal procedure" or Congress's exercise of it.

The judgment of the Court of Appeals is reversed, and the case is remanded for further proceedings.

*It is so ordered.*

# E. SUPPLEMENTAL JURISDICTION 28 USC 1367

13. To start litigation in a federal court the plaintiff must have a valid "key to the courthouse," such as admiralty, federal question, or diversity jurisdiction. Then once the plaintiff has successfully opened the door to the federal court, many other parties may follow into the courthouse, and join in the same suit because they also have an interest in the same case or controversy.

For example, in a case involving a car accident, plaintiff may sue the driver of the other car. Then that driver may implead the maker of the car, as a third-party defendant, if the defendant claims that some flaw in the design of the car prevented the defendant from stopping in time.

It makes sense to try all of the claims arising from the car accident at one time. So even though the plaintiff might not have been allowed to sue the maker of the car in federal court, (because both plaintiff and the car maker were from the same state, for example), the jurisdiction of the federal court will be expanded to allow the issues between the defendant and the car maker to be tried in the same suit as the claim by plaintiff against defendant. While the door to the federal courthouse is open anyway, various other parties are allowed to be brought into federal court if their claims involve the same case or controversy. [Adding additional claims and parties to an existing lawsuit will be discussed in more detail in Chapters 5 and 6.]

This expansion of jurisdiction was formerly called "ancillary" or "pendent" jurisdiction – depending on the specific facts involved. In 1990 Congress enacted 28 USC 1367, which specifically authorizes this sort of expansion of federal jurisdiction, which is now called *Supplemental jurisdiction.* So it is no longer necessary to try to distinguish between ancillary and pendent jurisdiction.

But there still are limits to how many additional issues and parties may be admitted to federal court based on Supplemental jurisdiction.

The following case was decided *before* 28 USC 1367 was enacted. But once you understand the following case you will see that the result would have been just the same under 28 USC 1367. Then it will be easier for you to understand the fairly complex provisions of 28 USC 1367(b).

98 S. CT. 2396
# SUPREME COURT OF THE UNITED STATES
## OWEN EQUIPMENT AND ERECTION COMPANY, PETITIONER,
### V.
## GERALDINE KROGER, RESPONDENT
## ADMINISTRATRIX OF THE ESTATE OF JAMES D. KROGER,
## DECEASED

DECIDED JUNE 21, 1978

Mr. Justice STEWART delivered the opinion of the Court.

In an action in which federal jurisdiction is based on diversity of citizenship, may the plaintiff assert a claim against a third-party defendant when there is no independent basis for federal jurisdiction over that claim? The Court of Appeals for the Eighth Circuit held in this case that such a claim is within the ancillary jurisdiction of the federal courts. We granted certiorari, because this decision conflicts with several recent decisions of other Courts of Appeals.

## I

On January 18, 1972, James Kroger was electrocuted when the boom of a steel crane next to which he was walking came too close to a high-tension electric power line. The respondent (his widow, who is the administratrix of his estate) filed a wrongful-death action in the United States District Court for the District of Nebraska against the Omaha Public Power District (OPPD). Her complaint alleged that OPPD's negligent construction, maintenance, and operation of the power line had caused Kroger's death. Federal jurisdiction was based on diversity of citizenship, since the respondent was a citizen of Iowa and OPPD was a Nebraska corporation.

OPPD then filed a third-party complaint pursuant to Fed.Rule Civ.Proc. 14(a) against the petitioner, Owen Equipment and Erection Co. (Owen), alleging that the crane was owned and operated by Owen, and that Owen's negligence had been the proximate cause of Kroger's death. OPPD later moved for summary judgment on the respondent's complaint against it. While this motion was pending, the respondent was granted leave to file an amended complaint naming Owen as an additional defendant. Thereafter, the District Court granted OPPD's motion for summary judgment. The case thus went to trial between the respondent and the petitioner alone.

The respondent's amended complaint alleged that Owen was "a Nebraska corporation with its principal place of business in Nebraska." Owen's answer admitted that it was "a corporation organized and existing under the laws of the State of Nebraska," and denied every other allegation of the complaint. On the third day of trial, however, it was disclosed that the petitioner's principal place of business was in Iowa, not Nebraska,[FN5] and that the petitioner and the respondent were thus both citizens of Iowa.[FN6] The petitioner then moved to dismiss the complaint for lack of jurisdiction. The District Court reserved decision on the motion, and the jury thereafter returned a verdict in favor of the respondent. In an unreported opinion issued after the trial, the District Court denied the petitioner's motion to dismiss the complaint.

FN5. The problem apparently was one of geography. Although the Missouri River generally marks the boundary between Iowa and Nebraska, Carter Lake, Iowa, where the accident occurred and where Owen had its main office, lies west of the river, adjacent to Omaha, Neb. Apparently the river once avulsed at one of its bends, cutting Carter Lake off from the rest of Iowa. [Avulsion, the sudden change of course by a river, does not change boundary lines determined by the prior location of the river.]

FN6. Title 28 U.S.C. § 1332(c) provides that "For the purposes of diversity jurisdiction . . ., a corporation shall be deemed a citizen of any State by which it has been incorporated and of the State where it has its principal place of business."

The judgment was affirmed on appeal.

## II

It is undisputed that there was no independent basis of federal jurisdiction over the respondent's state-law tort action against the petitioner, since both are citizens of Iowa. And although Fed.Rule Civ.Proc. 14(a) permits a plaintiff to assert a claim against a third-party defendant, it does not purport to say whether or not such a claim requires an independent basis of federal jurisdiction. Indeed, it could not determine that question, since it is axiomatic that the Federal Rules of Civil Procedure do not create or withdraw federal jurisdiction.

In affirming the District Court's judgment, the Court of Appeals relied upon the doctrine of ancillary jurisdiction, whose contours it believed were defined by this Court's holding in *Mine Workers v. Gibbs*. The *Gibbs* case differed from this one in that it involved pendent jurisdiction, which concerns the resolution of a plaintiff's federal and state-law claims against a single defendant in one action. By contrast, in this case there was no claim based upon substantive federal law, but rather state-law tort claims against two different defendants. Nonetheless, the Court of Appeals was correct in perceiving that *Gibbs* and this case are two species of the same generic problem: Under what circumstances may a federal court hear and decide a state-law claim arising between citizens of the same State? But we believe that the Court of Appeals failed to understand the scope of the doctrine of the *Gibbs* case.

The plaintiff in *Gibbs* alleged that the defendant union had violated the common law of Tennessee as well as the federal prohibition of secondary boycotts. This Court held that, although the parties were not of diverse citizenship, the District Court properly entertained the state-law claim as pendent to the federal claim.

It is apparent that *Gibbs* delineated the constitutional limits of federal judicial power. But even if it be assumed that the District Court in the present case had constitutional power to decide the respondent's lawsuit against the petitioner, it does not follow that the decision of the Court of Appeals was correct. Constitutional power is merely the first hurdle that must be overcome in determining that a federal court has jurisdiction over a particular controversy. For the jurisdiction of the federal courts is limited not only by the provisions of Art. III of the Constitution, but also by Acts of Congress.

Statutory law as well as the Constitution may limit a federal court's jurisdiction over nonfederal claims. [FN11]

> FN11. As used in this opinion, the term "nonfederal claim" means one as to which there is no independent basis for federal jurisdiction. Conversely, a "federal claim" means one as to which an independent basis for federal jurisdiction exists.

## III

The relevant statute in this case, 28 U.S.C. § 1332(a)(1), confers upon federal courts jurisdiction over "civil actions where the matter in controversy exceeds the sum or value of $10,000 . . . and is between . . . citizens of different States." This statute and its predecessors have consistently been held to require complete diversity of citizenship. That is, diversity jurisdiction does not exist unless *each* defendant is a citizen of a different State from *each* plaintiff. Over the years Congress has repeatedly re-enacted or amended the statute conferring diversity jurisdiction, leaving intact this rule of complete diversity. Whatever may have been the original purposes of diversity-of-citizenship jurisdiction, this subsequent history clearly demonstrates a congressional mandate that diversity jurisdiction is not to be available when any plaintiff is a citizen of the same State as any defendant.

Thus it is clear that the respondent could not originally have brought suit in federal court naming Owen and OPPD as codefendants, since citizens of Iowa would have been on both sides of the litigation. Yet the identical lawsuit resulted when she amended her complaint. Complete diversity was destroyed just as surely as if she had sued Owen initially. In either situation, in the plain language of the statute, the "matter in controversy" could not be "between . . . citizens of different States."

It is a fundamental precept that federal courts are courts of limited jurisdiction. The limits upon federal jurisdiction, whether imposed by the Constitution or by Congress, must be neither disregarded nor evaded. Yet under the reasoning of the Court of Appeals in this case, a plaintiff could defeat the statutory requirement of complete diversity by the simple expedient of suing only those defendants who were of diverse citizenship and waiting for them to implead nondiverse defendants. If, as the Court of Appeals thought, a "common nucleus of operative fact" were the only requirement for ancillary jurisdiction in a diversity case, there would be no principled reason why the respondent in this case could not have joined her cause of action against Owen in her original complaint as ancillary to her claim against OPPD. Congress' requirement of complete diversity would thus have been evaded completely.

The nonfederal claim here was asserted by the plaintiff, who voluntarily chose to bring suit upon a state-law claim in a federal court. By contrast, ancillary jurisdiction typically involves claims by a defending party haled into court against his will, or by another person whose rights might be irretrievably lost unless he could assert them in an ongoing action in a federal court. A plaintiff cannot complain if ancillary jurisdiction does not encompass all of his possible claims in a case such as this one, since it is he who has chosen the federal rather than the state forum and must thus accept its limitations. "The efficiency plaintiff seeks so avidly is available without question in the state courts." [20]

FN20. Whether Iowa's statute of limitations would now bar an action by the respondent in an Iowa court is, of course, entirely a matter of state law.

It is not unreasonable to assume that, in generally requiring complete diversity, Congress did not intend to confine the jurisdiction of federal courts so inflexibly that they are unable to protect legal rights or effectively to resolve an entire, logically entwined lawsuit. Those practical needs are the basis of the doctrine of ancillary jurisdiction. But neither the convenience of litigants nor considerations of judicial economy can suffice to justify extension of the doctrine of ancillary jurisdiction to a plaintiff's cause of action against a citizen of the same State in a diversity case.

Congress has established the basic rule that diversity jurisdiction exists under 28 U.S.C. § 1332 only when there is complete diversity of citizenship. To allow the requirement of complete diversity to be circumvented as it was in this case would simply flout the congressional command.[FN21]

> FN21. Our holding is that the District Court lacked power to entertain the respondent's lawsuit against the petitioner. Thus, the asserted inequity in the respondent's alleged concealment of its citizenship is irrelevant. Federal judicial power does not depend upon "prior action or consent of the parties."

Accordingly, the judgment of the Court of Appeals is reversed.

*It is so ordered.*

14. Taking time to read the full text of 28 USC 1367 might be useful at this time, although you will be able to get a fuller understanding of the usefulness of Supplemental jurisdiction after you have studied Chapters 5 and 6.

# CHAPTER 4

# CHANGING THE LOCATION OF THE LITIGATION

1. Initially, the plaintiff has the choice of courthouse. The plaintiff may prefer to be in a state court system or in the federal court system. In many cases, especially with a corporate defendant, the defendant may be subject to suit in a number of different states. So the plaintiff has the opportunity to select the court that is most likely to give plaintiff a favorable result.

Ideally, a lawsuit should come out the same way no matter where the case is heard. But trial lawyers usually feel that there is, in fact, a difference between different courts. Even within the same state some parts of the state may be considered to be friendlier to plaintiffs in particular types of cases. Within a given state experienced trial lawyers may prefer state courts over federal courts – or the reverse. That preference is based on human factors that simply cannot be learned in law school.

As you have already seen, there may be a definite difference between the law that would be applied in one state, compared to the law that would be applied in another state. *Keeton v. Hustler Magazine*, where the time allowed by the statute of limitations had run out in every state except New Hampshire, is a good example.

So plaintiff's choice of where to start the lawsuit might not be a choice that defendant feels comfortable with – for any number of reasons, including clear choice of law issues, and a myriad of human factors. Therefore, defendant may try to change the location of the trial by use of one of the techniques covered in this chapter – Removal, Transfer, Forum Non Conveniens, or Change of Venue.

# A. REMOVAL 28 USC 1441, 1446, 1447

2. When a defendant is sued in state court, and would prefer to have the litigation take place in federal court, (as in the case of *Lu Junhong v. Boeing*, for example), there are several techniques available. 28 USC 1441(a) provides that:

> "Except as otherwise expressly provided by Act of Congress, any civil action brought in a State court of which the district courts of the United States have original jurisdiction, may be removed by the defendant or the defendants, to the district court of the United States for the district and division embracing the place where such action is pending."

But there are limits to removal. Sec. 1441(b)(2) provides that when federal jurisdiction would be available only on the basis of diversity jurisdiction described in 1332(a), then the case cannot be removed to federal court if any defendant is a citizen of the state in which the action was originally brought.

This makes sense. If diversity jurisdiction is intended to overcome the "home town advantage" that a local plaintiff might have in state court over an out-of-state defendant, then if both plaintiff and defendant are from the same state, there should be no "home town advantage" on either side – and thus no need to try the case in the federal system.

Removal from state court to federal court must be done promptly – basically within 30 days of the time the defendant receives a copy of the complaint. (28 USC 1446(b). Then if plaintiff feels that the removal was improper, plaintiff must object within the next 30 days. (28 USC 1447(c)).

In the following case the issue of removal was considered to be so important that it made it all the way to the U.S. Supreme Court – more than two years after the suit had been filed. In all that time *no* court had heard any evidence, or taken any action on the merits of the case. The parties were still fighting as to whether the suit should be heard in state or federal court.

That might seem like a waste of time. Nevertheless, the result in the following case does provide a good description of how laws develop over time, and does clarify an important, larger issue as to the "citizenship" of a corporation. This will be important for future litigation.

SUPREME COURT OF THE UNITED STATES
THE HERTZ CORPORATION, PETITIONER
V.
MELINDA FRIEND ET AL.

DECIDED FEBRUARY 23, 2010

BREYER, J., delivered the opinion for a unanimous Court.

The federal diversity jurisdiction statute provides that "a corporation shall be deemed to be a citizen of any State by which it has been incorporated *and of the State where it has its principal place of business.*" 28 U.S.C. § 1332(c)(1) (emphasis added). We seek here to resolve different interpretations that the Circuits have given this phrase. In doing so, we place primary weight upon the need for judicial administration of a jurisdictional statute to remain as simple as possible. And we conclude that the phrase "principal place of business" refers to the place where the corporation's high level officers direct, control, and coordinate the corporation's activities. Lower federal courts have often metaphorically called that place the corporation's "nerve center." We believe that the "nerve center" will typically be found at a corporation's headquarters.

I

In September 2007, respondents Melinda Friend and John Nhieu, two California citizens, sued petitioner, the Hertz Corporation, in a California state court. They sought damages for what they claimed were violations of California's wage and hour laws. And they requested relief on behalf of a potential class composed of California citizens who had allegedly suffered similar harms.

Hertz filed a notice seeking removal to a federal court. Hertz claimed that the plaintiffs and the defendant were citizens of different States. §§ 1332(a)(1), (c)(1). Hence, the federal court possessed diversity-of-citizenship jurisdiction. Friend and Nhieu, however, claimed that the Hertz Corporation was a California citizen, like themselves, and that, hence, diversity jurisdiction was lacking.

To support its position, Hertz submitted a declaration by an employee relations manager that sought to show that Hertz's "principal place of business" was in New Jersey, not in California. The declaration stated, among other things, that Hertz operated facilities in 44 States; and that California -- which had about 12% of the Nation's population, Pet. for Cert. 8 -- accounted for 273 of Hertz's 1,606 car rental locations; about 2,300 of its 11,230 full-time employees; about $ 811 million of its $ 4.371 billion in annual revenue; and about 3.8 million of its approximately 21 million annual transactions, *i.e.*, rentals. The declaration also stated that the "leadership of Hertz and its domestic subsidiaries" is located at Hertz's "corporate headquarters" in Park Ridge, New Jersey; that its "core executive and administrative functions . . . are carried out" there and "to a lesser extent" in Oklahoma City, Oklahoma; and that its "major administrative operations . . . are found" at those two locations.

The District Court of the Northern District of California accepted Hertz's statement of the facts as undisputed. But it concluded that, given those facts, Hertz was a citizen of California.

The District Court consequently remanded the case to the state courts.

Hertz appealed the District Court's remand order. The Ninth Circuit affirmed in a brief memorandum opinion. Hertz filed a petition for certiorari. And, in light of differences among the Circuits in the application of the test for corporate citizenship, we granted the writ.

## II

At the outset, we consider a jurisdictional objection. Respondents point out that the statute permitting Hertz to appeal the District Court's remand order to the Court of Appeals, *28 U.S.C. § 1453(c)*, constitutes an exception to a more general jurisdictional rule that remand orders are "not reviewable on appeal." *§ 1447(d)*. They add that the language of *§ 1453(c)* refers only to "courts of appeals," not to the Supreme Court. The statute also says that if "a final judgment on the appeal" in a court of appeals "is not issued before the end" of 60 days (with a possible 10-day extension), "the appeal shall be denied." And respondents draw from these statutory circumstances the conclusion that Congress intended to permit review of a remand order only by a court of appeals, not by the Supreme Court (at least not if, as here, this Court's grant of certiorari comes after *§ 1453(c)*'s time period has elapsed).

This argument, however, makes far too much of too little. We normally do not read statutory silence as implicitly modifying or limiting Supreme Court jurisdiction that another statute specifically grants. Here, another, pre-existing federal statute gives this Court jurisdiction to "review writ of certiorari" cases that, like this case, are "in the courts of appeals" when we grant the writ. *28 U.S.C. § 1254*. This statutory jurisdictional grant replicates similar grants that yet older statutes provided. This history provides particularly strong reasons *not* to read *§ 1453(c)*'s silence or ambiguous language as modifying or limiting our pre-existing jurisdiction.

We thus interpret § 1453(c)'s "60-day" requirement as simply requiring a court of appeals to reach a decision within a specified time -- not to deprive this Court of subsequent jurisdiction to review the case.

## III

We begin our "principal place of business" discussion with a brief review of relevant history. The Constitution provides that the "judicial Power shall extend" to "Controversies . . . between Citizens of different States." Art. III, § 2. This language, however, does not automatically confer diversity jurisdiction upon the federal courts. Rather, it authorizes Congress to do so and, in doing so, to determine the scope of the federal courts' jurisdiction within constitutional limits.

Congress first authorized federal courts to exercise diversity jurisdiction in 1789 when, in the First Judiciary Act, Congress granted federal courts authority to hear suits "between a citizen of the State where the suit is brought, and a citizen of another State." § 11, 1 Stat. 78. The statute said nothing about corporations. In 1809, Chief Justice Marshall, writing for a unanimous Court, described a corporation as an "invisible, intangible, and artificial being" which was "certainly not a citizen." But the Court held that a corporation could invoke the federal courts' diversity jurisdiction based on a pleading that the corporation's shareholders were all citizens of a different State from the defendants, as "the term citizen ought to be understood as it is used in the constitution, and as it is used in other laws. That is, to describe the real persons who come into court, in this case, under their corporate name."

In *Louisville, C. & C. R. Co. v. Letson, 43 U.S. 497 (1844)*, the Court modified this initial approach. It held that a corporation was to be deemed an artificial person of the State by which it had been created, and its citizenship for jurisdictional purposes determined accordingly. Ten years later, the Court in *Marshall v. Baltimore & Ohio R. Co., 16 How. 314, (1854)*, held that the reason a corporation was a citizen of its State of incorporation was that, for the limited purpose of determining corporate citizenship, courts could conclusively (and artificially) presume that a corporation's *shareholders* were citizens of the State of incorporation. And it reaffirmed *Letson*. Whatever the rationale, the practical upshot was that, for diversity purposes, the federal courts considered a corporation to be a citizen of the State of its incorporation.

In 1928 this Court made clear that the "state of incorporation" rule was virtually absolute. It held that a corporation closely identified with State A could proceed in a federal court located in that State as long as the corporation had filed its incorporation papers in State B, perhaps a State where the corporation did no business at all. See *Black and White Taxicab & Transfer Co. v. Brown and Yellow Taxicab & Transfer*

*Co.*, *276 U.S. 518*, (refusing to question corporation's reincorporation motives and finding diversity jurisdiction). Subsequently, many in Congress and those who testified before it pointed out that this interpretation was at odds with diversity jurisdiction's basic rationale, namely, opening the federal courts' doors to those who might otherwise suffer from local prejudice against out-of-state parties. Through its choice of the State of incorporation, a corporation could manipulate federal-court jurisdiction, for example, opening the federal courts' doors in a State where it conducted nearly all its business by filing incorporation papers elsewhere. ("Since the Supreme Court has decided that a corporation is a citizen . . . it has become a common practice for corporations to be incorporated in one State while they do business in another. And there is no doubt but that it often occurs simply for the purpose of being able to have the advantage of choosing between two tribunals in case of litigation").

At the same time as federal dockets increased in size, many judges began to believe those dockets contained too many diversity cases. A committee of the Judicial Conference of the United States studied the matter.

Among its observations, the committee found a general need "to prevent frauds and abuses" with respect to jurisdiction. The committee recommended against eliminating diversity cases altogether. Instead it recommended, along with other proposals, a statutory amendment that would make a corporation a citizen both of the State of its incorporation and any State from which it received more than half of its gross income.

During the spring and summer of 1951 committee members circulated their report and attended circuit conferences at which federal judges discussed the report's recommendations. Reflecting those criticisms, the committee filed a new report in September, in which it revised its corporate citizenship recommendation. It now proposed that "'a corporation shall be deemed a citizen of the state of its original creation . . . and shall also be deemed a citizen of a state where it has its principal place of business,'" the source of the present-day statutory language. ...

The House Committee reprinted the Judicial Conference Committee Reports along with other reports and relevant testimony and circulated it to the general public "for the purpose of inviting further suggestions and comments." Subsequently, in 1958, Congress both codified the courts' traditional place of incorporation test and also enacted into law a slightly modified version of the Conference Committee's proposed "principal place of business" language. A corporation was to "be deemed a citizen of any State by which it has been incorporated and of the State where it has its principal place of business."

## IV

The phrase "principal place of business" has proved more difficult to apply than its originators likely expected.... Compare *Burdick v. Dillon, 144 F. 737, 738 (CA1 1906)* (holding that a corporation's "principal office, rather than a factory, mill, or mine . . . constitutes the 'principal place of business'"), with *Continental Coal Corp. v. Roszelle Bros., 242 F. 243, 247 (CA6 1917)* (identifying the "principal place of business" as the location of mining activities, rather than the "principal office")

After Congress' amendment, courts were similarly uncertain as to where to look to determine a corporation's "principal place of business" for diversity purposes. If a corporation's headquarters and executive offices were in the same State in which it did most of its business, the test seemed straightforward. The "principal place of business" was located in that State.

But suppose those corporate headquarters, including executive offices, are in one State, while the corporation's plants or other centers of business activity are located in other States? In 1959 a distinguished federal district judge, Edward Weinfeld, relied on the Second Circuit's interpretation of the Bankruptcy Act to answer this question in part:

> Where a corporation is engaged in far-flung and varied activities which are carried on in different states, its principal place of business is the nerve center from which it radiates out to its constituent parts and from which its officers direct, control and coordinate all activities without regard to locale, in the furtherance of the corporate objective. The test applied by our Court of Appeals, is that place where the corporation has an 'office from which its business was directed and controlled' -- the place where 'all of its business was under the supreme direction and control of its officers.' *Scot Typewriter Co., 170 F. Supp., at 865.*

Numerous Circuits have since followed this rule, applying the "nerve center" test for corporations with "far-flung" business activities.

*Scot*'s analysis, however, did not go far enough. For it did not answer what courts should do when the operations of the corporation are not "far-flung" but rather limited to only a few States. When faced with this question, various courts have focused more heavily on where a corporation's actual business activities are located.

Perhaps because corporations come in many different forms, involve many different kinds of business activities, and locate offices and plants for different reasons in different ways in different regions, a general "business activities" approach has proved unusually difficult to apply. Courts must decide which factors are more important than others: for example, plant location, sales or servicing centers; transactions, payrolls, or revenue generation.

The number of factors grew as courts explicitly combined aspects of the "nerve center" and "business activity" tests to look to a corporation's "total activities," sometimes to try to determine what treatises have described as the corporation's "center of gravity." Not surprisingly, different circuits (and sometimes different courts within a single circuit) have applied these highly general multifactor tests in different ways. (noting that the First Circuit "has never explained a basis for choosing between 'the center of corporate activity' test and the 'locus of operations' test"; the Second Circuit uses a "two-part test" similar to that of the Fifth, Ninth, and Eleventh Circuits involving an initial determination as to whether "a corporation's activities are centralized or decentralized" followed by an application of either the "place of operations" or "nerve center" test; the Third Circuit applies the "center of corporate activities" test searching for the "headquarters of a corporation's day-to-day activity"; the Fourth Circuit has "endorsed neither the 'nerve center' or 'place of operations' test to the exclusion of the other"; the Tenth Circuit directs consideration of the "total activity of the company considered as a whole").

This complexity may reflect an unmediated judicial effort to apply the statutory phrase "principal place of business" in light of the general purpose of diversity jurisdiction, *i.e.*, an effort to find the State where a corporation is least likely to suffer out-of-state prejudice when it is sued in a local court. But, if so, that task seems doomed to failure. After all, the relevant purposive concern -- prejudice against an out-of-state party -- will often depend upon factors that courts cannot easily measure, for example, a corporation's image, its history, and its advertising, while the factors that courts can more easily measure, for example, its office or plant location, its sales, its employment, or the nature of the goods or services it supplies, will sometimes bear no more than a distant relation to the likelihood of prejudice. At the same time, this approach is at war with administrative simplicity. And it has failed to achieve a nationally uniform interpretation of federal law, an unfortunate consequence in a federal legal system.

V

A

In an effort to find a single, more uniform interpretation of the statutory phrase, we have reviewed the Courts of Appeals' divergent and increasingly complex interpretations. Having done so, we now return to, and expand, Judge Weinfeld's approach, as applied in the Seventh Circuit. See, *e.g., Scot Typewriter Co. We* conclude that "principal place of business" is best read as referring to the place where a corporation's officers direct, control, and coordinate the corporation's activities. It is the place that Courts of Appeals have called the corporation's "nerve center." And in practice it should normally be the place where the corporation maintains its headquarters -- provided that the headquarters is the actual center of direction, control, and coordination, *i.e.*, the "nerve center," and not simply an office where the corporation holds its board meetings (for example, attended by directors and officers who have traveled there for the occasion).

Three sets of considerations, taken together, convince us that this approach, while imperfect, is superior to other possibilities. First, the statute's language supports the approach. The statute's text deems a corporation a citizen of the "State where it has its principal place of business." *28 U.S.C. § 1332(c)(1).* The word "place" is in the singular, not the plural. The word "principal" requires us to pick out the "main, prominent" or "leading" place. And the fact that the word "place" follows the words "State where" means that the "place" is a place *within* a State. It is not the State itself.

A corporation's "nerve center," usually its main headquarters, is a single place. The public often (though not always) considers it the corporation's main place of business. And it is a place within a State. By contrast, the application of a more general business activities test has led some courts, as in the present case, to look, not at a particular place within a State, but incorrectly at the State itself, measuring the total amount of business activities that the corporation conducts there and determining whether they are "significantly larger" than in the next-ranking State.

This approach invites greater litigation and can lead to strange results, as the Ninth Circuit has since recognized. Namely, if a "corporation may be deemed a citizen of California on the basis" of "activities that roughly reflect California's larger population nearly every national retailer -- no matter how far flung its operations -- will be deemed a citizen of California for diversity purposes." But why award or decline diversity jurisdiction on the basis of a State's population, whether measured directly, indirectly (say proportionately), or with modifications?

Second, administrative simplicity is a major virtue in a jurisdictional statute. (Eschewing "the sort of vague boundary that is to be avoided in the area of subject-matter jurisdiction wherever possible"). Complex jurisdictional tests complicate a case, eating up time and money as the parties litigate, not the merits of their claims, but which court is the right court to decide those claims. Complex tests produce appeals and reversals, encourage gamesmanship, and, again, diminish the likelihood that results and settlements will reflect a claim's legal and factual merits. Judicial resources too are at stake. Courts have an independent obligation to determine whether subject-matter jurisdiction exists, even when no party challenges it. So courts benefit from straightforward rules under which they can readily assure themselves of their power to hear a case.

Simple jurisdictional rules also promote greater predictability. Predictability is valuable to corporations making business and investment decisions. Predictability also benefits plaintiffs deciding whether to file suit in a state or federal court.

A "nerve center" approach, which ordinarily equates that "center" with a corporation's headquarters, is simple to apply *comparatively speaking*. The metaphor of a corporate "brain," while not precise, suggests a single location. By contrast, a corporation's general business activities more often lack a single principal place where they take place. That is to say, the corporation may have several plants, many sales locations, and employees located in many different places. If so, it will not be as easy to determine which of these different business locales is the "principal" or most important "place."

Third, the statute's legislative history, for those who accept it, offers a simplicity-related interpretive benchmark. The Judicial Conference provided an initial version of its proposal that suggested a numerical test. A corporation would be deemed a citizen of the State that accounted for more than half of its gross income. The Conference changed its mind in light of criticism that such a test would prove too complex and impractical to apply. That history suggests that the words "principal place of business" should be interpreted to be no more complex than the initial "half of gross income" test. A "nerve center" test offers such a possibility. A general business activities test does not.

B

We recognize that there may be no perfect test that satisfies all administrative and purposive criteria. We recognize as well that, under the "nerve center" test we adopt today, there will be hard cases. For example, in this era of telecommuting, some corporations may divide their command and coordinating functions among officers who work at several different locations, perhaps communicating over the Internet. That said, our test nonetheless points courts in a single direction, towards the center of overall direction, control, and coordination. Courts do not have to try to weigh corporate functions, assets, or revenues different in kind, one from the other. Our approach provides a sensible test that is relatively easier to apply, not a test that will, in all instances, automatically generate a result.

We also recognize that the use of a "nerve center" test may in some cases produce results that seem to cut against the basic rationale for *28 U.S.C. § 1332*. For example, if the bulk of a company's business activities visible to the public take place in New Jersey, while its top officers direct those activities just across the river in New York, the "principal place of business" is New York. Onc could arguc that members of the public in New Jersey would be *less* likely to be prejudiced against the corporation than persons in New York -- yet the corporation will still be entitled to remove a New Jersey state case to federal court. And note too that the same corporation would be unable to remove a New York state case to federal court, despite the New York public's presumed prejudice against the corporation.

We understand that such seeming anomalies will arise. However, in view of the necessity of having a clearer rule, we must accept them. Accepting occasionally counterintuitive results is the price the legal system must pay to avoid overly complex jurisdictional administration while producing the benefits that accompany a more uniform legal system.

The burden of persuasion for establishing diversity jurisdiction, of course, remains on the party asserting it. When challenged on allegations of jurisdictional facts, the parties must support their allegations by competent proof. And when faced with such a challenge, we reject suggestions such as, for example, the one made by petitioner that the mere filing of a form like the Securities and Exchange Commission's Form 10-K listing a corporation's "principal executive offices" would, without more, be sufficient proof to establish a corporation's "nerve center." ... Such possibilities would readily permit jurisdictional manipulation, thereby subverting a major reason for the insertion of the "principal place of business" language in the diversity statute. Indeed, if the record reveals attempts at manipulation -- for example, that the alleged "nerve center" is nothing more than a mail drop box, a bare office with a computer, or the location of an annual executive retreat -- the courts should instead take as the "nerve center" the place of actual direction, control, and coordination, in the absence of such manipulation.

## VI

Petitioner's unchallenged declaration suggests that Hertz's center of direction, control, and coordination, its "nerve center," and its corporate headquarters are one and the same, and they are located in New Jersey, not in California. Because respondents should have a fair opportunity to litigate their case in light of our holding, however, we vacate the Ninth Circuit's judgment and remand the case for further proceedings consistent with this opinion.

# B. TRANSFER 28 USC 1404 AND 1631

3. When a lawsuit is filed in a location that is seriously inconvenient for the parties and the witnesses, it may be transferred to another court *within the same court system* in the interests of justice. In the criminal system this happens when there is so much local prejudice within a particular community that it may be difficult to have a fair trial. So the defendant asks for a change of venue.

The same thing can happen in a civil case – usually not because of local prejudice, but simply because nearly all of the witnesses and evidence are located in a different place. For the convenience of the parties, the witnesses, and the courts, it may be best to transfer the case to a different location. Within the state court system a case may be transferred to a different location *within the same state.*

Once a case is in the federal court system – either because it was originally filed in the federal system or was removed by the defendant to federal court – the case can be transferred to any other appropriate trial court *within the federal system.* In other words, a case could be transferred from a U.S. District Court in Maine to a U.S. District Court in California.

The following case is a fascinating example of a *plaintiff* filing a case in a federal court in one state, and then asking that the case be transferred to a federal court in another state.

Just remember that transfers can only be made within the same court system. A case filed in state court can only be transferred to another court in that same state. Since all of the federal courts are within the *federal* system, a case filed in the federal court in one state can be transferred to a *federal* court in a different state.

## 110 S.CT. 1274
## SUPREME COURT OF THE UNITED STATES
## ALBERT J. FERENS, ET UX., PETITIONERS
### V.
### JOHN DEERE COMPANY

DECIDED MARCH 5, 1990

**Justice KENNEDY delivered the opinion of the Court.**

Section 1404(a) of Title 28 states: "For the convenience of parties and witnesses, in the interest of justice, a district court may transfer any civil action to any other district or division where it might have been brought." In *Van Dusen v. Barrack,* we held that, following a transfer under § 1404(a) initiated by a defendant, the transferee court must follow the choice-of-law rules that prevailed in the transferor court. We now decide that, when a plaintiff moves for the transfer, the same rule applies.

I

Albert Ferens lost his right hand when, the allegation is, it became caught in his combine harvester, manufactured by Deere & Company. The accident occurred while Ferens was working with the combine on his farm in Pennsylvania. For reasons not explained in the record, Ferens delayed filing a tort suit, and Pennsylvania's 2–year limitations period expired. In the third year, he and his wife sued Deere in the United States District Court for the Western District of Pennsylvania, raising contract and warranty claims as to which the Pennsylvania limitations period had not yet run. The District Court had diversity jurisdiction, as Ferens and his wife are Pennsylvania residents, and Deere is incorporated in Delaware with its principal place of business in Illinois.

Not to be deprived of a tort action, the Ferenses in the same year filed a second diversity suit against Deere in the United States District Court for the Southern District of Mississippi, alleging negligence and products liability. Diversity jurisdiction and venue were proper. The Ferenses sued Deere in the District Court in Mississippi because they knew that, under *Klaxon Co. v. Stentor Electric Mfg.* (1941), the federal court in the exercise of diversity jurisdiction must apply the same choice-of-law rules that Mississippi state courts would apply if they were deciding the case.

A Mississippi court would rule that Pennsylvania substantive law controls the personal injury claim but that Mississippi's own law governs the limitation period.

The Mississippi courts, as a result, would apply Mississippi's 6-year statute of limitations to the tort claim arising under Pennsylvania law and the tort action would not be time barred under the Mississippi statute.

The issue now before us arose when the Ferenses took their forum shopping a step further: having chosen the federal court in Mississippi to take advantage of the State's limitations period, they next moved, under § 1404(a), to transfer the action to the federal court in Pennsylvania on the ground that Pennsylvania was a more convenient forum. The Ferenses acted on the assumption that, after the transfer, the choice-of-law rules in the Mississippi forum, including a rule requiring application of the Mississippi statute of limitations, would continue to govern the suit.

Deere put up no opposition, and the District Court in Mississippi granted the § 1404(a) motion. The court accepted the Ferenses' arguments that they resided in Pennsylvania; that the accident occurred there; that the claim had no connection to Mississippi; that a substantial number of witnesses resided in the Western District of Pennsylvania but none resided in Mississippi; that most of the documentary evidence was located in the Western District of Pennsylvania but none was located in Mississippi; and that the warranty action pending in the Western District of Pennsylvania presented common questions of law and fact.

The District Court in Pennsylvania consolidated the transferred tort action with the Ferenses' pending warranty action but declined to honor the Mississippi statute of limitations as the District Court in Mississippi would have done. It ruled instead that, because the Ferenses had moved for transfer as plaintiffs, the rule in *Van Dusen* did not apply. Invoking the 2-year limitations period set by Pennsylvania law, the District Court dismissed their tort action.

The Court of Appeals for the Third Circuit affirmed.

We granted certiorari.

II

Section 1404(a) states only that a district court may transfer venue for the convenience of the parties and witnesses when in the interest of justice. It says nothing about choice of law and nothing about affording plaintiffs different treatment from defendants. We touched upon these issues in *Van Dusen*, but left open the question presented in this case. In *Van Dusen*, an airplane flying from Boston to Philadelphia crashed into Boston Harbor soon after takeoff. The personal representatives of the accident victims brought more than 100 actions in the District Court for the District of Massachusetts and more than 40 actions in the District Court for the Eastern District of Pennsylvania. When the defendants moved to transfer the actions brought in Pennsylvania to the federal court in Massachusetts, a number of the Pennsylvania plaintiffs objected because they lacked capacity under Massachusetts law to sue as representatives of the decedents. The plaintiffs also averred that the transfer would deprive them of the benefits of Pennsylvania's choice-of-law rules because the transferee forum would apply to their wrongful-death claims a different substantive rule. The plaintiffs obtained from the Court of Appeals a writ of mandamus ordering the District Court to vacate the transfer.

We reversed. After considering issues not related to the present dispute, we held that the Court of Appeals erred in its assumption that Massachusetts law would govern the action following transfer. The legislative history of § 1404(a) showed that Congress had enacted the statute because broad venue provisions in federal Acts often resulted in inconvenient forums and that Congress had decided to respond to this problem by permitting transfer to a convenient federal court under § 1404(a).

"This legislative background supports the view that § 1404(a) was not designed to narrow the plaintiff's venue privilege or to defeat the state-law advantages that might accrue from the exercise of this venue privilege but rather the provision was simply to counteract the inconveniences that flowed from the venue statutes by permitting transfer to a convenient federal court. The legislative history of § 1404(a) certainly does not justify the rather startling conclusion that one might 'get a change of a law as a bonus for a change of venue.' Indeed, an interpretation accepting such a rule would go far to frustrate the remedial purposes of § 1404(a). If a change in the law were in the offing, the parties might well regard the section primarily as a forum-shopping instrument. And, more importantly, courts would at least be reluctant to grant transfers, despite considerations of convenience, if to do so might conceivably prejudice the claim of a plaintiff who initially selected a permissible forum. We believe, therefore, that both the history and purposes of § 1404(a) indicate that it should be regarded as a federal judicial housekeeping measure, dealing with the placement of litigation in the federal courts and generally intended, on the basis of convenience and fairness, simply to authorize a change of courtrooms."

We thus held that the law applicable to a diversity case does not change upon a transfer initiated by a defendant.

## III (omitted)

### A

The policy that § 1404(a) should not deprive parties of state-law advantages, although perhaps discernible in the legislative history, has its real foundation in *Erie R. Co. v. Tompkins*. The *Erie* rule remains a vital expression of the federal system and the concomitant integrity of the separate States. We explained *Erie* in *Guaranty Trust Co. v. York*, 326 U.S. 99, 109(1945), as follows:

> In essence, the intent of the *Erie* decision was to insure that, in all cases where a federal court is exercising jurisdiction solely because of the diversity of citizenship of the parties, the outcome of the litigation in the federal court should be substantially the same, so far as legal rules determine the outcome of a litigation, as it would be if tried in a State court.

The nub of the policy that underlies *Erie R. Co. v. Tompkins* is that for the same transaction the accident of a suit by a non-resident litigant in a federal court instead of in a State court a block away should not lead to a substantially different result.

In *Hanna v. Plumer*, (1965), we held that Congress has the power to prescribe procedural rules that differ from state-law rules even at the expense of altering the outcome of litigation. This case does not involve a conflict.

The *Erie* policy had a clear implication for *Van Dusen*. The existence of diversity jurisdiction gave the defendants the opportunity to make a motion to transfer venue under § 1404(a), and if the applicable law were to change after transfer, the plaintiff's venue privilege and resulting state-law advantages could be defeated at the defendant's option. To allow the transfer and at the same time preserve the plaintiff's state-law advantages, we held that the choice-of-law rules should not change following a transfer initiated by a defendant.

Transfers initiated by a plaintiff involve some different considerations, but lead to the same result. Applying the transferor law, of course, will not deprive the plaintiff of any state-law advantages. A defendant, in one sense, also will lose no legal advantage if the transferor law controls after a transfer initiated by the plaintiff; the same law, after all, would have applied if the plaintiff had not made the motion. In another sense, however, a defendant may lose a nonlegal advantage. Deere, for example, would lose whatever advantage inheres in not having to litigate in Pennsylvania, or, put another way, in forcing the Ferenses to litigate in Mississippi or not at all.

We, nonetheless, find the advantage that the defendant loses slight. A plaintiff always can sue in the favorable state court or sue in diversity and not seek a transfer. By asking for application of the Mississippi statute of limitations following a transfer to Pennsylvania on grounds of convenience, the Ferenses are seeking to deprive Deere only of the advantage of using against them the inconvenience of litigating in Mississippi. The text of § 1404(a) may not say anything about choice of law, but we think it not the purpose of the section to protect a party's ability to use inconvenience as a shield to discourage or hinder litigation otherwise proper. The section exists to eliminate inconvenience without altering permissible choices under the venue statutes. This interpretation should come as little surprise. As in our previous cases, we think that "to construe § 1404(a) this way merely carries out its design, to protect litigants, witnesses and the public against unnecessary inconvenience and expense, not to provide a shelter for proceedings in costly and inconvenient forums." By creating an opportunity to have venue transferred between courts in different States on the basis of convenience, an option that does not exist absent federal jurisdiction, Congress, with respect to diversity, retained the *Erie* policy while diminishing the incidents of inconvenience.

Applying the transferee law, by contrast, would undermine the *Erie* rule in a serious way. It would mean that initiating a transfer under § 1404(a) changes the state law applicable to a diversity case. In general, we have seen § 1404(a) as a housekeeping measure that should not alter the state law governing a case under *Erie*. The Mississippi statute of limitations, which everyone agrees would have applied if the Ferenses had not moved for a transfer, should continue to apply in this case.

In any event, defendants in the position of Deere would not fare much better if we required application of the transferee law instead of the transferor law. True, if the transferee law were to apply, some plaintiffs would not sue these defendants for fear that they would have no choice but to litigate in an inconvenient forum. But applying the transferee law would not discourage all plaintiffs from suing. Some plaintiffs would prefer to litigate in an inconvenient forum with favorable law than to litigate in a convenient forum with unfavorable law or not to litigate at all. The Ferenses, no doubt, would have abided by their initial choice of the District Court in Mississippi had they known that the District Court in Pennsylvania would dismiss their action. If we were to rule for Deere in this case, we would accomplish little more than discouraging the occasional motions by plaintiffs to transfer inconvenient cases. Other plaintiffs would sue in an inconvenient forum with the expectation that the defendants themselves would seek transfer to a convenient forum, resulting in application of the transferor law under *Van Dusen*. In this case, for example, Deere might have moved for a transfer if the Ferenses had not.

B

*Van Dusen* also sought to fashion a rule that would not create opportunities for forum shopping. An opportunity for forum shopping exists whenever a party has a choice of forums that will apply different laws. The *Van Dusen* policy against forum shopping simply requires us to interpret § 1404(a) in a way that does not create an opportunity for obtaining a more favorable law by selecting a forum through a transfer of venue. In the *Van Dusen* case itself, this meant that we could not allow defendants to use a transfer to change the law.

No interpretation of § 1404(a), however, will create comparable opportunities for forum shopping by a plaintiff because, even without § 1404(a), a plaintiff already has the option of shopping for a forum with the most favorable law. The Ferenses, for example, had an opportunity for forum shopping in the state courts because both the Mississippi and Pennsylvania courts had jurisdiction and because they each would have applied a different statute of limitations. Diversity jurisdiction did not eliminate these forum shopping opportunities; instead, under *Erie,* the federal courts had to replicate them.

C

*Van Dusen* also made clear that the decision to transfer venue under § 1404(a) should turn on considerations of convenience rather than on the possibility of prejudice resulting from a change in the applicable law. We reasoned in *Van Dusen* that, if the law changed following a transfer initiated by the defendant, a district court "would at least be reluctant to grant transfers, despite considerations of convenience, if to do so might conceivably prejudice the claim of a plaintiff." The court, to determine the prejudice, might have to make an elaborate survey of the law, including statutes of limitations, burdens of proof, presumptions, and the like. This would turn what is supposed to be a statute for convenience of the courts into one expending extensive judicial time and resources. Because this difficult task is contrary to the purpose of the statute, in *Van Dusen* we made it unnecessary by ruling that a transfer of venue by the defendant does not result in a change of law. This same policy requires application of the transferor law when a plaintiff initiates a transfer.

If the law were to change following a transfer initiated by a plaintiff, a district court in a similar fashion would be at least reluctant to grant a transfer that would prejudice the defendant. Hardship might occur because plaintiffs may find as many opportunities to exploit application of the transferee law as they would find opportunities for exploiting application of the transferor law. If the transferee law were to apply, moreover, the plaintiff simply would not move to transfer unless the benefits of convenience outweighed the loss of favorable law.⏋

Some might think that a plaintiff should pay the price for choosing an inconvenient forum by being put to a choice of law versus forum. But this assumes that § 1404(a) is for the benefit only of the moving party. By the statute's own terms, it is not. Section 1404(a) also exists for the benefit of the witnesses and the interest of justice, which must include the convenience of the court. Litigation in an inconvenient forum does not harm the plaintiff alone. As Justice Jackson said:

> "Administrative difficulties follow for courts when litigation is piled up in congested centers instead of being handled at its origin. Jury duty is a burden that ought not to be imposed upon the people of a community which has no relation to the litigation. In cases which touch the affairs of many persons, there is reason for holding the trial in their view and reach rather than in remote parts of the country where they can learn of it by report only. There is a local interest in having localized controversies decided at home. There is an appropriateness too, in having the trial of a diversity case in a forum that is at home with the state law that must govern the case, rather than having a court in some other forum untangle problems in conflicts of laws, and in law foreign to itself." *Gulf Oil Corp. v. Gilbert* (1947).

The desire to take a punitive view of the plaintiff's actions should not obscure the systemic costs of litigating in an inconvenient place.

## IV

Some may object that a district court in Pennsylvania should not have to apply a Mississippi statute of limitations to a Pennsylvania cause of action. This point, although understandable, should have little to do with the outcome of this case. Congress gave the Ferenses the power to seek a transfer in § 1404(a), and our decision in *Van Dusen* already could require a district court in Pennsylvania to apply the Mississippi statute of limitations to Pennsylvania claims. Our rule may seem too generous because it allows the Ferenses to have both their choice of law and their choice of forum, or even to reward the Ferenses for conduct that seems manipulative. We nonetheless see no alternative rule that would produce a more acceptable result. Deciding that the transferee law should apply, in effect, would tell the Ferenses that they should have continued to litigate their warranty action in Pennsylvania and their tort action in Mississippi. Some might find this preferable, but we do not. We have made quite clear that "to permit a situation in which two cases involving precisely the same issues are simultaneously pending in different District Courts leads to the wastefulness of time, energy and money that § 1404(a) was designed to prevent."

From a substantive standpoint, two further objections give us pause but do not persuade us to change our rule. First, one might ask why we require the Ferenses to file in the District Court in Mississippi at all. Efficiency might seem to dictate a rule allowing plaintiffs in the Ferenses' position not to file in an inconvenient forum and then to return to a convenient forum though a transfer of venue, but instead simply to file in the convenient forum and ask for the law of the inconvenient forum to apply. Although our rule may invoke certain formality, one must remember that § 1404(a) does not provide for an automatic transfer of venue. The section, instead, permits a transfer only when convenient and "in the interest of justice." Plaintiffs in the position of the Ferenses must go to the distant forum because they have no guarantee, until the court there examines the facts, that they may obtain a transfer. No one has contested the justice of transferring this particular case, but the option remains open to defendants in future cases. Although a court cannot ignore the systemic costs of inconvenience, it may consider the course that the litigation already has taken in determining the interest of justice.

Second, one might contend that, because no *per se* rule requiring a court to apply either the transferor law or the transferee law will seem appropriate in all circumstances, we should develop more sophisticated federal choice-of-law rules for diversity actions involving transfers. To a large extent, however, state conflicts-of-law rules already ensure that appropriate laws will apply to diversity cases. Federal law, as a general matter, does not interfere with these rules. In addition, even if more elaborate federal choice-of-law rules would not run afoul of *Klaxon* and *Erie,* we believe that applying the law of the transferor forum effects the appropriate balance between fairness and simplicity.

For the foregoing reasons, we conclude that Mississippi's statute of limitations should govern the Ferenses' action. We reverse and remand for proceedings consistent with this opinion.

# C. FORUM NON CONVENIENS

4. The doctrine of forum non conveniens, (forum is not convenient), is another way a court can get rid of a case over which it technically has jurisdiction. Even though there is jurisdiction for a court to hear a particular case, it may be clear that the location selected by the plaintiff is simply an inappropriate place for trial – from a practical point of view. So the court is allowed to decline to exercise jurisdiction on the basis of forum non conveniens.

Within the federal court system, 28 USC 1404 now allows the original court to transfer the case to a more appropriate federal court. Before 28 USC 1404 was enacted, courts could use the doctrine of forum non conveniens – as illustrated by the following case. This case still sets the standard for the factors to be considered with forum non conveniens.

67 S. CT. 839
SUPREME COURT OF THE UNITED STATES
GULF OIL CORPORATION
V.
GILBERT.

DECIDED MARCH 10, 1947

Mr. Justice JACKSON delivered the opinion of the Court.

The questions are whether the United States District Court has inherent power to dismiss a suit pursuant to the doctrine of forum non conveniens and, if so, whether that power was abused in this case.

The plaintiff brought this action in the Southern District of New York, but resides at Lynchburg, Virginia, where he operated a public warehouse. He alleges that the defendant, in violation of the ordinances of Lynchburg, so carelessly handled a delivery of gasoline to his warehouse tanks and pumps as to cause an explosion and fire which consumed the warehouse building to his damage of $41,889.10, destroyed merchandise and fixtures to his damage of $3,602.40, caused injury to his business and profits of $20,038.27, and burned the property of customers in his custody under warehousing agreements to the extent of $300,000. He asks judgment of $365,529.77 with costs and disbursements, and interest from the date of fire. The action clearly is one in tort.

The defendant is a corporation organized under the laws of Pennsylvania, qualified to do business in both Virginia and New York, and it has designated officials of each state as agents to receive service of process. When sued in New York, the defendant, invoking the doctrine of forum non conveniens, claimed that the appropriate place for trial is Virginia where the plaintiff lives and defendant does business, where all events in litigation took place, where most of the witnesses reside, and where both state and federal courts are available to plaintiff and are able to obtain jurisdiction of the defendant.

The case, on its merits, involves no federal question and was brought in the United States District Court solely because of diversity in citizenship of the parties. Because of the character of its jurisdiction and the holdings of and under Erie Railroad Co. v. Tompkins, the District Court considered that the law of New York as to forum non conveniens applied and that it required the case to be left to Virginia courts. It therefore dismissed.

The Circuit Court of Appeals disagreed ...

## I.

It is conceded that the venue statutes of the United States permitted the plaintiff to commence his action in the Southern District of New York and empower that court to entertain it. But that does not settle the question whether it must do so. Indeed the doctrine of forum non conveniens can never apply if there is absence of jurisdiction or mistake of venue.

This Court, in one form of words or another, has repeatedly recognized the existence of the power to decline jurisdiction in exceptional circumstances. As formulated by Mr. Justice Brandeis the rule is: 'Obviously, the proposition that a court having jurisdiction must exercise it, is not universally true; else the admiralty court could never decline jurisdiction on the ground that the litigation is between foreigners. Nor is it true of courts administering other systems of our law. Courts of equity and of law also occasionally decline, in the interest of justice, to exercise jurisdiction, where the suit is between aliens or nonresidents, or where for kindred reasons the litigation can more appropriately be conducted in a foreign tribunal.'

We later expressly said that a state court 'may in appropriate cases apply the doctrine of forum non conveniens.' Even where federal rights binding on state courts under the Constitution are sought to be adjudged, this Court has sustained state courts in a refusal to entertain a litigation between a nonresident and a foreign corporation or between two foreign corporations. It has held the use of an inappropriate forum in one case an unconstitutional burden on interstate commerce. On substantially forum non conveniens grounds we have required federal courts to relinquish decision of cases within their jurisdiction where the court would have to participate in the administrative policy of a state.

## II

The principle of forum non conveniens is simply that a court may resist imposition upon its jurisdiction even when jurisdiction is authorized by the letter of a general venue statute. These statutes are drawn with a necessary generality and usually give a plaintiff a choice of courts, so that he may be quite sure of some place in which to pursue his remedy. But the open door may admit those who seek not simply justice but perhaps justice blended with some harassment. A plaintiff sometimes is under temptation to resort to a strategy of forcing the trial at a most inconvenient place for an adversary, even at some inconvenience to himself.

Many of the states have met misuse of venue by investing courts with a discretion to change the place of trial on various grounds, such as the convenience of witnesses and the ends of justice. The federal law contains no such express criteria to guide the district court in exercising its power. But the problem is a very old one affecting the administration of the courts as well as the rights of litigants, and both in England and in this country the common law worked out techniques and criteria for dealing with it.

Wisely, it has not been attempted to catalogue the circumstances which will justify or require either grant or denial of remedy. The doctrine leaves much to the discretion of the court to which plaintiff resorts, and experience has not shown a judicial tendency to renounce one's own jurisdiction so strong as to result in many abuses.

If the combination and weight of factors requisite to given results are difficult to forecast or state, those to be considered are not difficult to name. An interest to be considered, and the one likely to be most pressed, is the private interest of the litigant. Important considerations are the relative ease of access to sources of proof; availability of compulsory process for attendance of unwilling, and the cost of obtaining attendance of willing, witnesses; possibility of view of premises, if view would be appropriate to the action; and all other practical problems that make trial of a case easy, expeditious and inexpensive. There may also be questions as to the enforceability of a judgment if one is obtained. The court will weigh relative advantages and obstacles to fair trial. It is often said that the plaintiff may not, by choice of an inconvenient forum, 'vex,' 'harass,' or 'oppress' the defendant by inflicting upon him expense or trouble not necessary to his own right to pursue his remedy. But unless the balance is strongly in favor of the defendant, the plaintiff's choice of forum should rarely be disturbed.

Factors of public interest also have place in applying the doctrine. Administrative difficulties follow for courts when litigation is piled up in congested centers instead of being handled at its origin. Jury duty is a burden that ought not to be imposed upon the people of a community which has no relation to the litigation. In cases which touch the affairs of many persons, there is reason for holding the trial in their view and reach rather than in remote parts of the country where they can learn of it by report only. There is a local interest in having localized controversies decided at home. There is an appropriateness, too, in having the trial of a diversity case in a forum that is at home with the state law that must govern the case, rather than having a court in some other forum untangle problems in conflict of laws, and in law foreign to itself.

The law of New York as to the discretion of a court to apply the doctrine of forum non conveniens, and as to the standards that guide discretion is, so far as here involved, the same as the federal rule. It would not be profitable, therefore, to pursue inquiry as to the source from which our rule must flow.

## III

Turning to the question whether this is one of those rather rare cases where the doctrine should be applied, we look first to the interests of the litigants.

The plaintiff himself is not a resident of New York, nor did any event connected with the case take place there, nor does any witness with the possible exception of experts live there. No one connected with that side of the case save counsel for the plaintiff resides there, and he has candidly told us that he was retained by insurance companies interested presumably because of subrogation. His affidavits and argument are devoted to controverting claims as to defendant's inconvenience rather than to showing that the present forum serves any convenience of his own, with one exception. The only justification for trial in New York advanced here is one rejected by the district court and is set forth in the brief as follows: 'This Court can readily realize that an action of this type, involving as it does a claim for damages in an amount close to $400,000, is one which may stagger the imagination of a local jury which is surely unaccustomed to dealing with amounts of such a nature. Furthermore, removed from Lynchburg, the respondent will have an opportunity to try this case free from local influences and preconceived notions which make it difficult to procure a jury which has no previous knowledge of any of the facts herein.'

This unproven premise that jurors of New York live on terms of intimacy with $400,000 transactions is not an assumption we easily make. Nor can we assume that a jury from Lynchburg and vicinity would be 'staggered' by contemplating the value of a warehouse building that stood in their region, or of merchandise and fixtures such as were used there, nor are they likely to be staggered by the value of chattels which the people of that neighborhood put in storage. It is a strange argument on behalf of a Virginia plaintiff that the community which gave him patronage to make his business valuable is not capable of furnishing jurors who know the value of the goods they store, the building they are stored in, or the business their patronage creates. And there is no specification of any local influence, other than accurate knowledge of local conditions, that would make a fair trial improbable. The net of this is that we cannot say the District Court was bound to entertain a provincial fear of the provincialism of a Virginia jury. That leaves the Virginia plaintiff without even a suggested reason for transporting this suit to New York.

Defendant points out that not only the plaintiff, but every person who participated in the acts charged to be negligent, resides in or near Lynchburg. It also claims a need to interplead an alleged independent contractor which made the delivery of the gasoline and which is a Virginia corporation domiciled in Lynchburg, that it cannot interplead in New York. There also are approximately 350 persons residing in and around Lynchburg who stored with plaintiff the goods for the damage to which he seeks to recover. The extent to which they have left the community since the fire and the number of them who will actually be needed is in dispute. The complaint alleges that defendant's conduct violated Lynchburg ordinances. Conditions are said to require proof by firemen and by many others. The learned and experienced trial judge was not unaware that litigants generally manage to try their cases with fewer witnesses than they predict in such motions as this. But he was justified in concluding that this trial is likely to be long and to involve calling many witnesses, and that Lynchburg, some 400 miles from New York, is the source of all proofs for either side with possible exception of experts. Certainly to fix the place of trial at a point where litigants cannot compel personal attendance and may be forced to try their cases on deposition, is to create a condition not satisfactory to court, jury or most litigants. Nor is it necessarily cured by the statement of plaintiff's counsel that he will see to getting many of the witnesses to the trial and that some of them 'would be delighted to come to New York to testify.' There may be circumstances where such a proposal should be given weight. In others the offer may not turn out to be as generous as defendant or court might suppose it to be. Such matters are for the District Court to decide in exercise of a sound discretion.

The court likewise could well have concluded that the task of the trial court would be simplified by trial in Virginia. If trial was in a state court, it could apply its own law to events occurring there. The course of adjudication in New York federal court might be beset with conflict of laws problems all avoided if the case is litigated in Virginia where it arose.

We are convinced that the District Court did not exceed its powers or the bounds of its discretion in dismissing plaintiff's complaint and remitting him to the courts of his own community. The Circuit Court of Appeals took too restrictive a view of the doctrine as approved by this Court. Its judgment is reversed.

Reversed.

5. Now that transfers within a court system are authorized, notice the skillful use of various techniques in the following case – ending with a declaration of forum non conveniens.

**102 S.CT. 252**
**SUPREME COURT OF THE UNITED STATES**
**PIPER AIRCRAFT COMPANY, PETITIONER,**
**V.**
**GAYNELL REYNO, PERSONAL REPRESENTATIVE OF THE**
**ESTATE OF WILLIAM FEHILLY,**
**ET AL.**
**HARTZELL PROPELLER, INC., PETITIONER,**
**V.**
**GAYNELL REYNO, PERSONAL REPRESENTATIVE OF THE**
**ESTATE OF WILLIAM FEHILLY,**
**ET AL.**

DECIDED DECEMBER 8, 1981

Justice MARSHALL delivered the opinion of the Court.

These cases arise out of an air crash that took place in Scotland. Respondent, acting as representative of the estates of several Scottish citizens killed in the accident, brought wrongful-death actions against petitioners that were ultimately transferred to the United States District Court for the Middle District of Pennsylvania. Petitioners moved to dismiss on the ground of *forum non conveniens*. After noting that an alternative forum existed in Scotland, the District Court granted their motions. The United States Court of Appeals for the Third Circuit reversed. The Court of Appeals based its decision, at least in part, on the ground that dismissal is automatically barred where the law of the alternative forum is less favorable to the plaintiff than the law of the forum chosen by the plaintiff. Because we conclude that the possibility of an unfavorable change in law should not, by itself, bar dismissal, and because we conclude that the District Court did not otherwise abuse its discretion, we reverse.

I

A

In July 1976, a small commercial aircraft crashed in the Scottish highlands during the course of a charter flight from Blackpool to Perth. The pilot and five passengers were killed instantly. The decedents were all Scottish subjects and residents, as are their heirs and next of kin. There were no eyewitnesses to the accident. At the time of the crash the plane was subject to Scottish air traffic control.

The aircraft, a twin-engine Piper Aztec, was manufactured in Pennsylvania by petitioner Piper Aircraft Co. (Piper). The propellers were manufactured in Ohio by petitioner Hartzell Propeller, Inc. (Hartzell). At the time of the crash the aircraft was registered in Great Britain and was owned and maintained by Air Navigation and Trading Co., Ltd. (Air Navigation). It was operated by McDonald Aviation, Ltd. (McDonald), a Scottish air taxi service. Both Air Navigation and McDonald were organized in the United Kingdom. The wreckage of the plane is now in a hangar in Farnsborough, England.

The British Department of Trade investigated the accident shortly after it occurred. A preliminary report found that the plane crashed after developing a spin, and suggested that mechanical failure in the plane or the propeller was responsible. At Hartzell's request, this report was reviewed by a three-member Review Board, which held a 9-day adversary hearing attended by all interested parties. The Review Board found no evidence of defective equipment and indicated that pilot error may have contributed to the accident. The pilot, who had obtained his commercial pilot's license only three months earlier, was flying over high ground at an altitude considerably lower than the minimum height required by his company's operations manual.

In July 1977, a California probate court appointed respondent Gaynell Reyno administratrix of the estates of the five passengers. Reyno is not related to and does not know any of the decedents or their survivors; she was a legal secretary to the attorney who filed this lawsuit. Several days after her appointment, Reyno commenced separate wrongful-death actions against Piper and Hartzell in the Superior Court of California, claiming negligence and strict liability. Air Navigation, McDonald, and the estate of the pilot are not parties to this litigation. The survivors of the five passengers whose estates are represented by Reyno filed a separate action in the United Kingdom against Air Navigation, McDonald, and the pilot's estate. Reyno candidly admits that the action against Piper and Hartzell was filed in the United States because its laws regarding liability, capacity to sue, and damages are more favorable to her position than are those of Scotland. Scottish law does not recognize strict liability in tort. Moreover, it permits wrongful-death actions only when brought by a decedent's relatives. The relatives may sue only for "loss of support and society."

On petitioners' motion, the suit was removed to the United States District Court for the Central District of California. Piper then moved for transfer to the United States District Court for the Middle District of Pennsylvania, pursuant to 28 U.S.C. § 1404(a). Hartzell moved to dismiss for lack of personal jurisdiction, or in the alternative, to transfer.[5] In December 1977, the District Court quashed service on Hartzell and transferred the case to the Middle District of Pennsylvania. Respondent then properly served process on Hartzell.

## B

In May 1978, after the suit had been transferred, both Hartzell and Piper moved to dismiss the action on the ground of *forum non conveniens*. The District Court granted these motions in October 1979. It relied on the balancing test set forth by this Court in *Gulf Oil Corp. v. Gilbert.*

The District Court concluded that the relevant public interests pointed strongly towards dismissal. The court determined that Pennsylvania law would apply to Piper and Scottish law to Hartzell if the case were tried in the Middle District of Pennsylvania. As a result, "trial in this forum would be hopelessly complex and confusing for a jury." In addition, the court noted that it was unfamiliar with Scottish law and thus would have to rely upon experts from that country. The court also found that the trial would be enormously costly and time-consuming; that it would be unfair to burden citizens with jury duty when the Middle District of Pennsylvania has little connection with the controversy; and that Scotland has a substantial interest in the outcome of the litigation.

## C.

On appeal, the United States Court of Appeals for the Third Circuit reversed and remanded for trial.

## II

The Court of Appeals erred in holding that plaintiffs may defeat a motion to dismiss on the ground of *forum non conveniens* merely by showing that the substantive law that would be applied in the alternative forum is less favorable to the plaintiffs than that of the present forum. The possibility of a change in substantive law should ordinarily not be given conclusive or even substantial weight in the *forum non conveniens* inquiry.

By holding that the central focus of the *forum non conveniens* inquiry is convenience, *Gilbert* implicitly recognized that dismissal may not be barred solely because of the possibility of an unfavorable change in law. Under *Gilbert*, dismissal will ordinarily be appropriate where trial in the plaintiff's chosen forum imposes a heavy burden on the defendant or the court, and where the plaintiff is unable to offer any specific reasons of convenience supporting his choice. If substantial weight were given to the possibility of an unfavorable change in law, however, dismissal might be barred even where trial in the chosen forum was plainly inconvenient.

This Court's earlier *forum non conveniens* decisions have repeatedly emphasized the need to retain flexibility. In *Gilbert*, the Court refused to identify specific circumstances "which will justify or require either grant or denial of remedy." Similarly, in *Koster*, the Court rejected the contention that where a trial would involve inquiry into the internal affairs of a foreign corporation, dismissal was always appropriate. "That is one, but only one, factor which may show convenience." And in *Williams v. Green Bay & Western R. Co.* we stated that we would not lay down a rigid rule to govern discretion, and that "each case turns on its facts." If central emphasis were placed on any one factor, the *forum non conveniens* doctrine would lose much of the very flexibility that makes it so valuable.

In fact, if conclusive or substantial weight were given to the possibility of a change in law, the *forum non conveniens* doctrine would become virtually useless. Jurisdiction and venue requirements are often easily satisfied. As a result, many plaintiffs are able to choose from among several forums. Ordinarily, these plaintiffs will select that forum whose choice-of-law rules are most advantageous. Thus, if the possibility of an unfavorable change in substantive law is given substantial weight in the *forum non conveniens* inquiry, dismissal would rarely be proper.

The Court of Appeals' approach also poses substantial practical problems. If the possibility of a change in law were given substantial weight, deciding motions to dismiss on the ground of *forum non conveniens* would become quite difficult. Choice-of-law analysis would become extremely important, and the courts would frequently be required to interpret the law of foreign jurisdictions. First, the trial court would have to determine what law would apply if the case were tried in the chosen forum, and what law would apply if the case were tried in the alternative forum. It would then have to compare the rights, remedies, and procedures available under the law that would be applied in each forum. Dismissal would be appropriate only if the court concluded that the law applied by the alternative forum is as favorable to the plaintiff as that of the chosen forum. The doctrine of *forum non conveniens*, however, is designed in part to help courts avoid conducting complex exercises in comparative law. As we stated in *Gilbert*, the public interest factors point towards dismissal where the court would be required to "untangle problems in conflict of laws, and in law foreign to itself."

Upholding the decision of the Court of Appeals would result in other practical problems. At least where the foreign plaintiff named an American manufacturer as defendant, [a court could not dismiss the case on grounds of *forum non conveniens* where dismissal might lead to an unfavorable change in law.] The American courts, which are already extremely attractive to foreign plaintiffs, would become even more attractive. The flow of litigation into the United States would increase and further congest already crowded courts.

The Court of Appeals based its decision, at least in part, on an analogy between dismissals on grounds of *forum non conveniens* and transfers between federal courts pursuant to § 1404(a). However, § 1404(a) transfers are different than dismissals on the ground of *forum non conveniens*.

Congress enacted § 1404(a) to permit change of venue between federal courts. Although the statute was drafted in accordance with the doctrine of *forum non conveniens*, it was intended to be a revision rather than a codification of the common law. District courts were given more discretion to transfer under § 1404(a) than they had to dismiss on grounds of *forum non conveniens*.

We do not hold that the possibility of an unfavorable change in law should *never* be a relevant consideration in a *forum non conveniens* inquiry. Of course, if the remedy provided by the alternative forum is so clearly inadequate or unsatisfactory that it is no remedy at all, the unfavorable change in law may be given substantial weight; the district court may conclude that dismissal would not be in the interests of justice. In these cases, however, the remedies that would be provided by the Scottish courts do not fall within this category. Although the relatives of the decedents may not be able to rely on a strict liability theory, and although their potential damages award may be smaller, there is no danger that they will be deprived of any remedy or treated unfairly.

## III

We do not believe that the District Court abused its discretion in weighing the private and public interests.

## A

The District Court acknowledged that there is ordinarily a strong presumption in favor of the plaintiff's choice of forum, which may be overcome only when the private and public interest factors clearly point towards trial in the alternative forum. It held, however, that the presumption applies with less force when the plaintiff or real parties in interest are foreign.

The District Court's distinction between resident or citizen plaintiffs and foreign plaintiffs is fully justified. In *Koster*, the Court indicated that a plaintiff's choice of forum is entitled to greater deference when the plaintiff has chosen the home forum. When the home forum has been chosen, it is reasonable to assume that this choice is convenient. When the plaintiff is foreign, however, this assumption is much less reasonable. Because the central purpose of any *forum non conveniens* inquiry is to ensure that the trial is convenient, a foreign plaintiff's choice deserves less deference.

B

The *forum non conveniens* determination is committed to the sound discretion of the trial court. It may be reversed only when there has been a clear abuse of discretion; where the court has considered all relevant public and private interest factors, and where its balancing of these factors is reasonable, its decision deserves substantial deference.

(1)

In analyzing the private interest factors, the District Court stated that the connections with Scotland are "overwhelming." This characterization may be somewhat exaggerated. Particularly with respect to the question of relative ease of access to sources of proof, the private interests point in both directions. As respondent emphasizes, records concerning the design, manufacture, and testing of the propeller and plane are located in the United States. She would have greater access to sources of proof relevant to her strict liability and negligence theories if trial were held here. However, the District Court did not act unreasonably in concluding that fewer evidentiary problems would be posed if the trial were held in Scotland. A large proportion of the relevant evidence is located in Great Britain.

The Court of Appeals found that the problems of proof could not be given any weight because Piper and Hartzell failed to describe with specificity the evidence they would not be able to obtain if trial were held in the United States. It suggested that defendants seeking *forum non conveniens* dismissal must submit affidavits identifying the witnesses they would call and the testimony these witnesses would provide if the trial were held in the alternative forum. Such detail is not necessary. Piper and Hartzell have moved for dismissal precisely because many crucial witnesses are located beyond the reach of compulsory process, and thus are difficult to identify or interview. Requiring extensive investigation would defeat the purpose of their motion. Of course, defendants must provide enough information to enable the District Court to balance the parties' interests. Our examination of the record convinces us that sufficient information was provided here. Both Piper and Hartzell submitted affidavits describing the evidentiary problems they would face if the trial were held in the United States.

The District Court correctly concluded that the problems posed by the inability to implead potential third-party defendants clearly supported holding the trial in Scotland. Joinder of the pilot's estate, Air Navigation, and McDonald is crucial to the presentation of petitioners' defense. If Piper and Hartzell can show that the accident was caused not by a design defect, but rather by the negligence of the pilot, the plane's owners, or the charter company, they will be relieved of all liability. It is true, of course, that if Hartzell and Piper were found liable after a trial in the United States, they could institute an action for indemnity or contribution against these parties in Scotland. It would be far more convenient, however, to resolve all claims in one trial. Finding that trial in the plaintiff's chosen forum would be burdensome is sufficient to support dismissal on grounds of *forum non conveniens*.

(2)

The District Court's review of the factors relating to the public interest was also reasonable. On the basis of its choice-of-law analysis, it concluded that if the case were tried in the Middle District of Pennsylvania, Pennsylvania law would apply to Piper and Scottish law to Hartzell. It stated that a trial involving two sets of laws would be confusing to the jury. It also noted its own lack of familiarity with Scottish law. Consideration of these problems was clearly appropriate under *Gilbert*; in that case we explicitly held that the need to apply foreign law pointed towards dismissal. The Court of Appeals found that the District Court's choice-of-law analysis was incorrect, and that American law would apply to both Hartzell and Piper. Thus, lack of familiarity with foreign law would not be a problem. Even if the Court of Appeals' conclusion is correct, however, all other public interest factors favored trial in Scotland.

Scotland has a very strong interest in this litigation. The accident occurred in its airspace. All of the decedents were Scottish. Apart from Piper and Hartzell, all potential plaintiffs and defendants are either Scottish or English. As we stated in *Gilbert*, there is "a local interest in having localized controversies decided at home." Respondent argues that American citizens have an interest in ensuring that American manufacturers are deterred from producing defective products, and that additional deterrence might be obtained if Piper and Hartzell were tried in the United States, where they could be sued on the basis of both negligence and strict liability. However, the incremental deterrence that would be gained if this trial were held in an American court is likely to be insignificant. The American interest in this accident is simply not sufficient to justify the enormous commitment of judicial time and resources that would inevitably be required if the case were to be tried here.

## IV

The Court of Appeals erred in holding that the possibility of an unfavorable change in law bars dismissal on the ground of *forum non conveniens*. It also erred in rejecting the District Court's *Gilbert* analysis. The District Court properly decided that the presumption in favor of the respondent's forum choice applied with less than maximum force because the real parties in interest are foreign. It did not act unreasonably in deciding that the private interests pointed towards trial in Scotland. Nor did it act unreasonably in deciding that the public interests favored trial in Scotland. Thus, the judgment of the Court of Appeals is Reversed.

6. Forum non conveniens is now particularly useful in the international arena when the litigation is primarily between corporations, neither of whom may have particularly strong ties to the U.S., as illustrated by the following case.

## 127 S. CT. 1184
## SUPREME COURT OF THE UNITED STATES
## SINOCHEM INTERNATIONAL CO. LTD., PETITIONER,
## V.
## MALAYSIA INTERNATIONAL SHIPPING CORP., RESPONDENT

DECIDED MARCH 5, 2007

**Justice GINSBURG delivered the opinion for a unanimous Court.**

This case concerns the doctrine of *forum non conveniens,* under which a federal district court may dismiss an action on the ground that a court abroad is the more appropriate and convenient forum for adjudicating the controversy. We granted review to decide a question that has divided the Courts of Appeals: "whether a district court must first conclusively establish its own jurisdiction before dismissing a suit on the ground of *forum non conveniens?*" We hold that a district court has discretion to respond at once to a defendant's *forum non conveniens* plea, and need not take up first any other threshold objection. In particular, a court need not resolve whether it has authority to adjudicate the cause (subject-matter jurisdiction) or personal jurisdiction over the defendant if it determines that, in any event, a foreign tribunal is plainly the more suitable arbiter of the merits of the case.

# I

The underlying controversy concerns alleged misrepresentations by a Chinese corporation to a Chinese admiralty court resulting in the arrest of a Malaysian vessel in China. In 2003, petitioner Sinochem International Company Ltd. (Sinochem), a Chinese state-owned importer, contracted with Triorient Trading, Inc. (Triorient), a domestic corporation that is not a party to this suit, to purchase steel coils.

Triorient subchartered a vessel owned by respondent Malaysia International Shipping Corporation (Malaysia International), a Malaysian company, to transport the coils to China. Triorient then hired a stevedoring company to load the steel coils at the Port of Philadelphia.

On June 8, 2003, Sinochem petitioned the Guangzhou Admiralty Court in China for interim relief, *i.e.*, preservation of a maritime claim against Malaysia International and arrest of the vessel that carried the steel coils to China. In support of its petition, Sinochem alleged that the Malaysian company had falsely backdated the bill of lading. The Chinese tribunal ordered the ship arrested the same day.

Thereafter, on July 2, 2003, Sinochem timely filed a complaint against Malaysia International and others in the Guangzhou Admiralty Court. Sinochem's complaint repeated the allegation that the bill of lading had been falsified resulting in unwarranted payment. Malaysia International contested the jurisdiction of the Chinese tribunal. The admiralty court rejected Malaysia International's jurisdictional objection, and that ruling was affirmed on appeal by the Guangdong Higher People's Court.

On June 23, 2003, shortly after the Chinese court ordered the vessel's arrest, Malaysia International filed the instant action against Sinochem in the United States District Court for the Eastern District of Pennsylvania. Malaysia International asserted in its federal court pleading that Sinochem's preservation petition to the Guangzhou court negligently misrepresented the "vessel's fitness and suitability to load its cargo." As relief, Malaysia International sought compensation for the loss it sustained due to the delay caused by the ship's arrest. Sinochem moved to dismiss the suit on several grounds, including lack of subject-matter jurisdiction, lack of personal jurisdiction, *forum non conveniens,* and international comity.

The District Court first determined that it had subject-matter jurisdiction under 28 U.S.C. § 1333(1) (admiralty or maritime jurisdiction). The court next concluded that it lacked personal jurisdiction over Sinochem under Pennsylvania's long-arm statute. Nevertheless, the court conjectured, limited discovery might reveal that Sinochem's national contacts sufficed to establish personal jurisdiction under Federal Rule of Civil Procedure 4(k)(2). The court did not permit such discovery, however, because it determined that the case could be adjudicated adequately and more conveniently in the Chinese courts. No significant interests of the United States were involved, the court observed, and while the cargo had been loaded in Philadelphia, the nub of the controversy was entirely foreign: The dispute centered on the arrest of a foreign ship in foreign waters pursuant to the order of a foreign court. Given the proceedings ongoing in China, and the absence of cause "to second-guess the authority of Chinese law or the competence of Chinese courts," the District Court granted the motion to dismiss under the doctrine of *forum non conveniens.*

A panel of the Court of Appeals for the Third Circuit agreed there was subject-matter jurisdiction under § 1333(1), and that the question of personal jurisdiction could not be resolved *sans* discovery. Although the court determined that *forum non conveniens* is a nonmerits ground for dismissal, the majority nevertheless held that the District Court could not dismiss the case under the *forum non conveniens* doctrine unless and until it determined definitively that it had both subject-matter jurisdiction over the cause and personal jurisdiction over the defendant.

We granted certiorari, to resolve a conflict among the Circuits on whether *forum non conveniens* can be decided prior to matters of jurisdiction. Satisfied that *forum non conveniens* may justify dismissal of an action though jurisdictional issues remain unresolved, we reverse the Third Circuit's judgment.

## II

A federal court has discretion to dismiss a case on the ground of *forum non conveniens* "when an alternative forum has jurisdiction to hear the case, and ... trial in the chosen forum would establish ... oppressiveness and vexation to a defendant ... out of all proportion to plaintiff's convenience, or ... the chosen forum is inappropriate because of considerations affecting the court's own administrative and legal problems." (quoting *Piper Aircraft Co. v. Reyno).*

Dismissal for *forum non conveniens* reflects a court's assessment of a "range of considerations, most notably the convenience to the parties and the practical difficulties

that can attend the adjudication of a dispute in a certain locality." We have characterized *forum non conveniens* as, essentially, "a supervening venue provision, permitting
displacement of the ordinary rules of venue when, in light of certain conditions, the
trial court thinks that jurisdiction ought to be declined."

The common-law doctrine of *forum non conveniens* "has continuing application in
federal courts only in cases where the alternative forum is abroad," and perhaps in
rare instances where a state or territorial court serves litigational convenience best.
For the federal court system, Congress has codified the doctrine and has provided
for transfer, rather than dismissal, when a sister federal court is the more convenient
place for trial of the action. See 28 U.S.C. § 1404(a) ("For the convenience of parties
and witnesses, in the interest of justice, a district court may transfer any civil action
to any other district or division where it might have been brought.

A defendant invoking *forum non conveniens* ordinarily bears a heavy burden in
opposing the plaintiff's chosen forum. When the plaintiff's choice is not its home
forum, however, the presumption in the plaintiff's favor "applies with less force," for
the assumption that the chosen forum is appropriate is in such cases "less reasonable." *Piper Aircraft Co.*

## III

*Steel Co. v. Citizens for Better Environment*, 523 U.S. 83 (1998), clarified that a federal
court generally may not rule on the merits of a case without first determining that
it has jurisdiction over the category of claim in suit (subject-matter jurisdiction) and
the parties (personal jurisdiction). "Without jurisdiction the court cannot proceed
at all in any cause"; it may not assume jurisdiction for the purpose of deciding the
merits of the case.

While *Steel Co.* confirmed that jurisdictional questions ordinarily must precede
merits determinations in dispositional order, *Ruhrgas* held that there is no mandatory
"sequencing of jurisdictional issues." In appropriate circumstances, *Ruhrgas* decided,
a court may dismiss for lack of personal jurisdiction without first establishing subject-matter jurisdiction.

Both *Steel Co.* and *Ruhrgas* recognized that a federal court has leeway "to choose
among threshold grounds for denying audience to a case on the merits." Dismissal
short of reaching the merits means that the court will not "proceed at all" to an adjudication of the cause. Thus, a federal district court declining to adjudicate state-law
claims on discretionary grounds need not first determine whether those claims fall
within its pendent jurisdiction. Nor must a federal court decide whether the parties present an Article III case or controversy before abstaining under *Younger v.*

*Harris* (1971). The principle underlying these decisions was well stated by the Seventh Circuit: "Jurisdiction is vital only if the court proposes to issue a judgment on the merits."

## IV

A *forum non conveniens* dismissal denies audience to a case on the merits. It is a determination that the merits should be adjudicated elsewhere.

Of course a court may need to identify the claims presented and the evidence relevant to adjudicating those issues to intelligently rule on a *forum non conveniens* motion. Resolving a *forum non conveniens* motion does not entail any assumption by the court of substantive "law-declaring power."

Statements in this Court's opinion in *Gulf Oil Corp. v. Gilbert (1947)* account in large part for the Third Circuit's conclusion that *forum non conveniens* can come into play only after a domestic court determines that it has jurisdiction over the cause and the parties and is a proper venue for the action. The Court said in *Gulf Oil* that "the doctrine of *forum non conveniens* can never apply if there is absence of jurisdiction," and that "in all cases in which ... *forum non conveniens* comes into play, it presupposes at least two forums in which the defendant is amenable to process."

Those statements from *Gulf Oil*, perhaps less than "felicitously" crafted, draw their meaning from the context in which they were embedded. The question presented in *Gulf Oil* was whether a court fully competent to adjudicate the case, *i.e.*, one that plainly had jurisdiction over the cause and the parties and was a proper venue, could nevertheless dismiss the action under the *forum non conveniens* doctrine. The Court answered that question "yes."

As to the first statement—that "*forum non conveniens* can never apply if there is absence of jurisdiction"—it is of course true that once a court determines that jurisdiction is lacking, it can proceed no further and must dismiss the case on that account. In that scenario "*forum non conveniens* can never apply."

The second statement—that *forum non conveniens* "presupposes at least two forums" with authority to adjudicate the case—said nothing that would negate a court's authority to presume, rather than dispositively decide, the propriety of the forum in which the plaintiff filed suit.

In sum, *Gulf Oil* did not present the question we here address: whether a federal court can dismiss under the *forum non conveniens* doctrine before definitively ascertaining its own jurisdiction. Confining the statements we have quoted to the setting in which they were made, we find in *Gulf Oil* no hindrance to the decision we reach today.

The Third Circuit expressed the further concern that a court failing first to establish its jurisdiction could not condition a *forum non conveniens* dismissal on the defendant's waiver of any statute of limitations defense or objection to the foreign forum's jurisdiction. Unable so to condition a dismissal, the Court of Appeals feared, a court could not shield the plaintiff against a foreign tribunal's refusal to entertain the suit. Here, however, Malaysia International faces no genuine risk that the more convenient forum will not take up the case. Proceedings to resolve the parties' dispute are underway in China, with Sinochem as the plaintiff. Jurisdiction of the Guangzhou Admiralty Court has been raised, determined, and affirmed on appeal. We therefore need not decide whether a court conditioning a *forum non conveniens* dismissal on the waiver of jurisdictional or limitations defenses in the foreign forum must first determine its own authority to adjudicate the case.

## V

This is a textbook case for immediate *forum non conveniens* dismissal. The District Court's subject-matter jurisdiction presented an issue of first impression in the Third Circuit, and was considered at some length by the courts below. Discovery concerning personal jurisdiction would have burdened Sinochem with expense and delay. And all to scant purpose: The District Court inevitably would dismiss the case without reaching the merits, given its well-considered *forum non conveniens* appraisal. Judicial economy is disserved by continuing litigation in the Eastern District of Pennsylvania given the proceedings long launched in China. And the gravamen of Malaysia International's complaint—misrepresentations to the Guangzhou Admiralty Court in the course of securing arrest of the vessel in China—is an issue best left for determination by the Chinese courts.

If, however, a court can readily determine that it lacks jurisdiction over the cause or the defendant, the proper course would be to dismiss on that ground. In the mine run of cases, jurisdiction "will involve no arduous inquiry" and both judicial economy and the consideration ordinarily accorded the plaintiff's choice of forum "should impel the federal court to dispose of those issues first." But where subject-matter or personal jurisdiction is difficult to determine, and *forum non conveniens* considerations weigh heavily in favor of dismissal, the court properly takes the less burdensome course.

For the reasons stated, the judgment of the Court of Appeals is reversed, and the case is remanded for proceedings consistent with this opinion.

7. There are rules in both the state system and the federal system as to proper venue – the location in which a case should be brought when courts in several different areas would all have sufficient subject matter jurisdiction and personal jurisdiction to hear the case. The federal provision on venue, 28 USC 1391, includes fairly extensive details. Basically, in the federal system venue is proper in the district where the defendant resides, where the property is located, or where a substantial part of the events took place. A corporation is considered to be a *resident* wherever it has significant contacts.

Remember that under 28 USC 1332(c) a corporation is a *citizen* only of where it is incorporated, and where it has its principal place of business, (with some special rules for insurance companies). The fact that a corporation is usually a *citizen* of only two states makes it easier to get diversity jurisdiction over a corporation. The fact that a corporation is a *resident* essentially wherever it does business, makes it easier to find that *venue* is proper in a number of different places when a plaintiff brings suits against a corporation.

The majority of *venue* fights are probably within the state court systems. The following is an illustration of such a fight. What is it that makes Boulder so different from the rest of Colorado?

# D. CHANGE OF VENUE 28 USC 1391, 1404 AND SIMILAR STATE RULES

342 P.3D 427

SUPREME COURT OF COLORADO

IN RE DEANNA HAGAN AND SHANE HAGAN, PLAINTIFFS

V.

FARMERS INSURANCE EXCHANGE, DEFENDANT

IN RE CYNTHIA EWALD, PLAINTIFF

V.

FARMERS INSURANCE EXCHANGE, DEFENDANT

IN RE JAMES MAYFIELD, PLAINTIFF

V.

FARMERS INSURANCE EXCHANGE, DEFENDANT

JANUARY 26, 2015

JUSTICE HOOD delivered the Opinion of the Court.

These original proceedings involve plaintiffs who filed separate actions against the same defendant, Farmers Insurance Exchange ("Farmers"), in Boulder County District Court. In each case, Farmers moved to change venue under C.R.C.P. 98(f)(2), alleging that a change would promote "the convenience of witnesses and the ends of justice." Farmers supported its motions with attorney affidavits that purport to demonstrate—based on Google Maps printouts alone—that the transferee court is a more convenient venue for the plaintiffs and their medical treatment providers. The trial court granted the motions in all three cases.

The plaintiffs asked this court to issue a rule to show cause why the orders granting a change of venue should not be vacated and venue transferred back to Boulder County. Their petitions under C.A.R. 21 exposed an inconsistency in how judges within the same district have applied Rule 98. Recognizing the need to promote a uniform application of the venue rules, we issued our rules to show cause.

We now make our rules absolute. We hold that the trial courts abused their discretion when they changed the venue in these cases. First, Boulder County District Court is a proper venue for all three cases; under C.R.C.P. 98(c)(1), the plaintiffs were allowed to file their complaints in the county of their choice because Farmers is a nonresident defendant. Second, the trial courts granted the motions without the requisite evidentiary support. The affidavits that Farmers submitted improperly focus on convenience to the plaintiffs and do not satisfy the standard set forth in *Sampson v. District Court*, 197 Colo. 158 (1979). *Sampson* requires a party seeking to change venue under Rule 98(f)(2) to support the motion with evidence indicating "the identity of the witnesses, the nature, materiality and admissibility of their testimony, and how the witnesses would be better accommodated by the requested change in venue." Consequently, we direct the transferee courts to return the cases to Boulder County District Court.

## I. Facts and Procedural History

### A. Hagan and Ewald

In 2011, Deanna Hagan (a driver) and her mother-in-law, Cynthia Ewald (her passenger), were involved in a car accident in Weld County. A third party, Abdi Abdullahi, allegedly collided with them after running a red light. Both Hagan and Ewald were hurt in the collision and received medical treatment for their injuries. Hagan asserts that she incurred over $11,000 in medical expenses and lost income because of her injuries. Ewald asserts that she incurred almost $68,000 in medical expenses and also lost income because of her injuries.

Hagan and Ewald were insured by Farmers and had underinsured motorist ("UIM") coverage up to $250,000 and medical payments coverage up to $25,000. Abdullahi was insured by Young America Insurance, with a policy limit of $25,000. Young America paid Ewald $25,000 to settle her claim. It paid Hagan $15,000 to settle her claim and held $10,000 in reserve for additional exposure. Hagan and Ewald contend that they also were entitled to UIM benefits, which Farmers has refused to pay.

Represented by the same counsel, Hagan (together with her husband) and Ewald filed separate lawsuits against Farmers in Boulder County District Court on the same day. The lawsuits asserted claims for breach of contract, bad faith breach of insurance contract, and improper denial of insurance claims in violation of sections 10–3–1115(1)(a) and 10–3–1116(1), C.R.S. (2014).

In both cases, Farmers filed a motion to change the venue to Arapahoe County District Court under Rule 98(f)(2), emphasizing that "no potential witnesses have any connection to Boulder County." Farmers supported its motions with affidavits by its attorney, which contained Google Maps printouts and estimated distances and travel times for the plaintiffs and their potential witnesses.

The trial courts granted Farmers' motions to change venue. The trial court in Ewald's case ruled first. It determined that Boulder County was not a proper venue. Then, noting that Ewald's medical treatment providers were "substantially closer" to the transferee court, it concluded that "a change in venue would promote the convenience of witnesses and the ends of justice." Relying on the order in *Ewald,* the trial court in the Hagans' case followed suit.

## B. Mayfield

In 2012, James Mayfield was involved in a car accident in El Paso County with an underinsured motorist, Mark Merriman, who allegedly failed to stop at a traffic light. Mayfield was hurt in the collision and received medical treatment for his injuries. He asserts that he incurred over $73,000 in medical expenses, had to drop out of school, and suffered a loss of earning capacity and substantial non-economic losses.

Mayfield was insured by Farmers and had UIM coverage up to $100,000. Merriman was insured by GEICO, with liability coverage up to $100,000. Mayfield filed a lawsuit against Merriman and settled it for $95,000. Claiming that his damages far exceeded $100,000, Mayfield then sought UIM benefits from Farmers. Farmers offered him $15,000 and refused to pay more.

Represented by different counsel than the Hagans and Ewald, Mayfield filed a lawsuit against Farmers in Boulder County District Court. In response to a motion to change venue, Mayfield's counsel filed an affidavit in which he stated that "the reason that Plaintiff's Complaint was filed in Boulder was that Colorado's new Civil Access Pilot Project rules (CAPP) are not applicable in Boulder County District Court" and that he and his co-counsel "do not feel that this would be a good case to litigate under the CAPP rules." Mayfield asserted claims for breach of contract and improper denial of insurance claims in violation of sections 10–3–1115(1)(a) and 10–3–1116(1). Mayfield's case was assigned to the same trial judge as the Hagans' case.

Represented by the same defense counsel, Farmers filed a motion to change the venue to El Paso County District Court under Rule 98(f)(2), again emphasizing that "no potential witnesses have any connection to Boulder County." Farmers once more supported its motion with an attorney affidavit with attached Google Maps printouts and estimated distances and travel times for the plaintiff and his potential witnesses. The trial court granted the motion.

## II. Original Jurisdiction

Under C.A.R. 21, this court may exercise its original jurisdiction to review the trial courts' orders because they relate to venue. Venue refers to the place of trial or "the locality where an action may be properly brought." Review is appropriate under C.A.R. 21 because "issues involving venue directly affect the trial court's jurisdiction and authority to proceed with a case." Further, review of a venue determination serves to avoid the delay and expense involved in a re-trial should this court deem venue improper.

## III. Analysis

Generally, a plaintiff is entitled to choose the place of trial when venue in more than one county would be proper. The plaintiffs, absent C.R.C.P. 98(f)(2) concerns, are entitled to their choice of venue.") There is a "strong presumption" in favor of that choice.

The party seeking a change of venue bears the burden of proving the right to a change. A court may change the place of trial "on good cause shown" under two circumstances: "(1) When the county designated in the complaint is not the proper county; (2) When the convenience of witnesses and the ends of justice would be promoted by the change." C.R.C.P. 98(f). A trial court's decision on a motion to change venue is reviewed for an abuse of discretion. If the trial court grants a motion to change venue despite a defendant's failure to show that venue should be changed under the standard delineated in *Sampson,* this court will return the action to the original venue for trial.

To assess whether the trial courts abused their discretion in granting Farmers' requests for a change of venue, we ask two questions. First, was venue in Boulder County District Court proper? The answer to this question is yes. Second, can a defendant seeking a change of venue under Rule 98(f)(2) based on witness convenience and the ends of justice satisfy its burden by submitting an affidavit that focuses on the proximity of the respective venues to the plaintiff and the plaintiff's possible witnesses? The answer to this question is no.

### A. Rule 98(f)(1)

We first assess whether Boulder County is a "proper county" for these cases for purposes of Rule 98(f)(1) and conclude that it is.

Our inquiry begins with the language of Rule 98(c), which presents a series of alternative, and equally appropriate, venues in a tort, contract, or other action. At issue here, subsection (1) provides:

> An action shall be tried in the county in which the defendants, or any of them, may reside at the commencement of the action, or in the county where the plaintiff resides when service is made on the defendant in such county; or *if the defendant is a nonresident of this state,* the action may be tried in any county in which the defendant may be found in this state, *or in the county designated in the complaint,* and if any defendant is about to depart from the state, such action may be tried in any county where plaintiff resides, or where defendant may be found and service had.

Here, it is undisputed that [under Colorado state law] Farmers has its principal place of business in California and is not a resident of Colorado. Consequently, pursuant to the italicized language above, the Hagans, Ewald, and Mayfield were permitted to designate any county in their complaints, including Boulder County. The language of Rule 98(c) has been interpreted to permit trial of an action in the county of plaintiff's choice where no defendant is a resident of Colorado.

However, when the trial court granted Farmers' motion for a change of venue in Ewald's action, it deemed "Plaintiffs' designated venue of Boulder County" to be "improper under C.R.C.P. 98(c)." It reached this conclusion after quoting only a portion of Rule 98(c)(1), which omitted the key phrase "or in the county designated in the complaint." Following suit eight days later, the trial court in the Hagans' action incorporated the legal analysis in the *Ewald* order into its own order granting Farmers' motion for a change of venue—noting that it was "persuasive authority because the Court agrees with its logic."

The trial courts in the *Hagan* and *Ewald* lawsuits abused their discretion in holding that Boulder County was not a proper venue. Because Farmers is a nonresident of Colorado, the plaintiffs were permitted to designate any county in their complaints under Rule 98(c)(1). In choosing Boulder, the plaintiffs may well have engaged in "forum shopping" and ventured away from where these cases seem to have their roots. But Rule 98(c)(1) does not restrict the plaintiff's choice of venue when the defendant is a nonresident, and potential witnesses need not have a connection to Boulder, despite Farmers' insistence to the contrary.

B. Rule 98(f)(2)

We next assess whether a change of venue would promote "the convenience of witnesses and the ends of justice" as required by C.R.C.P. 98(f)(2)—focusing on the type
of evidence that a movant must present. We conclude that the attorney affidavits
that Farmers presented to the district court were insufficient under *Sampson* and its
progeny.

In *Sampson,* this court made clear that the party moving to change venue under
Rule 98(f)(2) must show, "through affidavit or evidence, the identity of the witnesses,
the nature, materiality and admissibility of their testimony, and how the witnesses
would be better accommodated by the requested change in venue."

This standard consolidates the varying requirements imposed in earlier cases,
which we cited in *Sampson.*

Conclusory statements do not satisfy this standard. In *Sampson,* for example,
this court explained that it was not enough for the movant to assert that the designated venue was remote and that witnesses would be inconvenienced. And in
*Ranger Insurance Co.,* this court concluded that the record was too limited to support
a change of venue when the movant summarily asserted that another venue would
be more convenient for the witnesses and would promote the ends of justice.

When the movant makes the requisite showing, the party opposing the change
"must at least balance the showing made by the moving party" or the court should
grant the motion. Farmers has not made the requisite showing in these cases, as the
attorney affidavits that it submitted in support of its motions to change venue do not
satisfy the *Sampson* standard.

In all three cases, Farmers' motions relied on affidavits by its attorney. Those affidavits primarily analyze (1) the distance the plaintiffs and their medical treatment
providers would have to travel to get to the proposed transferee court, as compared
to the original venue, and (2) the approximate travel time to each venue. Because
these travel distances and times are generally shorter for the proposed transferee
court, Farmers contends that the transferee court is necessarily a more convenient
venue under Rule 98(f)(2). We disagree.

The problem lies not in who provided the affidavits, but in their contents. The
deficiency is twofold.

First and foremost, Farmers' affidavits focus inordinately on the convenience of
the non-moving party. Farmers calculates (and compares) the distance and estimated
travel time, without traffic, from the plaintiffs' homes to the Boulder County and
Arapahoe County courthouses (in the *Hagan* and *Ewald* actions) and to the Boulder
County and El Paso County courthouses (in the *Mayfield* action). But a plaintiff's

convenience is not a defendant's concern. A defendant may not use a plaintiff's residential address (or a plaintiff's professional address) against him or her to attack a venue that is specifically permitted by Rule 98.

Second, to satisfy the standard set forth in *Sampson,* the affidavits must contain three categories of pertinent information: (1) "the identity of the witnesses"; (2) "the nature, materiality and admissibility of their testimony"; and (3) "how the witnesses would be better accommodated by the requested change in venue." No category is determinative; the trial court must assess the totality of the circumstances to assess whether a change of venue is necessary and appropriate.

We evaluate each category in turn. We do so against the backdrop of our case law, which provides examples of what types of evidence will (and will not) support a Rule 98(f)(2) motion, as well as guidance on the types of circumstances that may justify a change of venue. *Department of Highways,* for instance, provides an exemplar of an affidavit that contains the requisite information. There, a motorist who was injured in an accident due to a hole in the pavement on an exit ramp filed a negligence action against the Department of Highways in Denver County. The Department filed a motion to change venue to Kit Carson County, which it supported with an affidavit by its assistant maintenance superintendent, who investigated the accident. The affidavit listed the names and addresses of 15 witnesses whom the Department (not the plaintiff) intended to call at trial—six of whom were employees and all of whom resided in Kit Carson County. The affidavit contained a brief description of their testimony. It averred the Department operated with very few employees due to budget limitations and it would be impossible to maintain the local roads with these employees attending a trial in Denver, over 150 miles away; thus, the inconvenience was to the Department and not to the plaintiff. We deemed this affidavit sufficient to justify a change of venue.

### 1. The Identity of the Witnesses

We begin by evaluating whether Farmers' attorney affidavits sufficiently set forth "the identity of the witnesses."

Farmers lists the plaintiffs' own names and addresses, together with the names and addresses of their "treating medical providers" and the physicians who performed their independent medical evaluations. Farmers extracted this information from the plaintiffs' demand letters, which it attached to the affidavits. As explained above, the party plaintiffs' convenience is immaterial. Also, identification of the plaintiffs' medical treatment providers implicates the third prong, namely how witnesses would be affected.

The affidavits largely ignore Farmers' own employees, as well as potential third-party witnesses. Only the affidavit filed in Ewald's case—which lists "Heidi Hanson, the most recent claims handler on Plaintiff's claim"—identifies any of Farmers' own employee-witnesses by name. And only the affidavit in Mayfield's case lists a third-party witness—"the underlying tortfeasor, Mark Merriman."

Furthermore, Farmers lists numerous business names, without specifying a doctor or corporate representative. Although the demand letters (which contain some additional identifying information) are also attached in support of the motions, complete information for each witness should be apparent from the face of an affidavit (or other evidence) to facilitate the court's evaluation of the motion to change venue.

Because Farmers focuses almost exclusively on the plaintiffs and their medical treatment providers and omits its own potential witnesses, and because Farmers often provides business names only, its affidavits do not identify the witnesses sufficiently to justify a change of venue under Rule 98(f)(2).

### 2. The Nature, Materiality, and Admissibility of the Witnesses' Testimony

We next consider the second prong of the *Sampson* standard—whether Farmers' attorney affidavits address the nature, materiality, and admissibility of the potential witnesses' testimony. This requirement ensures that a motion to change venue does not engender a meaningless "battle of numbers," in which the parties compete by presenting the reviewing court with long lists of possible witnesses located in their preferred venues.

This court has applied this requirement (and deemed it fulfilled) in cases such as *Department of Highways*. But we have not yet expanded on what it takes to satisfy this requirement. We do so today, turning to commentary on 28 U.S.C. § 1404 (2014) (the federal counterpart to Rule 98) for guidance.

The party seeking a change of venue must provide at least "a general summary" of what the key witnesses' testimony will cover. That description should provide the reviewing court with enough information to understand whether the witnesses are important or peripheral. Consider, for example, a case in which one key nonparty witness is located in or near the original venue and another key nonparty witness is located in or near the proposed venue. The description should allow the court to make an informed judgment as to their respective importance. In addition, if the admissibility of a witness's testimony is in question (e.g., because it contains hearsay), the affidavit identifying that witness should briefly explain why his or her testimony will likely be admissible.

We recognize that motions to change venue are generally filed at the beginning stages of litigation, before the parties have engaged in discovery. But this timing should not preclude a movant from providing information at this most basic level.

Because Farmers' affidavits do not contain any information at all on the nature, materiality, and admissibility of the potential witnesses' testimony, they do not meet the second prong of the *Sampson* standard and do not justify a change of venue under Rule 98(f)(2).

### 3. How the Witnesses Would Be Affected

Last, we assess whether Farmers' attorney affidavits establish "how the witnesses would be better accommodated by the requested change in venue." In other words, how will the change affect the witnesses?

The affidavits do not establish how any witnesses would be better accommodated by the requested change of venue. Distance and travel time logically factor into convenience, but they are not dispositive. Farmers' assertion that trial in Boulder County would be inconvenient for witnesses is largely speculative.

Courts have expressed suspicion when a defendant advocates for the convenience of a plaintiff's witnesses. We share their apprehension. While the convenience of the plaintiffs' witnesses is relevant in assessing convenience under Rule 98(f)(2), the moving party should point to more than distance: Do the professional witnesses, such as treatment providers, actually object to the travel involved? If so, why?

The affidavits do not demonstrate that a single witness actually stated that it would be inconvenient for him or her to attend a trial in Boulder County, as compared to the transferee courts. Witness affidavits to this effect would help. *cf. Lopez v. Am. Standard Ins. Co.,* No. 14CV30476 (Colo.Dist.Ct. Aug. 7, 2014) (considering that three of plaintiff's witnesses provided an affidavit stating that Weld County would not be more convenient than Boulder County in denying insurance company's motion to change venue under Rule 98(f)(2)); *see also Jacobs v. Banks* (emphasizing that defendants "did not even indicate that they had contacted the nonparty witnesses, much less identify the specific inconveniences which might be incurred by the witnesses," rendering their moving papers insufficient as a matter of law).

It is also noteworthy that the affidavits do not contain the home addresses for the potential witnesses, except for the plaintiffs themselves. Without requiring that a movant include both work and home addresses for each witness identified, we note the possibility that the witnesses' homes might be closer to Boulder County, thereby rendering that venue more convenient for those witnesses traveling from home, not the workplace.

Further, it does not appear that the plaintiffs even intend to call the many witnesses enumerated in the affidavits, or (on the flip side) that Farmers' witness list is complete. By way of example, Mayfield advises the court that he does not intend to call the majority of the medical treatment providers that Farmers lists in its affidavit. He also notes that the expert witnesses whom he intends to call—who are not on Farmers' list—are closer to Boulder County than to El Paso County.

Finally, distance and travel time—while relevant—constitute a nebulous benchmark. Granted, this court has not hesitated to find inconvenience in cases involving significant travel differentials in the 150–mile to 200–mile range. *See Bacher*, 527 P.2d at 59 (vacating an order denying a motion to change venue, where the counties were remote and material witnesses would have had to travel approximately 200 miles to get to the designated venue). But when two closely situated counties are under scrutiny, no bright line separates convenience from inconvenience. For instance, assuming that the witnesses listed in Farmers' attorney affidavit in Mayfield's case actually will testify, where does a 76.5– to 97.6–mile difference fall on the convenience spectrum?

The split within the Boulder County District Court illustrates that no universal notion of convenience exists. The trial courts found Boulder County to be inconvenient here, but other judges in the same district have deemed extra travel time within the greater Denver area to be less consequential.

Because Farmers' evidence does not establish that the witnesses would be better accommodated by a move to another county, it does not justify a change of venue under Rule 98(f)(2).

### 4. The Ends of Justice

In addition to the convenience arguments advanced through the attorney affidavits, Farmers asserts that a change of venue would promote "the ends of justice" by (1) ensuring that "a jury of the majority of the vicinage of the witnesses pass upon their credibility"; (2) deterring plaintiffs from forum shopping to avoid CAPP districts; and (3) reducing witness costs for which Farmers will be responsible if it loses at trial. We reject these arguments.

"Vicinage" means "vicinity" or "proximity." In the context of juries, it is a somewhat anachronistic term referring to "the locality from which jurors will be drawn." In criminal cases, for instance, jurors must generally "be selected from a geographical district that includes the locality of the commission of the crime," without extending "too far beyond the general vicinity of that locality." There is no corresponding vicinage requirement in civil cases. Moreover, the venues under consideration here are all metropolitan areas along the Front Range; therefore, any difference in the jury's composition would likely be minimal.

Farmers' CAPP and costs-based arguments are likewise without merit. We decline to impose hurdles on a plaintiff's choice of venue that do not exist in the plain language of Rule 98 and section 13–16–122, C.R.S. (2014).

## IV. Conclusion

"Consistent with specific venue provisions, courts should attempt to accommodate the litigants and their witnesses to the greatest extent possible." Still, courts must do so within established parameters. Thirty-six years ago, in *Sampson*, this court outlined certain evidentiary requirements for a motion to change venue. The trial courts granted Farmers' motions to change venue without insisting upon the critical information that *Sampson* requires. It was an abuse of discretion for the trial courts to order a change of venue without adequate supporting affidavits or an evidentiary hearing. Consequently, we now make our rules to show cause absolute.

We hold that the trial courts abused their discretion when they changed the venue in these cases. First, Boulder County District Court is a proper venue for all three cases; under Rule 98(c)(1), the plaintiffs were allowed to file their complaints in the county of their choice because Farmers is a nonresident defendant. Second, the trial courts granted the motions without the requisite evidentiary support. The affidavits that Farmers submitted improperly focus on convenience to the plaintiffs and do not satisfy the standard set forth in *Sampson*. *Sampson* requires a party seeking to change venue under Rule 98(f)(2) to support the motion with evidence indicating "the identity of the witnesses, the nature, materiality and admissibility of their testimony, and how the witnesses would be better accommodated by the requested change in venue."

We direct the transferee courts to return the cases to Boulder County District Court.

# CHAPTER 5

# PLEADINGS

1. Now to get down to specifics. What must be included in the plaintiff's complaint and the defendant's answer? And what happens if it is clear from the pleadings that either of the parties is entitled, now, to summary judgment on one or more of the issues?

For the most part this book will concentrate on the Federal Rules of Civil Procedure – since those are the rules applicable in every state when suit is brought in one of the federal courts within the state. In addition, about half of the states have adopted some variety of the federal rules for their own *state* rules of civil procedure.

However, if you end up practicing in one of the states, such as California, that still uses the older style of procedural rules, call *Code Pleading*, you will need to make some adjustments. The major difference is that in a Code Pleading jurisdiction you need to be much more careful on exactly how you word the statements in the allegation of facts included in the complaint. Hint: If a case uses the word "demurrer" instead of the words, "fails to state a claim on which relief can be granted," you can be almost certain that the case was decided in a Code jurisdiction. The word "demurrer", (essentially meaning "so what?") is not used in the federal rules.

FRCP 7 lists only seven pleadings that are allowed under the federal rules. FRCP 8(a) states that the complaint – the pleading that starts the lawsuit – must contain:

> "(1) a short and plain statement of the grounds for the court's jurisdiction ...
> (2) a short and plain statement of the claim showing that the pleader is entitled to relief; and
> (3) a demand for the relief sought."

Now for a few cases which may make these rules more memorable.

# A. CLAIM FOR WHICH RELIEF CAN BE GRANTED – RULES 7, 8, 11, 12

135 S.CT. 346

SUPREME COURT OF THE UNITED STATES

TRACEY L. JOHNSON, ET AL.

V.

CITY OF SHELBY, MISSISSIPPI.

NOVEMBER 10, 2014

PER CURIAM.

Plaintiffs below, petitioners here, worked as police officers for the city of Shelby, Mississippi. They allege that they were fired by the city's board of aldermen, not for deficient performance, but because they brought to light criminal activities of one of the aldermen. Charging violations of their Fourteenth Amendment due process rights, they sought compensatory relief from the city. Summary judgment was entered against them in the District Court, and affirmed on appeal, for failure to invoke 42 U.S.C. § 1983 in their complaint.

We summarily reverse. Federal pleading rules call for "a short and plain statement of the claim showing that the pleader is entitled to relief," Fed. Rule Civ. Proc. 8(a)(2); they do not countenance dismissal of a complaint for imperfect statement of the legal theory supporting the claim asserted. (Federal Rules of Civil Procedure "are designed to discourage battles over mere form of statement"); 5 C. Wright & A. Miller, § 1215, p. 172 (3d ed. 2002) (Rule 8(a)(2) "indicates that a basic objective of the rules is to avoid civil cases turning on technicalities"). In particular, no heightened pleading rule requires plaintiffs seeking damages for violations of constitutional rights to invoke § 1983 expressly in order to state a claim. See *Leatherman v. Tarrant County Narcotics* (a federal court may not apply a standard "more stringent than the usual pleading requirements of Rule 8(a)" in "civil rights cases alleging municipal liability"); and *Swierkiewicz v. Sorema* (holding that imposing a "heightened pleading standard in employment discrimination cases conflicts with Federal Rule of Civil Procedure 8(a)(2)").

The Fifth Circuit defended its requirement that complaints expressly invoke § 1983 as "not a mere pleading formality." The requirement serves a notice function, the Fifth Circuit said, because "certain consequences flow from claims under § 1983, such as the unavailability of *respondeat superior* liability, which bears on the qualified immunity analysis." This statement displays some confusion in the Fifth Circuit's perception of petitioners' suit. No "qualified immunity analysis" is implicated here, as petitioners asserted a constitutional claim against the city only, not against any municipal officer. See *Owen v. Independence,* (a "municipality may not assert the good faith of its officers or agents as a defense to liability under § 1983").

Our decisions in *Bell Atlantic Corp. v. Twombly,* (2007), and *Ashcroft v. Iqbal,* (2009), are not in point, for they concern the *factual* allegations a complaint must contain to survive a motion to dismiss. A plaintiff, they instruct, must plead facts sufficient to show that her claim has substantive plausibility. Petitioners' complaint was not deficient in that regard. Petitioners stated simply, concisely, and directly events that, they alleged, entitled them to damages from the city. Having informed the city of the factual basis for their complaint, they were required to do no more to stave off threshold dismissal for want of an adequate statement of their claim. See Fed. Rules Civ. Proc. 8(a)(2) and (3), (d)(1), (e). For clarification and to ward off further insistence on a punctiliously stated "theory of the pleadings," petitioners, on remand, should be accorded an opportunity to add to their complaint a citation to § 1983. See 5 Wright & Miller ("The federal rules effectively abolish the restrictive theory of the pleadings doctrine, making it clear that it is unnecessary to set out a legal theory for the plaintiff's claim for relief." Fed. Rules Civ. Proc. 15(a)(2) ("The court should freely give leave [to amend a pleading] when justice so requires.").

For the reasons stated, the petition for certiorari is granted, the judgment of the United States Court of Appeals for the Fifth Circuit is reversed, and the case is remanded for further proceedings consistent with this opinion.

# B. AMENDING THE PLEADINGS - RULE 15

2. If a plaintiff does decide that he should amend the initial complaint, how long does he have to do so – and when will the amendment *relate back* to the date of the original complaint?

### 130 S.CT. 2485
### SUPREME COURT OF THE UNITED STATES
### WANDA KRUPSKI, PETITIONER,
### V.
### COSTA CROCIERE S. P. A.

DECIDED JUNE 7, 2010

**Justice SOTOMAYOR delivered the opinion of the Court.**

Rule 15(c) of the Federal Rules of Civil Procedure governs when an amended pleading "relates back" to the date of a timely filed original pleading and is thus itself timely even though it was filed outside an applicable statute of limitations. Where an amended pleading changes a party or a party's name, the Rule requires, among other things, that "the party to be brought in by amendment ... knew or should have known that the action would have been brought against it, but for a mistake concerning the proper party's identity." Rule 15(c)(1)(C). In this case, the Court of Appeals held that Rule 15(c) was not satisfied because the plaintiff knew or should have known of the proper defendant before filing her original complaint. The court also held that relation back was not appropriate because the plaintiff had unduly delayed in seeking to amend. We hold that relation back under Rule 15(c)(1)(C) depends on what the party to be added knew or should have known, not on the amending party's knowledge or its timeliness in seeking to amend the pleading. Accordingly, we reverse the judgment of the Court of Appeals.

I

On February 21, 2007, petitioner, Wanda Krupski, tripped over a cable and fractured her femur while she was on board the cruise ship Costa Magica. Upon her return home, she acquired counsel and began the process of seeking compensation for her injuries. Krupski's passenger ticket—which explained that it was the sole contract between each passenger and the carrier, included a variety of requirements for obtaining damages for an injury suffered on board one of the carrier's ships. The ticket identified the carrier as

"Costa Crociere S. p. A., an Italian corporation, and all Vessels and other ships owned, chartered, operated, marketed or provided by Costa Crociere, S. p. A., and all officers, staff members, crew members, independent contractors, medical providers, concessionaires, pilots, suppliers, agents and assigns onboard said Vessels, and the manufacturers of said Vessels and all their component parts."

The ticket required an injured party to submit "written notice of the claim with full particulars ... to the carrier or its duly authorized agent within 185 days after the date of injury." The ticket further required any lawsuit to be "filed within one year after the date of injury" and to be "served upon the carrier within 120 days after filing." For cases arising from voyages departing from or returning to a United States port in which the amount in controversy exceeded $75,000, the ticket designated the United States District Court for the Southern District of Florida in Broward County, Florida, as the exclusive forum for a lawsuit. The ticket extended the "defenses, limitations and exceptions ... that may be invoked by the CARRIER" to "all persons who may act on behalf of the CARRIER or on whose behalf the CARRIER may act," including "the CARRIER's parents, subsidiaries, affiliates, successors, assigns, representatives, agents, employees, servants, concessionaires and contractors" as well as "Costa Cruise Lines N. V.," identified as the "sales and marketing agent for the CARRIER and the issuer of this Passage Ticket Contract." The front of the ticket listed Costa Cruise Lines' address in Florida and stated that an entity called "Costa Cruises" was "the first cruise company in the world" to obtain a certain certification of quality.

On July 2, 2007, Krupski's counsel notified Costa Cruise Lines of Krupski's claims. On July 9, 2007, the claims administrator for Costa Cruise requested additional information from Krupski "in order to facilitate our future attempts to achieve a pre-litigation settlement." The parties were unable to reach a settlement, however, and on February 1, 2008—three weeks before the 1-year limitations period expired—Krupski filed a negligence action against Costa Cruise, invoking the diversity jurisdiction of the Federal District Court for the Southern District of Florida. The complaint alleged that Costa Cruise "owned, operated, managed, supervised and controlled" the ship on which Krupski had injured herself; that Costa Cruise had extended to its passengers an invitation to enter onto the ship; and that Costa Cruise owed Krupski a duty of care, which it breached by failing to take steps that would have prevented her accident. The complaint further stated that venue was proper under the passenger ticket's forum selection clause and averred that, by the July 2007 notice of her claims, Krupski had complied with the ticket's presuit requirements. Krupski served Costa Cruise on February 4, 2008.

Over the next several months—after the limitations period had expired—Costa Cruise brought Costa Crociere's existence to Krupski's attention three times. First, on February 25, 2008, Costa Cruise filed its answer, asserting that it was not the proper defendant, as it was merely the North American sales and marketing agent for Costa Crociere, which was the actual carrier and vessel operator. Second, on March 20, 2008, Costa Cruise listed Costa Crociere as an interested party in its corporate disclosure statement. Finally, on May 6, 2008, Costa Cruise moved for summary judgment, again stating that Costa Crociere was the proper defendant.

On June 13, 2008, Krupski responded to Costa Cruise's motion for summary judgment, arguing for limited discovery to determine whether Costa Cruise should be dismissed. According to Krupski, the following sources of information led her to believe Costa Cruise was the responsible party: The travel documents prominently identified Costa Cruise and gave its Florida address; Costa Cruise's Web site listed Costa Cruise in Florida as the United States office for the Italian company Costa Crociere; and the Web site of the Florida Department of State listed Costa Cruise as the only "Costa" company registered to do business in that State. Krupski also observed that Costa Cruise's claims administrator had responded to her claims notification without indicating that Costa Cruise was not a responsible party. With her response, Krupski simultaneously moved to amend her complaint to add Costa Crociere as a defendant.

On July 2, 2008, after oral argument, the District Court denied Costa Cruise's motion for summary judgment without prejudice and granted Krupski leave to amend, ordering that Krupski effect proper service on Costa Crociere by September 16, 2008. Complying with the court's deadline, Krupski filed an amended complaint on July 11, 2008, and served Costa Crociere on August 21, 2008. On that same date, the District Court issued an order dismissing Costa Cruise from the case pursuant to the parties' joint stipulation, Krupski apparently having concluded that Costa Cruise was correct that it bore no responsibility for her injuries.

Shortly thereafter, Costa Crociere—represented by the same counsel who had represented Costa Cruise, moved to dismiss, contending that the amended complaint did not relate back under Rule 15(c) and was therefore untimely. The District Court agreed. Rule 15(c), the court explained, imposes three requirements before an amended complaint against a newly named defendant can relate back to the original complaint. First, the claim against the newly named defendant must have arisen "out of the conduct, transaction, or occurrence set out—or attempted to be set out—in the original pleading." Second, "within the period provided by Rule 4(m) for serving the summons and complaint" (which is ordinarily 90 days from when the complaint is filed, see Rule 4(m)), the newly named defendant must have "received such notice of the action that it will not be prejudiced in defending on the merits." Finally, the plaintiff must show that, within the Rule 4(m) period, the newly named defendant "knew or should have known that the action would have been brought against it, but for a mistake concerning the proper party's identity." Rule 15(c)(1)(C)(ii).

The first two conditions posed no problem, the court explained: The claim against Costa Crociere clearly involved the same occurrence as the original claim against Costa Cruise, and Costa Crociere had constructive notice of the action and had not shown that any unfair prejudice would result from relation back. But the court found the third condition fatal to Krupski's attempt to relate back, concluding that Krupski had not made a mistake concerning the identity of the proper party. Relying on Eleventh Circuit precedent, the court explained that the word "mistake" should not be construed to encompass a deliberate decision not to sue a party whose identity the plaintiff knew before the statute of limitations had run. Because Costa Cruise informed Krupski that Costa Crociere was the proper defendant in its answer, corporate disclosure statement, and motion for summary judgment, and yet Krupski delayed for months in moving to amend and then in filing an amended complaint, the court concluded that Krupski knew of the proper defendant and made no mistake.

The Eleventh Circuit affirmed in an unpublished *per curiam* opinion.

We granted certiorari to resolve tension among the Circuits over the breadth of Rule 15(c)(1)(C)(ii), and we now reverse.

II

Under the Federal Rules of Civil Procedure, an amendment to a pleading relates back to the date of the original pleading when:

"(A) the law that provides the applicable statute of limitations allows relation back;

"(B) the amendment asserts a claim or defense that arose out of the conduct, transaction, or occurrence set out—or attempted to be set out—in the original pleading; or

"(C) the amendment changes the party or the naming of the party against whom a claim is asserted, if Rule 15(c)(1)(B) is satisfied and if, within the period provided by Rule 4(m) for serving the summons and complaint, the party to be brought in by amendment:

"(i) received such notice of the action that it will not be prejudiced in defending on the merits; and

"(ii) knew or should have known that the action would have been brought against it, but for a mistake concerning the proper party's identity." Rule 15(c)(1).

In our view, neither of the Court of Appeals' reasons for denying relation back under Rule 15(c)(1)(C)(ii) finds support in the text of the Rule. We consider each reason in turn.

A

The Court of Appeals first decided that Krupski either knew or should have known of the proper party's identity and thus determined that she had made a deliberate choice instead of a mistake in not naming Costa Crociere as a party in her original pleading. By focusing on Krupski's knowledge, the Court of Appeals chose the wrong starting point. The question under Rule 15(c)(1)(C)(ii) is not whether Krupski knew or should have known the identity of Costa Crociere as the proper defendant, but whether Costa Crociere knew or should have known that it would have been named as a defendant but for an error. Rule 15(c)(1)(C)(ii) asks what the prospective *defendant* knew or should have known during the Rule 4(m) period, not what the *plaintiff* knew or should have known at the time of filing her original complaint.

Information in the plaintiff's possession is relevant only if it bears on the defendant's understanding of whether the plaintiff made a mistake regarding the proper party's identity. For purposes of that inquiry, it would be error to conflate knowledge of a party's existence with the absence of mistake. A mistake is "an error, misconception, or misunderstanding; an erroneous belief." Black's Law Dictionary 1092 (9th ed.2009); see also Webster's Third New International Dictionary 1446 (2002) (defining "mistake" as "a misunderstanding of the meaning or implication of something"; "a wrong action or statement proceeding from faulty judgment, inadequate knowledge, or inattention"; "an erroneous belief"; or "a state of mind not in accordance with the facts"). That a plaintiff knows of a party's existence does not preclude her from making a mistake with respect to that party's identity. A plaintiff may know that a prospective defendant—call him party A—exists, while erroneously believing him to have the status of party B. Similarly, a plaintiff may know generally what party A does while misunderstanding the roles that party A and party B played in the "conduct, transaction, or occurrence" giving rise to her claim. If the plaintiff sues party B instead of party A under these circumstances, she has made a "mistake concerning the proper party's identity" notwithstanding her knowledge of the existence of both parties. The only question under Rule 15(c)(1)(C)(ii), then, is whether party A knew or should have known that, absent some mistake, the action would have been brought against him.

Respondent urges that the key issue under Rule 15(c)(1)(C)(ii) is whether the plaintiff made a deliberate choice to sue one party over another. We agree that making a deliberate choice to sue one party instead of another while fully understanding the factual and legal differences between the two parties is the antithesis of making a mistake concerning the proper party's identity. We disagree, however, with respondent's position that any time a plaintiff is aware of the existence of two parties and chooses to sue the wrong one, the proper defendant could reasonably believe that the plaintiff made no mistake. The reasonableness of the mistake is not itself at issue. As noted, a plaintiff might know that the prospective defendant exists but nonetheless harbor a misunderstanding about his status or role in the events giving rise to the claim at issue, and she may mistakenly choose to sue a different defendant based on that misimpression. That kind of deliberate but mistaken choice does not foreclose a finding that Rule 15(c)(1)(C)(ii) has been satisfied.

This reading is consistent with the purpose of relation back: to balance the interests of the defendant protected by the statute of limitations with the preference expressed in the Federal Rules of Civil Procedure in general, and Rule 15 in particular, for resolving disputes on their merits. A prospective defendant who legitimately believed that the limitations period had passed without any attempt to sue him has a strong interest in repose. But repose would be a windfall for a prospective defendant who understood, or who should have understood, that he escaped suit during the limitations period only because the plaintiff misunderstood a crucial fact about his identity. Because a plaintiff's knowledge of the existence of a party does not foreclose the possibility that she has made a mistake of identity about which that party should have been aware, such knowledge does not support that party's interest in repose.

Our reading is also consistent with the history of Rule 15(c)(1)(C). That provision was added in 1966 to respond to a recurring problem in suits against the Federal

Government, particularly in the Social Security context. Individuals who had filed timely lawsuits challenging the administrative denial of benefits often failed to name the party identified in the statute as the proper defendant—the current Secretary of what was then the Department of Health, Education, and Welfare—and named instead the United States; the Department of Health, Education, and Welfare itself; the nonexistent "Federal Security Administration"; or a Secretary who had recently retired from office. By the time the plaintiffs discovered their mistakes, the statute of limitations in many cases had expired, and the district courts denied the plaintiffs leave to amend on the ground that the amended complaints would not relate back. Rule 15(c) was therefore "amplified to provide a general solution" to this problem. It is conceivable that the Social Security litigants knew or reasonably should have known the identity of the proper defendant either because of documents in their administrative cases or by dint of the statute setting forth the filing requirements. Nonetheless, the Advisory Committee clearly meant their filings to qualify as mistakes under the Rule.

Respondent suggests that our decision in *Nelson v. Adams USA,* (2000), forecloses the reading of Rule 15(c)(1)(C)(ii) we adopt today. We disagree. In that case, Adams USA, Inc. (Adams), had obtained an award of attorney's fees against the corporation of which Donald Nelson was the president and sole shareholder. After Adams became concerned that the corporation did not have sufficient funds to pay the award, Adams sought to amend its pleading to add Nelson as a party and simultaneously moved to amend the judgment to hold Nelson responsible. The District Court granted both motions, and the Court of Appeals affirmed. We reversed, holding that the requirements of due process, as codified in Rules 12 and 15 of the Federal Rules of Civil Procedure, demand that an added party have the opportunity to respond before judgment is entered against him. In a footnote explaining that relation back does not deny the added party an opportunity to respond to the amended pleading, we noted that the case did not arise under the "mistake clause" of Rule 15(c): "Respondent Adams made no such mistake. It knew of Nelson's role and existence and, until it moved to amend its pleading, chose to assert its claim for costs and fees only against Nelson's company."

Contrary to respondent's claim, *Nelson* does not suggest that Rule 15(c)(1)(C)(ii) cannot be satisfied if a plaintiff knew of the prospective defendant's existence at the time she filed her original complaint. In that case, there was nothing in the initial pleading suggesting that Nelson was an intended party, while there was evidence in the record (of which Nelson was aware) that Adams sought to add him only after learning that the company would not be able to satisfy the judgment. This evidence countered any implication that Adams had originally failed to name Nelson because of any "mistake concerning the proper party's identity," and instead suggested that Adams decided to name Nelson only after the fact in an attempt to ensure that the fee award would be paid. The footnote merely observes that Adams had originally been under no misimpression about the function Nelson played in the underlying dispute. We said, after all, that Adams knew of Nelson's "role" as well as his existence. Read in context, the footnote in *Nelson* is entirely consistent with our understanding of the Rule: When the original complaint and the plaintiff's conduct compel the conclusion that the failure to name the prospective defendant in the original complaint was the result of a fully informed decision as opposed to a mistake concerning the proper defendant's identity, the requirements of Rule 15(c)(1)(C)(ii) are not met. This conclusion is in keeping with our rejection today of the Court of Appeals' reliance on the plaintiff's knowledge to deny relation back.

B

The Court of Appeals offered a second reason why Krupski's amended complaint did not relate back: Krupski had unduly delayed in seeking to file, and in eventually filing, an amended complaint. The Court of Appeals offered no support for its view that a plaintiff's dilatory conduct can justify the denial of relation back under Rule 15(c)(1)(C), and we find none. The Rule plainly sets forth an exclusive list of requirements for relation back, and the amending party's diligence is not among them. Moreover, the Rule mandates relation back once the Rule's requirements are satisfied; it does not leave the decision whether to grant relation back to the district court's equitable discretion. Rule 15(c)(1) ("An amendment ... *relates back* ... when" the three listed requirements are met (emphasis added)).

The mandatory nature of the inquiry for relation back under Rule 15(c) is particularly striking in contrast to the inquiry under Rule 15(a), which sets forth the circumstances in which a party may amend its pleading before trial. By its terms, Rule 15(a) gives discretion to the district court in deciding whether to grant a motion to amend a pleading to add a party or a claim. Following an initial period after filing a pleading during which a party may amend once "as a matter of course," "a party may amend its pleading only with the opposing party's written consent or the court's leave," which the court "should freely give ... when justice so requires." Rules 15(a)(1)-(2). We have previously explained that a court may consider a movant's "undue delay" or "dilatory motive" in deciding whether to grant leave to amend under Rule 15(a). As the contrast between Rule 15(a) and Rule 15(c) makes clear, however, the speed with which a plaintiff moves to amend her complaint or files an amended complaint after obtaining leave to do so has no bearing on whether the amended complaint relates back.

Rule 15(c)(1)(C) does permit a court to examine a plaintiff's conduct during the Rule 4(m) period, but not in the way or for the purpose respondent or the Court of Appeals suggests. As we have explained, the question under Rule 15(c)(1)(C)(ii) is what the prospective defendant reasonably should have understood about the plaintiff's intent in filing the original complaint against the first defendant. To the extent the plaintiff's postfiling conduct informs the prospective defendant's understanding of whether the plaintiff initially made a "mistake concerning the proper party's identity," a court may consider the conduct. ("Post-filing events occasionally can shed light on the plaintiff's state of mind at an earlier time" and "can inform *a defendant's* reasonable beliefs concerning whether her omission from the original complaint represented a mistake (as opposed to a conscious choice)"). The plaintiff's post-filing conduct is otherwise immaterial to the question whether an amended complaint relates back.

C

Applying these principles to the facts of this case, we think it clear that the courts below erred in denying relation back under Rule 15(c)(1)(C)(ii). The District Court held that Costa Crociere had "constructive notice" of Krupski's complaint within the Rule 4(m) period. Costa Crociere has not challenged this finding. Because the complaint made clear that Krupski meant to sue the company that "owned, operated, managed, supervised and controlled" the ship on which she was injured, and also indicated (mistakenly) that Costa Cruise performed those roles, Costa Crociere should have known, within the Rule 4(m) period, that it was not named as a defendant in that complaint only because of Krupski's misunderstanding about which "Costa" entity was in charge of the ship—clearly a "mistake concerning the proper party's identity."

Respondent contends that because the original complaint referred to the ticket's forum requirement and presuit claims notification procedure, Krupski was clearly aware of the contents of the ticket, and because the ticket identified Costa Crociere as the carrier and proper party for a lawsuit, respondent was entitled to think that she made a deliberate choice to sue Costa Cruise instead of Costa Crociere. As we have explained, however, that Krupski may have known the contents of the ticket does not foreclose the possibility that she nonetheless misunderstood crucial facts regarding the two companies' identities. Especially because the face of the complaint plainly indicated such a misunderstanding, respondent's contention is not persuasive. Moreover, respondent has articulated no strategy that it could reasonably have thought Krupski was pursuing in suing a defendant that was legally unable to provide relief.

Respondent also argues that Krupski's failure to move to amend her complaint during the Rule 4(m) period shows that she made no mistake in that period. But as discussed, any delay on Krupski's part is relevant only to the extent it may have informed Costa Crociere's understanding during the Rule 4(m) period of whether she made a mistake originally. Krupski's failure to add Costa Crociere during the Rule 4(m) period is not sufficient to make reasonable any belief that she had made a deliberate and informed decision not to sue Costa Crociere in the first instance. Nothing in Krupski's conduct during the Rule 4(m) period suggests that she failed to name Costa Crociere because of anything other than a mistake.

It is also worth noting that Costa Cruise and Costa Crociere are related corporate entities with very similar names; "crociera" even means "cruise" in Italian. Cassell's Italian Dictionary 137, 670 (1967). This interrelationship and similarity heighten the expectation that Costa Crociere should suspect a mistake has been made when Costa Cruise is named in a complaint that actually describes Costa Crociere's activities. Cf. *Morel v. DaimlerChrysler AG,* 565 F.3d 20, 27 (C.A.1 2009) (where complaint conveyed plaintiffs' attempt to sue automobile manufacturer and erroneously named the manufacturer as Daimler–Chrysler Corporation instead of the actual manufacturer, a legally distinct but related entity named DaimlerChrysler AG, the latter should have realized it had not been named because of plaintiffs' mistake). In addition, Costa Crociere's own actions contributed to passenger confusion over "the proper party" for a lawsuit. The front of the ticket advertises that "Costa Cruises" has achieved a certification of quality, without clarifying whether "Costa Cruises" is Costa Cruise Lines, Costa Crociere, or some other related "Costa" company. Indeed, Costa Crociere is evidently aware that the difference between Costa Cruise and Costa Crociere can be confusing for cruise ship passengers.

In light of these facts, Costa Crociere should have known that Krupski's failure to name it as a defendant in her original complaint was due to a mistake concerning the proper party's identity. We therefore reverse the judgment of the Court of Appeals for the Eleventh Circuit and remand the case for further proceedings consistent with this opinion.

## C. COUNTERCLAIMS AND CROSSCLAIMS - RULES 12 & 13

3. Once defendant has received a copy of plaintiff's complaint, defendant is required to file a response. This response may be *either* a motion under Rule 12, or an answer. A motion under Rule 12 will usually be a motion to dismiss on one of the grounds specified under Rule 12(b) - such as lack of subject matter jurisdiction or lack of personal jurisdiction – or the "catch all" 12(b)(6) "failure to state a claim on which relief can be granted."

If the response is filed in the form of an *answer*, the answer must, among other things, raise any affirmative defenses – such as the statute of limitations or various other affirmative defenses listed in Rule 8(c).

In addition, if defendant has a claim *against plaintiff* that arises from the same transaction as that described in plaintiff's complaint, then the defendant *must* include in her answer that claim against the plaintiff. This claim by the defendant against the plaintiff is called a *counterclaim*. See FRCP 13(a). Defendant *may* also include in her answer any other claim that she has against the plaintiff. See FRCP 13(b).

Once a case involves more than one plaintiff and one defendant, it can get messy. For example, if plaintiffs A and B sued defendants D and E, defendant D may have a counterclaim against plaintiff A. And defendant D may also have a claim against his co-defendant, E, which would be called a *crossclaim*. It may begin to look somewhat like a tennis game.

It is probably easiest if you picture all of the plaintiffs as being on one side of the net, and all of the defendants on the other side of the net. Plaintiffs A and B send a complaint across the net – and the complaint includes a claim against D and E. Defendants D and E then each send an answer back across the net, denying various allegations in the complaint, raising any available affirmative defenses, (as required by FRCP 8(c)), and also including a new claim, called a *counterclaim*, against plaintiff B. Then D and E begin to assert claims against each other, and these claims between the original parties to the lawsuit ( D & E), who are on the same side of the net, are called *crossclaims*. [Don't worry, C will come into the action in the next chapter.]

When something goes wrong with a construction project you are likely to have a welter of claims, counterclaims and crossclaims – with everyone trying to blame the problem on someone else. A situation like that is illustrated in the following case.

*Supplemental jurisdiction*, discussed in Chapter IV, is likely to extend to nearly all of the claims involved in the basic transaction – such as a construction project. The following case illustrates some of the issues.

Note that today, under 28 USC 1367, enacted in 1990, the result in this case would be the same as it was when the case was decided in 1977. The difference would be that the jurisdiction of the court would now be called *supplemental jurisdiction* instead of *ancillary jurisdiction*.

<br>

## 560 F.2D 1122
## UNITED STATES COURT OF APPEALS,
## THIRD CIRCUIT
## FAIRVIEW PARK EXCAVATING CO., INC.
## V.
## AL MONZO CONSTRUCTION COMPANY, INC., AND
## MARYLAND CASUALTY COMPANY, APPELLANTS, AND
## ROBINSON TOWNSHIP MUNICIPAL AUTHORITY.
## FAIRVIEW PARK EXCAVATING CO., INC.
## V.
## AL MONZO CONSTRUCTION COMPANY, INC., APPELLANT.

<br>

DECIDED JUNE 30, 1977

<br>

**GARTH, Circuit Judge.**

This appeal initially presented a jurisdictional question arising out of an action brought by the plaintiff subcontractor (Fairview) against its general contractor (Monzo) and a Pennsylvania municipal authority (Robinson Township) for which the construction work in issue was being performed. After Fairview's claim against the Township had been dismissed on state law grounds, the district court then dismissed Monzo's cross-claim against the Township for lack of an independent (diversity) basis for federal subject matter jurisdiction. Monzo contends in this appeal that the dismissal of its cross-claim against the Township was erroneous. We agree. However, because we have been informed that the relief sought in the cross-claim has since been obtained by Monzo in its subsequent state court proceedings, it is apparent that the issue before us has been mooted, and thus for this reason, the March 16, 1976 order of the district court dismissing Monzo's cross-claim will be affirmed.

## I.

Fairview Park Excavating Co., Inc., the plaintiff, is an Ohio corporation which as a subcontractor provided labor and materials under certain construction contracts for Robinson Township. Al Monzo Construction Company, Inc., a defendant, is a Pennsylvania corporation, which acted as general contractor to Robinson Township. Robinson Township Municipal Authority, another defendant, is a "citizen" of Pennsylvania. Maryland Casualty Co., a defendant, is a Maryland corporation which became a surety on Monzo's bond guaranteeing payment to subcontractors, laborers and materialmen.

Fairview completed its work as subcontractor but did not receive payment. Fairview then filed a diversity action in the United States District Court for the Western District of Pennsylvania joining Monzo, Maryland Casualty and the Township as defendants.

The Township denied any liability to Fairview, claiming that Fairview was not in contractual privity with it. The Township asserted that it had contracted only with Monzo as its contractor, and that any monies still owing to Monzo were being withheld by the Township only until Monzo completed certain restoration work.

Monzo and Maryland Casualty, replying together, denied liability, counterclaimed against Fairview, and cross-claimed against the Township. The Township counterclaimed against Monzo for damages caused by defective work. Trial without a jury was set for March 16, 1976.

On the first day of trial, however, the district court granted the Township's motion that Fairview's complaint against it be dismissed. The district court subsequently explained the basis for its dismissal of the Township as a defendant as follows:

Just prior to the commencement of trial on March 16, 1976, Robinson moved for dismissal on the ground that there was no contractual relationship between Fairview and Robinson, that the contract documents so provided and that there was no jurisdiction over the cross-claim of Monzo against Robinson because Robinson could not have been sued by Fairview in any event, citing *City of Philadelphia v. National Surety Corporation*. We considered that case controlling in its holding that under the law of Pennsylvania a municipal corporation is liable to a contractor but not to a subcontractor, materialman or laborer. While Robinson was a municipal authority and not a municipal corporation, we considered the proposition controlling.

With the Township no longer a "defendant" in Fairview's suit, its only remaining connection to the case was provided by Monzo's cross-claim. However, even this connection was short-lived. On the same date, March 16, 1976, the district court dismissed Monzo's cross-claim because of an absence of diversity between the two parties. In its Memorandum Opinion of June 1, 1976, the district court stated: "The various disputes between Monzo and Robinson were not properly before us and are, in fact, matters for state court jurisdiction, there being no diversity of citizenship between these parties."

At this juncture, only Fairview's claim against Monzo was left. After trial, judgment was entered for Fairview. Defendants Monzo and Maryland Casualty thereafter filed a "Motion for a New Trial." On June 2, 1976, the district court dismissed that motion, and the defendants filed a timely notice of appeal. It was only during oral argument that it appeared that Monzo had recovered a judgment against the Township in the Pennsylvania Court of Common Pleas and that the time for appeal of that judgment had expired.

II.

The primary complaint voiced by Monzo on this appeal is that the district court erred in dismissing its cross-claim against the Township on jurisdictional grounds. Monzo contends that, having once acquired jurisdiction over the Township as a defendant to its cross-claim, it could not be divested of jurisdiction by the Township's dismissal as a primary defendant to the plaintiff Fairview's claim if that dismissal was predicated (as it was) on nonjurisdictional grounds.

The Township's argument, in our view, is not to the contrary. In its brief, the Township quotes Professor Moore as follows:

> If the original bill or claim in connection with which the cross-claim arises is dismissed
> for lack of jurisdiction, it would seem, on analogy to cases concerning counterclaims,
> that the dismissal carries with it the cross-claim, unless the latter is supported by inde-
> pendent jurisdictional grounds.

However, reliance on that proposition affords little comfort to the Township, for here the original claim was dismissed on nonjurisdictional rather than jurisdictional grounds. As indicated earlier, the district court judge properly held that under

Pennsylvania law an absence of contractual privity between the plaintiff and the Township was fatal to Fairview's cause of action.

The basis for the distinction between jurisdictional and nonjurisdictional dismissals is readily apparent. If a federal court dismisses a plaintiff's claim for lack of subject matter jurisdiction, any cross-claims dependent upon ancillary jurisdiction must necessarily fall as well, because it is the plaintiff's claim to which the cross-claim is ancillary that provides the derivative source of jurisdiction for the cross-claim. Deviation from this rule would work an impermissible expansion of federal subject matter jurisdiction. Yet by the same token, once a district court judge has properly permitted a cross-claim under F.R.Civ.P. 13(g), as was the case here, the ancillary jurisdiction that results should not be defeated by a decision on the merits adverse to the plaintiff on the plaintiff's primary claim. As Judge Aldrich has stated:

> If (a defendant) had a proper cross-claim against its co-defendants this gave the court ancillary jurisdiction even though all the parties to the cross-claim were citizens of the same state. The termination of the original claim would not affect this. This is but one illustration of the elementary principle that jurisdiction which has once attached is not lost by subsequent events.

The contrary rule, which the Township urges here, would operate to make subject matter jurisdiction over every ancillary cross-claim dependent upon that claim's being resolved prior to the plaintiff's primary action. (Otherwise a judgment on the merits adverse to the plaintiff would drain the cross-claim of jurisdiction in every instance, a completely indefensible result.) Given that cross-claims necessarily involve co-defendants, a rule which would restrict the duration of federal court jurisdiction over cross-claims to the pendency of plaintiff's primary claim would be untenable: in many cases, cross-claims need not be heard until plaintiff has obtained a judgment on the merits. To permit the raising of a threat of a dismissal for want of jurisdiction at that point would destroy cross-claims otherwise properly maintainable by virtue of ancillary jurisdiction.

Hence, as this Court previously held in *Aetna Insurance Co. v. Newton,*

> (A) dismissal of the original complaint as to one of the defendants named therein does not operate as a dismissal of a cross-claim filed against such defendant by a codefendant.

The *Frommeyer* case cited in Aetna seems strikingly similar to the present one. The general contractor on a construction job, Wortmann, entered into a subcontract with

L. & R. Construction Co. for all concrete work on the job. L. & R., in turn entered into a subcontract with Frommeyer. Both Wortmann and L. & R. obtained sureties. When Frommeyer failed to receive payment from L. & R., it brought suit in federal district court against Wortmann, Wortmann's surety, L. & R., and L. & R.'s surety, American Surety Company ("American Surety"). Both Wortmann and Wortmann's surety cross-claimed against American Surety. American Surety subsequently moved to dismiss Frommeyer's complaint as to it for failure to state a cause of action, and the district court judge was constrained to agree. American Surety then sought dismissal of the cross-claims. That argument was rejected. The district court held that "Once proper, the cross-claims did not cease to be so because the party to whom they were addressed subsequently ceased to be a co-party."

As noted, *Frommeyer's* conclusion was adopted by this Court in *Aetna Insurance Co. v. Newton*, supra, and controls here.

## III.

Our conclusion that the district court should not have dismissed appellants' cross-claim would normally require a remand for the purpose of a trial on the merits of that claim. At oral argument, however, we were informed by counsel that after the dismissal of its cross-claim, Monzo filed a Pennsylvania state court action against the Township for the precise relief which it sought to obtain through its federal court cross-claim. That action has proceeded to judgment, and the time to appeal that judgment pursuant to Pennsylvania law has expired.

We requested counsel to submit a certified copy of the state court judgment. The docket entries for Al Monzo Construction Co. v. The Municipal Authority of the Township of Robinson, reveal that Monzo's complaint against the Township was filed April 30, 1976; that Monzo moved for summary judgment on October 5, 1976; and that summary judgment in favor of Monzo was granted on November 29, 1976, in the amount of $102,589.32 precisely the amount claimed in appellants' counterclaim against the same party, Robinson Township.

In light of this disclosure, it would accomplish nothing to remand this case to the district court for that court's determination as to whether it should award what would necessarily amount to duplicative relief for a single legal injury. Having received the only relief against the Township to which it is entitled, Monzo can have no cognizable interest in litigating its cross-claim.

The district court's dismissal of appellants' cross-claim must therefore be affirmed, not because the cross-claim lacked an independent basis of federal subject matter jurisdiction, but because the cross-claim has become moot.

## IV.

We have determined that the district court should not have dismissed appellants' cross-claim. However, we have also concluded that by reason of the state court events which have occurred since the district court's disposition of this issue, the case must be dismissed as moot.

The order of the district court dismissing Monzo's cross-claim will therefore be affirmed.

# D. SUMMARY JUDGMENT - RULE 56

4. When the pleadings are complete, any party may move for *Judgment on the Pleadings* under FRCP 12(c). If any matters outside the pleadings have been accepted by the court, then the proper procedure would be to file a *Motion for Summary Judgment*, under FRCP 56. A motion for summary judgment can be filed at any time during the discovery process, (which may go on for years), and for up to 30 days after discovery has closed. FRCP 56(b).

In the following case you will notice that a great deal of discovery has already taken place. Based on the pleadings, and all of that discovery, the trial judge appropriately granted plaintiff's motion for summary judgment on one of the major issues of the case.

**2013 WL 2634429**
**UNITED STATES DISTRICT COURT, DISTRICT OF VERMONT.**
**WENDIE DREVES, PLAINTIFF,**
**V.**
**HUDSON GROUP (HG) RETAIL, LLC, DEFENDANT.**

JUNE 12, 2013

OPINION AND ORDER

WILLIAM K. SESSIONS III, District Judge.

Wendie Dreves asserts that her former employer, Hudson Group ("Hudson") (1) violated federal and Vermont equal pay provisions by paying her male successor more than it paid her. [She also made three other claims.] Before the Court are Dreves's Motion for Partial Summary Judgment on her equal pay claim under the Vermont Fair Employment Practices Act ("VFEPA"), and Hudson's Motion for Summary Judgment on all pending claims.

# BACKGROUND

## I. Dreves's Employment

Hudson employed Dreves as the general manager of its retail operation at Burlington International Airport from September 22, 2003, until September 8, 2010, when Hudson terminated her and replaced her with Jarrod Dixon. At the time of her termination, Dreves was 58. Before her seven years with Hudson, Dreves spent 16 years in retail management: one year as assistant manager in a fabric store in Wasilla, Alaska; five years as an assistant manager and manager of Brooks pharmacy in Burlington and St. Albans, Vermont; two years as a manager of Jo–Ann Fabric in South Burlington, Vermont; five years as manager of Spencer Gifts, also in South Burlington; and three years as the general manager of the Burlington airport store that was acquired by Hudson in 2003.

When she joined Hudson, Dreves's initial base salary was $34,365, but she received several raises during her seven years with the company. The responsibilities of the general manager at Burlington International Airport grew during Dreves's tenure, most notably in 2007, when Hudson added two small stores behind the security checkpoint. In July 2007, after the additions, Hudson increased Dreves's salary to $45,505. Dreves's salary reached $48,230 in 2008, which is where it remained until she was terminated. Dreves did not receive a raise in 2010 because of a company-wide salary freeze.

## II. Dreves's Successor

While Hudson was preparing to terminate Dreves, two Hudson employees, Scorcia and Nieves identified Jarrod Dixon as the person they believed was best suited to assume her responsibilities in Burlington. Dixon, 42 years old at the time he replaced Dreves, started working at Hudson in 2004 as a magazine manager at Hudson's airport store in Manchester, New Hampshire. Hudson promoted Dixon first to warehouse manager and, in 2008, to assistant general manager. By 2010, Nieves and Scorcia considered Dixon to be the assistant general manager who was "next in line" for a promotion to general manager. Dixon had a strong record as an assistant manager in Manchester and also had direct experience with the Burlington operations from visits to evaluate and help address problems with Hudson's operation there.

Accordingly, Scorcia began preparing an offer to persuade Dixon to transfer to Burlington and assume the responsibilities of general manager. Scorcia began by taking Dixon's existing salary of $36,575 and attempting to calculate a comparable salary for Burlington. Hudson did not have any generally applicable policy or practice of equalizing the after-tax income of its employees to account for variations in state income rates, so Nieves assisted Scorcia by providing informal fact research to determine what differences existed between the two locations. Relying on a cost of living that was 12.6 percent higher in Burlington as well as a Vermont income tax rate of 9.5 percent where New Hampshire had none, Nieves calculated that Dixon's existing Manchester salary of $36,575 would have to be increased to $45,085 to give him a comparable salary in Burlington. That figure served as a starting point. Scorcia determined that more would be needed to induce Dixon to relocate his family, as his wife had a part-time job in Manchester and his children were in school there. Scorcia added approximately $5,000 and offered Dixon $50,000 per year if he took the job. Dixon turned down Scorcia's opening offer and told him that it was insufficient for him to move his family to Burlington. Dixon requested $55,000, but he and Scorcia met halfway and settled on a salary of $52,500. Hudson also compensated Dixon for $5,000 in moving expenses.

Nieves's tax calculations proved to be incorrect. The actual Vermont tax on Dixon's assistant manager salary of $36,575 would have been only $229, or 0.63 percent of his salary. How Nieves arrived at the cost-of-living assessment is unclear. Nieves states that he calculated it by comparing the house and food prices for Burlington and Manchester; however, he does not remember what websites he consulted nor does he have a record of how he made the calculation. Hudson conducted no inquiry into Dixon's wife's employment or her prospects for employment upon moving to Burlington.

Dreves received positive performance evaluations prior to 2009. One of Dreves's annual performance reviews employed male pronouns, a product of a default setting that automatically populated Hudson's forms with male, not female pronouns.

## DISCUSSION

Summary judgment is appropriate where "the movant shows that there is no genuine dispute as to any material fact and the movant is entitled to judgment as a matter of law." Fed.R.Civ.P. § 56(a). "At the summary judgment stage the judge's function is not himself to weigh the evidence and determine the truth of the matter but to determine whether there is a genuine issue for trial." While the Court must draw all inferences from the facts in the light most favorable to the non-moving party, that party may not "rely on mere speculation or conjecture as to the true nature of the facts to overcome a motion for summary judgment."

I. Equal Pay

"The Equal Pay Act, passed by Congress in 1963, prohibits employers from discriminating among employees on the basis of sex by paying higher wages to employees of the opposite sex for 'equal work on jobs the performance of which requires equal skill, effort, and responsibility, and which are performed under similar working conditions.' 29 U.S.C. § 206(d)(1). "The purpose behind the enactment of the EPA was to legislate out of existence a long-held, but outmoded societal view that a man should be paid more than a woman for the same work." To that end, Congress chose not to require individuals bringing equal pay claims to prove discriminatory intent. Unlike Title VII, the EPA does not require a plaintiff to establish an employer's discriminatory intent.

The Vermont Fair Employment Practices Act ("VFEPA") contains an equal pay provision that is virtually identical to the EPA. Vermont courts construe provisions of the VFEPA in accordance with the federal anti-discrimination laws on which they were modeled. Accordingly, this Court may avail itself of federal precedent when interpreting the equal pay provision of the VFEPA.

To state a *prima facie* case under both the federal and Vermont provisions, a plaintiff must show that " 'i) the employer pays different wages to employees of the opposite sex; ii) the employees perform equal work on jobs requiring equal skill, effort, and responsibility; and iii) the jobs are performed under similar working conditions.' Once a plaintiff has made a *prima facie* case, the burden shifts to the employer to establish one of four affirmative defenses: that the pay difference is due to a seniority system, a merit system, a system that measures quantity or quality of production, or "any factor other than sex."

To establish the factor-other-than-sex defense, an employer must show that "a *bona fide business-related reason* exists for using the gender-neutral factor that results in a wage differential." This requires demonstrating that the pay disparity was based *solely* on factors other than sex. The employer carries the burden of persuasion, not just production, in asserting this defense.

Hudson concedes that Dreves has established a prima facie case under the VFEPA; however, the parties dispute whether Hudson has presented the Court with a valid "factor other than sex" that explains the differential in pay between Dreves and her male successor, Dixon. To avoid summary judgment for Dreves, Hudson has the burden of showing that the facts viewed in its favor demonstrate that factors other than sex could explain the entirety of the pay disparity between Dreves and Dixon. The parties disagree vehemently about the extent of the pay disparity, but the question at this stage can be broken down into two straightforward components: First, what is the smallest disparity between what Hudson paid Dreves and what it paid Dixon that the facts, viewed in the light most favorable to Hudson, support? Second, has Hudson proffered valid factors other than sex that explain the entirety of that gap?

Dreves asks the Court to compare the difference between her starting salary in 2003 and Dixon's starting salary in 2010; however, the responsibilities of the general manager expanded in 2007. For that reason, Dreves's 2007 salary of $45,505 is the earliest one that reflects the exact responsibilities that Dixon assumed in 2010. Adjusting for inflation, Dreves's 2007 salary was $47,561 in 2010 dollars. The pay gap that must be explained by factors other than sex is $4,939, the difference between Dixon's starting salary of $52,500 and $47,561.

The Court is cognizant of the fact that Dreves's 2007 salary may also have taken into account her substantial experience as a general manager in Burlington, experience that Dixon did not have when he started in 2010. From this standpoint, the difference between Dreves's 2007 salary and Dixon's 2010 salary may very well understate the extent of the pay disparity between the two because it does not take into account the fact that she had much more experience. Because the Court must view the facts most favorably to Hudson, the Court makes no attempt to factor Dreves's greater experience at this juncture; however, Dreves is not foreclosed from arguing that her experience relative to Dixon should factor into a calculation of damages.

### 1. Experience

A comparator's past work experience does not justify a pay differential simply because those experiences make him well-suited for his position; rather, the comparator's experience must justify the employer's decision to pay the comparator more than another employee who is doing the same work. It is therefore the comparator's experience *vis-à-vis* the claimant that is salient.

In this case, Hudson argues that Dixon's six years of experience with the company in several managerial roles as well as his direct experience in Burlington made him the ideal candidate to replace Dreves as general manager of the Burlington operation. While Nieves and Scorcia may have recognized that Dixon's experience may have made him suited to replace Dreves, it does not justify paying Dreves less for the same work. Dreves had much more experience than Dixon. At the time she was fired, Dreves had spent 23 years in retail management, ten of which were as the general manager at Burlington International Airport. To the extent that Dreves and Dixon's relative experience justified a pay disparity, it should have favored Dreves, not Dixon. For this reason, Hudson has not met its burden of persuasion in establishing that the disparity between Dreves's and Dixon's pay is explained by its attempt to induce a more qualified employee to take a position.

## C. Negotiation

Finally, Hudson suggests that its salary negotiation with Dixon constitutes a factor other than sex that justifies paying him more than it paid Dreves. Hudson's use of its negotiation with Dixon as a defense has two shortcomings. First, it ignores the fact that Hudson's initial offer of $50,000 was itself unattributable to any factor other than sex. If Dixon had simply accepted that offer, the negotiation would have resulted in a salary that is unjustified by any of the other factors Hudson cites. It would be strange indeed if an indefensible disparity could be transformed to a defensible (and larger) one whenever a comparator asked for more money than was originally offered.

Second, there is simply no basis for the proposition that a male comparator's ability to negotiate a higher salary is a legitimate business-related justification to pay a woman less. To hold otherwise would eviscerate the federal and Vermont equal pay provisions. It would also require the Court to accept a theory that is essentially indistinguishable from the repudiated argument that employers are justified in paying men more than women because men command higher salaries in the marketplace. *See Corning Glass Works v. Brennan,* 417 U.S. 188, 205 (1974). ("That the company took advantage of a job market in which it could pay women less may be understandable as a matter of economics, but its differential nevertheless became illegal once Congress enacted into law the principle of equal pay for equal work."). Reliance on the difference in value that the market places on women and men "became illegal once Congress enacted into law the principle of equal work for equal pay."

In sum, Hudson has failed to meet its burden of establishing a factor other than sex or combination of factors other than sex that are sufficient to explain the pay disparity between Dreves and Dixon, even when all the facts and inferences are viewed in the light most favorable to Hudson. For that reason, Dreves is entitled to summary judgment on the issue of liability with respect to her equal pay claim under the VEFPA.[FN12] Nonetheless, factual disputes concerning Dreves's damages persist, so Dreves is not entitled to summary judgment on that portion of her claim.

FN12. Dreves did not move for summary judgment on her federal EPA claim even though the standard for liability is identical.

## CONCLUSION

For the reasons stated, the Court grants summary judgment to Dreves on the issue of Hudson's liability under her Vermont equal pay claim.

The heart of Dreves's complaint is that she was paid less than her male successor. Though the ultimate responsibility of this Court is to explain how Vermont and federal law bears on the particular facts of Dreves's case, the Court is not blind to the larger problem it reflects. The unequivocal promise of equal pay for equal work continues to go unrealized. In 2012, women's median weekly earnings were 81 percent of men's. Not all of that disparity is the product of discrimination, whether intentional or otherwise, but at least ten percentage points of the gap is unexplained by measurable differences in male and female educational attainment, work experience, choice of occupation, choice of industry, and other factors. Alarmingly, women who have earned professional degrees, work longer hours, or hold management positions are subject to some of the largest pay disparities.[FN17]

FN17. *See* Bureau of Labor Statistics, *Highlights of Women's Earnings in 2011,* http:// www.bls.gov/cps/cpswom2011.pdf, at (accessed June 6, 2013) (showing an earnings ratio of 74.9 between women and men who have earned a bachelors' degree or higher); (showing a pay ratio of 71.6% for women in management, professional, and related occupations)

In the fifty years since the passage of the Equal Pay Act, we have taken significant strides towards parity. In 1963, the female to male earnings ratio was 60 percent and many of the country's leading colleges and universities were admitting their first female students. Today, the gap is markedly smaller, and women outnumber men in higher education.

That progress justifies confidence but not complacency. The convergence of wages has slowed in recent years and in 2012, the wage gap actually increased slightly. Any gap in the pay of men and women, whether forty or ten or one percent, is an implicit statement to our children that we value the work of our daughters less than that of our sons. It sends a message that Congress, the Vermont General Assembly, and this Court reject.

In this case, Hudson has not identified factors that meet this standard. Even if the extent of the pay disparity between Dreves and her male successor is viewed in the light most favorable to Hudson, there is a gap of $4,939 that is unexplained by gender-neutral, *bona-fide,* and business-related factors. Though an employer may have valid reasons to offer an employee a higher salary to induce him or her to take a job, "inducement" in and of itself is not a sufficient defense. An employer may justify a pay disparity by showing that it sought to induce an employee with better qualifications or greater experience than the claimant, but the Court is not presented with those circumstances in this case. Finally, the fact that a male employee demanded and received a higher salary is not an acceptable justification for failing to provide a female employee with equal pay for equal work. When an employer defends a pay disparity as the product of either "market forces" or, as here, a discrete negotiation in which a man demands a higher salary that a woman, the result is the same: the employer does not have a legally valid defense and the employee is entitled to summary judgment.

# CHAPTER 6

# PARTIES

1. As you have seen in some of the earlier cases, there are times when a number of different parties may have an involvement with a particular fact situation. This chapter includes cases illustrating how various parties may get involved.

First, FRCP 17 states that every action "must be prosecuted in the name of the real party in interest." That sounds simple enough – but may turn out to be relatively complex. For example, an issue of subrogation may be involved. Here is how that works. Whenever an insurance company pays a claim for its insured, for example, the insurance company becomes subrogated to the rights of the insured. In other words, if A and B are in an auto accident, and A is insured by State Farm and suffers a loss covered by that insurance, State Farm will pay A. Then State Farm has the same right to go after B that A would have had. State Farm, because of subrogation, has the right to go after B to recover whatever amount State Farm has paid to A.

However, it is generally felt that an insurance company is not a particularly attractive plaintiff. A jury might be expected to be quite sympathetic to an elderly widow who had been injured by a careless driver. The jury would be expected to be much less concerned about an insurance company, trying to recoup the money that it has already paid to the elderly widow. So whenever possible, insurance companies try to bring suit in the name of the insured, (for example, the elderly widow), rather than in the name of the insurance company.

It then may become an issue as to who is the "real party in interest" – the elderly widow or the insurance company? Rule 17 requires that any suit be brought in the name of the real party in interest. The next case sets forth the basic rules for making that determination of who is the real party in interest. Under what circumstances will an insurance company be allowed to bring suit in the name of the insured?

# A. REAL PARTY IN INTEREST - RULE 17

485 F. 2D 78
UNITED STATES COURT OF APPEALS,
FOURTH CIRCUIT
VIRGINIA ELECTRIC AND POWER COMPANY, WHO SUES FOR
THE USE AND BENEFIT OF INSURANCE COMPANY OF NORTH
AMERICA, APPELLEE,
V.
WESTINGHOUSE ELECTRIC CORPORATION AND
STONE & WEBSTER ENGINEERING CORPORATION,
APPELLANTS.

DECIDED OCTOBER 3, 1973. (CERT. DENIED BY U.S. SUPREME COURT
2/19/74)

CRAVEN, Circuit Judge:

Virginia Electric and Power Company (VEPCO) brought this action on April 16, 1969, on its own behalf and on behalf of its insurer and partial subrogee, Insurance Company of North America (INA), to recover damages resulting from the failure of one of VEPCO's power generating stations. The defendants are Westinghouse Electric Corporation, builder of the station, and Stone and Webster Engineering Corporation, the engineers. Jurisdiction was founded on diversity of citizenship under 28 U. S.C. § 1332.

The defendants moved to dismiss the action urging that INA, by virtue of the subrogation, was the real party in interest under Fed.R.Civ.P. 17 and must prosecute the action as plaintiff. Since INA is a Pennsylvania corporation, its joinder as party plaintiff would destroy diversity jurisdiction and require dismissal because defendant Westinghouse is also a Pennsylvania corporation. Alternatively, the defendants urged that INA was an indispensable person who could not be made a party (because to do so would destroy diversity jurisdiction) and that under Fed.R.Civ.P. 19(b) the action should be dismissed. The district court denied the motion to dismiss and certified, under 28 U.S.C. § 1292(b), that a controlling question of law was involved as to which there existed a substantial ground for difference of opinion and that an immediate appeal would materially advance the litigation. We granted an interlocutory appeal to determine whether the district court properly concluded VEPCO could pursue this action for the entire loss and that the action could continue without joinder of INA. We think so, and affirm.

I

On January 22, 1967, a failure occurred at VEPCO's Mount Storm Generating Station, resulting in alleged losses of approximately $2,200,000. There was in effect an insurance policy issued by INA securing VEPCO against the risk of additional operating costs due to physical damage or loss to facilities. The policy contained a $100,000 deductible clause. Pursuant to the policy, INA originally paid VEPCO $1,900,000.

VEPCO then brought this action on its own behalf for $200,000 (the $100,000 loss uninsured under the deductible provision of the insurance policy plus $100,000 alleged expediting expenses) and for $1,900,000 for its insurer, INA. VEPCO also instituted a separate action against INA for an alleged balance owing under the insurance policy of approximately $200,000. VEPCO and INA settled that action, and VEPCO received an additional $50,000 from INA, leaving VEPCO with an unreimbursed loss of $150,000. In consideration of the settlement, VEPCO and INA agreed that INA would furnish counsel and have exclusive control over the present action and that INA would prosecute VEPCO's claims for the remaining uninsured loss.[FN1] Additionally, VEPCO executed a subrogation agreement whereby INA was subrogated to the rights of VEPCO against Westinghouse and Stone and Webster.[FN2]

FN1. VEPCO executed a cooperation agreement which provided in part:
Vepco also agrees that the conduct of the continuing action to recover against Westinghouse and/or S. & W. for such claims shall be under the exclusive direction and control of the Insurer . . . . (7) Vepco and I.N.A. further agree that counsel for I.N.A. shall represent its claims, if any, against Westinghouse and/or S. & W. for uninsured loss, claim for which is in the sum of $150,000.00, but it shall be under no obligation for costs and expenses incurred in the prosecution of such claims conjunctively with those to which I.N.A. is subrogated.

FN2. The subrogation instrument provided in relevant part:

... Vepco hereby subrogates the Insurer to all of its remaining rights of recovery against Westinghouse Electric Corporation and/or Stone & Webster Engineering Corporation ... for the losses and claims and damages resulting from an occurrence on January 22, 1967, at its Mount Storm Power Station, Mt. Storm, West Virginia.

The district court, construing the agreement of cooperation and the instrument of subrogation, found "that VEPCO has retained a pecuniary interest and that standing is retained by virtue of its intent to recover the uninsured loss." This finding is not contested on appeal. The district court then held that VEPCO as a real party in interest could proceed in the action to attempt to recover the full loss.[FN3]

> FN3. Counsel for INA has now represented to the court that INA is willing to execute an agreement binding it to any final judgment in this action.

## II

About the best that can be said for Fed.R.Civ.P. 17 is that it conveys a certain amount of correct information about naming plaintiffs. Originally intended to incorporate the more permissive practice of equity to permit persons having an equitable or beneficial interest to sue in their own names, it is now thought by some commentators to serve only to confuse the already complex problems of determining whether diversity of citizenship exists. Intended to expand the class of those who may sue to include persons having an equitable or beneficial interest, the rule is unfortunately susceptible to efforts to prevent prosecution of claims as illustrated by this appeal. Ingenious counsel are enabled to present yet another "decision point" resulting in extravagant expenditures of time and effort before ever reaching the merits.

"Rule 17(a) is a barnacle on the federal practice ship. It ought to be scraped away. ... Rules 19, 17(b) and substantive rules as to stating a claim for relief are adequate without interjecting the meaningless, logically inconsistent commands of the real party in interest rule ...." Kennedy, Federal Rule 17(a); Will the Real Party in Interest Please Stand?, 51 Minn.L.Rev. 675, 724 (1967).

The meaning and object of the real party in interest principle embodied in Rule 17 is that the action must be brought by a person who possesses the right to enforce the claim and who has a significant interest in the litigation. Whether a plaintiff is entitled to enforce the asserted right is determined according to the substantive law. In a diversity action such as this one, the governing substantive law is the law of the state. While the question of in whose name the action must be prosecuted is procedural, and thus governed by federal law, its resolution depends on the underlying substantive law of the state.

In the present case it appears that VEPCO has both a sufficient interest in the litigation and is entitled under the substantive law to recover for the entire loss resulting from the failure of its generating station. VEPCO retained a significant pecuniary interest in the litigation. Thus this is not a case where an insurer-subrogee has paid an *entire* loss suffered by the insured and is the only real party in interest who must sue in his own name.[FN8] In addition to having a sufficient interest in the litigation, VEPCO, as subrogor, is entitled under the substantive law to bring suit for its entire loss. VEPCO, being entitled to enforce the right, may bring this action even though INA will ultimately receive the major portion of any recovery.

> FN8. Where an insured has been fully recompensed but appears as a party, the insured is a nominal party only. The insured's citizenship is not considered for purposes of diversity of citizenship, and upon timely motion the insurer-subrogee must be substituted as the party plaintiff. *Link Aviation, Inc. v. Downs*. In the present case, the subrogation is only partial, and it is only the citizenship of the plaintiff, VEPCO, which is considered in determining diversity.

To allow VEPCO to maintain this action for the entire loss accords with the purposes of Rule 17. Under the common-law practice, a subrogee or assignee could enforce his rights only in the name of his subrogor or assignor. The original purpose of Rule 17 was to liberalize party rules, *i. e.,* to allow an assignee or subrogee to enforce his rights in his own name.

Where there is partial subrogation, there are two real parties in interest under Rule 17. Either party may bring suit–the insurer-subrogee to the extent it has reimbursed the subrogor, or the subrogor for either the entire loss or only its unreimbursed loss. If either the subrogor or subrogee brings suit, joinder is often appropriate upon proper motion by the defendant. But joinder is not appropriate, and certainly not required by Rule 17, for the purpose of destroying diversity jurisdiction and requiring dismissal. Even without joinder the partial subrogee is generally precluded from bringing a subsequent action against the defendants where a judgment has been rendered in a suit by the subrogor for the entire loss. Multiplicity of suits, one by the subrogor for his loss and one by the subrogee for the reimbursed loss, is thus prevented as fully as if joinder were compelled.

In the present case INA will clearly be precluded from subjecting Westinghouse and Stone and Webster to further suits. Under the cooperation agreement between

VEPCO and INA filed with the court, INA has full and exclusive control of the litigation. It is settled under the applicable substantive law that any judgment will have full res judicata effect as to INA in these circumstances.

Thus we conclude that the district court properly allowed the suit to continue with VEPCO as the party plaintiff. "It would result in unnecessary hardship and confusion to hold that such a company such as INA, entitled to partial subrogation, must go into a state court and try over again issues that will be settled in the federal court. There is nothing in modern practice which sanctions any such absurdity."

## III

Fed.R.Civ.P. 19 requires that certain parties be joined if feasible. It is clear that a partial subrogee is a person to be joined if feasible under Fed.R.Civ.P. 19(a). However, here the partial subrogee, INA, cannot be joined without destroying diversity jurisdiction, and Rule 19 by its own terms exhibits concern that the courts not be deprived of jurisdiction by unnecessary joinder. Fed.R.Civ.P. 19(a). In such a case the court must consider the four factors enumerated in Rule 19(b) to determine whether in equity and good conscience the action should proceed, or should be dismissed. Whether a particular lawsuit must be dismissed in the absence of that person, can only be determined in the context of particular litigation."

A review of the four interests which must be considered by the district court in its discretion demonstrates that the court below properly allowed the action to continue without joinder of INA. First, it is difficult to see how a judgment in this action might be prejudicial to either INA or the parties before the court. INA has control of the litigation and the opportunity to fully litigate its derivative rights arising out of subrogation. The defendants have failed to show how they would be prejudiced on the merits by nonjoinder of INA. Second, if any prejudice were shown, it can be avoided by the shaping of relief. Third, it is clear that a judgment rendered in INA's absence will be fully adequate to protect both INA and the parties and the public interest in the termination of disputes on the merits. The defendants have not sought any affirmative relief against VEPCO and do not suggest they would seek affirmative relief against INA if it were joined. Also because of INA's control of the suit, it will be bound by any judgment in favor of the defendants. Fourth, it is not clear that plaintiff would have an adequate remedy in the courts of either Virginia or another state against both Stone and Webster and Westinghouse.[FN22] INA, the partial subrogee, is thus clearly not an "indispensable" party to this litigation. The district court below correctly allowed the action to continue without joinder of INA.

FN22. It further appears that commencement of suit in another court may now be barred by the statute of limitations.

Accordingly, for the reasons stated, the decision of the district court is.
Affirmed.

# B. IMPLEADER - RULE 14 – THIRD-PARTY PRACTICE

2. Sometimes when A sues B it may be that B feels that if B is held liable, it may be because a third party, C, was wholly or partially at fault. For example, if A suffers food poising after eating sushi at B's restaurant, A may file suit against B. However B might claim that if the sushi really did cause the food poising, then C is to blame – since C delivered the sushi to the restaurant and all B did was take the sushi out of the box and put it on A's plate. In a situation like that as soon as A sues B, B will add C to the lawsuit by use of a technique called *impleader*. [B brings *in* another party by means of *impleader*.]

In the federal rules this is called *Third-Party Practice*. By means of rather cumbersome wording, FRCP 14 provides that "A defending party may, as a third-party plaintiff, serve a summons and complaint on a nonparty who is or may be liable to it for all or part of the claim against it." The defendant should implead the third party promptly, or the court may decide that it is too late to do so.

**2009 WL 2448440**

**UNITED STATES DISTRICT COURT,**

**N.D. TEXAS, DALLAS DIVISION**

**AMERICAN INTERNATIONAL SPECIALTY LINES INSURANCE**

**COMPANY, PLAINTIFF,**

**V.**

**7-ELEVEN, INC., DEFENDANT.**

*OL on last page
of this case.*

DECIDED AUGUST 7, 2009

MEMORANDUM OPINION AND ORDER

BARBARA M.G. LYNN, District Judge.

Before the Court is Defendant 7–Eleven, Inc.'s Motion for Leave to Join Responsible Third Party. For the following reasons, the Motion is **DENIED.**

**Background**

Plaintiff American International Specialty Lines Insurance Company ("AISLIC") filed this suit against 7–Eleven, Inc. ("7–Eleven") on May 12, 2008. AISLIC claims petroleum hydrocarbons leaked out of storage containers located under a 7–Eleven store, forming a "plume" that seeped into the soil and groundwater under an adjacent Diamond Shamrock gas station, the owners of which are insured by AISLIC. Under the direction of the Texas Commission on Environmental Quality ("TCEQ"), AISLIC, as indemnitor of the Diamond Shamrock property owner, was required to investigate and clean up the contamination. In this case, AISLIC seeks to recover from 7–Eleven costs it incurred during that effort. On June 5, 2009, 7–Eleven filed a motion seeking leave to file a third party complaint against Albertson's, LLC ("Albertson's"). 7–Eleven claims that a separate plume of petroleum and petroleum hydrocarbons formed under a nearby Albertson's Express store, which contributed to the contamination of the Diamond Shamrock property, thereby increasing the remediation costs AISLIC now seeks to recover from 7–Eleven. 7–Eleven's proposed third party complaint seeks to hold Albertson's liable for any remediation costs associated with Albertson's role. AISLIC opposes the Motion, arguing that it is futile and untimely, and that the addition of Albertson's would prejudice its efforts in preparing for trial.

## Legal Standard

A third party complaint may be filed against those who may be at least partially liable for the plaintiff's claims against the defendant. Where, as here, a defendant seeks to file a third party complaint more than ten days after serving its answer, it must obtain leave of court to do so, and the court is given "wide discretion" when deciding whether to allow a third party complaint. District courts considering whether to grant leave have considered factors such as possible prejudice to the other parties, undue delay by the third party plaintiff, and whether allowing the third party complaint would further the goals of Rule 14, by eliminating duplicative suits and promoting judicial economy.

There is little case law in the Fifth Circuit which examines what factors are properly considered when deciding whether to permit a third party complaint.

## Analysis

### I. Whether Albertson's is Potentially Liable to 7–Eleven

The Court first addresses whether Albertson's is potentially liable to 7–Eleven for the claims asserted by AISLIC. AISLIC argues that the TCEQ has determined that AISLIC is not responsible for remediating contamination on the Diamond Shamrock site caused by the Albertson's plume, and therefore, AISLIC has not incurred costs for such remediation.

AISLIC's position is based on the following facts. An October 31, 2007, report was authored by Titan Engineering, an environmental consulting firm hired to investigate contamination of the Diamond Shamrock site, and sent to the TCEQ ("the Titan Report"), and it informed the TCEQ that the Diamond Shamrock site was apparently also being contaminated, by leakage from the Albertson's property. On December 10, 2007, the TCEQ responded to the Titan Report, stating that "no further delineation of the Alberton's contamination will be necessary. The TCEQ will request further investigation from the Albertson's facility." Bart Gaskill, AISLIC's environmental consultant, testified that his firm identified Albertson's as a separate source of groundwater contamination on the Diamond Shamrock site and originally planned to clean up that contamination; however, once TCEQ was informed that Albertson's was the second source of pollution, TCEQ stated that Diamond Shamrock's owners were not responsible for cleaning up the Albertson's contamination, and therefore, no new cleanup costs for any Albertson's contamination were thereafter incurred by AISLIC. As of May 12, 2009, when Plaintiff's expert, Steve Larson, was deposed, Larson had not attempted to determine whether there had been a comingling of the Albertson's and 7–Eleven plumes.

7–Eleven asserts that although the TCEQ relieved AISLIC of further responsibility for remediation of contamination resulting from the Albertson's plume, AISLIC has not addressed Albertson's responsibility for all or part of AISLIC's costs incurred during past efforts to remediate the Diamond Shamrock site, costs which AISLIC now seeks to recover from 7–Eleven.

The proposed third party complaint seeks to hold Albertson's liable for the portion of the remediation costs caused by Albertson's. AISLIC seeks from 7–Eleven reimbursement for both past and future costs associated with the cleanup of the Diamond Shamrock site. As Albertson's is potentially liable for at least some of these costs, it would be properly joined as a third party defendant, if a request for such had been made in accordance with the timing established by the Court's Scheduling Order of September 22, 2008, which required that Motions to Join be filed by November 14, 2008.

II. Leave to Amend

### 1) Timing

7–Eleven argues that leave should be granted because it only recently learned the "full extent of the facts" associated with the Albertson's plume and how the Albertson's plume affected the Diamond Shamrock site. It cites the May 7, 2009, Gaskill deposition as "specifically confirming" that the Albertson's plume contaminated the Diamond Shamrock site and that Gaskill discussed the Titan Report and its reference to Albertson's possible involvement.

AISLIC's position is that the Motion is untimely. In response to 7–Eleven's argument that it did not know about the facts underlying Albertson's involvement until recently, AISLIC states that on September 28, 2007, AISLIC's counsel sent 7–Eleven's counsel a copy of the Affected Property Assessment Report for the Diamond Shamrock site, which identifies Albertson's as a potential off-site source of the Diamond Shamrock contamination. Similarly, on November 27, 2007, AISLIC's counsel sent a letter to 7–Eleven's counsel, attaching a copy of a letter Titan sent to TCEQ, identifying Albertson's as a source of contamination. AISLIC argues that these facts establish that 7–Eleven had notice of Albertson's possible involvement since the fall of 2007.

AISLIC further argues that 7–Eleven and its environmental consultants were aware that the TCEQ documents demonstrating Albertson's connection with the contamination were a matter of public record and available at any time, but that 7–Eleven apparently did not request them. AISLIC argues that once this suit was filed, 7–Eleven had a duty to investigate the possibility that other parties were responsible for the contamination, but did not do so. AISLIC also argues that 7–Eleven has failed to vigorously pursue Albertson's possible liability even after it learned of Albertson's involvement. Larson, 7–Eleven's expert, reported that he had reviewed the site's Affected Property Assessment Report, but he acknowledged during his deposition that he had neither attempted to determine whether the two plumes were comingled, nor tried to separate Albertson's part in the contamination from 7–Eleven's. AISLIC further notes that 7–Eleven did not serve discovery requests on AISLIC until April 7, 2009, thereby delaying its ability to use the discovery to find other responsible parties. Although the parties apparently had an agreement not to serve formal discovery requests until March 30, 2009, 7–Eleven is responsible for the effects of its decision to delay discovery on its ability to add parties after the date set in the Scheduling Order.

### 2) Prejudice

AISLIC also argues it would be prejudiced by the joinder of Albertson's at this time, because the parties have already conducted discovery, hired experts, and filed motions for summary judgment. The addition of Albertson's would force both sides to seek leave to conduct additional discovery and would likely require both parties to amend their expert reports, and perhaps to seek new grounds for summary judgment. 7–Eleven argues that AISLIC would not be prejudiced by the filing of the third party complaint because the trial is now set for December 7, 2009, and that the purposes of Rule 14 and the interests of judicial economy would be served by allowing the addition of factually-related claims.

### Analysis

The Court denies the Motion for Leave for several reasons. First, it is untimely. 7–Eleven knew, or should have known, of Albertson's potential liability in late 2007, when it was provided the Affected Property Assessment Report, and additionally when it received the November 26, 2007 letter from Titan to TCEQ. Further, all of TCEQ's files relating to the Diamond Shamrock site are available to the public, and a review of those documents would indicate that Albertson's is a potential source of contamination. 7–Eleven did not act expeditiously in pursuing these issues, even after it retained an expert.

Second, AISLIC would be prejudiced if the Court were to join Albertson's as a third party defendant, likely resulting in it engaging in new discovery and amending pleadings, all of which would increase AISLIC's costs, and prejudice its efforts to prepare for trial of this case. Further, 7–Eleven has not even argued, much less demonstrated, that it could not pursue Albertson's at a later time, so the prejudice to it resulting from a denial of its Motion is modest at best. Finally, the interests of judicial economy are not significantly advanced by the addition of Albertson's as a third party defendant at this late hour.

## Conclusion

The Motion for Leave to Join Albertson's is **DENIED.** AISLIC's Motion to Strike 7–Eleven's Reply Appendix Docket Entry # 56 is **DENIED AS MOOT.**

OL: Motion for leave ~~denied~~ to add Albertson's as ~~an~~ a 3rd party for supplemental underground contamination is denied on the grounds of untimeliness, likely prejudicing American and did not advance the interest of the judicial economy.

# C. INTERPLEADER - RULE 22 AND 28 USC 1335

3. Interpleader is used when there are several claimants to the same limited fund, such as a specific bank account. The bank, understandably, wants to be sure that *all* of the claimants to the bank account assert their claims in the same suit – so that the bank does not end up paying more than once. The technique that may be used by the bank to accomplish this goal is called *interpleader*.

In the federal system two types of interpleader are available: Rule 22 interpleader and Section 1335 interpleader. Section 1335 interpleader, authorized by 28 USC 1335, is by far the better way to go. Both types of interpleader will be explained below.

A. As you might guess from the number, 28 USC 1335 is actually a *key* to the federal courthouse – just as 1331 (federal question), 1332 (diversity), and 1333 (admiralty) are *keys* to the federal courthouse. The Sec. 1335 key is a two-sided key. Two factors are required.

The fund at issue must be worth at least $500 [yes, $500 – even today!]; and at least *one claimant* must be from a state different from at least one other *claimant*. In other words, if there is *minimum* diversity between any two *claimants,* and at least $500 in the fund, the federal court will accept jurisdiction – as soon as the bank has deposited the fund into the control of the court. The citizenship of the bank, frequently called the *stakeholder* is of no significance at all. So it is very easy to get this sort of litigation into federal court.

28 USC 1397 provides that an interpleader action under Sec. 1335 may be brought in any judicial district in which one or more *claimants* reside. And perhaps best of all, 28 USC 2361 provides for nation-wide service of process in a Sec. 1335 interpleader action.

> In any civil action ... under section 1335... a district court may issue its process for all claimants and enter its order restraining them from instituting or prosecuting any proceeding in any State or United States court affecting the property ... involved in the interpleader action.

B. Rule 22 interpleader is available when there is not *minimal* diversity between the claimants – when all of the claimants are from the same state – but the bank (stakeholder) is from a state that is different from the state of any one of the claimants. For example, if all of the claimants are from Colorado, but the bank is a citizen of Delaware, there would be *complete* diversity required by 1332, but there would *not* be the *minimal* diversity required for 1335 jurisdiction.

Remember that Rule 22 is *not* a key to the courthouse. It is just one of the Rules of Procedure directing how a case should be handled – once the federal courts have subject matter jurisdiction over the litigation. Once the plaintiff has gained admission to the courthouse - by use of the 1332 diversity key, or the 1331 federal question key, for example – then Rule 22 becomes applicable and authorizes the stakeholder to join all claimants in the same suit. Notice that the *plaintiff* in an interpleader action will normally be the *stakeholder,* since it is the stakeholder that wants all the claims to the limited fund to be asserted in one lawsuit. All of the *claimants* to the fund will normally be named as the *defendants.*

Here are some examples.

## 87 S.CT. 1199
## SUPREME COURT OF THE UNITED STATES
## STATE FARM FIRE & CASUALTY CO. ET AL., PETITIONERS,
## V.
## KATHRYN TASHIRE ET AL., RESPONDENTS

DECIDED APRIL 10, 1967

*OL on last page of case*

**Mr. Justice FORTAS delivered the opinion of the Court.**

Early one September morning in 1964, a Greyhound bus proceeding northward through Shasta County, California, collided with a southbound pickup truck. Two of the passengers aboard the bus were killed. Thirty-three others were injured, as were the bus driver, the driver of the truck and its lone passenger. One of the dead and 10 of the injured passengers were Canadians; the rest of the individuals involved were citizens of five American States. The ensuing litigation led to the present case, which raises important questions concerning administration of the interpleader remedy in the federal courts.

The litigation began when four of the injured passengers filed suit in California state courts, seeking damages in excess of $1,000,000. Named as defendants were Greyhound Lines, Inc., a California corporation; Theron Nauta, the bus driver; Ellis Clark, who drove the truck; and Kenneth Glasgow, the passenger in the truck who was apparently its owner as well. Each of the individual defendants was a citizen and resident of Oregon. Before these cases could come to trial and before other suits were filed in California or elsewhere, petitioner State Farm Fire & Casualty Company, an Illinois corporation, brought this action in the nature of interpleader in the United States District Court for the District of Oregon.

In its complaint State Farm asserted that at the time of the Shasta County collision it had in force an insurance policy with respect to Ellis Clark, driver of the truck, providing for bodily injury liability up to $10,000 per person and $20,000 per occurrence and for legal representation of Clark in actions covered by the policy. It asserted that actions already filed in California and others which it anticipated would be filed far exceeded in aggregate damages sought the amount of its maximum liability under the policy. Accordingly, it paid into court the sum of $20,000 and asked the court (1) to require all claimants to establish their claims against Clark and his insurer in this single proceeding and in no other, and (2) to discharge State Farm from all further obligations under its policy—including its duty to defend Clark in lawsuits arising from the accident. Alternatively, State Farm expressed its conviction that the policy issued to Clark excluded from coverage accidents resulting from his operation of a truck which belonged to another and was being used in the business of another. The complaint, therefore, requested that the court decree that the insurer owed no duty to Clark and was not liable on the policy, and it asked the court to refund the $20,000 deposit.

Joined as defendants were Clark, Glasgow, Nauta, Greyhound Lines, and each of the prospective claimants. Jurisdiction was predicated upon 28 U.S.C. s 1335, the federal interpleader statute, and upon general diversity, of citizenship, there being diversity between two or more of the claimants to the fund and between State Farm and all of the named defendants.

An order issued, requiring the defendants to show cause why they should not be restrained from filing or prosecuting "any proceeding in any state or United States Court affecting the property or obligation involved in this interpleader action, and specifically against the plaintiff and the defendant Ellis D. Clark." Personal service was effected on each of the American defendants, and registered mail was employed to reach the 11 Canadian claimants. Defendants Nauta, Greyhound, and several of the injured passengers responded, contending that the policy did cover this accident and advancing various arguments for the position that interpleader was either impermissible or inappropriate in the present circumstances. Greyhound, however, soon switched sides and moved that the court broaden any injunction to include Nauta and Greyhound among those who could not be sued except within the confines of the interpleader proceeding.

When a temporary injunction along the lines sought by State Farm was issued by the United States District Court for the District of Oregon, the present respondents moved to dismiss the action and, in the alternative, for a change of venue—to the Northern District of California, in which district the collision had occurred. After a hearing, the court declined to dissolve the temporary injunction, but continued the motion for a change of venue. The injunction was later broadened to include the protection sought by Greyhound, but modified to permit the filing—although not the prosecution—of [additional] suits. The injunction, therefore, provided that all suits against Clark, State Farm, Greyhound, and Nauta be prosecuted in the interpleader proceeding.

On interlocutory appeal, the Court of Appeals for the Ninth Circuit reversed. We granted certiorari.

I

Before considering the issues presented by the petition for certiorari, we find it necessary to dispose of a question neither raised by the parties nor passed upon by the courts below. Since the matter concerns our jurisdiction, we raise it on our own motion. The interpleader statute, 28 U.S.C. Sec. 1335, applies where there are "Two or more adverse claimants, of diverse citizenship." This provision has been uniformly construed to require only "minimal diversity," that is, diversity of citizenship between  two or more claimants, without regard to the circumstance that other rival claimants may be co-citizens. The language of the statute, the legislative purpose broadly to remedy the problems posed by multiple claimants to a single fund, and the consistent judicial interpretation tacitly accepted by Congress, persuade us that the statute requires no more. There remains, however, the question whether such a statutory construction is consistent with Article III of our Constitution, which extends the federal judicial power to "Controversies * * * between citizens of different States * * * and between a State, or the Citizens thereof, and foreign States, Citizens or Subjects." In *Strawbridge v. Curtiss* (1806), this Court held that the diversity of citizenship statute required "complete diversity:" where co-citizens appeared on both sides of a dispute, jurisdiction was lost. But Chief Justice Marshall there purported to construe only "The words of the act of congress," not the Constitution itself. And in a variety of contexts this Court and the lower courts have concluded that Article III poses no obstacle to the legislative extension of federal jurisdiction, founded on diversity, so long as any two adverse parties are not co-citizens. Accordingly, we conclude that the present case is properly in the federal courts.

## II

We do not agree with the Court of Appeals that, in the absence of a state law or contractual provision for "direct action" suits against the insurance company, the company must wait until persons asserting claims against its insured have reduced those claims to judgment before seeking to invoke the benefits of federal interpleader. Until the decision below, every court confronted by the question has concluded that the 1948 revision removed whatever requirement there might previously have been that the insurance company wait until at least two claimants reduced their claims to judgments. The commentators are in accord.

Considerations of judicial administration demonstrate the soundness of this view which, in any event, seems compelled by the language of the present statute, which is remedial and to be liberally construed. Were an insurance company required to await reduction of claims to judgment, the first claimant to obtain such a judgment or to negotiate a settlement might appropriate all or a disproportionate slice of the fund before his fellow claimants were able to establish their claims. The difficulties such a race to judgment pose for the insurer, and the unfairness which may result to some claimants, were among the principal evils the interpleader device was intended to remedy.

## III

The fact that State Farm had properly invoked the interpleader jurisdiction under Sec. 1335 did not, however, entitle it to an order both enjoining prosecution of suits against it outside the confines of the interpleader proceeding and also extending such protection to its insured, the alleged tortfeasor. Still less was Greyhound Lines entitled to have that order expanded so as to protect itself and its driver, also alleged to be tortfeasors, from suits brought by its passengers in various state or federal courts. Here, the scope of the litigation, in terms of parties and claims, was vastly more extensive than the confines of the "fund," the deposited proceeds of the insurance policy. In these circumstances, the mere existence of such a fund cannot, by use of interpleader, be employed to accomplish purposes that exceed the needs of orderly contest with respect to the fund.

There are situations, of a type not present here, where the effect of interpleader is to confine the total litigation to a single forum and proceeding. One such case is where a stakeholder, faced with rival claims to the fund itself, acknowledges—or denies—his liability to one or the other of the claimants. In this situation, the fund itself is the target of the claimants. It marks the outer limits of the controversy. It is, therefore, reasonable and sensible that interpleader, in discharge of its office to protect the fund, should also protect the stakeholder from vexatious and multiple litigation. In this context, the suits sought to be enjoined are squarely within the language of 28 U.S.C. Sec. 2361, which provides in part:

> In any civil action of interpleader or in the nature of interpleader under section 1335 of this title, a district court may issue its process for all claimants and enter its order restraining them from instituting or prosecuting any proceeding in any State or United States court affecting the property, instrument or obligation involved in the interpleader action.

But the present case is another matter. Here, an accident has happened. Thirty-five passengers or their representatives have claims which they wish to press against a variety of defendants: the bus company, its driver, the owner of the truck, and the truck driver. The circumstance that one of the prospective defendants happens to have an insurance policy is a fortuitous event which should not of itself shape the nature of the ensuing litigation. For example, a resident of California, injured in California aboard a bus owned by a California corporation should not be forced to sue that corporation anywhere but in California simply because another prospective defendant carried an insurance policy. And an insurance company whose maximum interest in the case cannot exceed $20,000 and who in fact asserts that it has no interest at all, should not be allowed to determine that dozens of tort plaintiffs must be compelled to press their claims—even those claims which are not against the insured and which in no event could be satisfied out of the meager insurance fund—in a single forum of the insurance company's choosing. There is nothing in the statutory scheme, and very little in the judicial and academic commentary upon that scheme, which requires that the tail be allowed to wag the dog in this fashion.

State Farm's interest in this case, which is the fulcrum of the interpleader procedure, is confined to its $20,000 fund. That interest receives full vindication when the court restrains claimants from seeking to enforce against the insurance company any judgment obtained against its insured, except in the interpleader proceeding itself. To the extent that the District Court sought to control claimants' lawsuits against the insured and other alleged tortfeasors, it exceeded the powers granted to it by the statutory scheme.

[We recognize, of course, that our view of interpleader means that it cannot be used to solve all the vexing problems of multiparty litigation arising out of a mass tort. But interpleader was never intended to perform such a function, to be an all-purpose "bill of peace." Had it been so intended, careful provision would necessarily have been made to insure that a party with little or no interest in the outcome of a complex controversy should not strip truly interested parties of substantial rights—such as the right to choose the forum in which to establish their claims, subject to generally applicable rules of jurisdiction, venue, service of process, removal, and change of venue.] None of the legislative and academic sponsors of a modern federal interpleader device viewed their accomplishment as a "bill of peace," capable of sweeping dozens of lawsuits out of the various state and federal courts in which they were brought and into a single interpleader proceeding.

In light of the evidence that federal interpleader was not intended to serve the function of a "bill of peace" in the context of multiparty litigation arising out of a mass tort, of the anomalous power which such a construction of the statute would give the stakeholder, and of the thrust of the statute and the purpose it was intended to serve, we hold that the interpleader statute did not authorize the injunction entered in the present case. Upon remand, the injunction is to be modified consistently with this opinion.

## IV

The judgment of the Court of Appeals is reversed, and the case is remanded to the United States District Court for proceedings consistent with this opinion.

4. Note: The reach of Section 1335 may not extend far enough to reach foreign claimants who can claim sovereign immunity. The following case will help you understand lots of important concepts in the international field, and will also be important to the issue of Required Parties, covered later in this chapter.

*OL: After the court held that federal jurisdiction was valid, they determined that all though State Farm properly invoked the interpleader jurisdiction, the injunction at question was improper because the insurer should not have the power to dictate forum and venue be a defendant had an insurance policy of theirs.*

## 128 S.CT. 2180
## SUPREME COURT OF THE UNITED STATES
## REPUBLIC OF THE PHILIPPINES, ET AL., PETITIONERS,
## V.
## JERRY S. PIMENTEL, TEMPORARY ADMINISTRATOR OF
## THE ESTATE OF MARIANO J. PIMENTEL, DECEASED, ET AL.,
## RESPONDENTS

DECIDED JUNE 12, 2008

**Justice KENNEDY delivered the opinion of the Court.**

This interpleader case turns on the interpretation and proper application of Rule 19 of the Federal Rules of Civil Procedure and requires us to address the Rule's operation in the context of foreign sovereign immunity.

This interpleader action was commenced to determine the ownership of property allegedly stolen by Ferdinand Marcos when he was the President of the Republic of the Philippines. Two entities named in the suit invoked sovereign immunity. They are the Republic of the Philippines and the Philippine Presidential Commission on Good Governance, referred to in turn as the Republic and the Commission. They were dismissed, but the interpleader action proceeded to judgment over their objection. Together with two parties who remained in the suit, the Republic and the Commission now insist it was error to allow the litigation to proceed. Under Rule 19, they contend, the action should have been dismissed once it became clear they could not be joined as parties without their consent.

The United States Court of Appeals for the Ninth Circuit, agreeing with the District Court, held the action could proceed without the Republic and the Commission as parties. Among the reasons the Court of Appeals gave was that the absent, sovereign entities would not prevail on their claims. We conclude the Court of Appeals gave insufficient weight to the foreign sovereign status of the Republic and the Commission, and that the court further erred in reaching and discounting the merits of their claims.

I

A

When the opinion of the Court of Appeals is consulted, the reader will find its quotations from Rule 19 do not accord with its text as set out here; for after the case was in the Court of Appeals and before it came here, the text of the Rule changed. The Rules Committee advised the changes were stylistic only.

As the substance and operation of the Rule both pre- and post–2007 are unchanged, we will refer to the present, revised version.

"Rule 19. Required Joinder of Parties.

(a) Persons Required to Be Joined if Feasible.

(1) *Required Party.* A person who is subject to service of process and whose joinder will not deprive the court of subject-matter jurisdiction must be joined as a party if:

"(A) in that person's absence, the court cannot accord complete relief among existing parties; or

"(B) that person claims an interest relating to the subject of the action and is so situated that disposing of the action in the person's absence may:
(i) as a practical matter impair or impede the person's ability to protect the interest; or
(ii) leave an existing party subject to a substantial risk of incurring double, multiple, or otherwise inconsistent obligations because of the interest.

(2) *Joinder by Court Order.* If a person has not been joined as required, the court must order that the person be made a party. A person who refuses to join as a plaintiff may be made either a defendant or, in a proper case, an involuntary plaintiff.

(3) *Venue.* If a joined party objects to venue and the joinder would make venue improper, the court must dismiss that party.

(b) When Joinder Is Not Feasible. If a person who is required to be joined if feasible cannot be joined, the court must determine whether, in equity and good conscience, the action should proceed among the existing parties or should be dismissed. The factors for the court to consider include:

(1) the extent to which a judgment rendered in the person's absence might prejudice that person or the existing parties;

(2) the extent to which any prejudice could be lessened or avoided by:
(A) protective provisions in the judgment;
(B) shaping the relief; or
(C) other measures;

(3) whether a judgment rendered in the person's absence would be adequate; and

(4) whether the plaintiff would have an adequate remedy if the action were dismissed for nonjoinder.

B

In 1972, Ferdinand Marcos, then President of the Republic, incorporated Arelma, S.A. (Arelma), under Panamanian law. Around the same time, Arelma opened a brokerage account with Merrill Lynch, Pierce, Fenner & Smith Inc. (Merrill Lynch) in New York, in which it deposited $2 million. As of the year 2000, the account had grown to approximately $35 million.

Alleged crimes and misfeasance by Marcos during his presidency became the subject of worldwide attention and protest. A class action by and on behalf of some 9,539 of his human rights victims was filed against Marcos and his estate, among others. The class action was tried in the United States District Court for the District of Hawaii and resulted in a nearly $2 billion judgment for the class. See *Hilao v. Estate of Marcos*. We refer to that litigation as the Pimentel case and to its class members as the Pimentel class. In a related action, the Estate of Roger Roxas and Golden Budha [*sic*] Corporation (the Roxas claimants) claim a right to execute against the assets to satisfy their own judgment against Marcos' widow, Imelda Marcos. See *Roxas v. Marcos*, 89 Hawai'i 91 (1998).

The Pimentel class claims a right to enforce its judgment by attaching the Arelma assets held by Merrill Lynch. The Republic and the Commission claim a right to the assets under a 1955 Philippine law providing that property derived from the misuse of public office is forfeited to the Republic from the moment of misappropriation.

After Marcos fled the Philippines in 1986, the Commission was created to recover any property he wrongfully took. Almost immediately the Commission asked the Swiss Government for assistance in recovering assets—including shares in Arelma— that Marcos had moved to Switzerland. In compliance, the Swiss Government froze certain assets and, in 1990, that freeze was upheld by the Swiss Federal Supreme Court. In 1991, the Commission asked the Sandiganbayan, a Philippine court of special jurisdiction over corruption cases, to declare forfeited to the Republic any property Marcos had obtained through misuse of his office. That litigation is still pending in the Sandiganbayan.

The Swiss assets were transferred to an escrow account set up by the Commission at the Philippine National Bank (PNB), pending the Sandiganbayan's decision as to their rightful owner. The Republic and the Commission requested that Merrill Lynch follow the same course and transfer the Arelma assets to an escrow account at PNB. Merrill Lynch did not do so. Facing claims from various Marcos creditors, including the Pimentel class, Merrill Lynch instead filed an interpleader action under 28 U.S.C. § 1335. The named defendants in the interpleader action were, among others, the Republic and the Commission, Arelma, PNB, and the Pimentel class (the respondents here).

The *Pimentel* case had been tried as a class action before Judge Manuel Real of the United States District Court for the Central District of California, who was sitting by designation in the District of Hawaii after the Judicial Panel on Multidistrict Litigation consolidated the various human rights complaints against Marcos in that court. Judge Real directed Merrill Lynch to file the interpleader action in the District of Hawaii, and he presided over the matter.

After being named as defendants in the interpleader action, the Republic and the Commission asserted sovereign immunity under the Foreign Sovereign Immunities Act of 1976 (FSIA), 28 U.S.C. § 1604. They moved to dismiss pursuant to Rule 19(b), based on the premise that the action could not proceed without them. Arelma and PNB also moved to dismiss pursuant to Rule 19(b). Without addressing whether they were entitled to sovereign immunity, Judge Real initially rejected the request by the Republic and the Commission to dismiss the interpleader action. They appealed, and the Court of Appeals reversed. It held the Republic and the Commission are entitled to sovereign immunity and that under Rule 19(a) they are required parties (or "necessary" parties under the old terminology).The Court of Appeals entered a stay pending the outcome of the litigation in the Sandiganbayan over the Marcos assets.

After concluding that the pending litigation in the Sandiganbayan could not determine entitlement to the Arelma assets, Judge Real vacated the stay, allowed the action to proceed, and awarded the assets to the Pimentel class. A week later, in the case initiated before the Sandiganbayan in 1991, the Republic asked that court to declare the Arelma assets forfeited, arguing the matter was ripe for decision. The Sandiganbayan has not yet ruled.

In the interpleader case the Republic, the Commission, Arelma, and PNB appealed the District Court's judgment in favor of the Pimentel claimants. This time the Court of Appeals affirmed. Dismissal of the interpleader suit, it held, was not warranted under Rule 19(b) because, though the Republic and the Commission were required ("necessary") parties under Rule 19(a), their claim had so little likelihood of success on the merits that the interpleader action could proceed without them. One of the reasons the court gave was that any action commenced by the Republic and the Commission to recover the assets would be barred by New York's 6–year statute of limitations for claims involving the misappropriation of public property. The court thus found it unnecessary to consider whether any prejudice to the Republic and the Commission might be lessened by some form of judgment or interim decree in the interpleader action. The court also considered the failure of the Republic and the Commission to obtain a judgment in the Sandiganbayan—despite the Arelma share certificates having been located and held in escrow at PNB since 1997–1998—to be an equitable consideration counseling against dismissal of the interpleader suit. The court further found it relevant that allowing the interpleader case to proceed would serve the interests of the Pimentel class, which, at this point, likely has no other available forum in which to enforce its judgment against property belonging to Marcos.

This Court granted certiorari.

## II

We begin with the question we asked the parties to address when we granted certiorari: Whether the Republic and the Commission, having been dismissed from the interpleader action based on their successful assertion of sovereign immunity, had the right to appeal the District Court's determination under Rule 19 that the action could proceed in their absence; and whether they have the right to seek this Court's review of the Court of Appeals' judgment affirming the District Court.

Without implying that respondents are correct in saying the Republic and the Commission could neither appeal nor become parties here, we conclude we need not rule on this point. Other parties before us, Arelma and PNB, also seek review of the Court of Appeals' decision affirming the District Court. As a general matter any party may move to dismiss an action under Rule 19(b). A court with proper jurisdiction may also consider *sua sponte* the absence of a required person and dismiss for failure to join.

Respondents argue, however, that Arelma and PNB have no standing to raise before this Court the question whether the action may proceed in the absence of the Republic and the Commission. Arelma and PNB lost on the merits of their underlying claims to the interpleaded assets in both the District Court and the Court of Appeals. By failing to petition for certiorari on that merits ruling, respondents contend, Arelma and PNB abandoned any entitlement to the interpleaded assets and therefore lack a concrete stake in the outcome of further proceedings. We disagree. Dismissal of the action under Rule 19(b) would benefit Arelma and PNB by vacating the judgment denying them the interpleaded assets. A party that seeks to have a judgment vacated in its entirety on procedural grounds does not lose standing simply because the party does not petition for certiorari on the substance of the order.

## III

We turn to the question whether the interpleader action could proceed in the District Court without the Republic and the Commission as parties.

In all events it is clear that multiple factors must bear on the decision whether to proceed without a required person. This decision "must be based on factors varying with the different cases, some such factors being substantive, some procedural, some compelling by themselves, and some subject to balancing against opposing interests."

## IV

We turn to Rule 19 as it relates to this case. The application of subdivision (a) of Rule 19 is not contested. The Republic and the Commission are required entities because "without them as parties in this interpleader action, their interests in the subject matter are not protected." All parties appear to concede this. The disagreement instead centers around the application of subdivision (b), which addresses whether the action may proceed without the Republic and the Commission, given that the Rule requires them to be parties.

The Court of Appeals erred in not giving the necessary weight to the absent entities' assertion of sovereign immunity. The court in effect decided the merits of the Republic and the Commission's claims to the Arelma assets. Once it was recognized that those claims were not frivolous, it was error for the Court of Appeals to address them on their merits when the required entities had been granted sovereign immunity. The action may not proceed.

A

In considering whether the Republic and the Commission would be prejudiced if the action were to proceed in their absence, the Court of Appeals gave insufficient weight to their sovereign status. The doctrine of foreign sovereign immunity has been recognized since early in the history of our Nation. It is premised upon the "perfect equality and absolute independence of sovereigns, and the common interest impelling them to mutual intercourse." *Schooner Exchange v. McFaddon*, (1812). The Court has observed that the doctrine is designed to "give foreign states and their instrumentalities some protection from the inconvenience of suit.

The privilege is codified by federal statute. FSIA, 28 U.S.C. §§ 1330, 1602–1611, provides that "a foreign state shall be immune from the jurisdiction of the courts of the United States and of the States except as provided in sections 1605 to 1607," absent existing international agreements to the contrary.

The District Court and the Court of Appeals failed to give full effect to sovereign immunity when they held the action could proceed without the Republic and the Commission. Giving full effect to sovereign immunity promotes the comity interests that have contributed to the development of the immunity doctrine. "Foreign sovereign immunity is a matter of grace and comity."

Comity and dignity interests take concrete form in this case. The claims of the Republic and the Commission arise from events of historical and political significance for the Republic and its people. The Republic and the Commission have a unique interest in resolving claims to the Arelma assets and in determining if, and how, the assets should be used to compensate those persons who suffered grievous injury under Marcos. There is a comity interest in allowing a foreign state to use its own courts for a dispute if it has a right to do so. The dignity of a foreign state is not enhanced if other nations bypass its courts without right or good cause. Then, too, there is the more specific affront that could result to the Republic and the Commission if property they claim is seized by the decree of a foreign court.

Where sovereign immunity is asserted, and the claims of the sovereign are not frivolous, dismissal of the action must be ordered where there is a potential for injury to the interests of the absent sovereign.

The Court of Appeals accordingly erred in undertaking to rule on the merits of the Republic and the Commission's claims. There may be cases where the person who is not joined asserts a claim that is frivolous. In that instance a court may have leeway under both Rule 19(a)(1), defining required parties, and Rule 19(b), addressing when a suit may go forward nonetheless, to disregard the frivolous claim. Here, the claims of the absent entities are not frivolous; and the Court of Appeals should not have proceeded on the premise that those claims would be determined against the sovereign entities that asserted immunity.

The Court of Appeals determined that the claims of the Republic and the Commission as to the assets would not succeed because a suit would be time barred in New York. This is not necessarily so. If the Sandiganbayan rules that the Republic owns the assets or stock of Arelma because Marcos did not own them and the property was forfeited to the Republic under Philippine law, then New York misappropriation rules might not be the applicable law. For instance, the Republic and the Commission, standing in for Arelma based upon the Sandiganbayan's judgment, might not pursue a misappropriation of public property suit, as the Court of Appeals assumed they would. They might instead, or in the alternative, file suit for breach of contract against Merrill Lynch. They would argue the statute of limitations would start to run if and when Merrill Lynch refused to hand over the assets ("In New York, a breach of contract cause of action accrues at the time of the breach"). Or the Republic and the Commission might bring an action either in state or federal court to enforce the Sandiganbayan's judgment. Merrill Lynch makes arguments why these actions would not succeed, see Brief for Merrill Lynch as *Amicus Curiae* 26–27, to which the Republic, the Commission, and the United States respond. We need not seek to predict the outcomes. It suffices that the claims would not be frivolous.

As these comments indicate, Rule 19 cannot be applied in a vacuum, and it may require some preliminary assessment of the merits of certain claims. For example, the Rule directs a court, in determining who is a required person, to consider whether complete relief can be afforded in their absence. Likewise, in the Rule 19(b) inquiry, a court must examine, to some extent, the claims presented and the interests likely to be asserted both by the joined parties and the absent entities or persons. Here, however, it was improper to issue a definitive holding regarding a nonfrivolous, substantive claim made by an absent, required entity that was entitled by its sovereign status to immunity from suit. That privilege is much diminished if an important and consequential ruling affecting the sovereign's substantial interest is determined, or at least assumed, by a federal court in the sovereign's absence and over its objection.

As explained above, the decision to proceed in the absence of the Republic and the Commission ignored the substantial prejudice those entities likely would incur. This most directly implicates Rule 19(b)'s first factor, which directs consideration of prejudice both to absent persons and those who are parties. We have discussed the absent entities. As to existing parties, we do not discount the Pimentel class' interest in recovering damages it was awarded pursuant to a judgment. Furthermore, combating public corruption is a significant international policy. The policy is manifested in treaties providing for international cooperation in recovering forfeited assets.

This policy does support the interest of the Pimentel class in recovering damages awarded to it. But it also underscores the important comity concerns implicated by the Republic and the Commission in asserting foreign sovereign immunity. The error is not that the District Court and the Court of Appeals gave too much weight to the interest of the Pimentel class, but that it did not accord proper weight to the compelling claim of sovereign immunity.

Based on these considerations we conclude the District Court and the Court of Appeals gave insufficient weight to the likely prejudice to the Republic and the Commission should the interpleader proceed in their absence.

B

As to the second Rule 19(b) factor—the extent to which any prejudice could be lessened or avoided by relief or measures alternative to dismissal,— there is no substantial argument to allow the action to proceed. No alternative remedies or forms of relief have been proposed to us or appear to be available. If the Marcos estate did not own the assets, or if the Republic owns them now, the claim of the Pimentel class likely fails; and in all events, if there are equally valid but competing claims, that too would require adjudication in a case where the Republic and the Commission are parties.

C

As to the third Rule 19(b) factor—whether a judgment rendered without the absent party would be adequate, Fed. Rule Civ. Proc. 19(b)(3)—the Court of Appeals understood "adequacy" to refer to satisfaction of the Pimentel class' claims. But adequacy refers to the "public stake in settling disputes by wholes, whenever possible." This "social interest in the efficient administration of justice and the avoidance of multiple litigation" is an interest that has "traditionally been thought to support compulsory joinder of absent and potentially adverse claimants." Going forward with the action without the Republic and the Commission would not further the public interest in settling the dispute as a whole because the Republic and the Commission would not be bound by the judgment in an action where they were not parties.

D

As to the fourth Rule 19(b) factor—whether the plaintiff would have an adequate remedy if the action were dismissed for nonjoinder—the Court of Appeals made much of what it considered the tort victims' lack of an alternative forum should this action be dismissed. This seems to assume the plaintiff in this interpleader action was the Pimentel class. It is Merrill Lynch, however, that has the statutory status of plaintiff as the stakeholder in the interpleader action.

It is true that, in an interpleader action, the stakeholder is often neutral as to the outcome, while other parties press claims in the manner of a plaintiff. That is insufficient, though, to overcome the statement in the interpleader statute that the stakeholder is the plaintiff. We do not ignore that, in context, the Pimentel class (and indeed all interpleader claimants) are to some extent comparable to the plaintiffs in noninterpleader cases. Their interests are not irrelevant to the Rule 19(b) equitable balance; but the other provisions of the Rule are the relevant ones to consult.

Merrill Lynch, as the stakeholder, makes the point that if the action is dismissed it loses the benefit of a judgment allowing it to disburse the assets and be done with the matter. Dismissal of the action, it urges, leaves it without an adequate remedy, for it "could potentially be forced ... to defend lawsuits by the various claimants in different jurisdictions, possibly leading to inconsistent judgments." A dismissal of the action on the ground of nonjoinder, however, will protect Merrill Lynch in some respects. That disposition will not provide Merrill Lynch with a judgment determining the party entitled to the assets, but it likely would provide Merrill Lynch with an effective defense against piecemeal litigation and inconsistent, conflicting judgments. As matters presently stand, in any later suit against it Merrill Lynch may seek to join the Republic and the Commission and have the action dismissed under Rule 19(b) should they again assert sovereign immunity. Dismissal for nonjoinder to some extent will serve the purpose of interpleader, which is to prevent a stakeholder from having to pay two or more parties for one claim.

Any prejudice to Merrill Lynch in this regard is outweighed by prejudice to the absent entities invoking sovereign immunity. Dismissal under Rule 19(b) will mean, in some instances, that plaintiffs will be left without a forum for definitive resolution of their claims. But that result is contemplated under the doctrine of foreign sovereign immunity. If a court determines that none of the exceptions to sovereign immunity applies, the plaintiff will be barred from raising his claim in any court in the United States.

V

In this case, the action must be dismissed. This leaves the Pimentel class, which has waited for years now to be compensated for grievous wrongs, with no immediate way to recover on its judgment against Marcos. And it leaves Merrill Lynch, the stakeholder, without a judgment.

The balance of equities may change in due course. One relevant change may occur if it appears that the Sandiganbayan cannot or will not issue its ruling within a reasonable period of time. Other changes could result when and if there is a ruling. If the Sandiganbayan rules that the Republic and the Commission have no right to the assets, their claims in some later interpleader suit would be less substantial than they are now. If the ruling is that the Republic and the Commission own the assets, then they may seek to enforce a judgment in our courts; or consent to become parties in an interpleader suit, where their claims could be considered; or file in some other forum if they can obtain jurisdiction over the relevant persons. We do note that if Merrill Lynch, or other parties, elect to commence further litigation in light of changed circumstances, it would not be necessary to file the new action in the District Court where this action arose, provided venue and jurisdictional requirements are satisfied elsewhere. The present action, however, may not proceed.

The judgment of the Court of Appeals for the Ninth Circuit is reversed, and the case is remanded with instructions to order the District Court to dismiss the interpleader action.

# D. INTERVENTION - RULE 24

4. Sometimes the existing parties to a lawsuit are perfectly happy to have the suit continue with only themselves, A and B, for example, as parties to the suit. But some outsider, C, insists that it must be allowed to join the suit. Enjoy the following case on intervention.

## 379 F.2D 818
## UNITED STATES COURT OF APPEALS FIFTH CIRCUIT.
## ATLANTIS DEVELOPMENT CORPORATION, LTD., APPELLANT,
## V.
## UNITED STATES OF AMERICA ET AL., APPELLEES

DECIDED JUNE 12, 1967

JOHN R. BROWN, Circuit Judge:

This case involves a little bit of nearly everything - a little bit of oceanography, a little bit of marine biology, a little bit of the tidelands oil controversy, a little bit of international law, a little bit of latter day Marco Polo exploration. But these do not command our resolution since the little bits are here controlled by the less exciting bigger, if not big, problem of intervention. The District Court declined to permit mandatory intervention as a matter of right or to allow intervention as permissive. As is so often true, a ruling made to avoid delay, complications, or expense turns out to have generated more of its own. With the main case being stayed by the District Court pending this appeal, it is pretty safe to assume that the case would long have been decided on its merits (or lack of them) had intervention of either kind been allowed. And this seems especially unfortunate since it is difficult to believe that the presence of the attempted intervenor would have added much to the litigation. All of this becomes the more ironic, if not unfortunate, since the intervenor and the Government sparring over why intervention ought or ought not to have been allowed, each try to persuade us the one was bound to win, the other lose on the merits which each proceeds to argue as though the parties were before or in the court. Adding to the problem, or perhaps more accurately, aiding in the solution of it, are the mid-1966 amendments to the Federal Rules of Civil Procedure including specifically those relating to intervention. We reverse.

What the jousting is all about is the ownership in, or right to control the use, development of and building on a number of coral reefs or islands comprising Pacific Reef, Ajax Reef, Long Reef, an unnamed reef and Triumph Reef which the intervenor has called the 'Atlantis Group' because of the name given them by Anderson, its predecessor in interest and the supposed discoverer. Discovery in the usual sense of finding a land area, continent or island heretofore unknown could hardly fit this case. For these reefs are, and have been for years, shown on Coast and Geodetic Charts and, more important, they are scarcely 4 1/2 miles off Elliott Key and 10 miles off the Coast of the Florida Mainland. Although the depth of water washing over them at mean low water is likely one of the factual controversies having some possible significance, it seems undisputed that frequently and periodically the bodies of these reefs become very apparent especially in rough seas when the rock or the top surface of the rock becomes plainly visible in the troughs of the seas.

Just how or in what manner these reefs were "discovered" is so far unrevealed. Some time in 1962 William T. Anderson discovered the reefs apparently by conceiving the idea of occupying them through the construction of facilities for a fishing club, marina, skin diving club, a hotel, and, perhaps as the chief lure, a gambling casino. Anderson made some sort of claim to it and with facilities unavailable to the adventurous explorers of the long past, he gave public notice of this in the United States and in England by newspaper advertisements in late 1962 and early 1963. These "rights" were acquired by Atlantis Development Corporation, Ltd., the proposed intervenor. Reflecting the desire manifested now by the persistent efforts to intervene to have legal rights ascertained in a peaceful fashion through established tribunals and not by self-help or the initiation of physical activities which would precipitate counter moves, physical or legal, or both, Atlantis (and predecessors) patiently sought permission from all governmental agencies, state and federal-just short of the United Nations- but to no avail. The State of Florida through the Trustees of the Internal Improvement Fund responding to a formal request stated that the property is "outside the Constitutional Boundaries of the State of Florida and therefore, not within the jurisdiction of the T.I.I.F." Undaunted, Atlantis turned to the Federal Government. To these entreaties of Department of Interior on September 14, 1962, replied: "The Department of the Interior has no jurisdiction over land that is outside the territorial limits of the United States. Questions concerning such land should be taken up with the Department of State." This was soon echoed by the answer of the Department of State on November 9, 1962, through the Assistant Legal Advisor. "The areas in question are outside of the jurisdiction of the United States and constitute a part of the high seas. The high seas are open to all nations and no state may validly subject any part of them to its sovereignty." Subsequently, Atlantis spent approximately $50,000 for surveys and the construction of four prefabricated buildings, three of which were destroyed by a hurricane in September 1963. Thereafter upon learning that the United States Corps of Engineers was asserting that permission was needed to erect certain structures on two of the reefs, Triumph and Long Reef, Atlantis commenced its long, but unrewarding, efforts either to convince the Corps of Engineers, the United States Attorney General, or both, that the island reefs were beyond the jurisdiction of United States control or to initiate litigation which would allow a judicial, peaceful resolution. The Engineers ultimately reaffirmed the earlier decision to require permits. In December 1964 on learning that the defendants in the main case had formally sought a permit from the Engineers, Atlantis notified the Government of its claim to ownership of the islands and the threatened unauthorized actions by the defendants. This precipitated further communications with the Department of Justice, with Atlantis importuning, apparently successfully, the Government to initiate the present action.

It was against this background that the litigation commenced. The suit is brought by the United States against the main defendants. The complaint was in two counts seeking injunctive relief. In the first the Government asserted that Triumph and Long Reefs are part of the bed of the Atlantic Ocean included in the Outer Continental Shelf subject to the jurisdiction, control and power of disposition of the United States. The action of the defendants in the erection of caissons on the reefs, the dredging of material from the seabed, and the depositing of the dredged material within the caissons without authorization was charged as constituting a trespass on government property. In the second count the Government alleged that the defendants were engaged in the erection of an artificial island or fixed structure on the Outer Continental Shelf in the vicinity of the reefs without a permit from the Secretary of the Army in violation of the Outer Continental Shelf Lands Act. Denying that the complaint stated a claim, F.R.Civ.P. 12(b), the defendants besides interposing a general denial asserted that the Secretary of the Army lacks jurisdiction to require a permit for construction on the Outer Continental Shelf and that the District Court lacks jurisdiction since the reefs and the defendants' actions thereon are outside the territorial limits of the United States. As thus framed, the issues in the main case are whether (1) the District Court has jurisdiction of subject matter, (2) the defendants are engaged in acts which constitute a trespass against government property, and (3) the defendants' construction activities without a permit violate various statutes.

Atlantis, seeking intervention by proposed answer and cross-claim against the defendants, admitted the jurisdiction of the District Court. It asserted that the United States has no territorial jurisdiction, dominion or ownership in or over the reefs and cannot therefore maintain the action for an injunction, and that conversely Atlantis has title to the property by discovery and occupation. In the cross-claim, Atlantis charged the defendants as trespassers against it. Appropriate relief was sought by the prayer.

The District Court without opinion declared in the order that intervenor "does not have such an interest in this cause as will justify its intervention, either as a matter of right or permissively."

The question of whether an intervention as a matter of right exists often turns on the unstated question of whether joinder of the intervenor was called for under new Rule 19. Were this the controlling inquiry, we find ample basis here to answer it in the affirmative. Atlantis - having formally informed the Government in detail of its claim of ownership to the very reefs in suit, that the defendants were trespassing against it, and having successfully urged the Government to institute suit against the defendants - seems clearly to occupy the position of a party who ought to have been joined as a defendant under new Rule 19(a)(2)(i).

When approached in this light, we think that both from the terms of Rule 24 Intervention, and Rule 19(a)(2)(i) Required Parties, intervention of right is called for here. Of course F.R.Civ.P. 24(a)(2) requires both the existence of an interest which may be impaired as a practical matter and an absence of adequate representation of the intervenor's interest by existing parties. There can be no difficulty here about the lack of representation. On the basis of the pleadings, Atlantis is without a friend in this litigation. The Government turns on the defendants and takes the same view both administratively and in its brief here toward Atlantis. The defendants, on the other hand, are claiming ownership in and the right to develop the very islands claimed by Atlantis.

Nor can there be any doubt that Atlantis "claims an interest relating to the property or transaction which is the subject of the action." The object of the suit is to assert the sovereign's exclusive dominion and control over two out of a group of islands publicly claimed by Atlantis. This identity with the very property at stake in the main case and with the particular transaction therein involved (the right to build structures with or without permission of the Corps of Engineers) is of exceptional importance.

This brings us then to the question whether these papers reflect that in the absence of Atlantis, a disposition of the main suit may as a practical matter impair of impede its ability to protect that interest - its claim to ownership and the right to control, use and develop without hindrance from the Government, the Department of Defense, or other agencies. Certain things are clear. Foremost, of course, is the plain proposition that the judgment itself as between Government and defendants cannot have any direct, immediate effect upon the rights of Atlantis, not a party to it.

But in a very real and practical sense is not the trial of this lawsuit the trial of Atlantis' suit as well? Quite apart from the contest of Atlantis' claim of sovereignty vis-a-vis the Government resulting from its "discovery" and occupation of the reefs, there are at least two basic substantial legal questions directly at issue, but not yet resolved in any Court at any time between the Government and the defendants which are inescapably present in the claim of Atlantis against the Government. One is whether these coral reefs built up by accretion of marine biology are "submerged lands" under the Outer Continental Shelf Lands Act. The second basic question is whether, assuming both from the standpoint of geographical location and their nature they constitute "lands," does the sovereignty of the United States extend to them with respect to any purposes not included in or done for the protection of the "exploring for, developing, removing, and transporting natural resources therefrom." Another, closely related, is whether the authority of the Secretary of the Army to prevent obstruction of navigation extended by § 1333(f) to "artificial islands and fixed structures," includes structures other than those "erected thereon for the purpose of exploring for, developing, removing, and transporting" mineral resources therefrom.

The Government would avoid all of these problems by urging us to rule as a matter of law on the face of the moving papers that the intervenors could not possibly win on the trial of the intervention and consequently intervention should be denied. In support it asserts that the claim that the reefs are beyond the jurisdiction of the United States is self-defeating, and under the plain meaning of the Outer Continental Shelf Lands Act and the facts revealed from the Coast and Geodetic Chart of which we must take judicial knowledge as proof of all facts shown.

The first is at least contingently answered by § 1333(b) which invests jurisdiction in the United States District Court of the nearest adjacent state. As to the others, it is, of course, conceivable that there will be some instances in which the total lack of merit is so evident from the face of the moving papers that denial of the right of intervention rests upon a complete lack of a substantial claim. But it hardly comports with good administration, if not due process, to determine the merits of a claim asserted in a pleading seeking an adjudication through an adversary hearing by denying access to the court at all. This seems especially important when dealing with interests in the outer Continental Shelf in view of the legislative history which reflected domestically the purpose of asserting a limited "horizontal jurisdiction" extending only to the seabed and subsoil, the limited nature of which was formally recognized by the International Convention on the Continental Shelf.

If in its claim against the defendants in the main suit these questions are answered favorably to the Government's position, the claim of Atlantis for all practical purposes is worthless. That statement assumes, of course, that such holding is either approved or made by this Court after an appeal to it and thereafter it is either affirmed, or not taken for review, on certiorari. It also assumes that in the subsequent separate trial of the claim of Atlantis against the Government the prior decision would be followed as a matter of stare decisis.

Do these assumptions have a realistic basis? Anyone familiar with the history of the Fifth Circuit could have but a single answer to that query. This Court, unlike some of our sister Circuit Courts who occasionally follow a different course, has long tried earnestly to follow the practice in which a decision announced by one panel of the Court is followed by all others until such time as it is reversed, either outright or by intervening decisions of the Supreme Court, or by the Court itself en banc. That means that if the defendants in the main action do not prevail upon these basic contentions which are part and parcel of the claim of Atlantis, the only way by which Atlantis can win is to secure a rehearing en banc with a successful overruling of the prior decision or, failing in either one or both of those efforts, a reversal of the earlier decision by the Supreme Court on certiorari. With the necessarily limited number of en banc hearings in this Circuit and with the small percentage of cases meriting certiorari, it is an understatement to characterize these prospects as formidable.

That is but a way of saying in a very graphic way that the failure to allow Atlantis an opportunity to advance its own theories both of law and fact in the trial (and appeal) of the pending case will if the disposition is favorable to the Government "as a practical matter impair or impede its ability to protect its interest."

Reversed.

# E. PARTIES WHO MUST BE INCLUDED - RULE 19

5. Several prior cases have discussed the issue of what parties *must* be included before litigation can proceed. Here is one more illustration of that problem – set in the context of World Cup soccer.

### 471 F.3D 377
### UNITED STATES COURT OF APPEALS, SECOND CIRCUIT
### MASTERCARD INTERNATIONAL INCORPORATED, PLAINTIFF–APPELLEE,
### FEDERATION INTERNATIONALE DE FOOTBALL ASSOCIATION, DEFENDANT–APPELLEE,
### V.
### VISA INTERNATIONAL SERVICE ASSOCIATION, INC., NON–PARTY–APPELLANT.

### DECIDED DECEMBER 18, 2006

POOLER, Circuit Judge.

Non-party movant-appellant Visa International Service Association ("Visa") moved to dismiss the underlying action contending that it is a necessary and indispensable party under Federal Rule of Civil Procedure 19. Visa also moved to intervene in the action under Federal Rule of Civil Procedure 24. Both motions were denied by the United States District Court for the Southern District of New York. Due to the expedited nature of these proceedings, this court issued an order indicating its disposition in this case on November 6, 2006. As we stated in our order, the appeal originally filed by Visa is dismissed for lack of jurisdiction and the district court's decision is otherwise affirmed. We now issue this opinion explaining our disposition.

## BACKGROUND

FIFA is the worldwide governing body of soccer (or football, as it is known outside the United States), and the organizer of the World Cup soccer tournament held every four years. The underlying lawsuit is a breach of contract action brought by MasterCard against FIFA seeking enforcement of an alleged contractual provision giving MasterCard "first right to acquire" exclusive sponsorship rights in its product category for the FIFA World Cup event in 2010 and 2014. MasterCard's complaint alleges that for the past sixteen years, MasterCard has had a contractual relationship with FIFA to act as a sponsor for the World Cup. MasterCard served as an official sponsor of the World Cup event in 1994, 1998, 2002, and 2006. Although soccer is still catching on among American television audiences, the World Cup is the most-viewed sporting event in the world. The 2002 World Cup drew a cumulative television audience of 28.8 billion viewers from over 200 countries.

In 2002, MasterCard and FIFA entered into a contract by which MasterCard acquired exclusive sponsorship rights in its product category for FIFA competitions between 2003 and 2006, including the 2006 World Cup ("the MasterCard Contract"). This contract also allegedly contained a "first right to acquire" provision that gave MasterCard a right of first refusal to sponsorship rights during the next FIFA sponsorship cycle, covering FIFA competitions from 2007—2010. According to MasterCard, under this provision, FIFA may not offer these sponsorship rights to another entity within MasterCard's product category without first providing MasterCard the opportunity to purchase these rights on comparable terms. Pursuant to this provision, FIFA allegedly offered MasterCard exclusive sponsorship rights for all FIFA competitions between 2007 and 2014, including the 2010 and 2014 World Cups. Negotiations between the parties continued over several months and allegedly culminated with FIFA sending MasterCard a 96–page "final" agreement on March 3, 2006, which MasterCard signed and returned to FIFA.

Meanwhile, FIFA was also in negotiations with Visa regarding these sponsorship rights. On March 30, 2006, MasterCard learned that FIFA had decided to finalize an agreement with Visa. On April 5, 2006, MasterCard received a letter from FIFA's president stating that FIFA had entered into a contract with Visa granting Visa the exclusive sponsorship rights to FIFA competitions, including the World Cup, through 2014 ("the Visa Contract"). The Visa Contract becomes effective January 1, 2007. Upon learning of the FIFA– Visa deal, MasterCard notified both FIFA and Visa that it considered FIFA's actions a violation of the right of first refusal provision in the MasterCard Contract and MasterCard would seek legal redress if FIFA went forward with the Visa Contract.

On April 10, 2006, Visa issued a press release announcing its contract with FIFA for exclusive sponsorship rights in the World Cup through 2014. On April 20, 2006, MasterCard filed suit in the Southern District of New York for breach of contract and sought injunctive relief "enjoining FIFA from consummating, effectuating or performing" any terms of the Visa Contract and ordering FIFA to perform its obligations under the alleged contract granting MasterCard exclusive rights through 2014. Federal jurisdiction is premised solely on diversity of citizenship.

On June 15, 2006, MasterCard filed a motion for a preliminary injunction. After FIFA's motion to dismiss for lack of personal jurisdiction and motion to compel arbitration were both denied, the district court scheduled the preliminary injunction hearing. Email communication produced in this case indicates that Visa has been in contact with FIFA regarding this litigation since the time it was filed. On September 11, 2006, two weeks before the preliminary injunction hearing, Visa sent a letter to the district court stating that it was a necessary and indispensable party to the litigation because of its contractual entitlement to the FIFA sponsorship rights. Visa claimed that because it was an indispensable party, the case must be dismissed for lack of subject matter jurisdiction. Since MasterCard and Visa are both incorporated under the laws of Delaware, Visa's joinder would destroy diversity jurisdiction—the sole basis for federal jurisdiction.

The district court construed Visa's letter submission as a motion to dismiss under Federal Rule of Civil Procedure 19, and denied the motion.

On September 25, 2006, Visa filed a motion for expedited appeal with this court. In addition, Visa filed in the district court a motion to intervene in the MasterCard–FIFA litigation under Federal Rule of Civil Procedure 24. The district court denied Visa's motion to stay. That same day, the district court held a telephonic hearing on Visa's motion to intervene, and denied that motion as well.

Meanwhile, also on September 25th, this court in response to Visa's emergency motion temporarily stayed the proceedings in the district court pending hearing of Visa's motion. After hearing oral argument, this court granted Visa's motion to stay the proceedings for the remainder of the appeal, set an expedited briefing schedule, and placed the appeal on the court's calendar for November 3, 2006. We heard oral argument as scheduled on November 3rd. Cognizant of the impending January 1, 2007 trigger date for the Visa Contract and the need for expeditious resolution of the underlying lawsuit, this court issued an order on November 6, 2006, indicating its disposition in this case, vacating the stay previously granted by this court, and remanding the matter to the district court. We now explain the basis of our decision.

## DISCUSSION

### I. Jurisdiction

Before we can discuss the merits of Visa's appeal, we must first establish that we have jurisdiction to do so. MasterCard contends that we lack jurisdiction to entertain Visa's original appeal of the Rule 19 Order because it is an uncertified interlocutory appeal. Visa, as a non-party to the underlying action, should not have been allowed to file a motion to dismiss in the district court. We find nothing in the text or notes to Rule 19 that would indicate strangers to an action may file motions to dismiss under that rule.

This is not to say, however, that the district court was prohibited from considering the issue of whether Visa was an indispensable party to the underlying litigation. Because Rule 19 protects the rights of an absentee party, both trial courts and appellate courts may consider this issue sua sponte even if it is not raised by the parties to the action. Both the trial court and the appellate court may take note of the nonjoinder of an indispensable party sua sponte. The Rule 19 issue "is sufficiently important that it can be raised at any stage of the proceedings—even sua sponte." Therefore, although the district court erroneously permitted non-party Visa to file a motion to dismiss under Rule 19, the district court was not precluded from considering the issue on its own accord. Since appellate courts have an equal duty to consider compulsory joinder issues sua sponte and ensure that indispensable parties are adequately protected, we will interpret the district court's decision to entertain Visa's "motion" as an exercise of its duty to examine Rule 19 issues on its own initiative and will reach the merits of the Rule 19 Order **if** appellate jurisdiction exists to review that Order.

We agree with MasterCard that the appeal of the Rule 19 Order originally filed by Visa is an uncertified interlocutory appeal that does not fit within the exception created by the collateral order doctrine. The denial of a motion to dismiss is not a final order and is therefore only appealable under the collateral order doctrine.

The collateral order doctrine is a "narrow exception to the general rule that interlocutory orders are not appealable as a matter of right." An interlocutory order is appealable under the collateral order doctrine only if it satisfies all of the following conditions: (1) it "conclusively determines the disputed question"; (2) it "resolves an important issue completely separate from the merits of the action;" and (3) it is "effectively unreviewable on appeal from a final judgment."). The appeal of the Rule 19 Order originally filed by Visa fails the third prong of this test. As Visa has amply demonstrated by its filing of a second appeal, the Rule 19 Order is not "effectively unreviewable on appeal from a final judgment."

The second appeal challenges the district court's denial of Visa's motion to intervene. "It is settled law that this Court has jurisdiction over an order denying intervention."

We therefore turn our attention to the second appeal filed by Visa. As indicated above, we have jurisdiction to review the denial of a motion to intervene. Once appellate jurisdiction is established, "we may simultaneously consider another issue not itself entitled to interlocutory review if the otherwise unappealable issue is inextricably intertwined with the appealable one, or if review of the otherwise unappealable issue is necessary to ensure meaningful review of the appealable one." We find review of the district court's Rule 19 Order is necessary to ensure meaningful review of the Rule 24 Order.

II. Rule 19 Order

We review the district court's failure to join a party under Rule 19 only for abuse of discretion.

### A. Rule 19(a)(1)

A party is necessary under Rule 19(a)(1) only if in that party's absence "complete relief cannot be accorded *among those already parties.*" Visa's absence will not prevent the district court from granting complete relief between MasterCard and FIFA. While there is no question that further litigation between Visa and FIFA, and perhaps MasterCard and Visa, is inevitable if MasterCard prevails in this lawsuit, Rule 19(a) (1) is concerned only with those who are already parties. MasterCard can obtain complete relief *as to FIFA* without Visa's presence in the case. If MasterCard prevails and is granted its requested relief, FIFA will be enjoined from awarding the sponsorship rights to another party, including Visa. This will resolve the dispute between MasterCard and FIFA, and Visa's presence is unnecessary to decide those questions. Thus, Visa is not a necessary party under Rule 19(a)(1).

### B. Rule 19(a)(2)(i)

We find no abuse of discretion in the district court's conclusion that Visa was not a necessary party under Rule 19(a)(2)(i). Visa claims that because MasterCard seeks to enjoin FIFA from performing the Visa Contract, its interests are clearly implicated and it is therefore entitled to appear in this litigation.

While the Visa Contract may be affected by this litigation, it is not the contract at issue in MasterCard's lawsuit. The underlying litigation involves the MasterCard Contract and whether MasterCard had a right of first refusal to the World Cup sponsorship rights. Even if MasterCard prevails and receives the relief it seeks, that does not render the Visa Contract invalid. It means that FIFA likely has breached the warranty provision of that contract, and Visa has the right to sue FIFA for that breach. Visa's ability to protect its interest in its contract with FIFA will not be impaired if is not joined here.

It is not enough under Rule 19(a)(2)(i) for a third party to have an interest, even a very strong interest, in the litigation. Nor is it enough for a third party to be adversely affected by the outcome of the litigation. Rather, necessary parties under Rule 19(a)(2)(i) are only those parties whose ability to protect their interests would be impaired *because of* that party's absence from the litigation. Thus, while Visa may have an interest that would be impaired by the outcome of this litigation, Visa still does not qualify as a necessary party under Rule 19(a)(2)(i) because the harm Visa may suffer is not *caused by* Visa's absence from this litigation. Any such harm would result from FIFA's alleged conduct in awarding Visa sponsorship rights it could not legally give.

## C. Rule 19(a)(2)(ii)

The district court's conclusion that Visa does not satisfy Rule 19(a)(2)(ii) is also not an abuse of discretion. Visa presents us with the following scenario: MasterCard prevails in the underlying lawsuit and is granted injunctive relief that prohibits FIFA from performing its obligations under the Visa Contract; Visa then sues FIFA for breach of the warranty provision in the Visa Contract seeking specific performance; Visa prevails and is granted specific performance requiring FIFA to perform its obligations under the Visa Contract. According to Visa, the possibility exists that FIFA could be under court order to perform the Visa Contract and under court order not to perform the Visa Contract, and this potential for inconsistent obligations renders Visa a necessary party to this litigation. Once again, Visa is ignoring a critical element in Rule 19(a)(2)(ii): the substantial risk of inconsistent obligations must be *caused by* the nonparty's absence in the case. Whether Visa is or is not a party in the underlying lawsuit, FIFA and Visa will litigate *their* dispute under *their* contract later on down the road if MasterCard prevails here.

We are also not persuaded that the scenario envisioned by Visa, in which the court below enjoins FIFA from performing the Visa Contract while a subsequent court orders FIFA to perform the Visa Contract, presents a "substantial risk" of inconsistent obligations, as required by Rule 19(a)(2)(ii). It is difficult to believe that a subsequent

tribunal faced with a party under a prior court-ordered injunction will nevertheless order that party to perform the very obligations a prior court has prohibited it
from performing. While Visa is correct that *it* will not be bound by any injunction
entered in the underlying litigation in its absence, FIFA is certainly bound by any
such injunction and a subsequent proceeding will have to recognize and respect the
injunction ordered by the district court in this case. It is worth noting that FIFA, the
party supposedly facing this grave predicament, has not advanced the argument that
it would be prejudiced by Visa's absence from this case. FIFA never raised the Rule 19
defense before the district court, it did not join in Visa's motion below, and it has not
participated in any way in the proceedings before this court. If FIFA actually believed
it would suffer prejudice if Visa is not a party in this case, it surely would have had
something to say on this point.

For these reasons, we cannot say that the district court's conclusion that Visa is
not a necessary party under Rule 19(a)(2)(ii) was an abuse of discretion. Having found
that Visa satisfies none of the three criteria for compulsory joinder, we affirm the
district court's decision that Visa is not a necessary party under Rule 19(a).

### D. Rule 19(b)

The district court also found that even assuming Visa were a necessary party, it
was not indispensable under Rule 19(b). Since we affirm the district court's conclusion that Visa is a not a necessary party, we need not discuss whether the district
court properly found that Visa was not an indispensable party. A party cannot be
indispensable unless it is a 'necessary party' under Rule 19(a)."). Accordingly, we
reject the challenge to the district court's subject matter jurisdiction over the underlying action.

### III. Rule 24 Order

We now turn to the district court's order denying Visa's motion to intervene under
Rule 24. Intervention as of right under Rule 24(a)(2) is granted when all four of the
following conditions are met: (1) the motion is timely; (2) the applicant asserts an
interest relating to the property or transaction that is the subject of the action; (3)
the applicant is so situated that without intervention, disposition of the action may,
as a practical matter, impair or impede the applicant's ability to protect its interest;
and (4) the applicant's interest is not adequately represented by the other parties. The
district court found that Visa's motion was untimely. The district court also noted

that, for the reasons stated at the hearing on the Rule 19 motion, Visa failed to satisfy the other conditions as well.

We find no abuse of discretion in the district court's decision to deny Visa's motion to intervene. First, even assuming Visa's motion was timely, if a party is not "necessary" under Rule 19(a), then it cannot satisfy the test for intervention as of right under Rule 24(a)(2). As Visa conceded during oral argument, these provisions contain overlapping language and thus if it failed to satisfy Rule 19(a), it could not satisfy Rule 24(a)(2). Rule 19(a)(2)(i) applies if a person "claims an interest relating to the subject of the action and is so situated that the disposition of the action in the person's absence may as a practical matter impair or impede the person's ability to protect that interest." Similarly, Rule 24(a)(2) provides for intervention as of right "when the applicant claims an interest relating to the property or transaction which is the subject of the action and the applicant is so situated that the disposition of the action may as a practical matter impair or impede the person's ability to protect that interest, unless the applicant's interest is adequately represented by existing parties." These rules are intended to mirror each other. Visa does not satisfy the definition of necessary party under Rule 19(a)(2)(i) because its absence from this litigation is not the cause of any harm to its interests. Nor will Visa's presence allow it to protect those interests. This finding also forecloses Visa's ability to intervene under Rule 24(a)(2). Visa must establish not only that it has an interest relating to the subject of the action but also that it "is so situated that *without intervention* the disposition of the action may, as a practical matter, impair or impede Visa's ability to protect its interest." Visa's ability to protect its interest will not be impaired or impeded *because* it is denied intervention in this case. As we have discussed, any harm to Visa's interests would result from FIFA's alleged conduct in breaching its contract with MasterCard and granting the sponsorship rights to Visa. And Visa cannot change this fact through intervention here since it is a stranger to the contractual dispute between MasterCard and FIFA.

Furthermore, we agree with the district court that Visa's motion to intervene was untimely. Factors to consider in determining timeliness include: "(a) the length of time the applicant knew or should have known of its interest before making the motion; (b) prejudice to existing parties resulting from the applicant's delay; (c) prejudice to the applicant if the motion is denied; and (d) the presence of unusual circumstances militating for or against a finding of timeliness. The district court properly found that these factors weigh against Visa. First, as the district court noted, Visa has known of MasterCard's position that it has prior claim to the sponsorship rights since the time this litigation began in April 2006. Visa has been in contact with FIFA throughout the course of this litigation, and MasterCard's complaint and other filings, including its motion for preliminary injunctive relief filed in June, are publicly available for anyone to access. Nevertheless, Visa did not file its motion to intervene until the eve of the preliminary injunction hearing.

Considering that Visa argued in support of its Rule 19 motion that it has a significant interest in this litigation that will be gravely prejudiced if the matter proceeds in its absence, the district court could properly find Visa's delay unjustified. Second, Visa's delay has resulted in prejudice to the existing parties because it has postponed resolution of the MasterCard–FIFA dispute, which, due to the impending January 1, 2007, trigger date for the Visa Contract, prejudices all parties. Finally, as we have discussed at length, Visa is not prejudiced if it is denied intervention since its absence from the litigation is not the cause of any harm Visa may suffer if MasterCard prevails in this lawsuit.

Accordingly, the district court could properly find Visa's motion to intervene untimely. For this reason, we also find no abuse of discretion in the district court's decision denying Visa permissive intervention. Thus, we affirm the district court's order denying Visa's motion to intervene under Rule 24.

## CONCLUSION

For the foregoing reasons, we dismiss the appeal originally filed by Visa of the district court's Rule 19 Order, reject Visa's argument that the district court lacks subject matter jurisdiction because Visa is a necessary and indispensable party, affirm the district court's Rule 24 Order, vacate the stay previously granted by this court, and remand the matter to the district court.

# CHAPTER 7

# CLASS ACTIONS

1. Class actions are an excellent way for plaintiffs to join together in one suit when each person has essentially the same claim against the same defendant, but it is not economically feasible for each plaintiff to bring an individual lawsuit. For example, if a utility provider has charged thousands of customers $500 more per year than allowed by law, it is simply not feasible for any one of those customers to sue for a refund. But If one person brings a *class action* suit on behalf of all of the utility's customers in one suit, that could make an impact.

Another situation in which a class action is highly useful is when an individual wants to challenge the constitutionality of a particular statute, but is unlikely to have the necessary "standing" long enough to see the case through to the end. For example, if a college student wants to challenge a state's "in-state-tuition" laws, the college student is unlikely to remain a college student for the full ten years it may take to litigate the case and see it through all final appeals. Once the individual graduates from college he will no longer have "standing" to litigate the case – so the case will become moot.

To solve both of these problems – injuries that are too small to justify individual suits, and wrongs for which no individual will have standing long enough to complete the litigation – bringing the litigation as a *class action* is an attractive alternative.

Once the court has *certified* that the case may proceed as a class action, the class action suit takes on a life of its own. It no longer matters if the particular members of the class stay the same, of if the legal principal involved no longer applies to the named plaintiff. The class action continues. And the named plaintiff is not allowed to settle or terminate the class action without the specific permission of the court. So courts are very careful about the initial decision on certification.

# A. STANDARD CLASS ACTIONS - RULE 23

95 S. CT. 553
SUPREME COURT OF THE UNITED STATES
CAROL MAUREEN SOSNA, ETC., APPELLANT,
V.
STATE OF IOWA ET AL., APPELLEES

DECIDED JANUARY 14, 1975

Mr. Justice REHNQUIST delivered the opinion of the Court.

Appellant Carol Sosna married Michael Sosna on September 5, 1964, in Michigan. They lived together in New York between October 1967 and August 1971, after which date they separated but continued to live in New York. In August 1972, appellant moved to Iowa with her three children, and the following month she petitioned the District Court of Jackson County, Iowa, for a dissolution of her marriage. Michael Sosna, who had been personally served with notice of the action when he came to Iowa to visit his children, made a special appearance to contest the jurisdiction of the Iowa court. The Iowa court dismissed the petition for lack of jurisdiction, finding that Michael Sosna was not a resident of Iowa and appellant had not been a resident of the State of Iowa for one year preceding the filing of her petition. In so doing the Iowa court applied the provisions of Iowa Code s 598.6 (1973) requiring that the petitioner in such an action be "for the last year a resident of the state."

Instead of appealing this ruling to the Iowa appellate courts, appellant filed a complaint in the United States District Court for the Northern District of Iowa asserting that Iowa's durational residency requirement for invoking its divorce jurisdiction violated the United States Constitution. She sought both injunctive and declaratory relief against the appellees in this case, one of whom is the State of Iowa, and the other of which is the judge of the District Court of Jackson County, Iowa, who had previously dismissed her petition.

A three-judge court held that the Iowa durational residency requirement was constitutional. We noted probable jurisdiction. For reasons stated in this opinion, we decide that this case is not moot, and hold that the Iowa durational residency requirement for divorce does not offend the United States Constitution.

## I

Appellant sought certification of her suit as a class action pursuant to Fed.Rule Civ. Proc. 23 so that she might represent the "class of those residents of the State of Iowa who have resided therein for a period of less than one year and who desire to initiate actions for dissolution of marriage or legal separation, and who are barred from doing so by the one-year durational residency requirement embodied in the Code of Iowa." The parties stipulated that there were in the State of Iowa "numerous people in the same situation as plaintiff," that joinder of those persons was impracticable, that appellant's claims were representative of the class, and that she would fairly and adequately protect the interests of the class. See Rule 23(a). This stipulation was approved by the District Court in a pretrial order. After the submission of briefs and proposed findings of fact and conclusions of law by the parties, the three-judge court by a divided vote upheld the constitutionality of the statute.

While the parties may be permitted to waive nonjurisdictional defects, they may not by stipulation invoke the judicial power of the United States in litigation which does not present an actual "case or controversy," and on the record before us we feel obliged to address the question of mootness before reaching the merits of appellant's claim. At the time the judgment of the three-judge court was handed down, appellant had not yet resided in Iowa for one year, and that court was clearly presented with a case or controversy in every sense contemplated by Art. III of the Constitution. By the time her case reached this Court, however, appellant had long since satisfied the Iowa durational residency requirement, and the Code no longer stood as a barrier to her attempts to secure dissolution of her marriage in the Iowa courts.[FN7] This is not an unusual development in a case challenging the validity of a durational residency requirement, for in many cases appellate review will not be completed until after the plaintiff has satisfied the residency requirement about which complaint was originally made.

FN7. Counsel for appellant disclosed at oral argument that appellant has in fact obtained a divorce in New York.

If appellant had sued only on her own behalf, both the fact that she now satisfies the one-year residency requirement and the fact that she has obtained a divorce elsewhere would make this case moot and require dismissal. But appellant brought this suit as a class action and sought to litigate the constitutionality of the durational residency requirement in a representative capacity. When the District Court certified the propriety of the class action, the class of unnamed persons described in the certification acquired a legal status separate from the interest asserted by appellant.[FN8] We are of the view that this factor significantly affects the mootness determination.

> FN8. The certification of a suit as a class action has important consequences for the unnamed members of the class. If the suit proceeds to judgment on the merits, it is contemplated that the decision will bind all persons who have been found at the time of certification to be members of the class. Once the suit is certified as a class action, it may not be settled or dismissed without the approval of the court. Rule 23(e).

In *Southern Pacific Terminal Co. v. ICC*, where a challenged ICC order had expired, and in *Moore v. Ogilvie*, where petitioners sought to be certified as candidates in an election that had already been held, the Court expressed its concern that the defendants in those cases could be expected again to act contrary to the rights asserted by the particular named plaintiffs involved, and in each case the controversy was held not to be moot because the questions presented were "capable of repetition, yet evading review." That situation is not presented in appellant's case, for the durational residency requirement enforced by Iowa does not at this time bar her from the Iowa courts. Unless we were to speculate that she may move from Iowa, only to return and later seek a divorce within one year from her return, the concerns that prompted this Court's holdings in *Southern Pacific* and *Moore* do not govern appellant's situation. But even though appellees in this proceeding might not again enforce the Iowa durational residency requirement against appellant, it is clear that they will enforce it against those persons in the class that appellant sought to represent and that the District Court certified. In this sense the case before us is one in which state officials will undoubtedly continue to enforce the challenged statute and yet, because of the passage of time, no single challenger will remain subject to its restrictions for the period necessary to see such a lawsuit to its conclusion.

This problem was present in *Dunn v. Blumstein*, and was there implicitly resolved in favor of the representative of the class. Respondent Blumstein brought a class action challenging the Tennessee law which barred persons from registering to vote unless, at the time of the next election, they would have resided in the State for a year and in a particular county for three months. By the time the District Court opinion was filed, Blumstein had resided in the county for the requisite three months, and the State contended that his challenge to the county requirement was moot. The District Court rejected this argument. Although the State did not raise a mootness argument in this Court, we observed that the District Court had been correct:

> Although appellee now can vote, the problem to voters posed by the Tennessee residence requirements is "capable of repetition, yet evading review."

> Although the Court did not expressly note the fact, by the time it decided the case Blumstein had resided in Tennessee for far more than a year.

The rationale of *Dunn* controls the present case. Although the controversy is no longer alive as to appellant *Sosna*, it remains very much alive for the class of persons she has been certified to represent. Like the other voters in *Dunn*, new residents of Iowa are aggrieved by an allegedly unconstitutional statute enforced by state officials. We believe that a case such as this, in which, as in *Dunn*, the issue sought to be litigated escapes full appellate review at the behest of any single challenger, does not inexorably become moot by the intervening resolution of the controversy as to the named plaintiffs.

We note, however, that the same exigency that justifies this doctrine serves to identify its limits. In cases in which the alleged harm would not dissipate during the normal time required for resolution of the controversy, the general principles of Art. III jurisdiction require that the plaintiff's personal stake in the litigation continue throughout the entirety of the litigation.

Our conclusion that this case is not moot in no way detracts from the firmly established requirement that the judicial power of Art. III courts extends only to "cases and controversies" specified in that Article. There must not only be a named plaintiff who has such a case or controversy at the time the complaint is filed, and at the time the class action is certified by the District Court pursuant to Rule 23, but there must be a live controversy at the time this Court reviews the case. The controversy may exist, however, between a named defendant and a member of the class represented by the named plaintiff, even though the claim of the named plaintiff has become moot.

In so holding, we disturb no principles established by our decisions with respect to class-action litigation. A named plaintiff in a class action must show that the threat of injury in a case such as this is "real and immediate," not "conjectural" or "hypothetical." A litigant must be a member of the class which he or she seeks to represent at the time the class action is certified by the district court. Appellant Sosna satisfied these criteria.

This conclusion does not automatically establish that appellant is entitled to litigate the interests of the class she seeks to represent, but it does shift the focus of examination from the elements of justiciability to the ability of the named representative to "fairly and adequately protect the interests of the class." Rule 23(a). Since it is contemplated that all members of the class will be bound by the ultimate ruling on the merits, Rule 23(c)(3), the district court must assure itself that the named representative will adequately protect the interests of the class. In the present suit, where it is unlikely that segments of the class appellant represents would have interests conflicting with those she has sought to advance, and where the interests of that class have been competently urged at each level of the proceeding, we believe that the test of Rule 23(a) is met. We therefore address ourselves to the merits of appellant's constitutional claim.

## II

The durational residency requirement under attack in this case is a part of Iowa's comprehensive statutory regulation of domestic relations, an area that has long been regarded as a virtually exclusive province of the States. Cases decided by this Court over a period of more than a century bear witness to this historical fact. In *Pennoyer v. Neff, (1878)*, the Court said: "The State has absolute right to prescribe the conditions upon which the marriage relation between its own citizens shall be created, and the causes for which it may be dissolved."

The imposition of a durational residency requirement for divorce is scarcely unique to Iowa, since 48 States impose such a requirement as a condition for maintaining an action for divorce. As might be expected, the periods vary among the States and range from six weeks to two years. The one-year period selected by Iowa is the most common length of time prescribed. Affirmed.

[The residency requirement was upheld.]

2. Now compare the *Sosna* case with the following case which was decided one month later by the U.S. Supreme Court.

## 95 S. CT. 848
## SUPREME COURT OF THE UNITED STATES
## THE BOARD OF SCHOOL COMMISSIONERS OF THE CITY OF
## INDIANAPOLIS ET AL., PETITIONERS,
## V.
## JEFF JACOBS ET AL., RESPONDENTS

### DECIDED FEBRUARY 18, 1975

PER CURIAM.

This action was brought in the District Court by six named plaintiffs seeking to have declared unconstitutional certain regulations and rules promulgated by the petitioner Board and to have the enforcement of those regulations and rules enjoined. In the complaint, the named plaintiffs stated that the action was brought as a class action pursuant to Fed.Rules Civ.Proc. 23(a) and (b)(2), and further stated that "plaintiff class members are all high school students attending schools managed, controlled, and maintained by the Board of School Commissioners of the City of Indianapolis." At the time this action was brought, plaintiffs were or had been involved in the publication and distribution of a student newspaper, and they alleged that certain actions taken by petitioner Board or its subordinates, as well as certain of its rules and regulations, interfered or threatened to interfere with the publication and distribution of the newspaper in violation of their First and Fourteenth Amendment rights. The plaintiffs prevailed on the merits of their action in the District Court, and the Court of Appeals affirmed. Defendants brought the case to this Court, and we granted certiorari. At oral argument, we were informed by counsel for petitioners that all of the named plaintiffs in the action had graduated from the Indianapolis school system; in these circumstances, it seems clear that a case or controversy no longer exists between the named plaintiffs and the defendants with respect to the validity of the rules at issue. The case is therefore moot unless it was duly certified as a class action pursuant to Fed.Rule Civ.Proc. 23, a controversy still exists between petitioners and the present members of the class, and the issue in controversy is such that it is capable of repetition yet evading review. Sosna v. Iowa. Because in our view there was inadequate compliance with the requirements of Rule 23(c), we have concluded that the case has become moot.

The only formal entry made by the District Court below purporting to certify this case as a class action is contained in that court's "Entry on Motion for Permanent

Injunction," wherein the court "concluded and ordered" that "the remaining named plaintiffs are qualified as proper representatives of the class whose interest they seek to protect." No other effort was made to identify the class or to certify the class action as contemplated by Rule 23(c)(1); nor does the quoted language comply with the requirement of Rule 23(c)(3) that "the judgment in an action maintained as a class action under subdivision . . . (b)(2) . . . shall include and describe those whom the court finds to be members of the class." The need for definition of the class purported to be represented by the named plaintiffs is especially important in cases like this one where the litigation is likely to become moot as to the initially named plaintiffs prior to the exhaustion of appellate review. Because the class action was never properly certified nor the class properly identified by the District Court, the judgment of the Court of Appeals is vacated and the case is remanded to that court with instructions to order the District Court to vacate its judgment and to dismiss the complaint.

So ordered.

**Mr. Justice DOUGLAS, dissenting.**

In *Sosna v. Iowa,* we found no mootness problem where a named plaintiff belatedly satisfied the durational residency requirement which she had initially sought to attack. Our holding to that effect was based upon three factors which we found present in that case: (1) a certification of the suit as a class action; (2) a continuing injury suffered by other members of the class; and (3) a time factor which made it highly probable that any single individual would find his claim inevitably mooted before the full course of litigation had been run. Applying those principles to the present case, I would hold that an Art. III controversy exists and that the parties are therefore entitled to a ruling on the merits.

This suit was instituted as a class action on behalf of all high school students attending Indianapolis public schools. The record does not contain any written order formally certifying the class, but the absence of such a written order is too slender a reed to support a holding of mootness, particularly in the face of the incontrovertible evidence that certification was intended and did, in fact, take place. At the close of the second day of the proceedings on plaintiffs' application for a temporary restraining order, the District Judge stated: "I will make a finding that this is an appropriate action, or a class action is appropriate insofar as this controversy is concerned." Later, in his written opinion, he stated that the two named plaintiffs who had not graduated by the time of these proceedings were "qualified as proper representatives of the class whose interest they seek to protect." At oral argument, moreover, counsel for the Board of School Commissioners stated, in response to a question from us, that there had been a declaration of certification of class action. The findings of the lower court, coupled with the representations of counsel for the petitioners, provide, in my view, a more than ample basis for holding that the first Sosna criterion has been met.

The Court today, however, purports to find this case distinguishable from *Sosna* in terms of the adequacy of compliance below with the requirements of Fed.Rule Civ.Proc. 23(c). A review of the record in *Sosna* discloses that the judgment entered by the District Court in that case does not in any way "include and describe those whom the court finds to be members of the class," as required by Rule 23(c)(3); nor is there anything in the record identifiable as a separate certification of the class in the sense which the Court finds to be contemplated by Rule 23(c)(1). The District Court in *Sosna,* in its pretrial order, adopted a stipulation of the parties to the effect that the prerequisites for a class action were met, and that there were numerous persons barred by Iowa's residency requirement from having their marriages dissolved; and in its final opinion, the District Court incorporated a bare reference to the fact that the suit was being treated as a class action. If these two factors alone were sufficient to establish proper certification of the class in *Sosna,* then I am at a loss to see why the factors catalogued earlier are not sufficient to establish proper certification in the instant case.

It is undoubtedly true that many federal district judges have been careless in their dealings with class actions, and have failed to comply carefully with the technical requirements of Rule 23. If we are to embark upon a program of scrupulous enforcement of compliance with those requirements, so be it; the end result may well be to avoid troublesome mootness problems of the sort which arose both here and in *Sosna.* Elementary principles of fairness to litigants suggest, however, that we should be reluctant to throw these respondents entirely out of court for their failure to induce the District Court to comply with technical requirements, when those requirements clearly were not being strictly enforced during the pendency of this litigation in the lower courts. And in particular, these principles of fairness suggest that the Court ought to provide a more reasoned explanation than it has given today for the difference in treatment which it has accorded to the appellants in *Sosna* and to the respondents herein.

With respect to the second *Sosna* criterion, it is clear that the Board intends to enforce the regulations struck down by the courts below unless it is flatly barred from doing so. A continuing dispute therefore exists between the Board and the members of the class, unless it can be said with some assurance that there are no class members who desire either to resurrect the "Corn Cob Curtain" or to distribute some comparable "underground" publication. The mere statement by counsel for the

Board that the Corn Cob Curtain "is no longer in existence" can hardly be deemed to provide that assurance; to the contrary, the Board's very insistence on the need for enforceable regulations reinforces the likelihood that the desire for unfettered expression will continue to breed clashes between Indianapolis high school students and the Board's proposed regulations. The inference of a continuing controversy is, in my view, just as strong as that which we found sufficient in *Sosna.*

The Court's readiness to find this controversy moot is particularly distressing in light of the issues at stake. True, there is no absolute time factor (such as that in *Sosna)* which will inevitably moot any future litigation over these regulations before it reaches a conclusion; it is conceivable that another plaintiff in a subsequent suit will be able to avoid the trap of mootness which the Court has sprung upon these unwitting parties. In remitting the underlying issues of this case to the course of some future, more expeditious lawsuit, however, we permit the Board to continue its enforcement, for an indefinite period of time, of regulations which have been held facially unconstitutional by both of the courts below. In allowing the Board to reimpose its system of prior restraints on student publications, we raise a very serious prospect of the precise sort of chilling effect which has long been a central concern in our First Amendment decisions. Any student who desires to express his views in a manner which may be offensive to school authorities is now put on notice that he faces not only a threat of immediate suppression of his ideas, but also the prospect of a long and arduous court battle if he is to vindicate his rights of free expression. Not the least inhibiting of all these factors will be the knowledge that all his efforts may come to naught as his claims are mooted by circumstances beyond his control.

In view of these likely consequences of today's decision, I am unable to join in the Court's rush to avoid resolving this case on the merits.

3. Very recently the U.S. Supreme Court had occasion to consider the issue of what happens if the defendant attempts to "buy off" the named plaintiff, by offering him a full settlement of his individual claims.

## 136 S.CT. 663
## SUPREME COURT OF THE UNITED STATES
## CAMPBELL–EWALD COMPANY, PETITIONER
## V.
## JOSE GOMEZ, RESPONDENT

DECIDED JANUARY 20, 2016. AS REVISED FEBRUARY 9, 2016.

**Justice GINSBURG delivered the opinion of the Court.**

Is an unaccepted offer to satisfy the named plaintiff's individual claim sufficient to render a case moot when the complaint seeks relief on behalf of the plaintiff and a class of persons similarly situated? We hold today, in accord with Rule 68 of the Federal Rules of Civil Procedure, that an unaccepted settlement offer has no force. Like other unaccepted contract offers, it creates no lasting right or obligation. With the offer off the table, and the defendant's continuing denial of liability, adversity between the parties persists.

This case presents a second question. The claim in suit concerns performance of the petitioner's contract with the Federal Government. Does the sovereign's immunity from suit shield the petitioner, a private enterprise, as well? We hold that the petitioner's status as a Government contractor does not entitle it to "derivative sovereign immunity," *i.e.*, the blanket immunity enjoyed by the sovereign.

I

The Telephone Consumer Protection Act (TCPA or Act) prohibits any person, absent the prior express consent of a telephone-call recipient, from "making any call using any automatic telephone dialing system to any telephone number assigned to a paging service or cellular telephone service." A text message to a cellular telephone, it is undisputed, qualifies as a "call" within the compass of the Act. For damages occasioned by conduct violating the TCPA, § 227(b)(3) authorizes a private right of action. A plaintiff successful in such an action may recover her "actual monetary loss" or $500 for each violation, "whichever is greater." Damages may be trebled if "the defendant willfully or knowingly violated" the Act.

Petitioner Campbell–Ewald Company (Campbell) is a nationwide advertising and marketing communications agency. Beginning in 2000, the United States Navy engaged Campbell to develop and execute a multimedia recruiting campaign. In 2005 and 2006, Campbell proposed to the Navy a campaign involving text messages sent to young adults, the Navy's target audience, encouraging them to learn more about the Navy. The Navy approved Campbell's proposal, conditioned on sending the messages only to individuals who had "opted in" to receipt of marketing solicitations on topics that included service in the Navy. In final form, the message read:

> "Destined for something big? Do it in the Navy. Get a career. An education. And a chance to serve a greater cause. For a FREE Navy video call [phone number]."

Campbell then contracted with Mindmatics LLC, which generated a list of cellular phone numbers geared to the Navy's target audience—namely, cellular phone users between the ages of 18 and 24 who had consented to receiving solicitations by text message. In May 2006, Mindmatics transmitted the Navy's message to over 100,000 recipients.

Respondent Jose Gomez was a recipient of the Navy's recruiting message. Alleging that he had never consented to receiving the message, that his age was nearly 40, and that Campbell had violated the TCPA by sending the message (and perhaps others like it), Gomez filed a class-action complaint in the District Court for the Central District of California in 2010. On behalf of a nationwide class of individuals who had received, but had not consented to receipt of, the text message, Gomez sought treble statutory damages, costs, and attorney's fees, also an injunction against Campbell's involvement in unsolicited messaging.

Prior to the agreed-upon deadline for Gomez to file a motion for class certification, Campbell proposed to settle Gomez's individual claim and filed an offer of judgment pursuant to Federal Rule of Civil Procedure 68. Campbell offered to pay Gomez his costs, excluding attorney's fees, and $1,503 per message for the May 2006 text message and any other text message Gomez could show he had received, thereby satisfying his personal treble-damages claim. Campbell also proposed a stipulated injunction in which it agreed to be barred from sending text messages in violation of the TCPA. The proposed injunction, however, denied liability and the allegations made in the complaint, and disclaimed the existence of grounds for the imposition of an injunction. The settlement offer did not include attorney's fees, Campbell observed, because the TCPA does not provide for an attorney's-fee award. Gomez did not accept the settlement offer and allowed Campbell's Rule 68 submission to lapse after the time, 14 days, specified in the Rule.

Campbell thereafter moved to dismiss the case pursuant to Federal Rule of Civil Procedure 12(b)(1) for lack of subject-matter jurisdiction. No Article III case or controversy remained, Campbell urged, because its offer mooted Gomez's individual claim by providing him with complete relief. Gomez had not moved for class certification before his claim became moot, Campbell added, so the putative class claims also became moot. The District Court denied Campbell's motion.

After limited discovery, Campbell moved for summary judgment on a discrete ground. The U.S. Navy enjoys the sovereign's immunity from suit under the TCPA, Campbell argued. The District Court granted the motion.

The Court of Appeals for the Ninth Circuit reversed the summary judgment entered for Campbell.

We granted certiorari to resolve a disagreement among the Courts of Appeals over whether an unaccepted offer can moot a plaintiff's claim, thereby depriving federal courts of Article III jurisdiction.

## II

Article III of the Constitution limits federal-court jurisdiction to "cases" and "controversies." U.S. Const., Art. III, § 2. We have interpreted this requirement to demand that "an actual controversy be extant at all stages of review, not merely at the time the complaint is filed." *Arizonans for Official English v. Arizona.* "If an intervening circumstance deprives the plaintiff of a 'personal stake in the outcome of the lawsuit,' at any point during litigation, the action can no longer proceed and must be dismissed as moot." A case becomes moot, however, "only when it is impossible for a court to grant any effectual relief whatever to the prevailing party." As long as the parties have a concrete interest, however small, in the outcome of the litigation, the case is not moot. Nothing in Rule 68 alters that basic principle.

Therefore, we now hold that Gomez's complaint was not effaced by Campbell's unaccepted offer to satisfy his individual claim.

Campbell's settlement offer proposed relief for Gomez alone, and it did not admit liability. Gomez rejected Campbell's settlement terms and the offer of judgment.

Under basic principles of contract law, Campbell's settlement bid and Rule 68 offer of judgment, once rejected, had no continuing efficacy. Absent Gomez's acceptance, Campbell's settlement offer remained only a proposal, binding neither Campbell nor Gomez. Having rejected Campbell's settlement bid, and given Campbell's continuing denial of liability, Gomez gained no entitlement to the relief Campbell previously offered. ("It is an undeniable principle of the law of contracts, that an offer of a bargain by one person to another, imposes no obligation upon the former, until it is accepted by the latter"). In short, with no settlement offer still operative, the parties remained adverse; both retained the same stake in the litigation they had at the outset.

The Federal Rule in point, Rule 68, hardly supports the argument that an unaccepted settlement offer can moot a complaint. An offer of judgment, the Rule provides, "is considered withdrawn" if not accepted within 14 days of its service. The sole built-in sanction: "If the ultimate judgment is not more favorable than the unaccepted offer, the offeree must pay the costs incurred after the offer was made." Rule 68(d).

When the settlement offer Campbell extended to Gomez expired, Gomez remained emptyhanded; his TCPA complaint, which Campbell opposed on the merits, stood wholly unsatisfied. Because Gomez's individual claim was not made moot by the expired settlement offer, that claim would retain vitality during the time involved in determining whether the case could proceed on behalf of a class. While a class lacks independent status until certified, see *Sosna v. Iowa*, a would-be class representative with a live claim of her own must be accorded a fair opportunity to show that certification is warranted.

In sum, an unaccepted settlement offer or offer of judgment does not moot a plaintiff's case, so the District Court retained jurisdiction to adjudicate Gomez's complaint. That ruling suffices to decide this case. We need not, and do not, now decide whether the result would be different if a defendant deposits the full amount of the plaintiff's individual claim in an account payable to the plaintiff, and the court then enters judgment for the plaintiff in that amount. That question is appropriately reserved for a case in which it is not hypothetical.

## III

The second question before us is whether Campbell's status as a federal contractor renders it immune from suit for violating the TCPA by sending text messages to unconsenting recipients. The United States and its agencies, it is undisputed, are not subject to the TCPA's prohibitions because no statute lifts their immunity. Do federal contractors share the Government's unqualified immunity from liability and litigation? We hold they do not.

Government contractors obtain certain immunity in connection with work which they do pursuant to their contractual undertakings with the United States. That immunity, however, unlike the sovereign's, is not absolute. Campbell asserts "derivative sovereign immunity," but can offer no authority for the notion that private persons performing Government work acquire the Government's embracive immunity. When a contractor violates both federal law and the Government's explicit instructions, as here alleged, no "derivative immunity" shields the contractor from suit by persons adversely affected by the violation.

At the pretrial stage of litigation, we construe the record in a light favorable to the party seeking to avoid summary disposition, here, Gomez. In opposition to summary judgment, Gomez presented evidence that the Navy authorized Campbell to send text messages only to individuals who had "opted in" to receive solicitations. A Navy representative noted the importance of ensuring that the message recipient list be "kosher" (*i.e.,* that all recipients had consented to receiving messages like the recruiting text), and made clear that the Navy relied on Campbell's representation that the list was in compliance. (Noting that Campbell itself encouraged the Navy to use only an opt-in list in order to meet national and local law requirements). In short, the current record reveals no basis for arguing that Gomez's right to remain message-free was in doubt or that Campbell complied with the Navy's instructions.

We do not overlook that subcontractor Mindmatics, not Campbell, dispatched the Navy's recruiting message to unconsenting recipients. But the Federal Communications Commission has ruled that, under federal common-law principles of agency, there is vicarious liability for TCPA violations. The Ninth Circuit deferred to that ruling, and we have no cause to question it. Campbell's vicarious liability for Mindmatics' conduct, however, in no way advances Campbell's contention that it acquired the sovereign's immunity from suit based on its contract with the Navy.

For the reasons stated, the judgment of the Court of Appeals for the Ninth Circuit is affirmed, and the case is remanded for further proceedings consistent with this opinion.

4. Clearly, this case would never have been brought except as a class action. When numerous small injuries can be combined into one class action, that will create enough of a fund from which the attorney representing the class can be paid. Individual members of the class may recover very little in the way of damages, but on the other hand, there is no way that the individual class members would have been willing to sue on their own. Without a class action the wrong might have continued unchallenged.

The next case, decided in 2016, illustrates another valuable use for class actions. When numerous employees are being short-changed by their employer, in relatively small amounts, it may well not be considered worthwhile for any employee to quit his or her job, bring suit individually, or go out on strike. Yet the action by the employer is wrong.

In 2011 in *Wal-mart v. Dukes*, the U.S. Supreme Court refused to allow a class action by employees challenging pay disparities. Why does the Supreme Court allow the following employee class action in 2016 when it refused to allow an employee class action in *Wal-mart* in 2011? What is the difference?

SUPREME COURT OF THE UNITED STATES

TYSON FOODS, INC., PETITIONER

V.

PEG BOUAPHAKEO, ET AL., INDIVIDUALLY AND ON BEHALF
OF ALL OTHERS SIMILARLY SITUATED, RESPONDENTS

DECIDED MARCH 22, 2016

KENNEDY, J., delivered the opinion of the Court, in which ROBERTS, C.J., and GINSBURG, BREYER, SOTOMAYOR, and KAGAN, JJ., joined. ROBERTS, C.J., filed a concurring opinion, in which ALITO, J., joined as to Part II. THOMAS, J., filed a dissenting opinion, in which ALITO, J., joined.

Justice KENNEDY delivered the opinion of the Court.

Following a jury trial, a class of employees recovered $2.9 million in compensatory damages from their employer for a violation of the Fair Labor Standards Act of 1938 (FLSA). The employees' primary grievance was that they did not receive statutorily mandated overtime pay for time spent donning and doffing protective equipment.

The employer seeks to reverse the judgment. It makes two arguments. Both relate to whether it was proper to permit the employees to pursue their claims as a class. First, the employer argues the class should not have been certified because the primary method of proving injury assumed each employee spent the same time donning and doffing protective gear, even though differences in the composition of that gear may have meant that, in fact, employees took different amounts of time to don and doff. Second, the employer argues certification was improper because the damages awarded to the class may be distributed to some persons who did not work any uncompensated overtime.

The Court of Appeals for the Eighth Circuit concluded there was no error in the District Court's decision to certify and maintain the class. This Court granted certiorari.

I

Respondents are employees at petitioner Tyson Foods' pork processing plant in Storm Lake, Iowa. They work in the plant's kill, cut, and retrim departments, where hogs are slaughtered, trimmed, and prepared for shipment. Grueling and dangerous, the work requires employees to wear certain protective gear. The exact composition of the gear depends on the tasks a worker performs on a given day.

Until 1998, employees at the plant were paid under a system called "gang-time." This compensated them only for time spent at their workstations, not for the time required to put on and take off their protective gear. In response to a federal-court injunction, and a Department of Labor suit to enforce that injunction, Tyson in 1998 began to pay all its employees for an additional four minutes a day for what it called "K-code time." The 4–minute period was the amount of time Tyson estimated employees needed to don and doff their gear. In 2007, Tyson stopped paying K-code time uniformly to all employees. Instead, it compensated some employees for between four and eight minutes but paid others nothing beyond their gang-time wages. At no point did Tyson record the time each employee spent donning and doffing.

Unsatisfied by these changes, respondents filed suit in the United States District Court for the Northern District of Iowa, alleging violations of the FLSA. The FLSA requires that a covered employee who works more than 40 hours a week receive compensation for excess time worked "at a rate not less than one and one-half times the regular rate at which he is employed." In 1947, nine years after the FLSA was first enacted, Congress passed the Portal–to–Portal Act, which clarified that compensable work does not include time spent walking to and from the employee's workstation or other "preliminary or postliminary activities." The FLSA, however, still requires employers to pay employees for activities "integral and indispensable" to their regular work, even if those activities do not occur at the employee's workstation. The FLSA also requires an employer to "make, keep, and preserve ... records of the persons employed by him and of the wages, hours, and other conditions and practices of employment."

In their complaint, respondents alleged that donning and doffing protective gear were integral and indispensable to their hazardous work and that petitioner's policy not to pay for those activities denied them overtime compensation required by the FLSA. Respondents also raised a claim under the Iowa Wage Payment Collection Law. This statute provides for recovery under state law when an employer fails to pay its employees "all wages due," which includes FLSA-mandated overtime.

Respondents sought certification of their Iowa law claims as a class action under Rule 23 of the Federal Rules of Civil Procedure. Rule 23 permits one or more individuals to sue as "representative parties on behalf of all members" of a class if certain preconditions are met. Respondents also sought certification of their federal claims as a "collective action" under 29 U.S.C. § 216. Section 216 is a provision of the FLSA that permits employees to sue on behalf of "themselves and other employees similarly situated."

Tyson objected to the certification of both classes on the same ground. It contended that, because of the variance in protective gear each employee wore, the employees' claims were not sufficiently similar to be resolved on a classwide basis. The District Court rejected that position. It concluded there were common questions susceptible to classwide resolution, such as "whether the donning and doffing of protective gear is considered work under the FLSA, whether such work is integral and indispensable, and whether any compensable work is *de minimis*." The District Court acknowledged that the workers did not all wear the same protective gear, but found that "when the putative plaintiffs are limited to those that are paid via a gang time system, there are far more factual similarities than dissimilarities." As a result, the District Court certified the following classes:

> "All current and former employees of Tyson's Storm Lake, Iowa, processing facility
> who have been employed at any time from February 7, 2004 [in the case of the FLSA
> collective action and February 7, 2005, in the case of the state-law class action], to the
> present, and who are or were paid under a 'gang time' compensation system in the
> Kill, Cut, or Retrim departments."

The only difference in definition between the classes was the date at which the class period began. The size of the class certified under Rule 23, however, was larger than that certified under § 216. This is because, while a class under Rule 23 includes all unnamed members who fall within the class definition, the "sole consequence of conditional certification under § 216 is the sending of court-approved written notice to employees ... who in turn become parties to a collective action only by filing written consent with the court." A total of 444 employees joined the collective action, while the Rule 23 class contained 3,344 members.

The case proceeded to trial before a jury. The parties stipulated that the employees were entitled to be paid for donning and doffing of certain equipment worn to protect from knife cuts. The jury was left to determine whether the time spent donning and doffing other protective equipment was compensable; whether Tyson was required to pay for donning and doffing during meal breaks; and the total amount of time spent on work that was not compensated under Tyson's gang-time system.

Since the employees' claims relate only to overtime, each employee had to show he or she worked more than 40 hours a week, inclusive of time spent donning and doffing, in order to recover. As a result of Tyson's failure to keep records of donning and doffing time, however, the employees were forced to rely on what the parties describe as "representative evidence." This evidence included employee testimony, video recordings of donning and doffing at the plant, and, most important, a study performed by an industrial relations expert, Dr. Kenneth Mericle. Mericle conducted 744 videotaped observations and analyzed how long various donning and doffing activities took. He then averaged the time taken in the observations to produce an estimate of 18 minutes a day for the cut and retrim departments and 21.25 minutes for the kill department.

Although it had not kept records for time spent donning and doffing, Tyson had information regarding each employee's gang-time and K-code time. Using this data, the employees' other expert, Dr. Liesl Fox, was able to estimate the amount of uncompensated work each employee did by adding Mericle's estimated average donning and doffing time to the gang-time each employee worked and then subtracting any K-code time. For example, if an employee in the kill department had worked 39.125 hours of gang-time in a 6–day workweek and had been paid an hour of K-code time, the estimated number of compensable hours the employee worked would be: 39.125 (individual number of gang-time hours worked) + 2.125 (the average donning and doffing hours for a 6–day week, based on Mericle's estimated average of 21.25 minutes a day) - 1 (K-code hours) = 40.25. That would mean the employee was being undercompensated by a quarter of an hour of overtime a week, in violation of the FLSA. On the other hand, if the employee's records showed only 38 hours of gang-time and an hour of K-code time, the calculation would be: 38 + 2.125 - 1 = 39.125. Having worked less than 40 hours, that employee would not be entitled to overtime pay and would not have proved an FLSA violation.

Using this methodology, Fox stated that 212 employees did not meet the 40–hour threshold and could not recover. The remaining class members, Fox maintained, had potentially been undercompensated to some degree.

Respondents proposed to bifurcate proceedings. They requested that, first, a trial be conducted on the questions whether time spent in donning and doffing was compensable work under the FLSA and how long those activities took to perform on average; and, second, that Fox's methodology be used to determine which employees suffered an FLSA violation and how much each was entitled to recover. Petitioner insisted upon a single proceeding in which damages would be calculated in the aggregate and by the jury. The District Court submitted both issues of liability and damages to the jury.

Petitioner did not move for a hearing regarding the statistical validity of respondents' studies under *Daubert v. Merrell Dow*, nor did it attempt to discredit the evidence with testimony from a rebuttal expert. Instead, as it had done in its opposition to class certification, petitioner argued to the jury that the varying amounts of time it took employees to don and doff different protective equipment made the lawsuit too speculative for classwide recovery. Petitioner also argued that Mericle's study overstated the average donning and doffing time. The jury was instructed that non-testifying members of the class could only recover if the evidence established they "suffered the same harm as a result of the same unlawful decision or policy."

Fox's calculations supported an aggregate award of approximately $6.7 million in unpaid wages. The jury returned a special verdict finding that time spent in donning and doffing protective gear at the beginning and end of the day was compensable work but that time during meal breaks was not. The jury more than halved the damages recommended by Fox. It awarded the class about $2.9 million in unpaid wages. That damages award has not yet been disbursed to the individual employees.

Tyson moved to set aside the jury verdict, arguing, among other things, that, in light of the variation in donning and doffing time, the classes should not have been certified. The District Court denied Tyson's motion, and the Court of Appeals for the Eighth Circuit affirmed the judgment and the award.

For the reasons that follow, this Court now affirms.

## II

Petitioner challenges the class certification of the state-law claims and the certification of the FLSA collective action. The parties do not dispute that the standard for certifying a collective action under the FLSA is no more stringent than the standard for certifying a class under the Federal Rules of Civil Procedure. This opinion assumes, without deciding, that this is correct. For purposes of this case then, if certification of respondents' class action under the Federal Rules was proper, certification of the collective action was proper as well.

Furthermore, the parties do not dispute that, in order to prove a violation of the Iowa statute, the employees had to do no more than demonstrate a violation of the FLSA. In this opinion, then, no distinction is made between the requirements for the class action raising the state-law claims and the collective action raising the federal claims.

## A

Federal Rule of Civil Procedure 23(b)(3) requires that, before a class is certified under that subsection, a district court must find that "questions of law or fact common to class members predominate over any questions affecting only individual members." The "predominance inquiry tests whether proposed classes are sufficiently cohesive to warrant adjudication by representation." This calls upon courts to give careful scrutiny to the relation between common and individual questions in a case. An individual question is one where "members of a proposed class will need to present evidence that varies from member to member," while a common question is one where "the same evidence will suffice for each member to make a prima facie showing or the issue is susceptible to generalized, class-wide proof." The predominance inquiry "asks whether the common, aggregation-enabling, issues in the case are more prevalent or important than the non-common, aggregation-defeating, individual issues." When "one or more of the central issues in the action are common to the class and can be said to predominate, the action may be considered proper under Rule 23(b)(3) even though other important matters will have to be tried separately, such as damages or some affirmative defenses peculiar to some individual class members."

Here, the parties do not dispute that there are important questions common to all class members, the most significant of which is whether time spent donning and doffing the required protective gear is compensable work under the FLSA. To be entitled to recovery, however, each employee must prove that the amount of time spent donning and doffing, when added to his or her regular hours, amounted to more than 40 hours in a given week. Petitioner argues that these necessarily person-specific inquiries into individual work time predominate over the common questions raised by respondents' claims, making class certification improper.

Respondents counter that these individual inquiries are unnecessary because it can be assumed each employee donned and doffed for the same average time observed in Mericle's sample. Whether this inference is permissible becomes the central dispute in this case. Petitioner contends that Mericle's study manufactures predominance by assuming away the very differences that make the case inappropriate for classwide resolution. Reliance on a representative sample, petitioner argues, absolves each employee of the responsibility to prove personal injury, and thus deprives petitioner of any ability to litigate its defenses to individual claims.

A representative or statistical sample, like all evidence, is a means to establish or defend against liability. Its permissibility turns not on the form a proceeding takes— be it a class or individual action—but on the degree to which the evidence is reliable in proving or disproving the elements of the relevant cause of action.

It follows that the Court would reach too far were it to establish general rules governing the use of statistical evidence, or so-called representative evidence, in all class-action cases. Evidence of this type is used in various substantive realms of the law. Whether and when statistical evidence can be used to establish classwide liability will depend on the purpose for which the evidence is being introduced and on "the elements of the underlying cause of action.

In many cases, a representative sample is "the only practicable means to collect and present relevant data" establishing a defendant's liability. Manual of Complex

Litigation § 11.493. In a case where representative evidence is relevant in proving a plaintiff's individual claim, that evidence cannot be deemed improper merely because the claim is brought on behalf of a class.

One way for respondents to show, then, that the sample relied upon here is a permissible method of proving classwide liability is by showing that each class member could have relied on that sample to establish liability if he or she had brought an individual action. If the sample could have sustained a reasonable jury finding as to hours worked in each employee's individual action, that sample is a permissible means of establishing the employees' hours worked in a class action.

The Court in *Mt. Clemens* held that when employers violate their statutory duty to keep proper records, and employees thereby have no way to establish the time spent doing uncompensated work, the "remedial nature of the FLSA and the great public policy which it embodies militate against making" the burden of proving uncompensated work "an impossible hurdle for the employee." Instead of punishing "the employee by denying him any recovery on the ground that he is unable to prove the precise extent of uncompensated work," the Court held "an employee has carried out his burden if he proves that he has in fact performed work for which he was improperly compensated and if he produces sufficient evidence to show the amount and extent of that work as a matter of just and reasonable inference." Under these circumstances, "the burden then shifts to the employer to come forward with evidence of the precise amount of work performed or with evidence to negative the reasonableness of the inference to be drawn from the employee's evidence."

In this suit, as in *Mt. Clemens,* respondents sought to introduce a representative sample to fill an evidentiary gap created by the employer's failure to keep adequate records. If the employees had proceeded with 3,344 individual lawsuits, each employee likely would have had to introduce Mericle's study to prove the hours he or she worked. Rather than absolving the employees from proving individual injury, the representative evidence here was a permissible means of making that very showing.

Reliance on Mericle's study did not deprive petitioner of its ability to litigate individual defenses. Since there were no alternative means for the employees to establish their hours worked, petitioner's primary defense was to show that Mericle's study was unrepresentative or inaccurate. When, as here, "the concern about the proposed class is not that it exhibits some fatal dissimilarity but, rather, a fatal similarity—[an alleged] failure of proof as to an element of the plaintiffs' cause of action—courts should engage that question as a matter of summary judgment, not class certification."

Petitioner's reliance on *Wal–Mart Stores, Inc. v. Dukes,* (2011), is misplaced. *Wal–Mart* does not stand for the broad proposition that a representative sample is an impermissible means of establishing classwide liability.

*Wal–Mart* involved a nationwide Title VII class of over 1 ½ million employees. In reversing class certification, this Court did not reach Rule 23(b)(3)'s predominance prong, holding instead that the class failed to meet even Rule 23(a)'s more basic requirement that class members share a common question of fact or law. The plaintiffs in *Wal–Mart* did not provide significant proof of a common policy of discrimination to which each employee was subject. "The only corporate policy that the plaintiffs' evidence convincingly established was Wal–Mart's 'policy' of allowing discretion by local supervisors over employment matters"; and even then, the plaintiffs could not identify "a common mode of exercising discretion that pervade[d] the entire company."

The plaintiffs in *Wal–Mart* proposed to use representative evidence as a means of overcoming this absence of a common policy. Under their proposed methodology, a "sample set of the class members would be selected, as to whom liability for sex discrimination and the backpay owing as a result would be determined in depositions supervised by a master." The aggregate damages award was to be derived by taking the "percentage of claims determined to be valid" from this sample and applying it to the rest of the class, and then multiplying the "number of (presumptively) valid claims" by "the average backpay award in the sample set." The Court held that this "Trial By Formula" was contrary to the Rules Enabling Act because it "'enlarged'" the class members' "'substantive rights'" and deprived defendants of their right to litigate statutory defenses to individual claims.

The Court's holding in the instant case is in accord with *Wal–Mart*. The underlying question in *Wal–Mart*, as here, was whether the sample at issue could have been used to establish liability in an individual action. Since the Court held that the employees were not similarly situated, none of them could have prevailed in an individual suit by relying on depositions detailing the ways in which other employees were discriminated against by their particular store managers. In Wal-Mart, by extension, if the employees had brought 1 ½million individual suits, there would be little or no role for representative evidence. Permitting the use of that sample in a class action, therefore, would have violated the Rules Enabling Act by giving plaintiffs and defendants different rights in a class proceeding than they could have asserted in an individual action.

In contrast, the study here could have been sufficient to sustain a jury finding as to hours worked if it were introduced in each employee's individual action. While the experiences of the employees in *Wal–Mart* bore little relationship to one another, in this case each employee worked in the same facility, did similar work, and was paid under the same policy. As *Mt. Clemens* confirms, under these circumstances the experiences of a subset of employees can be probative as to the experiences of all of them.

[This is not to say that all inferences drawn from representative evidence in an FLSA case are "just and reasonable." Representative evidence that is statistically inadequate or based on implausible assumptions could not lead to a fair or accurate estimate of the uncompensated hours an employee has worked.]Petitioner, however, did not raise a challenge to respondents' experts' methodology under *Daubert*; and, as a result, there is no basis in the record to conclude it was legal error to admit that evidence.

Once a district court finds evidence to be admissible, its persuasiveness is, in general, a matter for the jury. Reasonable minds may differ as to whether the average time Mericle calculated is probative as to the time actually worked by each employee. Resolving that question, however, is the near-exclusive province of the jury. The District Court could have denied class certification on this ground only if it concluded that no reasonable juror could have believed that the employees spent roughly equal time donning and doffing. The District Court made no such finding, and the record here provides no basis for this Court to second-guess that conclusion.

The Court reiterates that, while petitioner, respondents, or their respective *amici* may urge adoption of broad and categorical rules governing the use of representative and statistical evidence in class actions, this case provides no occasion to do so. Whether a representative sample may be used to establish classwide liability will depend on the purpose for which the sample is being introduced and on the underlying cause of action. [In FLSA actions, inferring the hours an employee has worked from a study such as Mericle's has been permitted by the Court so long as the study is otherwise admissible. The fairness and utility of statistical methods in contexts other than those presented here will depend on facts and circumstances particular to those cases.]

B

In its petition for certiorari petitioner framed its second question presented as whether a class may be certified if it contains "members who were not injured and have no legal right to any damages." In its merits brief, however, petitioner reframes its argument. It now concedes that "the fact that federal courts lack authority to compensate persons who cannot prove injury does not mean that a class action (or collective action) can never be certified in the absence of proof that all class members were injured." In light of petitioner's abandonment of its argument from the petition, the Court need not, and does not, address it.

Petitioner's new argument is that, "where class plaintiffs cannot offer" proof that all class members are injured, "they must demonstrate instead that there is some mechanism to identify the uninjured class members prior to judgment and ensure that uninjured members (1) do not contribute to the size of any damage award and (2) cannot recover such damages." *Ibid.* Petitioner contends that respondents have not demonstrated any mechanism for ensuring that uninjured class members do not recover damages here.

Petitioner's new argument is predicated on the assumption that the damages award cannot be apportioned so that only those class members who suffered an FLSA violation recover. According to petitioner, because Fox's mechanism for determining who had worked over 40 hours depended on Mericle's estimate of donning and doffing time, and because the jury must have rejected Mericle's estimate when it reduced the damages award by more than half, it will not be possible to know which workers are entitled to share in the award.

As petitioner and its *amici* stress, the question whether uninjured class members may recover is one of great importance. It is not, however, a question yet fairly presented by this case, because the damages award has not yet been disbursed, nor does the record indicate how it will be disbursed.

Respondents allege there remain ways of distributing the award to only those individuals who worked more than 40 hours. For example, by working backwards from the damages award, and assuming each employee donned and doffed for an identical amount of time (an assumption that follows from the jury's finding that the employees suffered equivalent harm under the policy), it may be possible to calculate the average donning and doffing time the jury necessarily must have found, and then apply this figure to each employee's known gang-time hours to determine which employees worked more than 40 hours.

Whether that or some other methodology will be successful in identifying uninjured class members is a question that, on this record, is premature. Petitioner may raise a challenge to the proposed method of allocation when the case returns to the District Court for disbursal of the award.

Finally, it bears emphasis that this problem appears to be one of petitioner's own making. Respondents proposed bifurcating between the liability and damages phases of this proceeding for the precise reason that it may be difficult to remove uninjured individuals from the class after an award is rendered. It was petitioner who argued against that option and now seeks to profit from the difficulty it caused. Whether, in light of the foregoing, any error should be deemed invited, is a question for the District Court to address in the first instance.

The judgment of the Court of Appeals for the Eighth Circuit is affirmed, and the case is remanded for further proceedings consistent with this opinion.

5. Even with the efficacy of class actions, it may be impossible to bring adequate relief to injured people who are part of a very large class of similarly injured people. The attorneys for a class action normally get paid first out of any award recovered. Normally a class action requires the expenditure of a great deal of time by the attorneys for the class. Therefore, it may be that nearly all of the award made in the class action goes to the attorneys – not to the class members. Even when there is a good faith attempt to minimize the percentage of the award going to the attorneys, that may not be possible – as illustrated by the following case. What statutory modification might be helpful in alleviating this problem?

## 119 S. CT. 2295
## SUPREME COURT OF THE UNITED STATES
## ESTEBAN ORTIZ, ET AL., PETITIONERS,
## V.
## FIBREBOARD CORPORATION ET AL.

DECIDED JUNE 23, 1999

**SOUTER, J., delivered the opinion of the Court, in which REHNQUIST, C.J., and O'CONNOR, SCALIA, KENNEDY, THOMAS, and GINSBURG, JJ., joined.**

Justice SOUTER delivered the opinion of the Court.

This case turns on the conditions for certifying a mandatory settlement class on a limited fund theory under Federal Rule of Civil Procedure 23(b)(1)(B). We hold that applicants for contested certification on this rationale must show that the fund is limited by more than the agreement of the parties, and has been allocated to claimants belonging within the class by a process addressing any conflicting interests of class members.

I

This case is a class action prompted by the elephantine mass of asbestos cases, and our discussion will suffice to show how this litigation defies customary judicial administration and calls for national legislation.[FN1]

FN1. This is a tale of danger known in the 1930s, exposure inflicted upon millions of Americans in the 1940s and 1950s, injuries that began to take their toll in the 1960s, and a flood of lawsuits beginning in the 1970s." On the basis of past and current filing data, and because of a latency period that may last as long as 40 years for some asbestos related diseases, a continuing stream of claims can be expected. The final toll of asbestos related injuries is unknown. Predictions have been made of 200,000 asbestos disease deaths before the year 2000 and as many as 265,000 by the year 2015.

The most objectionable aspects of asbestos litigation can be briefly summarized: dockets in both federal and state courts continue to grow; long delays are routine; trials are too long; the same issues are litigated over and over; transaction costs exceed the victims' recovery by nearly two to one; exhaustion of assets threatens and distorts the process; and future claimants may lose altogether.

Respondent Fibreboard Corporation was a defendant in the 1967 action. Although it was primarily a timber company, from the 1920's through 1971 the company manufactured a variety of products containing asbestos, mainly for high-temperature industrial applications. As the tide of asbestos litigation rose, Fibreboard found itself litigating on two fronts. On one, plaintiffs were filing a stream of personal injury claims against it, swelling throughout the 1980's and 1990's to thousands of new claims for compensatory damages each year. On the second front, Fibreboard was battling for funds to pay its tort claimants. From May 1957 through March 1959, respondent Continental Casualty Company had provided Fibreboard with a comprehensive general liability policy with limits of $1 million per occurrence, $500,000 per claim, and no aggregate limit. Fibreboard also claimed that respondent Pacific Indemnity Company had insured it from 1956 to 1957 under a similar policy.

With asbestos case filings continuing unabated, and its secure insurance assets almost depleted, Fibreboard in 1988 began a practice of "structured settlement," paying plaintiffs 40 percent of the settlement figure up front with the balance contingent upon a successful resolution of the coverage dispute. By 1991, however, the pace of filings forced Fibreboard to start settling cases entirely with the assignments of its rights against Continental, with no initial payment. To reflect the risk that Continental might prevail in the coverage dispute, these assignment agreements generally carried a figure about twice the nominal amount of earlier settlements. Continental challenged Fibreboard's right to make unilateral assignments, but in 1992 a California state court ruled for Fibreboard in that dispute.

Meanwhile, in the aftermath of a 1990 Federal Judicial Center conference on the asbestos litigation crisis, Fibreboard approached a group of leading asbestos plaintiffs' lawyers, offering to discuss a "global settlement" of its asbestos personal-injury liability. Early negotiations bore relatively little fruit, save for the December 1992 settlement by assignment of a significant inventory of pending claims. This settlement brought Fibreboard's deferred settlement obligations to more than $1.2 billion, all contingent upon victory over Continental on the scope of coverage and the validity of the settlement assignments.

In February 1993, after Continental had lost on both issues at the trial level, and thus faced the possibility of practically unbounded liability, it too joined the global settlement negotiations. Because Continental conditioned its part in any settlement on a guarantee of "total peace," ensuring no unknown future liabilities, talks focused on the feasibility of a mandatory class action, one binding all potential plaintiffs and giving none of them any choice to opt out of the certified class. Negotiations continued throughout the spring and summer of 1993.

With the insurance companies' appeal of the consolidated coverage case set to be heard on August 27, the negotiating parties faced a motivating deadline, and about midnight before the argument, in a coffee shop in Tyler, Texas, the negotiators finally agreed upon $1.535 billion as the key term of a "Global Settlement Agreement." $1.525 billion of this sum would come from Continental and Pacific, while Fibreboard would contribute $10 million, all but $500,000 of it from other insurance proceeds.

The next day, as a hedge against the possibility that the Global Settlement Agreement might fail, plaintiffs' counsel insisted as a condition of that agreement that Fibreboard and its two insurers settle the coverage dispute by what came to be known as the "Trilateral Settlement Agreement." The two insurers agreed to provide Fibreboard with funds eventually set at $2 billion to defend against asbestos claimants.

On September 9, 1993, as agreed, a group of named plaintiffs filed an action in the United States District Court for the Eastern District of Texas, seeking certification for settlement purposes of a mandatory class comprising three groups: all persons with personal injury claims against Fibreboard for asbestos exposure who had not yet brought suit or settled their claims before the previous August 27; those who had dismissed such a claim but retained the right to bring a future action against Fibreboard; and "past, present and future spouses, parents, children, and other relatives" of class members exposed to Fibreboard asbestos.

The complaint pleaded personal injury claims against Fibreboard, and, as justification for class certification, relied on the shared necessity of ensuring insurance funds sufficient for compensation. After Continental and Pacific had obtained leave to intervene as party-defendants, the District Court provisionally granted class certification, enjoined commencement of further separate litigation against Fibreboard by class members, and appointed a guardian ad litem to review the fairness of the settlement to the class members.

As finally negotiated, the Global Settlement Agreement provided that in exchange for full releases from class members, Fibreboard, Continental, and Pacific would establish a trust to process and pay class members' asbestos personal injury and death claims. Claimants seeking compensation would be required to try to settle with the trust. If initial settlement attempts failed, claimants would have to proceed to mediation, arbitration, and a mandatory settlement conference. Only after exhausting that process could claimants go to court against the trust, subject to a limit of $500,000 per claim, with punitive damages and prejudgment interest barred. Claims resolved without litigation would be discharged over three years, while judgments would be paid out over a 5– to 10–year period. The Global Settlement Agreement also provided for paying more serious claims first in the event of a shortfall in any given year.

After an extensive campaign to give notice of the pending settlement to potential class members, the District Court allowed groups of objectors, including petitioners here, to intervene. After an 8–day fairness hearing, the District Court certified the class and approved the settlement as "fair, adequate, and reasonable" under Rule 23(e). Satisfied that the requirements of Rule 23(a) were met, the District Court certified the class under Rule 23(b)(1)(B).

On appeal, the Fifth Circuit affirmed. We granted certiorari, and now reverse.

## II

In contrast to class actions brought under subdivision (b)(3), in cases brought under subdivision (b)(1), Rule 23 does not provide for absent class members to receive notice and to exclude themselves from class membership as a matter of right. It is for this reason that such cases are often referred to as "mandatory" class actions.

One recurring type of such suits was the limited fund class action, aggregating "claims ... made by numerous persons against a fund insufficient to satisfy all claims." ("Classic" limited fund class actions "include claimants to trust assets, a bank account, insurance proceeds, company assets in a liquidation sale, proceeds of a ship sale in a maritime accident suit, and others").

## B

The cases forming this pedigree of the limited fund class action as understood by the drafters of Rule 23 have a number of common characteristics, despite the variety of circumstances from which they arose.

The first and most distinctive characteristic is that the totals of the aggregated liquidated claims and the fund available for satisfying them, set definitely at their maximums, demonstrate the inadequacy of the fund to pay all the claims. Second, the whole of the inadequate fund was to be devoted to the overwhelming claims. Third, the claimants identified by a common theory of recovery were treated equitably among themselves.

In sum, mandatory class treatment through representative actions on a limited fund theory was justified with reference to a "fund" with a definitely ascertained limit, all of which would be distributed to satisfy all those with liquidated claims based on a common theory of liability, by an equitable, pro rata distribution.

## C

If we needed further counsel against adventurous application of Rule 23(b)(1)(B), the Rules Enabling Act and the general doctrine of constitutional avoidance would jointly sound a warning of the serious constitutional concerns that come with any attempt to aggregate individual tort claims on a limited fund rationale. First, the certification of a mandatory class followed by settlement of its action for money damages obviously implicates the Seventh Amendment jury trial rights of absent class members. Since the merger of law and equity in 1938, it has become settled among the lower courts that "class action plaintiffs may obtain a jury trial on any legal issues they present." By its nature, however, a mandatory settlement-only class action with legal issues and future claimants compromises their Seventh Amendment rights without their consent.

Second, and no less important, mandatory class actions aggregating damages claims implicate the due process "principle of general application in Anglo–American jurisprudence that one is not bound by a judgment *in personam* in a litigation in which he is not designated as a party or to which he has not been made a party by service of process,"

Unlike Rule 23(b)(3) class members, objectors to the collectivism of a mandatory subdivision (b)(1)(B) action have no inherent right to abstain. The legal rights of absent class members (which in a class like this one would include claimants who by definition may be unidentifiable when the class is certified) are resolved regardless of either their consent, or, in a class with objectors, their express wish to the contrary. And in settlement-only class actions the procedural protections built into the Rule to protect the rights of absent class members during litigation are never invoked in an adversarial setting.

## IV

The record on which the District Court rested its certification of the class for the purpose of the global settlement did not support the essential premises of mandatory limited fund actions. It failed to demonstrate that the fund was limited except by the agreement of the parties, and it showed exclusions from the class and allocations of assets at odds with the concept of limited fund treatment and the structural protections of Rule 23(a).

## A

When a district court certifies for class action settlement only, the moment of certification requires "heightened attention," to the justifications for binding the class members. This is so because certification of a mandatory settlement class, however provisional technically, effectively concludes the proceeding save for the final fairness hearing. And a fairness hearing under Rule 23(e) is no substitute for rigorous adherence to those provisions of the Rule "designed to protect absentees.

In this case, since there was no adequate demonstration of one element required for limited fund treatment, the upper limit of the fund itself, no showing of insufficiency is possible.

The "fund" in this case comprised both the general assets of Fibreboard and the insurance assets provided by the two policies. As to Fibreboard's assets exclusive of the contested insurance, the District Court and the Fifth Circuit concluded that Fibreboard had a then-current sale value of $235 million that could be devoted to the limited fund. While that estimate may have been conservative,[FN28] at least the District Court heard evidence and made an independent finding at some point in the proceedings.

> FN28. The District Court based the $235 million figure on evidence provided by an investment banker regarding what a "financially prudent buyer" would pay to acquire Fibreboard free of its personal injury asbestos liabilities, less transaction costs. In 1997, however, Fibreboard was acquired for about $515 million.

The same, however, cannot be said for the value of the disputed insurance. The insurance assets would obviously be "limited" in the traditional sense if the total of demonstrable claims would render the insurers insolvent, or if the policies provided aggregate limits falling short of that total; calculation might be difficult, but the way to demonstrate the limit would be clear. Neither possibility is presented in this case, however. Instead, any limit of the insurance asset here had to be a product of potentially unlimited policy coverage discounted by the risk that Fibreboard would ultimately lose the coverage dispute litigation. This sense of limit as a value discounted by risk is of course a step removed from the historical model, but even on the assumption that it would suffice for limited fund treatment, there was no adequate finding of fact to support its application here. Instead of undertaking an independent evaluation of potential insurance funds, the District Court (and, later, the Court of Appeals), simply accepted the $2 billion Trilateral Settlement Agreement figure as representing the maximum amount the insurance companies could be required to pay tort victims, concluding that "where insurance coverage is disputed, it is appropriate to value the insurance asset at a settlement value."

Settlement value is not always acceptable, however. One may take a settlement amount as good evidence of the maximum available if one can assume that parties of equal knowledge and negotiating skill agreed upon the figure through arms-length bargaining, unhindered by any considerations tugging against the interests of the parties ostensibly represented in the negotiation. But no such assumption may be indulged in this case, or probably in any class action settlement with the potential for gigantic fees. [FN30] In this case, certainly, any assumption that plaintiffs' counsel could be of a mind to do their simple best in bargaining for the benefit of the settlement class is patently at odds with the fact that at least some of the same lawyers representing plaintiffs and the class had also negotiated the separate settlement of 45,000 pending claims, the full payment of which was contingent on a successful Global Settlement Agreement or the successful resolution of the insurance coverage dispute (either by litigation or by agreement, as eventually occurred in the Trilateral Settlement Agreement). Class counsel thus had great incentive to reach any agreement in the global settlement negotiations that they thought might survive a Rule 23(e) fairness hearing, rather than the best possible arrangement for the substantially unidentified global settlement class.

> FN30. In a strictly rational world, plaintiffs' counsel would always press for the limit of what the defense would pay. But with an already enormous fee within counsel's grasp, zeal for the client may relax sooner than it would in a case brought on behalf of one claimant.

B

The definition of the class excludes myriad claimants with causes of action, or foreseeable causes of action, arising from exposure to Fibreboard asbestos. While the class includes those with present claims never filed, present claims withdrawn without prejudice, and future claimants, it fails to include those who had previously settled with Fibreboard while retaining the right to sue again "upon development of an asbestos related malignancy," plaintiffs with claims pending against Fibreboard at the time of the initial announcement of the Global Settlement Agreement, and the plaintiffs in the "inventory" claims settled as a supposedly necessary step in reaching the global settlement

It is a fair question how far a natural class may be depleted by prior dispositions of claims and still qualify as a mandatory limited fund class, but there can be no question that such a mandatory settlement class will not qualify when in the very negotiations aimed at a class settlement, class counsel agree to exclude what could turn out to be as much as a third of the claimants that negotiators thought might eventually be involved, a substantial number of whom class counsel represent.

On the second element of equity within the class, the fairness of the distribution of the fund among class members, the settlement certification is likewise deficient.

First, it is obvious that a class divided between holders of present and future claims (some of the latter involving no physical injury and attributable to claimants not yet born) requires division into homogeneous subclasses under Rule 23(c)(4)(B), with separate representation to eliminate conflicting interests of counsel.

Second, the class included those exposed to Fibreboard's asbestos products both before and after 1959. The date is significant, for that year saw the expiration of Fibreboard's insurance policy with Continental, the one that provided the bulk of the insurance funds for the settlement. Pre–1959 claimants accordingly had more valuable claims than post–1959 claimants

Nor does it answer the settlement's failures to provide structural protections in the service of equity to argue that the certified class members' common interest in securing contested insurance funds for the payment of claims was so weighty as to diminish the deficiencies beneath recognition here.

C

A third contested feature of this settlement certification that departs markedly from the limited fund antecedents is the ultimate provision for a fund smaller than the assets understood by the Court of Appeals to be available for payment of the mandatory class members' claims; most notably, Fibreboard was allowed to retain virtually its entire net worth. Given our treatment of the two preceding deficiencies of the certification, there is of course no need to decide whether this feature of the agreement would alone be fatal to the Global Settlement Agreement. To ignore it entirely, however, would be so misleading that we have decided simply to identify the issue it raises, without purporting to resolve it at this time.

Fibreboard listed its supposed entire net worth as a component of the total (and allegedly inadequate) assets available for claimants, but subsequently retained all but $500,000 of that equity for itself.

The District Court in this case seems to have had a further point in mind, however. One great advantage of class action treatment of mass tort cases is the opportunity to save the enormous transaction costs of piecemeal litigation, an advantage to which the settlement's proponents have referred in this case. Although the District Court made no specific finding about the transaction cost saving likely from this class settlement, estimating the amount in the "hundreds of millions," it did conclude that the amount would exceed Fibreboard's net worth as the Court valued it, (Fibreboard's net worth of $235 million "is considerably less than the likely savings in defense costs under the Global Settlement"). If a settlement thus saves transaction costs that would never have gone into a class member's pocket in the absence of settlement, may a credit for some of the savings be recognized in a mandatory class action as an incentive to settlement? It is at least a legitimate question, which we leave for another day.

**V (omitted)**

**VI**

In sum, the applicability of Rule 23(b)(1)(B) to a fund and plan purporting to liquidate actual and potential tort claims is subject to question, and its purported application in this case was in any event improper.

Assuming, *arguendo,* that a mandatory, limited fund rationale could under some circumstances be applied to a settlement class of tort claimants it would be essential that the fund be shown to be limited independently of the agreement of the parties to the action, and equally essential under Rules 23(a) and (b)(1)(B) that the class include all those with claims unsatisfied at the time of the settlement negotiations, with intraclass conflicts addressed by recognizing independently represented subclasses. In this case, the limit of the fund was determined by treating the settlement agreement as dispositive, an error magnified by the representation of class members by counsel also representing excluded plaintiffs, whose settlements would be funded fully upon settlement of the class action on any terms that could survive final fairness review. Those separate settlements, together with other exclusions from the claimant class, precluded adequate structural protection by subclass treatment, which was not even afforded to the conflicting elements within the class as certified.

The judgment of the Court of Appeals, accordingly, is reversed, and the case is remanded for further proceedings consistent with this opinion.

# B. CLASS ACTION FAIRNESS ACT (CAFA) 28 USC 1332(D)

6. The Class Action Fairness Act, (CAFA), went into effect in 2005. Rather than making it a distinct statutory section, it is tacked onto the end of the diversity jurisdiction section, as 28 USC 1332(d). CAFA creates a key to the courthouse that might be described as a *five-sided* key. CAFA grants federal subject matter jurisdiction to a class action in which (1) There are at least 100 members of the class; (2) the amount in controversy exceeds $5 million; (3) *any* plaintiff is from a state different from *any* defendant; (4) at least 2/3rds of the members of the class of plaintiffs are *not* citizens of the same state as a *significant* defendant; and (5) no similar class action has been brought within the preceding three years.

Not surprisingly, very few CAFA cases have reached the U.S. Supreme Court to date, but *Dart Cherokee*, below, illustrates some of the fights that may take place when plaintiffs attempt to bring a case under CAFA.

Why is the defendant in this case claiming that the damages are likely to be very high?

## 135 S.CT. 547
## SUPREME COURT OF THE UNITED STATES
## DART CHEROKEE BASIN OPERATING COMPANY, LLC, ET AL., PETITIONERS
## V.
## BRANDON W. OWENS.

DECIDED DECEMBER 15, 2014

**Justice GINSBURG delivered the opinion of the Court.**

To remove a case from a state court to a federal court, a defendant must file in the federal forum a notice of removal "containing a short and plain statement of the grounds for removal." 28 U.S.C. § 1446(a). When removal is based on diversity of citizenship, an amount-in-controversy requirement must be met. Ordinarily, "the matter in controversy must exceed the sum or value of $75,000." § 1332(a). In class actions for which the requirement of diversity of citizenship is relaxed, § 1332(d)(2)(A)–(C), "the matter in controversy must exceed the sum or value of $5,000,000," § 1332(d)(2). If the plaintiff's complaint, filed in state court, demands monetary relief of a stated sum, that sum, if asserted in good faith, is "deemed to be the amount in controversy." § 1446(c)(2). When the plaintiff's complaint does not state the amount in controversy, the defendant's notice of removal may do so.

To assert the amount in controversy adequately in the removal notice, does it suffice to allege the requisite amount plausibly, or must the defendant incorporate into the notice of removal evidence supporting the allegation? The answer, we hold, is supplied by the removal statute itself. A statement "short and plain" need not contain evidentiary submissions.

I

Brandon W. Owens, plaintiff below, filed a putative class action in Kansas state court alleging that defendants Dart Cherokee and Cherokee Basin Pipeline, LLC (collectively, Dart), underpaid royalties owed to putative class members under certain oil and gas leases. The complaint sought "a fair and reasonable amount" to compensate putative class members for "damages" they sustained due to the alleged underpayments.

Invoking federal jurisdiction under the Class Action Fairness Act of 2005 (CAFA), Dart removed the case to the U.S. District Court for the District of Kansas. CAFA gives federal courts jurisdiction over certain class actions, defined in § 1332(d)(1), if the class has more than 100 members, the parties are minimally diverse, and the amount in controversy exceeds $5 million. Dart's notice of removal alleged that all three requirements were satisfied. With respect to the amount in controversy, Dart stated that the purported underpayments to putative class members totaled more than $8.2 million.

Owens moved to remand the case to state court. The notice of removal was "deficient as a matter of law," Owens asserted, because it included "no evidence" proving that the amount in controversy exceeded $5 million. In response, Dart submitted a declaration by one of its executive officers. The declaration included a detailed damages calculation indicating that the amount in controversy, *sans* interest, exceeded $11 million. Without challenging Dart's calculation, Owens urged that Dart's amount-in-controversy submission came too late. "The legally deficient notice of removal," Owens maintained, could not be cured by "post-removal evidence about the amount in controversy."

Reading Tenth Circuit precedent to require proof of the amount in controversy in the notice of removal itself, the District Court granted Owens' remand motion. Dart's declaration, the District Court held, could not serve to keep the case in federal court.

Ordinarily, remand orders "are not reviewable on appeal or otherwise." § 1447(d). There is an exception, however, for cases invoking CAFA. In such cases, "a court of appeals may accept an appeal from an order of a district court granting or denying a motion to remand." Citing this exception, Dart petitioned the Tenth Circuit for permission to appeal. The Tenth Circuit denied review.

Dart filed a petition for certiorari in this Court requesting resolution of the following question: "Whether a defendant seeking removal to federal court is required to include evidence supporting federal jurisdiction in the notice of removal, or is alleging the required 'short and plain statement of the grounds for removal' enough?"

## II

As noted above, a defendant seeking to remove a case to a federal court must file in the federal forum a notice of removal "containing a short and plain statement of the grounds for removal." § 1446(a). By design, § 1446(a) tracks the general pleading requirement stated in Rule 8(a) of the Federal Rules of Civil Procedure.

When a plaintiff invokes federal-court jurisdiction, the plaintiff's amount-in-controversy allegation is accepted if made in good faith. Similarly, when a defendant seeks federal-court adjudication, the defendant's amount-in-controversy allegation should be accepted when not contested by the plaintiff or questioned by the court.

If the plaintiff contests the defendant's allegation, § 1446(c)(2)(B) instructs: "Removal is proper on the basis of an amount in controversy asserted" by the defendant "if the district court finds, by the preponderance of the evidence, that the amount in controversy exceeds" the jurisdictional threshold. This provision, added to § 1446 as part of the Federal Courts Jurisdiction and Venue Clarification Act of 2011 (JVCA), clarifies the procedure in order when a defendant's assertion of the amount in controversy is challenged. In such a case, both sides submit proof and the court decides, by a preponderance of the evidence, whether the amount-in-controversy requirement has been satisfied. As the House Judiciary Committee Report on the JVCA observed:

"Defendants do not need to prove to a legal certainty that the amount in controversy requirement has been met. Rather, defendants may simply allege or assert that the jurisdictional threshold has been met. Discovery may be taken with regard to that question. In case of a dispute, the district court must make findings of jurisdictional fact to which the preponderance standard applies." H.R.Rep. No. 112–10, p. 16 (2011).

Of course, a dispute about a defendant's jurisdictional allegations cannot arise until *after* the defendant files a notice of removal containing those allegations.

In remanding the case to state court, the District Court relied, in part, on a purported "presumption" against removal. We need not here decide whether such a presumption is proper in mine-run diversity cases. It suffices to point out that no antiremoval presumption attends cases invoking CAFA, which Congress enacted to facilitate adjudication of certain class actions in federal court.

In sum, as specified in § 1446(a), a defendant's notice of removal need include only a plausible allegation that the amount in controversy exceeds the jurisdictional threshold. Evidence establishing the amount is required by § 1446(c)(2)(B) only when the plaintiff contests, or the court questions, the defendant's allegation.

## III

We find no jurisdictional barrier to our settlement of the question presented. The case was "in" the Court of Appeals because of Dart's leave-to-appeal application, and we have jurisdiction to review what the Court of Appeals did with that application.

Discretion to review a remand order is not rudderless. Matters of discretion are reviewable for abuse of discretion. A court "would necessarily abuse its discretion if it based its ruling on an erroneous view of the law." This case fits that bill.

The District Court erred in ruling that Dart's amount-in-controversy allegation failed for want of proof. "A defendant seeking removal under CAFA need only allege the jurisdictional amount in its notice of removal and must prove that amount only if the plaintiff challenges the allegation.

In the above-described circumstances, we find it an abuse of discretion for the Tenth Circuit to deny Dart's request for review.

For the reasons stated, the judgment of the U.S. Court of Appeals for the Tenth Circuit is vacated, and the case is remanded for further proceedings consistent with this opinion.

# CHAPTER 8

# MULTI-DISTRICT LITIGATION - 28 USC 1407

1. Frequently, numerous plaintiffs all around the country may be suing the same defendants over some product flaw, (such as automobile air bag design, or emissions controls), or some major tort case such as a plane or train crash. Some of the suits may be class actions; some may be suits by single plaintiffs. But all of them have a great deal in common – they are all against the same defendant(s) for the same basic reasons. The specific damages may be different in each case. But the basic issue of liability is the same, and the same documents will be sought by discovery.

   So 28 USC 1407 provides that the Judicial Panel on Multidistrict Litigation (JPML), on its own motion, may *transfer* all of such actions to any one specific district "for coordinated or consolidated pretrial proceedings." The individual plaintiffs and their lawyers have no choice in the matter. If the JPML decrees that the cases will be transferred, they will be transferred – to a specific judge chosen by the JPML. Then all of the cases will be consolidated for pretrial discovery – saving a great deal of time and money by having all of the discovery done as one piece – rather than the same discovery taking place in 100 different cases. *If* settlements have not been reached in all of the cases by the end of all of the discovery, then each case which still remains open will be remanded by the JPML to the court from which it was transferred, for trial on the merits.

   There are lots of specific rules with regard to multi-district litigation, and it is becoming more and more widely used. Since the inception of this process of consolidated multidistrict litigation, the Manual for Complex Litigation – describing just how lead counsel is selected, who sits where, etc. – has grown from a slim volume to a very large treatise.

   The following recent U.S. Supreme Court case gives just a glimpse of one of the many issues involved with multidistrict litigation.

# SUPREME COURT OF THE UNITED STATES
## ELLEN GELBOIM, ET AL., PETITIONERS
## V.
## BANK OF AMERICA CORPORATION ET AL., RESPONDENTS

DECIDED JANUARY 21, 2015

**GINSBURG, J., delivered the opinion for a unanimous Court.**

An unsuccessful litigant in a federal district court may take an appeal, as a matter of right, from a "final decision of the district court." 28 U.S.C. § 1291. The question here presented: Is the right to appeal secured by § 1291 affected when a case is consolidated for pretrial proceedings in multidistrict litigation (or MDL) authorized by 28 U.S.C. § 1407?

Petitioners Ellen Gelboim and Linda Zacher filed in the United States District Court for the Southern District of New York a class-action complaint raising a single claim. They alleged that a number of banks, acting in concert, had violated federal antitrust law. Their case was consolidated for pretrial proceedings together with some 60 other cases, commenced in different districts, raising "one or more common questions of fact," § 1407(a).

The defendant banks, respondents here, moved to dismiss the Gelboim–Zacher complaint on the ground that the plaintiffs had suffered no antitrust injury. The District Court granted the motion, denied leave to amend the complaint, and dismissed the case in its entirety. Other cases made part of the multidistrict pretrial proceedings, however, presented discrete claims and remained before the District Court.

The Court of Appeals for the Second Circuit, acting on its own motion, dismissed the appeal filed by Gelboim and Zacher for want of appellate jurisdiction. We reverse the Second Circuit's judgment and hold that the Gelboim–Zacher complaint retained its independent status for purposes of appellate jurisdiction under § 1291. Petitioners' right to appeal ripened when the District Court dismissed their case, not upon eventual completion of multidistrict proceedings in all of the consolidated cases.

I

Three legal prescriptions figure in this case: Title 28 U.S.C. §§ 1291 and 1407, and Federal Rule of Civil Procedure 54(b).

Section 1291 gives the courts of appeals jurisdiction over appeals from "all final decisions of the district courts of the United States." A "final decision" is one "by which a district court disassociates itself from a case." While decisions of this Court have accorded § 1291 a "practical rather than a technical construction," (*Cohen v. Beneficial Industrial Loan Corp.*), the statute's core application is to rulings that terminate an action.

Rule 54(b) permits district courts to authorize immediate appeal of dispositive rulings on separate claims in a civil action raising multiple claims:

> When an action presents more than one claim for relief ... or when multiple parties are involved, the court may direct entry of a final judgment as to one or more, but fewer than all, claims or parties only if the court expressly determines that there is no just reason for delay.

Rule 54(b) relaxes "the former general practice that, in multiple claims actions, *all* the claims had to be finally decided before an appeal could be entertained from a final decision upon any of them." The Federal Rules allow a plaintiff to "state [in one complaint] as many separate claims as it has." Rule 8(d)(3). Rule 54(b) was adopted in view of the breadth of the "civil action" the Rules allow, specifically "to avoid the possible injustice" of "delaying judgment on a distinctly separate claim pending adjudication of the entire case." The Rule thus aimed to augment, not diminish, appeal opportunity.

Section 1407 is of more recent vintage. Enacted in 1968 in response to a growing number of complex but related cases filed in multiple districts, § 1407 authorizes the Judicial Panel on Multidistrict Litigation (JPML) to transfer civil actions "involving one or more common questions of fact ... to any district for coordinated or consolidated pretrial proceedings" in order to "promote the just and efficient conduct of such actions."

Transfer under § 1407 aims to "eliminate duplication in discovery, avoid conflicting rulings and schedules, reduce litigation cost, and save the time and effort of the parties, the attorneys, the witnesses, and the courts." Manual for Complex Litigation § 20.131, p. 220 (4th ed. 2004). "Each action" transferred pursuant to § 1407, the provision instructs, "shall be remanded by the panel at or before the conclusion of ... pretrial proceedings to the district from which it was transferred unless it shall have been previously terminated." § 1407(a).

## II

The London InterBank Offered Rate (LIBOR) is a benchmark interest rate disseminated by the British Bankers' Association based on the rate at which certain banks predict they can borrow funds. LIBOR is a reference point in determining interest rates for financial instruments in the United States and globally.

In August 2011, the JPML (Judicial Panel on Multidistrict Litigation), established MDL No. 2262 (LIBOR MDL) for cases involving allegations that the banks named as defendants understated their borrowing costs, thereby depressing LIBOR and enabling the banks to pay lower interest rates on financial instruments sold to investors. Composing the LIBOR MDL, over 60 actions, commenced in California, Illinois, Iowa, Kansas, Massachusetts, Minnesota, New Jersey, New York, Ohio, Pennsylvania, Texas, Virginia, and Wisconsin, were coordinated or consolidated for pretrial proceedings in the United States District Court for the Southern District of New York.

In June 2012, the District Court entertained a motion to dismiss four categories of cases included in the MDL. The first three categories involved putative class actions, each with a single lead case: (1) the Gelboim–Zacher action, filed on behalf of purchasers of bonds with LIBOR-linked interest rates; (2) an action filed on behalf of purchasers of over-the-counter LIBOR-based instruments (OTC plaintiffs); (3) an action filed on behalf of purchasers of LIBOR-based instruments on exchanges (Exchange plaintiffs). The fourth category, not relevant here, comprised a set of individual actions filed by Charles Schwab Corporation and related entities. The Gelboim–Zacher complaint asserted a federal antitrust claim under § 1 of the Sherman Act, 15 U.S.C. § 1, and that claim only, while the complaints in the other actions asserted a federal antitrust claim in addition to other differently based federal and state claims.

Determining that no plaintiff could assert a cognizable antitrust injury, the District Court granted the banks' motion to dismiss plaintiffs' antitrust claims—the sole claim raised in the Gelboim–Zacher complaint. Assuming that the Gelboim–Zacher plaintiffs were entitled to an immediate appeal of right under § 1291 because their suit had been "dismissed in its entirety," the District Court granted Rule 54(b) certification.

On its own initiative, the Second Circuit dismissed the Gelboim–Zacher appeal because the "order appealed from did not dispose of all claims in the consolidated action."

We granted review of the Second Circuit's judgment dismissing the Gelboim–Zacher appeal. Before this Court, petitioners Gelboim and Zacher contend that the order dismissing their case in its entirety removed them from the consolidated proceeding, thereby triggering their right to appeal under § 1291. Respondent banks urge that consolidated cases proceed as one unit for the duration of the consolidation.

Consequently, they maintain, there is no appeal of right from an order dismissing fewer than all consolidated claims, thus the sole avenue for appeal while the consolidation continues is Rule 54(b). Agreeing with Gelboim and Zacher, we reverse the Court of Appeals' judgment.

## III

Cases consolidated for MDL pretrial proceedings ordinarily retain their separate identities, so an order disposing of one of the discrete cases in its entirety should qualify under § 1291 as an appealable final decision. Section 1407 refers to individual "actions" which may be transferred to a single district court, not to any monolithic multidistrict "action" created by transfer. § 1407 does not "imbue transferred actions with some new and distinctive character"). And Congress anticipated that, during the pendency of pretrial proceedings, final decisions might be rendered in one or more of the actions consolidated pursuant to § 1407. It specified that "at or before the conclusion of pretrial proceedings," each of the transferred actions must be remanded to the originating district *unless the action shall have been previously terminated.*" § 1407(a) (emphasis added).

The District Court's order dismissing the Gelboim–Zacher complaint for lack of antitrust injury, without leave to amend, had the hallmarks of a final decision. Ruling on the merits of the case, the District Court completed its adjudication of petitioners' complaint and terminated their action. As a result of the District Court's disposition, petitioners are no longer participants in the consolidated proceedings. Nothing about the initial consolidation of their civil action with other cases in the LIBOR MDL renders the dismissal of their complaint in any way tentative or incomplete. As is ordinarily the case, the § 1407 consolidation offered convenience for the parties and promoted efficient judicial administration, but did not meld the Gelboim–Zacher action and others in the MDL into a single unit.

The banks' view that, in a § 1407 consolidation, no appeal of right accrues until the consolidation ends would leave plaintiffs like Gelboim and Zacher in a quandary about the proper timing of their appeals. Under Federal Rule of Appellate Procedure 4, which this Court has called "jurisdictional," *Bowles v. Russell,* a notice of appeal in a civil case must be filed "within 30 days after entry of the judgment or order appealed from," Rule 4(a)(1)(A). If plaintiffs whose actions have been dismissed with prejudice by a district court must await the termination of pretrial proceedings in all consolidated cases, what event or order would start the 30–day clock? When pretrial consolidation concludes, there may be no occasion for the entry of any judgment. Orders may issue returning cases to their originating courts but an order of that genre would not qualify as the dispositive ruling Gelboim and Zacher seek to overturn on appeal. And surely would-be appellants need not await final disposition of all cases in their originating districts, long after pretrial consolidation under § 1407 could even arguably justify treating the cases as a judicial unit.

The sensible solution to the appeal-clock trigger is evident: When the transferee court overseeing pretrial proceedings in multidistrict litigation grants a defendant's dispositive motion "on all issues in some transferred cases, those cases become immediately appealable ... while cases where other issues remain would not be appealable at that time." Multidistrict Litigation Manual § 9:21, p. 312 (2014).

The banks express concern that plaintiffs with the weakest cases may be positioned to appeal because their complaint states only one claim, while plaintiffs with stronger cases will be unable to appeal simultaneously because they have other claims still pending. Rule 54(b) attends to this concern. District courts may grant certifications under that Rule, thereby enabling plaintiffs in actions that have not been dismissed in their entirety to pursue immediate appellate review. That is just what happened in this very case. The District Court granted Rule 54(b) certifications to two other groups of plaintiffs so they could appeal at the same time Gelboim and Zacher could. And if the MDL court believes that further proceedings might be relevant to a claim a defendant moves to dismiss, the court ordinarily can defer ruling on the motion, thus allowing all plaintiffs to participate in the ongoing MDL proceedings.

While Rule 54(b) can aid parties with multiple-claim complaints— the rule, properly read, is of no avail to Gelboim and Zacher. Rule 54(b) addresses orders finally adjudicating fewer than all claims presented in a civil action complaint. It "does not apply to a single claim action nor to a multiple claims action in which all of the claims have been finally decided." In short, Rule 54(b) is designed to permit acceleration of appeals in multiple-claim cases, not to retard appeals in single-claim cases.

Section 1292(b), the banks conceded at argument, is inapposite here. It allows district courts to designate for review *interlocutory orders* "not otherwise appealable," where immediate appeal "may materially advance the ultimate termination of the litigation." § 1292(b). The designation may be accepted or rejected in the discretion of the court of appeals. It suffices to note that there is nothing "interlocutory" about the dismissal order in the Gelboim–Zacher action.

For the reasons stated, we reverse the judgment of the U.S. Court of Appeals for the Second Circuit deeming the District Court's dismissal of the Gelboim–Zacher complaint unripe for appellate review, and we remand the case for further proceedings consistent with this opinion.

# CHAPTER 9

# DISCOVERY RULES 26 THROUGH 37

1. The most important part of any litigation is likely to be discovery. Yes, there may sometimes be some challenging issues of personal or subject matter jurisdiction, and some interesting issues of choice of law. But the fundamentals of discovery are usually at the heart of almost everything. What *are* defendant's minimum contacts with the jurisdiction? How much did the defendant know, in advance, about the dangers of a particular product? Were defendants' actions intentional, or merely negligent? What are the necessary facts to be proved to a judge or jury? What will be the most effective way of proving those facts?

   The vast majority of cases filed never get to trial. They are settled. Effective discovery is a major factor in securing a good settlement for your client.

   This chapter will introduce you to some of the major tools used for discovery. Several of the cases included in this chapter are U.S. Supreme Court cases. But many of the included cases are from the trial court level, because most discovery disputes do not make it all the way to the U.S. Supreme Court.

## A. PRIVILEGES

2. First, there is some information that is simply protected from discovery. You will not be able to get that information – no matter how useful it might be. The basic rule is that discussions between any attorney and her client are protected by the Attorney-Client privilege. Period.

# 1. ATTORNEY/CLIENT

### 118 S. CT. 2081
### SUPREME COURT OF THE UNITED STATES
### SWIDLER & BERLIN AND JAMES HAMILTON, PETITIONERS,
### V.
### UNITED STATES

DECIDED JUNE 25, 1998

**Chief Justice REHNQUIST delivered the opinion of the Court.**

Petitioner, James Hamilton, an attorney, made notes of an initial interview with a client shortly before the client's death. The Government, represented by the Office of Independent Counsel, now seeks his notes for use in a criminal investigation. We hold that the notes are protected by the attorney-client privilege.

This dispute arises out of an investigation conducted by the Office of the Independent Counsel into whether various individuals made false statements, obstructed justice, or committed other crimes during investigations of the 1993 dismissal of employees from the White House Travel Office. Vincent W. Foster, Jr., was Deputy White House Counsel when the firings occurred. In July 1993, Foster met with petitioner Hamilton, an attorney at petitioner Swidler & Berlin, to seek legal representation concerning possible congressional or other investigations of the firings. During a 2-hour meeting, Hamilton took three pages of handwritten notes. One of the first entries in the notes is the word "Privileged." Nine days later, Foster committed suicide.

In December 1995, a federal grand jury, at the request of the Independent Counsel, issued subpoenas to petitioners Hamilton and Swidler & Berlin for, *inter alia,* Hamilton's handwritten notes of his meeting with Foster. Petitioners filed a motion to quash, arguing that the notes were protected by the attorney-client privilege and by the work-product privilege. The District Court, after examining the notes *in camera,* concluded they were protected from disclosure by both doctrines and denied enforcement of the subpoenas.

The Court of Appeals for the District of Columbia Circuit reversed.

Petitioners sought review in this Court on both the attorney-client privilege and the work-product privilege.[FN1] We granted certiorari, and we now reverse.

FN1. Because we sustain the claim of attorney-client privilege, we do not reach the claim of work-product privilege.

The attorney-client privilege is one of the oldest recognized privileges for confidential communications. *Upjohn Co. v. United States.* The privilege is intended to encourage "full and frank communication between attorneys and their clients and thereby promote broader public interests in the observance of law and the administration of justice." *Upjohn.* The issue presented here is the scope of that privilege; more particularly, the extent to which the privilege survives the death of the client. Our interpretation of the privilege's scope is guided by "the principles of the common law as interpreted by the courts in the light of reason and experience."

The Independent Counsel argues that the attorney-client privilege should not prevent disclosure of confidential communications where the client has died and the information is relevant to a criminal proceeding. There is some authority for this position.

But other than these two decisions, cases addressing the existence of the privilege after death - most involving the testamentary exception* - uniformly presume the privilege survives, even if they do not so hold. Several State Supreme Court decisions expressly hold that the attorney-client privilege extends beyond the death of the client, even in the criminal context.

*[Editor's note: The testamentary exception is used frequently in probate. It allows an attorney who drafted a will to testify as to what the client really intended, if the words of the will are not clear, and the client has died.]

In *Glover v. Patten*, (1897), this Court, in recognizing the testamentary exception, expressly assumed that the privilege continues after the individual's death.

The great body of case law supports, either by holding or considered dicta, the position that the privilege does survive in a case such as the present one. Given the language of Rule 501, at the very least the burden is on the Independent Counsel to show that "reason and experience" require a departure from this rule.

Commentators on the law also recognize that the general rule is that the attorney-client privilege continues after death.

Despite the scholarly criticism, we think there are weighty reasons that counsel in favor of posthumous application. Knowing that communications will remain confidential even after death encourages the client to communicate fully and frankly with counsel. While the fear of disclosure, and the consequent withholding of information from counsel, may be reduced if disclosure is limited to posthumous disclosure in a criminal context, it seems unreasonable to assume that it vanishes altogether. Clients may be concerned about reputation, civil liability, or possible harm to friends or family. Posthumous disclosure of such communications may be as feared as disclosure during the client's lifetime.

Clients consult attorneys for a wide variety of reasons, only one of which involves possible criminal liability. Many attorneys act as counselors on personal and family matters, where, in the course of obtaining the desired advice, confidences about family members or financial problems must be revealed in order to assure sound legal advice. The same is true of owners of small businesses who may regularly consult their attorneys about a variety of problems arising in the course of the business. These confidences may not come close to any sort of admission of criminal wrongdoing, but nonetheless be matters which the client would not wish divulged.

In related cases, we have said that the loss of evidence admittedly caused by the privilege is justified in part by the fact that without the privilege, the client may not have made such communications in the first place. This is true of disclosure before and after the client's death. Without assurance of the privilege's posthumous application, the client may very well not have made disclosures to his attorney at all, so the loss of evidence is more apparent than real. In the case at hand, it seems quite plausible that Foster, perhaps already contemplating suicide, may not have sought legal advice from Hamilton if he had not been assured the conversation was privileged.

A "no harm in one more exception" rationale could contribute to the general erosion of the privilege, without reference to common-law principles or "reason and experience."

The Independent Counsel, relying on cases such as *United States v. Nixon*, and Branzenburg, urges that privileges be strictly construed because they are inconsistent with the paramount judicial goal of truth seeking. But both *Nixon* and *Branzenburg* dealt with the creation of privileges not recognized by the common law, whereas here we deal with one of the oldest recognized privileges in the law. And we are asked, not simply to "construe" the privilege, but to narrow it, contrary to the weight of the existing body of case law.

It has been generally, if not universally, accepted, for well over a century, that the attorney-client privilege survives the death of the client in a case such as this. While the arguments against the survival of the privilege are by no means frivolous, they are based in large part on speculation - thoughtful speculation, but speculation nonetheless - as to whether posthumous termination of the privilege would diminish a client's willingness to confide in an attorney. In an area where empirical information would be useful, it is scant and inconclusive.

Rule 501's direction to look to "the principles of the common law as they may be interpreted by the courts of the United States in the light of reason and experience" does not mandate that a rule, once established, should endure for all time. But here the Independent Counsel has simply not made a sufficient showing to overturn the common-law rule embodied in the prevailing caselaw. Interpreted in the light of reason and experience, that body of law requires that the attorney-client privilege prevent disclosure of the notes at issue in this case. The judgment of the Court of Appeals is *Reversed.*

## 2. WORK PRODUCT

3. Another very strong privilege that may protect certain documents from discovery is the Attorney – Work Product privilege, now described in FRCP 26(b)(3). *Hickman v. Taylor* continues to be the lead case on the Attorney-Work Product privilege.

**67 S.CT. 385**

**SUPREME COURT OF THE UNITED STATES**

**HICKMAN**

**V.**

**TAYLOR ET AL.**

DECIDED JANUARY 13, 1947

**Mr. Justice MURPHY delivered the opinion of the Court.**

This case presents an important problem as to the extent to which a party may inquire into oral and written statements of witnesses, or other information, secured by an adverse party's counsel in the course of preparation for possible litigation after a claim has arisen. Examination into a person's files and records, including those resulting from the professional activities of an attorney, must be judged with care. It is not without reason that various safeguards have been established to preclude unwarranted excursions into the privacy of a man's work. At the same time, public policy supports reasonable and necessary inquiries. Properly to balance these competing interests is a delicate and difficult task.

On February 7, 1943, the tug 'J. M. Taylor' sank while engaged in helping to tow a car float of the Baltimore & Ohio Railroad across the Delaware River at Philadelphia. The accident was apparently unusual in nature, the cause of it still being unknown. Five of the nine crew members were drowned. Three days later the tug owners and the underwriters employed a law firm, of which respondent Fortenbaugh is a member, to defend them against potential suits by representatives of the deceased crew members and to sue the railroad for damages to the tug.

A public hearing was held on March 4, 1943, before the United States Steamboat Inspectors, at which the four survivors were examined. This testimony was recorded and made available to all interested parties. Shortly thereafter, Fortenbaugh privately interviewed the survivors and took statements from them with an eye toward the anticipated litigation; the survivors signed these statements on March 29. Fortenbaugh also interviewed other persons believed to have some information relating to the accident and in some cases he made memoranda of what they told him. At the time when Fortenbaugh secured the statements of the survivors, representatives of two of the deceased crew members had been in communication with him. Ultimately claims were presented by representatives of all five of the deceased; four of the claims, however, were settled without litigation. The fifth claimant, petitioner herein, brought suit in a federal court under the Jones Act on November 26, 1943, naming as defendants the two tug owners, individually and as partners, and the railroad.

One year later, petitioner filed 39 interrogatories directed to the tug owners. The 38th interrogatory read:

> State whether any statements of the members of the crews of the Tugs 'J. M. Taylor' and 'Philadelphia' or of any other vessel were taken in connection with the towing of the car float and the sinking of the Tug 'John M. Taylor.'
> Attach hereto exact copies of all such statements if in writing, and if oral, set forth in detail the exact provisions of any such oral statements or reports.'

Supplemental interrogatories asked whether any oral or written statements, records, reports or other memoranda had been made concerning any matter relative to the towing operation, the sinking of the tug, the salvaging and repair of the tug, and the death of the deceased. If the answer was in the affirmative, the tug owners were then requested to set forth the nature of all such records, reports, statements or other memoranda.

The tug owners, through Fortenbaugh, answered all of the interrogatories except No. 38 and the supplemental ones just described. While admitting that statements of the survivors had been taken, they declined to summarize or set forth the contents. They did so on the ground that such requests called "for privileged matter obtained in preparation for litigation" and constituted "an attempt to obtain indirectly counsel's private files." It was claimed that answering these requests "would involve practically turning over not only the complete files, but also the telephone records and, almost, the thoughts of counsel."

In connection with the hearing on these objections, Fortenbaugh made a written statement and gave an informal oral deposition explaining the circumstances under which he had taken the statements. But he was not expressly asked in the deposition to produce the statements. The District Court for the Eastern District of

Pennsylvania, sitting en banc, held that the requested matters were not privileged. The court then decreed that the tug owners and Fortenbaugh, as counsel and agent for the tug owners forthwith "Answer Plaintiff's 38th interrogatory and supplemental interrogatories; produce all written statements of witnesses obtained by Mr. Fortenbaugh, as counsel and agent for Defendants; state in substance any fact concerning this case which Defendants learned through oral statements made by witnesses to Mr. Fortenbaugh whether or not included in his private memoranda and produce Mr. Fortenbaugh's memoranda containing statements of fact by witnesses or to submit these memoranda to the Court for determination of those portions which should be revealed to Plaintiff." Upon their refusal, the court adjudged them in contempt and ordered them imprisoned until they complied.

The Third Circuit Court of Appeals reversed the judgment of the District Court. It held that the information here sought was part of the "work product of the lawyer" and hence privileged from discovery under the Federal Rules of Civil Procedure.

We granted certiorari.

The pre-trial deposition-discovery mechanism established by Rules 26 to 37 is one of the most significant innovations of the Federal Rules of Civil Procedure. Under the prior federal practice, the pre-trial functions of notice-giving issue-formulation and fact-revelation were performed primarily and inadequately by the pleadings.[2] Inquiry into the issues and the facts before trial was narrowly confined and was often cumbersome in method. The new rules, however, restrict the pleadings to the task of general notice-giving and invest the deposition-discovery process with a vital role in the preparation for trial. The various instruments of discovery now serve (1) as a device, along with the pre-trial hearing under Rule 16, to narrow and clarify the basic issues between the parties, and as a device for ascertaining the facts, or information as to the existence or whereabouts of facts, relative to those issues. Thus civil trials in the federal courts no longer need be carried on in the dark. The way is now clear, consistent with recognized privileges, for the parties to obtain the fullest possible knowledge of the issues and facts before trial.

The deposition-discovery rules create integrated procedural devices. And the basic question at stake is whether any of those devices may be used to inquire into materials collected by an adverse party's counsel in the course of preparation for possible litigation.

In urging that he has a right to inquire into the materials secured and prepared by Fortenbaugh, petitioner emphasizes that the deposition-discovery portions of the Federal Rules of Civil Procedure are designed to enable the parties to discover the true facts and to compel their disclosure wherever they may be found. It is said that inquiry may be made under these rules, epitomized by Rule 26, as to any relevant matter which is not privileged; and since the discovery provisions are to be applied as broadly and liberally as possible, the privilege limitation must be restricted to its narrowest bounds. On the premise that the attorney-client privilege is the one involved in this case, petitioner argues that it must be strictly confined to confidential communications made by a client to his attorney. And since the materials here in issue were secured by Fortenbaugh from third persons rather than from his clients, the tug owners, the conclusion is reached that these materials are proper subjects for discovery under Rule 26.

As additional support for this result, petitioner claims that to prohibit discovery under these circumstances would give a corporate defendant a tremendous advantage in a suit by an individual plaintiff. Thus in a suit by an injured employee against a railroad or in a suit by an insured person against an insurance company the corporate defendant could pull a dark veil of secrecy over all the pertinent facts it can collect after the claim arises merely on the assertion that such facts were gathered by its large staff of attorneys and claim agents. At the same time, the individual plaintiff, who often has direct knowledge of the matter in issue and has no counsel until some time after his claim arises could be compelled to disclose all the intimate details of his case. By endowing with immunity from disclosure all that a lawyer discovers in the course of his duties, it is said, the rights of individual litigants in such cases are drained of vitality and the lawsuit becomes more of a battle of deception than a search for truth.

But framing the problem in terms of assisting individual plaintiffs in their suits against corporate defendants is unsatisfactory. Discovery concededly may work to the disadvantage as well as to the advantage of individual plaintiffs. Discovery, in other words, is not a one-way proposition. It is available in all types of cases at the behest of any party, individual or corporate, plaintiff or defendant. The problem thus far transcends the situation confronting this petitioner. And we must view that problem in light of the limitless situations where the particular kind of discovery sought by petitioner might be used.

We agree, of course, that the deposition-discovery rules are to be accorded a broad and liberal treatment. No longer can the time-honored cry of 'fishing expedition' serve to preclude a party from inquiring into the facts underlying his opponent's case. Mutual knowledge of all the relevant facts gathered by both parties is essential to proper litigation. To that end, either party may compel the other to disgorge whatever facts he has in his possession. The deposition-discovery procedure simply advances the stage at which the disclosure can be compelled from the time of trial to the period preceding it, thus reducing the possibility of surprise. But discovery, like all matters of procedure, has ultimate and necessary boundaries. Limitations inevitably arise when it can be shown that the examination is being conducted in bad faith or in such a manner as to annoy, embarrass or oppress the person subject to the inquiry. And as Rule 26(b) provides, further limitations come into existence when the inquiry touches upon the irrelevant or encroaches upon the recognized domains of privilege.

We also agree that the memoranda, statements and mental impressions in issue in this case fall outside the scope of the attorney-client privilege and hence are not protected from discovery on that basis. It is unnecessary here to delineate the content and scope of that privilege as recognized in the federal courts. For present purposes, it suffices to note that the protective cloak of this privilege does not extend to information which an attorney secures from a witness while acting for his client in anticipation of litigation. Nor does this privilege concern the memoranda, briefs, communications and other writings prepared by counsel for his own use in prosecuting his client's case; and it is equally unrelated to writings which reflect an attorney's mental impressions, conclusions, opinions or legal theories.

But the impropriety of invoking that privilege does not provide an answer to the problem before us. Petitioner has made more than an ordinary request for relevant, non-privileged facts in the possession of his adversaries or their counsel. He has sought discovery as of right of oral and written statements of witnesses whose identity is well known and whose availability to petitioner appears unimpaired. He has sought production of these matters after making the most searching inquiries of his opponents as to the circumstances surrounding the fatal accident, which inquiries were sworn to have been answered to the best of their information and belief. Interrogatories were directed toward all the events prior to, during and subsequent to the sinking of the tug. Full and honest answers to such broad inquiries would necessarily have included all pertinent information gleaned by Fortenbaugh through his interviews with the witnesses. Petitioner makes no suggestion, and we cannot assume, that the tug owners or Fortenbaugh were incomplete or dishonest in the framing of their answers. In addition, petitioner was free to examine the public testimony of the witnesses taken before the United States Steamboat Inspectors. We are thus dealing with an attempt to secure the production of written statements and mental impressions contained in the files and the mind of the attorney Fortenbaugh without any showing of necessity or any indication or claim that denial of such production would unduly prejudice the preparation of petitioner's case or cause him any hardship or injustice. For aught that appears, the essence of what petitioner seeks either has been revealed to him already through the interrogatories or is readily available to him direct from the witnesses for the asking.

The District Court, after hearing objections to petitioner's request, commanded Fortenbaugh to produce all written statements of witnesses and to state in substance any facts learned through oral statements of witnesses to him. Fortenbaugh was to submit any memoranda he had made of the oral statements so that the court might determine what portions should be revealed to petitioner. All of this was ordered without any showing by petitioner, or any requirement that he make a proper showing, of the necessity for the production of any of this material or any demonstration that denial of production would cause hardship or injustice. The court simply ordered production on the theory that the facts sought were material and were not privileged as constituting attorney-client communications.

In our opinion, neither Rule 26 nor any other rule dealing with discovery contemplates production under such circumstances. That is not because the subject matter is privileged or irrelevant, as those concepts are used in these rules. Here is simply an attempt, without purported necessity or justification, to secure written statements, private memoranda and personal recollections prepared or formed by an adverse party's counsel in the course of his legal duties. As such, it falls outside the arena of discovery and contravenes the public policy underlying the orderly prosecution and defense of legal claims. Not even the most liberal of discovery theories can justify unwarranted inquiries into the files and the mental impressions of an attorney.

Historically, a lawyer is an officer of the court and is bound to work for the advancement of justice while faithfully protecting the rightful interests of his clients. In performing his various duties, however, it is essential that a lawyer work with a certain degree of privacy, free from unnecessary intrusion by opposing parties and their counsel. Proper preparation of a client's case demands that he assemble information, sift what he considers to be the relevant from the irrelevant facts, prepare his legal theories and plan his strategy without undue and needless interference. That is the historical and the necessary way in which lawyers act within the framework of our system of jurisprudence to promote justice and to protect their clients' interests. This work is reflected, of course, in interviews, statements, memoranda, correspondence, briefs, mental impressions, personal beliefs, and countless other tangible and intangible ways—aptly though roughly termed by the Circuit Court of Appeals in this case as the 'Work product of the lawyer.' Were such materials open to opposing counsel on mere demand, much of what is now put down in writing would remain unwritten. An attorney's thoughts, heretofore inviolate, would not be his own. Inefficiency, unfairness and sharp practices would inevitably develop in the giving of legal advice and in the preparation of cases for trial. The effect on the legal profession would be demoralizing. And the interests of the clients and the cause of justice would be poorly served.

We do not mean to say that all written materials obtained or prepared by an adversary's counsel with an eye toward litigation are necessarily free from discovery in all cases. Where relevant and non-privileged facts remain hidden in an attorney's file and where production of those facts is essential to the preparation of one's case, discovery may properly be had. Such written statements and documents might, under certain circumstances, be admissible in evidence or give clues as to the existence or location of relevant facts. Or they might be useful for purposes of impeachment or corroboration. And production might be justified where the witnesses are no longer available or can be reached only with difficulty. Were production of written statements and documents to be precluded under such circumstances, the liberal ideals of the deposition-discovery portions of the Federal Rules of Civil Procedure would be stripped of much of their meaning. But the general policy against invading the privacy of an attorney's course of preparation is so well recognized and so essential to an orderly working of our system of legal procedure that a burden rests on the one who would invade that privacy to establish adequate reasons to justify production through a subpoena or court order. That burden, we believe, is necessarily implicit in the rules.

The rules give the trial judge the requisite discretion to make a judgment as to whether discovery should be allowed as to written statements secured from witnesses. But in the instant case there was no room for that discretion to operate in favor of the petitioner. No attempt was made to establish any reason why Fortenbaugh should be forced to produce the written statements. There was only a naked, general demand for these materials as of right and a finding by the District Court that no recognizable privilege was involved. That was insufficient to justify discovery under these circumstances and the court should have sustained the refusal of the tug owners and Fortenbaugh to produce.

But as to oral statements made by witnesses to Fortenbaugh, whether presently in the form of his mental impressions or memoranda, we do not believe that any showing of necessity can be made under the circumstances of this case so as to justify production. Under ordinary conditions, forcing an attorney to repeat or write out all that witnesses have told him and to deliver the account to his adversary gives rise to grave dangers of inaccuracy and untrustworthiness. No legitimate purpose is served by such production. The practice forces the attorney to testify as to what he remembers or what he saw fit to write down regarding witnesses' remarks. Such testimony could not qualify as evidence; and to use it for impeachment or corroborative purposes would make the attorney much less an officer of the court and much more an ordinary witness. The standards of the profession would thereby suffer.

Denial of production of this nature does not mean that any material, non-privileged facts can be hidden from the petitioner in this case. He need not be unduly hindered in the preparation of his case, in the discovery of facts or in his anticipation of his opponents' position. Searching interrogatories directed to Fortenbaugh and the tug owners, production of written documents and statements upon a proper showing and direct interviews with the witnesses themselves all serve to reveal the facts in Fortenbaugh's possession to the fullest possible extent consistent with public policy. Petitioner's counsel frankly admits that he wants the oral statements only to help prepare himself to examine witnesses and to make sure that he has overlooked nothing. That is insufficient under the circumstances to permit him an exception to the policy underlying the privacy of Fortenbaugh's professional activities. If there should be a rare situation justifying production of these matters, petitioner's case is not of that type.

We fully appreciate the wide-spread controversy among the members of the legal profession over the problem raised by this case. It is a problem that rests on what has been one of the most hazy frontiers of the discovery process. But until some rule or statute definitely prescribes otherwise, we are not justified in permitting discovery in a situation of this nature as a matter of unqualified right. When Rule 26 and the other discovery rules were adopted, this Court and the members of the bar in general certainly did not believe or contemplate that all the files and mental processes of lawyers were thereby opened to the free scrutiny of their adversaries. And we refuse to interpret the rules at this time so as to reach so harsh and unwarranted a result.

We therefore affirm the judgment of the Circuit Court of Appeals.

Mr. Justice JACKSON, concurring.

The primary effect of the practice advocated here would be on the legal profession itself. But it too often is overlooked that the lawyer and the law office are indispensable parts of our administration of justice. Law-abiding people can go nowhere else to learn the ever changing and constantly multiplying rules by which they must behave and to obtain redress for their wrongs. The welfare and tone of the legal profession is therefore of prime consequence to society, which would feel the consequences of such a practice as petitioner urges secondarily but certainly.

It seems clear and long has been recognized that discovery should provide a party access to anything that is evidence in his case. It seems equally clear that discovery should not nullify the privilege of confidential communication between attorney and client. But those principles give us no real assistance here because what is being sought is neither evidence nor is it a privileged communication between attorney and client.

Counsel for the petitioner candidly said on argument that he wanted this information to help prepare himself to examine witnesses, to make sure he overlooked nothing. But a common law trial is and always should be an adversary proceeding. Discovery was hardly intended to enable a learned profession to perform its functions either **without wits or on wits borrowed from the adversary.**

4. One inexpensive, but sometimes relatively slow means of discovering useful information may be through the Freedom of Information Act, (FOIA). With certain important exceptions, the federal government is required to disclose to anyone who asks, whatever information the government has collected on a particular topic. There may be some downsides to submitting a FOIA request, as illustrated by the following case.

To help you understand the next case, it may help to know that when a party requests certain information from the opponent, and the opponent claims that the information is privileged, the party from whom the information was requested may respond by submitting a privilege log – indicating categories of documents it has – but is not willing to disclose because it claims that the documents are privileged. Then the court can decide which documents are privileged – and which are not.

This case provides a very good description of when the attorney client privilege is – or is not – applicable to certain documents, and the extent of discovery allowed under Rule 26. Note how easy it is for an attorney, unintentionally, to waive the protections of attorney work product.

## 293 F.R.D. 539
## UNITED STATES DISTRICT COURT, S.D. NEW YORK.
## IN RE TERRORIST ATTACKS ON SEPTEMBER 11, 2001.
## THIS DECISION RELATES TO:
## ASHTON, ET AL. V. AL QAEDA ISLAMIC; BURNETT V. AL BARAKA; FEDERAL INSURANCE CO. V. AL QAIDA; O'NEILL V. AL BARAKA INVESTMENT & DEVEL. CORP.; CONTINENTAL CASUALTY CO. V. AL QAEDA; CANTOR FITZGERALD & CO. V. AKIDA BANK PRIVATE LTD.; EURO BROKERS, INC. V. AL BARAKA INVESTMENT & DEVEL. CORP.

### DECIDED JUNE 12, 2013

MEMORANDUM DECISION AND ORDER

FRANK MAAS, United States Magistrate Judge.

## I. Introduction and Background

This litigation, now in its tenth year, consolidates personal injury and property damage claims against various terrorist organizations, Islamic charities, and foreign banks, arising out of their alleged involvement in the terrorist attacks on September 11, 2001. The case has a complex and sprawling procedural history, which has seen a number of dismissals, default judgments, and two trips to the Court of Appeals. There has been no shortage of disputes regarding discovery, which continues to proceed at a deliberate pace.

In February, the Plaintiffs submitted a privilege log in response to the document requests of a number of the defendants. The Defendants have moved to compel production of two categories of documents identified in the log, which they contend have been improperly withheld from disclosure: (a) correspondence with government agencies relating to document requests the Plaintiffs made pursuant to the Freedom of Information Act ("FOIA"), and (b) documents deemed confidential that Plaintiffs' counsel obtained in connection with their representation of separate, unrelated parties in *Linde, et al. v. Arab Bank,* a case currently pending before Judge Gershon in the Eastern District of New York.

For reasons that are explained below, the motion is granted in part and denied in part.

## II. Analysis

### A. FOIA Correspondence

The FOIA correspondence consists of three types of documents: (1) letters from Plaintiffs' counsel to various government agencies requesting documents pursuant to FOIA ("FOIA Requests"), (2) letters or other communications from the government acknowledging and responding to the Plaintiffs' FOIA requests ("FOIA Responses"), and (3) the actual documents received in response to the Plaintiffs' FOIA requests ("Underlying Documents"). The Plaintiffs concede that the Underlying Documents are not privileged and have agreed to produce all such documents that have not already been disclosed. They take a different position with respect to the FOIA Requests and Responses, maintaining that those documents are exempt from disclosure because they contain details about their attorneys' mental impressions, thoughts, legal theories, and priorities concerning which documents and issues to pursue. Because the FOIA Requests and Responses allegedly tend to reveal counsels' confidential strategies about "which subjects to research, which documents to collect, and which documents and issues to prioritize," the Plaintiffs argue that requiring production would unfairly prejudice them by supplying the Defendants with a "roadmap" to their case.

The work product doctrine, originally articulated by the Supreme Court in *Hickman v. Taylor,* is codified in Rule 26(b)(3) of the Federal Rules of Civil Procedure. That rule excludes from discovery "materials 'prepared in anticipation of litigation' by a party or the party's representative, absent a showing of substantial need." The protection afforded by the work product rule provides a "zone of privacy in which a lawyer can prepare and develop legal theories and strategy 'with an eye toward litigation,' free from unnecessary intrusion by his adversaries." To avail itself of that protection, a party must demonstrate that the material at issue is "(1) a document or tangible thing, (2) that was prepared in anticipation of litigation, and (3) was prepared by or for a party, or by or for his representative." However, the work product rule is not absolute. Thus, even if a document qualifies as work product within the meaning of Rule 26(b)(3), a party may obtain its disclosure by showing that it has a "substantial need" for the document and cannot obtain the "substantial equivalent" through other means without "undue hardship." Rule 26 further distinguishes between "factual" work product—such as materials obtained through independent factual investigation—which requires the ordinary showing of "substantial need," and "opinion" work product—materials containing an attorney's mental impressions, conclusions, opinions, or legal theories—which receives special protection and is not discoverable absent a "highly persuasive" showing of need.

## 1. FOIA Requests

The Plaintiffs' FOIA Requests clearly are work product because they were created on the Plaintiffs' behalf by their lawyers as part of their factual investigation in connection with this litigation. Moreover, to the extent that the Requests are reflective of counsels' determinations about which subject matter, documents, or issues are important to their case, they provide a window into the Plaintiffs' confidential legal theories and strategies.

Ordinarily, that would be sufficient to end the inquiry. Here, however, the Plaintiffs voluntarily disclosed the work product information contained in their FOIA Requests to the government. When work product is shared with third parties in a manner that is either "inconsistent with maintaining secrecy against opponents or substantially increases the opportunity for a potential adversary to obtain the protected information," any applicable protection for those documents is waived. The Plaintiffs' decision to submit their FOIA Requests to the government means that they are now within the records of each agency to which they were sent and are therefore obtainable by anyone, including the Defendants, through an independent FOIA request. Not only is that kind of disclosure plainly inconsistent with the requirement that parties take reasonable steps to keep work product secret, but it also significantly raises the odds that such information might wind up in the hands of a litigation opponent.

The Plaintiffs contend that their sharing of work product information with various government agencies should not lead to any waiver because the government is not their adversary in this or any related proceeding. But even disclosure to non-adversaries waives work product protection if it materially increases the likelihood that an adversary can gain access to that information. The FOIA Requests are now widely available to the public through FOIA as a direct result of the Plaintiffs' decision to submit them to government agencies. Although work product protection might be preserved "where the disclosing party and the third party share a common interest," the government and the Plaintiffs have no relevant interests in common. Thus, even though the government might not be their adversary, the Plaintiffs' disclosures nonetheless have forfeited any work product protection that might otherwise be applicable.

The Plaintiffs argue that the FOIA correspondence should be afforded more extensive protection because the documents allegedly fall within the scope of the common law work product doctrine, which stems directly from *Hickman* and is somewhat broader than the privilege that is encompassed by Rule 26(b)(3). Application of the common law standard, however, would not alter the fact that the Plaintiffs disclosed their FOIA Requests to the government, thereby waiving any applicable protection.

Finally, the Plaintiffs' contention that their FOIA Requests may not necessarily be reachable through FOIA, finds no support in the law. Indeed, FOIA requires federal agencies to produce copies of *any* requested records unless one of nine statutory exemptions applies. The Plaintiffs cite Exemptions 4 and 5 as possible exemptions, but neither is remotely applicable to the documents at issue here. Exemption 4, which applies to privileged or confidential "trade secrets and commercial or financial information obtained from a person," is plainly inapposite because the Plaintiffs' FOIA Requests contain no such information. Exemption 5 relates to "inter-agency or intra-agency memorandums or letters which would not be available by law to a party other than an agency in litigation with the agency." In addition, Exemption 5 requires, among other things, that a government agency be the source of the documents at issue.

Since the FOIA Requests originated from the Plaintiffs and clearly are not "inter-agency or intra-agency memorandums or letters," Exemption 5 also is inapplicable. At any rate, even if any of the statutory exemptions were germane, the Plaintiffs have no right to enforce them in this action. The proper avenue for enjoining an agency from disclosing documents pursuant to FOIA is a reverse FOIA action, which would require the Plaintiffs to prove that the government's disclosure would be "arbitrary, capricious, an abuse of discretion, or otherwise not in accordance with the law." The Plaintiffs have not even come close to making that showing here.

## 2. FOIA Responses

The FOIA Responses are not work product because they were prepared by government officers as part of their statutory obligations under FOIA. The work product rule "does not extend to documents in an attorney's possession that were prepared by a third party in the ordinary course of business and would have been created in essentially similar form irrespective of any litigation anticipated by counsel." ("The work product rule has no application to a document prepared by and in the hands of a third person who is neither a party to nor interested in the action") The government is not the Plaintiffs' agent, nor has it been shown to have any interest in the outcome of the present litigation. The Responses therefore were improperly designated as attorney work product.

Moreover, the Supreme Court has held that a "written agency response to a FOIA request" constitutes a public disclosure. Thus, even if the government's FOIA Responses could properly be claimed as the Plaintiffs' work product, their public disclosure clearly would eliminate any basis for excluding them from discovery.

## 3. Relevance Objections

Regardless of whether work product protection applies, the Plaintiffs argue that the FOIA correspondence is irrelevant to the case and thus not discoverable under Rule 26 of the Federal Rules of Civil Procedure. The Plaintiffs further assert that it would be inappropriate to allow discovery because the documents might be determined to be inadmissible at trial due to their "highly prejudicial" nature. Given the expansive concept of relevance under Rule 26, however, both of these arguments are unavailing.

Rule 26(b)(1) allows discovery into "any nonprivileged matter that is relevant to any party's claim or defense." "This obviously broad rule is liberally construed." Here, the mere fact that the Plaintiffs have listed the FOIA correspondence on their privilege log suggests that it is responsive to the Defendants' requests and, therefore, at least discovery relevant. Moreover, as the Defendants correctly observe, the FOIA correspondence may contain highly relevant substantive information, such as the names and locations of witnesses, and consequently be of great significance to the Defendants. The subject matter and contents of these communications thus satisfies the minimal threshold for relevance required under Rule 26.

It is true that Federal Rule of Evidence 403 permits a judge to exclude relevant evidence at trial if its "probative value is substantially outweighed by the danger of unfair prejudice, confusion of the issues, or misleading the jury." Whether a document is admissible, however, is a separate issue from whether it is discoverable. "Admissibility is not a prerequisite to discoverability, and the scope of relevance under Rule 26 is broader than under the Rules of Evidence."

Indeed, Rule 26 specifically provides that "relevant information need not be admissible at trial if the discovery appears reasonably calculated to lead to the discovery of admissible evidence." Thus, even if the FOIA correspondence is ultimately deemed inadmissible at trial, that is not a valid basis for excluding it from discovery.

Accordingly, the FOIA correspondence is not exempt from disclosure and must be produced.

## B. Arab Bank Documents

The dispute concerning the *Arab Bank* documents arises out of the fact that the law firm representing certain of the plaintiffs in this case also represents a number of other parties in the *Arab Bank* suit. None of the plaintiffs in this case, however, are parties in the *Arab Bank* case. By way of background, the *Arab Bank* litigation involves claims against Arab Bank, PLC ("Arab Bank"), a large Jordanian bank, for monetary damages allegedly arising out of its involvement in the provision of financial services and other support to terrorist organizations in Israel between 1995 and 2004. During the course of discovery, Arab Bank has produced customer records and various other sensitive documents pursuant to a court-ordered confidentiality agreement, which forbids any party from using confidential information obtained in the *Arab Bank* litigation for any purpose unrelated to that case.

In responding to the discovery requests in this case, Plaintiffs' counsel determined that some of the documents that it had obtained in the *Arab Bank* litigation were responsive to the Defendants' production requests. The Plaintiffs withheld those documents from disclosure, however, because they were subject to the terms of the *Arab Bank* protective order. Nonetheless, Plaintiffs' counsel listed the *Arab Bank* documents on the Plaintiffs' privilege log. The Defendants argue that, in the course of doing so, the Plaintiffs unfairly and improperly considered or made use of the *Arab Bank* documents and, therefore, should be foreclosed from seeking to shield them from discovery by reason of the protective order. During a conference on April 16, 2013, I proposed that the parties jointly request that Judge Gershon modify the *Arab Bank* protective order so that any documents subject to that order could be disclosed in this case. Upon further reflection, however, I have concluded that the *Arab Bank* documents do not belong in this litigation at all—whether on a privilege log or otherwise.

The reason the *Arab Bank* documents must be excluded is more fundamental than the existence of the protective order. Rule 34 of the Federal Rules of Civil Procedure permits a party to obtain discovery of documents only to the extent that they are within a responding party's "possession, custody, or control." Because the *Arab Bank* documents were produced only to the parties in the *Arab Bank* litigation, they are not and never have been within the Plaintiffs' possession, custody, or control. The fact that attorneys for the Plaintiffs also happen to represent parties in *Arab Bank* is irrelevant, since "attorneys have numerous clients and the documents of one client do not simply come within the control of another merely because both clients have retained the services of the same lawyer or law firm." ("The mere fact ... that the attorney for a party has possession of a document does not make his possession of the document the possession of the party").

Thus, although the Plaintiffs may be correct that the *Arab Bank* documents contain information relevant to the Defendants' discovery requests, the documents are not ones that they have the ability either to produce or withhold. Indeed, a document in an attorney's possession is within a party's possession or control only if the attorney "comes into possession of the document as *attorney for that party.*"

Nor do the Plaintiffs have any legal means to obtain those documents since it would be a material breach of the *Arab Bank* protective order for Plaintiffs' counsel to disclose them to the Plaintiffs for use in this litigation.

The *Arab Bank* documents therefore were improperly identified as responsive and should not have been included on the privilege log. All entries relating to the *Arab Bank* documents consequently should be removed.

## III. Conclusion

For the foregoing reasons, the Defendants' motion is granted in part and denied in part. The Plaintiffs shall have until June 24, 2013, to produce the FOIA documents and correspondence and to delete any privilege log entries related to the *Arab Bank* documents. Also by that date, Plaintiffs' counsel shall provide certification they have produced all Underlying Documents responsive to the Defendants' requests.

In anticipation of the Court's ruling, the Plaintiffs have asked that any order of production be reciprocal, so that the Defendants will be required to produce all FOIA correspondence of their own that has been withheld from disclosure. The Defendants have voiced no objection to that request. Accordingly, the Defendants are directed to produce any responsive FOIA communications that they previously have withheld on the basis that they are protected by the work product doctrine. All such documents shall be produced by June 24, 2013.

# B. DISCOVERY TOOLS

## 1. INTERROGATORIES RULE 33

5. Interrogatories, under Rule 33, may be addressed *only to parties*. They may not be used to collect information from witnesses. Because of serious abuses in the past, interrogatories are now limited to 25 – but that limit may be expanded by the court. Interrogatories are written questions, and are a good way to collect specific data. But they are generally *not* a good way of ascertaining who will be an effective witness. Although interrogatories are addressed to an opposing party, they will actually be answered – very carefully - by the party's attorney.

Note that under Rule 33(a)(2) an interrogatory may properly ask about opinions and contentions. Notice, too, that Rule 33(d) gives a party the option of saying "Come and find it for yourself," if the answers to the interrogatories are in the responding party's business records, and the burden of shifting through the records would be substantially the same for either party. There are, of course, huge risks in allowing the opposing party access to all of the business records.

The following case is part of a malpractice suit against a law firm by an unhappy former client. Notice the type of information the unhappy client is trying to collect. The case itself is just intended to illustrate some of the rather mundane, but time consuming fights that may arise over interrogatories. Don't worry about specifics – just read the case for a small glimpse of the realities of discovery.

277 F.R.D. 642

UNITED STATES DISTRICT COURT,

D. KANSAS

ALTINA POUNCIL, ADMINISTRATOR OF THE ESTATE OF

WILLIE SUE CLAY, PLAINTIFF,

V.

BRANCH LAW FIRM, ET AL., DEFENDANTS.


DECIDED DECEMBER 13, 2011

MEMORANDUM AND ORDER


**DAVID J. WAXSE, United States Magistrate Judge.**

Before the Court is Plaintiff's Motion to Compel Defendants to Fully Comply with Second Set of Interrogatories and Second Requests for Production (ECF No. 74). Plaintiff requests an order under Fed.R.Civ.P. 37(a) compelling Defendants to provide full and complete responses to her Second Set of Interrogatory Nos. 26–32 and Second Request for Production Nos. 2–4 and 7. The motion is granted.

## I. Background Facts

Plaintiff Altina Pouncil, Administrator of the Estate of Willie Sue Clay ("Estate"), filed suit against Defendants Turner Branch and the Branch Law Firm, asserting claims for legal malpractice, negligence, and breach of fiduciary duty. After Willie Sue Clay died while taking the pharmaceutical drug Vioxx, Plaintiff retained Defendants to represent the Estate in its claim against the drug manufacturer, Merck & Co., Inc. The Estate's claim against Merck ended when the Estate was barred from recovery under the Vioxx settlement agreement because the claim failed to meet the eligibility requirements. Plaintiff's claims against Defendants arise from the events surrounding the Estate's failed claim against Merck.

Plaintiff filed this action on September 15, 2010. She served her First Set of Interrogatories on Defendants, consisting of interrogatories numbered Nos. 1 through 25, and First Requests for Production on December 22, 2010. Defendants served their responses and objections to Plaintiff's First Set of Interrogatories and First Requests for Production on March 23, 2011.

On May 12, 2011, Plaintiff supplemented her discovery requests and served her Second Set of Interrogatories (Nos. 26 through 32) and Second Requests for Production (Nos. 1 through 7) on Defendants. Defendants served their discovery responses on June 27, 2011, after Plaintiff granted Defendants a two-week extension of time to serve their responses. Defendants objected to the Second Set of Interrogatories and Second Requests for Production. After attempting to confer to resolve the discovery disputes as required by Fed.R.Civ.P. 37(a)(1). Plaintiff filed the instant motion to compel.

## II. Objection that Interrogatories Exceed Numerical Limit

Defendants argue that they should not be compelled to respond to Plaintiff's Second Set of Interrogatories at all because Plaintiff, in her First Set of Interrogatories, has served more than the 40 interrogatories allowed by the Scheduling Order. Specifically, Defendants contend that Plaintiff's First Interrogatory Nos. 6, 16, 18, and 20 should each be counted as multiple interrogatories.

Federal Rule of Civil Procedure 33(a)(1) imposes a limit on the number of allowable interrogatories. Under this rule, a party may serve a maximum of 25 written interrogatories upon any other party, including all discrete subparts, unless the parties otherwise stipulate or the Court allows more. The advisory committee notes to the 1993 amendments note that parties should not evade this presumptive limit through using question subparts to seek information about discrete separate subjects. This Court has noted the difficulty in identifying discrete subparts in *Williams v. Board of County Commissioners of the Unified Government of Wyandotte County and Kansas City, Kansas:*

> Interrogatories often contain subparts. Some are explicit and separately numbered or lettered, while others are implicit and not separately numbered or lettered. Extensive use of subparts, whether explicit or implicit, could defeat the purposes of the numerical limit contained in Rule 33(a), or in a scheduling order, by rendering it meaningless unless each subpart counts as a separate interrogatory. On the other hand, if all subparts count as separate interrogatories, the use of interrogatories might be unduly restricted or requests for increases in the numerical limit might become automatic.

As this Court has noted in numerous decisions since *Williams,* the advisory committee provided the following guidance for when subparts should count as separate interrogatories:

Each party is allowed to serve 25 interrogatories upon any other party, but must secure leave of the court (or stipulation from the opposing party) to serve a larger number. Parties cannot evade this presumptive limitation through the device of joining as "subparts" questions that seek information about discrete separate subjects. However, a question asking about communications of a particular type should be treated as a single interrogatory even though it requests that the time, place, persons present, and contents be stated separately for each such communication.

*Federal Practice and Procedure* commentators Wright, Miller and Marcus have construed the advisory committee's guidance to mean that "an interrogatory containing subparts directed at eliciting details concerning a common theme should be considered a single question," while an interrogatory with "subparts inquiring into discrete areas is likely to be counted as more than one for purposes of the limitation." The Court has previously applied these "common theme" standards in determining whether interrogatories exceed the numerical limit. With this common theme standard and its previous applications in mind, this Court makes the following specific findings with regard to the disputed interrogatories:

A. First Interrogatory No. 6

Defendants assert that Interrogatory No. 6 of Plaintiff's First Set of Interrogatories should be counted as seven interrogatories because it asks for facts supporting seven allegations in the complaint. Interrogatory No. 6 requests that Defendants "identify each fact which you claim supports your denial of the allegation contained in paragraph 32 of the Complaint and identify all documents relied on to support such denial. Please provide a response for each subsection of paragraph 32 of the Complaint." Paragraph 32 of the Complaint alleges the following:

32. Defendants breached the duty to exercise ordinary care, skill, and knowledge of a reasonably competent attorney in one or more of the following respects:
a. Defendants failed to properly prepare Claims Forms including, but not limited to, providing erroneous information.
b. Defendants failed to make timely and adequate submissions of documentation to the Vioxx Settlement Agreement Claims Administrator.
c. Defendants failed to determine the reasons for, or take reasonable actions to respond to, the Notices of Ineligibility issued by the Vioxx Settlement Agreement Claims Administrator and Gate Committee.

d. Defendants failed to provide adequate or timely counsel to Plaintiff regarding the Estate's claims and decision making throughout the Vioxx Settlement Agreement process.

e. Defendants failed to properly consult with and advise Plaintiff before making the decision to appeal the Gate Committee's Notice of Ineligibility to the Special Master.

f. Defendants failed to properly supervise non-attorney employees of Branch Law Firm and allowed such non-attorney employees to exercise an improper amount of autonomy and responsibility over aspects of administration of the Estate's Vioxx Settlement Agreement claim.

g. Defendants, through their conduct, failed to exercise the ordinary care, skill, and knowledge of a reasonably competent attorney in representing and advising the Estate.

The Court agrees with Defendants and finds that Interrogatory No. 6 should be counted as seven separate interrogatories. Although the information sought may arguably relate to the common theme of Defendants' alleged negligence in the administration and prosecution of the Estate's Vioxx claim, the Court finds the allegations are sufficiently different and require Defendants to identify a different set of facts. They should therefore be counted as separate interrogatories. Interrogatory No. 6 will be counted as seven interrogatories for purposes of the interrogatory limit.

B. First Interrogatory No. 16

Defendants assert that Plaintiff's First Interrogatory No. 16 should be counted as four interrogatories. It requests that Defendants "identify each fact which you claim supports your affirmative defense contained in paragraph J of the Affirmative Defenses section of the Answer and identify all documents relied on to support such affirmative defense." Paragraph J of Defendants' Answer states that Plaintiff's claims are barred by the doctrines of unclean hands, laches, estoppel, and/or waiver.

The Court concludes that Interrogatory No. 16 should not be counted as four separate interrogatories. The four affirmative defenses asserted by Defendants are closely related equitable doctrines that pertain to alleged actions taken by Plaintiff that would relieve Defendants of liability on her claim. The closely related nature of these equitable defenses satisfies the common theme analysis because their success depends upon certain alleged conduct of Plaintiff with respect to asserting her claim. Moreover, these defenses appear to be boilerplate defenses that are commonly asserted together in an answer. It is therefore appropriate for Plaintiff to inquire as to the facts supporting them in one interrogatory. Interrogatory No. 16 should therefore be counted as only one interrogatory.

## C. First Interrogatory No. 18

Defendants assert that Interrogatory No. 18 should be counted as three interrogatories. It asks the following:

> At the time Ms. Pouncil entered the Estate of Willie Sue Clay's Vioxx Claim into the Vioxx Settlement Agreement please state whether you advised Ms. Pouncil to enter the Estate of Willie Sue Clay's Vioxx Claim into the Vioxx Settlement Agreement and whether you believed the Clay Claim was eligible for recovery under the Vioxx Settlement Agreement. If you believe the Clay Claim was eligible for recovery under the Vioxx Settlement Agreement, why do you believe the Clay Claim was denied? If you do not believe the Clay Claim was eligible for recovery under the Vioxx Settlement Agreement, why was the Clay Claim appealed to the Vioxx Settlement Agreement Special Master?

The Court concludes that Interrogatory No. 18 does not contain three discrete subparts that should be treated as separate interrogatories. All of the information sought in this interrogatory pertains to the common theme of the Clay Claim being entered into the Vioxx Settlement Agreement. Requesting specific information about Defendants' beliefs regarding the claim and its entry into the Vioxx Settlement Agreement does not enlarge the interrogatory beyond the bounds of its common theme. Accordingly, Interrogatory No. 18 will be counted as one interrogatory.

## D. First Interrogatory No. 20

Defendants assert that Interrogatory No. 20 should be counted as three interrogatories. Interrogatory No. 20 asks Defendant to identify:

> Any and all persons who worked on, assisted with, or participated in any aspect of the representation of the Clay Claim and for such individuals please identify (1) whether such person is employed by Branch Law Firm or another entity, (2) what role such person played in the representation of the Clay Claim including, without limitation, such persons duties and responsibilities, (3) whether such person has medical education or training, and (4) what role, if any, such person played in determining the injury indicated on the Claims Form.

The Court concludes that Interrogatory No. 20 does not contain discrete subparts that should be treated as separate interrogatories. This interrogatory is limited to the common theme of who worked on the Clay Claim during Defendants' representation of Plaintiff. Each asserted discrete subpart requests pertinent, specific information related to those persons, and it does not exceed the common theme. Again, there is no indication that this interrogatory is abusive or meant to skirt the interrogatory limit. Instead, it merely asks for enumerated details regarding persons who worked on the Estate's Vioxx claim. Accordingly, Interrogatory No. 20 will be counted as one interrogatory.

In summary, the Court counts Plaintiff's First Interrogatory No. 6 as seven interrogatories and counts Nos. 16, 18 and 20 each as a single interrogatory. Even with Interrogatory No. 6 constituting seven interrogatories, Plaintiff's Second Set of Interrogatories (Nos. 26 through 32) does not exceed the 40–interrogatory limit imposed by the Scheduling Order. Accordingly, Defendants are not relieved of their obligation to respond to Plaintiff's Second Set of Interrogatories based upon the Second Set exceeding the interrogatory limit.

### III. Specific Objections to Plaintiff's Second Set of Interrogatories and Requests for Production

A. Second Interrogatory Nos. 26–28

Interrogatory Nos. 26 through 28 ask Defendants for the following information:

> Please indicate whether or not you contend Willie Sue Clay suffered a myocardial infarction prior to beginning her use of Vioxx pursuant to the provisions of Exhibit 3.2.1 of the Vioxx Settlement Agreement. If so, please identify each fact which you claim supports this contention and identify all documents you believe support your contention. (Interrogatory No. 26)

> Please indicate whether or not you contend Willie Sue Clay's family history is ambiguous or unambiguous pursuant to the provisions of Exhibit 3.2.1 of the Vioxx Settlement Agreement. If so, please identify each fact which you claim supports this contention and identify all documents you believe support this contention. (Interrogatory No. 27)

> Please indicate whether or not you contend Willie Sue Clay's injury is less than "Level 1–Death" pursuant to the provisions of Exhibit 3.2.1 of the Vioxx Settlement

Agreement. If so, identify each fact which you claim supports this contention and identify all documents you believe support this contention. (Interrogatory No. 28)

Defendants object to these interrogatories as seeking the mental impressions, conclusions, opinions, and legal theories of their counsel, which are protected from discovery as attorney opinion work product. They also object that these interrogatories are premature contention interrogatories and they should not be compelled to respond until discovery is complete and the experts have been deposed.

### 1. Work Product Objection

The work product doctrine, first recognized by the Supreme Court in *Hickman v. Taylor*, is governed by the uniform federal standard set forth in Fed.R.Civ.P. 26(b)(3). Under Rule 26(b)(3)(A), the work product doctrine applies to "documents and tangible things that are prepared in anticipation of litigation or for trial by or for another party or its representative." Subsection (B) further provides that the court "must protect against the disclosure of the mental impressions, conclusions, opinions, or legal theories of a party's attorney or other representative concerning the litigation." Thus, although Rule 26(b)(3)(A) is confined to the discovery of "documents and tangible things," the doctrine has been expanded to reach information sought through interrogatories when the interrogatory seeks the mental impressions or legal conclusions of an attorney. A party claiming work product protection has the burden of establishing that the material sought to be protected as work product comes within the doctrine. "A mere allegation that the work product doctrine applies is insufficient."

In the context of an objection to an interrogatory, this Court has held that unless the interrogatory (1) specifically inquiries into an attorney's mental impressions, conclusions, or legal theories, or (2) asks for the content of a document protectable as work product, it is inappropriate to raise a work product objection. The work product doctrine also does not provide any protection for "facts concerning the creation of work product or facts contained within work product." In a similar vein, it has held that the work product doctrine does not prevent a party from propounding an interrogatory asking about "the existence or nonexistence of documents, even though the documents themselves may not be subject to discovery."

The Court finds that Interrogatory Nos. 26–28 do not specifically request or inquire into the mental impressions, conclusions, or legal theories of defense counsel. Nor do they ask for the content of any documents or materials that Defendants have shown to be protected work product. The interrogatories ask for Defendants' contentions with respect to the factual issues of whether Willie Sue Clay suffered a myocardial infarction prior to beginning her use of Vioxx, whether her family history is ambiguous, and whether her injury is less than "Level 1–Death." The interrogatories also request that Defendants identify the facts and documents supporting their contentions. Defendants, who have the burden of supporting their work product objection, have not shown that answering these interrogatories would reveal the mental impressions, conclusions, opinions, or legal theories of their counsel. Accordingly, Defendants' work product objection to Interrogatory Nos. 26–28 is overruled.

### 2. Objection as Premature Contention Interrogatories

Defendants also object to the interrogatories as premature contention interrogatories. Fed.R.Civ.P. 33(a)(2) allows certain contention interrogatories. It provides that an interrogatory "may relate to any matter that may be inquired into under Rule 26(b). An interrogatory is not objectionable merely because it asks for an opinion or contention that relates to fact or the application of law to fact," Interrogatory Nos. 26–28 appear to be asking for Defendants' contentions that relate to certain facts. Those facts include whether Willie Sue Clay suffered a myocardial infarction prior to beginning her use of Vioxx, whether her family history is ambiguous, and whether her injury is less than "Level 1–Death." These contention interrogatories provide Plaintiff with the opportunity to determine what proof is necessary to effectively refute Defendants' position on these issues. Plaintiff is permitted to serve contention interrogatories.

In addition to their other objections, Defendants ask, at a minimum, that the Court permit them to delay answering Interrogatory Nos. 26–28 until the completion of discovery. It is within the court's discretion to "order that the interrogatory need not be answered until designated discovery is complete." Here, the Court finds no persuasive reason for Defendants to defer their answers to Interrogatory Nos. 26–28. Defendants should answer these interrogatories as fully as they can, keeping in mind their continuing obligation to supplement their discovery responses as additional or different information becomes available. Although Defendants have not yet deposed Plaintiff's expert witness, Plaintiff has already provided Defendants with her expert's report. Accordingly, the Court denies Defendants' request to defer compelling responses to Interrogatory Nos. 26–28 as premature contention interrogatories. Plaintiff's motion to compel Defendants to answer Second Interrogatory Nos. 26–28 is granted.

## B. Second Interrogatory Nos. 29–32

Plaintiff's Second Interrogatory No. 29 asks for the number of Vioxx claimants Defendants represented at the end of each month during the period of February 2008 to July 2009. Interrogatory No. 30 seeks the number of Vioxx claimants in which a certain employee worked on, assisted with, or participated in any aspect of the representation as of the end of each month. Interrogatory No. 31 requests the number of people employed by Defendants at the end of each month for the period February 2008 to July 2009. Interrogatory No. 32 asks Defendants to "indicate how many of Defendants' employees, exclusively or for a majority of their time (more than half of their working time), worked on, assisted with, or participated in any aspect of the representation of Vioxx claimants as of the end of each month. Of those employees, please indicate how many were attorneys, how many were paralegals, and how many were employees other than attorneys or paralegals."

### 1. Relevance Objection

Defendants object to Interrogatories Nos. 29–32 as not reasonably calculated to lead to the discovery of admissible evidence. It argues that the information requested in the interrogatories bears no relationship to the claims and defenses in this case.

Federal Rule of Civil Procedure 26(b)(1) sets the scope of discovery. It provides that "parties may obtain discovery regarding any nonprivileged matter that is relevant to any party's claim or defense." The court construes relevance broadly at the discovery stage of litigation, and a "request for discovery should be considered relevant if there is 'any possibility' that the information sought may be relevant to the claim or defense of any party."

The Court finds that these interrogatories request relevant information. The interrogatories request information regarding the number of clients Defendants represented during the time in question, Defendants' case management procedures, and details regarding how Defendants oversaw employees who worked on Vioxx claims. All of this information is relevant to and probative of Plaintiff's claim that Defendants breached a professional duty of care and were negligent in handling the Estate's Vioxx claim. Defendants' relevance objection to Interrogatory Nos. 29–32 is overruled.

## 2. Mootness

Defendants also argue that Plaintiff's motion to compel information responsive to Interrogatory Nos. 29–32 is moot because Plaintiff was able to elicit the information sought during depositions of Defendant Branch and several employees of the law firm. The Court has reviewed the deposition transcripts submitted and concludes that Interrogatory Nos. 29–32 are not moot as argued by Defendants. Although the depositions briefly addressed the general themes of the disputed interrogatories, they are insufficient as a substitute for answering the specific interrogatories at issue here. The Court finds that the deposition testimony does not sufficiently answer the interrogatories and therefore does not render Plaintiff's motion to compel moot. Accordingly, Defendants shall provide responsive answers to these interrogatories. Plaintiff's motion to compel Defendants to answer Second Interrogatory Nos. 29–32 is granted.

## C. Second Request for Production Nos. 2 and 3

Request No. 2 asks for "all documents relating to any form of advertising which were used or publicized in the State of Kansas at any time by Defendants soliciting the representation of persons injured as a result of using Vioxx including, but not limited to, television, radio, and print." Request No. 3 similarly requests information "relating to any form of advertising used by third-parties at any time who were retained by Defendants or who referred clients or potential clients to Defendants." These Requests thus seek television, radio and print advertising—whether directly by Defendants or through third parties—in the state of Kansas that solicited the representation of persons injured as a result of using Vioxx.

Defendants argue that these Requests are not properly oriented in time or tailored to the issues in this matter because they are not limited to a time frame in which Plaintiff or other heirs of the Estate would have allegedly seen advertisements before retaining Defendants. Defendants cite no authority to support this objection, although it is apparently akin to arguing the disputed Requests are overly broad and unduly burdensome. The Court has reviewed Request Nos. 2 and 3 and concludes that they are narrowly tailored to a reasonable time frame. Consequently, the Court denies Defendants' objections regarding the alleged failure to properly orient or tailor the requests to the issues in this matter.

Although the requests ask for "all documents related to any form of advertising" and contain no explicit time limitation, they are not overly broad in terms of time. They are limited to advertising to potential clients regarding injuries sustained as a result of using Vioxx; this is a sufficient limitation in terms of both time and substance. Defendants assert that they only advertised regarding Vioxx injuries in the state of Kansas during a limited period of time. Due to the explicit limitation to Vioxx-related advertising, Request Nos. 2 and 3 are necessarily limited to this time frame. Because this period would not extend for an overly burdensome period of time or cover an overly burdensome amount of material, Defendants' objection to the requests for failure to tailor or orient in time is without merit.

Despite their objections, Defendants state that they have already produced the only documents responsive to these Requests. In her reply, Plaintiff disputes that the newsletters produced by Defendants are responsive to the Requests. She claims that Defendants have not produced any documents related to advertising from other law firms with whom Defendants had agreements with to conduct advertising and refer clients. To the extent that Defendants have in their possession, custody or control any documents related to advertising for Vioxx-related-injuries from other law firms with whom they had agreements, Defendants shall produce these documents within 30 days of the date of this Memorandum and Order. Plaintiff's motion to compel Defendants to produce documents responsive to Second Request Nos. 2 and 3 is granted.

D. Second Request for Production No. 4

Request No. 4 seeks "all documents relating to agreements of any kind, which Defendants had with other law firms or attorneys regarding fee sharing arrangements related to the representation of the Estate of Willie Sue Clay." Defendants object to the Request as not reasonably calculated to lead to the discovery of admissible evidence. They argue that fee arrangements between Defendants and other firms or attorneys bear no relation to the claims and defenses in this matter, and they should not be compelled to produce any such documents. They also assert that the motion to compel is moot with regard to Request No. 4 as they have produced responsive documents and Plaintiff's counsel has already questioned Defendant Branch regarding the fee arrangements at his deposition.

**1. Relevance Objection**

The Court finds that the documents sought by Request No. 4. are directly relevant to Plaintiff's claims. Request for Production No. 4 seeks information regarding Defendants' fee arrangements with other law firms that could bear directly on the representations allegedly made to potential clients, including the Estate. Defendants' fee sharing agreements with other law firms relating the representation of the Estate's Vioxx claim are relevant to Plaintiff's malpractice, negligence, and breach of fiduciary duty claims. More specifically, the information is relevant to whether the fee arrangements provided a financial incentive for Defendants to accept more Vioxx clients than they could competently handle. Defendants' relevancy objection to Request No. 4 is overruled.

### 2. Mootness

Defendants also assert that Plaintiff's motion to compel is moot because they have produced documents responsive to the Request and Plaintiff's counsel has already deposed Defendant Branch regarding the fee arrangements. In her reply, Plaintiff argues that the motion to compel on this Request is not moot. She argues that Defendants cannot avoid their obligation to produce documents responsive to a request for production by lodging baseless objections and then claiming they are moot because Plaintiff later had the opportunity to question a witness in a deposition about a related topic. Plaintiff maintains that she is entitled to receive all documents that are responsive to this request.

The Court has reviewed the excerpted portions of Defendant Branch's deposition transcript and concludes that the motion to compel as to Request No. 4 is not moot. Although Defendant Branch was questioned about the fee arrangement with the Estate, he did not testify regarding any fee sharing arrangements that Defendants had with other law firms or attorneys. Moreover, this testimony is not the same as actually producing the agreements and other responsive documents. Defendant Branch's deposition testimony does not render Plaintiff's motion to compel on Request No. 4 moot. Plaintiff's motion to compel Defendants to produce documents responsive to Second Request No. 4 is granted.

### E. Second Request for Production No. 7

Request for Production No. 7 asks Defendants to produce "all calendars, appointment books, or other logs of dates and/or events that Defendant Turner Branch maintained at any time for the period from February 14, 2008, to July 20, 2009." Defendants object to the request on the grounds the information is protected by the attorney-client privilege and the work product doctrine, and is not relevant. They further point out that Plaintiff's counsel had an opportunity to question Defendant Branch during his deposition and that it would be redundant to require production of documents responsive to Request No. 7.

## 1. Attorney–Client Privilege Objection

The standards for evaluating the attorney-client privilege are well-established. "In federal court, the determination of what is privileged depends upon the dictates of Rule 501 of the Federal Rules of Evidence." Subject-matter jurisdiction in this case is based on diversity; therefore, "state law supplies the rule of decision."

Under Kansas law, the essential elements of the attorney-client privilege are:

> (1) Where legal advice is sought (2) from a professional legal advisor in his capacity as such, (3) the communications made in the course of that relationship (4) made in confidence (5) by the client (6) are permanently protected (7) from disclosures by the client, the legal advisor, or any other witness (8) unless privilege is waived.

The existence of the privilege is determined on a case-by-case basis. The party seeking to assert the attorney-client privilege as a bar to discovery has the burden of establishing that it applies. Moreover, a party must make a "clear showing" that the privilege applies.

With these rules in mind, the Court finds that Defendants have failed to make a clear showing that the requested documents are protected by the attorney-client privilege. Defendants' lone, unsupported statement that producing responsive documents will likely require disclosure of Defendant Branch's confidential communications with other clients is not sufficient to meet their burden. Defendants' objection that Request No. 7 calls for the production of documents or information protected by the attorney-client privilege is overruled.

## 2. Work Product Objection

Defendants also argue that the calendars and appointment books sought are protected from disclosure as work product because they would disclose Defendant Branch's mental impressions regarding matters in which he represents other clients. Like their attorney-client privilege objection above, the Court finds that Defendants have not met their burden of establishing that Defendant Branch's calendars, appointment books, or other logs of dates and events contain information that would constitute the protected mental impressions of Defendant Branch relating to other clients. Defendants, as the party with the burden of supporting their work product objection, have not shown that the documents requested contain information that would reveal the mental impressions, conclusions, opinions, or legal theories of Defendant Branch. Accordingly, Defendants' work product objection to Request No. 7 is overruled.

### 3. Relevance Objection

Defendants also object to Request No. 7 as not reasonably calculated to lead to the discovery of admissible evidence. They argue that because the relevancy of the Request is not apparent on its face, Plaintiff must establish the relevancy of the documents sought. The Court agrees that Plaintiff has the burden to show the relevancy of Defendant Branch's calendars, appointment books, or other logs of dates and events.

Plaintiff argues that the information regarding Defendants' schedule during the requested time period is relevant because Defendants assert that Turner Branch made the final decision on all aspects of Plaintiff's claim. Plaintiff points out that Defendants, in their Supplemental Response to Interrogatory Nos. 19 and 20, state that Defendant Branch "oversaw all individuals working on the claim; all individuals were under his control and no dispositive steps were taken on the claim without Mr. Branch's knowledge and input." According to Plaintiff, this response demonstrates that Defendants are claiming that Defendant Branch had an extensive and intimate involvement with the representation of Plaintiff in relation to her Vioxx claim and that no major decision was made on the claim without Mr. Branch's direct involvement. Based on this alleged extensive involvement, Defendant Branch's schedule during the relevant time period of Defendants' representation of the Estate is relevant as to whether Mr. Branch was, in fact, present and available during such time period to provide the type of involvement that Mr. Branch claims that he provided in Plaintiff's representation.

Plaintiff has convinced the Court that Request No. 7 for Defendant Branch's calendars, appointment books, or other logs of dates and events seeks information relevant to the issue of whether Defendant Branch was present and available during the relevant time period he claims that he was involved in the Estate's Vioxx claim. Accordingly, Defendants' objection based on the relevancy of the discovery request is denied.

### 4. Objection That Information Sought is Redundant

Defendants' final argument is that it would be redundant to require them to produce documents responsive to Request No. 7 because Plaintiff's counsel had the opportunity to question Defendant Branch during his deposition about his schedule during the Vioxx litigation. They assert that Defendant Branch testified that his time between November 2007 and 2009 was primarily spent on Vioxx matters, including frequent travel to New Jersey, Houston, and New Orleans.

The Court does not find Request No. 7 to be unreasonably duplicative or cumulative of Defendant Branch's deposition testimony. The documents requested could contradict or support his deposition testimony. Plaintiff's motion to compel Defendants to produce documents responsive to Second Request No. 7 is granted.

## IV. EXPENSES

### A. Expenses Related to this Motion

Under Fed.R.Civ.P. 37(a)(5)(A), if a motion to compel is granted, the court "must, after providing an opportunity to be heard, require the party ... whose conduct necessitated the motion ... to pay the movant's reasonable expenses incurred in making the motion, including attorney's fees." The court must not order payment, however, if the opposing party's response or objection was substantially justified or other circumstances make an award of expenses unjust. In this case, Plaintiff requests that the Court assess her costs and fees related to the motion against Defendants. Upon a review of the briefing, the Court concludes that the parties should bear their own fees and expenses. Although the Court is granting Plaintiff's motion to compel, Defendants were substantially justified in lodging their supernumerary objections to the second set of interrogatories. Plaintiff's request for expenses related to this motion is denied.

### B. Expenses Related to Future Discovery and Depositions

Plaintiff additionally requests that the Court require Defendants to pay for any costs incurred in deposing Defendants for a second time. Because Plaintiff did not have all of the relevant information when she first deposed Defendants, the theory proceeds, it might be necessary to take a second deposition after Defendants comply with this Order. Prospectively assessing these costs, however, is not necessary. If Plaintiff determines the information disclosed by Defendants pursuant to this Order requires additional depositions to be taken, then she will be free to move the Court for leave to depose Defendants and with any associated expenses at that time. For the time being, Plaintiff's request for prospective costs related to secondary depositions is accordingly denied.

IT IS THEREFORE ORDERED that Plaintiff's Motion to Compel Defendants to Fully Comply with Second Set of Interrogatories and Second Requests for Production (ECF No. 74) is granted. *Within thirty (30) days of this Memorandum and Order,* Defendants shall serve, without objection, their answers to Plaintiff's Second Set of

Interrogatories Nos. 26–32 and produce documents responsive to Plaintiff's Second Request for Production Nos. 2–4, and 7.

IT IS FURTHER ORDERED THAT each party shall bear its own fees and expenses related to this motion.

## 2. DEPOSITION RULES 27, 30, 31 AND 32

6. Depositions are the best discovery tool available for getting a sense of how effective a particular person may be as a witness. Depositions are also a good way of pinning a potential witness down to a particular statement of the facts. If, at trial, the witness says something that conflicts with what the witness said at a deposition two years earlier, then the conflict in statements can be used for impeachment purposes. "On May 1, 2016 at your deposition you said 'X'; now you are saying 'Y.' Which one of your two conflicting statements is actually true?"

There are a total of 6 rules regarding depositions, (Rules 27, 28, 29, 30, 31 and 32). That is some indication of the variety of situations in which depositions may be useful. Rules 27, 30 and 31 are the most important rules for depositions.

Rule 27 allows a deposition to be taken even before a suit is filed – if it looks as if the proposed witness might not be available later – because of age or some other reason.

Rule 31 allows for a deposition to be taken by written questions, if it might be too expensive to take a deposition in person, relative to the amount of information likely to be obtained.

But most depositions are Depositions by Oral Examination, under Rule 30. In the past, an oral deposition of a single individual might go on for days. Now Rule 30(d)(1) provides that no single deposition may last longer than 1 day, for 7 hours, unless the court provides otherwise.

The witness, the person who is answering the questions at a deposition, is called the deponent. Lawyers for both sides are present at the deposition and they take turns asking questions, just as they would at trial. The lawyer who has called for the deposition will go first. Then the other lawyer will have a chance to ask questions. Then each side may be allowed follow-up questions.

There will be a court reporter present to make an exact transcript of everything that was said by any person at the deposition. Or the deposition may be recorded by some other means. Everyone who testifies will be under oath, and statements made at a deposition can later be used for impeachment purposes – or if the witness is unavailable at the time of trial.

But unlike a trial, no judge is present at a deposition, and the range of inquiry is much broader than it would be at trial. Some parts of a deposition may be to some extent a "fishing expedition" – trying to find out areas in which there may be valuable information. Part of a deposition is also to try to ascertain how effective the deponent may be as a witness at trial – how well does he or she stand up to pressure? How effective is he or she at telling the story?

A deposition is also intended to get information.

When plaintiff is suing a big company, plaintiff may have no idea which person within the company will have the information necessary to answer the questions in specific parts of the deposition. So Rule 30(b)(6) provides that the person seeking to take a deposition of someone in the company should describe the matter at issue, and then it is the responsibility of the company to provide a person who will be able to answer that specific set of questions at the deposition.

Note the attorney's responsibility in this matter.

**2013 WL 3833065**

**UNITED STATES DISTRICT COURT, D. MINNESOTA.**

**AVIVA SPORTS, INC., PLAINTIFF,**

**V.**

**FINGERHUT DIRECT MARKETING, INC., MENARD, INC.,
KMART CORPORATION, WAL–MART STORES, INC., AND
MANLEY TOYS, LTD., DEFENDANTS.**

DECIDED JULY 23, 2013

JOAN N. ERICKSEN, District Judge.

## I. BACKGROUND

The factual background underlying this issue was thoroughly set forth in the magistrate judge's March 20, 2013 Order, and the Court will not repeat it at length here. In summary, Aviva had originally noticed a Rule 30(b)(6) deposition of Manley for January 11, 2011. Aviva's attorney traveled to Hong Kong for the deposition. Manley identified Chan Siu Lun ("Chan") as its corporate deponent, and Manley's counsel participated by telephone. Chan was not prepared to testify, and in April 2011, Aviva moved to compel Manley to produce a properly prepared Rule 30(b)(6) witness. On January 3, 2012, the Court concluded that Manley's corporate designee was "woefully unprepared" to respond to numerous topics and ordered Manley to produce a properly prepared Rule 30(b)(6) witness and pay the costs of a translator if one would be needed. The Court also warned that if Manley again produces an unprepared witness, the Court will entertain a motion for sanctions against Manley.

On June 7, 2012, Manley produced Richard Toth as its Rule 30(b)(6) witness. Toth was not adequately prepared to testify as to each of the identified topics at that time. Due to Toth's schedule, the deposition had to be continued on December 11, 2012. Aviva informed Lobbin that at least the six-month delay would give Toth time to become better prepared. In December 2012, however, Toth was still grossly unprepared to provide meaningful testimony as to several of the identified deposition topics. Aviva, believing that another motion to compel would be futile, instead moved for an award of fees and costs incurred in connection with the failed depositions and in bringing its motion for sanctions.

As this Court noted in its May 3, 2013 Order, the magistrate judge correctly found that Toth was unprepared to testify as Manley's corporate designee. For example, Toth—the President of Manley Toys *Direct* (*not* Manley Toys, *Ltd.*, the Defendant in this case)—did not know how Manley Toys, *Ltd.* does business or why his company was even called "Manley," and he denied knowing anything about Manley Toys, *Ltd.* He could not provide any testimony regarding the organizational structure of Manley Toys, Ltd. other than the names of the individuals who own the company. He had no information regarding the revenues, units, costs and profits received from the sales of the products at issue. It appears that Manley's Chinese counsel, Walter Fong, prepared brief (and only slightly responsive) answers to the identified deposition topics, and Toth was completely unprepared to answer any follow-up questions related to those topics. Generally speaking, if the answer to Aviva's question was not on the notes provided to him by Fong, Toth could not answer the question.

In the magistrate judge's March 20 Order, affirmed in part by this Court, the magistrate judge imposed sanctions against Manley under both Rule 37 of the Federal Rules of Civil Procedure and 28 U.S.C. § 1927, finding that "Manley's decision to send Toth to the deposition armed with little knowledge beyond the notes prepared by Fong is indefensible." The magistrate judge also concluded that Lobbin played a "key role" in the failure of the second deposition and that he knew or should have known that Toth was unprepared. "Any lawyer acting with a reasonable amount of skill and diligence would have recognized that Toth was not the right deponent and the fault for failing to adequately prepare Toth lies with Manley and its counsel." The magistrate judge found that Lobbin willfully disregarded the Court's order regarding Manley's Rule 30(b)(6) deposition. As examples, the magistrate judge explained that Lobbin attempted to justify Toth's "dismal performance" by citing the need for an English-proficient deponent, despite the fact that the Court explicitly provided that Manley could produce a non-English-speaking deponent so long as it paid for a translator. Lobbin emphasized the "convenience" of having Toth testify—presumably because Toth lives in the United States. The magistrate judge concluded that "counsel's conduct in the deposition was objectively reckless and so egregious that it amounted to bad faith" and "unnecessarily prolonged these proceedings by putting Aviva through the time and expense of participating in this useless deposition."

## II. DISCUSSION

"A court may require counsel to satisfy personally attorneys' fees reasonably incurred by an opposing party when counsel's conduct 'multiplies the proceedings in any case unreasonably and vexatiously.'" 28 U.S.C. § 1927).

Section 1927 provides:

> "Any attorney or other person admitted to conduct cases in any court of the United States who so multiplies the proceedings in any case unreasonably and vexatiously may be required by the court to satisfy personally the excess costs, expenses, and attorneys' fees reasonably incurred because of such conduct.

The statute permits sanctions when an attorney's conduct, 'viewed objectively, manifests either intentional or reckless disregard of the attorney's duties to the court.'

Federal Rule of Civil Procedure 37(b) authorizes sanctions for failure to comply with discovery orders. If the Court finds that there has been a failure to comply with a discovery order, "the court must order the disobedient party, the attorney advising that party, or both to pay the reasonable expenses, including attorney's fees, caused by the failure, unless the failure was substantially justified or other circumstances make an award of expenses unjust." Rule 37 sanctions are permissible where there is "an order compelling discovery, a willful violation of that order, and prejudice to the other party."

These sanctions "must be applied diligently both "to penalize those whose conduct may be deemed to warrant such a sanction, and to deter those who might be tempted to such conduct in the absence of such a deterrent."

Lobbin makes four arguments as to why sanctions against him are unwarranted; the Court will address each argument in turn. First, Lobbin points to his "honorable credentials," "unblemished 18–year professional record" and "reasonable personal and professional disposition." The Court does not question Lobbin's credentials, record or disposition. None of these things, however, provide any justification or explanation for Lobbin's reckless disregard of his duties to the court in this matter. 'All attorneys, as 'officers of the court,' owe duties of complete candor and primary loyalty to the court before which they practice." Lobbin's eighteen years of experience as an attorney should have made him acutely aware of his professional duties and his obligation to ensure that his client complied with the Court's discovery orders. Further, his experience should have provided him with ample understanding of discovery procedures and proper deposition preparedness.

Lobbin next points to the fact that Aviva requested a sanction against Manley, rather than against Manley's attorney. As Lobbin acknowledges, the Court may order sanctions *sua sponte,* which is precisely why this matter is currently before the Court. Whether or not Aviva chose to seek sanctions against Manley, Lobbin, or both does not factor into this Court's analysis as to whether such sanctions against Lobbin are, in fact, warranted. As an attorney, Lobbin owes a duty to the Court, and it is for the Court to determine whether that duty has been neglected.

Lobbin also contends that the Court should not consider misconduct on the part of Manley's prior counsel in assessing whether sanctions against Lobbin are appropriate. As Lobbin correctly notes, Manley has switched lead counsel numerous times during the course of this litigation; Lobbin did not begin representing Manley until early May 2012, a month before Toth's first deposition. Before Lobbin entered this litigation, the Court on several occasions had warned or reprimanded Manley's previous counsel. The Court assures Lobbin that he is not being "penalized personally for conduct that occurred before he ever got involved in the litigation." The fact that former counsel had been repeatedly warned regarding Manley's noncompliance with discovery orders, however, should have served as notice to Lobbin that he was assuming representation of a potentially noncompliant client that had previously engaged in discovery misconduct. Lobbin had access to the electronic record in this case and assumed representation of Manley with full knowledge of the events that had already transpired. Thus, while Lobbin is not personally responsible for the conduct that occurred prior to May 2012, he was at least on notice of Manley's obvious contempt for the judicial system and this Court's orders and that the Court was not letting Manley's attorneys off the hook for Manley's misconduct.

Next, Lobbin asserts that he should not be personally sanctioned for the failed Rule 30(b)(6) deposition because he was not authorized to select or prepare the witness and he did not assume representation of Manley until May 2012, shortly before Toth's June deposition. He contends that because he was not authorized to select or prepare the corporate deponent, he could not cause the "deposition testimony to be any different or better than it was" and "that it could not have gone better no matter what I did." Walter Fong, Manley's Chinese counsel, submitted a declaration in which he states that although Lobbin's "input" regarding the deposition was "welcomed," it was Fong who took responsibility for selecting and preparing Toth. The Court identifies several problems with this argument.

First, although Lobbin had only recently begun representing Manley prior to Toth's first deposition in June 2012, Lobbin had ample time to correct Toth's deficiencies prior to the continuation of Toth's deposition in December 2012. Lobbin provides no evidence or argument as to what steps he took or attempted to take between the failed June deposition and the failed December deposition. Lobbin states that "perhaps I could have personally conducted the witness selection and preparation process, and traveled to China for that purpose; however, I was assured repeatedly in discussions with Manley's representative that the designated Rule 30(b)(6) witness would be fully prepared to provide information in response to the deposition topics." Even giving Lobbin the benefit of the doubt that he did not have enough time to become involved in the preparation of the 30(b)(6) witness prior to the June deposition and that he reasonably relied on his client's assurances that the witness would be prepared, there is no excuse for Lobbin's failure to intervene between the two deposition dates. By the conclusion of the June deposition, Lobbin was certainly on notice that Toth was inadequately prepared. At that point, it was unreasonable for Lobbin to rely on any further assurances from Manley that the deficiencies would be corrected by December.[FN4] (An attorney "may rely on assertions by the client and on communications with other counsel in the case *as long as that reliance is appropriate under the circumstances*" and "what is reasonable is a matter for the court to decide on the totality of the circumstances."

> FN4. It is questionable whether Lobbin's reliance on Manley's assurances was *ever* reasonable, given his own acknowledgment that Manley is a "challenging litigation client" and his awareness of Manley's other previous discovery abuses. A quick glance at the ECF record in this case reveals a docket littered with motions and orders for sanctions against Manley. Lobbin should have been that much more diligent in his attempts to make sure Manley complied with this Court's discovery orders, and given Manley's history of noncompliance and disobedience, a reasonable attorney would have been wary of Manley's assurances in the first place.

As the attorney advising Manley's conduct and as an officer of the Court, Lobbin was required to do *something* to try to assure Manley's compliance. If he was not aware that Manley's designated 30(b)(6) witness was unprepared prior to the June deposition, he certainly should have been aware of this fact after the deposition. There is no evidence that Lobbin attempted to take any steps to further prepare Toth or otherwise ensure that Manley produced an adequately prepared 30(b)(6) witness for deposition during the six-month interval. For example, there is no indication that Lobbin ever traveled to China to assist in discovery or personally engage with his Chinese client, nor is there any suggestion that he spoke with Toth between the two depositions to assess Toth's preparation and adequacy to testify. Lobbin's late entry into this litigation does not explain his complete disregard for this Court's discovery orders as evidenced by Toth's continued dismal performance in December 2012. While perhaps Lobbin could have been excused from responsibility for the failed June deposition, he offers nothing to excuse his actions—or lack thereof—leading up to the December deposition.

It is also apparent from Lobbin's statements during Toth's deposition and from Lobbin's subsequent submissions to the Court that he took the absurd position that Toth *was* adequately prepared for the deposition. During the deposition, Lobbin asserted that Toth's "general knowledge" of the identified topics was sufficient, despite the magistrate judge's January 3 Order contemplating testimony from a corporate deponent who could testify specifically on the identified topics. In his objections to the magistrate judge's imposition of sanctions, Lobbin repeatedly asserted that Toth was a proper and prepared witness. The only reason he does not continue to make this assertion now is because this Court expressly stated that it will not further entertain that argument in connection with this matter. The Court recognizes that Lobbin has a duty to zealously advocate for his client, but even that advocacy must be "within the bounds of the law." Model Rules of Professional Conduct. (2013). Here, Lobbin not only asserted that Toth was an adequately prepared deponent in connection with his advocacy for his client, he also made this assertion in his own objections to the magistrate judge's order of sanctions against him personally.

It is difficult for the Court to characterize Lobbin's conduct simply as "competent, good-faith advocacy" on behalf of his client, in light of Lobbin's previous statements and submissions.

Lobbin appears to believe that the fact that Manley's Chinese counsel took responsibility for the selection and preparation of Manley's 30(b)(6) witness somehow absolves him of any wrongdoing. He is mistaken. Lobbin is Manley's United States counsel and the counsel of record in this case, and he has a professional responsibility not only to his client, but also to the Court. "An attorney's duty to a client can never outweigh his or her responsibility to see that our system of justice functions smoothly." "This concept is as old as common law jurisprudence itself." Lobbin cannot stick his head in the sand and cower behind his client's disobedient conduct. Lobbin may be held responsible for Manley's discovery violations, even if he did not personally instigate the conduct.

The phrase "attorney advising such conduct" does not ... exclude either an attorney's willful blindness or his acquiescence to the misfeasance of his client; to the contrary, the phrase instructs that when an attorney advises a client in discovery matters, he assumes a responsibility for the professional disposition of that portion of a lawsuit and may be held accountable for positions taken or responses filed during that process. Sanctions exist, in part, to remind attorneys that service to their clients must coexist with their responsibilities toward the court, toward the law and toward their brethren at the bar.

Even if the Court accepted that Lobbin acted in good faith and truly believed that Manley—despite having clearly shown complete and utter disregard for this Court's discovery orders throughout the course of this four-year litigation—would take the steps it needed to take to adequately prepare its designated 30(b)(6) witness, Lobbin's subjective good faith alone is not enough to absolve him of all responsibility for this fiasco. "Subjective good faith ought not to be an infinitely expansive safe harbor to protect an attorney" who behaves in a way "that a competent attorney could not under any conceivable justification reasonably believe" to be appropriate. "Although subjective good faith on the part of a non-attorney party may in some instances excuse otherwise unreasonable conduct, we are entitled to demand that an attorney exhibit some judgment." To excuse objectively unreasonable conduct by an attorney would be to state that one who acts "with an empty head and a pure heart" is not responsible for the consequences.

Based on the extensive record in this case, Lobbin's unreasonable reliance on Manley's assurances, and his failure to make any diligent attempt to comply with the Court's discovery order prior to the disastrous December deposition, the Court finds that Lobbin's behavior, when viewed objectively, constituted intentional or reckless disregard of his duties, at best characterized as a willful blindness toward his client's disdain for the judicial process. Lobbin's utter failure to attempt to discharge his duties as an officer of the Court unreasonably and vexatiously multiplied the proceedings in this case and amounted to bad faith. There was a discovery order compelling Manley's production of a prepared 30(b)(6) deponent, a willful violation of that order, and Aviva was prejudiced by that violation—both in the time and money expended on the failed deposition and in Aviva's inability to acquire through discovery the information it needed to pursue its claims. There is nothing to show that the failure to comply with the discovery order was substantially justified or that there are any other circumstances that would make an award of expenses unjust. "This conduct amounts to a near total dereliction of professional responsibility" and such abusive conduct should not, cannot, and will not be cost-free." Sanctions against

Lobbin under Federal Rule of Civil Procedure 37(b) or 28 U.S.C. § 1927 are warranted. Lobbin shall be jointly and severally liable for Aviva's reasonable expenses—including attorneys' fees—incurred in connection with the failed depositions and in bringing the motion for sanctions.

"The most useful starting point for determining the amount of a reasonable fee is the number of hours reasonably expended on the litigation multiplied by a reasonable hourly rate." Hours that are excessive, redundant or otherwise unnecessary are not "reasonably expended" and should be excluded from the calculation.

Aviva's attorney, Keith Sorge ("Sorge"), submitted an affidavit stating that he spent at least 69.9 hours in connection with preparing for and attending the two Toth depositions and the motion for sanctions. Sorge's billing rate is $400 per hour, resulting in claimed fees of $27,960.00. Sorge's affidavit also states that attorney Ryan Sorge ("Ryan Sorge") spent 5.5 hours reviewing and identifying documents to be used at the deposition, at a billing rate of $225 per hour. Sorge also claims costs totaling $103.00. Manley submitted a response, objecting to the number of hours claimed by Keith Sorge as unreasonable. Manley does not object to the billing rates of $400 and $225 per hour, the 5.5 hours expended by Ryan Sorge, or the claimed costs.

The Court finds that the attorneys' fees incurred by Ryan Sorge ($1,237.50), the claimed costs ($103.00), and Keith Sorge's hourly rate of $400 per hour are reasonable. The Court also finds, despite Manley's objection, that the twelve hours Sorge claims for actually deposing Toth and preparing for and participating in the motion hearing is reasonable. Toth's two depositions together lasted approximately seven hours, and the hearing on the motion for sanctions lasted approximately one hour. Factoring in transit and reasonable preparation time, the Court does not find twelve hours expended on the depositions and hearing to be unreasonable.

Sorge also states that he spent approximately fourteen hours preparing for *each* of the two Toth depositions, including time spent reviewing documents, researching Manley, and drafting questions; Manley objects that the twenty-eight hours is unreasonable because the second Toth deposition was merely a continuation of the first deposition and did not require significant additional preparation. Given the numerous documents involved in this case, the Court finds that it was reasonable for Sorge to spend fourteen hours preparing for the first Toth deposition. It was not, however, reasonable to spend an *additional* fourteen hours preparing for what should have been a continuation of the first deposition. The Court finds that seven hours is a reasonable time to have spent in preparation for the second of the two depositions.

Finally, Sorge claims to have spent twenty-nine hours drafting the submissions in support of Aviva's motion for sanctions and responding to Manley's opposition to that motion, including time spent reviewing Toth's deposition. The Court finds this amount of time to be excessive. [Aviva's memorandum in support of its motion was only sixteen pages and was not factually or legally complex. Aviva's barely-four-page reply brief contained no new factual information and included no citations to law. Throughout both briefs, Aviva primarily relied on citations to and quotes from Toth's deposition—and although that deposition transcript was approximately three-hundred pages long, the Court does not find that it should have required more than a few hours to read. The Court finds twenty-nine hours to be an unreasonable amount of time to read through the deposition, draft the motion papers, and read and respond to Manley's objections. Instead, fifteen hours represents a reasonable amount of time necessary to conduct these activities.]

[In sum, the Court finds that Sorge reasonably expended forty-eight hours in connection with the two Toth depositions and motion hearing. At a rate of $400 per hour, this amounts to attorneys' fees of $19,200. Upon adding this amount to the $1,237.50 fees incurred by Ryan Sorge and the costs of $103.00, the Court finds that Manley and Lobbin are jointly and severally liable for $20,540.50 in reasonable fees and costs incurred in connection with this discovery misconduct.]

7. There may be many other problems with depositions. For example, what if a named plaintiff in a particular class action simply does not show up for his own deposition? What might be appropriate penalties?

In the following case how do you suppose a defendant might decide which of 100 members of a plaintiff class should be deposed? What is the potential for abuse in that situation?

2015 WL 1969984
UNITED STATES DISTRICT COURT,
DISTRICT OF COLUMBIA.
KENNETH CAMPBELL, ET AL., PLAINTIFFS,
V.
NATIONAL RAILROAD PASSENGER CORPORATION,
DEFENDANT.

SIGNED MAY 4, 2015
SYNOPSIS

**Background:** Current and former employees brought action under Title VII against railroad alleging class-wide racial discrimination in employment. Railroad moved for sanctions based on failure of two employees to appear for depositions during class-discovery phase of litigation.

Emmet G. Sullivan, United States District Judge

When a plaintiff files a lawsuit, he takes on certain responsibilities, including the duty to participate in discovery in good faith. A component of this duty is that parties must appear for properly noticed depositions. Robert Guerra and Terrence Whitesides, two named plaintiffs in this putative class action against the National Railroad Passenger Corporation ("Amtrak"), failed to appear for their depositions during the class-discovery phase of litigation. Pending before the Court is Amtrak's motion for relief under Federal Rule of Civil Procedure 37(d), which seeks exclusion of the legal claims of Guerra and Whitesides and an award of costs and attorneys' fees.

The failure of Guerra and Whitesides to appear for depositions is disturbing and the Court finds itself required by Rule 37(d) to award Amtrak some of the expenses incurred as a result of that failure. Nevertheless, the Court "has the right, if not the duty, to temper justice with understanding." Because the existing record does not provide detail regarding the plaintiffs' claimed inability to pay or the amount of costs and fees that Amtrak seeks to recover, the Court requires more information before fashioning an appropriate monetary sanction. In view of the fact that any prejudice caused by plaintiffs' actions can be cured by striking the evidence they submitted in support of class certification, the Court concludes that dismissal of their legal claims would be excessive. Accordingly, upon consideration of Amtrak's motion, the response and reply thereto, the applicable law, and the entire record, the Court GRANTS IN PART AND DENIES IN PART Amtrak's motion.

## I. Background

On March 1, 2012, the Court entered an Amended Scheduling Order. That Order provided that Amtrak would be permitted to depose "any individual who submits an affidavit, declaration, or statement in support of Plaintiff's Motion for Class Certification." Plaintiffs Guerra and Whitesides each submitted declarations in support of plaintiffs' motion for class certification. Rather than deposing everyone who submitted a declaration, Amtrak selected forty-one individuals, including Guerra and Whitesides. In addition to the issues with Guerra and Whitesides, scheduling issues arose regarding other depositions, persuading the Court to grant two extensions of the deposition deadline, for a total extension of twenty-four days.

### A. Mr. Guerra Fails to Appear for a Deposition.

After significant difficulty scheduling Mr. Guerra's deposition, plaintiffs' counsel informed Amtrak on June 6, 2012 that Mr. Guerra could be available for a deposition on June 7, 2012. Mr. Guerra's deposition was noticed for 9:00 a.m. on June 7, 2012 in Washington, D.C. Shortly after 9:00 a.m., plaintiffs' counsel informed defendant's counsel by phone that Mr. Guerra would not be attending. Plaintiffs' counsel explained the reasons more fully in an email later that morning:

> We understand that Robert Guerra decided not to appear for his deposition this morning out of his personal concerns and fears of retaliation, including possible retribution by former co-workers if he were to testify at this time. We recognize that the court reporter appearance fee must be paid. We will tender that payment forthwith if Amtrak will agree not to pursue any other monetary sanction against Mr. Guerra or Plaintiffs' counsel.

Amtrak's counsel had prepared for the deposition before it was cancelled.

### B. Mr. Whitesides Fails to Appear for a Deposition.

Plaintiffs' counsel suggested that Mr. Whitesides be deposed in New York City on May 2, 2012 at 2:00 p.m. A deposition notice for that date, time, and location was issued. At 9:00 p.m. on May 1, 2012, plaintiffs' counsel informed defendant's counsel that the deposition could not go forward. Plaintiffs' counsel had "just received a phone call from Terrence Whitesides" who "experienced a death in his family this evening, apparently a relative to whom he was close."

Plaintiffs' counsel later proposed that the deposition take place on May 23, 2012 at 2:00 p.m. in Washington, D.C. Amtrak issued a deposition notice for that date, time, and location. On May 22, 2012, plaintiffs' counsel cancelled Mr. Whitesides's deposition, due to their inability to contact Mr. Whitesides. ("Plaintiffs' counsel were unable to contact Whitesides after repeated attempts. We kept trying, without success, right up to the day before the deposition."). Due to the short notice of each cancellation, Amtrak's attorneys had twice begun preparing for Mr. Whitesides's deposition.

## C. Amtrak Moves for Relief Under Rule 37(d).

Currently pending before the Court—and scheduled to be argued on June 15, 2015—are plaintiffs' motion for class certification and defendant's motion for partial summary judgment on the plaintiffs' disparate-impact claims. Amtrak has also moved to strike the individual claims of plaintiffs Guerra and Whitesides, and for payment of attorney's fees and costs in connection with those plaintiffs' failure to appear for depositions. Plaintiffs oppose the motion, and Amtrak has filed a reply brief. Because Amtrak's motion to exclude raises a discrete issue that is distinct from the motions to be argued on June 15th, the Court finds that it is efficient to address the motion separately. Because the parties' positions on the motion to exclude are clear from their pleadings, oral argument is unnecessary.

## II. Analysis

The Court's authority to sanction parties for discovery violations derives from Federal Rule of Civil Procedure 37, which permits the Court, "on motion, to order sanctions if: (i) a party fails, after being served with proper notice, to appear for that person's deposition." Fed.R.Civ.P. 37(d)(1)(A). There is no dispute that Guerra and Whitesides failed to appear for properly noticed depositions. The dispute is over the appropriate sanction.

Amtrak asserts that the only effective sanction would be dismissal with prejudice, as well as an award of the attorney's fees and costs incurred by Amtrak in preparing for the cancelled depositions and litigating this motion. Plaintiffs argue that dismissal is not warranted because lesser sanctions would mitigate any prejudice to Amtrak, and that an award of costs and fees is not warranted because of the inability of Guerra and Whitesides to pay.

The central requirement of Rule 37 is that "any sanction must be just," which requires in cases involving severe sanctions that the district court consider whether lesser sanctions would be more appropriate for the particular violation. Rule 37 contains a non-exhaustive list of potential sanctions, which include the establishment of adverse findings of fact, striking pleadings, and dismissing a case or entering a default judgment. *See* Fed.R.Civ.P. 37(b)(2)(A).

## A. Dismissal Is Not Warranted.

Dismissal under Rule 37 is an extremely harsh sanction. It is to be taken only after unfruitful resort to lesser sanctions. ("Particularly in the context of litigation-ending sanctions, we have insisted that since our system favors the disposition of cases on the merits, dismissal is a sanction of last resort to be applied only after less dire alternatives have been explored without success or would obviously prove futile.")

"Dismissal is warranted when (1) the other party has been 'so prejudiced by the misconduct that it would be unfair to require the party to proceed further in the case,' (2) the party's misconduct has put 'an intolerable burden' on the court by requiring the court to modify its own docket and operations in order to accommodate the delay, *or* (3) the court finds it necessary "to sanction conduct that is disrespectful to the court and to deter similar misconduct in the future." In this case, an Order striking the declarations submitted by Guerra and Whitesides in support of class certification would cure any prejudice to Amtrak. The burden on the Court may in no way be characterized as "intolerable." Finally, although deterrence is an important concern, it must also be proportional to the party's action and the striking of the declarations of Guerra and Whitesides, combined with a partial award of expenses, will suffice.

### 1. Prejudice

"In determining whether a party's misconduct prejudices the other party so severely as to make it unfair to require the other party to proceed with the case, courts look to whether the aggrieved party has cited specific facts demonstrating actual prejudice, such as the loss of key witnesses." This generally requires a showing that "the errant party's behavior 'has severely hampered the other party's ability to present his case.'" Prejudice will not be found merely because a plaintiff's behavior caused the defendant "to waste time and money while defending this action."

To be sure, Amtrak is clearly prejudiced by its inability to examine Guerra and Whitesides regarding the facts they proffered in their declarations in support of the plaintiffs' motion for class certification. *Cf.* Reply at 4 (noting that "Amtrak went to great lengths to determine who it would depose based on the declarants' specific personal allegations and their purported knowledge of facts to support Plaintiffs' class-based allegations"). The Court does not doubt that the inability to cross-examine a witness regarding a material fact within that witness's personal knowledge could prejudice a party. Here, however, any prejudice arising from Amtrak's inability to examine Guerra and Whitesides may be fully cured by striking the declarations submitted by Guerra and Whitesides.

### 2. Burden on the Court

The Court may also order dismissal when "the delay or misconduct would require the court to expend considerable judicial resources in the future in addition to those it has already wasted, thereby inconveniencing many other innocent litigants in the presentation of *their* cases." (Dismissal may be appropriate when the burden placed on the Court is 'intolerable.')

### 3. Deterrence

The Court may also resort to dismissal when necessary for its deterrent value. "A discovery sanction imposed for its deterrent effect 'must be calibrated to the gravity of the misconduct,' and courts should avoid 'pointless exactions of retribution.'" Deterrence may support a case-dispositive sanction where, for example, noncompliance with discovery was a strategic decision. *See Founding Church of Scientology,* 802 F.2d at 1458 (upholding dismissal as sanction for failure of leader of a plaintiff-organization to appear for a deposition based in part upon "substantial evidence that the arrangement by which Hubbard could communicate with the Church only at his initiative was in fact designed to shield Hubbard from legal process").

Amtrak asserts that the deterrent value of lesser sanctions would be insufficient because "if Guerra and Whitesides are not dismissed, it essentially allows Plaintiffs to pick and choose which declarants should be deposed, depending on the strength and veracity of their claims." This overstates the misconduct that is actually at issue. No evidence has been proffered to suggest that plaintiffs' counsel or any other plaintiff was involved in the decisions of Guerra and Whitesides not to appear. A different result might be warranted if the record permitted the Court to infer that the failure to appear was due not to the reasons given, but to a strategic decision.

That is not to approve of either plaintiff's actions. There were ways to address Mr. Guerra's concern without violating his duty to appear for a properly noticed deposition. Had he expressed concerns in advance, his counsel could have sought to reach an agreement with Amtrak regarding additional protections, moved for a protective order, or otherwise assuaged his concerns. Although Mr. Whitesides's first failure to appear is eminently understandable—he suffered a death in the family the evening before his deposition was scheduled and promptly notified his lawyer—his second failure to appear is unexplained. Mr. Guerra's failure to appear and Mr. Whitesides's second failure to appear warrant a sanction to deter similar conduct in the future. Consistent with the Court's duty to "consider whether lesser sanctions would be more appropriate for the particular violation," the Court concludes that deterrence is served by: (1) striking the declarations of Guerra and Whitesides; and (2) a partial award of expenses, as discussed below.

B. The Court Will Award Some Expenses.

Rule 37 requires the Court to order "the party failing to act, the attorney advising that party, or both to pay the reasonable expenses, including attorney's fees, caused by the failure, unless the failure was substantially justified or other circumstances make an award of expenses unjust." Fed.R.Civ.P. 37(d)(3). Plaintiffs bear the burden of proving that their failure was "substantially justified" or that circumstances render an award "unjust." Plaintiffs argue that an award of expenses would be unjust because "neither Guerra nor Whitesides have the personal financial resources to pay." ("Both Mr. Guerra and Mr. Whitesides have limited financial means and would be unable, or it would be a hardship for them, to pay Amtrak's attorneys' fees or costs"). They therefore suggest an award of only the costs attributable to the court-reporter cancellation fees. Amtrak subsequently advised the Court that those fees have been waived.

The Court begins with the proposition that "a flat per se policy against the imposition of sanctions under Rule 37 upon any party who is financially indigent does not accord with the purposes of that rule and would open the door to many possible abuses." Such a holding would grant a party *carte blanche* to abuse the discovery process. Nonetheless, a party's inability to pay a sanction is a factor that the Court may consider. There may well be situations in which financial indigency will tilt against the imposition of Rule 37 sanctions. (Monetary sanction not warranted where a plaintiff's "Application to Proceed In Forma Pauperis suggests that she is not able to pay sanctions in any amount.").

In this case, declining to award any expenses would leave largely unpunished the unacceptable behavior of two plaintiffs who voluntarily invoked this Court's authority by joining this lawsuit. Striking their declarations will cure any prejudice to Amtrak, but carries a relatively minimal deterrent value as there remain 100 other declarations in support of class certification. Accordingly, the Court concludes that a monetary sanction is appropriate to deter future discovery violations—both by Guerra and Whitesides and by others.

The Court does not have an appropriate record on which to decide precisely what monetary sanction to award, however. Plaintiffs assert that Guerra and Whitesides "would be unable, or it would be a hardship for them, to pay Amtrak's attorneys' fees or costs." This vague disjunctive statement is not sufficiently detailed to assist the Court in balancing the need to fashion a sanction that would provide appropriate deterrence against the need to avoid being unjustly punitive. Amtrak asks for all costs and attorneys' fees regarding the deposition preparation and litigation of this motion, but did not provide an accounting of these fees and costs. Accordingly, the Court holds only that Rule 37(d) requires that the Court award at a minimum the non-attorney-fee costs attributable directly to the May 23 and June 7 depositions. After the parties submit pleadings with sufficiently detailed information to permit the Court to fashion an award that is both reasonable and proportional, the Court will decide whether this award is sufficient, or whether an award of some portion of the attorneys' fees attributable to the May 23 and June 7 depositions and the litigation of this motion is also warranted.

## III. Conclusion

For the foregoing reasons, the Court GRANTS IN PART AND DENIES IN PART Amtrak's motion for exclusion of plaintiffs Guerra and Whitesides and for related costs. An appropriate Order accompanies this Memorandum Opinion.

SO ORDERED.

8. Today probably the vast majority of important information is stored electronically. That Electronically Stored Information, (ESI), is of course discoverable to the
same extent that any other information would be discoverable.

It is important that when ESI is disclosed to the other party that it be disclosed
in its original, electronic form, rather than being printed out and sent to the other
party. Keeping ESI in its electronic form is important for at least two major reasons.

First, ESI is normally searched by "key word" searches. Vast quantities of material can be searched rapidly by telling the computer to pull out all documents that
contain certain words or phrases. Designing an effective "key word" search is an
art. And of course many different words and phrases are searched, in an attempt to
come up with everything that might be important to the case.

Second, an e-mail, for example, in its electronic format, contains lots of important data (metadata), that will be lost if the e-mail is converted to printed form.

"The MIT Media Lab recently developed a tool demonstrating the significance
of email metadata. The tool analyzes the metadata from the user's Gmail account
and visualizes that data, revealing who the user talked to, how often, and when,
among other things. Printing paper copies of emails and permanently deleting the
electronic data, then, deprives those emails of a significant amount of their evidentiary value. Several courts have acknowledged the significant advantages of producing electronic documents in their native format. *See, e.g., Covad Comm'cns Co.
v. Revonet, Inc.,* ("it is improper to take an electronically searchable document and
either destroy or degrade the document's ability to be searched"); *Covad Comm'cns
Co. v. Revonet,* (ordering the production of emails in electronic format after opposing party produced such emails in hard copy form). Moreover, the Advisory
Committee Notes to Rule 34 reinforces the importance of maintaining electronic
data in electronic form. *See* Fed.R.Civ.P. 34, Advisory Committee Note. ('The option
to produce in a reasonably usable form does not mean that a responding party
is free to convert electronically stored information from the form in which it is
ordinarily maintained to a different form that makes it more difficult or burdensome for the requesting party to use the information efficiently in the litigation.
If the responding party ordinarily maintains the information it is producing in a
way that makes it searchable by electronic means, the information should not be
produced in a form that removes or significantly degrades this feature.')" *Sekisui
v. Hart, fn. 71.*

The litigation involved in the following case, *Zubulake v. UBS,* set the standard
still applicable to parties – and their attorneys – with regard to preservation and

disclosure of ESI. Note that statements made during various depositions led to the discovery of previously undisclosed ESI – and were a contributing factor to the sanctions imposed for destruction of some ESI.

**229 F.R.D. 422**
**UNITED STATES DISTRICT COURT,**
**S.D. NEW YORK.**
**LAURA ZUBULAKE, PLAINTIFF,**
**V.**
**UBS WARBURG LLC, UBS WARBURG, AND UBS AG,**
**DEFENDANTS.**

DECIDED JULY 20, 2004

SCHEINDLIN, District Judge.

Commenting on the importance of speaking clearly and listening closely, Phillip Roth memorably quipped, "The English language is a form of communication! ... Words aren't only bombs and bullets—no, they're little gifts, containing meanings!" What is true in love is equally true at law: Lawyers and their clients need to communicate clearly and effectively with one another to ensure that litigation proceeds efficiently. When communication between counsel and client breaks down, conversation becomes "just crossfire," and there are usually casualties.

## I. INTRODUCTION

This is the fifth written opinion in this case, a relatively routine employment discrimination dispute in which discovery has now lasted over two years. Laura Zubulake is once again moving to sanction UBS for its failure to produce relevant information and for its tardy production of such material. In order to decide whether sanctions are warranted, the following question must be answered: Did UBS fail to preserve and timely produce relevant information and, if so, did it act negligently, recklessly, or willfully?

This decision addresses counsel's obligation to ensure that relevant information is preserved by giving clear instructions to the client to preserve such information and, perhaps more importantly, a client's obligation to heed those instructions. Early on in this litigation, UBS's counsel—both in-house and outside—instructed UBS personnel to retain relevant electronic information. Notwithstanding these instructions, certain UBS employees deleted relevant e-mails. Other employees never produced relevant information to counsel. As a result, many discoverable e-mails were not produced to Zubulake until recently, even though they were responsive to a document request propounded on June 3, 2002. In addition, a number of e-mails responsive to that document request were deleted and have been lost altogether.

Counsel, in turn, failed to request retained information from one key employee and to give the litigation hold instructions to another. They also failed to adequately communicate with another employee about how she maintained her computer files. Counsel also failed to safeguard backup tapes that might have contained some of the deleted e-mails, and which would have mitigated the damage done by UBS's destruction of those e-mails.

The conduct of both counsel and client thus calls to mind the now-famous words of the prison captain in *Cool Hand Luke:* "What we've got here is a failure to communicate." Because of this failure by *both* UBS and its counsel, Zubulake has been prejudiced. As a result, sanctions are warranted.

## II. FACTS

Zubulake is an equities trader who is suing her former employer for gender discrimination, failure to promote, and retaliation under federal, state, and city law.

## A. Background

Zubulake filed an initial charge of gender discrimination with the EEOC on August 16, 2001. Well before that, however—as early as April 2001—UBS employees were on notice of Zubulake's impending court action. After she received a right-to-sue letter from the EEOC, Zubulake filed this lawsuit on February 15, 2002.

Fully aware of their common law duty to preserve relevant evidence, UBS's in-house attorneys gave oral instructions in August 2001—immediately after Zubulake filed her EEOC charge—instructing employees not to destroy or delete material potentially relevant to Zubulake's claims, and in fact to segregate such material into separate files for the lawyers' eventual review. This warning pertained to both electronic and hard-copy files, but did *not* specifically pertain to so-called "backup tapes," maintained by UBS's information technology personnel. In particular, UBS's in-house counsel, Robert L. Salzberg, "advised relevant UBS employees to preserve and turn over to counsel all files, records or other written memoranda or documents concerning the allegations raised in the EEOC charge or any aspect of Zubulake's employment." Subsequently—but still in August 2001—UBS's outside counsel met with a number of the key players in the litigation and reiterated Mr. Salzberg's instructions, reminding them to preserve relevant documents, "including e-mails." Salzberg reduced these instructions to writing in e-mails dated February 22, 2002 - immediately after Zubulake filed her complaint—and September 25, 2002. Finally, in August 2002, after Zubulake propounded a document request that specifically called for e-mails stored on backup tapes, UBS's outside counsel instructed UBS information technology personnel to stop recycling backup tapes. *Every* UBS employee mentioned in this Opinion (with the exception of Mike Davies) either personally spoke to UBS's outside counsel about the duty to preserve e-mails, or was a recipient of one of Salzberg's e-mails.

B. Procedural History (omitted)

C. The Instant Dispute

The essence of the current dispute is that during the re-depositions required by *Zubulake IV,* Zubulake learned about more deleted e-mails and about the existence of e-mails preserved on UBS's active servers that were, to that point, never produced. In sum, Zubulake has now presented evidence that UBS personnel deleted relevant e-mails, some of which were subsequently recovered from backup tapes (or elsewhere) and thus produced to Zubulake long after her initial document requests, and some of which were lost altogether. Zubulake has also presented evidence that some UBS personnel did not produce responsive documents to counsel until recently, depriving Zubulake of the documents for almost two years.

### 1. Deleted E–Mails

Notwithstanding the clear and repeated warnings of counsel, Zubulake has proffered evidence that a number of key UBS employees—Orgill, Hardisty, Holland, Chapin, Varsano, and Amone—failed to retain e-mails germane to Zubulake's claims. Some of the deleted e-mails were restored from backup tapes (or other sources) and have been produced to Zubulake, others have been altogether lost, though there is strong evidence that they once existed. Although I have long been aware that certain e-mails were deleted, the re-depositions demonstrate the scope and importance of those documents.

*a. At Least One E–Mail Has Never Been Produced*

At least one e-mail has been irretrievably lost; the existence of that e-mail is known only because of oblique references to it in other correspondence. It has already been shown that Chapin—the alleged primary discriminator—deleted relevant e-mails. In addition to those e-mails, Zubulake has evidence suggesting that Chapin deleted at least one other e-mail that has been lost *entirely.*

Although Zubulake has only been able to present concrete evidence that this one e-mail was irretrievably lost, there may well be others. Zubulake has presented extensive proof, detailed below, that UBS personnel were deleting relevant e-mails. Many of those e-mails were recovered from backup tapes. The UBS record retention policies called for monthly backup tapes to be retained for three years. The tapes covering the relevant time period (circa August 2001) should have been available to UBS in August 2002, when counsel instructed UBS's information technology personnel that backup tapes were also subject to the litigation hold.

Nonetheless, many backup tapes for the most relevant time periods are missing.

*b. Many E–Mails Were Deleted and Only Later Recovered from Alternate Sources*

Other e-mails were deleted in contravention of counsel's "litigation hold" instructions, but were subsequently recovered from alternative sources—such as backup tapes—and thus produced to Zubulake, albeit almost two years after she propounded her initial document requests.

These are merely examples. The proof is clear: UBS personnel unquestionably deleted relevant e-mails from their computers after August 2001, even though they had received at least two directions from counsel not to. Some of those e-mails were recovered (Zubulake has pointed to at least 45), but some—and no one can say how many—were not. And even those e-mails that were recovered were produced to Zubulake well after she originally asked for them.

### 2. Retained, But Unproduced, E–Mails

Separate and apart from the deleted material are a number of e-mails that were absent from UBS's initial production even though they were not deleted. These e-mails existed in the active, on-line files of two UBS employees—Kim and Tong—but were not produced to counsel and thus not turned over to Zubulake until she learned of their existence as a result of her counsel's questions at deposition. Indeed, these e-mails were not produced until after Zubulake had conducted thirteen depositions and four re-depositions.

During her February 19, 2004, deposition, Kim testified that she was *never* asked to produce her files regarding Zubulake to counsel, nor did she ever actually produce them, although she was asked to retain them. One week after Kim's deposition, UBS produced seven new e-mails. The obvious inference to be drawn is that, subsequent to the deposition, counsel for the first time asked Kim to produce her files.

On March 29, 2004, UBS produced several new e-mails, and three new e-mail retention policies, from Tong's active files. At her deposition two weeks earlier, Tong explained (as she had at her first deposition, a year previous) that she kept a separate "archive" file on her computer with documents pertaining to Zubulake. UBS admits that until the March 2004 deposition, it misunderstood Tong's use of the word "archive" to mean backup tapes; after her March 2004 testimony, it was clear that she meant active data. Again, the inference is that UBS's counsel then, for the first time, asked her to produce her active computer files.

Davies testified that he was unaware of Zubulake's EEOC charge when he spoke with Orgill. The timing of his e-mails, however—the newly produced e-mail that acknowledges receiving Zubulake's EEOC charge coming three hours before the e-mail beginning "I spoke to Brad"—strongly undercuts this claim. The new e-mail, therefore, is circumstantial evidence that could support the inference that Davies knew about the EEOC charge when he spoke with Orgill, and suggests that Orgill knew about the EEOC charge when the decision was made to terminate Zubulake. Its relevance to Zubulake's retaliation claim is unquestionable, and yet it was not produced until April 20, 2004.

Zubulake now moves for sanctions as a result of UBS's purported discovery failings. In particular, she asks that an adverse inference instruction be given to the jury that eventually hears this case.

## III. LEGAL STANDARD

Spoliation is "the destruction or significant alteration of evidence, or the failure to preserve property for another's use as evidence in pending or reasonably foreseeable litigation." "The determination of an appropriate sanction for spoliation, if any, is confined to the sound discretion of the trial judge, and is assessed on a case-by-case basis." The authority to sanction litigants for spoliation arises jointly under the Federal Rules of Civil Procedure and the court's inherent powers.

The spoliation of evidence germane "to proof of an issue at trial can support an inference that the evidence would have been unfavorable to the party responsible for its destruction." A party seeking an adverse inference instruction (or other sanctions) based on the spoliation of evidence must establish the following three elements: (1) that the party having control over the evidence had an obligation to preserve it at the time it was destroyed; (2) that the records were destroyed with a "culpable state of mind" and (3) that the destroyed evidence was "relevant" to the party's claim or defense such that a reasonable trier of fact could find that it would support that claim or defense.

In this circuit, a "culpable state of mind" for purposes of a spoliation inference includes ordinary negligence. When evidence is destroyed in bad faith (*i.e.*, intentionally or willfully), that fact alone is sufficient to demonstrate relevance. By contrast, when the destruction is negligent, relevance must be proven by the party seeking the sanctions.

In the context of a request for an adverse inference instruction, the concept of "relevance" encompasses not only the ordinary meaning of the term, but also that the destroyed evidence would have been favorable to the movant. "This corroboration requirement is even more necessary where the destruction was merely negligent, since in those cases it cannot be inferred from the conduct of the spoliator that the evidence would even have been harmful to him." This is equally true in cases of gross negligence or recklessness; only in the case of *willful* spoliation does the degree of culpability give rise to a presumption of the relevance of the documents destroyed.

## IV. DISCUSSION

In *Zubulake IV,* I held that UBS had a duty to preserve its employees' active files as early as April 2001, and certainly by August 2001, when Zubulake filed her EEOC charge. Zubulake has thus satisfied the first element of the adverse inference test. As noted, the central question implicated by this motion is whether UBS and its counsel took all necessary steps to guarantee that relevant data was both preserved and produced.

### A. Counsel's Duty to Monitor Compliance

In *Zubulake IV,* I summarized a litigant's preservation obligations:

> Once a party reasonably anticipates litigation, it must suspend its routine document retention/destruction policy and put in place a "litigation hold" to ensure the preservation of relevant documents. As a general rule, that litigation hold does not apply to inaccessible backup tapes (*e.g.,* those typically maintained solely for the purpose of

disaster recovery), which may continue to be recycled on the schedule set forth in the company's policy. On the other hand, if backup tapes are accessible (*i.e.,* actively used for information retrieval), then such tapes *would* likely be subject to the litigation hold.

A party's discovery obligations do not end with the implementation of a "litigation hold"—to the contrary, that's only the beginning. Counsel must oversee compliance with the litigation hold, monitoring the party's efforts to retain and produce the relevant documents. Proper communication between a party and her lawyer will ensure (1) that all relevant information (or at least all sources of relevant information) is discovered, (2) that relevant information is retained on a continuing basis; and (3) that relevant non-privileged material is produced to the opposing party.

### 1. Counsel's Duty to Locate Relevant Information

Once a "litigation hold" is in place, a party and her counsel must make certain that all sources of potentially relevant information are identified and placed "on hold." To do this, counsel must become fully familiar with her client's document retention policies, as well as the client's data retention architecture. This will invariably involve speaking with information technology personnel, who can explain system-wide backup procedures and the actual (as opposed to theoretical) implementation of the firm's recycling policy. It will also involve communicating with the "key players" in the litigation, in order to understand how they stored information. In this case, for example, some UBS employees created separate computer files pertaining to Zubulake, while others printed out relevant e-mails and retained them in hard copy only. Unless counsel interviews each employee, it is impossible to determine whether all potential sources of information have been inspected. A brief conversation with counsel, for example, might have revealed that Tong maintained "archive" copies of e-mails concerning Zubulake, and that "archive" meant a separate on-line computer file, not a backup tape. Had that conversation taken place, Zubulake might have had relevant e-mails from that file two years ago.

To the extent that it may not be feasible for counsel to speak with every key player, given the size of a company or the scope of the lawsuit, counsel must be more creative. It may be possible to run a system-wide keyword search; counsel could then preserve a copy of each "hit." Although this sounds burdensome, it need not be. Counsel does not have to review these documents, only see that they are retained. For example, counsel could create a broad list of search terms, run a search for a limited time frame, and then segregate responsive documents. When the opposing party propounds its document requests, the parties could negotiate a list of search terms to be used in identifying responsive documents, and counsel would only be obliged to review documents that came up as "hits" on the second, more restrictive search. The initial broad cut merely guarantees that relevant documents are not lost.

In short, it is *not* sufficient to notify all employees of a litigation hold and expect that the party will then retain and produce all relevant information. Counsel must take affirmative steps to monitor compliance so that all sources of discoverable information are identified and searched. This is not to say that counsel will necessarily succeed in locating all such sources, or that the later discovery of new sources is evidence of a lack of effort. But counsel and client must take *some reasonable steps* to see that sources of relevant information are located.

### 2. Counsel's Continuing Duty to Ensure Preservation

Once a party and her counsel have identified all of the sources of potentially relevant information, they are under a duty to retain that information and to produce information responsive to the opposing party's requests. Rule 26 creates a "duty to supplement" those responses. Although the Rule 26 duty to supplement is nominally the party's, it really falls on counsel. As the Advisory Committee explains,

> Although the party signs the answers, it is his lawyer who understands their significance and bears the responsibility to bring answers up to date. In a complex case all sorts of information reaches the party, who little understands its bearing on answers previously given to interrogatories. In practice, therefore, the lawyer under a continuing burden must periodically recheck all interrogatories and canvass all new information.

To ameliorate this burden, the Rules impose a continuing duty to supplement responses to discovery requests *only* when "a party, or more frequently his lawyer, obtains actual knowledge that a prior response is incorrect. This exception does not impose a duty to check the accuracy of prior responses, but it prevents knowing concealment by a party or attorney."

The *continuing* duty to supplement disclosures strongly suggests that parties also have a duty to make sure that discoverable information is not lost. Indeed, the notion of a "duty to preserve" connotes an ongoing obligation. Obviously, if information is lost or destroyed, it has not been preserved.

A lawyer cannot be obliged to monitor her client like a parent watching a child. At some point, the client must bear responsibility for a failure to preserve. At the same time, counsel is more conscious of the contours of the preservation obligation;

a party cannot reasonably be trusted to receive the "litigation hold" instruction once and to fully comply with it without the active supervision of counsel.

*First,* counsel must issue a "litigation hold" at the outset of litigation or whenever litigation is reasonably anticipated. The litigation hold should be periodically re-issued so that new employees are aware of it, and so that it is fresh in the minds of all employees.

*Second,* counsel should communicate directly with the "key players" in the litigation, *i.e.,* the people identified in a party's initial disclosure and any subsequent supplementation thereto. Because these "key players" are the "employees likely to have relevant information," it is particularly important that the preservation duty be communicated clearly to them. As with the litigation hold, the key players should be periodically reminded that the preservation duty is still in place.

*Finally,* counsel should instruct all employees to produce electronic copies of their relevant active files. Counsel must also make sure that all backup media which the party is required to retain is identified and stored in a safe place. In cases involving a small number of relevant backup tapes, counsel might be advised to take physical possession of backup tapes. In other cases, it might make sense for relevant backup tapes to be segregated and placed in storage. Regardless of what particular arrangement counsel chooses to employ, the point is to separate relevant backup tapes from others. One of the primary reasons that electronic data is lost is ineffective communication with information technology personnel. By taking possession of, or otherwise safeguarding, all potentially relevant backup tapes, counsel eliminates the possibility that such tapes will be inadvertently recycled.

### 3. What Happened at UBS After August 2001?

As more fully described above, UBS's in-house counsel issued a litigation hold in August 2001 and repeated that instruction several times from September 2001 through September 2002. Outside counsel also spoke with some (but not all) of the key players in August 2001. Nonetheless, certain employees unquestionably deleted e-mails. Although many of the deleted e-mails were recovered from backup tapes, a number of backup tapes—and the e-mails on them—are lost forever. Other employees, notwithstanding counsel's request that they produce their files on Zubulake, did not do so.

UBS's counsel—both in-house and outside—repeatedly advised UBS of its discovery obligations. In fact, counsel came very close to taking the precautions laid out above.

To be sure, counsel did not fully comply with the standards set forth above. Nonetheless, under the standards existing at the time, counsel acted reasonably to the extent that they directed UBS to implement a litigation hold. Yet notwithstanding the clear instructions of counsel, UBS personnel failed to preserve plainly relevant e-mails.

*b. Counsel's Failings*

On the other hand, UBS's counsel are not entirely blameless. With respect to locating relevant information, counsel failed to adequately communicate with Tong about how she stored data. Although counsel determined that Tong kept her files on Zubulake in an "archive," they apparently made no effort to learn what that meant. A few simple questions—like the ones that Zubulake's counsel asked at Tong's re-deposition—would have revealed that she kept those files in a separate *active* file on her computer.

With respect to making sure that relevant data was retained, counsel failed in a number of important respects. *First,* neither in-house nor outside counsel communicated the litigation hold instructions to Mike Davies, a senior human resources employee who was intimately involved in Zubulake's termination. *Second,* even though the litigation hold instructions were communicated to Kim, no one ever asked her to produce her files. And *third,* counsel failed to protect relevant backup tapes; had they done so, Zubulake might have been able to recover some of the e-mails that UBS employees deleted.

In addition, if Varsano's deposition testimony is to be credited, he turned over "all of the e-mails that he received concerning Ms. Zubulake." If Varsano turned over these e-mails, then counsel must have failed to produce some of them.

In sum, while UBS personnel deleted e-mails, copies of many of these e-mails were lost or belatedly produced as a result of counsel's failures.

*c. Summary*

Counsel failed to communicate the litigation hold order to all key players. They also failed to ascertain each of the key players' document management habits. By the same token, UBS employees—for unknown reasons—ignored many of the instructions that counsel gave. This case represents a failure of communication, and that failure falls on counsel and client alike.

At the end of the day, however, the duty to preserve and produce documents rests on the party. Once that duty is made clear to a party, either by court order or by instructions from counsel, that party is on notice of its obligations and acts at its own peril. Though more diligent action on the part of counsel would have mitigated some of the damage caused by UBS's deletion of e-mails, UBS deleted the e-mails in defiance of explicit instructions not to.

Because UBS personnel continued to delete relevant e-mails, Zubulake was denied access to e-mails to which she was entitled. Even those e-mails that were deleted but ultimately salvaged from other sources (*e.g.*, backup tapes or Tong and Kim's active files) were produced 22 months after they were initially requested. The effect of losing potentially relevant e-mails is obvious, but the effect of late production cannot be underestimated either. The extent of UBS's spoliation was uncovered by Zubulake during court-ordered re-depositions.

I therefore conclude that UBS acted willfully in destroying potentially relevant information, which resulted either in the absence of such information or its tardy production. Because UBS's spoliation was willful, the lost information is presumed to be relevant.

## B. Remedy

Having concluded that UBS was under a duty to preserve the e-mails and that it deleted presumably relevant e-mails willfully, I now consider the full panoply of available sanctions. In doing so, I recognize that a major consideration in choosing an appropriate sanction—along with punishing UBS and deterring future misconduct—is to restore Zubulake to the position that she would have been in had UBS faithfully discharged its discovery obligations. That being so, I find that the following sanctions are warranted.

*First,* the jury empaneled to hear this case will be given an adverse inference instruction with respect to e-mails deleted after August 2001, and in particular, with respect to e-mails that were irretrievably lost when UBS's backup tapes were recycled. No one can ever know precisely what was on those tapes, but the content of e-mails recovered from other sources—along with the fact that UBS employees willfully deleted e-mails—is sufficiently favorable to Zubulake that I am convinced that the contents of the lost tapes would have been similarly, if not more, favorable.

*Second,* UBS is ordered to pay the costs of any depositions or re-depositions required by the late production.

*Third,* UBS is ordered to pay the costs of this motion.

Finally, I note that UBS's belated production has resulted in a self-executing sanction. Not only was Zubulake unable to question UBS's witnesses using the newly produced e-mails, but UBS was unable to prepare those witnesses with the aid of those e-mails. Some of UBS's witnesses, not having seen these e-mails, have already given deposition testimony that seems to contradict the newly discovered evidence. Zubulake is, of course, free to use this testimony at trial.

These sanctions are designed to compensate Zubulake for the harm done to her by the loss of or extremely delayed access to potentially relevant evidence. They should also stem the need for any further litigation over the backup tapes.

UBS must pay for the restoration and production of relevant e-mails from Varsano's August 2001 backup tape, and pay for any re-deposition of Tong or Varsano that is necessitated by new e-mails found on that tape.

## V. CONCLUSION

In sum, counsel has a duty to effectively communicate to her client its discovery obligations so that all relevant information is discovered, retained, and produced. In particular, once the duty to preserve attaches, counsel must identify sources of discoverable information. This will usually entail speaking directly with the key players in the litigation, as well as the client's information technology personnel. In addition, when the duty to preserve attaches, counsel must put in place a litigation hold and make that known to all relevant employees by communicating with them directly. The litigation hold instructions must be reiterated regularly and compliance must be monitored. Counsel must also call for employees to produce copies of relevant electronic evidence, and must arrange for the segregation and safeguarding of any archival media (*e.g.,* backup tapes) that the party has a duty to preserve.

Once counsel takes these steps (or once a court order is in place), a party is fully on notice of its discovery obligations. If a party acts contrary to counsel's instructions or to a court's order, it acts at its own peril.

UBS failed to preserve relevant e-mails, even after receiving adequate warnings from counsel, resulting in the production of some relevant e-mails almost two years after they were initially requested, and resulting in the complete destruction of others. For that reason, Zubulake's motion is granted and sanctions are warranted. UBS is ordered to:

1. Pay for the re-deposition of relevant UBS personnel, limited to the subject of the newly-discovered e-mails;

2. Restore and produce relevant documents from Varsano's August 2001 backup tape;

3. Pay for the re-deposition of Varsano and Tong, limited to the new material produced from Varsano's August 2001 backup tape; and

4. Pay all "reasonable expenses, including attorney's fees," incurred by Zubulake in connection with the making of this motion.

In addition, I will give the following instruction to the jury that hears this case:

You have heard that UBS failed to produce some of the e-mails sent or received by UBS personnel in August and September 2001. Plaintiff has argued that this evidence was in defendants' control and would have proven facts material to the matter in controversy.

If you find that UBS could have produced this evidence, and that the evidence was within its control, and that the evidence would have been material in deciding facts in dispute in this case, you are permitted, but not required, to infer that the evidence would have been unfavorable to UBS.

In deciding whether to draw this inference, you should consider whether the evidence not produced would merely have duplicated other evidence already before you. You may also consider whether you are satisfied that UBS's failure to produce this information was reasonable. Again, any inference you decide to draw should be based on all of the facts and circumstances in this case.

The Clerk is directed to close this motion [number 43 on the docket sheet]. Fact discovery shall close on October 4, 2004. A final pretrial conference is scheduled for 4:30 PM on October 13, 2004, in Courtroom 15C. If either party believes that a dispositive motion is appropriate, that date will be converted to a pre-motion conference.

## VI. POSTSCRIPT

The subject of the discovery of electronically stored information is rapidly evolving. When this case began more than two years ago, there was little guidance from the judiciary, bar associations or the academy as to the governing standards. Much has changed in that time. There have been a flood of recent opinions—including a number from appellate courts—and there are now several treatises on the subject. In addition, professional groups such as the American Bar Association and the Sedona Conference have provided very useful guidance on thorny issues relating to the discovery of electronically stored information. Many courts have adopted, or are considering adopting, local rules addressing the subject. Most recently, the Standing Committee on Rules and Procedures has approved for publication and public comment a proposal for revisions to the Federal Rules of Civil Procedure designed to address many of the issues raised by the discovery of electronically stored information.

Now that the key issues have been addressed and national standards are developing, parties and their counsel are fully on notice of their responsibility to preserve and produce electronically stored information. The tedious and difficult fact finding encompassed in this opinion and others like it is a great burden on a court's limited resources. The time and effort spent by counsel to litigate these issues has also been time-consuming and distracting. This Court, for one, is optimistic that with the guidance now provided it will not be necessary to spend this amount of time again. It is hoped that counsel will heed the guidance provided by these resources and will work to ensure that preservation, production and spoliation issues are limited, if not eliminated.

SO ORDERED.

9. Many years after *Zubulake* set the standard for ESI discovery the same judge, Shira Scheindlin, issued another important order in the following case regarding the importance of preserving and disclosing ESI.

## 945 F. SUPP. 2D 494
## UNITED STATES DISTRICT COURT, S.D. NEW YORK
## SEKISUI AMERICAN CORPORATION AND SEKISUI MEDICAL CO. LTD., PLAINTIFFS,
## V.
## RICHARD HART AND MARIE LOUISE TRUDEL-HART, DEFENDANTS.

AUGUST 15, 2013

SHIRA A. SCHEINDLIN, District Judge.

A decade ago, I issued a series of opinions regarding the scope of a litigant's duty to preserve electronic documents and the consequences of a failure to preserve such documents falling within the scope of that duty. At its simplest, that duty requires a party anticipating litigation to refrain from deleting electronically stored information ("ESI") that may be relevant to that litigation. Such obligation should, at this point, be quite clear-especially to the party planning to sue. Here, I consider the appropriate penalty for a party that-with full knowledge of the likelihood of litigation-intentionally and permanently destroyed the email files of several key players in this action.[FN2] I also consider how to determine an appropriate remedy for the injured party when it remains unclear whether the destroyed evidence would, in fact, be favorable to that party.

> FN2. The imposition of sanctions for the spoliation of evidence is a relatively rare occurrence. While this is the third case in which I have given an adverse inference instruction based on the spoliation of ESI, this number is miniscule considering that I have presided over approximately 4,000 civil cases during my tenure as a United States District Judge.

## I. INTRODUCTION

Sekisui brings this action for breach of contract against Richard Hart and Marie Louise Trudel-Hart (collectively, "the Harts") in relation to Sekisui's acquisition of America Diagnostica, Inc. ("ADI"), a medical diagnostic products manufacturer of which Hart was president. During discovery, Sekisui revealed that ESI in the form of email files belonging to certain ADI employees—including Hart—had been deleted or were otherwise missing. In March 2013, it became clear that Sekisui did not institute a litigation hold until more than fifteen months after sending a Notice of Claim to the Harts. In the meantime, Sekisui permanently deleted the ESI of Hart and former ADI employee Leigh Ayres. In light of these developments, the Harts requested that this Court impose sanctions on Sekisui for the spoliation of evidence. Specifically, the Harts requested: (1) an adverse inference jury instruction based on the destruction of Hart's and Ayres' ESI; and (2) sanctions for spoliation based on the alleged or actual loss of the email folders of several other ADI employees.

## II. BACKGROUND

### A. The Present Action

Sekisui expressed interest in acquiring ADI from the Harts in late 2008. The purchase agreement governing the sale of ADI to Sekisui contained a number of representations and warranties, including: (1) that ADI complied with all relevant federal regulations; (2) that its facilities were sufficient to conduct its business activities; and (3) that ADI's products contained no material defects. Not satisfied that ADI was complying with the Representations, Sekisui fired Hart and sent the Harts a Notice of Claim on October 14, 2010, evidencing Sekisui's intent to file a lawsuit. Sekisui then filed its Complaint on May 2, 2012, alleging that the Harts breached the contract of sale by violating the specific representations in the purchase agreement.

### B. The Destruction of Hart's ESI

On February 8, 2013, counsel for Sekisui revealed to the Harts that Hart's email files were deleted in March 2011, five months after the Harts received the Notice of Claim. In response to questioning by the Harts, Sekisui revealed that a litigation hold was put into place in January 2012, about fifteen months after the Notice of Claim was sent to the Harts. Sekisui did not notify Northeast Computer Services, (NSC), the vendor in charge of managing Sekisui's information technology systems, of the duty to preserve until July 2012, three months after the Complaint was filed. In the interim, Hart's email folder was permanently deleted by NCS at the directive of former ADI employee Dicey Taylor, who was ADI's head of Human Resources. Sekisui initially represented that no other ESI was missing besides Hart's and that of a few other former ADI employees, none of whom were considered relevant custodians.

Further investigation by the Harts revealed that days before filing the Complaint, the NCS employee who deleted Hart's ESI emailed another NCS employee regarding Taylor's directive. According to the email:

"Several months ago, maybe in the summer, Taylor told me to delete Hart's mailbox. I followed this by "are you sure? are you sure? are you sure?" She was very certain that she wanted it deleted, apparently she thought that there wasn't any more useful information or whatever they needed they captured. I would have personally archived it.... This is not 100% certain, but I thought I heard that Hart's email had been combed through by the Sekisui lawyers before Taylor told me to delete it."

In June 2012, Doug LeMasurier—the NCS employee in charge of the ADI account—confirmed that Hart's email was permanently deleted and irretrievable. LeMasurier stated: "There is no backup of this file. We recommended that it not be deleted, but we were instructed by an ADI employee to delete the file."

By way of explanation, Sekisui maintains that the destruction of Hart's ESI was "largely due to the actions of a single former employee acting without direction from Sekisui," i.e., Taylor. Sekisui further asserts that Taylor made the unilateral decision to delete Hart's email in order to free up space on the ADI server after determining that Hart was no longer receiving work-related email. Before directing NCS to permanently delete Hart's ESI, Taylor apparently "identified and printed any emails that she deemed pertinent to the company," which emails have been produced to the Harts. Even those emails deemed "pertinent to the company" do not appear to have been backed up before being deleted by NCS; they were merely printed by Taylor in hard copy. Sekisui searched several alternative sources and eventually produced about 36,000 emails to and from Hart. Sekisui also maintains that, according to current and former ADI employees, Hart "used email sparingly," often used his personal email account, and took a work computer from ADI on which he retained copies of his work email, and which he never returned. It is impossible to say how many emails were permanently deleted and remain unrecoverable. Because of a cognitive disorder, Hart cannot testify or be deposed in this action.

## C. The Destruction of Ayres' ESI

Sekisui initially denied the Harts' assertion that Ayres' emails had also been deleted, assuring that "Sekisui has maintained the email folders for custodians including Ayres and there is no basis to accuse Sekisui of the improper deletion" of Ayres' ESI. However, the Harts uncovered evidence establishing that, in fact, Taylor instructed

NCS to delete Ayres' email files in October 2011. Ayres was the ADI employee responsible for ensuring compliance with FDA regulations, and the deletion of her ESI was carried out with the apparent approval of ADI's then-President and chief operating officer, Kevin Morrissey. Taylor directed LeMasurier to "delete Leigh Ayres from the … server—totally into cyberspace. Do not archive. Kevin Morrissey has approved this removal." Taylor's request apparently responded to another ADI employee's suggestion that Ayres' email *address* be deleted since Ayres was no longer an employee and had only been receiving junk mail. Instead, more than a year after the duty to preserve arose, Taylor ordered the permanent destruction of Ayres' ESI with apparent permission from (and at least awareness of) of ADI's then-President.

Sekisui maintains that the deletion of Ayres' email files was done "for the sole purpose of removing emails that were unnecessary for the continued operation of ADI's business." Sekisui was able to produce nearly 7,000 emails and attachments "from Ms. Ayres's archived email files, plus several thousand more Ayres emails from other custodians' files." There is, again, no way to determine how much ESI was deleted permanently and remains unrecoverable. Sekisui also emphasizes that it has maintained and produced thousands of relevant documents—including non-email electronic files-of both Hart and Ayres. Accordingly, Sekisui argues that the missing emails would be of only marginal relevance in this action.

## IV. APPLICABLE LAW

The controlling case in this Circuit regarding adverse inference instructions is *Residential Funding Corp. v. DeGeorge Financial Corp.* The court there held:

> A party seeking an adverse inference instruction based on the destruction of evidence must establish (1) that the party having control over the evidence had an obligation to preserve it at the time it was destroyed; (2) that the records were destroyed with a culpable state of mind; and (3) that the destroyed evidence was relevant to the party's claim or defense such that a reasonable trier of fact could find that it would support that claim or defense.

> Rule 37 "authorizes a wide range of sanctions for discovery abuses." If the district court determines that a party wrongfully withheld or destroyed evidence, it may tell the jury "those facts and nothing more; or it might add that the jury could, but need not, draw inferences against the spoliators based on those facts; or that the jury *should* draw adverse inferences against the spoliators based on those facts; or that the jury should render a verdict for the innocent party."

## A. Establishing a Culpable State of Mind

"The culpable state of mind factor is satisfied by a showing that the evidence was destroyed knowingly, even if without intent to breach a duty to preserve it, or negligently." "The sanction of an adverse inference may be appropriate in some cases involving the negligent destruction of evidence because each party should bear the risk of its own negligence." This is because the adverse inference provides the necessary mechanism for restoring the evidentiary balance. The inference is adverse to the destroyer not because of any finding of moral culpability, but because the risk that the evidence would have been detrimental rather than favorable should fall on the party responsible for its loss.

It follows that gross negligence also satisfies the culpability requirement. This circuit follows a "case-by-case approach to the failure to produce relevant evidence" because "such failures occur along a continuum of fault-ranging from innocence through the degrees of negligence to intentionality."

## B. Establishing Relevance

"Relevant" in the context of an adverse inference instruction means that the party seeking an adverse inference must adduce sufficient evidence from which a reasonable trier of fact could infer that "the destroyed or unavailable evidence would have been of the nature alleged by the party affected by its destruction, i.e., that the destroyed evidence would have been helpful to the movant." Yet "courts must take care not to hold the prejudiced party to too strict a standard of proof regarding the likely contents of the destroyed or unavailable evidence, because doing so would subvert the purposes of the adverse inference, and would allow parties who have destroyed evidence to profit from that destruction."

When evidence is destroyed willfully, the destruction alone is sufficient circumstantial evidence from which a reasonable fact finder could conclude that the missing evidence was unfavorable to that party. The intentional destruction of relevant records, either paper or electronic, after the duty to preserve has attached, is willful. Similarly, a showing of gross negligence in the destruction of evidence will in some circumstances suffice, standing alone, to support a finding that the evidence was unfavorable to the grossly negligent party. Accordingly, where a party seeking an adverse inference adduces evidence that its opponent destroyed potential evidence in bad faith or through gross negligence (satisfying the "culpable state of mind" factor), that same evidence will frequently also be sufficient to permit a jury to conclude that the missing evidence is favorable to the party (satisfying the "relevance" factor).

## C. Prejudice

When evidence is destroyed willfully or through gross negligence, prejudice to the innocent party may be presumed because that party is "deprived of what the court can assume would have been evidence relevant to the innocent party's claims or defenses." That is, prejudice is presumed precisely because relevant evidence, *i.e.,* evidence presumed to be unfavorable to the spoliating party, has been intention-ally destroyed and is no longer available to the innocent party. When, however, the destruction of evidence is merely negligent, the burden falls on the innocent party to prove prejudice. This circuit has "repeatedly held that a case-by-case approach to the failure to produce relevant evidence, at the discretion of the district court, is appropriate." The failure to adopt good preservation practices is "one factor in the determination of whether discovery sanctions should issue."

## V. DISCUSSION

### A. Culpable State of Mind

#### 1. The Destruction of Hart's ESI

Hart's ESI was willfully destroyed. It is undisputed that Taylor directed an NCS employee to permanently delete Hart's ESI. Indeed, Taylor was apparently "very cer-tain" that the ESI should be deleted and, notably, demanded the destruction despite the fact that the NCS employee recommended against such action. Moreover, no back-up tapes were made of the data deleted, and even the emails that Taylor *did* print are of significantly less evidentiary value given that their metadata is no longer available. The law does not require a showing of malice to establish intentionality with respect to the spoliation of evidence. In the context of an adverse inference analysis, there is no analytical distinction between destroying evidence in bad faith, *i .e.,* with a malevolent purpose, and destroying it willfully. That Sekisui provides a good faith explanation for the destruction of Hart's ESI—suggesting that Taylor's directive was given in order to save space on the server—does not change the fact that the ESI was willfully destroyed.

#### 2. The Destruction of Ayres' ESI

As discussed earlier, even a good faith explanation for the willful destruction of ESI when the duty to preserve has attached does not alter the finding of willfulness.

Here, the deletion of Ayres' ESI was intentional: not only was potentially relevant ESI destroyed at the behest of an ADI employee after the duty to preserve had attached but such direction was given with *at least* the knowledge of ADI's then-President, Kevin Morrissey, if not his outright approval.

### 3. Sekisui's Failure to Ensure Preservation of Relevant Documents

Such failure constitutes gross negligence in these circumstances. While the failure to timely institute a litigation hold does not constitute gross negligence per se, the facts here are egregious and establish that Sekisui was grossly negligent. *First,* no litigation hold was issued by Sekisui until fifteen months after the Notice of Claim was sent to the Harts. Such failure is inexcusable given that Sekisui is the plaintiff in this action and, as such, had full knowledge of the possibility of future litigation. *Second,* once a litigation hold was issued, it took Sekisui another six months to notify its IT vendor-*i.e.,* the company responsible for actually preserving the relevant documents-of that duty to preserve. And, in the meantime, the ESI of *at least* two significant former ADI employees was destroyed at ADI's direction. As such, I find that (1) Sekisui's destruction of the Hart and Ayres ESI was intentional, and (2) its further failure to meet even the most basic document preservation obligations constitutes gross negligence.

## B. Relevance

There is no question that Hart's and Ayres' ESI is relevant. Ayres' ESI would be relevant because "Ayres previously had been the ADI employee responsible for ensuring ADI's compliance with FDA regulations." Indeed, there can be no doubt that Hart's and Ayres' ESI is relevant based solely on *whose* data was destroyed. *First,* Hart is not only a defendant in this action, but also is unable to testify on his own behalf due to a cognitive disorder. *Second,* Ayres' position at ADI is directly related to the claim in this action: Sekisui makes a claim for breach of contract, in part, on the basis that the Harts breached the Representation relating to FDA compliance, and Ayres was the ADI employee responsible for such compliance. Sekisui appears to concede the relevance of Hart's and Ayres' ESI in any event. Indeed, the real argument here has always been whether the destruction of that ESI prejudices the Harts.

## C. Prejudice

When evidence is destroyed intentionally, such destruction is sufficient evidence from which to conclude that the missing evidence was unfavorable to that party As such, once willfulness is established, no burden is imposed on the innocent party to point to now-destroyed evidence which is no longer available *because the other party destroyed it.* Rather, the "risk that the evidence would have been detrimental rather than favorable to the spoliator should fall on the party responsible for its loss." To shift the burden to the innocent party to describe or produce what has been lost as a result of the opposing party's willful or grossly negligent conduct is inappropriate because it incentivizes bad behavior on the part of would-be spoliators. That is, it "would allow parties who have destroyed evidence to profit from that destruction." Prejudice is presumed for the purposes of determining whether to give an adverse inference instruction when, as here, evidence is willfully destroyed by the spoliating party. As a result of the destruction of Hart's and Ayres' ESI, the Harts are left without an untold amount of contemporaneous evidence of ADI's operations prior to purchase by Sekisui. Despite the fact that Sekisui has made a real effort to minimize the harm done by that destruction, it is unable to rebut the presumption of prejudice because an unknowable amount of ESI of Hart, Ayres, and potentially others, was permanently destroyed and remains irretrievable. The Harts' inability to use the missing emails to attempt to prove "routine compliance" with FDA regulations may be as prejudicial to the Harts as depriving a party of access to a "smoking gun" document. The destruction of Hart's and Ayres' ESI was willful and prejudice is therefore presumed. I emphasize that prejudice is only presumed when determining *whether* an adverse inference instruction will be given. The jury may still determine that the Harts were not prejudiced by Sekisui's willful destruction of ESI and decline to draw any adverse inference.

## B. Sanctions Imposed

Accordingly, the Harts' request for an adverse inference jury instruction is granted. I will give the following jury charge:

> The Harts have shown that Sekisui destroyed relevant evidence. This is known as the "spoliation of evidence."

> Spoliation is the destruction of evidence or the failure to preserve property for another's use as evidence in pending or reasonably foreseeable litigation.

To demonstrate that spoliation occurred, several elements must be proven by a preponderance of the evidence:

*First,* that relevant evidence was destroyed after the duty to preserve arose.

*Second,* that the evidence lost would have been favorable to the Harts.

As to the first element I instruct you, as a matter of law, that Sekisui failed to preserve relevant evidence after its duty to preserve arose. This failure resulted from an employee's intentional directive given to ADI's information technology vendor to destroy the email files of—at least—Richard Hart and Leigh Ayres. Moreover, this failure resulted from Sekisui's gross negligence in performing its discovery obligations. I direct you that I have already found as a matter of law that this lost evidence is relevant to the issues in this case.

As to the second element, you may presume, if you so choose, that such lost evidence would have been favorable to the Harts. In deciding whether to adopt this presumption, you may take into account the egregiousness of the plaintiffs' conduct in failing to preserve the evidence.

Sekisui offered evidence that, although evidence was lost and it may have been relevant, nevertheless such evidence would not have been favorable to the Harts.

If you decline to presume that the lost evidence would have been favorable to the Harts, then your consideration of the lost evidence is at an end, and you will *not* draw any inference arising from the lost evidence.

However, if you decide to presume that the lost evidence would have been favorable to the Harts, you must next decide whether Sekisui rebutted that presumption. If you determine that Sekisui *rebutted* the presumption that the lost evidence was favorable to the Harts, you will *not* draw any inference arising from the lost evidence against Sekisui. If, on the other hand, you determine that Sekisui has *not rebutted* the presumption that the lost evidence was favorable to the Harts, you may draw an inference against Sekisui and in favor of the Harts-namely that the lost evidence would have been favorable to the Harts.

In addition, Sekisui is subject to monetary sanctions. The Harts are entitled to an award of reasonable costs, including attorneys' fees, associated with bringing this motion. The Harts shall submit a reasonable fee application to this Court for approval.

Sekisui's argument that the Harts were not prejudiced by the destruction of this ESI is not lost on this Court. Nor is the fact that Sekisui has recovered thousands of Hart's and Ayres' emails and thousands of other non-email documents. Sekisui remains free to make this argument to the jury and the jury remains free to accept that argument should it find, by a preponderance of the evidence, that the Harts were not prejudiced by Sekisui's failure to meet its discovery obligations.

## VI. CONCLUSION

In light of the foregoing, the Harts' request for sanctions in the form of an adverse inference jury instruction is granted

## 4. SANCTIONS RULE 37

10. When a party flagrantly disregards its discovery obligation, the court has inherent power, and power under Rule 37, to impose severe sanctions.

11. The first case in this section, *Antero v. Strudley,* perhaps has to do with something more moderate than a Rule 37 sanction. It discusses something called a "Lone Pine Order" that is available in federal courts, but not accepted by many state courts. There is no question that discovery can get out of hand. A large company may demand so much discovery from a small company that the small company simply folds. It is just too expensive for the small company to continue with the litigation – no matter what the merits may be.

    On the other side, a plaintiff may bring an essentially frivolous suit against a large company, assuming that the large company would rather just settle for a moderate amount, rather than going through the delay and expense caused by litigation. Rule 11 provides for sanctions, against any party, lawyer, or lawyer's law firm that files a frivolous suit. Rule 12 allows a court to grant a motion to dismiss right at the beginning of litigation if it is clear on the pleadings that the plaintiff has no case. When matters outside the pleadings are considered by a court, and the answer seems totally clear, the court may grant summary judgment to one side or the other under Rule 56.

    Yet federal courts, in some circumstances, are also allowed to use an additional tool, called a "Lone Pine Order" to try to help end inappropriate litigation. After initial disclosures have been made by both sides to the litigation, but before discovery begins, federal courts are allowed to issue Lone Pine Orders in some circumstances. Many state courts, including Colorado, do not permit the use of Lone Pine Orders, for the reasons explained below.

347 P.3D 149

SUPREME COURT OF COLORADO

ANTERO RESOURCES CORPORATION, ANTERO RESOURCES
PICEANCE CORPORATION, CALFRAC WELL SERVICES
CORPORATION, AND FRONTIER DRILLING LLC,
PETITIONERS

V.

WILLIAM G. STRUDLEY AND BETH E. STRUDLEY,
INDIVIDUALLY, AND AS THE PARENTS AND NATURAL
GUARDIANS OF WILLIAM STRUDLEY, A MINOR, AND
CHARLES STRUDLEY, A MINOR, RESPONDENTS

DECIDED APRIL 20, 2015

JUSTICE HOBBS delivered the Opinion of the Court.

We granted certiorari to consider whether a specialized type of modified case management order known as a "*Lone Pine* order" is authorized under the Colorado Rules of Civil Procedure and, if so, to assess whether the trial court abused its discretion by entering such an order in this case. *Lone Pine* orders developed from an unpublished opinion of the Superior Court of New Jersey, *Lore v. Lone Pine Corp.*, 1986 WL 637507 (N.J.Super. Ct. Law Div. Nov. 18, 1986). Entered after initial disclosures but before discovery, *Lone Pine* orders require plaintiffs in toxic tort cases to provide evidence sufficient to establish a prima facie case of injury, exposure, and causation, or else face dismissal of their claims. Federal Rule of Civil Procedure 16(c) authorizes their use in complex federal cases to reduce potential burdens on defendants, particularly in mass tort litigation.

After the initial exchange of Rule 26 disclosures, Antero Resources Corporation, Antero Resources Piceance Corporation, Calfrac Well Services Corporation, and Frontier Drilling LLC (collectively "Antero Resources") asked the trial court to enter a modified case management order requiring the plaintiffs ("the Strudleys") to present prima facie evidence that they suffered injuries attributable to the natural gas drilling operations of Antero Resources. The trial court granted the motion and issued a *Lone Pine* order that directed the Strudleys to provide prima facie evidence to support their allegations of exposure, injury, and causation before the court would allow full discovery. The trial court determined that the Strudleys failed to present sufficient evidence and dismissed their case with prejudice. The court of appeals reversed, concluding that, as a matter of first impression, *Lone Pine* orders "are not permitted as a matter of Colorado law." We agree with the court of appeals.

We hold that Colorado's Rules of Civil Procedure do not allow a trial court to issue a modified case management order, such as a *Lone Pine* order, that requires a plaintiff to present prima facie evidence in support of a claim before a plaintiff can exercise its full rights of discovery under the Colorado Rules. Although the comments to C.R.C.P. 16 promote active judicial case management, the rule does not provide a trial court with authority to fashion its own summary judgment-like filter and dismiss claims during the early stages of litigation.

I

William G. Strudley and Beth E. Strudley, individually, and as the parents of two minor children, sued Antero Resources, claiming they suffered physical injuries and property damage due to Antero Resources' natural gas drilling operations near their home. Specifically, the Strudleys allege that pollutants from the drilling site contaminated the air, water, and ground near their home, causing them to suffer burning eyes and throats, rashes, headaches, nausea, coughing, and bloody noses. Initial construction of the drilling operations began in August 2010, and the Strudleys assert that the pollution forced the family to move shortly thereafter, in January 2011. While the complaint identified several chemicals that allegedly polluted the property, it did not causally connect specific chemicals to actual injuries.

Both parties exchanged initial disclosures as required by the presumptive case management order in place under C.R.C.P. 16(b) and C.R.C.P. 26. Antero Resources then moved for a modified case management order under C.R.C.P. 16(c), requesting that the trial court issue a *Lone Pine* order requiring the Strudleys to present prima facie evidence to support their claims before discovery could continue. In support of its argument that there was substantial doubt as to whether the Strudleys could make a prima facie showing of exposure, injury, and causation, Antero Resources submitted a Colorado Oil and Gas Conservation Commission report finding no "oil & gas related impacts to the Strudleys' well." Additionally, Antero Resources submitted sworn testimony that it operated the wells in compliance with all applicable laws. Antero Resources expressed concern that discovery would be costly and burdensome for the defendant companies. The Strudleys objected contesting that under Colorado law and existing statutory procedures they had a right to engage in discovery central to their claims before the court could test the merits of their case.

Seeking to promote efficiency in what it determined to be a "complex toxic tort action involving numerous claims," the trial court issued a modified case management order. The order provided for evaluating the merits of the case at an early stage, requiring a prima facie showing—through expert opinions in the form of affidavits, studies and reports, and medical records—of each plaintiff's exposure to toxic chemicals as a result of Antero Resources' activities, as well as evidence of causation specific to those toxins for each plaintiff. It also required identification and quantification of the contamination of the Strudleys' real property attributable to the companies' operations. The order prohibited the Strudleys from conducting discovery until they made this prima facie showing of exposure and medical causation for each plaintiff.

Specifically, the modified case management order required the Strudleys to provide, within 105 days:

> i. Expert opinions provided by way of sworn affidavits, with supporting data and facts that establish *for each Plaintiff* (a) the identity of each hazardous substance from Defendants' activities to which he or she was exposed and which Plaintiff claims caused him or her injury; (b) whether any and each of these substances can cause the type(s) of disease or illness that Plaintiffs claim (general causation); (c) the dose or other quantitative measurement of the concentration, timing and duration of his/her exposure to each substance; (d) if other than the Plaintiffs' residence, the precise location of any exposure; (e) an identification, by way of reference to a medically recognized diagnosis, of the specific disease or illness from which each Plaintiff allegedly suffers or for which medical monitoring is purportedly necessary; and (f) a conclusion that such illness was in fact caused by such exposure (specific causation).

> ii. Each and every study, report and analysis that contains any finding of contamination on Plaintiffs' property or at the point of each Plaintiffs' claimed exposure.

> iii. A list of the name and last known address and phone number of each health care provider who provided each Plaintiff with health services along with a release authorizing the health care providers to provide Plaintiffs' and Defendants' counsel with all of each Plaintiff's medical records, in the form of Exhibit A hereto, within twenty-one days of the date of this Court's entry of this Modified Case Management Order.

> iv. Identification and quantification of contamination of the Plaintiffs' real property attributable to Defendants' operations.

The trial court noted that its requirement did not prejudice the Strudleys "because ultimately they will need to come forward with this data and expert opinions in order to establish their claims."

In response to the modified case management order, the Strudleys provided a variety of maps, photos, medical records, and air and water sample analysis reports. Additionally, the Strudleys submitted a letter from John G. Huntington, Ph.D. ("Dr. Huntington"), about the results of a water sample test conducted on December 7, 2011—nearly a year after the Strudleys had moved. Dr. Huntington stated that the water contained chemicals in amounts above the recommended concentrations but did not make conclusions as to the danger of the amounts or whether the chemicals caused the alleged injuries. The Strudleys also submitted an affidavit from Thomas L. Kurt, MD, MPH ("Dr. Kurt"), who, based on a description of the family's symptoms and color photographs of rashes and bloody noses, concluded that sufficient evidence existed to warrant further investigation. Dr. Kurt did not render an opinion as to whether chemical exposure caused the alleged injuries. The Strudleys did not provide an expert opinion concluding that they had been exposed to dangerous chemicals or that Antero Resources' conduct caused the alleged injuries and harm to the property.

Subsequently, Antero Resources filed a motion to dismiss, or in the alternative, for summary judgment, asserting that the Strudleys failed to comply with the modified case management order. The trial court granted the motion, rejecting the Strudleys' showing as insufficient and dismissing the action with prejudice presumably under C.R.C.P. 37, although the trial court did not cite any rule of civil procedure. In its analysis, the trial court relied heavily on *Lore v. Lone Pine Corp.*, the namesake unpublished opinion that created this type of modified case management order.

The Strudleys appealed. The court of appeals concluded that the trial court had exceeded its authority as a matter of law by issuing the *Lone Pine* order and that in the alternative the trial court erred by entering the *Lone Pine* order under the circumstances of this case. The court of appeals reversed the trial court's *Lone Pine* order along with the order of dismissal and reinstated the Strudleys' claims. We granted certiorari to resolve whether our Rules of Civil Procedure authorize the use of *Lone Pine* orders and, if so, whether the trial court in this case acted within its discretion in entering and enforcing such an order.

II

We hold that Colorado's Rules of Civil Procedure do not allow a trial court to issue a modified case management order, such as a *Lone Pine* order, that requires a plaintiff to present prima facie evidence in support of a claim before a plaintiff can exercise its full rights of discovery under the Colorado Rules. Although the comments to C.R.C.P. 16 promote active judicial case management, the rule does not provide a trial court with authority to fashion its own summary judgment-like filter and dismiss claims during the early stages of litigation.

A. Standard of Review (omitted)

B. Lone Pine Orders

*Lone Pine* orders under the Federal Rules are designed to manage complex issues and mitigate potential burdens on defendants and the court during the course of litigation. Colorado appellate courts have never authorized their use. In contrast, federal courts rely on Fed.R.Civ.P. 16(c)(2)(L) as authority to "adopt special procedures for managing potentially difficult or protracted actions that may involve complex issues, multiple parties, difficult legal questions, or unusual proof problems." The federal courts have discretion to use such orders in complex cases when discovery would likely be challenging, protracted, and expensive. *See, e.g., Acuna*, 200 F.3d at 340 (authorizing Lone Pine orders in a case involving 1600 plaintiffs suing over 100 defendants for a range of injuries occurring over a forty-year period).

Federal courts considering whether to issue *Lone Pine* orders seek to balance efficiency and equity. A court may decline to issue a *Lone Pine* order even in a complex case when other procedural devices can accommodate the unique issues of the litigation. Or it may decide to issue a *Lone Pine* order after extensive discovery. *See Vioxx*, (noting that after ten years and millions of pages of discovery, "it is not too much to ask a plaintiff to provide some kind of evidence to support his or her claim").

Only a handful of state courts have issued *Lone Pine* or similar orders. Even in jurisdictions where state courts have authority to issue *Lone Pine* orders, their use at an early stage of discovery may constitute an abuse of discretion.

C. Comparison of C.R.C.P. 16 and Fed.R.Civ.P. 16

While many Colorado Rules are patterned from Federal Rules, C.R.C.P. 16 contains critical differences from Fed.R.Civ.P. 16. When a Colorado Rule is modeled on a Federal Rule of Civil Procedure, we look to federal authority for guidance in construing the Colorado rule.

In revising C.R.C.P. 16 in 2002, we did not adopt a counterpart to Fed. R. Civ. P. 16(c), which explicitly grants trial courts substantial discretion to adopt procedures to streamline complex litigation in its early stages, "at any pretrial conference." Of importance here, Fed.R.Civ.P. 16(c)(2)(L) authorizes trial courts to "consider and take appropriate action" by "adopting special procedures for managing potentially difficult or protracted actions that may involve complex issues, multiple parties, difficult legal questions, or unusual proof problems." In addition, Fed.R.Civ.P. 16(c)(2)(A) grants trial courts authority to "formulate and simplify the issues, and eliminate frivolous claims or defenses." More generally, Fed.R.Civ.P. 16(c)(2)(P) authorizes trial courts to "facilitate in other ways the just, speedy, and inexpensive disposition of the action."

The language of C.R.C.P. 16 is markedly different from the language of Fed.R.Civ.P. 16. On its face, C.R.C.P. 16 does not contain a grant of authority for complex cases or otherwise afford trial courts the authority to require a plaintiff to make a prima facie showing before the plaintiff fully exercises discovery rights under the Colorado Rules. Instead, C.R.C.P. 16 primarily addresses basic scheduling matters. For instance, C.R.C.P. 16(b) creates a timeline of key trial-related events applicable to presumptive case management orders, including the "at issue date" for purposes of calculating deadlines; "meet and confer" date for counsel; trial setting; service of C.R.C.P. 26(a)(1) initial disclosures; disclosure of expert testimony in accordance with C.R.C.P. 26(a)(2); timing of initial settlement discussions; deadlines for joining additional parties, amending pleadings, and filing pretrial motions; and discovery schedule. Thus C.R.C.P. 16(c) accords the parties and the trial court flexibility to modify the presumptive order upon a showing of good cause "to allow the parties an appropriate amount of time to meet case management deadlines, including discovery, expert disclosures, and the filing of summary judgment motions." Rule 16(c) concludes by stating that "*the amounts of time allowed shall be within the discretion of the court* on a case-by-case basis"—indicating that any modifications would relate to time and schedule.

Neither subsection 16(b) nor 16(c) of our rules addresses a party's disclosure or discovery obligations beyond establishing deadlines and referencing C.R.C.P. 26, which contains general provisions governing discovery and disclosure. In the context of explaining Rule 16's goal of eliminating " 'hide-the-ball' and 'hardball' tactics" and to curtail abuses of the rules, the comments emphasize that trial judges are expected to "assertively lead the management of cases to ensure that justice is served."

In Colorado, case management orders under our Rule 16, whether presumptive or modified, are instruments courts employ to streamline litigation and ensure a just progression of a case. We amended the rule to "emphasize and foster professionalism and to de-emphasize sanctions for non-compliance," purposefully leaving adequate enforcement provisions in place. Indeed, an additional stated purpose of C.R.C.P. 16 is "to encourage cooperation among counsel and parties to facilitate disclosure, discovery, pretrial and trial procedures."

Together with amended Rule 26, our amended Rule 16 provides a tool for the court to manage discovery while efficiently advancing the litigation toward resolution, reflecting the development away from the seemingly unrestricted discovery that courts often endorsed in the past. Rule 16 does not, however, authorize a trial court to condition discovery upon the plaintiff establishing a prima facie case. In sum, when revising Rule 16 in 2002, we did not pattern our rule on Fed.R.Civ.P. 16(c).

## D. Other Colorado Rules of Civil Procedure

Colorado Rules of Civil Procedure other than Rule 16 allow trial courts to dispose of non-meritorious claims and issue sanctions for abuses. For example, C.R.C.P. 11 allows a trial court to sanction attorneys and their clients for filing pleadings that are not "well grounded in fact" or "warranted by existing law or a good faith argument for the extension, modification, or reversal of existing law," or pleadings that are "interposed for any improper purpose." C.R.C.P. 12(b)(5) allows a court to dismiss a claim for "failure to state a claim upon which relief can be granted." C.R.C.P. 56 allows defendants to challenge the sufficiency of a claim before trial through a motion for summary judgment. Additionally, expert disclosures required under Rule 26(a)(2) and all of the discovery-related rules, especially Rules 30, 33, 34, and 36, ensure that the discovery process operates within clearly defined limits. Likewise, Rule 37 allows a trial court to sanction a party for failure to make a disclosure or cooperate in discovery.

Thus, Colorado trial courts have a range of tools other than *Lone Pine* orders by which to actively manage cases.

## E. Colorado Case Law

Recently, we analyzed the scope of a party's right to discovery, explaining that the changes to the rules, including to C.R.C.P. 16, "reflect a growing effort to require active judicial management of pretrial matters" to reduce the cost of litigation. We construed the amended rules as narrowing the scope of discovery that parties are entitled to conduct. We held that C.R.C.P. 16 and 26 require a court to exercise control over discovery to prevent unnecessary or abusive discovery.

*DCP Midstream* is consistent with our previous acknowledgment that the rules vest trial courts with discretion to manage discovery in a way that balances competing goals: endeavoring to reduce discovery costs, simplify the issues, and promote expeditious settlement of cases, while also promoting the discovery of relevant evidence.

In *Direct Sales*, we looked at whether the plaintiff was entitled to certain financial information upon the mere filing of an unfair competition complaint. We held that, except where privilege applies, a plaintiff is entitled to the information, and it would be an abuse of discretion to require the plaintiff to establish a prima facie case of liability. Further, we emphasized that "the adoption of a prima facie case requirement would be contrary to the basic principles governing discovery," namely that "discovery rules should be construed liberally to effectuate the full extent of their truth-seeking purpose" and "in close cases, the balance must be struck in favor of allowing discovery."

F. Application to This Case

This case involves only four family members, four defendants, and one parcel of land, yet the trial court labeled it a "complex toxic tort action." The trial court made clear that focusing on the Strudleys' "admissible evidence concerning exposure and causation" might "*eliminate* or sharply curtail this case" (emphasis added). With this threat looming, and without the benefit of fully exercising their right to discovery under the rules, the Strudleys submitted evidence to the trial court in an attempt to comply with the order. The trial court compared that evidence with the evidence submitted in *Lone Pine* and concluded that the same "adequacy issues" plagued both cases.

But because no statute, rule, or past Colorado case recognizes authority for trial courts to enter *Lone Pine* orders, we conclude that the trial court lacked authority to enter a *Lone Pine* order in this case. Whether presumptive or modified, case management orders under Rule 16 are instruments courts employ to streamline litigation and ensure the just progression of a case—not to eliminate claims or dismiss a case independent of mechanisms for eliminating claims and dismissing cases under the rules. We share the concerns of other courts that have found *Lone Pine* orders unauthorized by their existing rules. Indeed, if a *Lone Pine* order cuts off or severely limits the litigant's right to discovery, the order closely resembles summary judgment, albeit without the safeguards supplied by the Rules of Civil Procedure. In Colorado, existing rules and procedural safeguards provide sufficient protection against frivolous or unsupported claims and burdensome discovery. Like the court in *Roth*, "we find it preferable to yield to the consistency and safeguards of the rules of civil procedure, as well as the court's own flexibility and discretion to address discovery disputes as they arise, as opposed to entering a rigid and exacting *Lone Pine* order."

The Colorado Rules of Civil Procedure grant courts flexibility and discretion to address discovery disputes as they arise. But this judicial authority is limited; it does not allow a court to require a plaintiff to establish a prima facie case in the early stages of litigation while simultaneously barring discovery that might expose the very support sought to prove a claim. C.R.C.P. 16 does not currently authorize *Lone*

*Pine* orders. Interpreting Rule 16 to allow *Lone Pine* orders would interfere with the rights provided to litigants and produce consequences unintended by our rules by forcing dismissal before affording plaintiffs the opportunity to establish the merits of their cases.

Accordingly, we affirm the judgment of the court of appeals.

12. Now for some entertaining cases on really bad discovery abuses – and the sanctions imposed.


### 633 F. SUPP. 2D 124
### UNITED STATES DISTRICT COURT, S.D. NEW YORK
### ARISTA RECORDS LLC, ATLANTIC RECORDING CORPORATION, BMG MUSIC, CAPITOL RECORDS, LLC, CAROLINE RECORDS, INC., ELEKTRA ENTERTAINMENT GROUP INC., INTERSCOPE RECORDS, LAFACE RECORDS LLC, MAVERICK RECORDING COMPANY, SONY BMG MUSIC ENTERTAINMENT, UMG RECORDS, INC., VIRGIN RECORDS AMERICA, INC., WARNER BROS. RECORDS, INC., AND ZOMBA RECORDING LLC, PLAINTIFFS,
### V.
### USENET.COM, INC., SIERRA CORPORATE DESIGN, INC., AND GERALD REYNOLDS, DEFENDANTS.


DECIDED JUNE 30, 2009


**HAROLD BAER, JR., District Judge.**

This action arises out of allegations of widespread infringement of copyrights in sound recordings owned by Plaintiffs Arista Records LLC; Atlantic Recordings Corporation; BMG Music; Capitol Records, LLC; Caroline Records; Elektra Entertainment Group Inc.; Interscope Records; LaFace Records LLC; Maverick Recording Company; Sony BMG Music Entertainment; UMG Recordings, Inc; Virgin Records America, Inc.; Warner Bros. Records Inc; and Zomba Recording LLC ("Plaintiffs"), copies of which are available for download by accessing a network of computers called the USENET through services provided by Defendants Usenet.com, Inc. ("UCI"), Sierra Corporate

Design, Inc. ("Sierra"), and spearheaded by their director and sole shareholder, Gerald Reynolds ("Reynolds") (collectively, "Defendants"). Specifically, Plaintiffs brought this action alleging (1) direct infringement of the Plaintiffs' exclusive right of distribution under 17 U.S.C. § 106(3); (2) inducement of copyright infringement; (3) contributory copyright infringement; and (4) vicarious copyright infringement. There are two motions by Plaintiffs before me-one for termination due to discovery abuse, and another for summary judgment-with a cross-motion for summary judgment from the Defendants. Defendants' [FN3] cross-motion for summary judgment argues that they are entitled to the safe harbor protections of § 512(c) of the Digital Millennium Copyright Act ("DMCA"). All parties filed numerous additional motions to exclude certain testimony, as well as voluminous evidentiary objections. Plaintiffs opine that their motion for terminating sanctions alleges discovery abuse sufficient to require that I strike the Defendants' answer and enter a default judgment in their favor ("Terminating Sanctions Motion"). For the reasons set forth below, Plaintiffs' Terminating Sanctions Motion is granted to the extent discussed in this opinion, though not in its entirety; Plaintiffs' motion for summary judgment is granted with respect to all claims; and Defendants' motion for summary judgment is dismissed as moot.

FN3. On May 21, 2009, Sierra filed a Suggestion of Bankruptcy in this matter advising the Court that it has filed a petition pursuant to chapter 7 of the Bankruptcy Code in the District of North Dakota. Pursuant to 11 U.S.C. § 362, an automatic stay is therefore in place with respect to Sierra, and it is not subject to the Court's Order and Opinion.

## II. MOTION FOR TERMINATING SANCTIONS

### A. Factual Background Relating to Spoliation of Evidence and Discovery Misconduct

As noted earlier, Defendants have once been sanctioned for spoliation of certain relevant and potentially highly incriminating data. However, upon the close of discovery and after having learned of certain even more egregious discovery violations, Plaintiffs filed their Terminating Sanctions Motion, this time seeking entry of a default judgment against Defendants based on widespread spoliation of evidence and gross discovery misconduct.

Plaintiffs allege that despite numerous requests for production, Defendants continually "stonewalled" discovery by failing to produce responsive documents or identify critical witnesses. Defendants' constant refrain was that they had produced all responsive documents. Only upon deposing Defendants' former assistant newsmaster and email administrator, Jessica Heiberg, did Plaintiffs experience what they characterize as a "watershed moment" in the case. Heiberg's testimony confirmed that Defendants' employees regularly used internal email for work-related matters, that a significant number of Defendants' employees stored their emails on their local computer hard drives, and that she had personally checked employees' work stations to ensure they were implementing proper email retention policies. Heiberg also identified other key internal documents that Defendants had not produced.

### 1. The Seven "Wiped" Hard Drives

Based on the revelation of this new evidence, Plaintiffs promptly filed a motion to compel production of responsive documents stored on Defendants' employee hard drives. A hearing was held. At this hearing, Defendants' counsel acknowledged for the first time that he was in possession of seven computer hard drives that had belonged to Defendants' employees (the "Seven Hard Drives"). Initially, Defendants conceded that four of the Seven Hard Drives had had their contents deleted or "wiped" and suggested they would produce documents from the remaining three drives. Later, Defendants admitted that the remaining three drives had the majority of their contents deleted, as well. Defendants hired a forensic expert to examine the drives, and were able to extract approximately 300,000 file fragments from the remaining three drives. These files consisted largely of fragments of deleted files and were largely unusable; however, Plaintiffs' forensic expert's analysis revealed that the file fragments contained pieces of incriminating documents, including emails and word processing documents that had been stored on the hard drives.

Over time, Defendants have proffered numerous explanations for the "wiping" of the hard drives. First, Defendants represented that the hard drives had been found in storage, and that they had been purchased blank on eBay and never used. Defendants later recanted this position and admitted that the Seven Hard Drives had all been pulled directly from the active workstations of Defendants' employees in June 2008, at the direction of Reynolds.

In opposing the Terminating Sanctions Motion, Defendants now espouse a different story-they now contend that the drives "would have appeared wiped" as a result of Defendants having upgraded all employee computers to the new Windows Vista operating system in early 2008. Analysis by Plaintiffs' forensic expert reveals that this explanation simply is not plausible.

In addition to the Seven Hard Drives that were purposefully wiped, the record evidence indicates that Defendants purposefully ensured that other of its work-issued computers became unavailable for production. For example, in March 2008, at the outset of discovery, Defendants terminated several key employees, including its chief technology officer Miro Stoichev and Jessica Heiberg and rather than preserving the data on their computers, Defendants allowed these and other terminated employees to take their computers with them, as "parting gifts." This was without making certain that the material was preserved.

### 4. Litigation Misconduct

In addition to these allegations of stonewalling and spoliation, Plaintiffs also allege that Defendants engaged in other misconduct to "pursue a clear strategy to prevent plaintiffs from discovering evidence demonstrating the true extent to which defendants fostered copyright infringement." First, Plaintiffs allege that at the time they began to serve third-party subpoenas, only five individuals were still employed by Sierra, other than Reynolds, all of whom were potentially significant witnesses. Plaintiffs allege that Defendants engineered these witnesses' unavailability during the height of discovery by causing them to travel to Europe on an expense-paid vacation to avoid being deposed. Defendants do not deny sending their employees out of the country during this critical period, but note that the employees returned from Europe in mid-August, a full two months before the end of the initial discovery period. However, Plaintiffs' information suggests that Defendants attempted to persuade the employees to remain out of the jurisdiction for a longer period, illustrating one more in what appears to be a series of bad faith tactics. Further, upon the employees' return, two of them-Leidholm and Richter-allegedly evaded service. Further, Reynolds, testifying as a Rule 30(b)(6) designee, provided misleading information concerning these witnesses' contact information and employment status. Plaintiffs allege that Defendants went to great lengths to shield former President Kraft from discovery by providing misleading information as to her employment and whereabouts. Although Ms. Kraft ultimately was deposed, Plaintiffs cite these actions as further evidence of bad faith.

In addition to witness misconduct, Plaintiffs also allege that Defendants knowingly served false responses to interrogatories. Specifically, Plaintiffs allege that Defendants never identified two employees - Ina Danova and Jolene Goldade - who together made up Sierra's marketing department, and who Plaintiffs later learned drafted incriminating promotional "essays," at Reynolds's request.

## B. Legal Standard

Terminating sanctions are used "only in extreme circumstances, usually after consideration of alternative, less drastic sanctions." However, "in this day of burgeoning, costly and protracted litigation courts should not shrink from imposing harsh sanctions where they are clearly warranted."

Lesser sanctions have been found to be ill-suited to cases involving bad faith irretrievable spoliation of likely important documents.

## C. Analysis

While I agree that Plaintiffs' evidence credibly illustrates a pattern of destruction of critical evidence, a failure to preserve other relevant documents and communications, and at best dilatory (and at worst, bad-faith) tactics with respect to Defendants' conduct during discovery, I am not prepared to impose the ultimate sanction.

### 3. Appropriate Sanction

Having determined that the imposition of sanctions is warranted in this case, the Court must next determine the appropriate remedy. As noted, tailoring an appropriate sanction lies within the sound discretion of the trial court, and is to be assessed on a case-by-case basis.

In the interest of saving trees (an interest the parties apparently do not share), I will not rule on each motion individually. Rather, I assure the parties that I am fully capable of separating the wheat from the chaff, and will consider only the evidence-both testimony and exhibits-admissible on summary judgment.

Accordingly, the record evidence reveals no genuine issue of material fact as to any of Plaintiffs' theories of direct or secondary liability for copyright infringement on the part of Defendants UCI and Reynolds. Plaintiffs are therefore entitled to summary judgment as a matter of law, and the only remaining question is the extent of Defendants' liability for damages.

13. The next case may be referred to as the "whack-a-mole" case.

## 776 F.3D 1
## UNITED STATES COURT OF APPEALS,
## DISTRICT OF COLUMBIA CIRCUIT
## WASHINGTON METROPOLITAN AREA TRANSIT COMMISSION,
## APPELLEE
## V.
## RELIABLE LIMOUSINE SERVICE, LLC AND PAUL BENJAMIN
## RODBERG, APPELLANTS.

DECIDED JANUARY 13, 2015

KAREN LECRAFT HENDERSON, Circuit Judge:

> The Wise do at once what the Fool does at last.
>
> —Baltasar Gracian
> *The Art of Worldly Wisdom*, cclxvii

Paul Rodberg operated a limousine business in the District of Columbia metropolitan area (District) for many years without authorization from the Washington Metropolitan Area Transit Commission (WMATC). WMATC eventually sued Rodberg and his company in district court, seeking an injunction to shut down his illegal limousine operation. After Rodberg failed to participate in discovery, the district court entered default judgment against him. Not to be outfoxed, Rodberg ignored the default judgment and continued operating his limousine business under a different name. The district court issued yet another order, making perfectly clear that *all* of Rodberg's companies were enjoined from transporting passengers in the District without a license. Rodberg now appeals the default judgment and the subsequent order. We affirm the district court's default judgment and lack jurisdiction to consider the subsequent order.

## I. BACKGROUND

Rodberg is in the limousine business. He has owned several iterations of a company providing limousine service in the District. From 1996 to 2009, Rodberg operated Reliable Limousine, Inc. (RLI). RLI repeatedly failed to pay its federal taxes. The Internal Revenue Service eventually caught up with Rodberg but, instead of paying the taxes owed, Rodberg shifted his limousine business to a new company: Reliable

Limousine Service, LLC (RLS). RLS operated from 2009 to 2011 but it too failed to pay taxes. The IRS again pursued and Rodberg again shifted his business to a new company: Reliable Limousine and Bus Service, LLC (RLBS). The United States sued Rodberg, RLI, RLS and RLBS in the District of Maryland, seeking injunctive relief to force their compliance with the tax laws. At one point in the litigation, the district court held Rodberg in contempt for "willfully and deliberately" refusing to participate in discovery. Rodberg and the United States ultimately settled.

Rodberg's legal woes did not end there. His limousine companies not only failed to pay their taxes but also transported passengers within the District without a license. In April 2012, WMATC sued Rodberg and RLS in the district court here, seeking an injunction to shut down Rodberg's limousine operation. The district court originally set the discovery deadline for November 2012. In October 2012, WMATC served Rodberg with interrogatories and document requests. Rodberg never responded. In December, the district court ordered Rodberg to participate in discovery, extended the discovery deadline to January 2013 and set the case for trial in March 2013. Rodberg remained non-compliant. He claimed he was not participating in discovery because he was at that point applying for a WMATC license. In February 2013, the district court rejected Rodberg's excuse and sanctioned him by awarding WMATC a default judgment. The default judgment included a permanent injunction that prohibited Rodberg and RLS from transporting passengers for hire in the District.[2]

But WMATC's victory was short-lived. It soon discovered what the IRS knew all too well: pursuing Rodberg was like playing whack-a-mole. Rodberg continued to provide limousine service in the District via *RLBS,* not *RLS.* This prompted WMATC to return to district court to seek a contempt citation. Instead, the district court decided to "clarify" its February injunction. *WMATC v. Reliable Limo. Serv., LLC,* 985 F.Supp.2d 23, 31–32 (D.D.C.2013). In October 2013, it issued an order expressly placing RLBS under the February 2013 injunction's prohibition on transporting passengers for hire.

Rodberg appealed.

## II. ANALYSIS

Rodberg contests the district court's entry of default judgment as a sanction for his discovery lapse. Although he does not dispute that his conduct was sanctionable, Rodberg argues that the punishment does not fit the crime.

We review the district court's imposition of discovery sanctions, including a default judgment award, for abuse of discretion. We then conduct an independent review to determine whether the district court abused its discretion. Because the parties do not dispute Rodberg's willfulness, we turn to the district court's choice of sanction.

To determine whether the district court abused its discretion by entering default judgment as a discovery sanction, we evaluate the following factors: (1) prejudice to the opposing party, (2) prejudice to the judicial system and (3) the need for punishment and deterrence. These factors are non-exhaustive and we must consider "all the relevant circumstances" surrounding the entry of default judgment. Still, we pay "great deference" to the district court's decision because it has "a better 'feel' for the litigation and the remedial actions most appropriate under the circumstances presented." After a careful review of the *Shea* factors, we are convinced that the district court did not abuse its discretion by entering default judgment against Rodberg.

## Prejudice to the Opposing Party

Rodberg's recalcitrance prejudiced WMATC in a direct and obvious manner. Each day of delay was another day that Rodberg illegally operated his limousine business. Granted, delay that merely prolongs litigation "is not a sufficient basis for establishing prejudice." But, here, there was more: in transporting passengers in the District without a license, Rodberg jeopardized the public safety. The first *Shea* factor weighs in favor of the district court's decision.

## Prejudice to the Judicial System

Rodberg also interfered with the district court's ability to manage its docket. In February 2013—one month before trial—Rodberg had not responded to any of WMATC's requested discovery. The district court was thus faced with a choice: enter default judgment or postpone the trial. We have described such a choice as "intolerable." Litigants do not exist in a vacuum; misconduct like Rodberg's can reverberate throughout the judicial system. "Litigants who are willful in halting the discovery process in this era of crowded dockets deprive other litigants of an opportunity to use the courts as a serious dispute-settlement mechanism. This is not a case in which the district court could have addressed Rodberg's misconduct by simply granting a continuance. The district court had already moved the discovery deadline twice. The district court had no reason to expect that, if it granted yet another continuance, Rodberg would meet his discovery responsibilities. *See Automated Datatron, Inc. v. Woodcock,*("It was not an abuse of discretion to rule that two weeks short of trial was too late to take certain action when the court had directed the litigant to take that action half a year earlier."); *Lee v. Max Int'l, LLC,* ("Three strikes are more than enough to allow the district court to call a litigant out."). Accordingly, the second *Shea* factor also weighs in favor of the district court's decision.

Deterrence and Punishment

Discovery sanctions serve two purposes: punishing disobedient parties and deterring others from emulating their behavior. On the spectrum of discovery misconduct, Rodberg's behavior was egregious. His refusal to participate in discovery was not only willful but appeared to be a calculated move to delay for the sake of delay. This factor weighs most strongly in favor of the district court's decision.

Notably, Rodberg has yet to offer a plausible excuse for his failure to participate in discovery. He claimed in district court that he was not participating because he first wanted to hear from WMATC about his license application. The district court correctly rejected this excuse. Litigants cannot pick and choose the legal proceedings they want to participate in at any given time. *See Harrington v. City of Chicago,* ("the pendency of other cases did not justify the litigant's failure to respond to written discovery requests throughout the discovery period"). Rodberg's non-excuse suggests that his motivation was far from bona fide and thus deserving of harsh sanctions.

In addition, Rodberg is a discovery repeat offender. In 2012, the District of Maryland held Rodberg in contempt for deliberately ignoring the IRS's discovery requests. Rodberg's history of discovery misconduct indicates that his lawlessness needs the harshest sanction to make him comply. *See Johnson v. CIR,* ("Dogged good-faith persistence in bad conduct becomes sanctionable once the guilty party learns or should have learned that it is sanctionable. Moreover, Rodberg ignored his discovery obligations in the IRS litigation while he was represented by different counsel, manifesting that Rodberg *himself* is the person responsible for his discovery delicts. This is not a case in which "an unwitting litigant is made to suffer for the sins of her attorney." ("We look disfavorably upon dismissals as sanctions for attorney misconduct or delay *unless the client himself has been made aware of the problem, usually through notice from the trial court.*" Rodberg's history of self-directed discovery misconduct plainly supports the district court's sanction of default judgment in this case.

Rodberg offers two responses, both unpersuasive. He claims that the district court violated two hard-and-fast rules in entering default judgment against him. Neither "rule," however, exists under our case law.

First, Rodberg argues that the district court had a duty to impose a lesser sanction before opting for default judgment. We have repeatedly rejected this proposition. Although the district court must *explain* why a lesser sanction is inadequate, it has no duty to impose it first, entering default judgment only after the lesser sanction fails.

Second, Rodberg contends that the district court erroneously entered default judgment based on a *single* violation of the discovery rules. Rodberg is mistaken, both legally and factually. We have never held that a district court cannot enter default judgment based on a single discovery violation. Granted, we have said that "under certain circumstances, dismissal may be an unduly severe sanction for a single episode of misconduct." But we have also affirmed a dismissal based on "a single incident of misconduct" if a "disruption of the judicial system" or "clear client responsibility for the misconduct" occurred. As noted, both factors—disruption of the judicial system and clear client responsibility—are present here.

In any event, Rodberg wrongly argues that he has committed only one discovery violation. Rodberg violated the discovery rules in January 2013 when he ignored the district court's order compelling discovery. Two months earlier, however, Rodberg also violated the discovery rules by failing to respond to WMATC's interrogatories. A litigant can be sanctioned for failing to respond to interrogatories even without a court order. Indeed, we have emphasized the heightened need for a sanction that bites in this context:

> If parties are allowed to flout their discovery obligations, choosing to wait to make a response to interrogatories until a trial court has lost patience with them, the effect will be to embroil trial judges in day-to-day supervision of discovery, a result directly contrary to the overall scheme of the federal discovery rules.

Additionally, as noted, Rodberg previously committed discovery violations in the IRS litigation. The district court properly took his earlier misconduct into account, even though it occurred in a different case and in a different federal court.

For these reasons, we conclude that the district court did not abuse its discretion when it entered default judgment against Rodberg as a sanction for his total discovery lapse. We therefore affirm the district court's February 2013 order awarding permanent injunctive relief.

14. Now watch the bodies fall in this next case. Note what happens to three of the attorneys involved.

111 S.CT. 2123
SUPREME COURT OF THE UNITED STATES
G. RUSSELL CHAMBERS, PETITIONER,
V.
NASCO, INC.

DECIDED JUNE 6, 1991

**Justice WHITE delivered the opinion of the Court.**

This case requires us to explore the scope of the inherent power of a federal court
to sanction a litigant for bad-faith conduct. Specifically, we are asked to determine
whether the District Court, sitting in diversity, properly invoked its inherent power
in assessing as a sanction for a party's bad-faith conduct attorney's fees and related
expenses paid by the party's opponent to its attorneys. We hold that the District
Court acted within its discretion, and we therefore affirm the judgment of the Court
of Appeals.

I

This case began as a simple action for specific performance of a contract, but it did
not remain so. Petitioner G. Russell Chambers was the sole shareholder and director of Calcasieu Television and Radio, Inc. (CTR), which operated television station
KPLC–TV in Lake Charles, Louisiana. On August 9, 1983, Chambers, acting both in
his individual capacity and on behalf of CTR, entered into a purchase agreement to
sell the station's facilities and broadcast license to respondent NASCO, Inc., for a purchase price of $18 million. The agreement was not recorded in the parishes in which
the two properties housing the station's facilities were located. Consummation of the
agreement was subject to the approval of the Federal Communications Commission
(FCC); both parties were obligated to file the necessary documents with the FCC no
later than September 23, 1983. By late August, however, Chambers had changed his
mind and tried to talk NASCO out of consummating the sale. NASCO refused. On
September 23, Chambers, through counsel, informed NASCO that he would not file
the necessary papers with the FCC.

NASCO decided to take legal action. On Friday, October 14, 1983, NASCO's counsel informed counsel for Chambers and CTR that NASCO would file suit the following Monday in the United States District Court for the Western District of Louisiana,

seeking specific performance of the agreement, as well as a temporary restraining order (TRO) to prevent the alienation or encumbrance of the properties at issue. NASCO provided this notice in accordance with Federal Rule of Civil Procedure 65 and Rule 11 of the District Court's Local Rules, both of which are designed to give a defendant in a TRO application notice of the hearing and an opportunity to be heard.

The reaction of Chambers and his attorney, A.J. Gray III, was later described by the District Court as having "emasculated and frustrated the purposes of these rules and the powers of the District Court by utilizing this notice to prevent NASCO's access to the remedy of specific performance." On Sunday, October 16, 1983, the pair acted to place the properties at issue beyond the reach of the District Court by means of the Louisiana Public Records Doctrine. Because the purchase agreement had never been recorded, they determined that if the properties were sold to a third party, and if the deeds were recorded before the issuance of a TRO, the District Court would lack jurisdiction over the properties.

To this end, Chambers and Gray created a trust, with Chambers' sister as trustee and Chambers' three adult children as beneficiaries. The pair then directed the president of CTR, who later became Chambers' wife, to execute warranty deeds conveying the two tracts at issue to the trust for a recited consideration of $1.4 million. Early Monday morning, the deeds were recorded. The trustee, as purchaser, had not signed the deeds; none of the consideration had been paid; and CTR remained in possession of the properties. Later that morning, NASCO's counsel appeared in the District Court to file the complaint and seek the TRO. With NASCO's counsel present, the District Judge telephoned Gray. Despite the judge's queries concerning the possibility that CTR was negotiating to sell the properties to a third person, Gray made no mention of the recordation of the deeds earlier that morning. That afternoon, Chambers met with his sister and had her sign the trust documents and a $1.4 million note to CTR. The next morning, Gray informed the District Court by letter of the recordation of the deeds the day before and admitted that he had intentionally withheld the information from the court.

Within the next few days, Chambers' attorneys prepared a leaseback agreement from the trustee to CTR, so that CTR could remain in possession of the properties and continue to operate the station. The following week, the District Court granted a preliminary injunction against Chambers and CTR and entered a second TRO to prevent the trustee from alienating or encumbering the properties. At that hearing, the District Judge warned that Gray's and Chambers' conduct had been unethical.

Despite this early warning, Chambers, often acting through his attorneys, continued to abuse the judicial process. In November 1983, in defiance of the preliminary injunction, he refused to allow NASCO to inspect CTR's corporate records.

The ensuing civil contempt proceedings resulted in the assessment of a $25,000 fine against Chambers personally.

Undeterred, Chambers proceeded with "a series of meritless motions and pleadings and delaying actions." These actions triggered further warnings from the court. At one point, acting *sua sponte,* the District Judge called a status conference to find out why bankers were being deposed. When informed by Chambers' counsel that the purpose was to learn whether NASCO could afford to pay for the station, the court canceled the depositions consistent with its authority under Federal Rule of Civil Procedure 26(g).

At the status conference nine days before the April 1985 trial date, [FN2] the District Judge again warned counsel that further misconduct would not be tolerated.[FN3] Finally, on the eve of trial, Chambers and CTR stipulated that the purchase agreement was enforceable and that Chambers had breached the agreement on September 23, 1983, by failing to file the necessary papers with the FCC. At trial, the only defense presented by Chambers was the Public Records Doctrine.

FN2. The trial date itself reflected delaying tactics. Trial had been set for February 1985, but in January, Gray, on behalf of Chambers, filed a motion to recuse the judge. The motion was denied, as was the subsequent writ of mandamus filed in the Court of Appeals.

FN3. To make his point clear, the District Judge gave counsel copies of Judge Schwarzer's then-recent article, Sanctions Under the New Federal Rule 11—A Closer Look, 104 F.R.D. 181 (1985).

In the interlude between the trial and the entry of judgment during which the District Court prepared its opinion, Chambers sought to render the purchase agreement meaningless by seeking permission from the FCC to build a new transmission tower for the station and to relocate the transmission facilities to that site, which was not covered by the agreement. Only after NASCO sought contempt sanctions did Chambers withdraw the application.

The District Court entered judgment on the merits in NASCO's favor, finding that the transfer of the properties to the trust was a simulated sale and that the deeds purporting to convey the property were "null, void, and of no effect." Chambers' motions, filed in the District Court, the Court of Appeals, and this Court, to stay the judgment pending appeal were denied. Undeterred, Chambers convinced CTR officials to file formal oppositions to NASCO's pending application for FCC approval of the transfer of the station's license, in contravention of both the District Court's injunctive orders and its judgment on the merits. NASCO then sought contempt sanctions for a third time, and the oppositions were withdrawn.

When Chambers refused to prepare to close the sale, NASCO again sought the court's help. A hearing was set for July 16, 1986, to determine whether certain equipment was to be included in the sale. At the beginning of the hearing, the court informed Chambers' new attorney, Edwin A. McCabe,[FN4] that further sanctionable conduct would not be tolerated. When the hearing was recessed for several days, Chambers, without notice to the court or NASCO, removed from service at the station all of the equipment at issue, forcing the District Court to order that the equipment be returned to service.

FN4. Gray had resigned as counsel for Chambers and CTR several months previously.

Immediately following oral argument on Chambers' appeal from the District Court's judgment on the merits, the Court of Appeals, ruling from the bench, found the appeal frivolous. The court imposed appellate sanctions in the form of attorney's fees and double costs, pursuant to Federal Rule of Appellate Procedure 38, and remanded the case to the District Court with orders to fix the amount of appellate sanctions and to determine whether further sanctions should be imposed for the manner in which the litigation had been conducted.

On remand, NASCO moved for sanctions, invoking the District Court's inherent power, Fed.Rule Civ.Proc. 11, and 28 U.S.C. § 1927. After full briefing and a hearing, the District Court determined that sanctions were appropriate "for the manner in which this proceeding was conducted in the district court from October 14, 1983, the time that plaintiff gave notice of its intention to file suit to this date." At the end of an extensive opinion recounting what it deemed to have been sanctionable conduct during this period, the court imposed sanctions against Chambers in the form of attorney's fees and expenses totaling $996,644.65, which represented the entire amount of NASCO's litigation costs paid to its attorneys.[FN5] In so doing, the court rejected Chambers' argument that he had merely followed the advice of counsel, labeling him "the strategist," behind a scheme devised "first, to deprive this Court of jurisdiction and, second, to devise a plan of obstruction, delay, harassment, and expense sufficient to reduce NASCO to a condition of exhausted compliance."

FN5. The court also sanctioned other individuals, who are not parties to the action in this Court. Chambers' sister, the trustee, was sanctioned by a reprimand; **attorney Gray was disbarred and prohibited from seeking readmission for three years; attorney Richard A. Curry, who represented the trustee, was suspended from**

**practice before the court for six months; and attorney McCabe was suspended for five years.** Although these sanctions did not affect the bank accounts of these individuals, they were nevertheless substantial sanctions and were as proportionate to the conduct at issue as was the monetary sanction imposed on Chambers. *Indeed, in the case of the disbarment of attorney Gray, the court recognized that the penalty was among the harshest possible sanctions and one which derived from its authority to supervise those admitted to practice before it.*

In imposing the sanctions, the District Court first considered Federal Rule of Civil Procedure 11. It noted that the alleged sanctionable conduct was that Chambers and the other defendants had "(1) attempted to deprive this Court of jurisdiction by acts of fraud, nearly all of which were performed outside the confines of this Court, (2) filed false and frivolous pleadings, and (3) attempted, by other tactics of delay, oppression, harassment and massive expense to reduce plaintiff to exhausted compliance." The court recognized that the conduct in the first and third categories could not be reached by Rule 11, which governs only papers filed with a court. As for the second category, the court explained that the falsity of the pleadings at issue did not become apparent until after the trial on the merits, so that it would have been impossible to assess sanctions at the time the papers were filed. Consequently, the District Court deemed Rule 11 "insufficient" for its purposes. The court likewise declined to impose sanctions under § 1927,[FN6] both because the statute applies only to attorneys, and therefore would not reach Chambers, and because the statute was not broad enough to reach "acts which degrade the judicial system," including "attempts to deprive the Court of jurisdiction, fraud, misleading and lying to the Court." The court therefore relied on its inherent power in imposing sanctions, stressing that "the wielding of that inherent power is particularly appropriate when the offending parties have practiced a fraud upon the court."

FN6. That statute provides:

**"Any attorney ... who so multiplies the proceedings in any case unreasonably and vexatiously may be required by the court to satisfy personally the excess costs, expenses, and attorneys' fees reasonably incurred because of such conduct." 28 U.S.C. § 1927.**

The Court of Appeals affirmed. Because of the importance of these issues, we granted certiorari.

# II

Chambers maintains that 28 U.S.C. § 1927 and the various sanctioning provisions in the Federal Rules of Civil Procedure reflect a legislative intent to displace the inherent power. At least, he argues that they obviate or foreclose resort to the inherent power in this case. We agree with the Court of Appeals that neither proposition is persuasive.

## A

It has long been understood that "certain implied powers must necessarily result to our Courts of justice from the nature of their institution," powers "which cannot be dispensed with in a Court, because they are necessary to the exercise of all others." For this reason, "Courts of justice are universally acknowledged to be vested, by their very creation, with power to impose silence, respect, and decorum, in their presence, and submission to their lawful mandates." These powers are "governed not by rule or statute but by the control necessarily vested in courts to manage their own affairs so as to achieve the orderly and expeditious disposition of cases."

Prior cases have outlined the scope of the inherent power of the federal courts. For example, the Court has held that a federal court has the power to control admission to its bar and to discipline attorneys who appear before it. While this power "ought to be exercised with great caution," it is nevertheless "incidental to all Courts."

In addition, it is firmly established that "the power to punish for contempts is inherent in all courts." This power reaches both conduct before the court and that beyond the court's confines, for "the underlying concern that gave rise to the contempt power was not merely the disruption of court proceedings. Rather, it was disobedience to the orders of the Judiciary, regardless of whether such disobedience interfered with the conduct of trial."

Of particular relevance here, the inherent power also allows a federal court to vacate its own judgment upon proof that a fraud has been perpetrated upon the court. This "historic power of equity to set aside fraudulently begotten judgments," is necessary to the integrity of the courts, for "tampering with the administration of justice in this manner involves far more than an injury to a single litigant. It is a wrong against the institutions set up to protect and safeguard the public." Moreover, a court has the power to conduct an independent investigation in order to determine whether it has been the victim of fraud.

There are other facets to a federal court's inherent power. The court may bar from the courtroom a criminal defendant who disrupts a trial. It may dismiss an action on grounds of *forum non conveniens, Gulf Oil Corp. v. Gilbert;* and it may act *sua sponte* to dismiss a suit for failure to prosecute.

Because of their very potency, inherent powers must be exercised with restraint and discretion. A primary aspect of that discretion is the ability to fashion an appropriate sanction for conduct which abuses the judicial process. As we recognized in *Roadway Express,* outright dismissal of a lawsuit, which we had upheld in *Link,* is a particularly severe sanction, yet is within the court's discretion. Consequently, the "less severe sanction" of an assessment of attorney's fees is undoubtedly within a court's inherent power as well.

Indeed, "there are ample grounds for recognizing that in narrowly defined circumstances federal courts have inherent power to assess attorney's fees against counsel," even though the so-called "American Rule" prohibits fee shifting in most cases. In this regard, if a court finds "that fraud has been practiced upon it, or that the very temple of justice has been defiled," it may assess attorney's fees against the responsible party, as it may when a party "shows bad faith by delaying or disrupting the litigation or by hampering enforcement of a court order." The imposition of sanctions in this instance transcends a court's equitable power concerning relations between the parties and reaches a court's inherent power to police itself, thus serving the dual purpose of "vindicating judicial authority without resort to the more drastic sanctions available for contempt of court and making the prevailing party whole for expenses caused by his opponent's obstinacy."

B

We discern no basis for holding that the sanctioning scheme of the statute and the rules displaces the inherent power to impose sanctions for the bad-faith conduct described above. These other mechanisms, taken alone or together, are not substitutes for the inherent power, for that power is both broader and narrower than other means of imposing sanctions. First, whereas each of the other mechanisms reaches only certain individuals or conduct, the inherent power extends to a full range of litigation abuses. At the very least, the inherent power must continue to exist to fill in the interstices.

It is true that the exercise of the inherent power of lower federal courts can be limited by statute and rule, for "these courts were created by act of Congress." Nevertheless, "we do not lightly assume that Congress has intended to depart from established principles" such as the scope of a court's inherent power. Thus, as the Court of Appeals for the Ninth Circuit has recognized, Rule 11 "does not repeal or modify existing authority of federal courts to deal with abuses under the court's inherent power."

The Court's prior cases have indicated that the inherent power of a court can be invoked even if procedural rules exist which sanction the same conduct. In *Link,* it was recognized that a federal district court has the inherent power to dismiss a case *sua sponte* for failure to prosecute, even though the language of Federal Rule of Civil Procedure 41(b) appeared to require a motion from a party.

There is, therefore, nothing in the other sanctioning mechanisms or prior cases interpreting them that warrants a conclusion that a federal court may not, as a matter of law, resort to its inherent power to impose attorney's fees as a sanction for bad-faith conduct. This is plainly the case where the conduct at issue is not covered by one of the other sanctioning provisions. But neither is a federal court forbidden to sanction bad-faith conduct by means of the inherent power simply because that conduct could also be sanctioned under the statute or the Rules. A court must, of course, exercise caution in invoking its inherent power, and it must comply with the mandates of due process, both in determining that the requisite bad faith exists and in assessing fees. Furthermore, when there is bad-faith conduct in the course of litigation that could be adequately sanctioned under the Rules, the court ordinarily should rely on the Rules rather than the inherent power. But if in the informed discretion of the court, neither the statute nor the Rules are up to the task, the court may safely rely on its inherent power.

Like the Court of Appeals, we find no abuse of discretion in resorting to the inherent power in the circumstances of this case. It is true that the District Court could have employed Rule 11 to sanction Chambers for filing "false and frivolous pleadings," and that some of the other conduct might have been reached through other Rules. Much of the bad-faith conduct by Chambers, however, was beyond the reach of the Rules; his entire course of conduct throughout the lawsuit evidenced bad faith and an attempt to perpetrate a fraud on the court, and the conduct sanctionable under the Rules was intertwined within conduct that only the inherent power could address. In circumstances such as these in which all of a litigant's conduct is deemed sanctionable, requiring a court first to apply Rules and statutes containing sanctioning provisions to discrete occurrences before invoking inherent power to address remaining instances of sanctionable conduct would serve only to foster extensive and needless satellite litigation, which is contrary to the aim of the Rules themselves.

## III

Chambers asserts that even if federal courts can use their inherent power to assess attorney's fees as a sanction in some cases, they are not free to do so when they sit in diversity, unless the applicable state law recognizes the "bad-faith" exception to the general rule against fee shifting.

We agree with NASCO that the limitation on a court's inherent power described there applies only to fee-shifting rules that embody a substantive policy, such as a statute which permits a prevailing party in certain classes of litigation to recover fees.

Only when there is a conflict between state and federal substantive law are the concerns of *Erie R. Co. v. Tompkins* applicable. As we explained in *Hanna v. Plumer,* the "outcome determinative" test of *Erie* and *Guaranty Trust Co. v. York,* "cannot be read without reference to the twin aims of the *Erie* rule: discouragement of forum-shopping and avoidance of inequitable administration of the laws." Despite Chambers' protestations to the contrary, neither of these twin aims is implicated by the assessment of attorney's fees as a sanction for bad-faith conduct before the court which involved disobedience of the court's orders and the attempt to defraud the court itself.

As Chambers has recognized, in the case of the bad-faith exception to the American Rule, "the underlying rationale of 'fee shifting' is, of course, punitive." "The award of attorney's fees for bad faith serves the same purpose as a remedial fine imposed for civil contempt," because "it vindicates the District Court's authority over a recalcitrant litigant."

Chambers argues that because the primary purpose of the sanction is punitive, assessing attorney's fees violates the State's prohibition on punitive damages. Under Louisiana law, there can be no punitive damages for breach of contract, even when a party has acted in bad faith in breaching the agreement. Indeed, "as a general rule attorney's fees are not allowed a successful litigant in Louisiana except where authorized by statute or by contract." It is clear, though, that this general rule focuses on the award of attorney's fees because of a party's success on the underlying claim. This substantive state policy is not implicated here, where sanctions were imposed for conduct during the litigation.

Here, the District Court did not attempt to sanction petitioner for breach of contract, but rather imposed sanctions for the fraud he perpetrated on the court and the bad faith he displayed toward both his adversary and the court throughout the course of the litigation. We agree with the Court of Appeals that "we do not see how the district court's inherent power to tax fees for that conduct can be made subservient to any state policy without transgressing the boundaries set out in *Erie, Guaranty Trust Co.,* and *Hanna,* for fee-shifting here is not a matter of substantive remedy, but of vindicating judicial authority.

## IV

We review a court's imposition of sanctions under its inherent power for abuse of discretion. Based on the circumstances of this case, we find that the District Court acted within its discretion in assessing as a sanction for Chambers' bad-faith conduct the entire amount of NASCO's attorney's fees.

Finally, Chambers claims the award is not "personalized," because the District Court failed to conduct any inquiry into whether he was personally responsible for the challenged conduct. This assertion is flatly contradicted by the District Court's detailed factual findings concerning Chambers' involvement in the sequence of events at issue. Indeed, the court specifically held that "the extraordinary amount of costs and expenses expended in this proceeding were caused not by lack of diligence or any delays in the trial of this matter by NASCO, NASCO's counsel or the Court, but solely by the relentless, repeated, fraudulent and brazenly unethical efforts of Chambers" and the others. The Court of Appeals saw no reason to disturb this finding. Neither do we.

For the foregoing reasons, the judgment of the Court of Appeals for the Fifth Circuit is *Affirmed.*

# CHAPTER 10

# DECLINING JURISDICTION

1. It is possible to file the same lawsuit in both federal court and state court at the same time. That may well be a good idea when it is not certain that the federal court will have jurisdiction, for example. Plaintiff will be entitled to get only one recovery. But until final judgment is entered in one suit or the other, both suits may proceed in parallel, at the same time.

Regardless of whether or not the plaintiff has filed the same suit in two different jurisdictions, there are times when a federal court, even though it has jurisdiction, abstains from exercising that jurisdiction. The two primary types of abstention for federal courts are called *Younger* abstention, (from the case of *Younger v. Harris),* and *Pullman* abstention, (from the case of *Pullman v. U.S.).* *Younger* abstention requires that federal courts abstain when state courts are already involved in a parallel criminal proceeding. *Pullman* abstention requires that federal courts abstain if the case is already in state court, with both state law and Constitutional issues, and solution of the state law issues in state court may obviate the need for a decision on the Constitutional issue.

In addition, federal courts may abstain from exercising jurisdiction on the basis of *"comity"* in order to avoid interfering with the sovereignty of a foreign country, or the sovereignty of a state. Abstention on the basis of *comity* is decided on a case by case basis.

The rules for *Younger* and *Pullman* abstention are more specific

# A. ABSTENTION

## 134 S.CT. 584
## SUPREME COURT OF THE UNITED STATES
## SPRINT COMMUNICATIONS, INC., PETITIONER
## V.
## ELIZABETH S. JACOBS ET AL.

DECIDED DECEMBER 10, 2013

Justice GINSBURG delivered the opinion for a unanimous Court.

This case involves two proceedings, one pending in state court, the other in federal court. Each seeks review of an Iowa Utilities Board (IUB or Board) order. And each presents the question whether Windstream Iowa Communications, Inc. (Windstream), a local telecommunications carrier, may impose on Sprint Communications, Inc. (Sprint), intrastate access charges for telephone calls transported via the Internet. Federal-court jurisdiction over controversies of this kind was confirmed in *Verizon v. Public Serv.* (2002). Invoking *Younger v. Harris,* 401 U.S. 37 (1971), the U.S. District Court for the Southern District of Iowa abstained from adjudicating Sprint's complaint in deference to the parallel state-court proceeding, and the Court of Appeals for the Eighth Circuit affirmed the District Court's abstention decision.

We reverse the judgment of the Court of Appeals. In the main, federal courts are obliged to decide cases within the scope of federal jurisdiction. Abstention is not in order simply because a pending state-court proceeding involves the same subject matter. *New Orleans Public Service, Inc. v. Council of City of New Orleans,* 491 U.S. 350 (1989) (*NOPSI*) ("There is no doctrine that ... pendency of state judicial proceedings excludes the federal courts."). This Court has recognized, however, certain instances in which the prospect of undue interference with state proceedings counsels against federal relief.

*Younger* exemplifies one class of cases in which federal-court abstention is required: When there is a parallel, pending state criminal proceeding, federal courts must refrain from enjoining the state prosecution. This Court has extended *Younger* abstention to particular state civil proceedings that are akin to criminal prosecutions, or that implicate a State's interest in enforcing the orders and judgments of its courts. We have cautioned, however, that federal courts ordinarily should entertain and resolve on the merits an action within the scope of a jurisdictional grant, and should not "refuse to decide a case in deference to the States."

Circumstances fitting within the *Younger* doctrine, we have stressed, are "exceptional"; they include, as catalogued in *NOPSI*, "state criminal prosecutions," "civil enforcement proceedings," and "civil proceedings involving certain orders that are uniquely in furtherance of the state courts' ability to perform their judicial functions." Because this case presents none of the circumstances the Court has ranked as "exceptional," the general rule governs: "The pendency of an action in a state court is no bar to proceedings concerning the same matter in the Federal court having jurisdiction."

I

Sprint, a national telecommunications service provider, has long paid intercarrier access fees to the Iowa communications company Windstream for certain long distance calls placed by Sprint customers to Windstream's in-state customers. In 2009, however, Sprint decided to withhold payment for a subset of those calls, classified as Voice over Internet Protocol (VoIP), after concluding that the Telecommunications Act of 1996 preempted intrastate regulation of VoIP traffic. In response, Windstream threatened to block all calls to and from Sprint customers.

Sprint filed a complaint against Windstream with the IUB asking the Board to enjoin Windstream from discontinuing service to Sprint. In Sprint's view, Iowa law entitled it to withhold payment while it contested the access charges and prohibited Windstream from carrying out its disconnection threat. In answer to Sprint's complaint, Windstream retracted its threat to discontinue serving Sprint, and Sprint moved, successfully, to withdraw its complaint. Because the conflict between Sprint and Windstream over VoIP calls was "likely to recur," however, the IUB decided to continue the proceedings to resolve the underlying legal question, *i.e.*, whether VoIP calls are subject to intrastate regulation. The question retained by the IUB, Sprint argued, was governed by federal law, and was not within the IUB's adjudicative jurisdiction. The IUB disagreed, ruling that the intrastate fees applied to VoIP calls.

Seeking to overturn the Board's ruling, Sprint commenced two lawsuits. First, Sprint sued the members of the IUB (respondents here) in their official capacities in the United States District Court for the Southern District of Iowa. In its *federal-court* complaint, Sprint sought a declaration that the Telecommunications Act of 1996 pre-empted the IUB's decision; as relief, Sprint requested an injunction against enforcement of the IUB's order. Second, Sprint petitioned for review of the IUB's order in Iowa *state* court. The state petition reiterated the preemption argument Sprint made in its federal-court complaint; in addition, Sprint asserted state law and procedural due process claims. Because Eighth Circuit precedent effectively required a plaintiff to exhaust state remedies before proceeding to federal court, Sprint urges that it filed the state suit as a protective measure. Failing to do so, Sprint explains, risked losing the opportunity to obtain any review, federal or state, should the federal court decide to abstain after the expiration of the Iowa statute of limitations.

As Sprint anticipated, the IUB filed a motion asking the Federal District Court to abstain in light of the state suit, citing *Younger v. Harris.* The District Court granted the IUB's motion and dismissed the suit. The IUB's decision, and the pending state-court review of it, the District Court said, composed one "uninterruptible process" implicating important state interests. On that ground, the court ruled, *Younger* abstention was in order.

For the most part, the Eighth Circuit agreed with the District Court's judgment. Recognizing the "possibility that the parties might return to federal court," however, the Court of Appeals vacated the judgment dismissing Sprint's complaint. In lieu of dismissal, the Eighth Circuit remanded the case, instructing the District Court to enter a stay during the pendency of the state-court action.

We granted certiorari to decide whether, consistent with our delineation of cases encompassed by the *Younger* doctrine, abstention was appropriate here.

## II

### A

Neither party has questioned the District Court's jurisdiction to decide whether federal law preempted the IUB's decision, and rightly so.

Federal courts, it was early and famously said, have "no more right to decline the exercise of jurisdiction which is given, than to usurp that which is not given." *Cohens v. Virginia,* (1821). Jurisdiction existing, this Court has cautioned, a federal court's "obligation" to hear and decide a case is "virtually unflagging." Parallel state-court proceedings do not detract from that obligation.

In *Younger,* we recognized a "far-from-novel" exception to this general rule. The plaintiff in *Younger* sought federal-court adjudication of the constitutionality of the California Criminal Syndicalism Act. Requesting an injunction against the Act's enforcement, the federal-court plaintiff was at the time the defendant in a pending state criminal prosecution under the Act. In those circumstances, we said, the federal court should decline to enjoin the prosecution, absent bad faith, harassment, or a patently invalid state statute. Abstention was in order, we explained, under "the basic doctrine of equity jurisprudence that courts of equity should not act to restrain a criminal prosecution, when the moving party has an adequate remedy at law and will not suffer irreparable injury if denied equitable relief." We explained as well that this doctrine was "reinforced" by the notion of "'comity,' that is, a proper respect for state functions."

We have since applied *Younger* to bar federal relief in certain civil actions. *Huffman v. Pursue,* is the pathmarking decision. There, Ohio officials brought a civil action in state court to abate the showing of obscene movies in Pursue's theater. Because the State was a party and the proceeding was "in aid of and closely related to the State's criminal statutes," the Court held *Younger* abstention appropriate.

More recently, in *NOPSI,* (1989), the Court had occasion to review and restate our *Younger* jurisprudence. *NOPSI* addressed and rejected an argument that a federal court should refuse to exercise jurisdiction to review a state council's ratemaking decision. "Only exceptional circumstances," we reaffirmed, "justify a federal court's refusal to decide a case in deference to the States." Those "exceptional circumstances" exist, the Court determined after surveying prior decisions, in three types of proceedings. First, *Younger* precluded federal intrusion into ongoing state criminal prosecutions. Second, certain "civil enforcement proceedings" warranted abstention. Finally, federal courts refrained from interfering with pending "civil proceedings involving certain orders ... uniquely in furtherance of the state courts' ability to perform their judicial functions. We have not applied *Younger* outside these three "exceptional" categories, and today hold, in accord with *NOPSI,* that they define *Younger*'s scope.

B

The IUB does not assert that the Iowa state court's review of the Board decision, considered alone, implicates *Younger*. Rather, the initial administrative proceeding justifies staying any action in federal court, the IUB contends, until the state review process has concluded. The same argument was advanced in *NOPSI*. We will assume without deciding, as the Court did in *NOPSI,* that an administrative adjudication and the subsequent state court's review of it count as a "unitary process" for *Younger* purposes. The question remains, however, whether the initial IUB proceeding is of the "sort entitled to *Younger* treatment."

The IUB proceeding, we conclude, does not fall within any of the three exceptional categories described in *NOPSI* and therefore does not trigger *Younger* abstention. The first and third categories plainly do not accommodate the IUB's proceeding. That proceeding was civil, not criminal in character, and it did not touch on a state court's ability to perform its judicial function.

Nor does the IUB's order rank as an act of civil enforcement of the kind to which *Younger* has been extended. Our decisions applying *Younger* to instances of civil enforcement have generally concerned state proceedings "akin to a criminal prosecution" in "important respects."

The IUB proceeding does not resemble the state enforcement actions this Court has found appropriate for *Younger* abstention. It is not "akin to a criminal prosecution." Nor was it initiated by "the State in its sovereign capacity." A private corporation, Sprint, initiated the action. No state authority conducted an investigation into Sprint's activities, and no state actor lodged a formal complaint against Sprint.

In its brief, the IUB emphasizes Sprint's decision to withdraw the complaint that commenced proceedings before the Board. At that point, the IUB argues, Sprint was no longer a willing participant, and the proceedings became, essentially, a civil enforcement action. The IUB's adjudicative authority, however, was invoked to settle a civil dispute between two private parties, not to sanction Sprint for commission of a wrongful act. Although Sprint withdrew its complaint, administrative efficiency, not misconduct by Sprint, prompted the IUB to answer the underlying federal question. By determining the intercarrier compensation regime applicable to VoIP calls, the IUB sought to avoid renewed litigation of the parties' dispute. Because the underlying legal question remained unsettled, the Board observed, the controversy was "likely to recur." Nothing here suggests that the IUB proceeding was "more akin to a criminal prosecution than are most civil cases."

The Court of Appeals and the IUB attribute to this Court's decision in *Middlesex* extraordinary breadth. We invoked *Younger* in *Middlesex* to bar a federal court from entertaining a lawyer's challenge to a New Jersey state ethics committee's pending investigation of the lawyer. Unlike the IUB proceeding here, the state ethics committee's hearing in *Middlesex* was indeed "akin to a criminal proceeding." As we noted, an investigation and formal complaint preceded the hearing, an agency of the State's Supreme Court initiated the hearing, and the purpose of the hearing was to determine whether the lawyer should be disciplined for his failure to meet the State's standards of professional conduct. The three *Middlesex* conditions recited above were not dispositive; they were, instead, *additional* factors appropriately considered by the federal court before invoking *Younger*.

Divorced from their quasi-criminal context, the three *Middlesex* conditions would extend *Younger* to virtually all parallel state and federal proceedings, at least where a party could identify a plausibly important state interest. That result is irreconcilable with our dominant instruction that, even in the presence of parallel state proceedings, abstention from the exercise of federal jurisdiction is the "exception, not the rule." In short, to guide other federal courts, we today clarify and affirm that *Younger* extends to the three "exceptional circumstances" identified in *NOPSI,* but no further.

For the reasons stated, the judgment of the United States Court of Appeals for the Eighth Circuit is Reversed.

2. There may be additional times when it is appropriate for the federal courts to abstain from exercising jurisdiction. One such ground for appropriate abstention is the *"Political Question Doctrine."*

But if the question at issue is really just a dispute as to whether or not Congress has authority under the Constitution to enact a particular statute, then that is an appropriate matter for the federal courts, and they need not abstain.

---

132 S.CT. 1421
SUPREME COURT OF THE UNITED STATES
MENACHEM BINYAMIN ZIVOTOFSKY, BY HIS PARENTS AND GUARDIANS,
ARI Z. AND NAOMI SIEGMAN ZIVOTOFSKY, PETITIONER
V.
HILLARY RODHAM CLINTON, SECRETARY OF STATE.

DECIDED MARCH 26, 2012

Chief Justice ROBERTS delivered the opinion of the Court.

Congress enacted a statute providing that Americans born in Jerusalem may elect to have "Israel" listed as the place of birth on their passports. The State Department declined to follow that law, citing its longstanding policy of not taking a position on the political status of Jerusalem. When sued by an American who invoked the statute, the Secretary of State argued that the courts lacked authority to decide the case because it presented a political question. The Court of Appeals so held.

We disagree. The courts are fully capable of determining whether this statute may be given effect, or instead must be struck down in light of authority conferred on the Executive by the Constitution.

I

A

In 2002, Congress enacted the Foreign Relations Authorization Act. Section 214 of the Act is entitled "United States Policy with Respect to Jerusalem as the Capital of Israel." The first two subsections express Congress's "commitment" to relocating the United States Embassy in Israel to Jerusalem. The third bars funding for the publication of official Government documents that do not list Jerusalem as the capital of Israel. The fourth and final provision, § 214(d), is the only one at stake in this case. Entitled "Record of Place of Birth as Israel for Passport Purposes," it provides that "for purposes of the registration of birth, certification of nationality, or issuance of a passport of a United States citizen born in the city of Jerusalem, the Secretary shall, upon the request of the citizen or the citizen's legal guardian, record the place of birth as Israel."

The State Department's Foreign Affairs Manual states that "where the birthplace of the applicant is located in territory disputed by another country, the city or area of birth may be written in the passport." 7 Foreign Affairs Manual § 1383.5–2. The manual specifically directs that passport officials should enter "JERUSALEM" and should "not write Israel or Jordan" when recording the birthplace of a person born in Jerusalem on a passport.

Section 214(d) sought to override this instruction by allowing citizens born in Jerusalem to have "Israel" recorded on their passports if they wish. In signing the Foreign Relations Authorization Act into law, President George W. Bush stated his belief that § 214 "impermissibly interferes with the President's constitutional authority to conduct the Nation's foreign affairs and to supervise the unitary executive branch." He added that if the section is "construed as mandatory," then it would "interfere with the President's constitutional authority to formulate the position of the United States, speak for the Nation in international affairs, and determine the terms on which recognition is given to foreign states." He concluded by emphasizing that "U.S. policy regarding Jerusalem has not changed." The President made no specific reference to the passport mandate in § 214(d).

B

Petitioner Menachem Binyamin Zivotofsky was born in Jerusalem on October 17, 2002, shortly after § 214(d) was enacted. Zivotofsky's parents were American citizens and he accordingly was as well, by virtue of congressional enactment. 8 U.S.C. § 1401(c); (foreign-born children of American citizens acquire citizenship at birth through "congressional generosity"). Zivotofsky's mother filed an application for a consular report of birth abroad and a United States passport. She requested that his place of birth be listed as "Jerusalem, Israel" on both documents. U.S. officials informed Zivotofsky's mother that State Department policy prohibits recording "Israel" as Zivotofsky's place of birth. Pursuant to that policy, Zivotofsky was issued a passport and consular report of birth abroad listing only "Jerusalem."

Zivotofsky's parents filed a complaint on his behalf against the Secretary of State. Zivotofsky sought a declaratory judgment and a permanent injunction ordering the Secretary to identify his place of birth as "Jerusalem, Israel" in the official documents. The District Court granted the Secretary's motion to dismiss the complaint on the grounds that Zivotofsky lacked standing and that his complaint presented a nonjusticiable political question.

The Court of Appeals for the D.C. Circuit reversed. It therefore remanded the case to the District Court.

The District Court again found that the case was not justiciable. It explained that "resolving Zivotofsky's claim on the merits would necessarily require the Court to decide the political status of Jerusalem." Concluding that the claim therefore presented a political question, the District Court dismissed the case for lack of subject matter jurisdiction.

The D.C. Circuit affirmed. Zivotofsky petitioned for certiorari, and we granted review.

## II

The lower courts concluded that Zivotofsky's claim presents a political question and therefore cannot be adjudicated. We disagree.

In general, the Judiciary has a responsibility to decide cases properly before it, even those it "would gladly avoid." *Cohens v. Virginia* (1821). Our precedents have identified a narrow exception to that rule, known as the "political question" doctrine. We have explained that a controversy "involves a political question ... where there is 'a textually demonstrable constitutional commitment of the issue to a coordinate political department; or a lack of judicially discoverable and manageable standards for resolving it.' " *Nixon v. United States* (1993). In such a case, we have held that a court lacks the authority to decide the dispute before it.

The lower courts ruled that this case involves a political question because deciding Zivotofsky's claim would force the Judicial Branch to interfere with the President's exercise of constitutional power committed to him alone. The District Court understood Zivotofsky to ask the courts to "decide the political status of Jerusalem." This misunderstands the issue presented. Zivotofsky does not ask the courts to determine whether Jerusalem is the capital of Israel. He instead seeks to determine whether he may vindicate his statutory right, under § 214(d), to choose to have Israel recorded on his passport as his place of birth.

For its part, the D.C. Circuit treated the two questions as one and the same. That court concluded that "only the Executive—not Congress and not the courts—has the power to define U.S. policy regarding Israel's sovereignty over Jerusalem," and also to "decide how best to implement that policy." Because the Department's passport rule was adopted to implement the President's "exclusive and unreviewable constitutional power to keep the United States out of the debate over the status of Jerusalem," the validity of that rule was itself a "nonjusticiable political question" that "the Constitution leaves to the Executive alone." Indeed, the D.C. Circuit's opinion does not even mention § 214(d) until the fifth of its six paragraphs of analysis, and then only to dismiss it as irrelevant: "That Congress took a position on the status of Jerusalem and gave Zivotofsky a statutory cause of action is of no moment to whether the judiciary has the authority to resolve this dispute."

The existence of a statutory right, however, is certainly relevant to the Judiciary's power to decide Zivotofsky's claim. The federal courts are not being asked to supplant a foreign policy decision of the political branches with the courts' own unmoored determination of what United States policy toward Jerusalem should be. Instead, Zivotofsky requests that the courts enforce a specific statutory right. To resolve his claim, the Judiciary must decide if Zivotofsky's interpretation of the statute is correct, and whether the statute is constitutional. This is a familiar judicial exercise.

Moreover, because the parties do not dispute the interpretation of § 214(d), the only real question for the courts is whether the statute is constitutional. At least since *Marbury v. Madison* (1803), we have recognized that when an Act of Congress is alleged to conflict with the Constitution, "it is emphatically the province and duty of the judicial department to say what the law is." That duty will sometimes involve the "resolution of litigation challenging the constitutional authority of one of the three branches," but courts cannot avoid their responsibility merely "because the issues have political implications."

In this case, determining the constitutionality of § 214(d) involves deciding whether the statute impermissibly intrudes upon Presidential powers under the Constitution. If so, the law must be invalidated and Zivotofsky's case should be dismissed for failure to state a claim. If, on the other hand, the statute does not trench on the President's powers, then the Secretary must be ordered to issue Zivotofsky a passport that complies with § 214(d). Either way, the political question doctrine is not implicated. "No policy underlying the political question doctrine suggests that Congress or the Executive ... can decide the constitutionality of a statute; that is a decision for the courts."

The Secretary contends that "there is 'a textually demonstrable constitutional commitment'" to the President of the sole power to recognize foreign sovereigns and, as a corollary, to determine whether an American born in Jerusalem may choose to have Israel listed as his place of birth on his passport. Perhaps. But there is, of course, no exclusive commitment to the Executive of the power to determine the constitutionality of a statute. The Judicial Branch appropriately exercises that authority, including in a case such as this, where the question is whether Congress or the Executive is "aggrandizing its power at the expense of another branch."

Our precedents have also found the political question doctrine implicated when there is "a lack of judicially discoverable and manageable standards for resolving" the question before the court. *Nixon, supra.* Framing the issue as the lower courts did, in terms of whether the Judiciary may decide the political status of Jerusalem, certainly raises those concerns. They dissipate, however, when the issue is recognized to be the more focused one of the constitutionality of § 214(d). Indeed, both sides offer detailed legal arguments regarding whether § 214(d) is constitutional in light of powers committed to the Executive, and whether Congress's own powers with respect to passports must be weighed in analyzing this question.

For example, the Secretary reprises on the merits her argument on the political question issue, claiming that the Constitution gives the Executive the exclusive power to formulate recognition policy. She roots her claim in the Constitution's declaration that the President shall "receive Ambassadors and other public Ministers." U.S. Const., Art. II, § 3. According to the Secretary, "centuries-long Executive Branch practice, congressional acquiescence, and decisions by this Court" confirm that the "receive Ambassadors" clause confers upon the Executive the exclusive power of recognition.

The Secretary observes that "President Washington and his cabinet unanimously decided that the President could receive the ambassador from the new government of France without first consulting Congress." (Citing Letter from George Washington to the Cabinet (Apr. 18, 1793). She notes, too, that early attempts by the Legislature to affect recognition policy were regularly "rejected in Congress as inappropriate incursions into the Executive Branch's constitutional authority." And she cites precedents from this Court stating that "political recognition is exclusively a function of the Executive."

The Secretary further contends that § 214(d) constitutes an impermissible exercise of the recognition power because "the decision as to how to describe the place of birth operates as an official statement of whether the United States recognizes a state's sovereignty over a territorial area." The Secretary will not "list as a place of birth a country whose sovereignty over the relevant territory the United States does not recognize." Therefore, she claims, "listing 'Israel' as the place of birth would constitute an official decision by the United States to begin to treat Jerusalem as a city located within Israel."

For his part, Zivotofsky argues that, far from being an exercise of the recognition power, § 214(d) is instead a "legitimate and permissible" exercise of Congress's "authority to legislate on the form and content of a passport." He points the Court to Professor Louis Henkin's observation that "'in the competition for power in foreign relations,' Congress has 'an impressive array of powers expressly enumerated in the Constitution.'" Zivotofsky suggests that Congress's authority to enact § 214(d) derives specifically from its powers over naturalization, U.S. Const., Art. I, § 8, cl. 4, and foreign commerce. According to Zivotofsky, Congress has used these powers to pass laws regulating the content and issuance of passports since 1856.

Zivotofsky contends that § 214(d) fits squarely within this tradition. He notes that the State Department's designated representative stated in her deposition for this litigation that the "place of birth" entry is included *only* as "an element of identification." (Deposition of Catherine Barry, Deputy Assistant Secretary of State for Overseas Citizens Services). Moreover, Zivotofsky argues, the "place of birth" entry cannot be taken as a means for recognizing foreign sovereigns, because the State Department authorizes recording unrecognized territories—such as the Gaza Strip and the West Bank—as places of birth.

Further, Zivotofsky claims that even if § 214(d) does implicate the recognition power, that is not a power the Constitution commits exclusively to the Executive. Zivotofsky argues that the Secretary is overreading the authority granted to the President in the "receive Ambassadors" clause. He observes that in the Federalist Papers, Alexander Hamilton described the power conferred by this clause as "more a matter of dignity than of authority," and called it "a circumstance, which will be without consequence in the administration of the government." The Federalist No. 69. Zivotofsky also points to other clauses in the Constitution, such as Congress's power to declare war, that suggest some congressional role in recognition. He cites, for example, an 1836 message from President Jackson to Congress, acknowledging that it is unclear who holds the authority to recognize because it is a power "nowhere expressly delegated" in the Constitution, and one that is "necessarily involved in some of the great powers given to Congress." Message from the President of the United States Upon the Subject of the Political, Military, and Civil Condition of Texas.

Zivotofsky argues that language from this Court's precedents suggesting the recognition power belongs exclusively to the President is inapplicable to his claim, because that language appeared in cases where the Court was asked to alter recognition policy developed by the Executive in the absence of congressional opposition. Finally, Zivotofsky contends that even if the "receive Ambassadors" clause confers some exclusive recognition power on the President, simply allowing a choice as to the "place of birth" entry on a passport does not significantly intrude on that power.

Recitation of these arguments—which sound in familiar principles of constitutional interpretation—is enough to establish that this case does not "turn on standards that defy judicial application." Resolution of Zivotofsky's claim demands careful examination of the textual, structural, and historical evidence put forward by the parties regarding the nature of the statute and of the passport and recognition powers. This is what courts do. The political question doctrine poses no bar to judicial review of this case.

## III

To say that Zivotofsky's claim presents issues the Judiciary is competent to resolve is not to say that reaching a decision in this case is simple. Because the District Court and the D.C. Circuit believed that review was barred by the political question doctrine, we are without the benefit of thorough lower court opinions to guide our analysis of the merits. Ours is "a court of final review and not first view." Ordinarily, "we do not decide in the first instance issues not decided below." In particular, when we reverse on a threshold question, we typically remand for resolution of any claims the lower courts' error prevented them from addressing. We see no reason to depart from this approach in this case. Having determined that this case is justiciable, we leave it to the lower courts to consider the merits in the first instance.

The judgment of the Court of Appeals for the D.C. Circuit is vacated, and the case is remanded for further proceedings consistent with this opinion.

# B. PREEMPTION

3. There are numerous areas in which the federal government has authority to pre-empt state law – generally as part of the power given to Congress by the *"Commerce Clause"* of the Constitution. It is the job of the courts to decide when, and to what extent state laws have been pre-empted by federal law when Congress has made no specific statement about pre-emption. The following case provides a very good description of the two basic types of federal pre-emption, "field" pre-emption and "conflict" pre-emption.

135 S.CT. 1591

SUPREME COURT OF THE UNITED STATES

ONEOK, INC., ET AL., PETITIONERS

V.

LEARJET, INC., ET AL.

DECIDED APRIL 21, 2015

**Justice BREYER delivered the opinion of the Court.**

[In this case, a group of manufacturers, hospitals, and other institutions that buy natural gas directly from interstate pipelines sued the pipelines, claiming that they engaged in behavior that violated state antitrust laws. The pipelines' behavior affected *both* federally regulated *wholesale* natural-gas prices *and* nonfederally regulated *retail* natural-gas prices. The question is whether the federal Natural Gas Act pre-empts these lawsuits. We have said that, in passing the Act, "Congress occupied the field of matters relating to wholesale sales and transportation of natural gas in interstate commerce." Nevertheless, for the reasons given below, we conclude that the Act does not pre-empt the state-law antitrust suits at issue here.]

## I

### A

The Supremacy Clause provides that "the Laws of the United States" (as well as treaties and the Constitution itself) "shall be the supreme Law of the Land any Thing in the Constitution or Laws of any state to the Contrary notwithstanding." Art. VI, cl. 2. Congress may consequently pre-empt, *i.e.*, invalidate, a state law through federal legislation. It may do so through express language in a statute. But even where, as here, a statute does not refer expressly to pre-emption, Congress may implicitly pre-empt a state law, rule, or other state action.

It may do so either through "field" pre-emption or "conflict" pre-emption. As to the former, Congress may have intended "to foreclose any state regulation in the *area*," irrespective of whether state law is consistent or inconsistent with "federal standards." *Arizona v. United States,* (2012). In such situations, Congress has forbidden the State to take action in the *field* that the federal statute pre-empts.

By contrast, conflict pre-emption exists where "compliance with both state and federal law is impossible," or where "the state law 'stands as an obstacle to the accomplishment and execution of the full purposes and objectives of Congress.'" In either situation, federal law must prevail.

No one here claims that any relevant federal statute expressly pre-empts state antitrust lawsuits. Nor have the parties argued at any length that these state suits conflict with federal law. Rather, the interstate pipeline companies (petitioners here) argue that Congress implicitly "'occupied *the field of matters* relating to wholesale sales and transportation of natural gas in interstate commerce.'" And they contend that the state antitrust claims advanced by their direct-sales customers (respondents here) fall within that field. The United States, supporting the pipelines, argues similarly. Since the parties have argued this case almost exclusively in terms of field pre-emption, we consider only the field pre-emption question.

### B

#### 1

Federal regulation of the natural-gas industry began at a time when the industry was divided into three segments. First, natural-gas producers sunk wells in large oil and gas fields (such as the Permian Basin in Texas and New Mexico). They gathered the gas, brought it to transportation points, and left it to interstate gas pipelines to transport the gas to distant markets. Second, interstate pipelines shipped the gas from the field to cities and towns across the Nation. Third, local gas distributors bought the gas from the interstate pipelines and resold it to business and residential customers within their localities.

Originally, the States regulated all three segments of the industry. But in the early 20th century, this Court held that the Commerce Clause forbids the States to regulate the second part of the business—*i.e.,* the interstate shipment and sale of gas to local distributors for resale. These holdings left a regulatory gap. Congress enacted the Natural Gas Act to fill it.

The Act, in § 5(a), gives rate-setting authority to the Federal Energy Regulatory Commission (FERC, formerly the Federal Power Commission (FPC)). That authority allows FERC to determine whether "any rate, charge, or classification collected by any natural-gas company in connection with any transportation or sale of natural gas, *subject to the jurisdiction of FERC*," or "any rule, regulation, practice, or contract affecting *such* rate, charge, or classification is unjust, unreasonable, unduly discrimi-natory, or preferential." As the italicized words make clear, § 5(a) limits the scope of FERC's authority to activities "in connection with any transportation or sale of natural gas, *subject to the jurisdiction of the Commission*." (Emphasis added). And the Act, in § 1(b), limits FERC's "jurisdiction" to (1) "the transportation of natural gas in interstate commerce," (2) "the sale in interstate commerce of natural gas for resale," and (3) "natural-gas companies engaged in such transportation or sale." § 717(b). The Act leaves regulation of other portions of the industry—such as production, local dis-tribution facilities, and direct sales—to the States. (Section 1(b) of the Act "expressly" provides that "States retain jurisdiction over *intrastate* transportation, local distribu-tion, and distribution facilities, and over 'the production or gathering of natural gas.'"

To simplify our discussion, we shall describe the firms that engage in *interstate* transportation as "jurisdictional sellers" or "*interstate* pipelines" (though various bro-kers and others may also fall within the Act's jurisdictional scope). Similarly, we shall refer to the sales over which FERC has jurisdiction as "*jurisdictional sales*" or "*wholesale sales.*"

2

Until the 1970's, natural-gas regulation roughly tracked the industry model we described above.

Deregulation of the natural-gas industry, however, brought about changes in FERC's approach. In the 1950's, this Court had held that the Natural Gas Act required regulation of prices at the interstate pipelines' *buying* end—*i.e.,* the prices at which field producers sold natural gas to interstate pipelines. By the 1970's, many in Congress thought that such efforts to regulate field prices had jeopardized natural-gas supplies in an industry already dependent "on the caprice of nature." (Recognizing that "the wealth of Midas and the wit of man cannot produce a natural gas field"). Hoping to avoid future shortages, Congress enacted forms of field price deregulation designed to rely upon competition, rather than regulation, to keep field prices low.

FERC promulgated new regulations designed to further this process of deregulation. Most important here, FERC adopted an approach that relied on the competitive marketplace, rather than classical regulatory rate-setting, as the main mechanism for keeping *wholesale* natural-gas rates at a reasonable level.

After the issuance of this order, FERC's oversight of the natural-gas market largely consisted of (1) ex ante examinations of *jurisdictional* sellers' market power, and (2) the availability of a complaint process under § 717d(a). The new system also led many large gas consumers—such as industrial and commercial users—to buy their own gas directly from gas producers, and to arrange (and often pay separately) for transportation from the field to the place of consumption.

The free-market system for setting interstate pipeline rates turned out to be less than perfect. Interstate pipelines, distributing companies, and many of the customers who bought directly from the pipelines found that they had to rely on privately published price indices to determine appropriate prices for their natural-gas contracts. These indices listed the prices at which natural gas was being sold in different (presumably competitive) markets across the country. The information on which these indices were based was voluntarily reported by natural-gas traders.

In 2003, FERC found that the indices were inaccurate, in part because much of the information that natural-gas traders reported had been *false*. FERC found that false reporting had involved "inflating the volume of trades, omitting trades, and adjusting the price of trades." That is, sometimes those who reported information simply fabricated it. Other times, the information reported reflected "wash trades," *i.e., "prearranged* pairs of trades of the same good between the same parties, involving no economic risk and no net change in beneficial ownership." FERC concluded that these "efforts to manipulate price indices compiled by trade publications" had helped raise "to extraordinary levels" the prices of both *jurisdictional* sales (that is, interstate pipeline sales for resale) and *nonjurisdictional* direct sales to ultimate consumers.

After issuing its final report on price manipulation in western markets, FERC issued a Code of Conduct. That code amended all blanket certificates to prohibit *jurisdictional* sellers "from engaging in actions without a legitimate business purpose that manipulate or attempt to manipulate market conditions, including wash trades and collusion." The code also required *jurisdictional* companies, when they provided information to natural-gas index publishers, to "provide accurate and factual information, and not knowingly submit false or misleading information or omit material information to any such publisher." At the same time, FERC issued a policy statement setting forth "minimum standards for creation and publication of any energy price index," and "for reporting transaction data to index developers." Finally, FERC, after finding that certain *jurisdictional* sellers had "engaged in wash trading that resulted in the manipulation of natural-gas prices," terminated those sellers' blanket marketing certificates.

Congress also took steps to address these problems. In particular, it passed the Energy Policy Act of 2005, which gives FERC the authority to issue rules and regulations to prevent "any manipulative or deceptive device or contrivance" by "any entity in connection with the purchase or sale of natural gas or the purchase or sale of transportation services subject to the jurisdiction of" FERC, 15 U.S.C. § 717c–1.

## C

We now turn to the cases before us. Respondents, as we have said, bought large quantities of natural gas directly from interstate pipelines for their own consumption. They believe that they overpaid in these transactions due to the interstate pipelines' manipulation of the natural-gas indices. Based on this belief, they filed state-law antitrust suits against petitioners in state and federal courts.

The pipelines removed all the state cases to federal court, where they were consolidated and sent for pretrial proceedings to the Federal District Court for the District of Nevada.

The pipelines then moved for summary judgment on the ground that the Natural Gas Act pre-empted respondents' state-law antitrust claims. The District Court granted their motion. It concluded that the pipelines were "*jurisdictional* sellers," *i.e.,* "natural gas companies engaged in" the "transportation of natural gas in interstate commerce." And it held that respondents' claims, which were "aimed at" these sellers' "alleged practices of false price reporting, wash trades, and anticompetitive collusive behavior" were *pre-empted* because such practices not only affected *nonjurisdictional* direct-sale prices but also "directly affected" *jurisdictional* (*i.e., wholesale*) rates.

The Ninth Circuit reversed.

The pipelines sought certiorari. They asked us to resolve confusion in the lower courts as to whether the Natural Gas Act pre-empts retail customers' *state* antitrust law challenges to practices that also affect *wholesale* rates. We granted the petition.

## II

Petitioners, supported by the United States, argue that their customers' state anti-trust lawsuits are within the field that the Natural Gas Act pre-empts. They point out that respondents' antitrust claims target anticompetitive activities that affected wholesale (as well as retail) rates. They add that the Natural Gas Act expressly grants FERC authority to keep wholesale rates at reasonable levels. (citing 15 U.S.C. §§ 717(b), 717d(a)). In exercising this authority, FERC has prohibited the very kind of anti-competitive conduct that the state actions attack. And, petitioners contend, letting these actions proceed will permit state antitrust courts to reach conclusions about that conduct that differ from those that FERC might reach or has already reached. Accordingly, petitioners argue, respondents' state-law antitrust suits fall within the pre-empted field.

### A.

Petitioners' arguments are forceful, but we cannot accept their conclusion. As we have repeatedly stressed, the Natural Gas Act "was drawn with meticulous regard for the continued exercise of state power, not to handicap or dilute it in any way." Accordingly, where (as here) a *state* law can be applied to *nonjurisdictional* as well as jurisdictional sales, we must proceed cautiously, finding pre-emption only where detailed examination convinces us that a matter falls within the pre-empted field as defined by our precedents.

Those precedents emphasize the importance of considering the *target* at which the state law *aims* in determining whether that law is pre-empted. Here the lawsuits are directed at practices affecting *retail* rates—which are "firmly on the *States'* side of that dividing line."

Antitrust laws, like blue sky laws, are not aimed at natural-gas companies in par-ticular, but rather all businesses in the marketplace. This broad applicability of state antitrust law supports a finding of no pre-emption here.

### B (omitted)

### C

To the extent any *conflicts* arise between state antitrust law proceedings and the federal rate-setting process, the doctrine of *conflict* pre-emption should prove suf-ficient to address them. But as we have noted, see Part I–A, *supra,* the parties have not argued conflict pre-emption. (Solicitor General agrees that he has not "analyzed this case under a conflict preemption regime"). We consequently leave conflict pre-emption questions for the lower courts to resolve in the first instance.]

D

We note that petitioners and the Solicitor General have argued that we should defer to FERC's determination that field pre-emption bars the respondents' claims. But they have not pointed to a specific FERC determination that state antitrust claims fall within the field pre-empted by the Natural Gas Act. Rather, they point only to the fact that FERC has promulgated detailed rules governing manipulation of price indices. [Because there is no determination by FERC that its regulation pre-empts the field into which respondents' state-law antitrust suits fall, we need not consider what legal effect such a determination might have. And we conclude that the detailed federal regulations here do not offset the other considerations that weigh against a finding of pre-emption in this context.

For these reasons, the judgment of the Court of Appeals for the Ninth Circuit is affirmed.]

OL: Federal law, or the natural gas act, does not fit the field pre-emption standard defined by precedent, as it regulates intrastate wholesale natural gas trade but not the retail sales of natural gas, which is dictated by state antitrust laws and not to be diluted by the NGA.

# C. SPECIFIC LIMITS ON FEDERAL JURISDICTION

4. On the opposite side of federal pre-emption are various statutes enacted by Congress which *specifically* prohibit federal courts from taking jurisdiction over various matters – which Congress has determined should be left to the states. The Tax Injunction Act is one such statute, which specifically provides that federal courts "shall not enjoin, suspend or restrain the assessment, levy or collection of any tax under State law."

The following case also mentions that even when a federal court is not specifically prohibited from taking jurisdiction it might decline to do so on the basis of "comity."

### 135 S.CT. 1124
### SUPREME COURT OF THE UNITED STATES
### DIRECT MARKETING ASSOCIATION, PETITIONER
### V.
### BARBARA BROHL, EXECUTIVE DIRECTOR, COLORADO DEPARTMENT OF REVENUE.

DECIDED MARCH 3, 2015

Justice THOMAS delivered the opinion for a unanimous Court.

In an effort to improve the collection of sales and use taxes for items purchased online, the State of Colorado passed a law requiring retailers that do not collect Colorado sales or use tax to notify Colorado customers of their use-tax liability and to report tax-related information to customers and the Colorado Department of Revenue. We must decide whether the Tax Injunction Act, which provides that federal district courts "shall not enjoin, suspend or restrain the assessment, levy or collection of any tax under State law," 28 U.S.C. § 1341, bars a suit to enjoin the enforcement of this law. We hold that it does not.

## I

## A

Like many States, Colorado has a complementary sales-and-use tax regime. Colorado imposes both a 2.9 percent tax on the sale of tangible personal property within the State, and an equivalent use tax for any property stored, used, or consumed in Colorado on which a sales tax was not paid to a retailer. Retailers with a physical presence in Colorado must collect the sales or use tax from consumers at the point of sale and remit the proceeds to the Colorado Department of Revenue (Department). But under our negative Commerce Clause precedents, Colorado may not require retailers who lack a physical presence in the State to collect these taxes on behalf of the Department. *Quill Corp. v. North Dakota,* (1992). Thus, Colorado requires its consumers who purchase tangible personal property from a retailer that does not collect these taxes (a "noncollecting retailer") to fill out a return and remit the taxes to the Department directly.

Voluntary compliance with the latter requirement is relatively low, leading to a significant loss of tax revenue, especially as Internet retailers have increasingly displaced their brick-and-mortar kin. In the decade before this suit was filed in 2010, e-commerce more than tripled. With approximately 25 percent of taxes unpaid on Internet sales, Colorado estimated in 2010 that its revenue loss attributable to noncompliance would grow by more than $20 million each year.

In hopes of stopping this trend, Colorado enacted legislation in 2010 imposing notice and reporting obligations on noncollecting retailers whose gross sales in Colorado exceed $100,000. Three provisions of that Act, along with their implementing regulations, are at issue here.

First, noncollecting retailers must "notify Colorado purchasers that sales or use tax is due on certain purchases and that the state of Colorado requires the purchaser to file a sales or use tax return." The retailer must provide this notice during each transaction with a Colorado purchaser, and is subject to a penalty of $5 for each transaction in which it fails to do so.

Second, by January 31 of each year, each noncollecting retailer must send a report to all Colorado purchasers who bought more than $500 worth of goods from the retailer in the previous year. That report must list the dates, categories, and amounts of those purchases. It must also contain a notice stating that Colorado "requires a sales or use tax return to be filed and sales or use tax paid on certain Colorado purchases made by the purchaser from the retailer." The retailer is subject to a penalty of $10 for each report it fails to send.

Finally, by March 1 of each year, noncollecting retailers must send a statement to the Department listing the names of their Colorado customers, their known addresses, and the total amount each Colorado customer paid for Colorado purchases in the prior calendar year. A noncollecting retailer that fails to make this report is subject to a penalty of $10 for each customer that it should have listed in the report.

B

Petitioner Direct Marketing Association is a trade association of businesses and organizations that market products directly to consumers, including those in Colorado, via catalogs, print advertisements, broadcast media, and the Internet. Many of its members have no physical presence in Colorado and choose not to collect Colorado sales and use taxes on Colorado purchases. As a result, they are subject to Colorado's notice and reporting requirements.

In 2010, Direct Marketing Association brought suit in the United States District Court for the District of Colorado against the Executive Director of the Department, alleging that the notice and reporting requirements violate provisions of the United States and Colorado Constitutions. As relevant here, Direct Marketing Association alleged that the provisions (1) discriminate against interstate commerce and (2) impose undue burdens on interstate commerce, all in violation of this Court's negative Commerce Clause precedents. At the request of both parties, the District Court stayed all challenges except these two, in order to facilitate expedited consideration. It then granted partial summary judgment to Direct Marketing Association and permanently enjoined enforcement of the notice and reporting requirements.

Exercising appellate jurisdiction under 28 U.S.C. § 1292(a)(1), the United States Court of Appeals for the Tenth Circuit reversed. Without reaching the merits, the Court of Appeals held that the District Court lacked jurisdiction over the suit because of the Tax Injunction Act (TIA), 28 U.S.C. § 1341. Acknowledging that the suit "differs from the prototypical TIA case," the Court of Appeals nevertheless found it barred by the TIA because, if successful, it "would limit, restrict, or hold back the state's chosen method of enforcing its tax laws and generating revenue."

We granted certiorari, and now reverse.

II

Enacted in 1937, the TIA provides that federal district courts "shall not enjoin, suspend or restrain the assessment, levy or collection of any tax under State law where a plain, speedy and efficient remedy may be had in the courts of such State." § 1341. The question before us is whether the relief sought here would "enjoin, suspend or restrain the assessment, levy or collection of any tax under State law." Because we conclude that it would not, we need not consider whether "a plain, speedy and efficient remedy may be had in the courts of" Colorado.

A

The District Court enjoined state officials from enforcing the notice and reporting requirements. Because an injunction is clearly a form of equitable relief barred by the TIA, the question becomes whether the enforcement of the notice and reporting requirements is an act of "assessment, levy or collection." We need not comprehensively define these terms to conclude that they do not encompass enforcement of the notice and reporting requirements at issue.

To begin, the Federal Tax Code has long treated information gathering as a phase of tax administration procedure that occurs before assessment, levy, or collection.

These terms do not encompass Colorado's enforcement of its notice and reporting requirements. The Executive Director does not seriously contend that the provisions at issue here involve a "levy"; instead she portrays them as part of the process of assessment and collection. But the notice and reporting requirements precede the steps of "assessment" and "collection." The notice given to Colorado consumers, for example, informs them of their use-tax liability and prompts them to keep a record of taxable purchases that they will report to the State at some future point. The annual summary that the retailers send to consumers provides them with a reminder of that use-tax liability and the information they need to fill out their annual returns. And the report the retailers file with the Department facilitates audits to determine tax deficiencies. After each of these notices or reports is filed, the State still needs to take further action to assess the taxpayer's use-tax liability and to collect payment from him.

Enforcement of the notice and reporting requirements may improve Colorado's ability to assess and ultimately collect its sales and use taxes from consumers, but the TIA is not keyed to all activities that may improve a State's ability to assess and collect taxes. Such a rule would be inconsistent not only with the text of the statute, but also with our rule favoring clear boundaries in the interpretation of jurisdictional statutes. The TIA is keyed to the acts of assessment, levy, and collection themselves, and enforcement of the notice and reporting requirements is none of these.

## B

Apparently concluding that enforcement of the notice and reporting requirements was not itself an act of "assessment, levy or collection," the Court of Appeals did not rely on those terms to hold that the TIA barred the suit. Instead, it adopted a broad definition of the word "restrain" in the TIA, which bars not only suits to "enjoin assessment, levy or collection" of a state tax but also suits to "suspend or restrain" those activities. Specifically, the Court of Appeals concluded that the TIA bars any suit that would "limit, restrict, or hold back" the assessment, levy, or collection of state taxes. Because the notice and reporting requirements are intended to facilitate collection of taxes, the Court of Appeals reasoned that the relief Direct Marketing Association sought and received would "limit, restrict, or hold back" the Department's collection efforts. That was error.

"Restrain," standing alone, can have several meanings. One is the broad meaning given by the Court of Appeals, which captures orders that merely *inhibit* acts of "assessment, levy and collection." Another, narrower meaning, however, is "to prohibit from action; to put compulsion upon ... to enjoin," which captures only those orders that stop (or perhaps compel) acts of "assessment, levy and collection."

To resolve this ambiguity, we look to the context in which the word is used. As used in the TIA, "restrain" acts on a carefully selected list of technical terms—"assessment, levy, collection"—not on an all-encompassing term, like "taxation." To give "restrain" the broad meaning selected by the Court of Appeals would be to defeat the precision of that list, as virtually any court action related to any phase of taxation might be said to "hold back" "collection." Such a broad construction would thus render "assessment and levy"—not to mention "enjoin and suspend"—mere surplusage, a result we try to avoid.

Finally, adopting a narrower definition is consistent with the rule that "jurisdictional rules should be clear." *Grable v. Darue* (2005). The question—at least for negative injunctions—is whether the relief to some degree stops "assessment, levy or collection," not whether it merely inhibits them.

Applying the correct definition, a suit cannot be understood to "restrain" the "assessment, levy or collection" of a state tax if it merely inhibits those activities.

# III

We take no position on whether a suit such as this one might nevertheless be barred under the "comity doctrine," which "counsels lower federal courts to resist engagement in certain cases falling within their jurisdiction." Under this doctrine, federal courts refrain from "interfering with the fiscal operations of the state governments in all cases where the Federal rights of the persons could otherwise be preserved unimpaired."

Unlike the TIA, the comity doctrine is nonjurisdictional. And here, Colorado did not seek comity from either of the courts below. Accordingly, we leave it to the Tenth Circuit to decide on remand whether the comity argument remains available to Colorado.

Because the TIA does not bar petitioner's suit, we reverse the judgment of the Court of Appeals. Like the Court of Appeals, we express no view on the merits of those claims and remand the case for further proceedings consistent with this opinion.

*It is so ordered.*

**Justice KENNEDY, concurring.**

The opinion of the Court has my unqualified join and assent, for in my view it is complete and correct. It does seem appropriate, and indeed necessary, to add this separate statement concerning what may well be a serious, continuing injustice faced by Colorado and many other States.

There is a powerful case to be made that a retailer doing extensive business within a State has a sufficiently "substantial nexus" to justify imposing some minor tax-collection duty, even if that business is done through mail or the Internet. After all, "interstate commerce may be required to pay its fair share of state taxes." This argument has grown stronger, and the cause more urgent, with time. When the Court decided *Quill*, mail-order sales in the United States totaled $180 billion. But in 1992, the Internet was in its infancy. By 2008, e-commerce sales alone totaled $3.16 trillion per year in the United States.

Because of *Quill* and *Bellas Hess*, States have been unable to collect many of the taxes due on these purchases. California, for example, has estimated that it is able to collect only about 4% of the use taxes due on sales from out-of-state vendors. The result has been a startling revenue shortfall in many States, with concomitant unfairness to local retailers and their customers who do pay taxes at the register. The facts of this case exemplify that trend: Colorado's losses in 2012 are estimated to be around

$170 million. States' education systems, healthcare services, and infrastructure are weakened as a result.

The Internet has caused far-reaching systemic and structural changes in the economy, and, indeed, in many other societal dimensions. Although online businesses may not have a physical presence in some States, the Web has, in many ways, brought the average American closer to most major retailers. A connection to a shopper's favorite store is a click away—regardless of how close or far the nearest storefront. Nearly 70% of American consumers shopped online in 2011. Today buyers have almost instant access to most retailers via cell phones, tablets, and laptops. As a result, a business may be present in a State in a meaningful way without that presence being physical in the traditional sense of the term.

Given these changes in technology and consumer sophistication, it is unwise to delay any longer a reconsideration of the Court's holding in *Quill*. A case questionable even when decided, *Quill* now harms States to a degree far greater than could have been anticipated earlier. It should be left in place only if a powerful showing can be made that its rationale is still correct.

The instant case does not raise this issue in a manner appropriate for the Court to address it. It does provide, however, the means to note the importance of reconsidering doubtful authority. The legal system should find an appropriate case for this Court to reexamine *Quill* and *Bellas Hess*.

# CHAPTER 11

# DAMAGES

States may well have a limit on how much a punitive damages award can be – compared to the actual damages involved. To date the federal courts do not have such a limit – except in Admiralty cases, or as part of specific statutes. Here are two of the famous U.S. Supreme Court cases on punitive damages.

## 116 S.CT. 1589
## SUPREME COURT OF THE UNITED STATES
## BMW OF NORTH AMERICA, INC., PETITIONER,
## V.
## IRA GORE, JR., RESPONDENT

DECIDED MAY 20, 1996

Justice STEVENS delivered the opinion of the Court.

The Due Process Clause of the Fourteenth Amendment prohibits a State from imposing a "grossly excessive" punishment on a tortfeasor. The wrongdoing involved in this case was the decision by a national distributor of automobiles not to advise its dealers, and hence their customers, of predelivery damage to new cars when the cost of repair amounted to less than 3 percent of the car's suggested retail price. The question presented is whether a $2 million punitive damages award to the purchaser of one of these cars exceeds the constitutional limit.

OL:

I

In January 1990, Dr. Ira Gore, Jr. (respondent), purchased a black BMW sports sedan for $40,750.88 from an authorized BMW dealer in Birmingham, Alabama. After driving the car for approximately nine months, and without noticing any flaws in its appearance, Dr. Gore took the car to "Slick Finish," an independent detailer, to make it look "snazzier than it normally would appear." Mr. Slick, the proprietor, detected evidence that the car had been repainted.[FN1] Convinced that he had been cheated, Dr. Gore brought suit against petitioner BMW of North America (BMW), the American distributor of BMW automobiles. Dr. Gore alleged, *inter alia*, that the failure to disclose that the car had been repainted constituted suppression of a material fact. The complaint prayed for $500,000 in compensatory and punitive damages, and costs.

> FN1. The top, hood, trunk, and quarter panels of Dr. Gore's car were repainted at
> BMW's vehicle preparation center in Brunswick, Georgia. The parties presumed that
> the damage was caused by exposure to acid rain during transit between the manufac-
> turing plant in Germany and the preparation center.

At trial, BMW acknowledged that it had adopted a nationwide policy in 1983 concerning cars that were damaged in the course of manufacture or transportation. If the cost of repairing the damage exceeded 3 percent of the car's suggested retail price, the car was placed in company service for a period of time and then sold as used. If the repair cost did not exceed 3 percent of the suggested retail price, however, the car was sold as new without advising the dealer that any repairs had been made. Because the $601.37 cost of repainting Dr. Gore's car was only about 1.5 percent of its suggested retail price, BMW did not disclose the damage or repair to the Birmingham dealer.

Dr. Gore asserted that his repainted car was worth less than a car that had not been refinished. To prove his actual damages of $4,000, he relied on the testimony of a former BMW dealer, who estimated that the value of a repainted BMW was approximately 10 percent less than the value of a new car that had not been damaged and repaired.[FN4] To support his claim for punitive damages, Dr. Gore introduced evidence that since 1983 BMW had sold 983 refinished cars as new, including 14 in Alabama, without disclosing that the cars had been repainted before sale at a cost of more than $300 per vehicle. Using the actual damage estimate of $4,000 per vehicle, Dr. Gore argued that a punitive award of $4 million would provide an appropriate penalty for selling approximately 1,000 cars for more than they were worth.

FN4. The dealer who testified to the reduction in value is the former owner of the Birmingham dealership sued in this action. He sold the dealership approximately one year before the trial.

In defense of its disclosure policy, BMW argued that it was under no obligation to disclose repairs of minor damage to new cars and that Dr. Gore's car was as good as a car with the original factory finish. It disputed Dr. Gore's assertion that the value of the car was impaired by the repainting and argued that this good-faith belief made a punitive award inappropriate. BMW also maintained that transactions in jurisdictions other than Alabama had no relevance to Dr. Gore's claim.

The jury returned a verdict finding BMW liable for compensatory damages of $4,000. In addition, the jury assessed $4 million in punitive damages, based on a determination that the nondisclosure policy constituted "gross, oppressive or malicious" fraud.

BMW filed a post-trial motion to set aside the punitive damages award. The company introduced evidence to establish that its nondisclosure policy was consistent with the laws of roughly 25 States defining the disclosure obligations of automobile manufacturers, distributors, and dealers. The most stringent of these statutes required disclosure of repairs costing more than 3 percent of the suggested retail price; none mandated disclosure of less costly repairs. Relying on these statutes, BMW contended that its conduct was lawful in these States and therefore could not provide the basis for an award of punitive damages.

BMW also drew the court's attention to the fact that its nondisclosure policy had never been adjudged unlawful before this action was filed. Just months before Dr. Gore's case went to trial, the jury in a similar lawsuit filed by another Alabama BMW purchaser found that BMW's failure to disclose paint repair constituted fraud. *Yates v. BMW of North America.*[FN8] Before the judgment in this case, BMW changed its policy by taking steps to avoid the sale of any refinished vehicles in Alabama and two other States. When the $4 million verdict was returned in this case, BMW promptly instituted a nationwide policy of full disclosure of all repairs, no matter how minor.

FN8. While awarding a comparable amount of compensatory damages, the *Yates* jury awarded no punitive damages at all. In *Yates,* the plaintiff also relied on the 1983 nondisclosure policy, but instead of offering evidence of 983 repairs costing more than $300 each, he introduced a bulk exhibit containing 5,856 repair bills to show that petitioner had sold over 5,800 new BMW vehicles without disclosing that they had been repaired.

In response to BMW's arguments, Dr. Gore asserted that the policy change demonstrated the efficacy of the punitive damages award. He noted that while no jury had held the policy unlawful, BMW had received a number of customer complaints relating to undisclosed repairs and had settled some lawsuits. Finally, he maintained that the disclosure statutes of other States were irrelevant because BMW had failed to offer any evidence that the disclosure statutes supplanted, rather than supplemented, existing causes of action for common-law fraud.

The trial judge denied BMW's post-trial motion, holding, *inter alia,* that the award was not excessive. On appeal, the Alabama Supreme Court also rejected BMW's claim that the award exceeded the constitutionally permissible amount. The Alabama Supreme Court did, however, rule in BMW's favor on one critical point: The court found that the jury improperly computed the amount of punitive damages by multiplying Dr. Gore's compensatory damages by the number of similar sales in other jurisdictions. Having found the verdict tainted, the court held that "a constitutionally reasonable punitive damages award in this case is $2,000,000," and therefore ordered a remittitur in that amount.

Because we believed that a review of this case would help to illuminate "the character of the standard that will identify unconstitutionally excessive awards" of punitive damages, we granted certiorari.

II

Punitive damages may properly be imposed to further a State's legitimate interests in punishing unlawful conduct and deterring its repetition. In our federal system, States necessarily have considerable flexibility in determining the level of punitive damages that they will allow in different classes of cases and in any particular case. Most States that authorize exemplary damages afford the jury similar latitude, requiring only that the damages awarded be reasonably necessary to vindicate the State's legitimate interests in punishment and deterrence. Only when an award can fairly be categorized as "grossly excessive" in relation to these interests does it enter the zone of arbitrariness that violates the Due Process Clause of the Fourteenth Amendment. For that reason, the federal excessiveness inquiry appropriately begins with an identification of the state interests that a punitive award is designed to serve. We therefore focus our attention first on the scope of Alabama's legitimate interests in punishing BMW and deterring it from future misconduct.

We may assume, *arguendo,* that it would be wise for every State to adopt Dr. Gore's preferred rule, requiring full disclosure of every presale repair to a car, no matter how trivial and regardless of its actual impact on the value of the car. But while we do not doubt that Congress has ample authority to enact such a policy for the entire Nation, it is clear that no single State could do so, or even impose its own policy choice on neighboring States.

We think it follows from these principles of state sovereignty and comity that a State may not impose economic sanctions on violators of its laws with the intent of changing the tortfeasors' lawful conduct in other States. By attempting to alter BMW's nationwide policy, Alabama would be infringing on the policy choices of other States. To avoid such encroachment, the economic penalties that a State such as Alabama inflicts on those who transgress its laws, whether the penalties take the form of legislatively authorized fines or judicially imposed punitive damages, must be supported by the State's interest in protecting its own consumers and its own economy. Alabama may insist that BMW adhere to a particular disclosure policy in that State. Alabama does not have the power, however, to punish BMW for conduct that was lawful where it occurred and that had no impact on Alabama or its residents. Nor may Alabama impose sanctions on BMW in order to deter conduct that is lawful in other jurisdictions.

## III

Elementary notions of fairness enshrined in our constitutional jurisprudence dictate that a person receive fair notice not only of the conduct that will subject him to punishment, but also of the severity of the penalty that a State may impose. Three guideposts, each of which indicates that BMW did not receive adequate notice of the magnitude of the sanction that Alabama might impose for adhering to the nondisclosure policy adopted in 1983, lead us to the conclusion that the $2 million award against BMW is grossly excessive: the degree of reprehensibility of the nondisclosure; the disparity between the harm or potential harm suffered by Dr. Gore and his punitive damages award; and the difference between this remedy and the civil penalties authorized or imposed in comparable cases. We discuss these considerations in turn.

### Degree of Reprehensibility

Perhaps the most important indicium of the reasonableness of a punitive damages award is the degree of reprehensibility of the defendant's conduct. In this case, none of the aggravating factors associated with particularly reprehensible conduct is present.

Dr. Gore's second argument for treating BMW as a recidivist is that the company should have anticipated that its actions would be considered fraudulent in some, if not all, jurisdictions. This contention overlooks the fact that actionable fraud requires a *material* misrepresentation or omission. This qualifier invites line-drawing of just the sort engaged in by States with disclosure statutes and by BMW. We do not think it can be disputed that there may exist minor imperfections in the finish of a new car that can be repaired (or indeed, left unrepaired) without materially affecting the car's value. There is no evidence that BMW acted in bad faith when it sought to establish the appropriate line between presumptively minor damage and damage requiring disclosure to purchasers. For this purpose, BMW could reasonably rely on state disclosure statutes for guidance. In this regard, it is also significant that there is no evidence that BMW persisted in a course of conduct after it had been adjudged unlawful on even one occasion, let alone repeated occasions.

Finally, the record in this case discloses no deliberate false statements, acts of affirmative misconduct, or concealment of evidence of improper motive.

Ratio

The second and perhaps most commonly cited indicium of an unreasonable or excessive punitive damages award is its ratio to the actual harm inflicted on the plaintiff. The principle that exemplary damages must bear a "reasonable relationship" to compensatory damages has a long pedigree. Scholars have identified a number of early English statutes authorizing the award of multiple damages for particular wrongs. Some 65 different enactments during the period between 1275 and 1753 provided for double, treble, or quadruple damages. Our decisions endorsed the proposition that a comparison between the compensatory award and the punitive award is significant.

The $2 million in punitive damages awarded to Dr. Gore by the Alabama Supreme Court is 500 times the amount of his actual harm as determined by the jury. Moreover, there is no suggestion that Dr. Gore or any other BMW purchaser was threatened with any additional potential harm by BMW's nondisclosure policy.

Of course, we have consistently rejected the notion that the constitutional line is marked by a simple mathematical formula, even one that compares actual *and potential* damages to the punitive award. Indeed, low awards of compensatory damages may properly support a higher ratio than high compensatory awards, if, for example, a particularly egregious act has resulted in only a small amount of economic damages. A higher ratio may also be justified in cases in which the injury is hard to detect or the monetary value of noneconomic harm might have been difficult to determine. It is appropriate, therefore, to reiterate our rejection of a categorical approach. We need not, and indeed we cannot, draw a mathematical bright line between the constitutionally acceptable and the constitutionally unacceptable that would fit every case.

We can say, however, that a general concern of reasonableness properly enters into the constitutional calculus. In most cases, the ratio will be within a constitutionally acceptable range, and remittitur will not be justified on this basis. When the ratio is a breathtaking 500 to 1, however, the award must surely "raise a suspicious judicial eyebrow."

Sanctions for Comparable Misconduct

Comparing the punitive damages award and the civil or criminal penalties that could be imposed for comparable misconduct provides a third indicium of excessiveness.

The maximum civil penalty authorized by the Alabama Legislature for a violation of its Deceptive Trade Practices Act is $2,000; other States authorize more severe sanctions, with the maxima ranging from $5,000 to $10,000. Significantly, some statutes draw a distinction between first offenders and recidivists.

The sanction imposed in this case cannot be justified on the ground that it was necessary to deter future misconduct without considering whether less drastic remedies could be expected to achieve that goal. The fact that a multimillion dollar penalty prompted a change in policy sheds no light on the question whether a lesser deterrent would have adequately protected the interests of Alabama consumers. In the absence of a history of noncompliance with known statutory requirements, there is no basis for assuming that a more modest sanction would not have been sufficient to motivate full compliance with the disclosure requirement imposed by the Alabama Supreme Court in this case.

## IV

The fact that BMW is a large corporation rather than an impecunious individual does not diminish its entitlement to fair notice of the demands that the several States impose on the conduct of its business. Indeed, its status as an active participant in the national economy implicates the federal interest in preventing individual States from imposing undue burdens on interstate commerce. While each State has ample power to protect its own consumers, none may use the punitive damages deterrent as a means of imposing its regulatory policies on the entire Nation.

We are not prepared to draw a bright line marking the limits of a constitutionally acceptable punitive damages award. Whether the appropriate remedy requires a new trial or merely an independent determination by the Alabama Supreme Court of the award necessary to vindicate the economic interests of Alabama consumers is a matter that should be addressed by the state court in the first instance.

[The judgment is reversed, and the case is remanded for further proceedings not inconsistent with this opinion.]

## 128 S.CT. 2605
## SUPREME COURT OF THE UNITED STATES
## EXXON SHIPPING COMPANY, ET AL., PETITIONERS,
## V.
## GRANT BAKER ET AL.

DECIDED JUNE 25, 2008

**Justice SOUTER delivered the opinion of the Court.**

[There are three questions of maritime law before us: whether a shipowner may be liable for punitive damages without acquiescence in the actions causing harm, whether punitive damages have been barred implicitly by federal statutory law making no provision for them, and whether the award of $2.5 billion in this case is greater than maritime law should allow in the circumstances. We are equally divided on the owner's derivative liability, and hold that the federal statutory law does not bar a punitive award on top of damages for economic loss, but that the award here should be limited to an amount equal to compensatory damages.]

I

[On March 24, 1989, the supertanker *Exxon Valdez* grounded on Bligh Reef off the Alaskan coast, fracturing its hull and spilling millions of gallons of crude oil into Prince William Sound. The owner, petitioner Exxon Shipping Co. (now SeaRiver Maritime, Inc.), and its owner, petitioner Exxon Mobil Corp. (collectively, Exxon), have settled state and federal claims for environmental damage, with payments exceeding $1 billion, and this action by respondent Baker and others, including commercial fishermen and native Alaskans, was brought for economic losses to individuals dependent on Prince William Sound for their livelihoods.]

A

The tanker was over 900 feet long and was used by Exxon to carry crude oil from the end of the Trans–Alaska Pipeline in Valdez, Alaska, to the lower 48 States. On the night of the spill it was carrying 53 million gallons of crude oil, or over a million barrels. Its captain was one Joseph Hazelwood, who had completed a 28–day alcohol treatment program while employed by Exxon, as his superiors knew, but dropped out of a prescribed followup program and stopped going to Alcoholics Anonymous meetings. According to the District Court, "there was evidence presented to the jury that after Hazelwood was released from residential treatment, he drank in bars, parking lots, apartments, airports, airplanes, restaurants, hotels, at various ports, and aboard Exxon tankers." The jury also heard contested testimony that Hazelwood drank with Exxon officials and that members of the Exxon management knew of his relapse. Although Exxon had a clear policy prohibiting employees from serving onboard within four hours of consuming alcohol, Exxon presented no evidence that it monitored Hazelwood after his return to duty or considered giving him a shoreside assignment. Witnesses testified that before the *Valdez* left port on the night of the disaster, Hazelwood downed at least five double vodkas in the waterfront bars of Valdez, an intake of about 15 ounces of 80–proof alcohol, enough "that a non-alcoholic would have passed out."

The ship sailed at 9:12 p.m. on March 23, 1989, guided by a state-licensed pilot for the first leg out, through the Valdez Narrows. At 11:20 p.m., Hazelwood took active control and, owing to poor conditions in the outbound shipping lane, radioed the Coast Guard for permission to move east across the inbound lane to a less icy path. Under the conditions, this was a standard move, which the last outbound tanker had also taken, and the Coast Guard cleared the *Valdez* to cross the inbound lane. The tanker accordingly steered east toward clearer waters, but the move put it in the path of an underwater reef off Bligh Island, thus requiring a turn back west into the shipping lane around Busby Light, north of the reef.

Two minutes before the required turn, however, Hazelwood left the bridge and went down to his cabin in order, he said, to do paperwork. This decision was inexplicable. There was expert testimony that, even if their presence is not strictly necessary, captains simply do not quit the bridge during maneuvers like this, and no paperwork could have justified it. And in fact the evidence was that Hazelwood's presence was required, both because there should have been two officers on the bridge at all times and his departure left only one, and because he was the only person on the entire ship licensed to navigate this part of Prince William Sound. To make matters worse, before going below Hazelwood put the tanker on autopilot, speeding it up, making the turn trickier, and any mistake harder to correct.

As Hazelwood left, he instructed the remaining officer, third mate Joseph Cousins, to move the tanker back into the shipping lane once it came abeam of Busby Light. Cousins, unlicensed to navigate in those waters, was left alone with helmsman Robert Kagan, a nonofficer. For reasons that remain a mystery, they failed to make the turn at Busby Light, and a later emergency maneuver attempted by Cousins came too late. The tanker ran aground on Bligh Reef, tearing the hull open and spilling 11 million gallons of crude oil into Prince William Sound.

After Hazelwood returned to the bridge and reported the grounding to the Coast Guard, he tried but failed to rock the *Valdez* off the reef, a maneuver which could have spilled more oil and caused the ship to founder. The Coast Guard's nearly immediate response included a blood test of Hazelwood showing a blood-alcohol level of .061, 11 hours after the spill. Experts testified that to have this much alcohol in his bloodstream so long after the accident, Hazelwood at the time of the spill must have had a blood-alcohol level of around .241, three times the legal limit for driving in most States.

In the aftermath of the disaster, Exxon spent around $2.1 billion in cleanup efforts. The United States charged the company with criminal violations of the Clean Water Act, the Refuse Act of 1899, the Migratory Bird Treaty Act, the Ports and Waterways Safety Act, and the Dangerous Cargo Act. Exxon pleaded guilty to violations of the Clean Water Act, the Refuse Act, and the Migratory Bird Treaty Act and agreed to pay a $150 million fine, later reduced to $25 million plus restitution of $100 million. A civil action by the United States and the State of Alaska for environmental harms ended with a consent decree for Exxon to pay at least $900 million toward restoring natural resources, and it paid another $303 million in voluntary settlements with fishermen, property owners, and other private parties.

B

The remaining civil cases were consolidated into this one against Exxon, Hazelwood, and others. The District Court for the District of Alaska divided the plaintiffs seeking compensatory damages into three classes: commercial fishermen, Native Alaskans, and landowners. At Exxon's behest, the court also certified a mandatory class of all plaintiffs seeking punitive damages, whose number topped 32,000. Respondents here, to whom we will refer as Baker for convenience, are members of that class.

For the purposes of the case, Exxon stipulated to its negligence in the *Valdez* disaster and its ensuing liability for compensatory damages. The court designed the trial accordingly: Phase I considered Exxon and Hazelwood's recklessness and thus their potential for punitive liability; Phase II set compensatory damages for commercial fishermen and Native Alaskans; and Phase III determined the amount of punitive damages for which Hazelwood and Exxon were each liable. (A contemplated Phase IV, setting compensation for still other plaintiffs, was obviated by settlement.)

In Phase II the jury awarded $287 million in compensatory damages to the commercial fishermen. After the Court deducted released claims, settlements, and other payments, the balance outstanding was $19,590,257. Meanwhile, most of the Native Alaskan class had settled their compensatory claims for $20 million, and those who opted out of that settlement ultimately settled for a total of around $2.6 million.

In Phase III, the jury heard about Exxon's management's acts and omissions arguably relevant to the spill. At the close of evidence, the court instructed the jurors on the purposes of punitive damages, emphasizing that they were designed not to provide compensatory relief but to punish and deter the defendants. The court charged the jury to consider the reprehensibility of the defendants' conduct, their financial condition, the magnitude of the harm, and any mitigating facts. The jury awarded $5,000 in punitive damages against Hazelwood and $5 billion against Exxon.

On appeal, the Court of Appeals for the Ninth Circuit remanded twice for adjustments in light of this Court's due process cases before ultimately itself remitting the award to $2.5 billion.

We granted certiorari to consider whether maritime law allows corporate liability for punitive damages on the basis of the acts of managerial agents, whether the Clean Water Act forecloses the award of punitive damages in maritime spill cases, and whether the punitive damages awarded against Exxon in this case were excessive as a matter of maritime common law. We now vacate and remand.

**[Parts II and III omitted.]**

**IV**

Finally, Exxon raises an issue of first impression about punitive damages in maritime law, which falls within a federal court's jurisdiction to decide in the manner of a common law court, subject to the authority of Congress to legislate otherwise if it disagrees with the judicial result. ("Admiralty law is judge-made law to a great extent"); Exxon challenges the size of the remaining $2.5 billion punitive-damages award. The claim goes to our understanding of the place of punishment in modern civil law and reasonable standards of process in administering punitive law, subjects that call for starting with a brief account of the history behind today's punitive damages.

A

The modern Anglo–American doctrine of punitive damages dates back at least to 1763, when a pair of decisions by the Court of Common Pleas recognized the availability of damages "for more than the injury received." In *Wilkes v. Wood*, (1763) one of the foundations of the Fourth Amendment, exemplary damages awarded against the Secretary of State, responsible for an unlawful search of John Wilkes's papers, were a spectacular £4,000. And in *Huckle v. Money*, (K.B.1763), the same judge who is recorded in *Wilkes* gave an opinion upholding a jury's award of £300 (against a government officer again) although "if the jury had been confined by their oath to consider the mere personal injury only, perhaps £20 damages would have been thought damages sufficient."

Awarding damages beyond the compensatory was not, however, a wholly novel idea even then, legal codes from ancient times through the Middle Ages having called for multiple damages for certain especially harmful acts. See, *e.g.*, Code of Hammurabi, (tenfold penalty for stealing the goat of a freed man). Punitive damages were a common law innovation untethered to strict numerical multipliers, and the doctrine promptly crossed the Atlantic, to become widely accepted in American courts by the middle of the 19th century.

B

Regardless of the alternative rationales over the years, the consensus today is that punitives are aimed not at compensation but principally at retribution and deterring harmful conduct. This consensus informs the doctrine in most modern American jurisdictions, where juries are customarily instructed on twin goals of punitive awards. The prevailing rule in American courts also limits punitive damages to cases of what the Court in *Day*, spoke of as "enormity," where a defendant's conduct is "outrageous," owing to "gross negligence," "willful, wanton, and reckless indifference for the rights of others," or behavior even more deplorable.

Regardless of culpability, however, heavier punitive awards have been thought to be justifiable when wrongdoing is hard to detect (increasing chances of getting away with it), see, *e.g.*, *BMW of North America, Inc. v. Gore* (1996) And, with a broadly analogous object, some regulatory schemes provide by statute for multiple recovery in order to induce private litigation to supplement official enforcement that might fall short if unaided. See, *e.g.*, *Reiter v. Sonotone Corp.*, (1979) (discussing antitrust treble damages).

C

State regulation of punitive damages varies. A few States award them rarely, or not at all. Nebraska bars punitive damages entirely, on state constitutional grounds. Four others permit punitive damages only when authorized by statute: Louisiana, Massachusetts, and Washington as a matter of common law, and New Hampshire by statute codifying common law tradition. Michigan courts recognize only exemplary damages supportable as compensatory, rather than truly punitive, while Connecticut courts have limited what they call punitive recovery to the "expenses of bringing the legal action, including attorney's fees, less taxable costs."

As for procedure, in most American jurisdictions the amount of the punitive award is generally determined by a jury in the first instance, and that "determination is then reviewed by trial and appellate courts to ensure that it is reasonable. Many States have gone further by imposing statutory limits on punitive awards, in the form of absolute monetary caps, see, e.g., Va.Code ($350,000 cap), a maximum ratio of punitive to compensatory damages; Ohio Rev.Code (2:1 ratio in most tort cases); or, frequently, some combination of the two, see, e.g., Alaska Stat. (greater of 3:1 ratio or $500,000 in most actions). The States that rely on a multiplier have adopted a variety of ratios, ranging from 5:1 to 1:1.

Despite these limitations, punitive damages overall are higher and more frequent in the United States than they are anywhere else.

For further contrast with American practice, Canada and Australia allow exemplary damages for outrageous conduct, but awards are considered extraordinary and rarely issue. Noncompensatory damages are not part of the civil-code tradition and thus unavailable in such countries as France, Germany, Austria, and Switzerland. And some legal systems not only decline to recognize punitive damages themselves but refuse to enforce foreign punitive judgments as contrary to public policy. See refusals to enforce judgments by Japanese, Italian, and German courts. "American parties should not anticipate smooth sailing when seeking to have a domestic punitive damages award recognized and enforced in other countries".

D

American punitive damages have been the target of audible criticism in recent decades, but the most recent studies tend to undercut much of it. A survey of the literature reveals that discretion to award punitive damages has not mass-produced runaway awards, and although some studies show the dollar amounts of punitive-damages awards growing over time, even in real terms, by most accounts the median ratio of punitive to compensatory awards has remained less than 1:1. Nor do the data substantiate a marked increase in the percentage of cases with punitive awards over the past several decades. The figures thus show an overall restraint and suggest that in many instances a high ratio of punitive to compensatory damages is substantially greater than necessary to punish or deter.

The real problem, it seems, is the stark unpredictability of punitive awards. Courts of law are concerned with fairness and consistency, and evidence that the median ratio of punitive to compensatory awards falls within a reasonable zone, or that punitive awards are infrequent, fails to tell us whether the spread between high and low individual awards is acceptable.

Starting with the premise of a punitive-damages regime, these ranges of variation might be acceptable or even desirable if they resulted from judges' and juries' refining their judgments to reach a generally accepted optimal level of penalty and deterrence in cases involving a wide range of circumstances, while producing fairly consistent results in cases with similar facts. But anecdotal evidence suggests that nothing of that sort is going on. One of our own leading cases on punitive damages, with a $4 million verdict by an Alabama jury, noted that a second Alabama case with strikingly similar facts produced "a comparable amount of compensatory damages" but "no punitive damages at all." See *Gore.* As the Supreme Court of Alabama candidly explained, "the disparity between the two jury verdicts was a reflection of the inherent uncertainty of the trial process." We are aware of no scholarly work pointing to consistency across punitive awards in cases involving similar claims and circumstances.

E

The Court's response to outlier punitive-damages awards has thus far been confined by claims at the constitutional level, and our cases have announced due process standards that every award must pass. Although "we have consistently rejected the notion that the constitutional line is marked by a simple mathematical formula," we have determined that "few awards exceeding a single-digit ratio between punitive and compensatory damages, to a significant degree, will satisfy due process," *State Farm.*

Today's enquiry differs from due process review because the case arises under federal maritime jurisdiction, and we are reviewing a jury award for conformity with maritime law, rather than the outer limit allowed by due process; we are examining the verdict in the exercise of federal maritime common law authority, which precedes and should obviate any application of the constitutional standard.

Our review of punitive damages today, then, considers not their intersection with the Constitution, but the desirability of regulating them as a common law remedy for which responsibility lies with this Court as a source of judge-made law in the absence of statute. Whatever may be the constitutional significance of the unpredictability of high punitive awards, this feature of happenstance is in tension with the function of the awards as punitive, just because of the implication of unfairness that an eccentrically high punitive verdict carries in a system whose commonly held notion of law rests on a sense of fairness in dealing with one another. Thus, a penalty should be reasonably predictable in its severity, so that even Justice Holmes's "bad man" can look ahead with some ability to know what the stakes are in choosing one course of action or another. And when the bad man's counterparts turn up from time to time, the penalty scheme they face ought to threaten them with a fair probability of suffering in like degree when they wreak like damage. The common sense of justice would surely bar penalties that reasonable people would think excessive for the harm caused in the circumstances.

V

Applying this standard to the present case, we take for granted the District Court's calculation of the total relevant compensatory damages at $507.5 million. See *In re Exxon Valdez.* A punitive-to-compensatory ratio of 1:1 thus yields maximum punitive damages in that amount.

We therefore vacate the judgment and remand the case for the Court of Appeals to remit the punitive-damages award accordingly.

# CHAPTER 12

# EFFECT OF PRIOR LITIGATION

1. Once litigation goes to conclusion, and all rights of appeal have terminated, that is the end of the cause of action. The plaintiff is barred from bringing that suit in any other court, at any time. The rules of *res judicata*, (also known as *claim preclusion*), and *collateral estoppel*, (also known as *issue preclusion*), are designed to put an end to the controversy.

However, as might be expected, complications arise. The following case, *Taylor v. Sturgell*, contains an excellent explanation of the doctrine of *claim preclusion* – as it may – or may not – affect a person who was not actually a party to a prior suit seeking exactly the same remedy, against exactly the same defendant as that now sought by the new plaintiff.

Because this is a recent U.S. Supreme Court case it is an especially valuable discussion of the whole area of claim preclusion. As with so many other situations in the law, notice how the particular circumstances of a case will affect the outcome.

It is easy to state the basic rule that, "No person is bound by a judgment in litigation to which he was not a party." But as you will see from *Taylor v. Sturgell*, that is not actually the rule. There are, in fact, many situations in which a person will be bound by a judgment in a case to which he or she was not a party.

It is important to notice the many different situations discussed in *Taylor*, and the other important cases described in *Taylor*. The area of res judicata, (also called claim preclusion), can be more complex than it might at first appear to be.

# A. RES JUDICATA (CLAIM PRECLUSION)

### 128 S. CT. 2161
### SUPREME COURT OF THE UNITED STATES
### BRENT TAYLOR, PETITIONER
### V.
### ROBERT A. STURGELL, ACTING ADMINISTRATOR, FEDERAL
### AVIATION ADMINISTRATION, ET AL., RESPONDENTS

DECIDED JUNE 12, 2008.

Justice Ginsburg delivered the opinion for a unanimous Court.

"It is a principle of general application in Anglo-American jurisprudence that one is not bound by a judgment *in personam* in a litigation in which he is not designated as a party or to which he has not been made a party by service of process." *Hansberry v. Lee, (1940)*. Several exceptions, recognized in this Court's decisions, temper this basic rule. In a class action, for example, a person not named as a party may be bound by a judgment on the merits of the action, if she was adequately represented by a party who actively participated in the litigation. In this case, we consider for the first time whether there is a "virtual representation" exception to the general rule against precluding non-parties. Adopted by a number of courts, including the courts below in the case now before us, the exception so styled is broader than any we have so far approved.

The virtual representation question we examine in this opinion arises in the following context. Petitioner Brent Taylor filed a lawsuit under the Freedom of Information Act seeking certain documents from the Federal Aviation Administration. Greg Herrick, Taylor's friend, had previously brought an unsuccessful suit seeking the same records. The two men have no legal relationship, and there is no evidence that Taylor controlled, financed, participated in, or even had notice of Herrick's earlier suit. Nevertheless, the D. C. Circuit held Taylor's suit precluded by the judgment against Herrick because, in that court's assessment, Herrick qualified as Taylor's "virtual representative."

We disapprove the doctrine of preclusion by "virtual representation," and hold, based on the record as it now stands, that the judgment against Herrick does not bar Taylor from maintaining this suit.

## I

The Freedom of Information Act (FOIA) accords "any person" a right to request any records held by a federal agency. No reason need be given for a FOIA request, and unless the requested materials fall within one of the Act's enumerated exemptions, see § 552(a)(3)(E), (b), the agency must "make the records promptly available" to the requester. If an agency refuses to furnish the requested records, the requester may file suit in federal court and obtain an injunction "ordering the production of any agency records improperly withheld." § 552(a)(4)(B).

The courts below held the instant FOIA suit barred by the judgment in earlier litigation seeking the same records. Because the lower courts' decisions turned on the connection between the two lawsuits, we begin with a full account of each action.

## A

The first suit was filed by Greg Herrick, an antique aircraft enthusiast and the owner of an F-45 airplane, a vintage model manufactured by the Fairchild Engine and Airplane Corporation (FEAC) in the 1930's. In 1997, seeking information that would help him restore his plane to its original condition, Herrick filed a FOIA request asking the Federal Aviation Administration (FAA) for copies of any technical documents about the F-45 contained in the agency's records.

To gain a certificate authorizing the manufacture and sale of the F-45, FEAC had submitted to the FAA's predecessor, the Civil Aeronautics Authority, detailed specifications and other technical data about the plane. Hundreds of pages of documents produced by FEAC in the certification process remain in the FAA's records. The FAA denied Herrick's request, however, upon finding that the documents he sought are subject to FOIA's exemption for "trade secrets and commercial or financial information obtained from a person and privileged or confidential," § 552(b)(4). In an administrative appeal, Herrick urged that FEAC and its successors had waived any trade-secret protection. The FAA thereupon contacted FEAC's corporate successor, respondent Fairchild Corporation (Fairchild). Because Fairchild objected to release of the documents, the agency adhered to its original decision.

Herrick then filed suit in the U. S. District Court for the District of Wyoming. Challenging the FAA's invocation of the trade-secret exemption, Herrick placed heavy weight on a 1955 letter from FEAC to the Civil Aeronautics Authority. The letter authorized the agency to lend any documents in its files to the public "for use in making repairs or replacement parts for aircraft produced by Fairchild." This broad authorization, Herrick maintained, showed that the F-45 certification records held by the FAA could not be regarded as "secret" or "confidential" within the meaning of § 552(b)(4).

Rejecting Herrick's argument, the District Court granted summary judgment to the FAA. The 1955 letter, the court reasoned, did not deprive the F-45 certification documents of trade-secret status, for those documents were never in fact released pursuant to the letter's blanket authorization. The court also stated that even if the 1955 letter had waived trade-secret protection, Fairchild had successfully "reversed" the waiver by objecting to the FAA's release of the records to Herrick.

On appeal, the Tenth Circuit agreed with Herrick that the 1955 letter had stripped the requested documents of trade-secret protection. But the Court of Appeals upheld the District Court's alternative determination--i.e., that Fairchild had restored trade-secret status by objecting to Herrick's FOIA request. On that ground, the appeals court affirmed the entry of summary judgment for the FAA.

B

The Tenth Circuit's decision issued on July 24, 2002. Less than a month later, on August 22, petitioner Brent Taylor--a friend of Herrick's and an antique aircraft enthusiast in his own right--submitted a FOIA request seeking the same documents Herrick had unsuccessfully sued to obtain. When the FAA failed to respond, Taylor filed a complaint in the U. S. District Court for the District of Columbia. Like Herrick, Taylor argued that FEAC's 1955 letter had stripped the records of their trade-secret status. But Taylor also sought to litigate the two issues concerning recapture of protected status that Herrick had failed to raise in his appeal to the Tenth Circuit.

After Fairchild intervened as a defendant, the District Court in D. C. concluded that Taylor's suit was barred by claim preclusion; accordingly, it granted summary judgment to Fairchild and the FAA. The court acknowledged that Taylor was not a party to Herrick's suit, however, it held that a nonparty may be bound by a judgment if she was "virtually represented" by a party.

The Eighth Circuit's seven-factor test for virtual representation, adopted by the District Court in Taylor's case, requires an "identity of interests" between the person to be bound and a party to the judgment.

The record before the District Court in Taylor's suit revealed the following facts about the relationship between Taylor and Herrick: Taylor is the president of the

Antique Aircraft Association, an organization to which Herrick belongs; the two men are "close associates," Herrick asked Taylor to help restore Herrick's F-45, though they had no contract or agreement for Taylor's participation in the restoration; Taylor was represented by the lawyer who represented Herrick in the earlier litigation; and Herrick apparently gave Taylor documents that Herrick had obtained from the FAA during discovery in his suit.

Fairchild and the FAA conceded that Taylor had not participated in Herrick's suit. The D. C. District Court determined, however, that Herrick ranked as Taylor's virtual representative because the facts fit each of the other six indicators on the Eighth Circuit's list. Accordingly, the District Court held Taylor's suit, seeking the same documents Herrick had requested, barred by the judgment against Herrick.

The D. C. Circuit affirmed.

We granted certiorari to resolve the disagreement among the Circuits over the permissibility and scope of preclusion based on 'virtual representation."

## II

The preclusive effect of a federal-court judgment is determined by federal common law. For judgments in federal-question cases--for example, Herrick's FOIA suit-- federal courts participate in developing "uniform federal rules" of res judicata, which this Court has ultimate authority to determine and declare.[4] The federal common law of preclusion is, of course, subject to due process limitations.

4 For judgments in diversity cases, federal law incorporates the rules of preclusion applied by the State in which the rendering court sits.

Taylor's case presents an issue of first impression in this sense: Until now, we have never addressed the doctrine of "virtual representation" adopted (in varying forms) by several Circuits and relied upon by the courts below. Our inquiry, however, is guided by well-established precedent regarding the propriety of nonparty preclusion. We review that precedent before taking up directly the issue of virtual representation.

## A

The preclusive effect of a judgment is defined by claim preclusion which is also referred to as "res judicata." Under the doctrine of claim preclusion, a final judgment forecloses "successive litigation of the very same claim, whether or not relitigation of the claim raises the same issues as the earlier suit." Issue preclusion, in contrast, bars "successive litigation of an issue of fact or law actually litigated and resolved in a valid court determination essential to the prior judgment," even if the issue recurs in the context of a different claim

A person who was not a party to a suit generally has not had a "full and fair opportunity to litigate" the claims and issues settled in that suit. The application of claim and issue preclusion to nonparties thus runs up against the "deep-rooted historic tradition that everyone should have his own day in court." Indicating the strength of that tradition, we have often repeated the general rule that "one is not bound by a judgment *in personam* in a litigation in which he is not designated as a party or to which he has not been made a party by service of process."

B

Though hardly in doubt, the rule against nonparty preclusion is subject to exceptions. For present purposes, the recognized exceptions can be grouped into six categories.

First, "a person who agrees to be bound by the determination of issues in an action between others is bound in accordance with the terms of his agreement." For example, "if separate actions involving the same transaction are brought by different plaintiffs against the same defendant, all the parties to all the actions may agree that the question of the defendant's liability will be definitely determined, one way or the other, in a 'test case.'"

Second, nonparty preclusion may be justified based on a variety of pre-existing "substantive legal relationships" between the person to be bound and a party to the judgment. Qualifying relationships include, but are not limited to, preceding and succeeding owners of property, bailee and bailor, and assignee and assignor. These exceptions originated "as much from the needs of property law as from the values of preclusion by judgment."

Third, we have confirmed that, "in certain limited circumstances," a nonparty may be bound by a judgment because she was "adequately represented by someone with the same interests who was a party" to the suit. Representative suits with preclusive effect on nonparties include properly conducted class actions, and suits brought by trustees, guardians, and other fiduciaries.

Fourth, a nonparty is bound by a judgment if she "assumed control" over the litigation in which that judgment was rendered. Because such a person has had "the opportunity to present proofs and argument," he has already "had his day in court" even though he was not a formal party to the litigation.

Fifth, a party bound by a judgment may not avoid its preclusive force by relitigating through a proxy. Preclusion is thus in order when a person who did not participate in a litigation later brings suit as the designated representative of a person who was a party to the prior adjudication. And although our decisions have not addressed the issue directly, it also seems clear that preclusion is appropriate when a nonparty later brings suit as an agent for a party who is bound by a judgment.

Sixth, in certain circumstances a special statutory scheme may "expressly foreclose successive litigation by nonlitigants if the scheme is otherwise consistent with due process." Examples of such schemes include bankruptcy and probate proceedings, and *quo warranto* actions or other suits that, "under the governing law, may be brought only on behalf of the public at large."

## III

### A (omitted)

### B

A diffuse balancing approach to nonparty preclusion would likely create more headaches than it relieves. Most obviously, it could significantly complicate the task of district courts faced in the first instance with preclusion questions. An all-things-considered balancing approach might spark wide-ranging, time-consuming, and expensive discovery tracking factors potentially relevant under seven- or five-prong tests. And after the relevant facts are established, district judges would be called upon to evaluate them under a standard that provides no firm guidance. Preclusion doctrine, it should be recalled, is intended to reduce the burden of litigation on courts and parties. "In this area of the law," we agree, "'crisp rules with sharp corners' are preferable to a round-about doctrine of opaque standards."

### C

*Stare decisis* will allow courts swiftly to dispose of repetitive suits brought in the same circuit. Even when *decisis stare* is not dispositive, "the human tendency not to waste money will deter the bringing of suits based on claims or issues that have already been adversely determined against others." This intuition seems to be borne out by experience: The FAA has not called our attention to any instances of abusive FOIA suits in the Circuits that reject the virtual representation theory respondents advocate here.

## IV

For the foregoing reasons, we disapprove the theory of virtual representation on which the decision below rested. The preclusive effects of a judgment in a federal-question case decided by a federal court should instead be determined according to the established grounds for nonparty preclusion described in this opinion.

Although references to "virtual representation" have proliferated in the lower courts, our decision is unlikely to occasion any great shift in actual practice. Many opinions use the term "virtual representation" in reaching results at least arguably defensible on established grounds. In these cases, dropping the "virtual representation" label would lead to clearer analysis with little, if any, change in outcomes. ("The term 'virtual representation' has cast more shadows than light on the problem of nonparty preclusion.")

In some cases, however, lower courts have relied on virtual representation to extend nonparty preclusion beyond the latter doctrine's proper bounds. We now turn back to Taylor's action to determine whether his suit is such a case, or whether the result reached by the courts below can be justified on one of the recognized grounds for nonparty preclusion.

### A

It is uncontested that four of the six grounds for nonparty preclusion have no application here: There is no indication that Taylor agreed to be bound by Herrick's litigation, that Taylor and Herrick have any legal relationship, that Taylor exercised any control over Herrick's suit, or that this suit implicates any special statutory scheme limiting relitigation. Neither the FAA nor Fairchild contends otherwise.

It is equally clear that preclusion cannot be justified on the theory that Taylor was adequately represented in Herrick's suit. Nothing in the record indicates that Herrick understood himself to be suing on Taylor's behalf, that Taylor even knew of Herrick's suit, or that the Wyoming District Court took special care to protect Taylor's interests. Under our pathmarking precedent, therefore, Herrick's representation was not "adequate."

That leaves only the fifth category: preclusion because a nonparty to an earlier litigation has brought suit as a representative or agent of a party who is bound by the prior adjudication. Taylor is not Herrick's legal representative and he has not purported to sue in a representative capacity. He concedes, however, that preclusion would be appropriate if respondents could demonstrate that he is acting as Herrick's "undisclosed agent."

Respondents argue here, as they did below, that Taylor's suit is a collusive attempt to relitigate Herrick's action. The D. C. Circuit considered a similar question in addressing the "tactical maneuvering" prong of its virtual representation test. The Court of Appeals did not, however, treat the issue as one of agency, and it expressly declined to reach any definitive conclusions due to "the ambiguity of the facts." We therefore remand to give the courts below an opportunity to determine whether Taylor, in pursuing the instant FOIA suit, is acting as Herrick's agent. Taylor concedes that such a remand is appropriate.

We have never defined the showing required to establish that a nonparty to a prior adjudication has become a litigating agent for a party to the earlier case. Because the issue has not been briefed in any detail, we do not discuss the matter elaborately here. We note, however, that courts should be cautious about finding preclusion on this basis. A mere whiff of "tactical maneuvering" will not suffice; instead, principles of agency law are suggestive. They indicate that preclusion is appropriate only if the putative agent's conduct of the suit is subject to the control of the party who is bound by the prior adjudication. ("A principal has the right to control the conduct of the agent with respect to matters entrusted to him.").

B

On remand, Fairchild suggests, Taylor should bear the burden of proving he is not acting as Herrick's agent. Fairchild justifies this proposed burden-shift on the ground that "it is unlikely an opposing party will have access to direct evidence of collusion."

We reject Fairchild's suggestion. Claim preclusion, like issue preclusion, is an affirmative defense. See *Fed. Rule Civ. Proc. 8(c)* Ordinarily, it is incumbent on the defendant to plead and prove such a defense, and we have never recognized claim preclusion as an exception to that general rule. ("A party asserting preclusion must carry the burden of establishing all necessary elements."). We acknowledge that direct evidence justifying nonparty preclusion is often in the hands of plaintiffs rather than defendants. But "very often one must plead and prove matters as to which his adversary has superior access to the proof." In these situations, targeted interrogatories or deposition questions can reduce the information disparity. We see no greater cause here than in other matters of affirmative defense to disturb the traditional allocation of the proof burden.

For the reasons stated, the judgment of the United States Court of Appeals for the District of Columbia Circuit is vacated, and the case is remanded for further proceedings consistent with this opinion.

2. Some years after all this litigation, Fairchild finally decided to release the specifications.

3. In the following 2001 case Justice Scalia creates some federal common law to govern what sort of state dismissals will have claim preclusive effect in federal courts sitting in a state different from the state in which the original judgment was issued.

121 S.CT. 1021

SUPREME COURT OF THE UNITED STATES

SEMTEK INTERNATIONAL INCORPORATED, PETITIONERS,

V.

LOCKHEED MARTIN CORPORATION, ET AL., RESPONDENTS

DECIDED FEBRUARY 27, 2001

SCALIA, J., delivered the opinion for a unanimous Court.

This case presents the question whether the claim-preclusive effect of a federal judgment dismissing a diversity action on statute-of-limitations grounds is determined by the law of the State in which the federal court sits.

I

Petitioner filed a complaint against respondent in California state court, alleging inducement of breach of contract and various business torts. Respondent removed the case to the United States District Court for the Central District of California on the basis of diversity of citizenship, and successfully moved to dismiss petitioner's claims as barred by California's 2–year statute of limitations. In its order of dismissal, the District Court, adopting language suggested by respondent, dismissed petitioner's claims "in their entirety on the merits and with prejudice." Without contesting the District Court's designation of its dismissal as "on the merits," petitioner appealed to the Court of Appeals for the Ninth Circuit, which affirmed the District Court's order. Petitioner also brought suit against respondent in the State Circuit Court for Baltimore City, Maryland, alleging the same causes of action, which were not time barred under Maryland's 3–year statute of limitations. Respondent sought injunctive relief against this action from the California federal court under the All Writs Act, 28 U.S.C. § 1651, and removed the action to the United States District Court for the District of Maryland on federal-question grounds (diversity grounds were not available because Lockheed "is a Maryland citizen.") The California federal court denied the relief requested, and the Maryland federal court remanded the case to state court because the federal question arose only by way of defense. Following a hearing, the Maryland state court granted respondent's motion to dismiss on the ground of res judicata. Petitioner then returned to the California federal court and the Ninth Circuit, unsuccessfully moving both courts to amend the former's earlier order so as to indicate that the dismissal was not "on the merits." Petitioner also appealed the Maryland trial court's order of dismissal to the Maryland Court of Special Appeals. The Court of Special Appeals affirmed, holding that, regardless of whether California would have accorded claim-preclusive effect to a statute-of-limitations dismissal by one of its own courts, the dismissal by the California federal court barred the complaint filed in Maryland, since the res judicata effect of federal diversity judgments is prescribed by federal law, under which the earlier dismissal was on the merits and claim preclusive. After the Maryland Court of Appeals declined to review the case, we granted certiorari.

## II

Petitioner contends that the outcome of this case is controlled by *Dupasseur v. Rochereau,* (1874), which held that the res judicata effect of a federal diversity judgment "is such as would belong to judgments of the State courts rendered under similar circumstances," and may not be accorded any "higher sanctity or effect." Since, petitioner argues, the dismissal of an action on statute-of-limitations grounds by a California state court would not be claim preclusive, it follows that the similar dismissal of this diversity action by the California federal court cannot be claim preclusive. While we agree that this would be the result demanded by *Dupasseur,* the case is not dispositive because it was decided under the Conformity Act of 1872, which required federal courts to apply the procedural law of the forum State in nonequity cases. That arguably affected the outcome of the case.

Respondent, for its part, contends that the outcome of this case is controlled by Federal Rule of Civil Procedure 41(b), which provides as follows:

> Involuntary Dismissal: Effect Thereof. For failure of the plaintiff to prosecute or to comply with these rules or any order of court, a defendant may move for dismissal

of an action or of any claim against the defendant. Unless the court in its order for dismissal otherwise specifies, a dismissal under this subdivision and any dismissal not provided for in this rule, other than a dismissal for lack of jurisdiction, for improper venue, or for failure to join a party under Rule 19, operates as an adjudication upon the merits.

Since the dismissal here did not "otherwise specify" (indeed, it specifically stated that it *was* "on the merits"), and did not pertain to the excepted subjects of jurisdiction, venue, or joinder, it follows, respondent contends, that the dismissal "is entitled to claim preclusive effect."

Implicit in this reasoning is the unstated minor premise that all judgments denominated "on the merits" are entitled to claim-preclusive effect. That premise is not necessarily valid. The original connotation of an "on the merits" adjudication is one that actually "passes directly on the substance of a particular claim" before the court. That connotation remains common to every jurisdiction of which we are aware. ("The prototypical judgment on the merits is one in which the merits of a party's claim are in fact adjudicated for or against the party after trial of the substantive issues"). And it is, we think, the meaning intended in those many statements to the effect that a judgment "on the merits" triggers the doctrine of res judicata or claim preclusion. See, *e.g., Parklane Hosiery Co. v. Shore.*

But over the years the meaning of the term "judgment on the merits" "has gradually undergone change," and it has come to be applied to some judgments (such as the one involved here) that do *not* pass upon the substantive merits of a claim and hence do *not* (in many jurisdictions) entail claim-preclusive effect. That is why the Restatement of Judgments has abandoned the use of the term—"because of its possibly misleading connotations."

In short, it is no longer true that a judgment "on the merits" is necessarily a judgment entitled to claim-preclusive effect; and there are a number of reasons for believing that the phrase "adjudication upon the merits" does not bear that meaning in Rule 41(b). To begin with, Rule 41(b) sets forth nothing more than a default rule for determining the import of a dismissal (a dismissal is "upon the merits," with the three stated exceptions, unless the court "otherwise specifies"). This would be a highly peculiar context in which to announce a federally prescribed rule on the complex question of claim preclusion, saying in effect, "All federal dismissals (with three specified exceptions) preclude suit elsewhere, unless the court otherwise specifies."

And even apart from the purely default character of Rule 41(b), it would be peculiar to find a rule governing the effect that must be accorded federal judgments by other courts ensconced in rules governing the internal procedures of the rendering court itself. Indeed, such a rule would arguably violate the jurisdictional limitation of the Rules Enabling Act: that the Rules "shall not abridge, enlarge or modify any substantive right." In the present case, for example, if California law left petitioner free to sue on this claim in Maryland even after the California statute of limitations had expired, the federal court's extinguishment of that right (through Rule 41(b)'s mandated claim-preclusive effect of its judgment) would seem to violate this limitation.

Moreover, as so interpreted, the Rule would in many cases violate the federalism principle of *Erie R. Co. v. Tompkins,* by engendering " 'substantial' variations in outcomes between state and federal litigation" which would "likely influence the choice of a forum," *Hanna v. Plumer, Guaranty Trust.* With regard to the claim-preclusion issue involved in the present case, for example, the traditional rule is that expiration of the applicable statute of limitations merely bars the remedy and does not extinguish the substantive right, so that dismissal on that ground does not have claim-preclusive effect in other jurisdictions with longer, unexpired limitations periods. See Restatement (Second) of Conflict of Laws §§ 142(2), 143 (1969); Restatement of Judgments § 49, Comment *a* (1942). Out-of-state defendants sued on stale claims in California and in other States adhering to this traditional rule would systematically remove state-law suits brought against them to federal court—where, unless otherwise specified, a statute-of-limitations dismissal would bar suit everywhere.

Finally, if Rule 41(b) did mean what respondent suggests, we would surely have relied upon it in our cases recognizing the claim-preclusive effect of federal judgments in federal-question cases. Yet for over half a century since the promulgation of Rule 41(b), we have not once done so.

We think the key to a more reasonable interpretation of the meaning of "operates as an adjudication upon the merits" in Rule 41(b) is to be found in Rule 41(a), which, in discussing the effect of voluntary dismissal by the plaintiff, makes clear that an "adjudication upon the merits" is the opposite of a "dismissal without prejudice":

> Unless otherwise stated in the notice of dismissal or stipulation, the dismissal is
> without prejudice, except that a notice of dismissal operates as an adjudication upon
> the merits when filed by a plaintiff who has once dismissed in any court of the United
> States or of any state an action based on or including the same claim.

The primary meaning of "dismissal without prejudice," we think, is dismissal without barring the plaintiff from returning later, to the same court, with the same underlying claim. That will also ordinarily (though not always) have the consequence of not barring the claim from *other* courts, but its primary meaning relates to the dismissing court itself. Thus, Black's Law Dictionary (7th ed.1999) defines "dismissed without prejudice" as "removed from the court's docket in such a way that the plaintiff may refile the same suit on the same claim," and defines "dismissal without prejudice" as "a dismissal that does not bar the plaintiff from refiling the lawsuit within the applicable limitations period."

We think, then, that the effect of the "adjudication upon the merits" default provision of Rule 41(b)—and, presumably, of the explicit order in the present case that used the language of that default provision—is simply that, unlike a dismissal "without prejudice," the dismissal in the present case barred refiling of the same claim in the United States District Court for the Central District of California. That is undoubtedly a necessary condition, but it is not a sufficient one, for claim-preclusive effect in other courts.

## III

Having concluded that the claim-preclusive effect, in Maryland, of this California federal diversity judgment is dictated neither by *Dupasseur v. Rochereau,* as petitioner contends, nor by Rule 41(b), as respondent contends, we turn to consideration of what determines the issue. Neither the Full Faith and Credit Clause, U.S. Const., Art. IV, § 1, nor the full faith and credit statute, 28 U.S.C. § 1738, addresses the question. By their terms they govern the effects to be given only to state-court judgments (and, in the case of the statute, to judgments by courts of territories and possessions). And no other federal textual provision, neither of the Constitution nor of any statute, addresses the claim-preclusive effect of a judgment in a federal diversity action.

It is also true, however, that no federal textual provision addresses the claim-preclusive effect of a federal-court judgment in a federal-question case, yet we have long held that States cannot give those judgments merely whatever effect they would give their own judgments, but must accord them the effect that this Court prescribes. The reasoning of that line of cases suggests, moreover, that even when States are allowed to give federal judgments (notably, judgments in diversity cases) no more than the effect accorded to state judgments, that disposition is by direction of *this* Court, which has the last word on the claim-preclusive effect of *all* federal judgments:

> "It is true that for some purposes and within certain limits it is only required that the judgments of the courts of the United States shall be given the same force and effect as are given the judgments of the courts of the States wherein they are rendered; but it is equally true that whether a Federal judgment has been given due force and effect in the state court is a Federal question reviewable by this court, which will determine for itself whether such judgment has been given due weight or otherwise.

In other words, in *Dupasseur* the State was allowed (indeed, required) to give a federal diversity judgment no more effect than it would accord one of its own judgments only because reference to state law was *the federal rule that this Court deemed appropriate.* In short, federal common law governs the claim-preclusive effect of a dismissal by a federal court sitting in diversity.

It is left to us, then, to determine the appropriate federal rule. And despite the sea change that has occurred in the background law since *Dupasseur* was decided—not only repeal of the Conformity Act but also the watershed decision of this Court in *Erie*—we think the result decreed by *Dupasseur* continues to be correct for diversity cases. Since state, rather than federal, substantive law is at issue there is no need for a uniform federal rule. And indeed, nationwide uniformity in the substance of the matter is better served by having the same claim-preclusive rule (the state rule) apply whether the dismissal has been ordered by a state or a federal court. This is, it seems to us, a classic case for adopting, as the federally prescribed rule of decision, the law that would be applied by state courts in the State in which the federal diversity court sits. As we have alluded to above, any other rule would produce the sort of "forum-shopping and inequitable administration of the laws" that *Erie* seeks to avoid, since filing in, or removing to, federal court would be encouraged by the divergent effects that the litigants would anticipate from likely grounds of dismissal.

This federal reference to state law will not obtain, of course, in situations in which the state law is incompatible with federal interests. If, for example, state law did not accord claim-preclusive effect to dismissals for willful violation of discovery orders, federal courts' interest in the integrity of their own processes might justify a contrary federal rule. No such conflict with potential federal interests exists in the present case. Dismissal of this state cause of action was decreed by the California federal court only because the California statute of limitations so required; and there is no conceivable federal interest in giving that time bar more effect in other courts than the California courts themselves would impose.

Because the claim-preclusive effect of the California federal court's dismissal "upon the merits" of petitioner's action on statute-of-limitations grounds is governed by a federal rule that in turn incorporates California's law of claim preclusion (the content of which we do not pass upon today), the Maryland Court of Special Appeals erred in holding that the dismissal necessarily precluded the bringing of this action in the Maryland courts. The judgment is reversed, and the case remanded for further proceedings not inconsistent with this opinion.

# B. COLLATERAL ESTOPPEL (ISSUE PRECLUSION)

4. *Collateral Estoppel*, also known as *issue preclusion,* applies when a particular *issue*, (though not the whole case), has been determined by prior litigation. For example, if A sued B in state court, and there were three issues involved, issues R, S and T, if A won on issue R, then in later litigation between A and B in either state or federal court, in a suit involving issues R and W, the second court, (either state or federal), would not allow re-litigation of issue R. Once a valid tribunal had decided issue R, no subsequent court would allow re-litigation of that same issue by the same parties. Both A and B would be *estopped*, (prohibited), from re-litigating issue R. Note that issue *W* could probably still go forward in the second tribunal – if it had not been a *compulsory* claim or counterclaim in the first litigation.

In the following case the question is whether collateral estoppel, (Issue preclusion), should be applied when an *administrative* tribunal rules on the issue of "*confusion*," and then in a later suit between the same two parties a jury makes a different determination on the issue of "*confusion*." Does the first ruling on "*confusion*" have issue preclusive effect on the later litigation before a jury?

135 S.CT. 1293
SUPREME COURT OF THE UNITED STATES
B & B HARDWARE, INC., PETITIONER
V.
HARGIS INDUSTRIES, INC., DBA SEALTITE BUILDING
FASTENERS, DBA EAST TEXAS FASTENERS ET AL.,
RESPONDENTS

DECIDED MARCH 24, 2015

Justice ALITO delivered the opinion of the Court.

Sometimes two different tribunals are asked to decide the same issue. When that happens, the decision of the first tribunal usually must be followed by the second, at least if the issue is really the same. Allowing the same issue to be decided more than once wastes litigants' resources and adjudicators' time, and it encourages parties who lose before one tribunal to shop around for another. The doctrine of collateral estoppel or issue preclusion is designed to prevent this from occurring.

This case concerns the application of issue preclusion in the context of trademark law. Petitioner, B & B Hardware, Inc. (B & B), and respondent Hargis Industries, Inc. (Hargis), both use similar trademarks; B & B owns SEALTIGHT while Hargis owns SEALTITE. Under the Lanham Act, an applicant can seek to register a trademark through an administrative process within the United States Patent and Trademark Office (PTO). But if another party believes that the PTO should not register a mark because it is too similar to its own, that party can oppose registration before the Trademark Trial and Appeal Board (TTAB). Here, Hargis tried to register the mark SEALTITE, but B & B opposed SEALTITE's registration. After a lengthy proceeding, the TTAB agreed with B & B that SEALTITE should not be registered.

In addition to permitting a party to object to the registration of a mark, the Lanham Act allows a mark owner to sue for trademark infringement. Both a registration proceeding and a suit for trademark infringement, more-over, can occur at the same time. In this case, while the TTAB was deciding whether SEALTITE should be registered, B & B and Hargis were also litigating the SEALTIGHT versus SEALTITE dispute in federal court. In both registration proceedings and infringement litigation, the tribunal asks whether a likelihood of confusion exists between the mark sought to be protected (here, SEALTIGHT) and the other mark (SEALTITE).

The question before this Court is whether the District Court in this case should have applied issue preclusion to the TTAB's decision that SEALTITE is confusingly similar to SEALTIGHT. Here, the Eighth Circuit rejected issue preclusion for reasons that would make it difficult for the doctrine ever to apply in trademark disputes. We disagree with that narrow understanding of issue preclusion. Instead, consistent with principles of law that apply in innumerable contexts, we hold that a court should give preclusive effect to TTAB decisions if the ordinary elements of issue preclusion are met. We therefore reverse the judgment of the Eighth Circuit and remand for further proceedings.

I.

A

Trademark law has a long history, going back at least to Roman times. The principle underlying trademark protection is that distinctive marks—words, names, symbols, and the like—can help distinguish a particular artisan's goods from those of others. One who first uses a distinct mark in commerce thus acquires rights to that mark. Those rights include preventing others from using the mark.

Though federal law does not create trademarks, Congress has long played a role in protecting them. In 1946, Congress enacted the Lanham Act, the current federal trademark scheme. As relevant here, the Lanham Act creates at least two adjudicative mechanisms to help protect marks. First, a trademark owner can register its mark with the PTO. Second, a mark owner can bring a suit for infringement in federal court.

Registration is significant. The Lanham Act confers "important legal rights and benefits" on trademark owners who register their marks. Registration, for instance, serves as "constructive notice of the registrant's claim of ownership" of the mark. It also is "prima facie evidence of the validity of the registered mark and of the registration of the mark, of the owner's ownership of the mark, and of the owner's exclusive right to use the registered mark in commerce on or in connection with the goods or services specified in the certificate." And once a mark has been registered for five years, it can become "incontestable."

To obtain the benefits of registration, a mark owner files an application with the PTO. § 1051. The application must include, among other things, "the date of the applicant's first use of the mark, the date of the applicant's first use of the mark in commerce, the goods in connection with which the mark is used, and a drawing of the mark." § 1051(a)(2). The usages listed in the application—i.e., those goods on which the mark appears along with, if applicable, their channels of distribution—are critical.

The PTO generally cannot register a mark which "so resembles" another mark "as to be likely, when used on or in connection with the goods of the applicant, to cause confusion, or to cause mistake, or to deceive."

If a trademark examiner believes that registration is warranted, the mark is published in the Official Gazette of the PTO. At that point, "any person who believes that he would be damaged by the registration" may "file an opposition." Opposition proceedings occur before the TTAB.

Opposition proceedings before the TTAB are in many ways "similar to a civil action in a federal district court." These proceedings, for instance, are largely governed by the Federal Rules of Civil Procedure and Evidence. The TTAB also allows discovery and depositions. The party opposing registration bears the burden of proof, and if that burden cannot be met, the opposed mark must be registered.

The primary way in which TTAB proceedings differ from ordinary civil litigation is that "proceedings before the Board are conducted in writing, and the Board's actions in a particular case are based upon the written record therein." In other words, there is no live testimony. Even so, the TTAB allows parties to submit transcribed testimony, taken under oath and subject to cross-examination, and to request oral argument.

When a party opposes registration because it believes the mark proposed to be registered is too similar to its own, the TTAB evaluates likelihood of confusion by applying some or all of the 13 factors set out in *In re E.I. DuPont DeNemours & Co.* After the TTAB decides whether to register the mark, a party can seek review in the U.S. Court of Appeals for the Federal Circuit, or it can file a new action in district court. In district court, the parties can conduct additional discovery and the judge resolves registration *de novo*.

The Lanham Act, of course, also creates a federal cause of action for trademark infringement. The owner of a mark, whether registered or not, can bring suit in federal court if another is using a mark that too closely resembles the plaintiff's. The court must decide whether the defendant's use of a mark in commerce "is likely to cause confusion, or to cause mistake, or to deceive" with regards to the plaintiff's mark. In infringement litigation, the district court considers the full range of a mark's usages, not just those in the application.

B

Petitioner B & B and respondent Hargis both manufacture metal fasteners. B & B manufactures fasteners for the aerospace industry, while Hargis manufactures fasteners for use in the construction trade. Although there are obvious differences between space shuttles and A-frame buildings, both aerospace and construction engineers prefer fasteners that seal things tightly. Accordingly, both B & B and Hargis want their wares associated with tight seals. A feud of nearly two decades has sprung from this seemingly commonplace set of facts.

In 1993 B & B registered SEALTIGHT for "threaded or unthreaded metal fasteners and other related hardware; namely, self-sealing nuts, bolts, screws, rivets and washers, all having a captive o-ring, for use in the aerospace industry." In 1996, Hargis sought to register SEALTITE for "self-piercing and self-drilling metal screws for use in the manufacture of metal and post-frame buildings." B & B opposed Hargis' registration because, although the two companies sell different products, it believes that SEALTITE is confusingly similar to SEALTIGHT.

The twists and turns in the SEALTIGHT versus SEALTITE controversy are labyrinthine. The question whether either of these marks should be registered, and if so, which one, has bounced around within the PTO for about two decades; related infringement litigation has been before the Eighth Circuit three times; and two separate juries have been empaneled and returned verdicts. The full story could fill a long, unhappy book.

For purposes here, we pick up the story in 2002, when the PTO published SEALTITE in the Official Gazette. This prompted opposition proceedings before the TTAB, complete with discovery, including depositions. B & B argued that SEALTITE could not be registered because it is confusingly similar to SEALTIGHT. B & B explained, for instance, that both companies have an online presence, the largest distributor of fasteners sells both companies' products, and consumers sometimes call the wrong company to place orders. Hargis rejoined that the companies sell different products, for different uses, to different types of consumers, through different channels of trade.

Invoking a number of the *DuPont* factors, the TTAB sided with B & B. The Board considered, for instance, whether SEALTIGHT is famous (it's not, said the Board), how the two products are used (differently), how much the marks resemble each other (very much), and whether customers are actually confused (perhaps sometimes). Concluding that "the most critical factors in its likelihood of confusion analysis are the similarities of the marks and the similarity of the goods," the TTAB determined that SEALTITE—when "used in connection with 'self-piercing and self-drilling metal screws for use in the manufacture of metal and post-frame buildings' "—could not be registered because it "so resembles" SEALTIGHT when "used in connection with fasteners that provide leakproof protection from liquids and gases, fasteners that have a captive o-ring, and 'threaded or unthreaded metal fastners and other related hardware ... for use in the aerospace industry' as to be *likely to cause confusion*." Despite a right to do so, Hargis did not seek judicial review in either the Federal Circuit or District Court.

All the while, B & B had sued Hargis for infringement. Before the District Court ruled on likelihood of confusion, however, the TTAB announced its decision. After a series of proceedings not relevant here, B & B argued to the District Court that Hargis could not contest likelihood of confusion because of the preclusive effect of the TTAB decision. The District Court disagreed, reasoning that the TTAB is not an Article III court. The *jury* returned a verdict for Hargis, *finding no likelihood of confusion.*

B & B appealed to the Eighth Circuit. The panel majority affirmed. After calling for the views of the Solicitor General, we granted certiorari.

## II

The first question that we must address is whether an agency decision can ever ground issue preclusion. The District Court rejected issue preclusion because agencies are not Article III courts.

This Court has long recognized that "the determination of a question directly involved in one action is conclusive as to that question in a second suit." *Cromwell v. County of Sac,* (1877). The idea is straightforward: Once a court has decided an issue, it is "forever settled as between the parties," thereby "protecting" against "the expense and vexation attending multiple lawsuits, conserving judicial resources, and fostering reliance on judicial action by minimizing the possibility of inconsistent verdicts." In short, "a losing litigant deserves no rematch after a defeat fairly suffered."

Although the idea of issue preclusion is straightforward, it can be challenging to implement. The Court, therefore, regularly turns to the Restatement (Second) of Judgments for a statement of the ordinary elements of issue preclusion. The Restatement explains that subject to certain well-known exceptions, the general rule is that "when an issue of fact or law is actually litigated and determined by a valid and final judgment, and the determination is essential to the judgment, the determination is conclusive in a subsequent action between the parties, whether on the same or a different claim." Restatement (Second) of Judgments § 27. (Listing exceptions such as whether appellate review was available or whether there were "differences in the quality or extensiveness of the procedures followed").

Both this Court's cases and the Restatement make clear that issue preclusion is not limited to those situations in which the same issue is before two *courts.* Rather, where a single issue is before a court and an administrative agency, preclusion also often applies. Indeed, this Court has explained that because the principle of issue preclusion was so "well established" at common law, in those situations in which

Congress has authorized agencies to resolve disputes, "courts may take it as given that Congress has legislated with the expectation that the principle of issue preclusion will apply except when a statutory purpose to the contrary is evident." This reflects the Court's longstanding view that "when an administrative agency is acting in a judicial capacity and resolves disputed issues of fact properly before it which the parties have had an adequate opportunity to litigate, the courts have not hesitated to apply res judicata to enforce repose."

Hargis argues that we should not read the Lanham Act (or, presumably, many other federal statutes) as authorizing issue preclusion. Otherwise, Hargis warns, the Court would have to confront "grave and doubtful questions" as to the Lanham Act's consistency with the Seventh Amendment and Article III of the Constitution. We are not persuaded.

At the outset, we note that Hargis does not argue that giving issue preclusive effect to the TTAB's decision would be unconstitutional. Instead, Hargis contends only that we should read the Lanham Act narrowly because a broad reading *might* be unconstitutional. The likely reason that Hargis has not directly advanced a constitutional argument is that, at least as to a jury trial right, Hargis did not even list the Seventh Amendment as an authority in its appellee brief to the Eighth Circuit. Moreover, although Hargis pressed an Article III argument below, in its opposition to certiorari in this Court, Hargis seemingly conceded that TTAB decisions *can sometimes* ground issue preclusion, though it now protests otherwise. To the extent, if any, that there could be a meritorious constitutional objection, it is not before us.

We reject Hargis' statutory argument that we should jettison administrative preclusion in whole or in part to avoid potential constitutional concerns. As to the Seventh Amendment, for instance, the Court has already held that the right to a jury trial does not negate the issue-preclusive effect of a judgment, even if that judgment was entered by a juryless tribunal. See *Parklane Hosiery Co. v. Shore.* It would seem to follow naturally that although the Seventh Amendment creates a jury trial right in suits for trademark damages, TTAB decisions still can have preclusive effect in such suits. Hargis disputes this reasoning even though it admits that in 1791 "'a party was not entitled to have a jury determine issues that had been previously adjudicated by a chancellor in equity.'" Instead, Hargis contends that issue preclusion should not apply to TTAB registration decisions because there were no agencies at common law. But our precedent holds that the Seventh Amendment does not strip competent tribunals of the power to issue judgments with preclusive effect; that logic would not seem to turn on the nature of the competent tribunal. And at the same time, adopting Hargis' view would dramatically undercut agency preclusion, despite what the Court has already said to the contrary. Nothing in Hargis' avoidance argument is weighty enough to overcome these weaknesses.

The claim that we should read the Lanham Act narrowly to avoid Article III concerns is equally unavailing—and for similar reasons. Hargis argues that because it might violate Article III if an agency could make a decision with preclusive effect in a later proceeding before a federal court, we should conclude, as a statutory matter, that issue preclusion is unavailable. Such a holding would not fit with our precedent. To be sure, the Court has never addressed whether such preclusion offends Article III. But because this Court's cases are so clear, there is no ambiguity for this Court to sidestep through constitutional avoidance.

## III

The next question is whether there is an "evident" reason why Congress would not want TTAB decisions to receive preclusive effect, even in those cases in which the ordinary elements of issue preclusion are met. We conclude that nothing in the Lanham Act bars the application of issue preclusion in such cases.

The Lanham Act's text certainly does not forbid issue preclusion. Nor does the Act's structure. Granted, one can seek judicial review of a TTAB registration decision in a *de novo* district court action, and some courts have concluded from this that Congress does not want unreviewed TTAB decisions to ground issue preclusion. But that conclusion does not follow. Ordinary preclusion law teaches that if a party to a court proceeding does not challenge an adverse decision, that decision can have preclusive effect in other cases, even if it would have been reviewed *de novo*. cf. *Federated Department Stores, Inc. v. Moitie.*

This case is also unlike *Astoria,* where a plaintiff claiming discrimination first went to an agency and then sued in court about the same alleged conduct. The Court concluded, quite sensibly, that the structure of that scheme indicated that the agency decision could not ground issue preclusion. When exhausting an administrative process is a prerequisite to suit in court, giving preclusive effect to the agency's determination in that very administrative process could render the judicial suit "strictly *pro forma.*" Here, if a party urged a district court reviewing a TTAB registration decision to give preclusive effect to the very TTAB decision under review, *Astoria* would apply. But that is not this case.

What matters here is that registration is not a prerequisite to an infringement action. Rather, it is a separate proceeding to decide separate rights. Neither is issue preclusion a one-way street. When a district court, as part of its judgment, decides an issue that overlaps with part of the TTAB's analysis, the TTAB gives preclusive effect to the court's judgment. (Giving preclusive effect to the District Court's earlier decision regarding SEALTIGHT's distinctiveness because the issue "was actually litigated and necessarily determined").

Hargis also argues that allowing TTAB decisions to have issue-preclusive effect will adversely affect the registration process. Because of the TTAB's "'limited jurisdiction'" and "'the narrowness of the issues'" before it, Hargis contends, the Court should infer that TTAB proceedings are supposed to be more streamlined than infringement litigation. But, the argument goes, if TTAB decisions can have issue-preclusive effect in infringement litigation, parties may spend more time and energy before the TTAB, thus bogging down the registration process. This concern does not change our conclusion. Issue preclusion is available unless it is "evident," that Congress does not want it. Here, if a streamlined process in all registration matters was particularly dear to Congress, it would not have authorized *de novo* challenges for those "dissatisfied" with TTAB decisions. Plenary review serves many functions, but ensuring a streamlined process is not one of them. Moreover, as explained below, for a great many registration decisions issue preclusion obviously will not apply because the ordinary elements will not be met. For those registrations, nothing we say today is relevant.

## IV

At last we turn to whether there is a categorical reason why registration decisions can never meet the ordinary elements of issue preclusion. Although many registrations will not satisfy those ordinary elements, that does not mean that none will. We agree with Professor McCarthy that issue preclusion applies where "the issues in the two cases are indeed identical and the other rules of collateral estoppel are carefully observed."

### A

It does not matter that registration and infringement are governed by different statutory provisions. Often a single standard is placed in different statutes; that does not foreclose issue preclusion. Neither does it matter that the TTAB and the Eighth Circuit use different factors to assess likelihood of confusion. For one thing, the factors are not fundamentally different, and "minor variations in the application of what is in essence the same legal standard do not defeat preclusion." More important, if federal law provides a single standard, parties cannot escape preclusion simply by litigating anew in tribunals that apply that one standard differently. A contrary rule would encourage the very evils that issue preclusion helps to prevent.

The real question, therefore, is whether likelihood of *confusion* for purposes of *registration* is the same standard as likelihood of *confusion* for purposes of *infringement*. We conclude it is, for at least three reasons. First, the operative language is essentially the same; the fact that the registration provision separates "likely" from "to cause confusion, or to cause mistake, or to deceive" does not change that reality. Second, the likelihood-of-confusion language that Congress used in these Lanham Act provisions has been central to trademark registration since at least 1881. That could hardly have been by accident. And third, district courts can cancel registrations during infringement litigation, just as they can adjudicate infringement in suits seeking judicial review of registration decisions. There is no reason to think that the same district judge in the same case should apply two separate standards of likelihood of confusion.

B

Hargis also argues that registration is categorically incompatible with issue preclusion because the TTAB uses procedures that differ from those used by district courts. Granted, "redetermination of issues is warranted if there is reason to doubt the quality, extensiveness, or fairness of procedures followed in prior litigation." But again, this only suggests that sometimes issue preclusion might be inappropriate, not that it always is.

Here, there is no categorical "reason to doubt the quality, extensiveness, or fairness," of the agency's procedures. In large part they are exactly the same as in federal court. For instance, although "the scope of discovery in Board proceedings is generally narrower than in court proceedings"—reflecting the fact that there are often fewer usages at issue—the TTAB has adopted almost the whole of Federal Rule of Civil Procedure 26. It is conceivable, of course, that the TTAB's procedures may prove ill-suited for a particular issue in a particular case, *e.g.,* a party may have tried to introduce material evidence but was prevented by the TTAB from doing so, or the TTAB's bar on live testimony may materially prejudice a party's ability to present its case. The ordinary law of issue preclusion, however, already accounts for those "rare" cases where a "compelling showing of unfairness" can be made.

C

Hargis also contends that the stakes for registration are so much lower than for infringement that issue preclusion should never apply to TTAB decisions. Issue preclusion may be inapt if "the amount in controversy in the first action was so small in relation to the amount in controversy in the second that preclusion would be plainly unfair." After all, "few litigants would spend $50,000 to defend a $5,000 claim." Hargis is wrong, however, that this exception to issue preclusion applies to every registration. To the contrary: When registration is opposed, there is good reason to think that both sides will take the matter seriously.

The benefits of registration are substantial. Registration is "prima facie evidence of the validity of the registered mark," and is a precondition for a mark to become "incontestable." Incontestability is a powerful protection.

The importance of registration is undoubtedly why Congress provided for *de novo* review of TTAB decisions in district court. It is incredible to think that a district court's adjudication of particular usages would not have preclusive effect in another district court. Why would unchallenged TTAB decisions be different? Congress' creation of this elaborate registration scheme, with so many important rights attached and backed up by plenary review, confirms that registration decisions can be weighty enough to ground issue preclusion.

V

For these reasons, the Eighth Circuit erred in this case. On remand, the court should apply the following rule: So long as the other ordinary elements of issue preclusion are met, when the usages adjudicated by the TTAB are materially the same as those before the district court, issue preclusion should apply.

The judgment of the United States Court of Appeals for the Eighth Circuit is reversed, and the case is remanded for further proceedings consistent with this opinion.

5. The next case, *Parklane*, is a famous case. In this case the Supreme Court authorizes the use of *offensive* collateral estoppel. Why is it called *offensive*? Because the plaintiff, (who is on *offense*), uses collateral estoppel against a defendant who has lost on the issue of "materially false and misleading" in a prior suit – against a *different* plaintiff!

# 99 S.CT. 645
## SUPREME COURT OF THE UNITED STATES
## PARKLANE HOSIERY COMPANY, INC., ET AL., PETITIONERS,
## V.
## LEO M. SHORE, RESPONDENT

DECIDED JANUARY 9, 1979

Mr. Justice STEWART delivered the opinion of the Court.

This case presents the question whether a party who has had issues of fact adjudicated adversely to it in an equitable action may be collaterally estopped from relitigating the same issues before a jury in a subsequent legal action brought against it by a new party.

The respondent brought this stockholder's class action against the petitioners in a Federal District Court. The complaint alleged that the petitioners, Parklane Hosiery Co., Inc. (Parklane), and 13 of its officers, directors, and stockholders, had issued a materially false and misleading proxy statement in connection with a merger. The proxy statement, according to the complaint, had violated §§ 14(a), 10(b), and 20(a) of the Securities Exchange Act of 1934, 48 Stat. 895, 891, 899, as amended, 15 U.S.C. §§ 78n(a), 78j(b), and 78t(a), as well as various rules and regulations promulgated by the Securities and Exchange Commission (SEC). The complaint sought damages, rescission of the merger, and recovery of costs.

Before this action came to trial, the SEC filed suit against the same defendants in the Federal District Court, alleging that the proxy statement that had been issued by Parklane was materially false and misleading in essentially the same respects as those that had been alleged in the respondent's complaint. Injunctive relief was requested. After a 4-day trial, the District Court found that the proxy statement was materially false and misleading in the respects alleged, and entered a declaratory judgment to that effect. *SEC v. Parklane Hosiery Co.* The Court of Appeals for the Second Circuit affirmed this judgment.

The respondent in the present case then moved for partial summary judgment against the petitioners, asserting that the petitioners were collaterally estopped from relitigating the issues that had been resolved against them in the action brought by the SEC. The District Court denied the motion on the ground that such an application of collateral estoppel would deny the petitioners their Seventh Amendment right to a jury trial. The Court of Appeals for the Second Circuit reversed, holding that a party who has had issues of fact determined against him after a full and fair opportunity to litigate in a nonjury trial is collaterally estopped from obtaining a subsequent jury trial of these same issues of fact. We granted certiorari.

## I

The threshold question to be considered is whether, quite apart from the right to a jury trial under the Seventh Amendment, the petitioners can be precluded from relitigating facts resolved adversely to them in a prior equitable proceeding with another party under the general law of collateral estoppel. Specifically, we must determine whether a litigant who was not a party to a prior judgment may nevertheless use that judgment "offensively" to prevent a defendant from relitigating issues resolved in the earlier proceeding.

### A

Collateral estoppel, like the related doctrine of res judicata, has the dual purpose of protecting litigants from the burden of relitigating an identical issue with the same party or his privy and of promoting judicial economy by preventing needless litigation. Until relatively recently, however, the scope of collateral estoppel was limited by the doctrine of mutuality of parties. Under this mutuality doctrine, neither party could use a prior judgment as an estoppel against the other unless both parties were bound by the judgment. Based on the premise that it is somehow unfair to allow a party to use a prior judgment when he himself would not be so bound, the mutuality requirement provided a party who had litigated and lost in a previous action an opportunity to relitigate identical issues with new parties.

By failing to recognize the obvious difference in position between a party who has never litigated an issue and one who has fully litigated and lost, the mutuality requirement was criticized almost from its inception. Recognizing the validity of this criticism, the Court in *Blonder-Tongue* abandoned the mutuality requirement, at least in cases where a patentee seeks to relitigate the validity of a patent after a federal court in a previous lawsuit has already declared it invalid.

### B

The *Blonder-Tongue* case involved defensive use of collateral estoppel—a plaintiff was estopped from asserting a claim that the plaintiff had previously litigated and lost against another defendant. The present case, by contrast, involves offensive use of collateral estoppel—a plaintiff is seeking to estop a defendant from relitigating the issues which the defendant previously litigated and lost against another plaintiff. In both the offensive and defensive use situations, the party against whom estoppel is asserted has litigated and lost in an earlier action. Nevertheless, several reasons have been advanced why the two situations should be treated differently.

First, offensive use of collateral estoppel does not promote judicial economy in the same manner as defensive use does. Defensive use of collateral estoppel precludes a plaintiff from relitigating identical issues by merely "switching adversaries." Thus defensive collateral estoppel gives a plaintiff a strong incentive to join all potential defendants in the first action if possible. Offensive use of collateral estoppel, on the other hand, creates precisely the opposite incentive. Since a plaintiff will be able to rely on a previous judgment against a defendant but will not be bound by that judgment if the defendant wins, the plaintiff has every incentive to adopt a "wait and see" attitude, in the hope that the first action by another plaintiff will result in a favorable judgment. Thus offensive use of collateral estoppel will likely increase rather than decrease the total amount of litigation, since potential plaintiffs will have everything to gain and nothing to lose by not intervening in the first action.

A second argument against offensive use of collateral estoppel is that it may be unfair to a defendant. If a defendant in the first action is sued for small or nominal damages, he may have little incentive to defend vigorously, particularly if future suits are not foreseeable. (Application of offensive collateral estoppel denied where defendant did not appeal an adverse judgment awarding damages of $35,000 and defendant was later sued for over $7 million). Allowing offensive collateral estoppel may also be unfair to a defendant if the judgment relied upon as a basis for the estoppel is itself inconsistent with one or more previous judgments in favor of the defendant. Still another situation where it might be unfair to apply offensive estoppel is where the second action affords the defendant procedural opportunities unavailable in the first action that could readily cause a different result.

## C

We have concluded that the preferable approach for dealing with these problems in the federal courts is not to preclude the use of offensive collateral estoppel, but to grant trial courts broad discretion to determine when it should be applied. The general rule should be that in cases where a plaintiff could easily have joined in the earlier action or where, either for the reasons discussed above or for other reasons, the application of offensive estoppel would be unfair to a defendant, a trial judge should not allow the use of offensive collateral estoppel.

In the present case, however, none of the circumstances that might justify reluctance to allow the offensive use of collateral estoppel is present. The application of offensive collateral estoppel will not here reward a private plaintiff who could have joined in the previous action, since the respondent probably could not have joined in the injunctive action brought by the SEC even had he so desired. Similarly, there is no unfairness to the petitioners in applying offensive collateral estoppel in this case. First, in light of the serious allegations made in the SEC's complaint against the petitioners, as well as the foreseeability of subsequent private suits that typically follow a successful Government judgment, the petitioners had every incentive to litigate the SEC lawsuit fully and vigorously. Second, the judgment in the SEC action was not inconsistent with any previous decision. Finally, there will in the respondent's action be no procedural opportunities available to the petitioners that were unavailable in the first action of a kind that might be likely to cause a different result.

We conclude, therefore, that none of the considerations that would justify a refusal to allow the use of offensive collateral estoppel is present in this case. Since the petitioners received a "full and fair" opportunity to litigate their claims in the SEC action, the contemporary law of collateral estoppel leads inescapably to the conclusion that the petitioners are collaterally estopped from relitigating the question of whether the proxy statement was materially false and misleading.

II

The question that remains is whether, notwithstanding the law of collateral estoppel, the use of offensive collateral estoppel in this case would violate the petitioners' Seventh Amendment right to a jury trial.

A

"The thrust of the Seventh Amendment was to preserve the right to jury trial as it existed in 1791." At common law, a litigant was not entitled to have a jury determine issues that had been previously adjudicated by a chancellor in equity.

Recognition that an equitable determination could have collateral-estoppel effect in a subsequent legal action was the major premise of this Court's decision in *Beacon Theatres, Inc. v. Westover.*

It is thus clear that the Court in the *Beacon Theatres* case thought that if an issue common to both legal and equitable claims was first determined by a judge, relitigation of the issue before a jury might be foreclosed by res judicata or collateral estoppel. To avoid this result, the Court held that when legal and equitable claims are joined in the same action, the trial judge has only limited discretion in determining the sequence of trial and "that discretion must, wherever possible, be exercised to preserve jury trial."

Thus the Court recognized that an equitable determination can have collateral-estoppel effect in a subsequent legal action and that this estoppel does not violate the Seventh Amendment.

## B

Despite the strong support to be found both in history and in the recent decisional law of this Court for the proposition that an equitable determination can have collateral-estoppel effect in a subsequent legal action, the petitioners argue that application of collateral estoppel in this case would nevertheless violate their Seventh Amendment right to a jury trial. The petitioners contend that since the scope of the Amendment must be determined by reference to the common law as it existed in 1791, and since the common law permitted collateral estoppel only where there was mutuality of parties, collateral estoppel cannot constitutionally be applied when such mutuality is absent.

The petitioners have advanced no persuasive reason, however, why the meaning of the Seventh Amendment should depend on whether or not mutuality of parties is present. A litigant who has lost because of adverse factual findings in an equity action is equally deprived of a jury trial whether he is estopped from relitigating the factual issues against the same party or a new party. In either case, the party against whom estoppel is asserted has litigated questions of fact, and has had the facts determined against him in an earlier proceeding. In either case there is no further fact finding function for the jury to perform, since the common factual issues have been resolved in the previous action. ("No one is entitled in a civil case to trial by jury, unless and except so far as there are issues of fact to be determined").

The Seventh Amendment has never been interpreted in the rigid manner advocated by the petitioners. On the contrary, many procedural devices developed since 1791 that have diminished the civil jury's historic domain have been found not to be inconsistent with the Seventh Amendment. See *Galloway v. United States.*

"The Amendment did not bind the federal courts to the exact procedural incidents or details of jury trial according to the common law in 1791, any more than it tied them to the common-law system of pleading or the specific rules of evidence then prevailing. Nor were 'the rules of the common law' then prevalent, including those relating to the procedure by which the judge regulated the jury's role on questions of fact, crystalized in a fixed and immutable system.

"The more logical conclusion, we think, and the one which both history and the previous decisions here support, is that the Amendment was designed to preserve the basic institution of jury trial in only its most fundamental elements, not the great mass of procedural forms and details, varying even then so widely among common-law jurisdictions."

The law of collateral estoppel, like the law in other procedural areas defining the scope of the jury's function, has evolved since 1791. Under the rationale of the *Galloway* case, these developments are not repugnant to the Seventh Amendment simply for the reason that they did not exist in 1791. Thus if, as we have held, the law of collateral estoppel forecloses the petitioners from relitigating the factual issues determined against them in the SEC action, nothing in the Seventh Amendment dictates a different result, even though because of lack of mutuality there would have been no collateral estoppel in 1791.

The judgment of the Court of Appeals is
Affirmed.

# CHAPTER 13

# POST TRIAL RELIEF

## A. BY MOTION FEDERAL RULES 59 AND 60

1. When a party wins after a long trial, the judgment may still not be final. If something has gone seriously wrong during the trial, Federal Rule 59 states that within 28 days after the end of the trial either party may file a motion for a new trial. Or the court, on its own, may order a new trial. That rarely happens.

Federal Rule 60 allows the court to order relief from a final judgment, (usually just within one year, but sometimes longer), if the judgment was the result of fraud, or for various other reasons. That is also very unlikely to happen.

What does happen, after almost every trial, is that there is an appeal.

## B. BY APPEAL 28 USC 1291 AND 28 USC 1292

2. When the judgment of a trial court is final, there is no question that there is a right to appeal. The difficulty arises when there is an important issue that has been decided by the trial court, but the entire trial has not yet been completed. The following cases illustrate the problem. Under what circumstances should a party be able to bring an appeal *before* the entire trial has been completed?

Normally appeals from <u>final</u> judgments are brought under 28 USC 1291, which provides that "The courts of appeals ... shall have jurisdiction of appeals from all final decisions of the district courts of the United States..."

28 USC 1292 has a multitude of provisions regarding <u>interlocutory</u> decisions.

Under the provisions of 28 USC 1292(b) a district court judge has the discretion to certify a particular order for an interlocutory appeal, before a final judgment has been reached.

In addition, the U.S. Supreme Court has recognized a limited expansion of 28 USC 1291, in order to allow an interlocutory appeal even when the district court judge has not certified an appeal under the provisions of 28 USC 1292.

The case which established this right to an interlocutory appeal under Sec. 1291 was *Cohen v. Beneficial Industrial Loan Corp. ((1949).* Under *Cohen,* if the district court makes a final decision on an important issue that is separable from the main action, is too important to be denied review, and for which review need not deferred until the whole case is completed, then the appellate court may permit an interlocutory appeal under Sec. 1291.

3. Even though the attorney-client privilege is one of the most important privileges known to the law, an adverse ruling on that issue is not automatically entitled to an immediate appeal, according to the following recent U.S. Supreme Court case.

130 S. CT. 599
SUPREME COURT OF THE UNITED STATES
MOHAWK INDUSTRIES, INC., PETITIONER
V.
NORMAN CARPENTER

DECIDED DECEMBER 8, 2009

**Justice Sotomayor delivered the opinion of the Court.**

*Section 1291* of the Judicial Code confers on federal courts of appeals jurisdiction to review "final decisions of the district courts." *28 U.S.C. § 1291.* Although "final decisions" typically are ones that trigger the entry of judgment, they also include a small set of prejudgment orders that are "collateral to" the merits of an action and "too important" to be denied immediate review. *Cohen v. Beneficial Industrial Loan Corp. (1949).* In this case, petitioner Mohawk Industries, Inc., attempted to bring a collateral order appeal after the District Court ordered it to disclose certain confidential materials on the ground that Mohawk had waived the attorney-client privilege. The Court of Appeals dismissed the appeal for want of jurisdiction.

The question before us is whether disclosure orders adverse to the attorney-client privilege qualify for immediate appeal under the collateral order doctrine. Agreeing with the Court of Appeals, we hold that they do not. Post judgment appeals, together with other review mechanisms, suffice to protect the rights of litigants and preserve the vitality of the attorney-client privilege.

I

In 2007, respondent Norman Carpenter, a former shift supervisor at a Mohawk manufacturing facility, filed suit in the United States District Court for the Northern District of Georgia, alleging that Mohawk had terminated him in violation of *42 U.S.C. § 1985(2)* and various Georgia laws. According to Carpenter's complaint, his termination came after he informed a member of Mohawk's human resources department in an e-mail that the company was employing undocumented immigrants. At the time, unbeknownst to Carpenter, Mohawk stood accused in a pending class-action lawsuit of conspiring to drive down the wages of its legal employees by knowingly hiring undocumented workers in violation of federal and state racketeering laws. Company officials directed Carpenter to meet with the company's retained counsel in the *Williams* case, and counsel allegedly pressured Carpenter to recant his statements. When he refused, Carpenter alleges, Mohawk fired him under false pretenses.

After learning of Carpenter's complaint, the plaintiffs in the *Williams* case sought an evidentiary hearing to explore Carpenter's allegations. In its response to their motion, Mohawk described Carpenter's accusations as "pure fantasy" and recounted the "true facts" of Carpenter's dismissal. According to Mohawk, Carpenter himself had "engaged in blatant and illegal misconduct" by attempting to have Mohawk hire an undocumented worker. The company "commenced an immediate investigation," during which retained counsel interviewed Carpenter. Because Carpenter's "efforts to cause Mohawk to circumvent federal immigration law" "blatantly violated Mohawk policy," the company terminated him.

As these events were unfolding in the *Williams* case, discovery was underway in Carpenter's case. Carpenter filed a motion to compel Mohawk to produce information concerning his meeting with retained counsel and the company's termination decision. Mohawk maintained that the requested information was protected by the attorney-client privilege.

The District Court agreed that the privilege applied to the requested information, but it granted Carpenter's motion to compel disclosure after concluding that

Mohawk had implicitly waived the privilege through its representations in the *Williams* case. The court declined to certify its order for interlocutory appeal under *28 U.S.C. § 1292(b)*. But, recognizing "the seriousness of its waiver finding," it stayed its ruling to allow Mohawk to explore other potential "avenues to appeal, such as a petition for mandamus or appealing this Order under the collateral order doctrine."

Mohawk filed a notice of appeal and a petition for a writ of mandamus to the Eleventh Circuit. The Court of Appeals dismissed the appeal for lack of jurisdiction under *28 U.S.C. § 1291*. We granted certiorari to resolve a conflict among the Circuits concerning the availability of collateral appeals in the attorney-client privilege context.

II

A

By statute, Courts of Appeals "have jurisdiction of appeals from all final decisions of the district courts of the United States . . . except where a direct review may be had in the Supreme Court." *28 U.S.C. § 1291*. A "final decision" is typically one "by which a district court disassociates itself from a case." This Court, however, "has long given" *§ 1291* a "practical rather than a technical construction." As we held in *Cohen*, the statute encompasses not only judgments that "terminate an action," but also a "small class" of collateral rulings that, although they do not end the litigation, are appropriately deemed "final." "That small category includes only decisions that are conclusive, that resolve important questions separate from the merits, and that are effectively unreviewable on appeal from the final judgment in the underlying action."

In applying *Cohen*'s collateral order doctrine, we have stressed that it must "never be allowed to swallow the general rule that a party is entitled to a single appeal, to be deferred until final judgment has been entered." Our admonition reflects a healthy respect for the virtues of the final-judgment rule. Permitting piecemeal, prejudgment appeals, we have recognized, undermines "efficient judicial administration" and encroaches upon the prerogatives of district court judges, who play a "special role" in managing ongoing litigation. The district judge can better exercise his or her responsibility to police the prejudgment tactics of litigants if the appellate courts do not repeatedly intervene to second-guess prejudgment rulings".

The justification for immediate appeal must therefore be sufficiently strong to overcome the usual benefits of deferring appeal until litigation concludes. This requirement finds expression in two of the three traditional *Cohen* conditions. The second condition insists upon "*important* questions separate from the merits." More significantly, "the third *Cohen* question, whether a right is 'adequately vindicable' or 'effectively reviewable,' simply cannot be answered without a judgment about the value of the interests that would be lost through rigorous application of a final judgment requirement." That a ruling "may burden litigants in ways that are only imperfectly reparable by appellate reversal of a final district court judgment has never sufficed." Instead, the decisive consideration is whether delaying review until the entry of final judgment "would imperil a substantial public interest" or "some particular value of a high order."

In making this determination, we do not engage in an "individualized jurisdictional inquiry." Rather, our focus is on "the entire category to which a claim belongs." As long as the class of claims, taken as a whole, can be adequately vindicated by other means, "the chance that the litigation at hand might be speeded, or a 'particular injustice' averted," does not provide a basis for jurisdiction under § *1291*.

B

Mohawk contends, however, that rulings implicating the attorney-client privilege differ in kind from run-of-the-mill discovery orders because of the important institutional interests at stake. According to Mohawk, the right to maintain attorney-client confidences--the *sine qua non* of a meaningful attorney-client relationship--is "irreparably destroyed absent immediate appeal" of adverse privilege rulings.

We readily acknowledge the importance of the attorney-client privilege, which "is one of the oldest recognized privileges for confidential communications." *Swidler & Berlin v. United States.* By assuring confidentiality, the privilege encourages clients to make "full and frank" disclosures to their attorneys, who are then better able to provide candid advice and effective representation. *Upjohn Co. v. United States.* This, in turn, serves "broader public interests in the observance of law and administration of justice."

The crucial question, however, is not whether an interest is important in the abstract; it is whether deferring review until final judgment so imperils the interest as to justify the cost of allowing immediate appeal of the entire class of relevant orders.

We reach a similar conclusion here. In our estimation, post judgment appeals generally suffice to protect the rights of litigants and assure the vitality of the attorney-client privilege. Appellate courts can remedy the improper disclosure of privileged material in the same way they remedy a host of other erroneous evidentiary rulings: by vacating an adverse judgment and remanding for a new trial in which the protected material and its fruits are excluded from evidence.

Dismissing such relief as inadequate, Mohawk emphasizes that the attorney-client privilege does not merely "prohibit use of protected information at trial"; it provides a "right not to disclose the privileged information in the first place." Mohawk is undoubtedly correct that an order to disclose privileged information intrudes on the confidentiality of attorney-client communications. But deferring review until final judgment does not meaningfully reduce the *ex ante* incentives for full and frank consultations between clients and counsel.

One reason for the lack of a discernible chill is that, in deciding how freely to speak, clients and counsel are unlikely to focus on the remote prospect of an erroneous disclosure order, let alone on the timing of a possible appeal. Whether or not immediate collateral order appeals are available, clients and counsel must account for the possibility that they will later be required by law to disclose their communications for a variety of reasons--for example, because they misjudged the scope of the privilege, because they waived the privilege, or because their communications fell within the privilege's crime-fraud exception. Most district court rulings on these matters involve the routine application of settled legal principles. They are unlikely to be reversed on appeal, particularly when they rest on factual determinations for which appellate deference is the norm. The breadth of the privilege and the narrowness of its exceptions will thus tend to exert a much greater influence on the conduct of clients and counsel than the small risk that the law will be misapplied.

Moreover, were attorneys and clients to reflect upon their appellate options, they would find that litigants confronted with a particularly injurious or novel privilege ruling have several potential avenues of review apart from collateral order appeal. First, a party may ask the district court to certify, and the court of appeals to accept, an interlocutory appeal pursuant to *28 U.S.C. § 1292(b)*. The preconditions for *§ 1292(b)* review--"a controlling question of law," the prompt resolution of which "may materially advance the ultimate termination of the litigation"--are most likely to be satisfied when a privilege ruling involves a new legal question or is of special consequence, and district courts should not hesitate to certify an interlocutory appeal in such cases. Second, in extraordinary circumstances --*i.e.*, when a disclosure order "amounts to a judicial usurpation of power or a clear abuse of discretion," or otherwise works a manifest injustice--a party may petition the court of appeals for a writ of mandamus. While these discretionary review mechanisms do not provide relief in every case, they serve as useful "safety valves" for promptly correcting serious errors.

3 Mohawk itself petitioned the Eleventh Circuit for a writ of mandamus. It has not asked us to review the Court of Appeals' denial of that relief.

Another long-recognized option is for a party to defy a disclosure order and incur court-imposed sanctions. District courts have a range of sanctions from which to choose, including "directing that the matters embraced in the order or other designated facts be taken as established for purposes of the action," "prohibiting the disobedient party from supporting or opposing designated claims or defenses," or "striking pleadings in whole or in part." *Fed. Rule Civ. Proc. 37(b)(2)(A)(i)-(iii)*. Such sanctions allow a party to obtain post judgment review without having to reveal its privileged information. Alternatively, when the circumstances warrant it, a district court may hold a noncomplying party in contempt. The party can then appeal directly from that ruling, at least when the contempt citation can be characterized as a criminal punishment.

These established mechanisms for appellate review not only provide assurances to clients and counsel about the security of their confidential communications; they also go a long way toward addressing Mohawk's concern that, absent collateral order appeals of adverse attorney-client privilege rulings, some litigants may experience severe hardship. Mohawk is no doubt right that an order to disclose privileged material may, in some situations, have implications beyond the case at hand. But the same can be said about many categories of pretrial discovery orders for which collateral order appeals are unavailable. As with these other orders, rulings adverse to the privilege vary in their significance; some may be momentous, but others are more mundane. *Section 1292(b)* appeals, mandamus, and appeals from contempt citations facilitate immediate review of some of the more consequential attorney-client privilege rulings. Moreover, protective orders are available to limit the spillover effects of disclosing sensitive information. That a fraction of orders adverse to the attorney-client privilege may nevertheless harm individual litigants in ways that are "only imperfectly reparable" does not justify making all such orders immediately appealable as of right under *§ 1291*.

In short, the limited benefits of applying "the blunt, categorical instrument of *§ 1291* collateral order appeal" to privilege-related disclosure orders simply cannot justify the likely institutional costs. Permitting parties to undertake successive, piecemeal appeals of all adverse attorney-client rulings would unduly delay the resolution of district court litigation and needlessly burden the Courts of Appeals.

C

In concluding that sufficiently effective review of adverse attorney-client privilege rulings can be had without resort to the *Cohen* doctrine, we reiterate that the class of collaterally appealable orders must remain "narrow and selective in its membership."

We expect that the combination of standard post judgment appeals, *§ 1292(b)* appeals, mandamus, and contempt appeals will continue to provide adequate protection to litigants ordered to disclose materials purportedly subject to the attorney-client privilege. Any further avenue for immediate appeal of such rulings should be furnished, if at all, through rulemaking, with the opportunity for full airing it provides.

In sum, we conclude that the collateral order doctrine does not extend to disclosure orders adverse to the attorney-client privilege. Effective appellate review can be had by other means. Accordingly, we affirm the judgment of the Court of Appeals for the Eleventh Circuit.

4. The extent of the legal rights of people who are claimed to have entered the U.S. illegally is also an important issue. As the following case explains, when the government undertakes a deportation process an Immigration Judge will make the first judicial decision. Then the immigrant may ask the Board of Immigration Appeals to reopen the case, or the Board may do so on its own motion. Next, there is a right to appeal to the appropriate court of appeals. However, the process may be complex.

Note that in the following case the government declined to defend the actions of the Court of Appeals for the Fifth Circuit when the matter reached the U.S. Supreme Court, so the U.S. Supreme Court appointed an *amicus curiae* to defend the position of the 5th Circuit so that both the government and the immigrant would be properly represented when the U.S. Supreme Court considered the important issues of the case.

## 135 S.CT. 2150
## SUPREME COURT OF THE UNITED STATES
## NOEL REYES MATA, PETITIONER
## V.
## LORETTA E. LYNCH, ATTORNEY GENERAL.

DECIDED JUNE 15, 2015

**Justice KAGAN delivered the opinion of the Court.**

An alien ordered to leave the country has a statutory right to file a motion to reopen his removal proceedings. If immigration officials deny that motion, a federal court of appeals has jurisdiction to consider a petition to review their decision.

Notwithstanding that rule, the court below declined to take jurisdiction over such an appeal because the motion to reopen had been denied as untimely. We hold that was error.

I

The Immigration and Nationality Act (INA), and its implementing regulations set out the process for removing aliens from the country. An immigration judge (IJ) conducts the initial proceedings; if he orders removal, the alien has the opportunity to appeal that decision to the Board of Immigration Appeals (BIA or Board). "Every alien ordered removed" also "has a right to file one motion" with the IJ or Board to "reopen his or her removal proceedings." Subject to exceptions not relevant here, that motion to reopen "shall be filed within 90 days" of the final removal order. Finally, the BIA's regulations provide that, separate and apart from acting on the alien's motion, the BIA may reopen removal proceedings "on its own motion"—or, in Latin, *sua sponte*—at any time.

Petitioner Noel Reyes Mata is a Mexican citizen who entered the United States unlawfully almost 15 years ago. In 2010, he was convicted of assault under the Texas Penal Code. The federal Department of Homeland Security (DHS) immediately initiated removal proceedings against him, and in August 2011 an IJ ordered him removed. Mata's lawyer then filed a notice of appeal with the BIA, indicating that he would soon submit a written brief stating grounds for reversing the IJ's decision. But the attorney never filed the brief, and the BIA dismissed the appeal in September 2012.

More than a hundred days later, Mata (by then represented by new counsel) filed a motion with the Board to reopen his case. DHS opposed the motion, arguing in part that Mata had failed to file it, as the INA requires, within 90 days of the Board's decision. Mata responded that the motion was "not time barred" because his first lawyer's "ineffective assistance" counted as an "exceptional circumstance" excusing his lateness. In addressing those arguments, the Board reaffirmed prior decisions holding that it had authority to equitably toll the 90–day period in certain cases involving ineffective representation. But the Board went on to determine that Mata was not entitled to equitable tolling because he could not show prejudice from his attorney's deficient performance; accordingly, the Board found Mata's motion untimely. And in closing, the Board decided as well that Mata's case was not one "that would warrant reopening as an exercise of" its *sua sponte* authority, stating that "the power to reopen on our own motion is not meant to be used as a general cure for filing defects."

Mata petitioned the Court of Appeals for the Fifth Circuit to review the BIA's denial of his motion to reopen, arguing that he was entitled to equitable tolling. The Fifth Circuit, however, declined to "address the merits of Mata's equitable-tolling claim." It stated instead that "in this circuit, an alien's request to the BIA for equitable tolling on the basis of ineffective assistance of counsel is construed as an invitation for the BIA to exercise its discretion to reopen the removal proceeding *sua sponte*." And circuit precedent held that courts have no jurisdiction to review the BIA's refusal to exercise its *sua sponte* power to reopen cases. The Court of Appeals thus dismissed Mata's appeal for lack of jurisdiction.

Every other Circuit that reviews removal orders has affirmed its jurisdiction to decide an appeal, like Mata's, that seeks equitable tolling of the statutory time limit to file a motion to reopen a removal proceeding. We granted certiorari to resolve this conflict. And because the Federal Government agrees with Mata that the Fifth Circuit had jurisdiction over his appeal, we appointed an *amicus curiae* to defend the judgment below. We now reverse.

II

As we held in *Kucana v. Holder,* circuit courts have jurisdiction when an alien appeals from the Board's denial of a motion to reopen a removal proceeding. The INA, in combination with a statute cross-referenced there, gives the courts of appeals jurisdiction to review "final orders of removal." That jurisdiction, as the INA expressly contemplates, encompasses review of decisions refusing to reopen or reconsider such orders. See 8 U.S.C. § 1252(b)(6) ("Any review sought of a motion to reopen or reconsider a removal order shall be consolidated with the review of the underlying order").

Indeed, as we explained in *Kucana*, courts have reviewed those decisions for nearly a hundred years; and even as Congress curtailed other aspects of courts' jurisdiction over BIA rulings, it left that authority in place.

Nothing changes when the Board denies a motion to reopen because it is untimely—nor when, in doing so, the Board rejects a request for equitable tolling. Under the INA, as under our century-old practice, the reason for the BIA's denial makes no difference to the jurisdictional issue. Whether the BIA rejects the alien's motion to reopen because it comes too late or because it falls short in some other respect, the courts have jurisdiction to review that decision.

Similarly, that jurisdiction remains unchanged if the Board, in addition to denying the alien's statutorily authorized motion, states that it will not exercise its separate *sua sponte* authority to reopen the case. In *Kucana*, we declined to decide whether courts have jurisdiction to review the BIA's use of that discretionary power. Courts of Appeals, including the Fifth Circuit, have held that they generally lack such authority. Assuming *arguendo* that is right, it means only that judicial review ends after the court has evaluated the Board's ruling on the alien's motion. That courts lack jurisdiction over one matter (the *sua sponte* decision) does not affect their jurisdiction over another (the decision on the alien's request).

It follows, as the night the day, that the Court of Appeals had jurisdiction over this case. Recall: As authorized by the INA, Mata filed a motion with the Board to reopen his removal proceeding. The Board declined to grant Mata his proposed relief, thus conferring jurisdiction on an appellate court under *Kucana*. The Board did so for timeliness reasons, holding that Mata had filed his motion after 90 days had elapsed and that he was not entitled to equitable tolling. But as just explained, the reason the Board gave makes no difference: Whenever the Board denies an alien's statutory motion to reopen a removal case, courts have jurisdiction to review its decision. In addition, the Board determined not to exercise its *sua sponte* authority to reopen. But once again, that extra ruling does not matter. The Court of Appeals did not lose jurisdiction over the Board's denial of Mata's motion just because the Board also declined to reopen his case *sua sponte*.

Nonetheless, the Fifth Circuit dismissed Mata's appeal for lack of jurisdiction. That decision, as described earlier, hinged on "construing" Mata's motion as something it was not: "an invitation for the BIA to exercise" its *sua sponte* authority. After all, courts often treat a request for "categorically unavailable" relief as instead "seeking relief that may be available." And here (*amicus* concludes) that meant construing Mata's request for equitable tolling as a request for *sua sponte* reopening—even though that caused the Fifth Circuit to lose its jurisdiction.

But that conclusion is wrong even on the assumption—and it is only an assumption—that its core premise about equitable tolling is true. If the INA precludes Mata from getting the relief he seeks, then the right course on appeal is to take jurisdiction over the case, explain why that is so, and affirm the BIA's decision not to reopen. The jurisdictional question (whether the court has power to decide if tolling is proper) is of course distinct from the merits question (whether tolling is proper). The absence of a valid cause of action does not implicate subject-matter jurisdiction. The Fifth Circuit thus retains jurisdiction even if Mata's appeal lacks merit. And when a federal court has jurisdiction, it also has a "virtually unflagging obligation ... to exercise" that authority. *Colorado River Water Conservation Dist. v. United States.* Accordingly, the Court of Appeals should have asserted jurisdiction over Mata's appeal and addressed the equitable tolling question.

Contrary to *amicus*'s view, the practice of recharacterizing pleadings so as to offer the possibility of relief cannot justify the Court of Appeals' alternative approach. True enough (and a good thing too) that courts sometimes construe one kind of filing as another: If a litigant misbrands a motion, but could get relief under a different label, a court will often make the requisite change. See, *e.g.*, 12 J. Moore, Moore's Federal Practice, § 59.11[4] (3 ed. 2015) (explaining how courts treat untimely Rule 59 motions as Rule 60 motions because the latter have no time limit). But that established practice does not entail sidestepping the judicial obligation to exercise jurisdiction. And it results in identifying a route to relief, not in rendering relief impossible. That makes all the difference between a court's generously reading pleadings and a court's construing away adjudicative authority.

And if, as *amicus* argues, that construal rests on an underlying merits decision—that the INA precludes any equitable tolling—then the Court of Appeals has effectively insulated a circuit split from our review. Putting the Fifth Circuit to the side, all appellate courts to have addressed the matter have held that the Board may sometimes equitably toll the time limit for an alien's motion to reopen. Assuming the Fifth Circuit thinks otherwise, that creates the kind of split of authority we typically think we need to resolve. But the Fifth Circuit's practice of recharacterizing appeals like Mata's as challenges to the Board's *sua sponte* decisions and then declining to exercise jurisdiction over them prevents that split from coming to light. Of course, the Court of Appeals may reach whatever conclusion it thinks best as to the availability of equitable tolling; we express no opinion on that matter. What the Fifth Circuit may not do is to wrap such a merits decision in jurisdictional garb so that we cannot address a possible division between that court and every other.

For the foregoing reasons, we reverse the judgment of the Court of Appeals and remand the case for further proceedings consistent with this opinion.

# CHAPTER 14

# ARBITRATION 9 USC 1 ᴇᴛ sᴇǫ.

1. It was once hoped that arbitration would provide an effective means to resolve disputes between parties relatively quickly and inexpensively. Perhaps that has sometimes been the case. In many cases, however, the early hopes have not been fulfilled.

There is growing suspicion that many contracts to arbitrate disputes may not, in fact, have been the result of informed negotiations between the parties, but rather the result of the stronger party having put an arbitration clause in a standard, form contract.

One important goal of arbitration was to avoid the delay and expense of litigation in the courts. Unfortunately, there has been a significant amount of litigation – in the courts – on the issue of what is, or is not subject to arbitration.

### 130 S.CT. 2772
### SUPREME COURT OF THE UNITED STATES
### RENT-A-CENTER, WEST, INC., PETITIONER
### V.
### ANTONIO JACKSON

DECIDED JUNE 21, 2010

JUSTICE SCALIA delivered the opinion of the Court.

We consider whether, under the Federal Arbitration Act (FAA or Act), *9 U.S.C. §§ 1-16*, a district court may decide a claim that an arbitration agreement is unconscionable, where the agreement explicitly assigns that decision to the arbitrator.

# I

On February 1, 2007, plaintiff, Antonio Jackson, filed an employment-discrimination suit under 42 *U.S.C. § 1981*, against his former employer in the United States District Court for the District of Nevada. The defendant, Rent-A-Center, West, Inc., filed a motion under the FAA to dismiss or stay the proceedings, and to compel arbitration. Rent-A-Center argued that the Mutual Agreement to Arbitrate Claims (Agreement), which Jackson signed on February 24, 2003 as a condition of his employment there, precluded Jackson from pursuing his claims in court. The Agreement provided for arbitration of all "past, present or future" disputes arising out of Jackson's employment with Rent-A-Center, including "claims for discrimination" and "claims for violation of any federal law." It also provided that "the Arbitrator, and not any federal, state, or local court or agency, shall have exclusive authority to resolve any dispute relating to the interpretation, applicability, enforceability or formation of this Agreement including, but not limited to any claim that all or any part of this Agreement is void or voidable."

Jackson opposed the motion to compel arbitration on the ground that "the arbitration agreement in question is clearly unenforceable in that it is unconscionable" under Nevada law. Rent-A-Center responded that Jackson's unconscionability claim was not properly before the court because Jackson had expressly agreed that the arbitrator would have exclusive authority to resolve any dispute about the enforceability of the Agreement. It also disputed the merits of Jackson's unconscionability claims.

The District Court granted Rent-A-Center's motion to dismiss the proceedings and to compel arbitration. The Court of Appeals for the Ninth Circuit reversed in part, affirmed in part, and remanded.

We granted certiorari.

# II

## A

The FAA reflects the fundamental principle that arbitration is a matter of contract. *Section 2*, the "primary substantive provision of the Act," provides:

> A written provision in a contract evidencing a transaction involving commerce to
> settle by arbitration a controversy thereafter arising out of such contract shall be valid,
> irrevocable, and enforceable, save upon such grounds as exist at law or in equity for
> the revocation of any contract. *9 U.S.C. § 2.*

The FAA thereby places arbitration agreements on an equal footing with other contracts, and requires courts to enforce them according to their terms. Like other contracts, however, they may be invalidated by "generally applicable contract defenses, such as fraud, duress, or unconscionability."

The Act also establishes procedures by which federal courts implement § 2's substantive rule. Under § 3, a party may apply to a federal court for a stay of the trial of an action "upon any issue referable to arbitration under an agreement in writing for such arbitration." Under § 4, a party "aggrieved" by the failure of another party "to arbitrate under a written agreement for arbitration" may petition a federal court "for an order directing that such arbitration proceed in the manner provided for in such agreement." The court "shall" order arbitration "upon being satisfied that the making of the agreement for arbitration or the failure to comply therewith is not in issue."

The Agreement here contains multiple "written provisions" to "settle by arbitration a controversy," § 2. Two are relevant to our discussion. First, the section titled "Claims Covered By The Agreement" provides for arbitration of all "past, present or future" disputes arising out of Jackson's employment with Rent-A-Center. Second, the section titled "Arbitration Procedures" provides that "the Arbitrator shall have exclusive authority to resolve any dispute relating to the enforceability of this Agreement including, but not limited to any claim that all or any part of this Agreement is void or voidable." The current "controversy" between the parties is whether the Agreement is unconscionable. It is the second provision, which delegates resolution of that controversy to the arbitrator, that Rent-A-Center seeks to enforce. Adopting the terminology used by the parties, we will refer to it as the delegation provision.

The delegation provision is an agreement to arbitrate threshold issues concerning the arbitration agreement. We have recognized that parties can agree to arbitrate "gateway" questions of "arbitrability," such as whether the parties have agreed to arbitrate or whether their agreement covers a particular controversy. This line of cases merely reflects the principle that arbitration is a matter of contract. An agreement to arbitrate a gateway issue is simply an additional, antecedent agreement the party seeking arbitration asks the federal court to enforce, and the FAA operates on this additional arbitration agreement just as it does on any other. The additional agreement is valid under § 2 "save upon such grounds as exist at law or in equity for the revocation of any contract," and federal courts can enforce the agreement by staying federal litigation under § 3 and compelling arbitration under § 4. The question before us, then, is whether the delegation provision is valid under § 2.

## B

There are two types of validity challenges under § 2: "One type challenges specifically the *validity of the agreement to arbitrate*," and "the other challenges the *contract as a whole*, either on a ground that directly affects the entire agreement (*e.g.*, the agreement was fraudulently induced), or on the ground that the illegality of one of the contract's provisions renders the whole contract invalid." In a line of cases neither party has asked us to overrule, we held that only the first type of challenge is relevant to a court's determination whether the arbitration agreement at issue is enforceable. That is because § 2 states that a "written provision" "to settle by arbitration a controversy" is "valid, irrevocable, and enforceable" *without mention* of the validity of the contract in which it is contained. Thus, a party's challenge to another provision of the contract, or to the contract as a whole, does not prevent a court from enforcing a specific agreement to arbitrate. "As a matter of substantive federal arbitration law, an arbitration provision is severable from the remainder of the contract."

But that agreements to arbitrate are severable does not mean that they are unassailable. If a party challenges the validity under § 2 of the precise agreement to arbitrate at issue, the federal court must consider the challenge before ordering compliance with that agreement under § 4. In *Prima Paint*, for example, if the claim had been "fraud in the inducement of the arbitration clause itself," then the court would have considered it. "To immunize an arbitration agreement from judicial challenge on the ground of fraud in the inducement would be to elevate it over other forms of contract." In some cases the claimed basis of invalidity for the contract as a whole will be much easier to establish than the same basis as applied only to the severable agreement to arbitrate. Thus, in an employment contract many elements of alleged unconscionability applicable to the entire contract (outrageously low wages, for example) would not affect the agreement to arbitrate alone. But even where that is not the case -- as in *Prima Paint* itself, where the alleged fraud that induced the whole contract equally induced the agreement to arbitrate which was part of that contract -- we nonetheless require the basis of challenge to be directed specifically to the agreement to arbitrate before the court will intervene.

Here, the "written provision to settle by arbitration a controversy," that Rent-A-Center asks us to enforce is the delegation provision -- the provision that gave the arbitrator "exclusive authority to resolve any dispute relating to the enforceability of this Agreement," The "remainder of the contract," is the rest of the agreement to arbitrate claims arising out of Jackson's employment with Rent-A-Center. To be sure this case differs from *Prima Paint*, *Buckeye*, and *Preston*, in that the arbitration provisions sought to be enforced in those cases were contained in contracts unrelated to arbitration -- contracts for consulting services, see *Prima Paint,* check-cashing services, see *Buckeye,* and "personal management" or "talent agent" services, see *Preston.* In this case, the underlying contract is itself an arbitration agreement. But that makes no difference. Application of the severability rule does not depend on the substance of the remainder of the contract. *Section 2* operates on the specific "written provision" to "settle by arbitration a controversy" that the party seeks to enforce. Accordingly, unless Jackson challenged the delegation provision specifically, we must treat it as valid under § 2, and must enforce it under §§ 3 and 4, leaving any challenge to the validity of the Agreement as a whole for the arbitrator.

C

The District Court correctly concluded that Jackson challenged only the validity of the contract as a whole. Nowhere in his opposition to Rent-A-Center's motion to compel arbitration did he even mention the delegation provision. Rent-A-Center noted this fact in its reply: "Jackson's response fails to rebut or otherwise address in any way Rent-A-Center's argument that the Arbitrator must decide Jackson's challenge to the enforceability of the Agreement. *Thus, Rent-A-Center's argument is uncontested.*"

The arguments Jackson made in his response to Rent-A-Center's motion to compel arbitration support this conclusion. Jackson stated that "the *entire agreement* seems drawn to provide Rent-A-Center with undue advantages should an employment-related dispute arise." At one point, he argued that the limitations on discovery "further support his contention that the *arbitration agreement as a whole* is substantively unconscionable." And before this Court, Jackson describes his challenge in the District Court as follows: He "opposed the motion to compel on the ground that the *entire arbitration agreement,* including the delegation clause, was unconscionable." That is an accurate description of his filings.

As required to make out a claim of unconscionability under Nevada law, he contended that the Agreement was both procedurally and substantively unconscionable. It was procedurally unconscionable, he argued, because it "was imposed as a condition of employment and was non-negotiable." But we need not consider that claim because none of Jackson's substantive unconscionability challenges was specific to the delegation provision. First, he argued that the Agreement's coverage was one sided in that it required arbitration of claims an employee was likely to bring -- contract, tort, discrimination, and statutory claims -- but did not require arbitration of claims Rent-A-Center was likely to bring -- intellectual property, unfair competition, and trade secrets claims. This one-sided-coverage argument clearly did not go to the validity of the delegation provision.

Jackson's other two substantive unconscionability arguments assailed arbitration procedures called for by the contract -- the fee-splitting arrangement and the limitations on discovery -- procedures that were to be used during arbitration under *both* the agreement to arbitrate employment-related disputes *and* the delegation provision. It may be that had Jackson challenged the delegation provision by arguing that these common procedures *as applied* to the delegation provision rendered *that provision* unconscionable, the challenge should have been considered by the court. To make such a claim based on the discovery procedures, Jackson would have had to argue that the limitation upon the number of depositions causes the arbitration of his claim that the Agreement is unenforceable to be unconscionable. That would be, of course, a much more difficult argument to sustain than the argument that the same limitation renders arbitration of his factbound employment-discrimination claim unconscionable. Likewise, the unfairness of the fee-splitting arrangement may be more difficult to establish for the arbitration of enforceability than for arbitration of more complex and fact-related aspects of the alleged employment discrimination. Jackson, however, did not make any arguments specific to the delegation provision; he argued that the fee-sharing and discovery procedures rendered the *entire* Agreement invalid.

Jackson's appeal to the Ninth Circuit confirms that he did not contest the validity of the delegation provision in particular.

Jackson repeated that argument before this Court. At oral argument, counsel stated: "There are certain elements of the arbitration agreement that are unconscionable and, under Nevada law, which would render the *entire arbitration agreement* unconscionable." And again, he stated, "we've got both certain provisions that are unconscionable, that under Nevada law render the *entire agreement* unconscionable, and that's what the Court is to rely on."

In his brief to this Court, Jackson made the contention, not mentioned below, that the delegation provision itself is substantively unconscionable because the *quid pro quo* he was supposed to receive for it -- that "in exchange for initially allowing an arbitrator to decide certain gateway questions," he would receive "plenary post-arbitration judicial review" -- was eliminated by the Court's subsequent holding in *Hall Street Associates, L. L. C. v. Mattel (2008)*, that the nonplenary grounds for judicial review in *§ 10 of the FAA* are exclusive. He brought this challenge to the delegation provision too late, and we will not consider it. [5]

5 *Hall Street Associates, L. L. C. v. Mattel, (2008)*, was decided after Jackson submitted his brief to the Ninth Circuit, but that does not change our conclusion that he forfeited the argument. Jackson could have submitted a supplemental brief during the *year and a half* between this Court's decision of *Hall Street* on March 25, 2008 and the Ninth

Circuit's judgment on September 9, 2009. Moreover, *Hall Street* affirmed a rule that had been in place in the Ninth Circuit since 2003.

We reverse the judgment of the Court of Appeals for the Ninth Circuit.

2. One of the major issues today is whether or not a party, by implication, gives up the right to *class action* arbitration if there is no specific provision about *class actions* in the contract. This is an especially important issue because in many cases there may be no effective way, financially, to present small individual claims unless they can be brought in a class action format.

## 130 S.CT. 1758
## SUPREME COURT OF THE UNITED STATES
## STOLT-NIELSEN S. A., ET AL., PETITIONERS
## V.
## ANIMALFEEDS INTERNATIONAL CORP.

### DECIDED APRIL 27, 2010

**JUSTICE ALITO delivered the opinion of the Court.**

We granted certiorari in this case to decide whether imposing class arbitration on parties whose arbitration clauses are "silent" on that issue is consistent with the Federal Arbitration Act (FAA), *9 U.S.C. § 1 et seq.*

I

A

Petitioners are shipping companies that serve a large share of the world market for parcel tankers -- seagoing vessels with compartments that are separately chartered to customers wishing to ship liquids in small quantities. One of those customers is AnimalFeeds International Corp. (hereinafter AnimalFeeds), which supplies raw ingredients, such as fish oil, to animal-feed producers around the world. AnimalFeeds ships its goods pursuant to a standard contract known in the maritime trade as a *charter party*.[1] Numerous charter parties are in regular use, and the charter party that

AnimalFeeds uses is known as the "Vegoilvoy" charter party. Petitioners assert, without contradiction, that charterers like AnimalFeeds, or their agents -- not the ship-owners -- typically select the particular charter party that governs their shipments.

> 1"Charter parties are commonly drafted using highly standardized forms specific to the particular trades and business needs of the parties." Adopted in 1950, the Vegoilvoy charter party contains the following arbitration clause:

> "Arbitration. Any dispute arising from the making, performance or termination of this Charter Party shall be settled in New York, Owner and Charterer each appointing an arbitrator, who shall be a merchant, broker or individual experienced in the shipping business; the two thus chosen, if they cannot agree, shall nominate a third arbitrator who shall be an Admiralty lawyer. Such arbitration shall be conducted in conformity with the provisions and procedure of the United States Arbitration Act [*i.e.*, the FAA], and a judgment of the Court shall be entered upon any award made by said arbitrator."

In 2003, a Department of Justice criminal investigation revealed that the ship owners (petitioners) were engaging in an illegal price-fixing conspiracy. When AnimalFeeds learned of this, it brought a putative class action against the ship owners (petitioners) in the District Court for the Eastern District of Pennsylvania, asserting antitrust claims for supracompetitive prices that the ship owners allegedly charged their customers over a period of several years.

Other charterers brought similar suits. In one of these, the District Court for the District of Connecticut held that the charterers' claims were not subject to arbitration under the applicable arbitration clause, but the Second Circuit reversed. While that appeal was pending, the Judicial Panel on Multidistrict Litigation ordered the consolidation of then-pending actions against the ship owners, including AnimalFeeds' action, in the District of Connecticut. The parties agree that as a consequence of these judgments and orders, AnimalFeeds and the ship owners must arbitrate their antitrust dispute.

B

In 2005, AnimalFeeds served petitioners with a demand for class arbitration, designating New York City as the place of arbitration and seeking to represent a class of "all direct purchasers of parcel tanker transportation services globally for bulk liquid chemicals, edible oils, acids, and other specialty liquids from the ship owners at any time during the period from August 1, 1998, to November 30, 2002." The parties entered into a supplemental agreement providing for the question of class arbitration to be submitted to a panel of three arbitrators.

The parties selected a panel of arbitrators and stipulated that the arbitration clause was "silent" with respect to class arbitration. Counsel for AnimalFeeds explained to the arbitration panel that the term "silent" did not simply mean that the clause made no express reference to class arbitration. Rather, he said, "all the parties agree that when a contract is silent on an issue there's been no agreement that has been reached on that issue."

After hearing argument and evidence, including testimony from petitioners' experts regarding arbitration customs and usage in the maritime trade, the arbitrators concluded that the arbitration clause allowed for class arbitration.

The arbitrators stayed the proceeding to allow the parties to seek judicial review, and the ship owners filed an application to vacate the arbitrators' award in the District Court for the Southern District of New York.

The District Court vacated the award.

AnimalFeeds appealed to the Court of Appeals, which reversed.

We granted certiorari.

## II

Instead of identifying and applying a rule of decision derived from the FAA or either maritime or New York law, the arbitration panel imposed its own policy choice and thus exceeded its powers. As a result, under *§ 10(b) of the FAA*, we must either "direct a rehearing by the arbitrators" or decide the question that was originally referred to the panel. Because we conclude that there can be only one possible outcome on the facts before us, we see no need to direct a rehearing by the arbitrators.

## III

### A

The arbitration panel thought that *Bazzle* "controlled" the "resolution" of the question whether the Vegoilvoy charter party "permits this arbitration to proceed on behalf of a class," but that understanding was incorrect.

*Bazzle* concerned contracts between a commercial lender (Green Tree) and its customers. These contracts contained an arbitration clause but did not expressly mention class arbitration. Nevertheless, an arbitrator conducted class arbitration proceedings and entered awards for the customers.

The South Carolina Supreme Court affirmed the awards.

When *Bazzle* reached this Court, no single rationale commanded a majority.

B

Unfortunately, the opinions in *Bazzle* appear to have baffled the parties in this case at the time of the arbitration proceeding.

As we have explained, however, *Bazzle* did not establish the rule to be applied in deciding whether class arbitration is permitted. The decision in *Bazzle* left that question open, and we turn to it now.

IV

While the interpretation of an arbitration agreement is generally a matter of state law, the FAA imposes certain rules of fundamental importance, including the basic precept that arbitration "is a matter of consent, not coercion,"

A

In 1925, Congress enacted the United States Arbitration Act, as the FAA was formerly known, for the express purpose of making "valid and enforceable written provisions or agreements for arbitration of disputes arising out of contracts, maritime transactions, or commerce among the States or Territories or with foreign nations." Reenacted and codified in 1947, the FAA provides, in pertinent part, that a "written provision in any maritime transaction" calling for the arbitration of a controversy arising out of such transaction "shall be valid, irrevocable, and enforceable, save upon such grounds as exist at law or in equity for the revocation of any contract," Under the FAA, a party to an arbitration agreement may petition a United States district court for an order directing that "arbitration proceed in the manner provided for in such agreement." § 4. Consistent with these provisions, we have said on numerous occasions that the central or "primary" purpose of the FAA is to ensure that "private agreements to arbitrate are enforced according to their terms."

Whether enforcing an agreement to arbitrate or construing an arbitration clause, courts and arbitrators must "give effect to the contractual rights and expectations of the parties." In this endeavor, "as with any other contract, the parties' intentions control." This is because an arbitrator derives his or her powers from the parties' agreement to forgo the legal process and submit their disputes to private dispute resolution. ("Arbitrators derive their authority to resolve disputes only because the parties have agreed in advance to submit such grievances to arbitration"); ("By agreeing to arbitrate, a party trades the procedures and opportunity for review of the courtroom for the simplicity, informality, and expedition of arbitration"); (an arbitrator "has no general charter to administer justice for a community which transcends the parties" but rather is "part of a system of self-government created by and confined to the parties").

Underscoring the consensual nature of private dispute resolution, we have held that parties are "'generally free to structure their arbitration agreements as they see fit.'" For example, we have held that parties may agree to limit the issues they choose to arbitrate, and may agree on rules under which any arbitration will proceed. They may choose who will resolve specific disputes.

We think it is also clear from our precedents and the contractual nature of arbitration that parties may specify *with whom* they choose to arbitrate their disputes. ("Nothing in the FAA authorizes a court to compel arbitration of any issues, *or by any parties*, that are not already covered in the agreement."

B

From these principles, it follows that a party may not be compelled under the FAA to submit to *class* arbitration unless there is a contractual basis for concluding that the party *agreed* to do so. In this case, however, the arbitration panel imposed class arbitration even though the parties concurred that they had reached no agreement on the issue. The critical point, in the view of the arbitration panel, was that petitioners did not "establish that the parties to the charter agreements intended to *preclude* class arbitration." Even though the parties are sophisticated business entities, even though there is no tradition of class arbitration under maritime law, and even though AnimalFeeds does not dispute that it is customary for the shipper to choose the charter party that is used for a particular shipment, the panel regarded the agreement's silence on the question of class arbitration as dispositive. The panel's conclusion is fundamentally at war with the foundational FAA principle that arbitration is a matter of consent.

In certain contexts, it is appropriate to presume that parties that enter into an arbitration agreement implicitly authorize the arbitrator to adopt such procedures as are necessary to give effect to the parties' agreement. Thus, we have said that "' "procedural" questions which grow out of the dispute and bear on its final disposition' are presumptively not for the judge, but for an arbitrator, to decide." This recognition is grounded in the background principle that "when the parties to a bargain sufficiently defined to be a contract have not agreed with respect to a term which is essential to a determination of their rights and duties, a term which is reasonable in the circumstances is supplied by the court."

An implicit agreement to authorize class-action arbitration, however, is not a term that the arbitrator may infer solely from the fact of the parties' agreement to arbitrate. This is so because class-action arbitration changes the nature of arbitration to such a degree that it cannot be presumed the parties consented to it by simply agreeing to submit their disputes to an arbitrator. In bilateral arbitration, parties forgo the procedural rigor and appellate review of the courts in order to realize the benefits of private dispute resolution: lower costs, greater efficiency and speed, and the ability to choose expert adjudicators to resolve specialized disputes.

The relative benefits of class-action arbitration are much less assured, giving reason to doubt the parties' mutual consent to resolve disputes through class-wide arbitration.

Consider just some of the fundamental changes brought about by the shift from bilateral arbitration to class-action arbitration. An arbitrator chosen according to an agreed-upon procedure, no longer resolves a single dispute between the parties to a single agreement, but instead resolves many disputes between hundreds or perhaps even thousands of parties. ("We believe domestic class members could be in the hundreds" and that "there could be class members that ship to and from the U.S. who are not domestic who we think would be covered"). Under the Class Rules, "the presumption of privacy and confidentiality" that applies in many bilateral arbitrations "shall not apply in class arbitrations." The arbitrator's award no longer purports to bind just the parties to a single arbitration agreement, but adjudicates the rights of absent parties as well. Cf. *Ortiz v. Fibreboard Corp.* And the commercial stakes of class-action arbitration are comparable to those of class-action litigation, even though the scope of judicial review is much more limited. We think that the differences between bilateral and class-action arbitration are too great for arbitrators to presume, consistent with their limited powers under the FAA, that the parties' mere silence on the issue of class-action arbitration constitutes consent to resolve their disputes in class proceedings.

V

For these reasons, the judgment of the Court of Appeals is reversed, and the case is remanded for further proceedings consistent with this opinion.

3. As this book goes to press there is discussion of an administrative order being promulgated to prohibit banks from including standard provisions in their contracts with consumers that require arbitration, and then direct that the consumer gives up the right to bring any class action against the banks. As demonstrated earlier, class actions are frequently the only feasible method for customers or employees to bring relatively small claims to the attention of the courts.

# CHAPTER 15

# REGULATING THE JUDICIARY

1. Judges play a very active role in all litigation. Decisions controlling discovery, granting or denying motions to dismiss or motions for summary judgment and the like are all crucial to the ultimate outcome of the litigation. So it is vital that all judges be impartial.

   Federal judges are appointed for life, in the hopes that that security will free them from political pressures and from the financial pressures caused by having to campaign for re-election.

   The following two cases illustrate some of the problems that may arise when a judge is required to campaign for election to office.

   In very rare instances it may be appropriate at the beginning of a trial to ask that a judge recuse himself or herself.

   Although the U.S. Supreme Court has generally avoided setting down hard and fast rules for judicial conduct, on June 9, 2016 it did declare that in criminal matters, "The Court now holds that under the Due Process Clause there is an impermissible risk of actual bias when a judge earlier had significant, personal involvement as a prosecutor in a critical decision regarding a defendant's case ... even if the judge in question did not cast a deciding vote." *Williams v. Pennsylvania,* 579 U.S. \_\_\_\_ (2016). In the *Williams* case, although it had been 26 years between the time that Ronald Castille, as Philadelphia District Attorney, had approved seeking the death-penalty against Williams, and the time that Ronald Castille, as Chief Justice of the Pennsylvania Supreme Court voted to uphold the conviction, the U.S. Supreme Court held that Justice Castille's refusal to recuse himself was an unconstitutional violation of Due Process – and not "harmless error." [Justice Castille's concurring opinion in the Pennsylvania Supreme Court case makes it clear that he still felt strongly about the case when he wrote that concurring opinion – 26 years after his initial involvement in the case.]

The following civil case seems quite mild, compared to the *Williams* case.

135 S.CT. 1656
SUPREME COURT OF THE UNITED STATES
LANELL WILLIAMS-YULEE, PETITIONER
V.
THE FLORIDA BAR.

DECIDED APRIL 29, 2015

ROBERTS, C.J., delivered the opinion of the Court, except as to Part II. BREYER, SOTOMAYOR, and KAGAN, JJ., joined that opinion in full, and GINSBURG, J., joined except as to Part II. BREYER, J., filed a concurring opinion. GINSBURG, J., filed an opinion concurring in part and concurring in the judgment, in which BREYER, J., joined as to Part II. SCALIA, J., filed a dissenting opinion, in which THOMAS, J., joined. KENNEDY, J., and ALITO, J., filed dissenting opinions.

Chief Justice ROBERTS delivered the opinion of the Court, except as to Part II.

Our Founders vested authority to appoint federal judges in the President, with the advice and consent of the Senate, and entrusted those judges to hold their offices during good behavior. The Constitution permits States to make a different choice, and most of them have done so. In 39 States, voters elect trial or appellate judges at the polls. In an effort to preserve public confidence in the integrity of their judiciaries, many of those States prohibit judges and judicial candidates from personally soliciting funds for their campaigns. We must decide whether the First Amendment permits such restrictions on speech.

We hold that it does. Judges are not politicians, even when they come to the bench by way of the ballot. And a State's decision to elect its judiciary does not compel it to treat judicial candidates like campaigners for political office. A State may assure its people that judges will apply the law without fear or favor—and without having personally asked anyone for money. We affirm the judgment of the Florida Supreme Court.

# I

## A

When Florida entered the Union in 1845, its Constitution provided for trial and appellate judges to be elected by the General Assembly. Florida soon followed more than a dozen of its sister States in transferring authority to elect judges to the voting public. The experiment did not last long in the Sunshine State. The war came, and Florida's 1868 Constitution returned judicial selection to the political branches. Over time, however, the people reclaimed the power to elect the state bench: Supreme Court justices in 1885 and trial court judges in 1942.

In the early 1970s, four Florida Supreme Court justices resigned from office following corruption scandals. Florida voters responded by amending their Constitution again. Under the system now in place, appellate judges are appointed by the Governor from a list of candidates proposed by a nominating committee—a process known as "merit selection." Then, every six years, voters decide whether to retain incumbent appellate judges for another term. Trial judges are still elected by popular vote, unless the local jurisdiction opts instead for merit selection.

Amid the corruption scandals of the 1970s, the Florida Supreme Court adopted a new Code of Judicial Conduct. In its present form, the first sentence of Canon 1 reads, "An independent and honorable judiciary is indispensable to justice in our society." Canon 1 instructs judges to observe "high standards of conduct" so that "the integrity and independence of the judiciary may be preserved." Canon 2 directs that a judge "shall act at all times in a manner that promotes public confidence in the integrity and impartiality of the judiciary." Other provisions prohibit judges from lending the prestige of their offices to private interests, engaging in certain business transactions, and personally participating in soliciting funds for nonprofit organizations.

Canon 7C(1) governs fundraising in judicial elections. The Canon, which is based on a provision in the American Bar Association's Model Code of Judicial Conduct, provides:

> A candidate, including an incumbent judge, for a judicial office that is filled by public election between competing candidates shall not personally solicit campaign funds, or solicit attorneys for publicly stated support, but may establish committees of responsible persons to secure and manage the expenditure of funds for the candidate's campaign and to obtain public statements of support for his or her candidacy. Such committees are not prohibited from soliciting campaign contributions and public support from any person or corporation authorized by law.

Florida statutes impose additional restrictions on campaign fundraising in judicial elections. Contributors may not donate more than $1,000 per election to a trial court candidate or more than $3,000 per retention election to a Supreme Court justice. Campaign committee treasurers must file periodic reports disclosing the names of contributors and the amount of each contribution.

Judicial candidates can seek guidance about campaign ethics rules from the Florida Judicial Ethics Advisory Committee. The Committee has interpreted Canon 7 to allow a judicial candidate to serve as treasurer of his own campaign committee, learn the identity of campaign contributors, and send thank you notes to donors.

Like Florida, most other States prohibit judicial candidates from soliciting campaign funds personally, but allow them to raise money through committees. According to the American Bar Association, 30 of the 39 States that elect trial or appellate judges have adopted restrictions similar to Canon 7C(1).

B

Lanell Williams–Yulee, who refers to herself as Yulee, has practiced law in Florida since 1991. In September 2009, she decided to run for a seat on the county court for Hillsborough County, a jurisdiction of about 1.3 million people that includes the city of Tampa. Shortly after filing paperwork to enter the race, Yulee drafted a letter announcing her candidacy. The letter described her experience and desire to "bring fresh ideas and positive solutions to the Judicial bench." The letter then stated:

> "An early contribution of $25, $50, $100, $250, or $500, made payable to 'Lanell Williams–Yulee Campaign for County Judge', will help raise the initial funds needed to launch the campaign and get our message out to the public. I ask for your support in meeting the primary election fund raiser goals. Thank you in advance for your support."

Yulee signed the letter and mailed it to local voters. She also posted the letter on her campaign Web site.

Yulee's bid for the bench did not unfold as she had hoped. She lost the primary to the incumbent judge. Then the Florida Bar filed a complaint against her. As relevant here, the Bar charged her with violating Rule 4–8.2(b) of the Rules Regulating the Florida Bar. That Rule requires judicial candidates to comply with applicable provisions of Florida's Code of Judicial Conduct, including the ban on personal solicitation of campaign funds in Canon 7C(1).

Yulee admitted that she had signed and sent the fundraising letter. But she argued that the Bar could not discipline her for that conduct because the First Amendment protects a judicial candidate's right to solicit campaign funds in an election. The Florida Supreme Court appointed a referee, who held a hearing and recommended a finding of guilt. As a sanction, the referee recommended that Yulee be publicly reprimanded and ordered to pay the costs of the proceeding ($1,860).

The Florida Supreme Court adopted the referee's recommendations.

The Florida Supreme Court acknowledged that some Federal Courts of Appeals—"whose judges have lifetime appointments and thus do not have to engage in fundraising"—had invalidated restrictions similar to Canon 7C(1). But the court found it persuasive that every State Supreme Court that had considered similar fundraising provisions—along with several Federal Courts of Appeals—had upheld the laws against First Amendment challenges. Florida's chief justice and one associate justice dissented. We granted certiorari.

## II

The First Amendment provides that Congress "shall make no law ... abridging the freedom of speech." The Fourteenth Amendment makes that prohibition applicable to the States. The parties agree that Canon 7C(1) restricts Yulee's speech on the basis of its content by prohibiting her from soliciting contributions to her election campaign. The parties disagree, however, about the level of scrutiny that should govern our review.

We have applied exacting scrutiny to laws restricting the solicitation of contributions to charity, upholding the speech limitations only if they are narrowly tailored to serve a compelling interest. As we have explained, noncommercial solicitation "is characteristically intertwined with informative and perhaps persuasive speech." Applying a lesser standard of scrutiny to such speech would threaten "the exercise of rights so vital to the maintenance of democratic institutions."

The principles underlying these charitable solicitation cases apply with even greater force here. Before asking for money in her fundraising letter, Yulee explained her fitness for the bench and expressed her vision for the judiciary. Her stated purpose for the solicitation was to get her "message out to the public." As we have long recognized, speech about public issues and the qualifications of candidates for elected office commands the highest level of First Amendment protection. Indeed, in our only prior case concerning speech restrictions on a candidate for judicial office, this Court and both parties assumed that strict scrutiny applied.

Here, Yulee does not claim that Canon 7C(1) violates her right to free association; she argues that it violates her right to free speech. And the Florida Bar can hardly dispute that the Canon infringes Yulee's freedom to discuss candidates and public issues—namely, herself and her qualifications to be a judge. The Bar's call to import the "closely drawn" test from the contribution limit context into a case about solicitation therefore has little avail.

In sum, we hold today what we assumed in *White*: A State may restrict the speech of a judicial candidate only if the restriction is narrowly tailored to serve a compelling interest.

## III

The Florida Bar faces a demanding task in defending Canon 7C(1) against Yulee's First Amendment challenge. We have emphasized that "it is the rare case" in which a State demonstrates that a speech restriction is narrowly tailored to serve a compelling interest. But those cases do arise. Here, Canon 7C(1) advances the State's compelling interest in preserving public confidence in the integrity of the judiciary, and it does so through means narrowly tailored to avoid unnecessarily abridging speech. This is therefore one of the rare cases in which a speech restriction withstands strict scrutiny.

### A

The interest served by Canon 7C(1) has firm support in our precedents. We have recognized the "vital state interest" in safeguarding "public confidence in the fairness and integrity of the nation's elected judges." *Caperton v. A.T. Massey Coal Co.* (2009). The importance of public confidence in the integrity of judges stems from the place of the judiciary in the government. Unlike the executive or the legislature, the judiciary "has no influence over either the sword or the purse; neither force nor will but merely judgment." The Federalist No. 78, (A. Hamilton). The judiciary's authority therefore depends in large measure on the public's willingness to respect and follow its decisions. As Justice Frankfurter once put it for the Court, "justice must satisfy the appearance of justice." It follows that public perception of judicial integrity is "a state interest of the highest order."

The vast majority of elected judges in States that allow personal solicitation serve with fairness and honor. But "even if judges were able to refrain from favoring donors, the mere possibility that judges' decisions may be motivated by the desire to repay campaign contributions is likely to undermine the public's confidence in the judiciary." In the eyes of the public, a judge's personal solicitation could result (even unknowingly) in "a possible temptation which might lead him not to hold the balance

nice, clear and true." That risk is especially pronounced because most donors are lawyers and litigants who may appear before the judge they are supporting.

The concept of public confidence in judicial integrity does not easily reduce to
precise definition, nor does it lend itself to proof by documentary record. But no one
denies that it is genuine and compelling. In short, it is the regrettable but unavoidable
appearance that judges who personally ask for money may diminish their integrity
that prompted the Supreme Court of Florida and most other States to sever the direct
link between judicial candidates and campaign contributors. As the Supreme Court
of Oregon explained, "the spectacle of lawyers or potential litigants directly handing
over money to judicial candidates should be avoided if the public is to have faith in
the impartiality of its judiciary." Moreover, personal solicitation by a judicial candidate "inevitably places the solicited individuals in a position to fear retaliation if
they fail to financially support that candidate." Potential litigants then fear that "the
integrity of the judicial system has been compromised, forcing them to search for an
attorney in part based upon the criteria of which attorneys have made the obligatory
contributions." A State's decision to elect its judges does not require it to tolerate
these risks. The Florida Bar's interest is compelling.

B

Yulee acknowledges the State's compelling interest in judicial integrity. She argues,
however, that the Canon's failure to restrict other speech equally damaging to judicial integrity and its appearance undercuts the Bar's position. In particular, she notes
that Canon 7C(1) allows a judge's campaign committee to solicit money, which arguably reduces public confidence in the integrity of the judiciary just as much as a
judge's personal solicitation. Yulee also points out that Florida permits judicial candidates to write thank you notes to campaign donors, which ensures that candidates
know who contributes and who does not.

It is always somewhat counterintuitive to argue that a law violates the First
Amendment by abridging *too little* speech. We have recognized, however, that underinclusiveness can raise "doubts about whether the government is in fact pursuing the
interest it invokes, rather than disfavoring a particular speaker or viewpoint."

Underinclusiveness can also reveal that a law does not actually advance a compelling interest. For example, a State's decision to prohibit newspapers, but not electronic media, from releasing the names of juvenile defendants suggested that the law
did not advance its stated purpose of protecting youth privacy.

Although a law's underinclusivity raises a red flag, the First Amendment imposes
no freestanding "underinclusiveness limitation."

Viewed in light of these principles, Canon 7C(1) raises no fatal underinclusivity concerns. The solicitation ban aims squarely at the conduct most likely to undermine public confidence in the integrity of the judiciary: personal requests for money by judges and judicial candidates. The Canon applies evenhandedly to all judges and judicial candidates, regardless of their viewpoint or chosen means of solicitation. And unlike some laws that we have found impermissibly underinclusive, Canon 7C(1) is not riddled with exceptions. Indeed, the Canon contains zero exceptions to its ban on personal solicitation.

In short, personal solicitation by judicial candidates implicates a different problem than solicitation by campaign committees. However similar the two solicitations may be in substance, a State may conclude that they present markedly different appearances to the public. Florida's choice to allow solicitation by campaign committees does not undermine its decision to ban solicitation by judges.

Likewise, allowing judicial candidates to write thank you notes to campaign donors does not detract from the State's interest in preserving public confidence in the integrity of the judiciary. Yulee argues that permitting thank you notes heightens the likelihood of actual bias by ensuring that judicial candidates know who supported their campaigns, and ensuring that the supporter knows that the candidate knows. Maybe so. But the State's compelling interest is implicated most directly by the candidate's personal solicitation itself. A failure to ban thank you notes for contributions not solicited by the candidate does not undercut the Bar's rationale.

In addition, the State has a good reason for allowing candidates to write thank you notes and raise money through committees. These accommodations reflect Florida's effort to respect the First Amendment interests of candidates and their contributors—to resolve the "fundamental tension between the ideal character of the judicial office and the real world of electoral politics."

C

In considering Yulee's tailoring arguments, we are mindful that most States with elected judges have determined that drawing a line between personal solicitation by candidates and solicitation by committees is necessary to preserve public confidence in the integrity of the judiciary. These considered judgments deserve our respect, especially because they reflect sensitive choices by States in an area central to their own governance—how to select those who "sit as their judges."

The desirability of judicial elections is a question that has sparked disagreement for more than 200 years. Hamilton believed that appointing judges to positions with life tenure constituted "the best expedient which can be devised in any government to secure a steady, upright, and impartial administration of the laws." The Federalist No. 78. Jefferson thought that making judges "dependent on none but themselves" ran counter to the principle of "a government founded on the public will." 12 The Works of Thomas Jefferson 5. The federal courts reflect the view of Hamilton; most States have sided with Jefferson. Both methods have given our Nation jurists of wisdom and rectitude who have devoted themselves to maintaining "the public's respect ... and a reserve of public goodwill, without becoming subservient to public opinion." Rehnquist, Judicial Independence, 38 U. Rich. L.Rev. 579, 596 (2004).

It is not our place to resolve this enduring debate. Our limited task is to apply the Constitution to the question presented in this case. Judicial candidates have a First Amendment right to speak in support of their campaigns. States have a compelling interest in preserving public confidence in their judiciaries. When the State adopts a narrowly tailored restriction like the one at issue here, those principles do not conflict. A State's decision to elect judges does not compel it to compromise public confidence in their integrity.

The judgment of the Florida Supreme Court is *Affirmed.*

2. The following case may remind you of a John Grisham novel that was published *before* this decision was announced, but that included a fact situation remarkably similar to this case.

**129 S.CT. 2252**
**SUPREME COURT OF THE UNITED STATES**
**HUGH M. CAPERTON, ET AL., PETITIONERS,**
**V.**
**A.T. MASSEY COAL CO., INC., ET AL.**

DECIDED JUNE 8, 2009

**Justice <u>KENNEDY</u> delivered the opinion of the Court.**

In this case the Supreme Court of Appeals of West Virginia reversed a trial court judgment, which had entered a jury verdict of $50 million. Five justices heard the case, and the vote to reverse was 3 to 2. The question presented is whether the Due Process Clause of the Fourteenth Amendment was violated when one of the justices in the majority denied a recusal motion. The basis for the motion was that the justice had received campaign contributions in an extraordinary amount from, and through the efforts of, the board chairman and principal officer of the corporation found liable for the damages.

Under our precedents there are objective standards that require recusal when "the probability of actual bias on the part of the judge or decisionmaker is too high to be constitutionally tolerable." Applying those precedents, we find that, in all the circumstances of this case, due process requires recusal.

## I

In August 2002 a West Virginia jury returned a verdict that found respondents A.T. Massey Coal Co. and its affiliates (hereinafter Massey) liable for fraudulent misrepresentation, concealment, and tortious interference with existing contractual relations. The jury awarded petitioners Hugh Caperton, Harman Development Corp., Harman Mining Corp., and Sovereign Coal Sales (hereinafter Caperton) the sum of $50 million in compensatory and punitive damages.

In June 2004 the state trial court denied Massey's post-trial motions challenging the verdict and the damages award, finding that Massey "intentionally acted in utter disregard of Caperton's rights and ultimately destroyed Caperton's businesses because, after conducting cost-benefit analyses, Massey concluded it was in its financial interest to do so." In March 2005 the trial court denied Massey's motion for judgment as a matter of law.

Don Blankenship is Massey's chairman, chief executive officer, and president. After the verdict but before the appeal, West Virginia held its 2004 judicial elections. Knowing the Supreme Court of Appeals of West Virginia would consider the appeal in the case, Blankenship decided to support an attorney who sought to replace Justice McGraw. Justice McGraw was a candidate for reelection to that court. The attorney who sought to replace him was Brent Benjamin.

In addition to contributing the $1,000 statutory maximum to Benjamin's campaign committee, Blankenship donated almost $2.5 million to "And For The Sake Of The Kids," a political organization formed under 26 U.S.C. § 527. The § 527 organization opposed McGraw and supported Benjamin. Blankenship's donations accounted for more than two-thirds of the total funds it raised. This was not all. Blankenship spent, in addition, just over $500,000 on independent expenditures—for direct mailings and letters soliciting donations as well as television and newspaper advertisements—" 'to support ... Brent Benjamin.' "

To provide some perspective, Blankenship's $3 million in contributions were more than the total amount spent by all other Benjamin supporters and three times the amount spent by Benjamin's own committee. Caperton contends that Blankenship spent $1 million more than the total amount spent by the campaign committees of both candidates combined.

Benjamin won. He received 382,036 votes (53.3%), and McGraw received 334,301 votes (46.7%).

In October 2005, before Massey filed its petition for appeal in West Virginia's highest court, Caperton moved to disqualify now-Justice Benjamin under the Due Process Clause and the West Virginia Code of Judicial Conduct, based on the conflict caused by Blankenship's campaign involvement. Justice Benjamin denied the motion in April 2006. He indicated that he "carefully considered the bases and accompanying exhibits proffered by the movants." But he found "no objective information … to show that this Justice has a bias for or against any litigant, that this Justice has prejudged the matters which comprise this litigation, or that this Justice will be anything but fair and impartial." In December 2006 Massey filed its petition for appeal to challenge the adverse jury verdict. The West Virginia Supreme Court of Appeals granted review.

In November 2007 that court reversed the $50 million verdict against Massey. The majority opinion, authored by then-Chief Justice Davis and joined by Justices Benjamin and Maynard, found that "Massey's conduct warranted the type of judgment rendered in this case." It reversed, nevertheless, based on two independent grounds—first, that a forum-selection clause contained in a contract to which Massey was not a party barred the suit in West Virginia, and, second, that res judicata barred the suit due to an out-of-state judgment to which Massey was not a party. Justice Starcher dissented, stating that the "majority's opinion is morally and legally wrong." Justice Albright also dissented, accusing the majority of "misapplying the law and introducing sweeping 'new law' into our jurisprudence that may well come back to haunt us."

Caperton sought rehearing, and the parties moved for disqualification of three of the five justices who decided the appeal. Photos had surfaced of Justice Maynard vacationing with Blankenship in the French Riviera while the case was pending. Justice Maynard granted Caperton's recusal motion. On the other side Justice Starcher granted Massey's recusal motion, apparently based on his public criticism of Blankenship's role in the 2004 elections. In his recusal memorandum Justice Starcher urged Justice Benjamin to recuse himself as well. He noted that "Blankenship's bestowal of his personal wealth, political tactics, and 'friendship' have created a cancer in the affairs of this Court." Justice Benjamin declined Justice Starcher's suggestion and denied Caperton's recusal motion.

The court granted rehearing. Justice Benjamin, now in the capacity of acting chief justice, selected Judges Cookman and Fox to replace the recused justices. Caperton moved a third time for disqualification, arguing that Justice Benjamin had failed to apply the correct standard under West Virginia law—*i.e.,* whether "a reasonable and prudent person, knowing these objective facts, would harbor doubts about Justice Benjamin's ability to be fair and impartial." Caperton also included the results of a public opinion poll, which indicated that over 67% of West Virginians doubted Justice Benjamin would be fair and impartial. Justice Benjamin again refused to withdraw, noting that the "push poll" was "neither credible nor sufficiently reliable to serve as the basis for an elected judge's disqualification."

In April 2008 a divided court again reversed the jury verdict, and again it was a 3-to-2 decision. Justice Davis filed a modified version of his prior opinion, repeating the two earlier holdings. She was joined by Justice Benjamin and Judge Fox. Justice Albright, joined by Judge Cookman, dissented: "Not only is the majority opinion unsupported by the facts and existing case law, but it is also fundamentally unfair. Sadly, justice was neither honored nor served by the majority." The dissent also noted "genuine due process implications arising under federal law" with respect to Justice Benjamin's failure to recuse himself.

Four months later—a month after the petition for writ of certiorari was filed in this Court—Justice Benjamin filed a concurring opinion. He defended the merits of the majority opinion as well as his decision not to recuse. He rejected Caperton's challenge to his participation in the case under both the Due Process Clause and West Virginia law. Justice Benjamin reiterated that he had no "'direct, personal, substantial, pecuniary interest' in this case." Adopting "a standard merely of 'appearances,'" he concluded, "seems little more than an invitation to subject West Virginia's justice system to the vagaries of the day—a framework in which predictability and stability yield to supposition, innuendo, half-truths, and partisan manipulations."

We granted certiorari.

## II

It is axiomatic that "a fair trial in a fair tribunal is a basic requirement of due process." As the Court has recognized, however, "most matters relating to judicial disqualification do not rise to a constitutional level." The early and leading case on the subject is *Tumey v. Ohio,* 273 U.S. 510, (1927). There, the Court stated that "matters of kinship, personal bias, state policy, remoteness of interest, would seem generally to be matters merely of legislative discretion."

The *Tumey* Court concluded that the Due Process Clause incorporated the common-law rule that a judge must recuse himself when he has "a direct, personal, substantial, pecuniary interest" in a case. This rule reflects the maxim that "no man is allowed to be a judge in his own cause; because his interest would certainly bias his judgment, and, not improbably, corrupt his integrity." The Federalist No. 10 (J. Madison). Under this rule, "disqualification for bias or prejudice was not permitted"; those matters were left to statutes and judicial codes. Personal bias or prejudice "alone would not be sufficient basis for imposing a constitutional requirement under the Due Process Clause."

As new problems have emerged that were not discussed at common law, however, the Court has identified additional instances which, as an objective matter, require recusal. These are circumstances "in which experience teaches that the probability of actual bias on the part of the judge or decisionmaker is too high to be constitutionally tolerable." *Withrow*. To place the present case in proper context, two instances where the Court has required recusal merit further discussion.

A

The first involved the emergence of local tribunals where a judge had a financial interest in the outcome of a case, although the interest was less than what would have been considered personal or direct at common law.

This was the problem addressed in *Tumey*. There, the mayor of a village had the authority to sit as a judge (with no jury) to try those accused of violating a state law prohibiting the possession of alcoholic beverages. Inherent in this structure were two potential conflicts. First, the mayor received a salary supplement for performing judicial duties, and the funds for that compensation derived from the fines assessed in a case. No fines were assessed upon acquittal. The mayor-judge thus received a salary supplement only if he convicted the defendant. Second, sums from the criminal fines were deposited to the village's general treasury fund for village improvements and repairs.

The Court held that the Due Process Clause required disqualification "both because of the mayor-judge's direct pecuniary interest in the outcome, and because of his official motive to convict and to graduate the fine to help the financial needs of the village." It so held despite observing that "there are doubtless mayors who would not allow such a consideration as $12 costs in each case to affect their judgment in it." The Court articulated the controlling principle:

"Every procedure which would offer a possible temptation to the average man as a judge to forget the burden of proof required to convict the defendant, or which might lead him not to hold the balance nice, clear and true between the State and the accused, denies the latter due process of law."

The Court was thus concerned with more than the traditional common-law prohibition on direct pecuniary interest. It was also concerned with a more general concept of interests that tempt adjudicators to disregard neutrality.

This concern with conflicts resulting from financial incentives was elaborated in *Ward v. Monroeville,* which invalidated a conviction in another mayor's court. In *Monroeville,* unlike in *Tumey,* the mayor received no money; instead, the fines the mayor assessed went to the town's general fisc. The Court held that "the fact that the mayor in *Tumey* shared directly in the fees and costs did not define the limits of the principle." The principle, instead, turned on the "'possible temptation'" the mayor might face; the mayor's "executive responsibilities for village finances may make him partisan to maintain the high level of contribution to those finances from the mayor's court." As the Court reiterated in another case that Term, "the judge's financial stake need not be as direct or positive as it appeared to be in *Tumey.*" See *Gibson v. Berryhill* (an administrative board composed of optometrists had a pecuniary interest of "sufficient substance" so that it could not preside over a hearing against competing optometrists).

The Court in *Lavoie* further clarified the reach of the Due Process Clause regarding a judge's financial interest in a case. There, a justice had cast the deciding vote on the Alabama Supreme Court to uphold a punitive damages award against an insurance company for bad-faith refusal to pay a claim. At the time of his vote, the justice was the lead plaintiff in a nearly identical lawsuit pending in Alabama's lower courts. His deciding vote, this Court surmised, "undoubtedly 'raised the stakes'" for the insurance defendant in the justice's suit.

The Court stressed that it was "not required to decide whether in fact the justice was influenced." The proper constitutional inquiry is "whether sitting on the case then before the Supreme Court of Alabama 'would offer a possible temptation to the average judge to lead him not to hold the balance nice, clear and true.'" The Court underscored that "what degree or kind of interest is sufficient to disqualify a judge from sitting 'cannot be defined with precision.' In the Court's view, however, it was important that the test have an objective component.

The *Lavoie* Court proceeded to distinguish the state court justice's particular interest in the case, which required recusal, from interests that were not a constitutional concern. For instance, "while the other justices might conceivably have had a slight pecuniary interest" due to their potential membership in a class-action suit against their own insurance companies, that interest is "'too remote and insubstantial to violate the constitutional constraints.'"

## B

The second instance requiring recusal that was not discussed at common law emerged in the criminal contempt context, where a judge had no pecuniary interest in the case but was challenged because of a conflict arising from his participation in an earlier proceeding. This Court characterized that first proceeding (perhaps pejoratively) as a "'one-man grand jury.'" *Murchison,* 349 U.S., at 133.

In that first proceeding, and as provided by state law, a judge examined witnesses to determine whether criminal charges should be brought. The judge called the two petitioners before him. One petitioner answered questions, but the judge found him untruthful and charged him with perjury. The second declined to answer on the ground that he did not have counsel with him, as state law seemed to permit. The judge charged him with contempt. The judge proceeded to try and convict both petitioners.

This Court set aside the convictions on grounds that the judge had a conflict of interest at the trial stage because of his earlier participation followed by his decision to charge them. The Due Process Clause required disqualification. The Court recited the general rule that "no man can be a judge in his own case," adding that "no man is permitted to try cases where he has an interest in the outcome." It noted that the disqualifying criteria "cannot be defined with precision. Circumstances and relationships must be considered." These circumstances and the prior relationship required recusal: "Having been a part of the one-man grand jury process a judge cannot be, in the very nature of things, wholly disinterested in the conviction or acquittal of those accused." That is because "as a practical matter it is difficult if not impossible for a judge to free himself from the influence of what took place in his 'grand-jury' secret session."

Following *Murchison* the Court held in *Mayberry v. Pennsylvania,* "that by reason of the Due Process Clause of the Fourteenth Amendment a defendant in criminal contempt proceedings should be given a public trial before a judge other than the one reviled by the contemnor." The Court reiterated that this rule rests on the relationship between the judge and the defendant: "A judge, vilified as was this Pennsylvania judge, necessarily becomes embroiled in a running, bitter controversy. No one so cruelly slandered is likely to maintain that calm detachment necessary for fair adjudication."

## III

Based on the principles described in these cases we turn to the issue before us. This problem arises in the context of judicial elections, a framework not presented in the precedents we have reviewed and discussed.

Caperton contends that Blankenship's pivotal role in getting Justice Benjamin elected created a constitutionally intolerable probability of actual bias. Though not a bribe or criminal influence, Justice Benjamin would nevertheless feel a debt of gratitude to Blankenship for his extraordinary efforts to get him elected. That temptation, Caperton claims, is as strong and inherent in human nature as was the conflict the Court confronted in *Tumey* and *Monroeville* when a mayor-judge (or the city) benefited financially from a defendant's conviction, as well as the conflict identified in *Murchison* and *Mayberry* when a judge was the object of a defendant's contempt.

Following accepted principles of our legal tradition respecting the proper performance of judicial functions, judges often inquire into their subjective motives and purposes in the ordinary course of deciding a case. This does not mean the inquiry is a simple one. "The work of deciding cases goes on every day in hundreds of courts throughout the land. Any judge, one might suppose, would find it easy to describe the process which he had followed a thousand times and more. Nothing could be farther from the truth." B. Cardozo, The Nature of the Judicial Process 9 (1921).

The judge inquires into reasons that seem to be leading to a particular result. Precedent and *stare decisis* and the text and purpose of the law and the Constitution; logic and scholarship and experience and common sense; and fairness and disinterest and neutrality are among the factors at work. To bring coherence to the process, and to seek respect for the resulting judgment, judges often explain the reasons for their conclusions and rulings. There are instances when the introspection that often attends this process may reveal that what the judge had assumed to be a proper, controlling factor is not the real one at work. If the judge discovers that some personal bias or improper consideration seems to be the actuating cause of the decision or to be an influence so difficult to dispel that there is a real possibility of undermining neutrality, the judge may think it necessary to consider withdrawing from the case.

The difficulties of inquiring into actual bias, and the fact that the inquiry is often a private one, simply underscore the need for objective rules. Otherwise there may be no adequate protection against a judge who simply misreads or misapprehends the real motives at work in deciding the case. The judge's own inquiry into actual bias, then, is not one that the law can easily superintend or review, though actual bias, if disclosed, no doubt would be grounds for appropriate relief. In lieu of exclusive reliance on that personal inquiry, or on appellate review of the judge's determination respecting actual bias, the Due Process Clause has been implemented by objective standards that do not require proof of actual bias. In defining these standards the Court has asked whether, "under a realistic appraisal of psychological tendencies and human weakness," the interest "poses such a risk of actual bias or prejudgment that the practice must be forbidden if the guarantee of due process is to be adequately implemented."

We turn to the influence at issue in this case. Not every campaign contribution by a litigant or attorney creates a probability of bias that requires a judge's recusal, but this is an exceptional case. We conclude that there is a serious risk of actual bias— based on objective and reasonable perceptions—when a person with a personal stake in a particular case had a significant and disproportionate influence in placing the judge on the case by raising funds or directing the judge's election campaign when the case was pending or imminent. The inquiry centers on the contribution's relative size in comparison to the total amount of money contributed to the campaign, the total amount spent in the election, and the apparent effect such contribution had on the outcome of the election.

Applying this principle, we conclude that Blankenship's campaign efforts had a significant and disproportionate influence in placing Justice Benjamin on the case. Blankenship contributed some $3 million to unseat the incumbent and replace him with Benjamin. His contributions eclipsed the total amount spent by all other Benjamin supporters and exceeded by 300% the amount spent by Benjamin's campaign committee. Caperton claims Blankenship spent $1 million more than the total amount spent by the campaign committees of both candidates combined.

Massey responds that Blankenship's support, while significant, did not cause Benjamin's victory. In the end the people of West Virginia elected him, and they did so based on many reasons other than Blankenship's efforts. Massey points out that every major state newspaper, but one, endorsed Benjamin. It also contends that then-Justice McGraw cost himself the election by giving a speech during the campaign, a speech the opposition seized upon for its own advantage.

Justice Benjamin raised similar arguments. He asserted that "the outcome of the 2004 election was due primarily to his own campaign's message," as well as McGraw's "devastating" speech in which he "made a number of controversial claims which became a matter of statewide discussion in the media, on the internet, and elsewhere."

Whether Blankenship's campaign contributions were a necessary and sufficient cause of Benjamin's victory is not the proper inquiry. Much like determining whether a judge is actually biased, proving what ultimately drives the electorate to choose a particular candidate is a difficult endeavor, not likely to lend itself to a certain conclusion. This is particularly true where, as here, there is no procedure for judicial factfinding and the sole trier of fact is the one accused of bias. Due process requires an objective inquiry into whether the contributor's influence on the election under all the circumstances "would offer a possible temptation to the average judge to lead him not to hold the balance nice, clear and true." In an election decided by fewer than 50,000 votes (382,036 to 334,301), Blankenship's campaign contributions—in comparison to the total amount contributed to the campaign, as well as the total amount spent in the election—had a significant and disproportionate influence on the electoral outcome. And the risk that Blankenship's influence engendered actual bias is sufficiently substantial that it "must be forbidden if the guarantee of due process is to be adequately implemented."

The temporal relationship between the campaign contributions, the justice's election, and the pendency of the case is also critical. It was reasonably foreseeable, when the campaign contributions were made, that the pending case would be before the newly elected justice. The $50 million adverse jury verdict had been entered before the election, and the Supreme Court of Appeals was the next step once the state trial court dealt with post-trial motions. So it became at once apparent that, absent recusal, Justice Benjamin would review a judgment that cost his biggest donor's company $50 million. Although there is no allegation of a *quid pro quo* agreement, the fact remains that Blankenship's extraordinary contributions were made at a time when he had a vested stake in the outcome. Just as no man is allowed to be a judge in his own cause, similar fears of bias can arise when—without the consent of the other parties—a man chooses the judge in his own cause. And applying this principle to the judicial election process, there was here a serious, objective risk of actual bias that required Justice Benjamin's recusal.

Justice Benjamin did undertake an extensive search for actual bias. But, as we have indicated, that is just one step in the judicial process; objective standards may also require recusal whether or not actual bias exists or can be proved. Due process "may sometimes bar trial by judges who have no actual bias and who would do their very best to weigh the scales of justice equally between contending parties." The failure to consider objective standards requiring recusal is not consistent with the imperatives of due process. We find that Blankenship's significant and disproportionate influence—coupled with the temporal relationship between the election and the pending case —"offer a possible temptation to the average ... judge to lead him not to hold the balance nice, clear and true." On these extreme facts the probability of actual bias rises to an unconstitutional level.

# IV

Our decision today addresses an extraordinary situation where the Constitution requires recusal. Massey and its *amici* predict that various adverse consequences will follow from recognizing a constitutional violation here—ranging from a flood of recusal motions to unnecessary interference with judicial elections. We disagree. The facts now before us are extreme by any measure. The parties point to no other instance involving judicial campaign contributions that presents a potential for bias comparable to the circumstances in this case.

It is true that extreme cases often test the bounds of established legal principles, and sometimes no administrable standard may be available to address the perceived wrong. But it is also true that extreme cases are more likely to cross constitutional limits, requiring this Court's intervention and formulation of objective standards. This is particularly true when due process is violated.

This Court's recusal cases are illustrative. In each case the Court dealt with extreme facts that created an unconstitutional probability of bias that cannot be defined with precision. Yet the Court articulated an objective standard to protect the parties' basic right to a fair trial in a fair tribunal. The Court was careful to distinguish the extreme facts of the cases before it from those interests that would not rise to a constitutional level. In this case we do nothing more than what the Court has done before.

One must also take into account the judicial reforms the States have implemented to eliminate even the appearance of partiality. Almost every State—West Virginia included—has adopted the American Bar Association's objective standard: "A judge shall avoid impropriety and the appearance of impropriety." ABA *Annotated Model Code of Judicial Conduct, Canon 2 (2004)*; The ABA Model Code's test for appearance of impropriety is "whether the conduct would create in reasonable minds a perception that the judge's ability to carry out judicial responsibilities with integrity, impartiality and competence is impaired." Canon 2A.

The West Virginia Code of Judicial Conduct also requires a judge to "disqualify himself or herself in a proceeding in which the judge's impartiality might reasonably be questioned." Canon 3E(1); see also 28 U.S.C. § 455(a) ("Any justice, judge, or magistrate judge of the United States shall disqualify himself in any proceeding in which his impartiality might reasonably be questioned"). Under Canon 3E(1), "'the question of disqualification focuses on whether an objective assessment of the judge's conduct produces a reasonable question about impartiality, not on the judge's subjective perception of the ability to act fairly.' ("Under 28 U.S.C. § 455(a), a judge should be disqualified only if it appears that he or she harbors an aversion, hostility or disposition of a kind that a fair-minded person could not set aside when judging the dispute").

Indeed, some States require recusal based on campaign contributions similar to those in this case.

These codes of conduct serve to maintain the integrity of the judiciary and the rule of law. The Conference of the Chief Justices has underscored that the codes are "the principal safeguard against judicial campaign abuses" that threaten to imperil "public confidence in the fairness and integrity of the nation's elected judges." Brief for Conference of Chief Justices as *Amicus Curiae*

> Courts, in our system, elaborate principles of law in the course of resolving disputes. The power and the prerogative of a court to perform this function rest, in the end, upon the respect accorded to its judgments. The citizen's respect for judgments depends in turn upon the issuing court's absolute probity. Judicial integrity is, in consequence, a state interest of the highest order.

It is for this reason that States may choose to "adopt recusal standards more rigorous than due process requires." The Due Process Clause demarks only the outer boundaries of judicial disqualifications. Congress and the states, of course, remain free to impose more rigorous standards for judicial disqualification than those we find mandated here today. Because the codes of judicial conduct provide more protection than due process requires, most disputes over disqualification will be resolved without resort to the Constitution. Application of the constitutional standard implicated in this case will thus be confined to rare instances.

The judgment of the Supreme Court of Appeals of West Virginia is reversed, and the case is remanded for further proceedings not inconsistent with this opinion.

# CHAPTER 16

# ATTORNEY'S FEES

1. The normal rule on attorney's fees in the United States is that each party pays his or her own attorney's fees – regardless of the outcome of the litigation. However, in a few situations, in an effort to persuade private attorneys to bring important litigation for clients who may not be able to pay attorney's fees, various state and federal statutes provide that a winning plaintiff is entitled to the award of attorney's fees. The specific wording of the statute is crucial, as illustrated by the two cases in this chapter.

130 S.CT. 2521
SUPREME COURT OF THE UNITED STATES
MICHAEL J. ASTRUE, COMMISSIONER OF SOCIAL SECURITY,
PETITIONER
V.
CATHERINE G. RATLIFF

DECIDED JUNE 14, 2010

THOMAS, J., delivered the opinion for a unanimous Court.

Section 204(d) of the Equal Access to Justice Act (EAJA), codified in *28 U.S.C. § 2412(d)*, provides in pertinent part that "a court shall award to a prevailing party fees and other expenses in any civil action brought by or against the United States unless the court finds that the position of the United States was substantially justified." We consider whether an award of "fees and other expenses" to a "prevailing party" under § 2412(d) is payable to the litigant or to his attorney. We hold that a § 2412(d) fees award is payable to the litigant and is therefore subject to a Government offset to satisfy a pre-existing debt that the litigant owes the United States.

## I

This case arises out of proceedings in which a Social Security claimant, Ruby Willows Kills Ree, prevailed on a claim for benefits against the United States. Respondent Catherine Ratliff was Ree's attorney in those proceedings. The District Court granted Ree's unopposed motion for a § 2412(d) fees award in the amount of $2,112.60. Before the United States paid the fees award, however, it discovered that Ree owed the Government a debt that predated the District Court's approval of the award. Accordingly, the United States sought an administrative offset against the fees award to satisfy part of that debt.

The Government's authority to use administrative offsets is statutory. See *31 U.S.C. §§ 3711(a), 3716(a)* (authorizing an agency whose debt collection attempts are unsuccessful to "collect the claim by administrative offset"). Congress has subjected to offset all "funds payable by the United States," *§ 3701(a)(1)*, to an individual who owes certain delinquent federal debts, see *§ 3701(b)*, unless, as relevant here, payment is exempted by statute. No such exemption applies to attorney's fees awards under *28 U.S.C. § 2412(d)(1)(A)*, which are otherwise subject to offset, and which, as of January 2005, are covered by the Treasury Offset Program (TOP) operated by the Treasury Department's Financial Management Service (FMS).

In this case, the Government, relying on the TOP, notified Ree that the Government would apply her § 2412(d) fees award to offset a portion of her outstanding federal debt. Ratliff intervened to challenge the offset on the grounds that § 2412(d) fees belong to a litigant's attorney and thus may not be used to offset or otherwise satisfy a litigant's federal debts. The District Court held that because § 2412(d) directs that fees be awarded to the prevailing party, not to her attorney, Ratliff lacked standing to challenge the Government's proposed offset.

The Court of Appeals for the Eighth Circuit reversed

We granted certiorari.

## II

*Subsection (d)(1)(A)* directs that courts "shall *award to a prevailing party* . . . fees and other expenses incurred by that party." We have long held that the term "prevailing party" in fee statutes is a "term of art" that refers to the prevailing litigant. This treatment reflects the fact that statutes that award attorney's fees to a prevailing party are exceptions to the "'American Rule'" that each *litigant* "bear his own attorney's fees." Nothing in EAJA supports a different reading. Indeed, other subsections within *§ 2412(d)* underscore that the term "prevailing party" in *subsection (d)(1)(A)* carries its usual and settled meaning -- prevailing litigant. Those other subsections clearly distinguish the party who receives the fees award (the litigant) from the attorney who performed the work that generated the fees.

Ratliff nonetheless asserts that *subsection (d)(1)(A)*'s use of the verb "award" renders *§ 2412(d)* fees payable directly to a prevailing party's attorney and thus protects the fees from a Government offset against the prevailing party's federal debts. We disagree.

The transitive verb "'award'" has a settled meaning in the litigation context: It means "to give or assign *by* sentence or judicial determination." The plain meaning of the word "award" in *subsection (d)(1)(A)* is thus that the court shall "give or assign by judicial determination" to the "prevailing party" (here, Ratliff's client Ree) attorney's fees in the amount sought and substantiated under, *inter alia, subsection (d)(1)(B)*.

## III

The Government's history of paying EAJA awards directly to attorneys in certain cases does not compel a different conclusion. The Government concedes that until 2006, it "frequently paid EAJA fees in Social Security cases directly to attorneys." But this fact does not alter our interpretation of *subsection (d)(1)(A)*'s "prevailing party" language or the Government's rights and obligations under the statute. As the Government explains, it most often paid EAJA fees directly to attorneys in cases in which the prevailing party had assigned its rights in the fees award to the attorney (which assignment would not be necessary if the statute rendered the fees award payable to the attorney in the first instance). The fact that some such cases involved a prevailing party with outstanding federal debts is unsurprising given that it was not until 2005 that the Treasury Department modified the TOP to require offsets against "miscellaneous" payments such as attorney's fees awards. And as Ratliff admits, the Government has since continued the direct payment practice only in cases where "the plaintiff does not owe a debt to the government and assigns the right to receive the fees to the attorney." The Government's decision to continue direct payments only in such cases is easily explained by the 2005 amendments to the TOP, and nothing about the Government's past payment practices altered the statutory text that governs this case or estopped the Government from conforming its payment practices to the Treasury Department's revised regulations. For all of these reasons, neither EAJA nor the SSA supports Ratliff's reading of *subsection (d)(1)(A)*.

Our cases interpreting and applying *42 U.S.C. § 1988*, which contains language virtually identical to the EAJA provision we address here, buttress this conclusion. Our most recent cases applying *§ 1988(b)*'s "prevailing party" language recognize the practical reality that attorneys are the beneficiaries and, almost always, the ultimate recipients of the fees that the statute awards to "prevailing parties." But these cases emphasize the nonstatutory (contractual and other assignment-based) rights that typically confer upon the attorney the entitlement to payment of the fees award the statute confers on the prevailing litigant. As noted above, these kinds of arrangements would be unnecessary if, as Ratliff contends, statutory fees language like that in *§ 1988(b)* and EAJA provides attorneys with a statutory right to direct payment of awards. Hence our conclusion that "the party, rather than the lawyer," is entitled to receive the fees" under *§ 1988(b)* and that the statute "controls what the losing defendant must pay, not what the prevailing plaintiff must pay his lawyer." See also *Evans v. Jeff D., 475 U.S. 717 (1986)*.

We reverse the Court of Appeals' judgment and remand the case for further proceedings consistent with this opinion.

2. The wording in the Civil Rights statutes is more favorable to attorneys. The following case also defines how the "Lodestar" method should be used in calculating attorney's fees.

# 130 S.CT. 1662
## SUPREME COURT OF THE UNITED STATES
## SONNY PERDUE, GOVERNOR OF GEORGIA, ET AL., PETITIONERS
## V.
## KENNY A., BY HIS NEXT FRIEND LINDA WINN, ET AL., RESPONDENTS

DECIDED APRIL 21, 2010

JUSTICE ALITO delivered the opinion of the Court.

This case presents the question whether the calculation of an attorney's fee, under federal fee-shifting statutes, based on the "lodestar," *i.e.*, the number of hours worked multiplied by the prevailing hourly rates, may be increased due to superior performance and results. We have stated in previous cases that such an increase is permitted in extraordinary circumstances, and we reaffirm that rule. But as we have also said in prior cases, there is a strong presumption that the lodestar is sufficient; factors subsumed in the lodestar calculation cannot be used as a ground for increasing an award above the lodestar; and a party seeking fees has the burden of identifying a factor that the lodestar does not adequately take into account and proving with specificity that an enhanced fee is justified. Because the District Court did not apply these standards, we reverse the decision below and remand for further proceedings consistent with this opinion.

## I

### A

Respondents (plaintiffs below) are children in the Georgia foster-care system and their next friends. They filed this class action on behalf of 3,000 children in foster care and named as defendants the Governor of Georgia and various state officials (petitioners in this case). Claiming that deficiencies in the foster-care system in two counties near Atlanta violated their federal and state constitutional and statutory rights, respondents sought injunctive and declaratory relief, as well as attorney's fees and expenses.

The United States District Court for the Northern District of Georgia eventually referred the case to mediation, where the parties entered into a consent decree, which the District Court approved. The consent decree resolved all pending issues other than the fees that respondents' attorneys were entitled to receive under *42 U.S.C. § 1988*.

Title *42 U.S.C. § 1988(b)* provides:

> In any action or proceeding to enforce a provision of sections 1981, 1981a, 1982, 1983, 1985, and 1986 of this title, the Religious Freedom Restoration Act of 1993, the Religious Land Use and Institutionalized Persons Act of 2000, title VI of the Civil Rights Act of 1964, or section 13981 of this title, the court, in its discretion, may allow the prevailing party, other than the United States, a reasonable attorney's fee as part of the costs.

B

Respondents submitted a request for more than $14 million in attorney's fees. Half of that amount was based on their calculation of the lodestar -- roughly 30,000 hours multiplied by hourly rates of $200 to $495 for attorneys and $75 to $150 for non-attorneys. In support of their fee request, respondents submitted affidavits asserting that these rates were within the range of prevailing market rates for legal services in the relevant market.

The other half of the amount that respondents sought represented a fee enhancement for superior work and results. Affidavits submitted in support of this request claimed that the lodestar amount "would be generally insufficient to induce lawyers of comparable skill, judgment, professional representation and experience" to litigate this case. Petitioners objected to the fee request, contending that some of the proposed hourly rates were too high, that the hours claimed were excessive, and that the enhancement would duplicate factors that were reflected in the lodestar amount.

The District Court awarded fees of approximately $10.5 million. The District Court found that the hourly rates proposed by respondents were "fair and reasonable," but that some of the entries on counsel's billing records were vague and that the hours claimed for many of the billing categories were excessive. The court therefore cut the non-travel hours by 15% and halved the hourly rate for travel hours. This resulted in a lodestar calculation of approximately $6 million.

The court then enhanced this award by 75%, concluding that the lodestar calculation did not take into account "(1) the fact that class counsel were required to advance case expenses of $ 1.7 million over a three-year period with no on-going reimbursement, (2) the fact that class counsel were not paid on an on-going basis as the work was being performed, and (3) the fact that class counsel's ability to recover a fee and expense reimbursement were completely contingent on the outcome of the case." The court stated that respondents' attorneys had exhibited "a higher degree of skill, commitment, dedication, and professionalism than the Court has seen displayed by the attorneys in any other case during its 27 years on the bench." The court also commented that the results obtained were "'extraordinary'" and added that "after 58 years as a practicing attorney and federal judge, the Court is unaware of any other case in which a plaintiff class has achieved such a favorable result on such a comprehensive scale." The enhancement resulted in an additional $4.5 million fee award.

Relying on prior Circuit precedent, a panel of the Eleventh Circuit affirmed.

We granted certiorari.

## II

The general rule in our legal system is that each party must pay its own attorney's fees and expenses, but Congress enacted *42 U.S.C. § 1988* in order to ensure that federal rights are adequately enforced. *Section 1988* provides that a prevailing party in certain civil rights actions may recover "a reasonable attorney's fee as part of the costs." Unfortunately, the statute does not explain what Congress meant by a "reasonable" fee, and therefore the task of identifying an appropriate methodology for determining a "reasonable" fee was left for the courts. ...

Although the lodestar method is not perfect, it has several important virtues. First, in accordance with our understanding of the aim of fee-shifting statutes, the lodestar looks to "the prevailing market rates in the relevant community." Developed after the practice of hourly billing had become widespread, the lodestar method produces an award that *roughly* approximates the fee that the prevailing attorney would have received if he or she had been representing a paying client who was billed by the hour in a comparable case. Second, the lodestar method is readily administrable, and thus cabins the discretion of trial judges, permits meaningful judicial review, and produces reasonably predictable results.

## III

Our prior decisions concerning the federal fee-shifting statutes have established six important rules that lead to our decision in this case.

First, a "reasonable" fee is a fee that is sufficient to induce a capable attorney to undertake the representation of a meritorious civil rights case. ("If plaintiffs find it possible to engage a lawyer based on the statutory assurance that he will be paid a 'reasonable fee,' the purpose behind the fee-shifting statute has been satisfied"); ("A reasonable attorney's fee is one that is adequate to attract competent counsel, but that does not produce windfalls to attorneys." *Section 1988*'s aim is to enforce the covered civil rights statutes, not to provide "a form of economic relief to improve the financial lot of attorneys."

Second, the lodestar method yields a fee that is presumptively sufficient to achieve this objective. Indeed, we have said that the presumption is a "strong" one.

Third, although we have never sustained an enhancement of a lodestar amount for performance, we have repeatedly said that enhancements may be awarded in "'rare'" and "'exceptional'" circumstances.

Fourth, we have noted that "the lodestar figure includes most, if not all, of the relevant factors constituting a 'reasonable' attorney's fee," and have held that an enhancement may not be awarded based on a factor that is subsumed in the lodestar calculation. We have thus held that the novelty and complexity of a case generally may not be used as a ground for an enhancement because these factors "presumably are fully reflected in the number of billable hours recorded by counsel." We have also held that the quality of an attorney's performance generally should not be used to adjust the lodestar "because considerations concerning the quality of a prevailing party's counsel's representation normally are reflected in the reasonable hourly rate."

Fifth, the burden of proving that an enhancement is necessary must be borne by the fee applicant.

Finally, a fee applicant seeking an enhancement must produce "specific evidence" that supports the award. (An enhancement must be based on "evidence that enhancement was necessary to provide fair and reasonable compensation"). This requirement is essential if the lodestar method is to realize one of its chief virtues, *i.e.*, providing a calculation that is objective and capable of being reviewed on appeal.

## IV

### A

In light of what we have said in prior cases, we reject any contention that a fee determined by the lodestar method may not be enhanced in any situation. The lodestar method was never intended to be conclusive in all circumstances. Instead, there is a "strong presumption" that the lodestar figure is reasonable, but that presumption may be overcome in those rare circumstances in which the lodestar does not adequately take into account a factor that may properly be considered in determining a reasonable fee.

B

In this case, we are asked to decide whether either the quality of an attorney's performance or the results obtained are factors that may properly provide a basis for an enhancement. We treat these two factors as one. When a plaintiff's attorney achieves results that are more favorable than would have been predicted based on the governing law and the available evidence, the outcome may be attributable to superior performance and commitment of resources by plaintiff's counsel. Or the outcome may result from inferior performance by defense counsel, unanticipated defense concessions, unexpectedly favorable rulings by the court, an unexpectedly sympathetic jury, or simple luck. Since none of these latter causes can justify an enhanced award, superior results are relevant only to the extent it can be shown that they are the result of superior attorney performance. Thus, we need only consider whether superior attorney performance can justify an enhancement. And in light of the principles derived from our prior cases, we inquire whether there are circumstances in which superior attorney performance is not adequately taken into account in the lodestar calculation. We conclude that there are a few such circumstances but that these circumstances are indeed "rare" and "exceptional," and require specific evidence that the lodestar fee would not have been "adequate to attract competent counsel."

First, an enhancement may be appropriate where the method used in determining the hourly rate employed in the lodestar calculation does not adequately measure the attorney's true market value, as demonstrated in part during the litigation.[5] This may occur if the hourly rate is determined by a formula that takes into account only a single factor (such as years since admission to the bar) or perhaps only a few similar factors. In such a case, an enhancement may be appropriate so that an attorney is compensated at the rate that the attorney would receive in cases not governed by the federal fee-shifting statutes. But in order to provide a calculation that is objective and reviewable, the trial judge should adjust the attorney's hourly rate in accordance with specific proof linking the attorney's ability to a prevailing market rate.

5 Respondents correctly note that an attorney's "brilliant insights and critical maneuvers" sometimes matter far more than hours worked or years of experience. But as we said in Blum, "in those cases, the special skill and experience of counsel should be reflected in the reasonableness of the hourly rates."

Second, an enhancement may be appropriate if the attorney's performance includes an extraordinary outlay of expenses and the litigation is exceptionally protracted. As Judge Carnes noted below, when an attorney agrees to represent a civil rights plaintiff who cannot afford to pay the attorney, the attorney presumably understands that no reimbursement is likely to be received until the successful resolution of the case, and therefore enhancements to compensate for delay in reimbursement for expenses must be reserved for unusual cases. In such exceptional cases, however, an enhancement may be allowed, but the amount of the enhancement must be calculated using a method that is reasonable, objective, and capable of being reviewed on appeal, such as by applying a standard rate of interest to the qualifying outlays of expenses.

Third, there may be extraordinary circumstances in which an attorney's performance involves exceptional delay in the payment of fees. An attorney who expects to be compensated under § 1988 presumably understands that payment of fees will generally not come until the end of the case, if at all. Compensation for this delay is generally made "either by basing the award on current rates or by adjusting the fee based on historical rates to reflect its present value." But we do not rule out the possibility that an enhancement may be appropriate where an attorney assumes these costs in the face of unanticipated delay, particularly where the delay is unjustifiably caused by the defense. In such a case, however, the enhancement should be calculated by applying a method similar to that described above in connection with exceptional delay in obtaining reimbursement for expenses.

We reject the suggestion that it is appropriate to grant performance enhancements on the ground that departures from hourly billing are becoming more common. As we have noted, the lodestar was adopted in part because it provides a rough approximation of general billing practices, and accordingly, if hourly billing becomes unusual, an alternative to the lodestar method may have to be found. However, neither respondents nor their *amici* contend that that day has arrived. Nor have they shown that permitting the award of enhancements on top of the lodestar figure corresponds to prevailing practice in the general run of cases.

We are told that, under an increasingly popular arrangement, attorneys are paid at a reduced hourly rate but receive a bonus if certain specified results are obtained, and this practice is analogized to the award of an enhancement such as the one in this case. The analogy, however, is flawed. An attorney who agrees, at the outset of the representation, to a reduced *hourly rate* in exchange for the opportunity to earn a performance bonus is in a position far different from an attorney in a § 1988 case who is compensated at the *full prevailing rate* and then seeks a performance enhancement in addition to the lodestar amount after the litigation has concluded. Reliance on these comparisons for the purposes of administering enhancements, therefore, is not appropriate.

# V

In the present case, the District Court did not provide proper justification for the large enhancement that it awarded. The court increased the lodestar award by 75% but, as far as the court's opinion reveals, this figure appears to have been essentially arbitrary. Why, for example, did the court grant a 75% enhancement instead of the 100% increase that respondents sought? And why 75% rather than 50% or 25% or 10%?

The District Court commented that the enhancement was the "minimum enhancement of the lodestar necessary to reasonably compensate respondents' counsel." But the effect of the enhancement was to increase the top rate for the attorneys to more than $ 866 per hour, and the District Court did not point to anything in the record that shows that this is an appropriate figure for the relevant market.

The District Court pointed to the fact that respondents' counsel had to make extraordinary outlays for expenses and had to wait for reimbursement, but the court did not calculate the amount of the enhancement that is attributable to this factor. Similarly, the District Court noted that respondents' counsel did not receive fees on an ongoing basis while the case was pending, but the court did not sufficiently link this factor to proof in the record that the delay here was outside the normal range expected by attorneys who rely on § 1988 for the payment of their fees or quantify the disparity. Nor did the court provide a calculation of the cost to counsel of any extraordinary and unwarranted delay. And the court's reliance on the contingency of the outcome contravenes our holding in *Dague*.

Finally, insofar as the District Court relied on a comparison of the performance of counsel in this case with the performance of counsel in unnamed prior cases, the District Court did not employ a methodology that permitted meaningful appellate review. Needless to say, we do not question the sincerity of the District Court's observations, and we are in no position to assess their accuracy. But when a trial judge awards an enhancement on an impressionistic basis, a major purpose of the lodestar method -- providing an objective and reviewable basis for fees, is undermined.

Determining a "reasonable attorney's fee" is a matter that is committed to the sound discretion of a trial judge, see *42 U.S.C. § 1988* (permitting court, "in its discretion," to award fees), but the judge's discretion is not unlimited. It is essential that the judge provide a reasonably specific explanation for all aspects of a fee determination, including any award of an enhancement. Unless such an explanation is given, adequate appellate review is not feasible, and without such review, widely disparate awards may be made, and awards may be influenced (or at least, may appear to be influenced) by a judge's subjective opinion regarding particular attorneys or the importance of the case. In addition, in future cases, defendants contemplating the possibility of settlement will have no way to estimate the likelihood of having to pay a potentially huge enhancement. Many a defendant would be unwilling to make a binding settlement offer on terms that left it exposed to liability for attorney's fees in whatever amount the court might fix on motion of the plaintiff.

*Section 1988* serves an important public purpose by making it possible for persons without means to bring suit to vindicate their rights. But unjustified enhancements that serve only to enrich attorneys are not consistent with the statute's aim. [8] In many cases, attorney's fees awarded under *§ 1988* are not paid by the individuals responsible for the constitutional or statutory violations on which the judgment is based. Instead, the fees are paid in effect by state and local taxpayers, and because state and local governments have limited budgets, money that is used to pay attorney's fees is money that cannot be used for programs that provide vital public services.

> 8 JUSTICE BREYER's opinion dramatically illustrates the danger of allowing a trial judge to award a huge enhancement not supported by any discernible methodology. That approach would retain the $4.5 million enhancement here so that respondents' attorneys would earn as much as the attorneys at some of the richest law firms in the country. These fees would be paid by the taxpayers of Georgia, where the annual per capita income is less than $34,000, and the annual salaries of attorneys employed by the State range from $48,000 for entry-level lawyers to $118,000 for the highest paid division chief. *Section 1988* was enacted to ensure that civil rights plaintiffs are adequately represented, not to provide such a windfall.

For all these reasons, the judgment of the Court of Appeals is reversed, and the case is remanded for proceedings consistent with this opinion.

# CHAPTER 17

# QUI TAM ACTIONS 31 USC 3729 ET SEQ.

1. There is a special form of civil action, called a *qui tam* action, that may be brought by any person, on behalf of the U.S. government, that sometimes results in massive amounts of money for the person brave enough to bring the action. Recently, payments of $48 to $58 *million* dollars *each* were expected to be paid to some whistle-blowers who had brought qui tam actions on behalf of the U.S. against the Bank of America under the False Claims Act, 31 USC 3729 et *seq.*

Here is how it works. An individual, working for the government, for a private company that has government contracts, or just for a private company, or as an individual, may have information that the government is being over-charged – that some person or entity is knowingly presenting a false or fraudulent claim to the government. 31 USC 3729(a)(1)(A). That individual is then entitled to file a claim, on behalf of the U.S. government.

The individual who files the claim is called the relator, (pronounced re LAY tor). The government has a certain amount of time to take over prosecution of the case. If it does not, the individual relator may continue with the prosecution on his own. In either case, the relator will be entitled to 15 percent to 30 percent of the final award – depending on the circumstances. So it is easy to see how a relator might walk away with a very large sum of money.

The reason that this process is beneficial to the government is that the relator is usually someone within the defendant company – such as an accountant or bookkeeper – who has inside knowledge of facts that the government would be unlikely to discover on its own.

All whistle-blowers are of course in real danger of losing their jobs. So some statutory protections are available to protect whistle-blowers in various situations. One such statutory protection is described in the last case in this chapter. After receipt of several million dollars by a qui tam relator, maybe the day job would not seem so important.

In any event, the first case in this chapter describes some of the technicalities involved with a qui tam action.

135 S.CT. 1970

SUPREME COURT OF THE UNITED STATES

KELLOGG BROWN & ROOT SERVICES, INC., ET AL.,
PETITIONERS

V.

UNITED STATES, EX REL. BENJAMIN CARTER.

DECIDED MAY 26, 2015

**Justice ALITO delivered the opinion for a unanimous Court.**

Wars have often provided "exceptional opportunities" for fraud on the United States Government. The False Claims Act was adopted in 1863 and signed into law by President Abraham Lincoln in order to combat rampant fraud in Civil War defense contracts. Predecessors of the Wartime Suspension of Limitations Act were enacted to address similar problems that arose during the First and Second World Wars.

In this case, we must decide two questions regarding those laws: first, whether the Wartime Suspension of Limitations Act applies only to criminal charges or also to civil claims; second, whether the False Claims Act's first-to-file bar keeps new claims out of court only while related claims are still alive or whether it may bar those claims in perpetuity.

I

A

The False Claims Act (FCA) imposes liability on any person who "knowingly presents ... a false or fraudulent claim for payment or approval," 31 U.S.C. § 3729(a)(1)(A), "to an officer or employee of the United States," 3729(b)(2)(A)(i). The FCA may be enforced not just through litigation brought by the Government itself, but also through civil *qui tam* actions that are filed by private parties, called relators, "in the name of the Government." § 3730(b).

In a *qui tam* suit under the FCA, the relator files a complaint under seal and serves the United States with a copy of the complaint and a disclosure of all material evidence.§ 3730(b)(2). After reviewing these materials, the United States may "proceed with the action, in which case the action shall be conducted by the Government," or it may "notify the court that it declines to take over the action, in which case the person bringing the action shall have the right to conduct the action." § 3730(b)(4). Regardless of the option that the United States selects, it retains the right at any time to dismiss the action entirely, §3730(c)(2)(A), or to settle the case, §3730(c)(2)(B).

The FCA imposes two restrictions on *qui tam* suits that are relevant here. One, the "first-to-file" bar, precludes a *qui tam* suit "based on the facts underlying a pending action." § 3730(b)(5). The other, the FCA's statute of limitations provision, states that a *qui tam* action must be brought within six years of a violation or within three years of the date by which the United States should have known about a violation. In no circumstances, however, may a suit be brought more than 10 years after the date of a violation. § 3731(b).

## B

The Wartime Suspension of Limitations Act (WSLA) suspends the statute of limitations for "any offense" involving fraud against the Federal Government. 18 U.S.C. § 3287. Before 2008, this provision was activated only "when the United States was at war." In 2008, however, this provision was made to apply as well whenever Congress has enacted "a specific authorization for the use of the Armed Forces, as described in section 5(b) of the War Powers Resolution (50 U.S.C. 1544(b))."

## II

Petitioners are defense contractors and related entities that provided logistical services to the United States military during the armed conflict in Iraq. From January to April 2005, respondent worked in Iraq for one of the petitioners as a water purification operator. He subsequently filed a *qui tam* complaint against petitioners (*Carter I*), alleging that they had fraudulently billed the Government for water purification services that were not performed or not performed properly. The Government declined to intervene.

In 2010, shortly before trial, the Government informed the parties about an earlier filed *qui tam* lawsuit, *United States ex rel. Thorpe v. Halliburton Co.* that arguably contained similar claims. This initiated a remarkable sequence of dismissals and filings.

The District Court held that respondent's suit was related to *Thorpe* and thus dismissed his case without prejudice under the first-to-file bar. Respondent appealed, and while his appeal was pending, *Thorpe* was dismissed for failure to prosecute. Respondent quickly filed a new complaint (*Carter II*), but the District Court dismissed this second complaint under the first-to-file rule because respondent's own earlier case was still pending on appeal. Respondent then voluntarily dismissed this appeal, and in June 2011, more than six years after the alleged fraud, he filed yet another complaint (*Carter III*), and it is this complaint that is now at issue.

Petitioners sought dismissal of this third complaint under the first-to-file rule, pointing to two allegedly related cases, one in Maryland and one in Texas, that had been filed in the interim between the filing of *Carter I* and *Carter III*. This time, the court dismissed respondent's complaint with prejudice. The court held that the latest complaint was barred under the first-to-file rule because the Maryland suit was already pending when that complaint was filed. The court also ruled that the WSLA applies only to criminal charges and thus did not suspend the time for filing respondent's civil claims. As a result, the court concluded, all but one of those claims were untimely because they were filed more than six years after the alleged wrongdoing.

The Fourth Circuit reversed. We granted certiorari.

## III

The text, structure, and history of the WSLA show that the Act applies only to criminal offenses.

### A

The WSLA's roots extend back to the time after the end of World War I. Concerned about war-related frauds, Congress in 1921 enacted a statute that extended the statute of limitations for such offenses. The new law provided as follows: "In offenses involving the defrauding or attempts to defraud the United States or any agency thereof ... and *now indictable under any existing statutes,* the period of limitations shall be six years." Since only crimes are "indictable," this provision quite clearly was limited to the filing of criminal charges.

In 1942, after the United States entered World War II, Congress enacted a similar suspension statute. This law, like its predecessor, applied to fraud "offenses now indictable under any existing statutes," but this time the law suspended "any existing statute of limitations" until the fixed date of June 30, 1945.

As that date approached, Congress decided to adopt a suspension statute which would remain in force for the duration of the war. Congress amended the 1942 WSLA in three important ways. First, Congress deleted the phrase "now indictable under any statute," so that the WSLA was made to apply simply to "any offense against the laws of the United States." Second, although previous versions of the WSLA were of definite duration, Congress now suspended the limitations period for the open-ended time frame of "three years after the termination of hostilities in the present war as proclaimed by the President or by a concurrent resolution of the two Houses of Congress." Third, Congress expanded the statute's coverage beyond offenses "involving defrauding or attempts to defraud the United States" to include other offenses pertaining to Government contracts and the handling and disposal of Government property.

Congress made more changes in 1948. From then until 2008, the WSLA's relevant language was as follows:

> When the United States is at war the running of any statute of limitations applicable to any offense (1) involving fraud or attempted fraud against the United States or any agency thereof in any manner, whether by conspiracy or not shall be suspended until three years after the termination of hostilities as proclaimed by the President or by a concurrent resolution of Congress.

> Act of June 25, 1948, § 3287, 62 Stat. 828.

In addition, Congress codified the WSLA in Title 18 of the United States Code, titled "Crimes and Criminal Procedure."

Finally, in 2008, Congress once again amended the WSLA, this time in two relevant ways. First, as noted, Congress changed the Act's triggering event, providing that tolling is available not only "when the United States is at war," but also when Congress has enacted a specific authorization for the use of military force. Second, Congress extended the suspension period from three to five years.

B

With this background in mind, we turn to the question whether the WSLA applies to civil claims as well as criminal charges. We hold that the Act applies only to the latter. We think it clear that the term "offense" in the WSLA applies solely to crimes.

But even if there were some ambiguity in the WSLA's use of that term, our cases instruct us to resolve that ambiguity in favor of the narrower definition. We have said that the WSLA should be "narrowly construed" and "interpreted in favor of repose."

Applying that principle here means that the term "offense" must be construed to refer only to crimes. Because this case involves civil claims, the WSLA does not suspend the applicable statute of limitations under either the 1948 or the 2008 version of the statute.

## IV

Petitioners acknowledge that respondent has raised other arguments that, if successful, could render at least one claim timely on remand. We therefore consider whether respondent's claims must be dismissed with prejudice under the first-to-file rule. We conclude that dismissal with prejudice was not called for.

The first-to-file bar provides that "when a person brings an action ... no person other than the Government may intervene or bring a related action based on the facts underlying the *pending* action." 31 U.S.C. § 3730(b)(5). The term "pending" means "remaining undecided; awaiting decision." Black's 1314 (10th ed. 2014). See also Webster's Third 1669 (1976) (defining "pending" to mean "not yet decided: in continuance: in suspense"). If the reference to a "pending" action in the FCA is interpreted in this way, an earlier suit bars a later suit while the earlier suit remains undecided but ceases to bar that suit once it is dismissed. We see no reason not to interpret the term "pending" in the FCA in accordance with its ordinary meaning.

Petitioners argue that Congress used the term "pending" in a very different—and very peculiar—way. In the FCA, according to petitioners, the term "pending" is used as a short-hand for the first filed action. Thus, as petitioners see things, the first-filed action remains "pending" even after it has been dismissed, and it forever bars any subsequent related action.

This interpretation does not comport with any known usage of the term "pending." Under this interpretation, *Marbury v. Madison,* 1 Cranch 137, 2 L.Ed. 60 (1803), is still "pending." So is the trial of Socrates.

Petitioners say that Congress used the term "pending" in the FCA as a sort of "short-hand," but a shorthand phrase or term is employed to provide a succinct way of expressing a concept that would otherwise require a lengthy or complex formulation. Here, we are told that "pending" is shorthand for "first-filed," a term that is neither lengthy nor complex. And if Congress had wanted to adopt the rule that petitioners favor, the task could have been accomplished in other equally economical ways—for example, by replacing "pending," with "earlier" or "prior."

Not only does petitioners' argument push the term "pending" far beyond the breaking point, but it would lead to strange results that Congress is unlikely to have wanted. Under petitioners' interpretation, a first-filed suit would bar all subsequent related suits even if that earlier suit was dismissed for a reason having nothing to do with the merits. Here, for example, the *Thorpe* suit, which provided the ground for the initial invocation of the first-to-file rule, was dismissed for failure to prosecute. Why would Congress want the abandonment of an earlier suit to bar a later potentially successful suit that might result in a large recovery for the Government?

Petitioners contend that interpreting "pending" to mean pending would produce practical problems, and there is some merit to their arguments. In particular, as petitioners note, if the first-to-file bar is lifted once the first-filed action ends, defendants may be reluctant to settle such actions for the full amount that they would accept if there were no prospect of subsequent suits asserting the same claims. Respondent and the United States argue that the doctrine of claim preclusion may protect defendants if the first-filed action is decided on the merits, but that issue is not before us in this case. The False Claims Act's *qui tam* provisions present many interpretive challenges, and it is beyond our ability in this case to make them operate together smoothly like a finely tuned machine. We hold that a *qui tam* suit under the FCA ceases to be "pending" once it is dismissed. We therefore agree with the Fourth Circuit that the dismissal with prejudice of respondent's one live claim was error.

The judgment of the United States Court of Appeals for the Fourth Circuit is reversed in part and affirmed in part, and the case is remanded for further proceedings consistent with this opinion.

---

### 135 S.CT. 913
### SUPREME COURT OF THE UNITED STATES
### DEPARTMENT OF HOMELAND SECURITY, PETITIONER
### V.
### ROBERT J. MACLEAN.

DECIDED JANUARY 21, 2015

**Chief Justice ROBERTS delivered the opinion of the Court.**

Federal law generally provides whistleblower protections to an employee who discloses information revealing "any violation of any law, rule, or regulation," or "a substantial and specific danger to public health or safety." 5 U.S.C. § 2302(b)(8)(A). An exception exists, however, for disclosures that are "specifically prohibited by law." Here, a federal air marshal publicly disclosed that the Transportation Security Administration (TSA) had decided to cut costs by removing air marshals from certain long-distance flights. The question presented is whether that disclosure was "specifically prohibited by law."

I

A

In 2002, Congress enacted the Homeland Security Act. As relevant here, that Act provides that the TSA "shall prescribe regulations prohibiting the disclosure of information obtained or developed in carrying out security if the Under Secretary decides that disclosing the information would be detrimental to the security of transportation."

Around the same time, the TSA promulgated regulations prohibiting the unauthorized disclosure of what it called "sensitive security information." The regulations described 18 categories of sensitive security information, including "specific details of aviation security measures such as information concerning specific numbers of Federal Air Marshals, deployments or missions, and the methods involved in such operations." Sensitive security information is not classified, so the TSA can share it with individuals who do not have a security clearance, such as airport employees.

B

Robert J. MacLean became a federal air marshal for the TSA in 2001. In that role, MacLean was assigned to protect passenger flights from potential hijackings.

On July 26, 2003, the Department of Homeland Security (DHS) issued a confidential advisory about a potential hijacking plot. The advisory said that members of the terrorist group al Qaeda were planning to attack passenger flights, and that they "considered suicide hijackings and bombings as the most promising methods to destroy aircraft in flight, as well as to strike ground targets." The advisory identified a number of potential targets, including the United Kingdom, Italy, Australia, and the east coast of the United States. Finally, the advisory warned that at least one of the attacks "could be executed by the end of the summer 2003."

The TSA soon summoned all air marshals (including MacLean) for face-to-face briefings about the hijacking plot. During MacLean's briefing, a TSA official told him that the hijackers were planning to "smuggle weapons in camera equipment or children's toys through foreign security," and then "fly into the United States into an airport that didn't require them to be screened." The hijackers would then board U.S.

flights, "overpower the crew or the Air Marshals and fly the planes into East Coast targets."

A few days after the briefing, MacLean received from the TSA a text message cancelling all overnight missions from Las Vegas until early August. MacLean, who was stationed in Las Vegas, believed that cancelling those missions during a hijacking alert was dangerous. He also believed that the cancellations were illegal, given that federal law required the TSA to put an air marshal on every flight that "presents high security risks," and provided that "nonstop, long distance flights, such as those targeted on September 11, 2001, should be a priority."

MacLean therefore asked a supervisor why the TSA had canceled the missions. The supervisor responded that the TSA wanted "to save money on hotel costs because there was no more money in the budget." MacLean also called the DHS Inspector General's Office to report the cancellations. But a special agent in that office told him there was "nothing that could be done."

Unwilling to accept those responses, MacLean contacted an MSNBC reporter and told him about the canceled missions. In turn, the reporter published a story about the TSA's decision, titled "Air Marshals pulled from key flights." The story reported that air marshals would "no longer be covering cross-country or international flights" because the agency did not want them "to incur the expense of staying overnight in hotels." The story also reported that the cancellations were "particularly disturbing to some" because they "coincided with a new high-level hijacking threat issued by the Department of Homeland Security."

After MSNBC published the story, several Members of Congress criticized the cancellations. Within 24 hours, the TSA reversed its decision and put air marshals back on the flights.

At first, the TSA did not know that MacLean was the source of the disclosure. In September 2004, however, MacLean appeared on NBC Nightly News to criticize the TSA's dress code for air marshals, which he believed made them too easy to identify. Although MacLean appeared in disguise, several co-workers recognized his voice, and the TSA began investigating the appearance. During that investigation, MacLean admitted that he had disclosed the text message back in 2003. Consequently, in April 2006, the TSA fired MacLean for disclosing sensitive security information without authorization.

MacLean challenged his firing before the Merit Systems Protection Board, arguing in relevant part that his disclosure was protected whistleblowing activity under 5 U.S.C. § 2302(b)(8)(A). The Board held that MacLean did not qualify for protection under that statute, however, because his disclosure was "specifically prohibited by law."

The Court of Appeals for the Federal Circuit vacated the Board's decision. We granted certiorari.

## II

Section 2302(b)(8) provides, in relevant part, that a federal agency may not take

> a personnel action with respect to any employee or applicant for employment because of
>
> (A) any disclosure of information by an employee or applicant which the employee or applicant reasonably believes evidences
> (i) any violation of any law, rule, or regulation, or
> (ii) gross mismanagement, a gross waste of funds, an abuse of authority, or a substantial and specific danger to public health or safety, "if such disclosure is not specifically prohibited by law and if such information is not specifically required by Executive order to be kept secret in the interest of national defense or the conduct of foreign affairs.

The Government argues that this whistleblower statute does not protect MacLean because his disclosure regarding the canceled missions was "specifically prohibited by law" in two ways. First, the Government argues that the disclosure was specifically prohibited by the TSA's regulations on sensitive security information. Second, the Government argues that the disclosure was specifically prohibited by 49 U.S.C. § 114(r)(1), which authorized the TSA to promulgate those regulations. We address each argument in turn.

### A

#### 1

In 2003, the TSA's regulations prohibited the disclosure of "specific details of aviation security measures such as information concerning specific numbers of Federal Air Marshals, deployments or missions, and the methods involved in such operations." MacLean does not dispute before this Court that the TSA's *regulations* prohibited his disclosure regarding the canceled missions. Thus, the question here is whether a disclosure that is specifically prohibited by *regulation* is also "specifically prohibited *by law*" under Section 2302(b)(8)(A).

The answer is no. Throughout Section 2302, Congress repeatedly used the phrase "law, rule, or regulation." For example, Section 2302(b)(1)(E) prohibits a federal agency from discriminating against an employee "on the basis of marital status or political affiliation, as prohibited under any law, rule, or regulation." For another example, Section 2302(b)(6) prohibits an agency from "granting any preference or advantage not authorized by law, rule, or regulation." And for a third example, Section 2302(b)(9)(A) prohibits an agency from retaliating against an employee for "the exercise of any appeal, complaint, or grievance right granted by any law, rule, or regulation."

In contrast, Congress did not use the phrase "law, rule, or regulation" in the statutory language at issue here; it used the word "law" standing alone. That is significant because Congress generally acts intentionally when it uses particular language in one section of a statute but omits it in another. Thus, Congress's choice to say "specifically prohibited by law" rather than "specifically prohibited by law, rule, or regulation" suggests that Congress meant to exclude rules and regulations.

The interpretive canon that Congress acts intentionally when it omits language included elsewhere applies with particular force here for two reasons. First, Congress used "law" and "law, rule, or regulation" in close proximity—indeed, in the same sentence. § 2302(b)(8)(A) (protecting the disclosure of "any violation of any law, rule, or regulation if such disclosure is not specifically prohibited by law"). Second, Congress used the broader phrase "law, rule, or regulation" repeatedly—nine times in Section 2302 alone. Those two aspects of the whistleblower statute make Congress's choice to use the narrower word "law" seem quite deliberate.

Another part of the statutory text points the same way. After creating an exception for disclosures "specifically prohibited by law," Section 2302(b)(8)(A) goes on to create a second exception for information "specifically required by Executive order to be kept secret in the interest of national defense or the conduct of foreign affairs." This exception is limited to action taken directly by the President. That suggests that the word "law" in the only other exception is limited to actions by Congress—after all, it would be unusual for the first exception to include action taken by executive agencies, when the second exception requires action by the President himself.

In addition, a broad interpretation of the word "law" could defeat the purpose of the whistleblower statute. If "law" included agency rules and regulations, then an agency could insulate itself from the scope of Section 2302(b)(8)(A) merely by promulgating a regulation that "specifically prohibited" whistleblowing. But Congress passed the whistleblower statute precisely because it did not trust agencies to regulate whistleblowers within their ranks. Thus, it is unlikely that Congress meant to include rules and regulations within the word "law."

The Government admits that some regulations fall outside the word "law" as used in Section 2302(b)(8)(A). As various examples show, Congress knew how to distinguish between regulations that had the force and effect of law and those that did not, but chose not to do so in Section 2302(b)(8)(A).

Although the Government argues here that the word "law" includes rules and regulations, it definitively rejected that argument in the Court of Appeals. At oral argument, a judge asked the Government's attorney the following question: "I thought I understood your brief to concede that the word "law" can't be a rule or regulation, it means statute. Am I wrong?" The Government's attorney responded: "You're not wrong your honor. I'll be as clear as I can. 'Specifically prohibited by law' here means statute." That concession reinforces our conclusion that the Government's proposed interpretations are unpersuasive.

In sum, when Congress used the phrase "specifically prohibited by law" instead of "specifically prohibited by law, rule, or regulation," it meant to exclude rules and regulations. We therefore hold that the TSA's regulations do not qualify as "law" for purposes of Section 2302(b)(8)(A).

B

We next consider whether MacLean's disclosure regarding the canceled missions was "specifically prohibited" by 49 U.S.C. § 114(r)(1) itself. As relevant here, that statute provides that the TSA "shall prescribe regulations prohibiting the disclosure of information obtained or developed in carrying out security if the Under Secretary decides that disclosing the information would be detrimental to the security of transportation." § 114(r)(1)(C).

This statute does not prohibit anything. On the contrary, it *authorizes* something— it authorizes the Under Secretary to "prescribe regulations." Thus, by its terms Section 114(r)(1) did not prohibit the disclosure at issue here.

The Government responds that Section 114(r)(1) did prohibit MacLean's disclosure by imposing a "legislative mandate" on the TSA to promulgate regulations to that effect. But the Government pushes the statute too far. It is the TSA's regulations—not the statute—that prohibited MacLean's disclosure. And as the dissent agrees, a regulation does not count as "law" under the whistleblower statute.

## III

Finally, the Government warns that providing whistleblower protection to individuals like MacLean would "gravely endanger public safety." That protection, the Government argues, would make the confidentiality of sensitive security information depend on the idiosyncratic judgment of each of the TSA's 60,000 employees. And those employees will "most likely lack access to all of the information that led the TSA to make particular security decisions." Thus, the Government says, we should conclude that Congress did not intend for Section 2302(b)(8)(A) to cover disclosures like MacLean's.

Those concerns are legitimate. But they are concerns that must be addressed by Congress or the President, rather than by this Court. Congress could, for example, amend Section 114(r)(1) so that the TSA's prohibitions on disclosure override the whistleblower protections in Section 2302(b)(8)(A). See, for example, 10 U.S.C. § 2640(h) ("the Secretary of Defense may (notwithstanding any other provision of law) withhold from public disclosure safety-related information that is provided to the Secretary voluntarily by an air carrier for the purposes of this section"). Congress could also exempt the TSA from the requirements of Section 2302(b)(8)(A) entirely, as Congress has already done for the Federal Bureau of Investigation, the Central Intelligence Agency, the Defense Intelligence Agency, the National Geospatial–Intelligence Agency, the National Security Agency, the Office of the Director of National Intelligence, and the National Reconnaissance Office.

Likewise, the President could prohibit the disclosure of sensitive security information by Executive order. Indeed, the Government suggested at oral argument that the President could "entirely duplicate" the regulations that the TSA has issued under Section 114(r)(1). Such an action would undoubtedly create an exception to the whistleblower protections found in Section 2302(b)(8)(A).

Although Congress and the President each has the power to address the Government's concerns, neither has done so. It is not our role to do so for them.

The judgment of the United States Court of Appeals for the Federal Circuit is
*Affirmed.*

9 781600 422942